The Civil War Battlefield Guide

Second
Edition

In great deeds something abides. On great fields something stays. Forms change and pass; bodies disappear; but spirits linger, to consecrate ground for the vision-place of souls. And reverent men and women from afar, and generations that know us not and that we know not of, heart-drawn to see where and by whom great things were suffered and done for them, shall come to this deathless field, to ponder and dream; and lo! the shadow of a mighty presence shall wrap them in its bosom, and the power of the vision pass into their souls.

— General Joshua Lawrence Chamberlain,
  Gettysburg, October 3, 1889

The Civil War Battlefield Guide

Second Edition

The Conservation Fund

Frances H. Kennedy

Editor and Principal Contributor

HOUGHTON MIFFLIN COMPANY · BOSTON · NEW YORK 1998

For information about permission to reproduce selections from
this book, write to Permissions, Houghton Mifflin Company,
215 Park Avenue South, New York, New York 10003.

Library of Congress Cataloging-in-Publication Data

The Civil War battlefield guide / Frances H. Kennedy, editor — 2nd ed.

p.   cm.

"The Conservation Fund."

Includes index.

ISBN 0-395-74012-6

1. United States — History— Civil War, 1861–1865 — Battlefields — Guidebooks.   2. United States — History — Civil War, 1861–1865 — Campaigns.
I. Kennedy, Frances H.   II. Conservation Fund (Arlington, Va.)

E641.C58   1998

973.7′3′025— dc21   98-7929 CIP

Printed in the United States of America

DOC 10 9 8 7 6 5 4 3 2 1

This book has been supported by a grant from
the National Endowment for the Humanities,
an independent federal agency.

Battlefield maps by John Marlin Murphy

Historical map captions by Richard W. Stephenson

Photograph captions by Brian C. Pohanka

Book design by David Ford

The Conservation Fund
dedicates this book to
Edwin C. Bearss
and its proceeds to the protection
of Civil War battlefields

This edition of
The Civil War Battlefield Guide
was made possible
by the generous support of
The Gilder Foundation
Heinz Family Foundation
Lindsay Young
Barbara and John Nau
The Phil Hardin Foundation
The Walt Disney Company
James S. and Lucia F. Gilliland
Texas Historical Commission

The Conservation Fund requests your
support of its Civil War Battlefield Campaign
and welcomes the partnership of citizen groups,
foundations, corporations, and public agencies
in battlefield protection.

———————

The Conservation Fund
1800 North Kent Street, Suite 1120
Arlington, Virginia 22209

Contents

●

Foreword   Patrick F. Noonan   xxiii

Preface   Frances H. Kennedy   xxv

Charleston Harbor: April 1861   1

Fort Sumter I, South Carolina (SC001),
Charleston County, April 12–14, 1861
James M. McPherson   1

**The Blockade of Chesapeake Bay and the
Potomac River: May–June 1861**   5

Sewell's Point, Virginia (VA001), Norfolk,
May 18–19, 1861   5

Aquia Creek, Virginia (VA002), Stafford County,
May 29–June 1, 1861   5

Big Bethel, Virginia (VA003), York County and
Hampton, June 10, 1861   6

West Virginia: June–December 1861   6

Philippi, West Virginia (WV001), Barbour
County, June 3, 1861   6

Rich Mountain, West Virginia (WV003),
Randolph County, July 11, 1861
Gary W. Gallagher   7

Kessler's Cross Lanes, West Virginia (WV004),
Nicholas County, August 26, 1861   9

Carnifex Ferry, West Virginia (WV006),
Nicholas County, September 10, 1861   9

Cheat Mountain, West Virginia (WV005),
Pocahontas County,
September 12–15, 1861   10

Greenbrier River, West Virginia (WV007),
Pocahontas County, October 3, 1861   10

Camp Allegheny, West Virginia (WV008),
Pocahontas County, December 13, 1861   10

Manassas Campaign: July 1861   11

Hoke's Run (Falling Waters), West Virginia
(WV002), Berkeley County, July 2, 1861   11

Blackburn's Ford, Virginia (VA004),
Prince William and Fairfax Counties,
July 18, 1861   11

First Manassas, Virginia (VA005),
Prince William County, July 21, 1861
William Glenn Robertson   11

The Staff Ride and Civil War Battlefields
William A. Stofft   16

**Northern Virginia: October–
December 1861**   18

Ball's Bluff, Virginia (VA006), Loudoun County,
October 21, 1861   18

Dranesville, Virginia (VA007), Fairfax County,
December 20, 1861   18

**Blockade of the Potomac River:
September 1861–March 1862**   18

Cockpit Point, Virginia (VA100), Prince William
County, January 3, 1862   18

Missouri: June–October 1861   19

Boonville, Missouri (MO001), Cooper County,
June 17, 1861   19

Carthage, Missouri (MO002), Jasper County,
July 5, 1861   20

Wilson's Creek, Missouri (MO004), Greene
and Christian Counties, August 10, 1861
Richard W. Hatcher III   21

Dry Wood Creek, Missouri (MO005),
Vernon County, September 2, 1861   23

Lexington I, Missouri (MO006), Lafayette
County, September 13–20, 1861   24

Liberty (Blue Mills Landing), Missouri
(MO003), Clay County, September 17, 1861   24

Fredericktown, Missouri (MO007),
Madison County, October 21, 1861   24

Springfield I, Missouri (MO008), Greene County,
October 25, 1861   25

**Grant on the Mississippi River:
November 1861**   26

Belmont, Missouri (MO009), Mississippi County,
November 7, 1861   26

**Missouri:
December 1861–January 1862**   27

Mount Zion Church, Missouri (MO010),
Boone County, December 28, 1861   27

Roan's Tan Yard, Missouri (MO011),
Randolph County, January 8, 1862   27

Florida: October 1861   27

Santa Rosa Island, Florida (FL001),
Escambia County, October 9, 1861   27

**Kentucky: September–
December 1861**   28

Barbourville, Kentucky (KY001), Knox County,
September 19, 1861   28

Camp Wildcat, Kentucky (KY002),
Laurel County, October 21, 1861   29

Ivy Mountain, Kentucky (KY003), Floyd County,
November 8–9, 1861   29

Rowlett's Station, Kentucky (KY004),
Hart County, December 17, 1861   29

Kentucky: January 1862   30

Middle Creek, Kentucky (KY005), Floyd County,
January 10, 1862   30

Mill Springs, Kentucky (KY006), Pulaski
and Wayne Counties, January 19, 1862
Kent Masterson Brown   30

**Indian Territory: November–
December 1861**   33

Round Mountain, Oklahoma (OK001), county
unknown, November 19, 1861   33

Chusto-Talasah, Oklahoma (OK002),
Tulsa County, December 9, 1861   33

Chustenahlah, Oklahoma (OK003),
Osage County, December 26, 1861   34

Pea Ridge, Arkansas: March 1862   34

Pea Ridge, Arkansas (AR001), Benton County,
March 6–8, 1862   *William L. Shea
and Earl J. Hess*   34

Arkansas: June–July 1862   38

St. Charles, Arkansas (AR002),
Arkansas County, June 17, 1862   38

Hill's Plantation, Arkansas (AR003),
Woodruff County, July 7, 1862   38

**Sibley's New Mexico Campaign:
February–March 1862**   39

Valverde, New Mexico (NM001), Socorro
County, February 20–21, 1862   39

Glorieta Pass, New Mexico (NM002), Santa Fe
and San Miguel Counties, March 26–28, 1862
Don E. Alberts   39

Contents

Cumberland and Tennessee Rivers:
February–June 1862   44

Fort Henry, Tennessee (TN001), Stewart County, February 6, 1862   44

Fort Donelson, Tennessee (TN002), Stewart County, February 12–16, 1862 *John Y. Simon*   45

Shiloh, Tennessee (TN003), Hardin County, April 6–7, 1862 *Stacy Allen*   48

Siege of Corinth, Mississippi (MS016), Alcorn County and Corinth, April 29–May 30, 1862   *T. Michael Parrish*   52

Middle Mississippi River:
February–June 1862   56

New Madrid/Island No. 10, Missouri (MO012), New Madrid, Missouri, and Lake County, Tennessee, February 28–April 8, 1862   56

Memphis I, Tennessee (TN004), Memphis, June 6, 1862   57

New Orleans: April–May 1862   58

Fort Jackson and Fort St. Philip, Louisiana (LA001), Plaquemines Parish, April 16–28, 1862   58

New Orleans, Louisiana (LA002), St. Bernard and Orleans Parishes, April 25–May 1, 1862   59

North Carolina: August 1861;
February–December 1862   59

Hatteras Inlet Forts, North Carolina (NC001), Dare County, August 28–29, 1861   59

Roanoke Island, North Carolina (NC002), Dare County, February 7–8, 1862   60

New Bern, North Carolina (NC003), Craven County, March 14, 1862   60

Fort Macon, North Carolina (NC004), Carteret County, March 23–April 26, 1862   61

South Mills, North Carolina (NC005), Camden County, April 19, 1862   61

Tranter's Creek, North Carolina (NC006), Pitt County, June 5, 1862   62

Kinston, North Carolina (NC007), Lenoir County, December 14, 1862   62

White Hall, North Carolina (NC008), Wayne County, December 16, 1862   62

Goldsboro Bridge, North Carolina (NC009), Wayne County, December 17, 1862   63

Fort Pulaski: April 1862   63

Fort Pulaski, Georgia (GA001), Chatham County, April 10–11, 1862   *Daniel A. Brown*   63

Charleston: June 1862   67

Secessionville, South Carolina (SC002), Charleston County, June 16, 1862 *Stephen R. Wise*   67

Simmons' Bluff, South Carolina (SC003), Charleston County, June 21, 1862   70

Mapping the Civil War
Richard W. Stephenson   71

Jackson Against the B & O Railroad:
January 1862   74

Hancock, Maryland (MD001), Washington County, Maryland, and Morgan County, West Virginia, January 5–6, 1862   74

Jackson's Shenandoah Valley Campaign:
March–June 1862   74

First Kernstown, Virginia (VA101), Frederick County and Winchester, March 23, 1862 *Thomas A. Lewis*   74

McDowell, Virginia (VA102), Highland County, May 8, 1862   *Robert G. Tanner*   78

Princeton Courthouse, West Virginia (WV009),
Mercer County, May 15–17, 1862   80

Front Royal, Virginia (VA103), Warren County,
May 23, 1862   80

First Winchester, Virginia (VA104),
Frederick County and Winchester,
May 25, 1862   81

Cross Keys, Virginia (VA105), Rockingham
County, June 8, 1862   *Donald C. Pfanz*   82

Port Republic, Virginia (VA106), Rockingham
County, June 9, 1862   *Donald C. Pfanz*   84

**Peninsula Campaign:
March–August 1862**   88

Hampton Roads, Virginia (VA008),
Hampton Roads, March 8–9, 1862   88

Siege of Yorktown, Virginia (VA009),
York County and Newport News,
April 5–May 4, 1862   88

Williamsburg, Virginia (VA010), York County
and Williamsburg, May 5, 1862   90

Eltham's Landing, Virginia (VA011),
New Kent County, May 7, 1862   91

Drewry's Bluff, Virginia (VA012),
Chesterfield County, May 15, 1862   91

Hanover Court House, Virginia (VA013),
Hanover County, May 27, 1862   91

Seven Pines, Virginia (VA014), Henrico County,
May 31–June 1, 1862   92

Oak Grove, Virginia (VA015), Henrico County,
June 25, 1862   93

Beaver Dam Creek (Mechanicsville/Ellerson's
Mill), Virginia (VA016), Hanover County,
June 26, 1862   93

Gaines' Mill, Virginia (VA017), Hanover County,
June 27, 1862   *Michael J. Andrus*   94

Garnett's and Golding's Farms, Virginia (VA018),
Henrico County, June 27–28, 1862   97

Savage's Station, Virginia (VA019),
Henrico County, June 29, 1862   98

Glendale, Virginia (VA020a), Henrico County,
June 30, 1862; White Oak Swamp, Virginia
(VA020b), Henrico County, June 30, 1862
Herman Hattaway and Ethan S. Rafuse   98

Malvern Hill, Virginia (VA021), Henrico County,
July 1, 1862   *Michael D. Litterst*   101

**Northern Virginia Campaign: August–
September 1862**   105

Cedar Mountain, Virginia (VA022), Culpeper
County, August 9, 1862   *Robert K. Krick*   105

Rappahannock River, Virginia (VA023),
Culpeper and Fauquier Counties,
August 22–25, 1862   107

Manassas Station/Junction, Virginia
(VA024), Prince William County,
August 26–27, 1862   108

Thoroughfare Gap, Virginia (VA025),
Prince William and Fauquier Counties,
August 28, 1862   108

Second Manassas, Virginia (VA026),
Prince William County, August 28–30, 1862
John J. Hennessy   108

Chantilly, Virginia (VA027), Fairfax County,
September 1, 1862   112

Maryland Campaign: September 1862   113

Harpers Ferry, West Virginia (WV010),
Jefferson County, September 12–15, 1862
Dennis E. Frye   113

South Mountain, Maryland (MD002),
Washington and Frederick Counties,
September 14, 1862   *Dennis E. Frye*   115

Antietam, Maryland (MD003),
Washington County, September 17, 1862
Stephen W. Sears   118

Shepherdstown, West Virginia (WV016),
Jefferson County, September 19–20, 1862   121

**Confederate Heartland Offensive:
June–October 1862**   122

Chattanooga I, Tennessee (TN005), Hamilton
County and Chattanooga, June 7–8, 1862   122

Murfreesboro I, Tennessee (TN006),
Rutherford County, July 13, 1862   122

Richmond, Kentucky (KY007),
Madison County, August 29–30, 1862   122

Munfordville (Battle for the Bridge),
Kentucky (KY008), Hart County,
September 14–17, 1862   123

Perryville, Kentucky (KY009), Boyle County,
October 8, 1862   *Paul Hawke*   124

A Civil War Legacy
William H. Webster   128

**Iuka and Corinth, Mississippi, Campaign:
September–October 1862**   129

Iuka, Mississippi (MS001), Tishomingo County,
September 19, 1862   129

Corinth, Mississippi (MS002), Alcorn County
and Corinth, October 3–4, 1862
George A. Reaves III   129

Davis Bridge (Hatchie Bridge), Tennessee
(TN007), Hardeman and McNairy Counties,
October 6, 1862   132

**Missouri and Oklahoma:
August–November 1862**   133

Kirksville, Missouri (MO013), Adair County,
August 6–9, 1862   133

Independence I, Missouri (MO014), Jackson
County, August 11, 1862   133

Lone Jack, Missouri (MO015), Jackson County,
August 15–16, 1862   133

Newtonia I, Missouri (MO016), Newton County,
September 30, 1862   134

Old Fort Wayne, Oklahoma (OK004), Delaware
County, October 22, 1862   134

Clark's Mill, Missouri (MO017), Douglas
County, November 7, 1862   134

**U.S.-Dakota Conflict of 1862:
August–September 1862**   135

Fort Ridgely, Minnesota (MN001), Nicollet
County, August 20–22, 1862   135

Wood Lake, Minnesota (MN002), Yellow
Medicine County, September 23, 1862   135

Louisiana: August–October 1862   136

Baton Rouge, Louisiana (LA003), East Baton
Rouge Parish, August 5, 1862   136

Donaldsonville I, Louisiana (LA004),
Ascension Parish, August 9, 1862   137

Georgia Landing, Louisiana (LA005),
Lafourche Parish, October 27, 1862   137

**Blockade of the Texas Coast:
September 1862–January 1863**   138

Sabine Pass I, Texas (TX001), Jefferson County,
September 24–25, 1862   138

Galveston I, Texas (TX002), Galveston County,
October 4, 1862   138

Galveston II, Texas (TX003), Galveston County,
January 1, 1863   138

Florida: June–October 1862   139

Tampa, Florida (FL002), Tampa, June 30–
July 1, 1862   139

St. Johns Bluff, Florida (FL003), Duval County,
October 1–3, 1862   139

Arkansas: November–December 1862   140

Cane Hill, Arkansas (AR004), Washington
County, November 28, 1862   140

Prairie Grove, Arkansas (AR005),
Washington County, December 7, 1862
William L. Shea   141

Fredericksburg: December 1862 144

Fredericksburg I, Virginia (VA028),
Spotsylvania County and Fredericksburg,
December 11–15, 1862 *A. Wilson Greene* 144

**Forrest's Raid into West Tennessee:
December 1862** 149

Jackson, Tennessee (TN009), Madison County,
December 19, 1862 149

Parker's Cross Roads, Tennessee (TN011),
Henderson County, December 31, 1862 149

**Stones River Campaign:
December 1862–January 1863** 150

Hartsville, Tennessee (TN008), Trousdale
County, December 7, 1862 150

Stones River, Tennessee (TN010), Rutherford
County, December 31, 1862–January 2, 1863
Grady McWhiney 151

**Vicksburg Campaign and Siege:
December 1862–July 1863** 154

Chickasaw Bayou, Mississippi (MS003),
Warren County, December 26–29, 1862
Terrence J. Winschel 154

Arkansas Post, Arkansas (AR006), Arkansas
County, January 9–11, 1863 157

Grand Gulf, Mississippi (MS004), Claiborne
County, April 29, 1863 157

Snyder's Bluff, Mississippi (MS005), Warren
County, April 29–May 1, 1863 158

Port Gibson, Mississippi (MS006), Claiborne
County, May 1, 1863 *Edwin C. Bearss* 158

Raymond, Mississippi (MS007), Hinds County,
May 12, 1863 *Edwin C. Bearss* 164

Jackson, Mississippi (MS008), Hinds County
and Jackson, May 14, 1863 167

Champion Hill, Mississippi (MS009), Hinds
County, May 16, 1863 *Edwin C. Bearss* 167

Big Black River Bridge, Mississippi (MS010),
Hinds and Warren Counties, May 17, 1863 170

Battle and Siege of Vicksburg, Mississippi
(MS011), Warren County and Vicksburg,
May 18–July 4, 1863 *Edwin C. Bearss* 171

Milliken's Bend, Louisiana (LA011), Madison
Parish, June 7, 1863 173

Goodrich's Landing, Louisiana (LA014), East
Carroll Parish, June 29–30, 1863 175

Helena, Arkansas (AR008), Phillips County,
July 4, 1863 175

**Streight's Raid Through Alabama:
April–May 1863** 176

Day's Gap, Alabama (AL001), Cullman County,
April 30, 1863 176

**Missouri and Arkansas:
January–May 1863** 177

Springfield II, Missouri (MO018),
Greene County, January 8, 1863 177

Hartville, Missouri (MO019), Wright County,
January 9–11, 1863 177

Cape Girardeau, Missouri (MO020),
Cape Girardeau, April 26, 1863 178

Chalk Bluff, Arkansas (AR007), Clay County,
May 1–2, 1863 178

West Louisiana: April 1863 179

Fort Bisland, Louisiana (LA006), St. Mary
Parish, April 12–13, 1863 179

Irish Bend, Louisiana (LA007), St. Mary Parish,
April 14, 1863 179

Vermillion Bayou, Louisiana (LA008),
Lafayette Parish, April 17, 1863 179

Louisiana: June–September 1863 180

Lafourche Crossing, Louisiana (LA012),
Lafourche Parish, June 20–21, 1863 180

Donaldsonville II, Louisiana (LA013),
Ascension Parish, June 28, 1863   180

Kock's Plantation, Louisiana (LA015),
Ascension Parish, July 12–13, 1863   180

Stirling's Plantation, Louisiana (LA016), Pointe
Coupee Parish, September 29, 1863   180

Siege of Port Hudson: May–July 1863   181

Plains Store, Louisiana (LA009), East Baton
Rouge Parish, May 21, 1863   181

Siege of Port Hudson, Louisiana (LA010),
East Baton Rouge and East Feliciana Parishes,
May 22–July 9, 1863
Lawrence Lee Hewitt   182

*"Making Free": African Americans and
the Civil War* James Oliver Horton   185

Black Medal of Honor Recipients   187

**Middle Tennessee:
February–April 1863**   189

Dover, Tennessee (TN012), Stewart County,
February 3, 1863   189

Thompson's Station, Tennessee (TN013),
Williamson County, March 4–5, 1863   189

Vaught's Hill, Tennessee (TN014),
Rutherford County, March 20, 1863   189

Brentwood, Tennessee (TN015),
Williamson County, March 25, 1863   190

Franklin I, Tennessee (TN016),
Williamson County and Franklin,
April 10, 1863   190

**Union Naval Attacks on Fort McAllister:
January–March 1863**   191

Fort McAllister I, Georgia (GA002), Bryan
County, January 27–March 3, 1863   191

Charleston: April–September 1863   191

Charleston Harbor I, South Carolina (SC004),
Charleston County, April 7, 1863   191

Fort Wagner I, Morris Island,
South Carolina (SC005), Charleston County,
July 10–11, 1863   192

Grimball's Landing, James Island,
South Carolina (SC006), Charleston County
July 16, 1863   192

Fort Wagner II, Morris Island, South Carolina
(SC007), Charleston County, July 18, 1863   192

Charleston Harbor II, South Carolina (SC009),
Charleston County, September 5–8, 1863   193

Fort Sumter II, South Carolina (SC008),
Charleston County, August 17–September 8,
1863   193

**Longstreet's Tidewater Campaign:
March–April 1863**   194

Fort Anderson, North Carolina (NC010),
Craven County, March 13–15, 1863   194

Washington, North Carolina (NC011), Beaufort
County, March 30–April 20, 1863   195

Suffolk I, Virginia (VA030), Suffolk,
April 13–15, 1863   195

Suffolk II (Hill's Point), Virginia (VA031),
Suffolk, April 19, 1863   195

**Cavalry Along the Rappahannock:
March 1863**   196

Kelly's Ford, Virginia (VA029), Culpeper County,
March 17, 1863   196

**Chancellorsville Campaign: April–
May 1863**   197

Chancellorsville, Virginia (VA032),
Spotsylvania County, April 30–May 6, 1863
Robert K. Krick   197

Fredericksburg II, Virginia (VA034),
Fredericksburg, May 3, 1863   199

Salem Church, Virginia (VA033), Spotsylvania
County, May 3–4, 1863   200

Preserving Civil War Battlefields
John Heinz   201

**Gettysburg Campaign:
June–July 1863**   202

Brandy Station, Virginia (VA035), Culpeper
County, June 9, 1863   *Clark B. Hall*   202

Second Winchester, Virginia (VA107), Frederick
County and Winchester, June 13–15, 1863   205

Aldie, Virginia (VA036), Loudoun County,
June 17, 1863   205

Middleburg, Virginia (VA037), Loudoun and
Fauquier Counties, June 17–19, 1863   205

Upperville, Virginia (VA038), Loudoun and
Fauquier Counties, June 21, 1863   206

Hanover, Pennsylvania (PA001), York County,
June 30, 1863   206

Gettysburg, Pennsylvania (PA002), Adams
County, July 1–3, 1863   *Harry W. Pfanz*   207

Williamsport, Maryland (MD004), Washington
County, July 6, 1863   212

Boonsboro–Funkstown–Falling Waters,
Maryland (MD006), Washington County,
July 8–14, 1863   213

Manassas Gap, Virginia (VA108), Warren and
Fauquier Counties, July 23, 1863   213

*The Gettysburg Address, November 19,
1863*   Abraham Lincoln   215

**Morgan's Indiana and Ohio Raid:
July 1863**   216

Corydon, Indiana (IN001), Harrison County,
July 9, 1863   216

Buffington Island, Ohio (OH001), Meigs County,
July 19, 1863   216

Salineville, Ohio (OH002), Columbiana County,
July 26, 1863   216

**Arkansas, Idaho, and Oklahoma:
January–September 1863;
February 1864**   217

Bear River, Idaho (ID001), Franklin County,
January 29, 1863   217

Cabin Creek, Oklahoma (OK006),
Mayes County, July 1–2, 1863   218

Honey Springs, Oklahoma (OK007), Muskogee
and McIntosh Counties, July 17, 1863
Bob L. Blackburn and LeRoy H. Fischer   219

Devil's Backbone, Arkansas (AR009),
Sebastian County, September 1, 1863   221

Middle Boggy, Oklahoma (OK005),
Atoka County, February 13, 1864   221

North Dakota: July–September 1863   222

Big Mound, North Dakota (ND001),
Kidder County, July 24, 1863   222

Dead Buffalo Lake, North Dakota (ND002),
Kidder County, July 26, 1863   222

Stony Lake, North Dakota (ND003),
Burleigh County, July 28, 1863   222

Whitestone Hill, North Dakota (ND004),
Dickey County, September 3–4, 1863   223

Kansas: August–October 1863   224

Lawrence, Kansas (KS001), Douglas County,
August 21, 1863   224

Baxter Springs, Kansas (KS002),
Cherokee County, October 6, 1863   224

Tullahoma Campaign: June 1863   225

Hoover's Gap, Tennessee (TN017), Bedford and
Rutherford Counties, June 24–26, 1863   225

**Chickamauga Campaign:
August–September 1863**   226

Chattanooga II, Tennessee (TN018), Hamilton
County and Chattanooga, August 21, 1863   226

Davis' Cross Roads, Georgia (GA003), Dade and
Walker Counties, September 10–11, 1863   227

Chickamauga, Georgia (GA004), Catoosa and
Walker Counties, September 18–20, 1863
William Glenn Robertson   227

**Blockade of the Texas Coast:
September 1863**   232

Sabine Pass II, Texas (TX006), Jefferson County,
September 8, 1863   232

Arkansas: September–October 1863   233

Bayou Fourche (Little Rock), Arkansas (AR010),
Pulaski County, September 10, 1863   233

Pine Bluff, Arkansas (AR011), Jefferson County,
October 25, 1863   233

Photography in the Civil War
David McCullough   234

**East Tennessee:
September–October 1863**   236

Blountville, Tennessee (TN019),
Sullivan County, September 22, 1863   236

Blue Springs, Tennessee (TN020),
Greene County, October 10, 1863   239

**Virginia & Tennessee Railroad:
November 1863**   240

Droop Mountain, West Virginia (WV012),
Pocahontas County, November 6, 1863   240

**Memphis & Charleston Railroad:
November 1863**   241

Collierville, Tennessee (TN022), Shelby County,
November 3, 1863   241

The Cracker Line: October 1863   241

Wauhatchie, Tennessee (TN021),
Hamilton, Marion, and Dade Counties,
October 28–29, 1863   241

**Chattanooga-Ringgold Campaign:
November 1863**   243

Chattanooga III, Tennessee (TN024),
Hamilton County and Chattanooga,
November 23–25, 1863   *Charles P. Roland*   243

Ringgold Gap, Georgia (GA005),
Catoosa County, November 27, 1863
Keith S. Bohannon   246

**Knoxville Campaign: November–
December 1863**   248

Campbell's Station, Tennessee (TN023),
Knox County, November 16, 1863   248

Fort Sanders, Tennessee (TN025), Knox County,
November 29, 1863   249

Bean's Station, Tennessee (TN026),
Grainger County, December 14, 1863   249

**East Tennessee: December 1863–
January 1864**   250

Mossy Creek, Tennessee (TN027),
Jefferson County, December 29, 1863   250

Dandridge, Tennessee (TN028),
Jefferson County, January 17, 1864   250

Fair Garden, Tennessee (TN029), Sevier County,
January 27–28, 1864   250

**Bristoe Campaign:
October–November 1863**   251

Auburn I, Virginia (VA039), Fauquier County,
October 13, 1863   251

Auburn II, Virginia (VA041), Fauquier County,
October 14, 1863   252

Bristoe Station, Virginia (VA040),
Prince William County, October 14, 1863
Jan Townsend   252

Buckland Mills, Virginia (VA042),
Fauquier County, October 19, 1863   254

Rappahannock Station, Virginia (VA043),
Culpeper and Fauquier Counties, November 7,
1863   255

**Mine Run Campaign:
November–December 1863**   255

Mine Run, Virginia (VA044), Orange County,
November 26–December 2, 1863
Richard Moe   255

**Rapidan River, Virginia:
February 1864**   260

Morton's Ford, Virginia (VA045), Orange and
Culpeper Counties, February 6–7, 1864   260

**Kilpatrick-Dahlgren Raid:
February–March 1864**   260

Walkerton, Virginia (VA125), King and
Queen County, March 2, 1864   260

Deep South: January–February 1864   261

Athens, Alabama (AL002), Limestone County,
January 26, 1864   261

Meridian, Mississippi (MS012), Lauderdale
County, February 14–20, 1864   261

Okolona, Mississippi (MS013), Chickasaw
County, February 22, 1864   261

Dalton I, Georgia (GA006), Whitfield County
and Dalton, February 22–27, 1864   262

**Florida: October 1863 and
February 1864**   263

Fort Brooke, Florida (FL004), Tampa,
October 16–18, 1863   263

Olustee, Florida (FL005), Baker County,
February 20, 1864   263

*Military Strategy, Politics, and
Economics: The Red River Campaign*
Ludwell H. Johnson   265

**Red River Campaign:
March–May 1864**   267

Fort DeRussy, Louisiana (LA017),
Avoyelles Parish, March 14, 1864   267

Mansfield, Louisiana (LA018), DeSoto Parish,
April 8, 1864   *Arthur W. Bergeron, Jr.*   267

Pleasant Hill, Louisiana (LA019), DeSoto
and Sabine Parishes, April 9, 1864
Arthur W. Bergeron, Jr.   269

Blair's Landing, Louisiana (LA020),
Red River Parish, April 12, 1864   271

Monett's Ferry, Louisiana (LA021),
Natchitoches Parish, April 23, 1864   271

Mansura, Louisiana (LA022), Avoyelles Parish,
May 16, 1864   272

Yellow Bayou, Louisiana (LA023),
Avoyelles Parish, May 18, 1864   272

**Camden, Arkansas, Expedition:
April–June 1864**   273

Elkin's Ferry, Arkansas (AR012), Clark and
Nevada Counties, April 3–4, 1864   273

Prairie D'Ane, Arkansas (AR013),
Nevada County, April 10–13, 1864   273

Poison Spring, Arkansas (AR014),
Ouachita County, April 18, 1864   273

Marks' Mills, Arkansas (AR015),
Cleveland County, April 25, 1864   274

Jenkins' Ferry, Arkansas (AR016), Grant County,
April 30, 1864   274

Ditch Bayou (Old River Lake),
Arkansas (AR017), Chicot County,
June 6, 1864   274

Forrest's Raid on Paducah and Fort Pillow:
March–April 1864 275

Paducah, Kentucky (KY010), McCracken
County, March 25, 1864 275

Fort Pillow, Tennessee (TN030), Lauderdale
County, April 12, 1864 275

North Carolina: April–May 1864 277

Plymouth, North Carolina (NC012),
Washington County, April 17–20, 1864 277

Albemarle Sound, North Carolina (NC013),
Chowan and Washington Counties,
May 5, 1864 277

Bermuda Hundred Campaign:
May 1864 278

Port Walthall Junction, Virginia (VA047),
Chesterfield County, May 6–7, 1864 278

Swift Creek and Fort Clifton, Virginia (VA050),
Chesterfield County, May 9, 1864 278

Chester Station, Virginia (VA051),
Chesterfield County, May 10, 1864 279

Proctor's Creek (Drewry's Bluff),
Virginia (VA053), Chesterfield County,
May 12–16, 1864 279

Ware Bottom Church and Howlett Line,
Virginia (VA054), Chesterfield County,
May 20, 1864 280

Grant's Overland Campaign:
May–June 1864 280

Wilderness, Virginia (VA046),
Spotsylvania County, May 5–6, 1864
Noah Andre Trudeau 280

Spotsylvania Court House, Virginia (VA048),
Spotsylvania County, May 8–21, 1864
William D. Matter 283

Yellow Tavern, Virginia (VA052),
Henrico County, May 11, 1864 286

North Anna, Virginia (VA055), Hanover
and Caroline Counties, May 23–26, 1864
J. Michael Miller 287

Wilson's Wharf, Virginia (VA056),
Charles City County, May 24, 1864 290

Haw's Shop, Virginia (VA058), Hanover County,
May 28, 1864 290

Totopotomoy Creek and Bethesda Church,
Virginia (VA057), Hanover County, May 28–30,
1864 290

Matadequin Creek (Old Church),
Virginia (VA059), Hanover County,
May 30, 1864 291

Cold Harbor, Virginia (VA062),
Hanover County, May 31–June 12, 1864
Richard J. Sommers 291

Trevilian Station, Virginia (VA099),
Louisa County, June 11–12, 1864 294

Samaria Church (Saint Mary's Church),
Virginia (VA112), Charles City County,
June 24, 1864 295

Southwest Virginia: May 1864 296

Cloyd's Mountain, Virginia (VA049),
Pulaski County, May 9, 1864
James I. Robertson, Jr. 296

Cove Mountain, Virginia (VA109),
Wythe County, May 10, 1864 297

Shenandoah Valley: May–June 1864 298

New Market, Virginia (VA110),
Shenandoah County, May 15, 1864
Joseph W. A. Whitehorne 298

Piedmont, Virginia (VA111), Augusta County,
June 5, 1864 *Joseph W. A. Whitehorne* 301

Lynchburg, Virginia (VA064),
Lynchburg, June 17–18, 1864 304

Early in Maryland, Pennsylvania, and the Shenandoah Valley: July–August 1864 305

Monocacy, Maryland (MD007), Frederick County, July 9, 1864   *Gary W. Gallagher* 305

Fort Stevens, District of Columbia (DC001), District of Columbia, July 11–12, 1864   308

Cool Spring, Virginia (VA114), Clarke County, July 17–18, 1864   309

Rutherford's Farm, Virginia (VA115), Frederick County and Winchester, July 20, 1864   309

Second Kernstown, Virginia (VA116), Frederick County and Winchester, July 24, 1864   *Joseph W. A. Whitehorne* 310

Folck's Mill, Maryland (MD008), Allegany County, August 1, 1864   312

Moorefield, West Virginia (WV013), Hardy County, August 7, 1864   313

Sheridan's Shenandoah Valley Campaign: August 1864–March 1865 313

Guard Hill, Virginia (VA117), Warren County, August 16, 1864   313

Summit Point and Cameron's Depot, West Virginia (WV014), Jefferson County, August 21, 1864   314

Smithfield Crossing, West Virginia (WV015), Jefferson and Berkeley Counties, August 28–29, 1864   314

Berryville, Virginia (VA118), Clarke County, September 3–4, 1864   315

Opequon (Third Winchester), Virginia (VA119), Frederick and Clarke Counties and Winchester, September 19, 1864   315

Fisher's Hill, Virginia (VA120), Shenandoah County, September 21–22, 1864   *Joseph W. A. Whitehorne* 316

Tom's Brook, Virginia (VA121), Shenandoah County, October 9, 1864   318

Cedar Creek, Virginia (VA122), Frederick, Shenandoah, and Warren Counties, October 19, 1864   *Joseph W. A. Whitehorne* 319

Waynesboro, Virginia (VA123), Augusta County, March 2, 1865   323

Hallowed Ground   Sam Nunn   325

Atlanta Campaign: May–September 1864 326

Rocky Face Ridge, Georgia (GA007), Whitfield County and Dalton, May 7–13, 1864   *Jay Luvaas* 326

Resaca, Georgia (GA008), Whitfield and Gordon Counties, May 13–15, 1864   *Jay Luvaas* 329

Adairsville, Georgia (GA009), Bartow and Gordon Counties, May 17, 1864   331

New Hope Church, Georgia (GA010), Paulding County, May 25–26, 1864; Pickett's Mill, Georgia (GA012), Paulding County, May 27, 1864; and Dallas, Georgia (GA011), Paulding County, May 28, 1864   *Jay Luvaas* 332

Lost Mountain–Brushy Mountain Line, Georgia (GA013), Paulding and Cobb Counties, June 9–18, 1864   335

Kolb's Farm, Georgia (GA014), Cobb County, June 22, 1864   336

Kennesaw Mountain, Georgia (GA015), Cobb County, June 27, 1864   *Jay Luvaas* 336

Peachtree Creek, Georgia (GA016), Fulton County, July 20, 1864   339

Atlanta, Georgia (GA017), Fulton and De Kalb Counties, July 22, 1864   340

Ezra Church, Georgia (GA018), Fulton County, July 28, 1864   341

Utoy Creek, Georgia (GA019), Fulton County, August 5–7, 1864   341

Dalton II, Georgia (GA020), Whitfield County
and Dalton, August 14–15, 1864   341

Lovejoy's Station, Georgia (GA021),
Clayton County, August 20, 1864   342

Jonesboro, Georgia (GA022), Clayton County,
August 31–September 1, 1864   342

**Morgan's Last Kentucky Raid:
June 1864**   344

Cynthiana, Kentucky (KY011), Harrison County,
June 11–12, 1864   344

**Forrest's Defense of Mississippi:
June–August 1864**   344

Brices Cross Roads, Mississippi (MS014),
Union, Prentiss, and Lee Counties, June 10, 1864
Edwin C. Bearss   344

Tupelo, Mississippi (MS015), Lee County
and Tupelo, July 14–15, 1864
Frank Allen Dennis   347

Memphis II, Tennessee (TN031),
Memphis, August 21, 1864   350

Dakota Territory: July 1864   351

Killdeer Mountain, North Dakota (ND005),
Dunn County, July 28–29, 1864   351

**Richmond-Petersburg Campaign:
June 1864–March 1865**   352

Petersburg I, Virginia (VA098),
Petersburg, June 9, 1864   352

Petersburg II, Virginia (VA063), Prince George
County and Petersburg, June 15–18, 1864   352

Jerusalem Plank Road, Virginia (VA065),
Dinwiddie County and Petersburg,
June 21–23, 1864   353

Staunton River Bridge, Virginia (VA113),
Halifax and Charlotte Counties,
June 25, 1864   354

Sappony Church, Virginia (VA067),
Sussex County, June 28, 1864   354

Reams Station I, Virginia (VA068), Dinwiddie
County, June 29, 1864   354

First Deep Bottom, Virginia (VA069),
Henrico County, July 27–29, 1864   355

The Crater, Virginia (VA070), Petersburg,
July 30, 1864   355

Second Deep Bottom, Virginia (VA071),
Henrico County, August 13–20, 1864
Robert E. L. Krick   356

Globe Tavern, Virginia (VA072), Dinwiddie
County, August 18–21, 1864   357

Reams Station II, Virginia (VA073),
Dinwiddie County, August 25, 1864
Christopher M. Calkins   360

Chaffin's Farm and New Market Heights,
Virginia (VA075), Henrico County,
September 29–30, 1864   362
  Chaffin's Farm   *David R. Ruth*   362
  New Market Heights
    William W. Gwaltney   364

Peebles' Farm, Virginia (VA074), Dinwiddie
County, September 30–October 2, 1864   368

Darbytown and New Market Roads, Virginia
(VA077), Henrico County, October 7, 1864   369

Darbytown Road, Virginia (VA078),
Henrico County, October 13, 1864   369

Boydton Plank Road, Virginia (VA079),
Dinwiddie County, October 27, 1864
Garrett C. Peck   369

Fair Oaks and Darbytown Road,
Virginia (VA080), Henrico County,
October 27–28, 1864   372

Hatcher's Run, Virginia (VA083), Dinwiddie
County, February 5–7, 1865   372

Fort Stedman, Virginia (VA084), Petersburg,
March 25, 1865   373

Mobile Bay: August 1864   374

Mobile Bay, Alabama (AL003), Mobile
and Baldwin Counties, August 2–23, 1864
Arthur W. Bergeron, Jr.   374

Pro-Confederate Activity in Missouri
James M. McPherson   377

**Price in Missouri and Kansas:
September–October 1864**   380

Pilot Knob, Missouri (MO021), Iron County,
September 26–28, 1864   *Albert Castel*   380

Glasgow, Missouri (MO022), Howard County,
October 15, 1864   382

Lexington II, Missouri (MO023), Lafayette
County, October 19, 1864   382

Little Blue River, Missouri (MO024), Jackson
County, October 21, 1864   382

Independence II, Missouri (MO025), Jackson
County, October 22, 1864   383

Big Blue River (Byram's Ford),
Missouri (MO026), Jackson County,
October 22–23, 1864   383

Westport, Missouri (MO027), Jackson County,
October 23, 1864   384

Marais des Cygnes, Kansas (KS004),
Linn County, October 25, 1864   384

Mine Creek, Kansas (KS003), Linn County,
October 25, 1864   384

Marmaton River, Missouri (MO028),
Vernon County, October 25, 1864   385

Newtonia II, Missouri (MO029),
Newton County, October 28, 1864
Albert Castel   385

**Southwest Virginia and East Tennessee:
September–December 1864**   387

Saltville I, Virginia (VA076), Smyth County,
October 2, 1864   387

Bull's Gap, Tennessee (TN033), Hamblen and
Greene Counties, November 11–14, 1864   387

Marion, Virginia (VA081), Smyth County,
December 16–18, 1864   388

Saltville II, Virginia (VA082), Smyth County,
December 20–21, 1864   388

**Forrest's Raid into West Tennessee:
October–November 1864**   389

Johnsonville, Tennessee (TN032), Benton
County, November 3–4, 1864   389

**Hood's March to Tennessee:
October–December 1864**   389

Allatoona, Georgia (GA023), Bartow County,
October 5, 1864   *William R. Scaife*   389

Dalton III, Georgia (GA024), Whitfield County
and Dalton, October 13, 1864   391

Decatur, Alabama (AL004), Morgan and
Limestone Counties, October 26–29, 1864   392

Columbia, Tennessee (TN034), Maury County,
November 24–29, 1864   392

Spring Hill, Tennessee (TN035), Maury County
and Spring Hill, November 29, 1864
Richard M. McMurry   392

Franklin II, Tennessee (TN036), Williamson
County and Franklin, November 30, 1864   395

Murfreesboro II, Tennessee (TN037), Rutherford
County, December 5–7, 1864   396

Nashville, Tennessee (TN038), Davidson
County, December 15–16, 1864   396

**Sand Creek, Colorado Territory:
November 1864**   398

Sand Creek, Colorado (CO001), Kiowa and/or
Cheyenne Counties, November 29, 1864   398

**Sherman's March to the Sea:
November–December 1864**   399

Griswoldville, Georgia (GA025), Twiggs and
Jones Counties, November 22, 1864   399

Buck Head Creek, Georgia (GA026),
Jenkins County, November 28, 1864   399

Honey Hill, South Carolina (SC010),
Jasper County, November 30, 1864   400

Waynesborough, Georgia (GA027),
Burke County, December 4, 1864   400

Fort McAllister II, Georgia (GA028),
Bryan County, December 13, 1864   400

**North Carolina: December 1864–
February 1865**   401

Fort Fisher I, North Carolina (NC014), New
Hanover County, December 7–27, 1864   401

Fort Fisher II, North Carolina (NC015), New
Hanover County, January 13–15, 1865   402

Wilmington, North Carolina (NC016), New
Hanover County, February 12–22, 1865   402

Second Inaugural Address, March 4, 1865
Abraham Lincoln   404

**Sherman's Carolina Campaign:
February–March 1865**   405

Rivers Bridge, South Carolina (SC011),
Bamberg County, February 2–3, 1865   405

Wyse Fork, North Carolina (NC017), Lenoir
County, March 7–10, 1865   406

Monroe's Cross Roads, North Carolina (NC018),
Hoke County, March 10, 1865   406

Averasboro, North Carolina (NC019), Harnett
and Cumberland Counties, March 16, 1865   407

Bentonville, North Carolina (NC020),
Johnston County, March 19–21, 1865
John G. Barrett   408

**Appomattox Campaign:
March–April 1865**   412

Lewis's Farm, Virginia (VA085), Dinwiddie
County, March 29, 1865   412

Dinwiddie Court House, Virginia (VA086),
Dinwiddie County, March 31, 1865   412

White Oak Road, Virginia (VA087), Dinwiddie
County, March 31, 1865   *David W. Lowe*   413

Five Forks, Virginia (VA088), Dinwiddie County,
April 1, 1865   *Christopher M. Calkins*   417

Petersburg III, Virginia (VA089), Dinwiddie
County and Petersburg, April 2, 1865
Emory Thomas   419

Sutherland Station, Virginia (VA090),
Dinwiddie County, April 2, 1865   423

Namozine Church, Virginia (VA124),
Amelia County, April 3, 1865   423

Amelia Springs, Virginia (VA091),
Amelia County, April 5, 1865   424

Sailor's Creek, Virginia (VA093), Amelia,
Nottaway, and Prince Edward Counties,
April 6, 1865   *Christopher M. Calkins*   424

Rice's Station, Virginia (VA092), Prince Edward
County, April 6, 1865   427

High Bridge, Virginia (VA095), Prince Edward
and Cumberland Counties, April 6–7, 1865   427

Cumberland Church, Virginia (VA094),
Cumberland County, April 7, 1865   428

Appomattox Station, Virginia (VA096),
Appomattox County, April 8, 1865   428

Appomattox Court House, Virginia (VA097),
Appomattox County, April 9, 1865
William C. Davis   429

Florida: March 1865   434

Natural Bridge, Florida (FL006), Leon County,
March 6, 1865   434

Mobile Campaign: March–April 1865   435

Spanish Fort, Alabama (AL005), Baldwin
County, March 27–April 8, 1865   435

Fort Blakely, Alabama (AL006), Baldwin County,
April 2–9, 1865   435

**Wilson's Raid in Alabama and Georgia:
March–May 1865**   436

Selma, Alabama (AL007), Dallas County,
April 2, 1865   436

Texas: May 1865   437

Palmito Ranch (TX005), Cameron County,
May 12–13, 1865   437

**Appendix 1: The 384 Principal
Battlefields**   440

**Appendix 2: An Excerpt from the *Civil War
Sites Advisory Commission Report on the
Nation's Civil War Battlefields***   457

**Appendix 3: Lost and Fragmented
Civil War Battlefields**   459

**Appendix 4: War Statistics
Robert W. Meinhard**   463

Glossary   464

About the Authors   467

Index   472

Foreword

○

The causes were complex — and distressingly simple — and the outcome was decisive. More than any other event in our nation's history, the Civil War set the direction for America's future. During the war almost 3 million Americans fought across battlefields that had been quiet farms, dusty roads, and country crossroads. In the four years of courage and despair, these battlefields earned somber distinction as hallowed ground.

For more than a hundred years, much of this hallowed ground was protected not by government but by private owners — often local farm families whose grandparents had seen the armies fight across their lands, and whose brothers and fathers had died at Manassas, Antietam, and Shiloh.

But our nation is changing. Cornfields and woodlands have become shopping malls; the country lanes are crowded highways. After more than a century our hallowed ground is threatened with desecration. In many places farmers are compelled to sell their property for development. Generations of stewardship are in peril.

Acknowledging this impending sea change in ownership, these dramatic changes in land use, Congress established the Civil War Sites Advisory Commission. The commission's 1993 landmark report, the basis for the second edition of *The Civil War Battlefield Guide*, helps communities set protection priorities.

Pressed from every side, community leaders are being asked to choose between apparently incompatible goals: battlefield preservation or economic development. That threat of incompatibility, however, is a myth. Communities that plan development to complement the historic treasures that battlefields represent benefit in many ways. Publicly and privately protected battlefields can function as "basic industries." They can generate jobs and local revenues. At the same time, they provide open space and help preserve the quality of life for residents — new and old.

Yet of the 384 battlefields included in this guide, most lack adequate protection. They are highly vulnerable to the pressures of unplanned and inappropriate development.

The Conservation Fund was established to work with public and private partners to protect America's special places — community open space, parkland, wildlife and waterfowl habitat, and important historic areas. Consequently, to preserve our ties to the history of our nation, The Conservation Fund launched the Civil War Battlefield Campaign in 1990. The multiyear project is aimed at safeguarding key Civil War sites through acquisition and increased public awareness. With our partners in the private and public sectors, we have been successful in acquiring property on twenty-eight battlefields in eleven states. These fifty-one protection projects, valued at more than $10.6 million, are complete. Yet our work continues.

With the loss of battlefield sites to sprawl, our generation must act today, so that Americans of tomorrow can walk the very ground where many of our nation's values were forged.

But our program does not stop with acquisition. To help residents protect the historic land that underlies their community's character, we have published a handbook: *The Dollar$ and Sense of Battlefield Preservation: The Economic Benefits of Protecting Civil War Battlefields.* We also worked with the state of Mississippi to develop and publish *A Guide to the Campaign and Siege of Vicksburg.* The publication helped launch a new initiative to preserve that state's Civil War heritage, increase tourism, and enhance economic growth.

To enable us to increase our acquisition and education programs, The Conservation Fund is actively seeking contributions from individuals, corporations, and foundations for the Battlefield Campaign. I believe future generations will praise our foresight, if we succeed, or curse our blindness, if we fail to act to protect these hallowed grounds.

Today you can stand at a score or more battlefields, including Antietam, at the edge of what is still a farm field, and visualize the waves of infantry, feel the urgency, capture for a moment the meaning of how that day changed our nation's history. The land is there as it was, and for a few minutes you are part of that terrible day, part of history. It is an unforgettable experience. In the years to come, generations of Americans will be able to share that experience. At the request of the National Park Service, the Richard King Mellon Foundation, assisted by The Conservation Fund, purchased the Cornfield and West Woods and donated them to Antietam National Battlefield. The foundation's other gifts to the nation include the historic land on the battlefields of Appomattox, Champion Hill, Five Forks, Gettysburg, Manassas, and the Wilderness.

Through the Battlefield Campaign, we are helping preserve that unique opportunity to be part of history, not just at Antietam but on land from Gettysburg to the Gulf, Glorieta to the Atlantic. Protecting these special places is not just our choice. It is our duty as a nation to the next generation. The second edition of *The Civil War Battlefield Guide*, with battlefield narratives and colorful, comprehensive maps, will help increase public awareness of the need to respect our hallowed ground. We urge local governments and historic preservation and conservation organizations to join in the effort by working in partnership with each other, private landowners, state agencies, the National Park Service, and The Conservation Fund to protect our Civil War battlefields.

At The Conservation Fund, we believe that by forming partnerships and by integrating economic development strategies and historical preservation policies, we demonstrate a new and more effective approach for America that will sustain our communities and build a better life for all our citizens.

It has been said that the United States as we know it today began not with the Revolution of 1776 but rather in the new nation that emerged from the Civil War. That turbulent beginning happened in places that have since become names in history but then were fields of battle for thousands of brave Americans. Our goal is to continue the tradition of stewardship that private ownership established. Our challenge is to do so in a way that will ensure that Americans of the coming century will know and understand the reasons for the Civil War. Our commitment must be to honor the unmatched valor of Americans of the past century, whose sacrifices built a new and stronger nation. I believe we can leave no greater legacy for Americans of the twenty-first century.

— Patrick F. Noonan
  Chairman, The Conservation Fund

Preface

❍

The goals of *The Civil War Battlefield Guide* are to celebrate the union of our states and the abolition of slavery, to honor those who fought and died in the war, and to provide readers with the best available information on the 384 principal battles of the Civil War. The Conservation Fund's intent is that the book will guide battlefield preservation as well as guide visitors to this hallowed ground, and we dedicate the book's royalties to battlefield preservation. This second edition includes the 384 principal battles designated by the *Civil War Sites Advisory Commission Report on the Nation's Civil War Battlefields.* This outstanding report was made possible by the partnership between Congress and the Department of the Interior, the commitment of the commissioners, and the diligence of the National Park Service American Battlefield Protection Program. Appendix 3 is an excerpt from the executive summary of the report, beginning with the names of the commissioners.

The battles in this *Guide* are presented in chronological order within the campaigns designated by the report, modified to assist the traveler. The campaigns are in chronological order, with some adjustments for the simultaneity of actions in different areas. The Contents can be used as a reference document for the (currently documented) location by county/city/state and, since it includes the date of each battle, for an overview of the war. The name of each battle is followed by a sequential reference number assigned by the commission. The eighty-one battles detailed in essays and shown on maps include the fifty the commission designated as the first priority for battlefield preservation as well as thirty-one additional battles that are central to our understanding of the war. The other 303 battles are de-

scribed in shorter summaries. There is information in the essays and in the summaries, in addition to the battle action, that provides background, links the battles within a campaign, and describes events that affect the progress of the war.

In the battle accounts, *US* or *CS* precedes each officer's rank, to help clarify the action for new students of the Civil War. The first time an officer is mentioned in each campaign and in each essay, his full name and rank are provided; for example: US Lieutenant General Ulysses S. Grant. After the first mention of an officer, only his last name is used until the next essay or summary; for example: Grant. When only the partial rank and name are given, for example, CS General Lee, it means that there was an account involving CS General Robert E. Lee in an earlier essay or summary in that campaign.

When there is more than one battle at a place, such as Manassas, we use the traditional name, First Manassas, Virginia. When the traditional name does not incorporate a number, we use a Roman numeral: Newtonia I, Missouri. For battles that are sieges we add that word to the name: Siege of Port Hudson. At the end of each battle essay are driving directions, the acres protected (if any), and mention of whether the battlefield is open to the public (as of 1997). Information about the protected land (if any) on the battlefields described in the 303 summaries is included at the end of each summary. When touring battlefields, visitors must remember that a small percentage of them are owned by public agencies and nonprofit organizations and are accessible to visitors. Most of the hallowed ground must be viewed from public roads. Visitors must not trespass. There is also privately owned land within the boundaries of many battlefield parks, so visitors should always stay on public roads and marked trails.

The maps that accompany the battle essays were drawn by John Murphy of Jackson, Mississippi, using U.S. Geological Survey maps as the base. The United States' forces are shown in blue and the Confederacy's in red. The officers are shown in five typefaces: the largest underlined typeface indicates the commander of several armies; the same typeface not underlined designates army commanders; a smaller underlined typeface indicates wing commanders; and the same typeface not underlined, corps commanders. To avoid too much complexity for the general reader, the smallest typeface, which is all capital letters, denotes all other officers. In some battles, a division commander has an independent command; he is shown in the corps commander typeface. The battle lines, as well as the advance and retreat arrows, show the areas of the action, but they do not always represent the exact size of the commands, such as corps, divisions, and brigades, since they can change during the span of the battle shown on the map. The battle action shown on the Spotsylvania Court House map, for example, shows nearly two weeks of action. The date on each battle map is the date of the action shown on it. The dates for the entire battle are given at the beginning of each essay. The combat strengths and the battle casualties (the total number of soldiers killed, wounded, missing, and taken prisoner) are estimated and based on the best available information. We welcome corrections and new data.

These maps can guide communities in protecting their battlefields as well as guide visitors. For those battles that do not have maps, The Conservation Fund will provide historic site information to interested landowners and community leaders, and will work in partnership with them to protect their battlefields. As research and battlefield preservation move forward, the Fund plans to expand the *Guide*'s detailed information on these battles. Appendix 1 is a list of the battles, alphabetized by state and then by county or city.

The maps that follow the list show the counties that include the terrain where one or more of the 384 battles was fought.

There are many people to whom I am grateful, beginning with my colleagues at The Conservation Fund, particularly the chairman, Patrick F. Noonan. The idea for the *Guide* was his. My special thanks to John F. Turner, the president, and Amy Gibson, Jack Lynn, Garrett Peck, Yvonne Romero, Sally Schreiber, Benjamin W. Sellers III, Megan Sussman, Jody Tick, and Kathy Turner. My thanks again to the advisers to the first edition of the *Guide:* Edwin C. Bearss, the late Edward C. Ezell, Gary W. Gallagher, Herbert M. Hart, James S. Hutchins, T. Destry Jarvis, Jay Luvaas, Robert W. Meinhard, Michael Musick, and Joseph W. A. Whitehorne.

My gratitude to the authors of the essays is boundless. They used their after-vocation time to write their essays and then contributed them pro bono. Their essays help us to learn about the past so that we can learn from it. In providing the details of battle tactics and strategy in their narratives, they have given life to those military terms while expanding our understanding of the Civil War and its meaning for us. There is information about them and their publications in the section About the Authors. I especially appreciate the additional labors undertaken by many of the essayists who, during these four years, joined me in crosschecking and rewriting sections of the book. First, of course, is Edwin C. Bearss, who read the entire book several times. His knowledge of the war and his willingness to share it made this book possible. My special thanks to James M. McPherson for his wise counsel. His book *Battle Cry of Freedom* is the superb one-volume history of the Civil War. My thanks, also, to the following essayists who gave hours of their time to write critiques of sections of the book and added important information: Stacy Allen, Michael J. Andrus, John G. Barrett, Arthur W. Bergeron, Jr., Bob L. Blackburn, Kent Masterson Brown, Christopher M. Calkins, Albert Castel, William C. Davis, Frank Allen Dennis, LeRoy H. Fischer,

Gary W. Gallagher, Clark B. Hall, Richard W. Hatcher III, John J. Hennessy, Lawrence Lee Hewitt, James Oliver Horton, Ludwell H. Johnson, Robert E. L. Krick, Robert K. Krick, David W. Lowe, Richard M. McMurry, T. Michael Parrish, Charles P. Roland, David R. Ruth, William R. Scaife, William L. Shea, Richard J. Sommers, Jan Townsend, Noah Andre Trudeau, Joseph W. A. Whitehorne, Terrence J. Winschel, and Stephen R. Wise. I am also grateful to William J. Cooper, Jr., William deBuys, Shan Holt, and Michael Zuckerman for correcting and guiding sections of the manuscript.

Because of the vision of our predecessors in preservation, America has outstanding professionals, agencies, and nonprofit organizations providing first-rate public history. They include the National Park Service, the state historic preservation offices, historical societies, and the growing number of state historic sites and parks. I am grateful for critiques of the manuscript, including valuable additions and corrections to the battle summaries that I wrote, by the following historians, listed by the state for which they provided information or the state in which they live. Alabama: Bill Rambo. Arkansas: Mark Christ and Jerry Russell. Colorado: W. Richard West, Jr. Florida: Dana C. Bryan, Paul Ghiotto, Bruce Graetz, and David P. Ogden. District of Columbia: Terrence J. Gough and Brigadier General John W. Mountcastle. Georgia: Dan Brown and Roger Durham. Idaho: Larry R. Jones, Brigham D. Madsen, and Katherine Spude. Kansas: Virgil Dean, Ramon Powers, and Dale Watts. Kentucky: Nadine G. Hawkins, David Morgan, Kenneth W. Noe, and Bobby Ray. Louisiana: Greg Potts. Maryland: Ted Alexander. Minnesota: John Crippen and Thomas R. Ellig. Mississippi: Michael Beard. Missouri: Jim Denny, William E. Farrand, Orvis N. Fitts, Tom Higdon, William Garrett Piston, David Roggensees, B. H. Rucker, and Connie Slaughter. New Mexico: Neil Mangum. North Carolina: Jim Bartley, Paul Branch, Win Dough, John C. Goode, Steve Harrison, Michael Hill, and Gehrig Spencer. North Dakota: Walter L. Bailey, Gerard Baker, Leonard Bruguier, and Merlan E.

Paaverud, Jr. Oklahoma: Whit Edwards, William B. Lees, and Neil Mangum. Pennsylvania: Gabor Boritt and Scott Hartwig. South Carolina: J. Tracy Power. Tennessee: Thomas Cartwright, Robert C. Mainfort, James Lee McDonough, James Ogden, Fred M. Prouty, Alethea D. Sayers, Wylie Sword, and Brian Steel Wills. Texas: Archie P. McDonald, James Steely, and Aaron P. Mahr Yanez. Virginia: Daniel J. Beattie, Brandon H. Beck, Kevin Foster, William J. Miller, Robert O'Neill, and John V. Quarstein. West Virginia: Phyllis Baxter, William M. Drennan, Jr., W. Hunter Lesser, Tim McKinney, Mark Mengele, Bruce J. Noble, Jr., and Michael A. Smith. I am grateful to Richard W. Stephenson for writing the captions for the historical maps from the Library of Congress collections; to Richard J. Sommers for his scholarly contributions to the glossary and for providing the historical names for the Virginia battles of Matadequin Creek and Samaria Church; to Brian C. Pohanka for writing the captions for the historical photographs; and to the historians at the Library of Congress, the National Archives, and the National Museum of American History for their assistance in our research. I extend my gratitude to Peg Anderson, to Margo Shearman for her fine work as manuscript editor, and to Harry Foster, friend as well as senior editor at Houghton Mifflin, for his wisdom and guidance.

I am honored to present the principal battles to my fellow Americans and to our visitors from other countries, and to celebrate the union of our states and the abolition of slavery. The *Guide*, as is evident by the many people named above, was made possible by a community effort: generous-spirited historians who shared their knowledge to increase readers' understanding of our Civil War. The remaining errors are mine. I invite our readers to join this community of historians by sending to me their corrections and additional information for the 303 battle summaries that I have written. Many of these battles are little known, but they are critical and merit additional research.

The National Park Service is a national treasure, to be honored by all Americans who care about our history as well as our natural areas. My thanks to the NPS professionals at the Civil War battlefields and to those who — with the people under contract to the Park Service — were the principal staff to the commission: Lawrence E. Aten, the executive director, Denise Dressel, Dale Floyd, Maureen Foster, John J. Knoerl, David W. Lowe, Kathleen Madigan, Marilyn W. Nickels, Katie Ryan, Rebecca Shrimpton, Jan Townsend, and Booker T. Wilson III.

My special thanks to my husband, Roger Kennedy, who, from the beginning of the *Guide* in 1988 to the completion of this second edition, read and cheered, listened and cared.

— Frances H. Kennedy
  Santa Fe, New Mexico,
  Memorial Day, 1998

The Civil War Battlefield Guide

*Second
Edition*

Charleston Harbor: April 1861

Fort Sumter I, South Carolina (SC001), Charleston County, April 12–14, 1861

James M. McPherson

Built to protect Charleston from foreign invasion, Fort Sumter fired its guns only against Americans. This was just one of several ironies associated with this state-of-the-art masonry fort, which, as the Civil War with its rifled artillery was to demonstrate, was already obsolete when it was occupied.

However, Sumter's most important role in the Civil War was not as a fort but as a symbol. By the time of Abraham Lincoln's inauguration as president on March 4, 1861, it was the most important piece of government property still held by United States forces in the seven states that had seceded to form the Confederate States of America. (The others were Fort Pickens, guarding the entrance to Pensacola harbor in Florida, and two minor forts on the Florida Keys.) For months national attention had centered on this huge pentagonal fortress controlling the entrance to Charleston harbor. On the day after Christmas 1860, US Major Robert Anderson had stealthily moved his garrison of 84 U.S. soldiers from ancient Fort Moultrie, adjacent to the mainland, to the five-foot-thick walls of Sumter, built on an artificial island at the mouth of the entrance to Charleston harbor. He had done so to reduce his men's vulnerability to attack by the South Carolina militia, which was swarming around them in the wake of the state's secession six days earlier. A Kentuckian who was married to a Georgian, Anderson deplored the possibility of war between North and South. Sympathetic to his region but loyal to the United States, he hoped that moving the garrison to Sumter would reduce tensions by lowering the possibility of attack. Instead, this action lit a slow fuse that exploded into war on April 12, 1861.

Southerners denounced Anderson's move as a violation of a presumed pledge by President James Buchanan not to violate the status quo in Charleston harbor. But northerners hailed Anderson as a hero. This stiffened the sagging determination of the Buchanan administration to maintain this symbol of national sovereignty in a "seceded" state, which the government and the northern people insisted had no constitutional right to secede. Maintaining that it *did* have such a right, South Carolina established artillery batteries around the harbor, pointing at Sumter. The national government decided to resupply and reinforce Anderson with 200 additional soldiers, to bring the garrison up to half the strength for which Fort Sumter had been designed. To minimize provocation, it chartered a civilian ship, *Star of the West*, instead of sending in a warship with the supplies and reinforcements. But the hotheaded Carolinians fired on *Star of the West* when it attempted to enter the harbor on January 9, 1861, forcing it to turn back and scurry out to sea. Lacking orders and loath to take responsibility for starting a war, Anderson did not return the fire. The guns of Sumter remained silent, and the United States remained at peace.

But this peace grew increasingly tense and fragile over the next three months. During that time six more southern states declared themselves out of the Union. As they seceded, they seized all federal property within their borders — arsenals, customhouses, mints, post offices, and forts — except Fort Sumter and the three other, less important forts. Delegates from the seven states met in Montgomery, Alabama, in February to adopt a constitution and create a government. Elected president of the new Confederate States of America, Jefferson Davis commissioned Pierre G. T. Beauregard as brigadier general and sent him to take command of the troops besieging the Union garrison at Fort Sumter. Meanwhile, all attempts by Congress and by a "peace convention" in Washington failed to come up with a compromise to restore the Union.

This was the situation that confronted Abraham Lincoln when he took the oath of office as

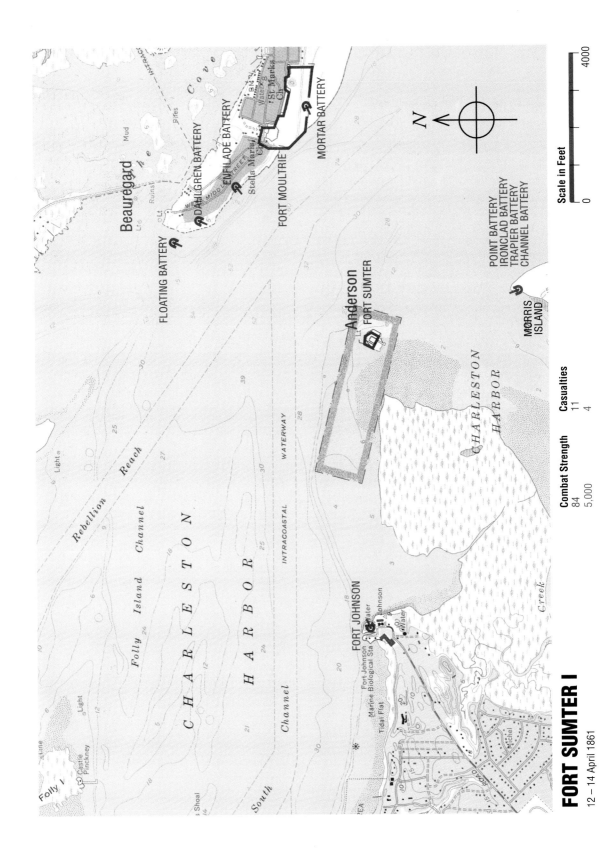

FORT SUMTER I

12 – 14 April 1861

Beauregard

Anderson

DAHLGREN BATTERY

ENFILADE BATTERY

FLOATING BATTERY

FORT MOULTRIE

MORTAR BATTERY

FORT SUMTER

FORT JOHNSON

MORRIS ISLAND

POINT BATTERY
IRONCLAD BATTERY
TRAPIER BATTERY
CHANNEL BATTERY

CHARLESTON HARBOR

CHARLESTON HARBOR

Rebellion Reach

Folly Island Channel

South Channel

INTRACOASTAL WATERWAY

Castle Pinckney

	Combat Strength	Casualties
	84	11
	5,000	4

Scale in Feet

0 — 4000

N

the sixteenth — and, some speculated, the last — president of the United States. In the first draft of his inaugural address, he expressed an intention to use "all the powers at my disposal" to "reclaim the public property and places which have fallen: to hold, occupy, and possess these, and all other property and places belonging to the government." Some of Lincoln's associates regarded the threat to reclaim federal property as too belligerent; they persuaded him to modify the address to state an intention only to "hold, occupy, and possess" government property. This meant primarily Fort Sumter. All eyes now focused on those 2.5 acres of federal real estate in Charleston harbor. Both sides saw it as a powerful emblem of sovereignty. As long as the American flag flew over Sumter, the United States could maintain its claim to be the legal government of South Carolina and the other seceded states. From the southern viewpoint, the Confederacy could not be considered a viable nation as long as a "foreign" power held a fort in one of its principal harbors.

Lincoln had balanced his inaugural vow to "hold, occupy, and possess" this symbol with expressions of peaceful intent in other respects. The peroration appealed to southerners as Americans sharing four score and five years of national history. "We are not enemies, but friends," said Lincoln. "Though passion may have strained, it must not break, our bonds of affection. The mystic chords of memory, stretching from every battlefield and patriot grave to every living heart and hearthstone all over this broad land, will yet swell the chorus of the Union when again touched, as surely they will be, by the better angels of our nature."

Lincoln hoped to buy time with his inaugural address — time for southern passions to cool; time for Unionists in the upper southern states that had not seceded to consolidate their control; time for the Unionists presumed to be in the majority even in seceded states to gain the upper hand. For all of this to happen, though, the status quo at Fort Sumter had to be preserved. If either side moved to change that status quo by force, it would start a war and probably provoke at least four more states into secession.

The day after his inauguration, Lincoln learned that time was running out. Major Anderson warned that his supplies could not last more than six weeks. By then the garrison would have to be resupplied or evacuated. The first option would be viewed by most southerners as provocation; the second would be viewed by the North as surrender.

Lincoln thus faced the most crucial decision of his career at the very beginning of his presidency. US General-in-Chief Winfield Scott advised him that it would take more military and naval power than the government then possessed to shoot its way into the harbor and reinforce Fort Sumter. Besides, this would put the onus of starting a war on the U.S. government. Secretary of State William H. Seward and a majority of the cabinet advised Lincoln to give up the fort in order to preserve the peace and prevent states in the upper South from joining their sister states in the Confederacy. But Montgomery Blair, Lincoln's postmaster general and a member of a powerful political family, insisted that this would be ruinous. It would constitute formal recognition of the Confederacy. It would mean the downfall of the Union, the end of a U.S. government with any claim of sovereignty over its constituent parts. Lincoln was inclined to agree. But what could he do about it? The press, political leaders of all factions, and the public showered reams of contradictory advice on the president. The pressure grew excruciating. Lincoln suffered sleepless nights and severe headaches; one morning he arose from bed and keeled over in a dead faint.

But amid the cacophony and the agony, Lincoln evolved a policy and made a decision. The key provision of his policy was to separate the question of reinforcement from that of resupply. The president decided to send in supplies but to hold troops and warships outside the harbor and authorize them to go into action only if the Confederates acted to stop the supply ships. And he would notify southern officials of his intentions. If Confederate artillery fired on the unarmed supply ships, the South would stand convicted of attacking "a mission of humanity," bringing "food for hungry men."

Lincoln's solution was a stroke of genius. It put the burden of deciding for peace or war on Jefferson Davis's shoulders. In effect, Lincoln flipped a coin and told Davis, "Heads I win; tails you lose." If Davis permitted the supplies to go in peacefully, the American flag would continue to fly over Fort Sumter. If he ordered Beauregard to stop them, the onus of starting a war would fall on the South.

Lincoln notified Governor Francis Pickens of South Carolina on April 6, 1861, that "an attempt will be made to supply Fort Sumter with provisions only, and that if such attempt be not resisted, no effort to throw in men, arms, or ammunition will be made without further notice, [except] in case of an attack on the fort." In response, the Confederate cabinet decided at a fateful meeting in Montgomery to open fire on Fort Sumter and force its surrender before the relief fleet arrived, if possible. Only Secretary of State Robert Toombs opposed this decision. He reportedly told Davis that it "will lose us every friend at the North. You will wantonly strike a hornets' nest. . . . Legions now quiet will swarm out and sting us to death. It is unnecessary. It puts us in the wrong. It is fatal."

Toombs was right. At 4:30 A.M. on April 12, the batteries around Charleston harbor opened fire. After thirty-three hours in which more than four thousand rounds were fired (only one thousand by the undermanned fort), the American flag was lowered in surrender on April 14. The news outraged and galvanized the northern people in the same way in which the Japanese attack on Pearl Harbor eighty years later galvanized the American people. On April 15 Lincoln called out the militia to suppress "insurrection." Northern men flocked to the recruiting offices; southern men did the same, and four more states joined the Confederacy.

By the time the U.S. flag rose again over the rubble that had been Fort Sumter, on April 14, 1865, 3 million men had fought in the armies and navies of the Union and Confederacy. At least 620,000 of them had died — nearly as many as in all the other wars fought by this country combined. Most of the things that we consider impor-

tant in that era of American history — the fate of slavery, the structure of society in both North and South, the direction of the American economy, the destiny of competing nationalisms in North and South, the definition of freedom, the very survival of the United States — rested on the shoulders of those weary men in blue and gray who fought it out during four years of ferocity unmatched in the Western world between the Napoleonic wars and World War I.

Estimated Casualties: 11 US, 4 CS

Fort Sumter National Monument, in Charleston harbor, includes 195 acres of the historic land.

The framers of our Constitution never exhausted so much labor, wisdom, and forbearance in its formation if it was intended to be broken up by every member of the [Union] at will. . . . It is idle to talk of secession. (January 1861)

Save in defense of my native State, I never desire again to draw my sword. (April 1861, following Virginia's secession)

— Robert E. Lee

We feel that our cause is just and holy. We protest solemnly in the face of mankind that we desire peace at any sacrifice save that of honor and independence; we seek no conquest, no aggrandizement, no concession of any kind of the States with which we were lately confederated. All we ask is to be let alone.

— President Jefferson Davis in his message to the special session of the Confederate Congress, April 29, 1861

The Blockade of Chesapeake Bay and the Potomac River: May–June 1861

Sewell's Point, Virginia (VA001), Norfolk, May 18–19, 1861

When the Civil War began, most people thought it would be a short, limited war. The Confederate states — South Carolina, Mississippi, Florida, Alabama, Georgia, Louisiana, Texas, Virginia, Arkansas, North Carolina, and Tennessee — had a population of only 9 million, 3.5 million of whom were slaves, compared with 23 million in the United States: Maine, Vermont, New Hampshire, Massachusetts, Connecticut, Rhode Island, New York, Pennsylvania, New Jersey, Ohio, Indiana, Michigan, Illinois, Wisconsin, Minnesota, Iowa, Oregon, California, and Kansas, admitted in January. (West Virginia was admitted as a free state in 1863 and Nevada in 1864.) The border slave states of Missouri, Kentucky, Delaware, and Maryland did not secede. The Confederacy had only about one-third as many miles of railroads as the North, which made the transportation of both soldiers and supplies more difficult in the South. The economy of the North was more diversified and was expanding, while in the South 80 percent of the labor force worked in agriculture, and cotton was king.

US General-in-Chief Winfield Scott proposed to President Abraham Lincoln a plan to bring the states back into the Union: cut the Confederacy off from the rest of the world instead of attacking its army in Virginia. His plan to blockade the Confederacy's coastline and control the Mississippi River valley with gunboats was dubbed the "Anaconda Plan" by those demanding immediate military action. Lincoln ordered a blockade of the southern seaboard from the South Carolina line to the Rio Grande on April 19 and on April 27 extended it to include the North Carolina and Virginia coasts. On April 20 the Federal navy burned and evacuated the Norfolk Navy Yard, destroying nine ships in the process. Occupation of Norfolk gave the Confederates their only major shipyard and thousands of heavy guns, but they held it for only one year. CS Brigadier General Walter Gwynn, who commanded the Confederate defenses around Norfolk, erected batteries at Sewell's Point, both to protect Norfolk and to control Hampton Roads.

The Union dispatched a fleet to Hampton Roads to enforce the blockade, and on May 18–19 the Federal gunboats *Monticello* and *Thomas Freeborn* exchanged fire with the batteries at Sewell's Point under CS Captain Peyton Colquitt, resulting in little damage to either side.

Estimated Casualties: 10 total

Aquia Creek, Virginia (VA002), Stafford County, May 29–June 1, 1861

In an attempt to close the Potomac to Union shipping, the Confederates constructed land batteries along the south bank of Aquia Creek, covering its confluence with the Potomac River near Stafford. The principal battery was commanded by CS Brigadier General Daniel Ruggles. It was at the foot of the wharf where it protected the northern terminus of the Richmond, Fredericksburg & Potomac Railroad from U.S. gunboats and threatened Union shipping.

On May 29 US Commander James H. Ward steamed downriver with the armed tug *Thomas Freeborn* to shell the works. Two days later he returned with four vessels of the Potomac Flotilla and exchanged fire with the battery until he ran out of ammunition. On June 1 the *Freeborn* and the *Pawnee* sailed to within two thousand yards of the forts. Most of the Confederate artillery fired over their targets and did little damage to the ships. That night the Confederates dug another earthwork north of the creek at Brent's Point. The U.S. vessels sailed away without silencing the batteries but had determined that the range of the Confederate guns was too short to stop Union shipping plying the wide Potomac River.

Estimated Casualties: 10 total

Big Bethel, Virginia (VA003), York County and Hampton, June 10, 1861

The Federals' control of Fort Monroe on the tip of the Virginia Peninsula between the York and James Rivers enabled them to occupy Hampton and Newport News. In order to block Union access up the peninsula from this stronghold, the Confederates dug a mile-long line of entrenchments north of Marsh Creek (now Brick Kiln Creek) near the village of Big Bethel. These were held by 1,200 troops commanded by CS Colonels John B. Magruder and Daniel Harvey Hill. A redoubt south of their line protected a bridge over the stream leading into the Confederate center.

On June 10 US Brigadier General Ebenezer W. Pierce led two infantry columns totaling 3,500 men from Hampton and Newport News to attack the Confederates at Big Bethel. The two columns were to join at the Big Bethel Road, just south of Little Bethel. However, the 7th New York mistook the 3rd New York, clad in gray uniforms, for the enemy. They thought the Confederates were behind as well as in front of them and opened fire. By the time Pierce sorted out his lines and was able to attack, he had lost the advantage of surprise.

While Pierce positioned his artillery opposite the Confederate redoubt covering the bridge, he sent US Major Theodore Winthrop downstream to cross a ford across Marsh Creek and maneuver around the enemy. He engaged the enemy left but deployed his troops piecemeal. The Confederates repulsed the attack, killed Winthrop, and forced the Federals to retreat to Hampton after only an hour of battle.

Estimated Casualties: 76 US, 8 CS

West Virginia: June–December 1861

Philippi, West Virginia (WV001), Barbour County, June 3, 1861

When the Virginia legislature voted to secede from the United States, most of the members from northwest Virginia voted no. There were few slaves in this mountainous region, and the area was more closely aligned with its northern neighbors, Ohio and Pennsylvania, than with the rest of Virginia. The region was strategic for both the United States and the Confederacy. The Baltimore & Ohio Railroad crossed it, linking the East with the Midwest; three major turnpikes ran through gaps in the Allegheny Mountains — the Northwestern, the Staunton to Parkersburg, and the James River and Kanawha; and the Great Kanawha Valley pointed toward Ohio, a potential invasion route. The Virginia Militia acted quickly to control the area and sent CS Colonel Thomas J. Jackson to Harpers Ferry to secure the armory and arsenal and to organize the militia assembling there. The Confederates disrupted the B & O Railroad and seized control of the turnpikes.

While the western Virginians moved toward secession from Virginia, the U.S. government moved in with military force. US Major General George B. McClellan assumed command of the Department of the Ohio to defend the Ohio River valley. US General-in-Chief Winfield Scott directed McClellan to move 20,000 troops into the area. When McClellan's forces occupied Grafton, an important junction on the railroad, the Confederates retreated eighteen miles to Philippi.

On June 2 US Brigadier General Thomas A. Morris marched two columns of five regiments to attack the enemy camped at Philippi. US Colonel Ebenezer Dumont moved south from Webster while US Colonel Benjamin Franklin Kelley's column marched from near Grafton. Converging, they launched a surprise attack the next day at dawn against CS Colonel George A. Porterfield's 775-man force. The Confederates fired a volley, then panicked. The battle became known as the

"Philippi Races" for the speed of the Confederates' retreat to Huttonsville. Philippi was the first land battle of the Civil War.

Estimated Casualties: 5 US, 6 CS

Rich Mountain, West Virginia (WV003), Randolph County, July 11, 1861

Gary W. Gallagher

Western Virginia experienced profound turmoil during June and July 1861. Home to about a quarter of the state's white population, the counties west of the Shenandoah Valley demonstrated little sympathy for secession. Western Virginians had long nursed grievances against their state government, which they believed favored the more heavily slaveholding areas of the Commonwealth. Virginia's decision to secede converted latent support for separate statehood into strident action that culminated in a unionist convention in Wheeling on June 11. The convention declared the Confederate government in Richmond unconstitutional, pronounced itself a "restored government" for the state, selected Francis Pierpont as the governor, and named a full slate of officials to replace those sympathizing with the Confederacy.

Eager to reward this evidence of unionist sentiment, Abraham Lincoln accepted the Wheeling government as legitimate. A legislature in Wheeling that spoke only for residents in the northwestern counties elected a pair of senators and three representatives who took their seats in the United States Congress in mid-July. In one of the war's many ironies western Virginia had taken

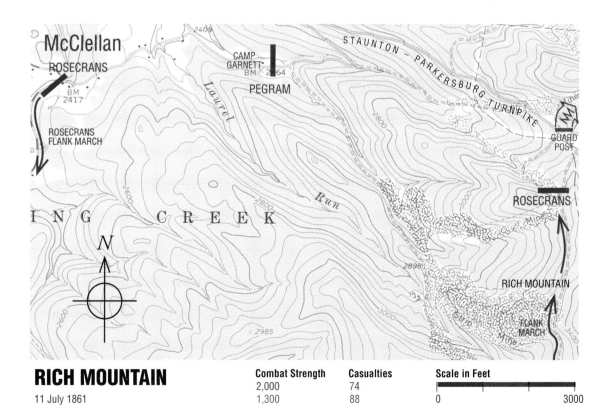

RICH MOUNTAIN

11 July 1861

Combat Strength	Casualties
2,000	74
1,300	88

Scale in Feet

0   3000

critical steps toward seceding from Confederate Virginia.

A military drama unfolded against this backdrop of constitutional struggle. By July 1, 1861, US Major General George B. McClellan commanded more than 20,000 Federal soldiers in northwestern Virginia. Just thirty-four years old, McClellan boasted a sterling reputation in the antebellum army, a daunting intellect, and an unbridled ego. He assured Unionists in the region that his soldiers were "enemies to none but armed rebels and those voluntarily giving them aid."

CS Brigadier General Robert Selden Garnett led the Confederates opposing McClellan. A Virginian, West Point graduate, and veteran of twenty years of antebellum military service, Garnett had been assigned command in northwestern Virginia in June. "They have not given me an adequate force," one witness recalled Garnett's stating just before he left to assume the post. "I can do nothing. They have sent me to my death." Although these words smack of embellishment, Garnett's force numbered only about 4,600 in early July.

Garnett faced a difficult situation. Federals had pressed Confederates southward from Grafton through Philippi toward Beverly, a crucial point on the eastern slope of Rich Mountain that had to be held if Garnett hoped to re-establish control over northwestern Virginia. Garnett placed troops at Buckhannon Pass, through which the Staunton-Parkersburg Turnpike traversed Rich Mountain near Beverly, as well as in the gap on Laurel Hill, which lay north of Beverly and sheltered the Grafton-Beverly Road. Most of the Confederates were with Garnett at Laurel Hill. CS Lieutenant Colonel John Pegram commanded about 1,300 at Rich Mountain, just west of Beverly and ten miles south of Laurel Hill.

McClellan coordinated an advance toward Beverly on July 6. US Brigadier General Thomas A. Morris marched his 4,000-man brigade from Philippi toward Garnett at Laurel Hill while McClellan directed three brigades totaling 8,000 men to concentrate opposite Pegram at Rich Mountain. Skirmishing on July 7–10 persuaded McClellan that he faced Confederates in considerable strength. On the night of July 10 US Brigadier General William S. Rosecrans, who led a Federal brigade at Rich Mountain, persuaded McClellan that he could use rough mountain paths to get around Pegram's left. McClellan instructed Rosecrans to make the flank march with 2,000 men the next morning. At the sound of firing from that column, the remaining Federals would assail Pegram's position from the west. Morris would keep watch on Garnett at Laurel Hill.

Pegram anticipated an attempt to flank his position on July 11 but thought it would be against his right. Noon approached on a rain-swept day when Confederate pickets reported Federals to the southeast. Rosecrans soon attacked in force down the crest of Rich Mountain, scattered some 310 men guarding the Confederate rear, and cut Pegram's command off from Beverly. McClellan failed to launch supporting assaults, however, fumbling an opportunity for more decisive results. During a confused retreat, Pegram's men split into several groups. Several hundred escaped to Staunton, but Pegram surrendered more than 550 exhausted soldiers on July 13.

The disaster at Rich Mountain isolated Garnett at Laurel Hill. Shelled by Morris's artillery during July 11, the Confederates expected to be attacked. Apprised that evening of Pegram's defeat, Garnett decided to retreat on the twelfth. Slogging through rain along horrible roads, the column moved northeast into the Cheat River valley. On July 13 elements of Morris's brigade attacked Garnett's force at Corricks Ford on Shavers Fork of the Cheat River. Mortally wounded while directing his rear guard, Garnett became the first general to die in the war. Most of his men eventually eluded the Federal pursuit.

The engagement at Rich Mountain yielded important results. Although Rosecrans deserved credit for the conception and execution of the Federal plan, northern newspapers lavished praise on his superior. McClellan overestimated Confederate numbers, vacillated when fighting began, and otherwise exhibited behavior for which he later would become notorious — but he basked in adulation from across the North and quickly moved to the forefront of Union military leaders. Politically the Confederate withdrawal left northwestern Virginia in Federal control and opened the way for another session of the Wheeling convention to vote for separate statehood in August. Many far larger battles of the war had fewer far-reaching consequences.

Estimated Casualties: 74 US, 88 CS

Rich Mountain Battlefield Civil War Site, which includes Camp Garnett, is five miles west of Beverly on Rich Mountain Road and is open to the public. The four hundred protected acres are managed by the Rich Mountain Battlefield Foundation and are owned by the foundation, the Randolph County Development Authority, and the Association for the Preservation of Civil War Sites.

Kessler's Cross Lanes, West Virginia (WV004), Nicholas County, August 26, 1861

On July 28 CS General Robert E. Lee left Richmond to oversee and coordinate the Confederate forces in northwest Virginia after their loss at Rich Mountain. They were commanded by four brigadier generals — one soldier (William W. Loring), one diplomat (Henry R. Jackson), and two former governors of Virginia (John B. Floyd and Henry A. Wise) — who would not cooperate.

Wise's force occupied Charleston until the loss at Rich Mountain prompted him to retreat to the Gauley River. Early on August 26, CS Brigadier General John B. Floyd's men crossed the Gauley River and attacked US Colonel Erastus Tyler's 7th Ohio Regiment at Kessler's Cross Lanes. In an hour's battle they routed the Federals, who escaped by various routes to Gauley Bridge. Floyd withdrew to a defensive position to control the important crossing of the Gauley River at Carnifex Ferry.

Estimated Casualties: 132 US, 40 CS

Carnifex Ferry, West Virginia (WV006), Nicholas County, September 10, 1861

When US General McClellan was named commander of the Army of the Potomac after his victory at Rich Mountain, US General Rosecrans assumed command of the Federal forces in northwest Virginia. After US Colonel Tyler's loss at Kessler's Cross Lanes, Rosecrans marched three brigades (5,000 men) south from Clarksburg on the Gauley Bridge–Weston Turnpike. They advanced against CS General Floyd's 1,740-man brigade at Carnifex Ferry on the afternoon of September 10. Rosecrans pushed Floyd's pickets in and penned the Confederates into their fortified camp in a bend in the river. Floyd's troops repelled the Federal assaults. The Confederates retreated from Carnifex to Big Sewell Mountain on the Fayette/Greenbrier County line and encamped on September 13. Three days later they withdrew sixteen miles to Meadow Bluff in Greenbrier County where CS General Lee joined them.

Floyd blamed the defeat on CS General Wise, who had delayed in sending Floyd adequate reinforcements. This increased the dissension among the Confederates. Both brigades retreated twenty miles to Sewell Mountain where each established its own defensive position.

Estimated Casualties: 158 US, 32 CS

Carnifex Ferry Battlefield State Park, twelve miles from Summersville near Route 129, includes about 156 acres of the historic battlefield.

Cheat Mountain, West Virginia (WV005), Pocahontas County, September 12–15, 1861

After their victory at Rich Mountain, the Federals concentrated their forces in two strategic locations to protect the two vital turnpikes. In the south 4,500 men protected Gauley Bridge, where the James River and Kanawha Turnpike crossed the Gauley just above its confluence with the New to form the Kanawha River. Seventy miles to the northeast the Federals constructed a strong fort on the east summit of Cheat Mountain to protect the Staunton-Parkersburg Turnpike. They massed 9,000–11,000 troops in the area. US Brigadier General Joseph J. Reynolds commanded 3,000 on Cheat Mountain.

CS General Loring commanded the 11,000-man Army of the Northwest at Valley Mountain. CS General Lee arrived to coordinate the assault, and the two generals devised a complicated plan to attack the Federals at Cheat Mountain. The main body under Lee and Loring advanced in a heavy rain through the Tygart Valley to defeat the Federals at Elkwater. A second force led by CS Brigadier General Samuel R. Anderson was to isolate and attack the entrenched Union position on the west summit of Cheat Mountain. CS Colonel Albert Rust was to begin the action by assaulting Cheat Summit Fort on the east side of Cheat Mountain. Despite the bad weather and a rugged march through the wilderness, Rust arrived undetected on the turnpike near the fort on September 12. He lost the element of surprise, however, when he blundered into Federal wagons one half mile from the fort. He was deterred by a small reconnaissance force led by US Colonel Nathan Kimball of the 14th Indiana, decided not to attack, and returned to his camp. Lee called off the attack after three days of skirmishing.

Lee withdrew to Valley Mountain on September 15 and returned to Richmond without a success on October 30. Wise was recalled to Richmond, and Floyd was sent to command Fort Donelson, Tennessee.

Estimated Casualties: 71 US, 100 CS

Greenbrier River, West Virginia (WV007), Pocahontas County, October 3, 1861

During the night of October 2–3 two brigades under US General Reynolds marched twelve miles down the Staunton-Parkersburg Turnpike from Cheat Mountain to Camp Bartow on the Greenbrier River to break up the camps of CS Brigadier General Henry R. Jackson's brigade. At 7:00 A.M. on October 3, Reynolds opened fire with artillery from across the river. During the morning he attempted to cross the river and flank Jackson's right and left. Both attacks were repulsed. Reynolds resumed his artillery bombardment for several hours but failed to dislodge the Confederates. The Federals retreated to Cheat Mountain that afternoon.

Estimated Casualties: 43 US, 52 CS

Camp Allegheny, West Virginia (WV008), Pocahontas County, December 13, 1861

CS Colonel Edward Johnson's forces occupied the summit of the 4,500-foot Allegheny Mountain to cover the Staunton-Parkersburg Turnpike. US Brigadier General Robert H. Milroy's force marched from Cheat Mountain and attacked Johnson on December 13. The Federals failed to coordinate their flank attacks in the rough terrain, so the Confederates were able to shift their troops to maintain a successful defense. By midafternoon Milroy had gained no advantage and withdrew. As a result of the battle Johnson was made a brigadier general and given the nom de guerre "Allegheny."

The five Confederate regiments at Camp Allegheny and the two at Lewisburg were the Confederacy's only troops in the area. Both sides suffered in the cold of their winter camps in the mountains.

Estimated Casualties: 137 US, 146 CS

Manassas Campaign: July 1861

Hoke's Run (Falling Waters), West Virginia (WV002), Berkeley County, July 2, 1861

The United States and the Confederacy both concentrated strong forces near Washington, D.C., during the late spring and early summer of 1861. The Confederates in northern Virginia under CS Brigadier General P. G. T. Beauregard deployed along Bull Run to protect the railroad at Manassas Junction. The Federals, commanded by US Brigadier General Irvin McDowell, gathered behind the capital's defenses. The first major offensive against the Confederacy was McDowell's attack on Beauregard's smaller army at Bull Run. McDowell ordered US Major General Robert Patterson's 18,000-man force to pen CS Brigadier General Joseph E. Johnston and his 11,000 Confederates in the Shenandoah Valley and prevent them from reinforcing Beauregard.

On July 2 Patterson crossed the Potomac River near Williamsport, Maryland, and marched along the Valley Pike to Martinsburg. Near Hoke's Run the brigades of US Colonels John J. Abercrombie and George H. Thomas encountered CS Colonel Thomas J. Jackson's regiments. Jackson followed orders to delay the Union advance and fell back slowly. On July 3 Patterson occupied Martinsburg, and on July 15 he marched to Bunker Hill. Instead of advancing on Johnston's headquarters at Winchester, Patterson turned east toward Charles Town and withdrew to Harpers Ferry. Patterson's withdrawal allowed Johnston's army to move out of the valley and reinforce Beauregard at First Manassas.

After the battle Jackson was promoted to brigadier general, effective June 17.

Estimated Casualties: 73 US, 25 CS

Blackburn's Ford, Virginia (VA004), Prince William and Fairfax Counties, July 18, 1861

On July 16 US General McDowell's untried army of 35,000 marched from the Washington defenses to battle CS General Beauregard's 21,000 men at the vital railroad junction at Manassas. Advancing southwest at a crawl through the July heat, McDowell reached Fairfax Court House on July 17 and tried to find a crossing of Bull Run so he could flank the Confederate army. Beauregard anticipated him and posted troops at seven crossings.

On July 18 McDowell sent his vanguard under US Brigadier General Daniel Tyler southeast from Centreville to reconnoiter the stream at Blackburn's Ford. Instead, Tyler attacked the Confederates guarding the ford. The brigades of CS Brigadier General James Longstreet and CS Colonel Jubal A. Early repulsed US Colonel Israel B. Richardson's brigade. This reconnaissance-in-force before the main battle at Manassas ruled out a head-on attack along Bull Run. McDowell decided to try to outflank the Confederates by crossing the stream beyond their left flank.

Estimated Casualties: 83 US, 68 CS

First Manassas, Virginia (VA005), Prince William County, July 21, 1861

William Glenn Robertson

When the Civil War began in April 1861, most Americans expected the conflict to be brief, with one titanic battle deciding the outcome. The placement of the Confederate capital at Richmond, Virginia, a hundred miles from Washington, D.C., virtually guaranteed a clash somewhere between the two cities before the end of summer. Needing a buffer zone around Washington, Federal units in late May crossed the Potomac River and secured the heights of Arlington and the town of Alexandria. Engineers immediately began construction of an extensive line of fortifications to protect the capital. Equally important, the works would provide a secure base for offensive operations against Richmond. Since US General-in-Chief Winfield Scott was too infirm to take the field in person, command of the army gathering behind the rising fortifications went to US Brigadier General Irvin McDowell. Upstream, a smaller force under US Major General Robert Patterson threatened the Shenandoah Valley.

South of Washington Confederate troops gathered around the important railroad center of Manassas Junction. In June CS Brigadier General P. G. T. Beauregard, victor of Fort Sumter, took command of the Manassas line, while a smaller force under CS Brigadier General Joseph E. Johnston guarded the Shenandoah Valley. Analyzing the terrain and the troop dispositions of both sides, Beauregard concluded that an advance against Manassas Junction was imminent. He decided to defend Manassas Junction along the line of Bull Run, three miles east of the rail center. He also believed that the widely scattered Confederate units would be defeated unless he and Johnston consolidated their forces before the Federals could strike. Since he could get no assurance that Johnston would be ordered to Manassas, he began to strengthen his line. The Confederacy did not expect to mount an offensive, only to repulse any Federal thrust against Manassas Junction.

Beauregard's analysis of Federal intentions was essentially correct. McDowell was under pressure from the politicians, the press, and the public to begin an advance. Unsure of himself and his green troops, he begged unsuccessfully for more time to prepare his army. Ordered to advance before the end of July, he planned a three-pronged movement against the Confederates defending Manassas Junction. The plan required Patterson to prevent Johnston's units from joining Beauregard at Manassas. By early July, Patterson's 18,000 troops had crossed the Potomac. Johnston's 11,000 Confederates fell back to Winchester, Virginia. If Patterson could maintain the pressure on Johnston, McDowell's 35,000 troops would have a very good chance of defeating Beauregard's 21,000 men at Manassas Junction.

Everything therefore depended on the two Federal armies acting in concert.

Although he was attempting to create and lead into battle the largest field army yet seen in North America, McDowell was not permitted to delay his advance beyond July 16. The populace demanded an "On to Richmond" movement, and it was McDowell's task to provide it. Consequently, in mid-July he organized his sixty separate regiments and batteries into brigades and divisions to facilitate their command and control. All of his five division commanders — Brigadier Generals Daniel Tyler and Theodore Runyon and Colonels David Hunter, Samuel P. Heintzelman, and Dixon Miles — were older than McDowell, and several had more experience, but none had ever seen, much less commanded, the numbers that would be following them to Bull Run.

Around Manassas Junction, Beauregard also struggled to equip and train enthusiastic but raw recruits. To accomplish that task, he divided his army into seven infantry brigades. All of his brigade commanders — Brigadier Generals Richard S. Ewell, James Longstreet, David R. Jones, and Milledge L. Bonham, and Colonels Nathan G. Evans, Philip St. George Cooke, and Jubal A. Early — were either West Point graduates or veterans of previous wars, or both. Deploying his troops on a six-mile front along the south bank of Bull Run, Beauregard concentrated the bulk of his infantry on his right center, where the Centreville-Manassas Road entered his lines. Bull Run itself was a modest defensive barrier, but there were far more crossing points than Beauregard could guard effectively.

Because of the heat and the lack of troop discipline, the Federal advance was glacially slow. Reaching Fairfax Court House at noon on July 17, McDowell rested his men while he looked for routes around the Confederate eastern flank. On July 18, he sent Tyler to seize Centreville and probe carefully beyond it. Unfortunately, Tyler blundered into an unproductive fight with the Confederates at Blackburn's Ford. Disconcerted by these setbacks, McDowell spent the next two days at Centreville, perfecting his organization

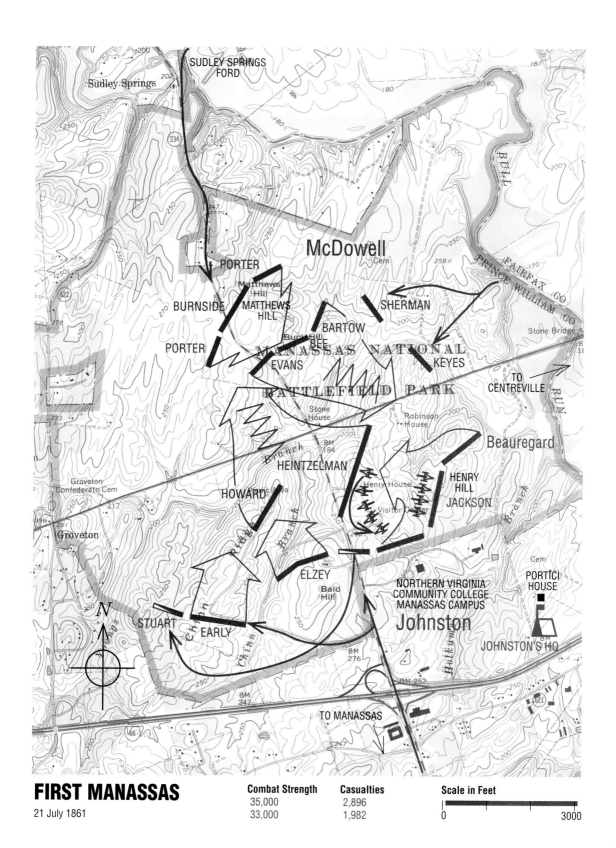

FIRST MANASSAS

21 July 1861

Combat Strength	Casualties
35,000	2,896
33,000	1,982

Scale in Feet

0   3000

and devising a new plan of attack. The new formulation envisioned a one-division feint at Stone Bridge on the Warrenton Turnpike while two divisions marched northwest to Sudley Ford, crossed Bull Run, and swept down on Beauregard's left. The attack was set for dawn on July 21.

McDowell's delay at Centreville gave Beauregard time to gather his scattered units. More important, on July 18 the Confederate government reluctantly permitted Johnston to evacuate Winchester and join Beauregard at Manassas Junction. Leaving a cavalry screen to deceive Patterson, Johnston marched toward Piedmont Station, where trains of the Manassas Gap Railroad awaited him. His leading brigade, led by CS Brigadier General Thomas J. Jackson, reached Beauregard on July 19; Johnston and parts of two other brigades arrived at Manassas Junction the next day. This exertion overtaxed the capacity of the railroad, however, so that parts of Johnston's army were left at Piedmont Station. Nevertheless, by virtue of his seniority, Johnston assumed command of the united Confederate forces.

Unaware that Patterson had withdrawn from Hoke's Run, permitting Johnston to leave the valley, McDowell ordered his army forward early on July 21. As before, things went wrong quickly. Tyler's men initially blocked the road to be used by the flanking divisions of Hunter and Heintzelman. When Tyler finally began his demonstration, his performance was so unconvincing that the opposing commander, Nathan Evans, began to suspect a ruse. When he learned from both pickets and signalmen that a Federal column was moving beyond his flank, Evans left four companies to deceive Tyler and took the remainder of his small brigade toward Sudley Ford. Arriving on Matthews Hill with little more than 900 men, Evans was just in time to block the advance of Hunter's 6,000 troops. He held his position alone until reinforced by the brigades of CS Brigadier General Barnard E. Bee and CS Colonel Francis F. Bartow, both from Johnston's army.

Eventually, sheer weight of numbers pushed Evans, Bee, and Bartow off Matthews Hill and into full retreat. Unfortunately, McDowell's green troops were slow to exploit their advantage. Beyond them the three shattered Confederate brigades climbed to the cleared plateau of Henry Hill. There they found Jackson's Brigade, which was just forming in line. Uttering the immortal remark "There is Jackson standing like a stone wall," Bee rallied his remnants behind Jackson. Others did likewise, and by early afternoon Beauregard and Johnston had gathered approximately 7,000 men along the rear edge of Henry Hill. Still, McDowell retained a significant strength advantage. After a one-hour lull in preparation for a final effort, he advanced two artillery batteries to suppress the defenders' fire. The batteries were devastated by Confederate artillery and a Confederate counterattack, but the infantry fight continued around the abandoned guns.

Early in the battle Beauregard and Johnston had agreed that the former would direct the battle line while the latter dispatched reinforcements from the rear. During the afternoon Johnston's efforts led to the arrival on the Confederate left of several fresh brigades. Under the pressure of these units, in late afternoon the Federal right began to crumble. At that moment Beauregard ordered a general advance, and the Confederate line swept forward. The Federal brigades gave way in confusion and could not be rallied, despite the best efforts of McDowell and other officers. Believing that the day was lost, thousands of Federal soldiers made their way to the rear as best they could. A few Confederate units followed a short distance toward Centreville, but Johnston's and Beauregard's men were in no condition to conduct a meaningful pursuit, and none was attempted.

Considering the number of troops available, the losses were not excessive on either side. McDowell had lost 2,896 (killed, wounded, or missing) from his army of approximately 35,000. He had also left behind twenty-seven cannons, nearly a hundred vehicles, several thousand shoulder arms, and great quantities of equipment. The Confederate victory cost Johnston and Beauregard 1,982 casualties from their combined forces of 33,000 officers and men. Both sides lost heavily in senior officers because of the need to lead the inexperienced troops by example.

Although Johnston had done more to achieve the Confederate victory, Beauregard received most of the adulation. In defeat, McDowell became the scapegoat for the mistakes of many besides himself. As for the men of both sides, most had acquitted themselves as well as could have been expected, given their inexperience.

The battle showed that those who expected a short war were utterly mistaken. It took four long years and a great many battles far more horrible than First Manassas to bring an end to the American Civil War.

Estimated Casualties: 2,896 US, 1,982 CS

Manassas National Battlefield Park, on Route 29 and Interstate 66 near Manassas, twenty-six miles southwest of Washington, D.C., includes 5,072 acres of the historic battlefield; 715 acres are privately owned.

The Staff Ride and Civil War Battlefields

William A. Stofft

If history is the memory of mankind, then military history is the memory of the profession of arms. First-rate armies have consistently required their leaders to undertake the systematic study of military history. This has been true, with brief exceptions, throughout the history of the U.S. Army. As the success of our deterrent strategy lengthens the period of peace and broadens the gap between training and battle experience, military history plays a greater role in the training and education of army leaders as a legitimate and necessary experience in preparation for national defense.

As Dwight David Eisenhower, general of the army and president of the United States, stated in his foreword to *The West Point Atlas of American Wars:*

> Through a careful and objective study of the significant campaigns of the world, a professional officer acquires a knowledge of military experience which he himself could not otherwise accumulate. The facts of a given battle may no longer serve any practical purpose except as a framework on which to base an analysis; but when the serious student of the military art delves into the reasons for the failure of a specific attack — or soberly analyzes the professional qualities of one of the responsible commanders of the past — he is, by this very activity, preparing for a day in which he, under different circumstances, may be facing decisions of vital consequence to his country.

The staff ride is a long-standing tradition in our army. Revisiting battlefields in a thoughtful and structured way helps connect today's officers to military history. In 1906 the assistant commander of the Staff College at Fort Leavenworth, Kansas, took twelve student officers to the Civil War battlefields of Georgia. Up through the 1930s these staff rides played an important role in the Leavenworth curriculum. They were begun again in the late 1960s and early 1970s by the Army War College at Carlisle, Pennsylvania, the Command and General Staff College at Leavenworth, and the United States Military Academy at West Point.

Today the U.S. Army tramps battlefields around the world wherever American soldiers are stationed. In 1987 army organizations reported well over three hundred staff rides, an average of nearly one per day, illustrating the importance of the ride as a teaching technique.

There are three basic phases of the staff ride. The preliminary study phase may take various forms, depending upon the available time. Through formal classroom instruction, individual study, or a combination of both, students learn the purpose of the exercise and acquire a basic knowledge of the campaign and battle by studying memoirs, after-action reports, and secondary sources.

In the field study phase, having read extensively about the battle, the students follow the course of the action on the field. At various places the leader stops to make significant points. Some individuals may play out the roles of the actual staff officers and commanders. Discussion of both facts and interpretation is encouraged. What happened? How did it happen? Why did it happen that way?

The final phase, integration, takes place on the battlefield immediately after the field study. The staff ride leader moderates the discussion, placing the battlefield just visited in the context of today's army and its problems.

The lessons learned on former battlefields are endless. At Gettysburg, for example, the student officers, including lieutenants and four-star generals, learn to appreciate the importance of terrain and understand the influence of technology on warfare, the functioning of the military staff, the role of logistics, and the necessity for good intelligence and communications. Leadership examples abound; one of the most moving is that of Colonel Joshua Lawrence Chamberlain, the professor from Maine, whose leadership at Little Round Top during the battle of Gettysburg provides inspiration even today.

The use today by the U.S. Army of our national battlefield parks underscores the foresight of those who in the 1890s campaigned successfully to have Congress enact legislation to establish the nation's first five battlefield parks. The legislated mission of these parks was to preserve and protect the hallowed ground on which these great battles were fought, to commemorate the battle participants, and to provide field classrooms for the U.S. military officer corps.

Northern Virginia: October–December 1861

Ball's Bluff, Virginia (VA006), Loudoun County, October 21, 1861

On October 21 US Brigadier General Charles P. Stone oversaw a poorly coordinated attempt to cross the Potomac River into Virginia at Harrison's Island and to advance on Leesburg. The demonstration that was designed to give US Major General George B. McClellan a quick victory by compelling the Confederates to evacuate Leesburg erupted into a bitter engagement. US Colonel Edward D. Baker, a senator from Oregon and friend of President Abraham Lincoln, did not order a reconnaissance before he led his brigade across the river and attacked. CS Brigadier General Nathan G. "Shanks" Evans's men were well positioned inland from a seventy-foot bluff. In their counterattack the Confederates drove the Federals into the river, took more than 700 prisoners, and killed Baker.

The Union rout and rumors of incompetence led to the establishment of the Congressional Joint Committee on the Conduct of War. Stone was arrested even though the disaster was the result of Baker's inept leadership.

Estimated Casualties: 921 US, 149 CS

Dranesville, Virginia (VA007), Fairfax County, December 20, 1861

On December 20 CS Brigadier General J. E. B. Stuart led four infantry regiments, a company of artillery, and cavalry to protect a foraging expedition near Dranesville. When he reached Dranesville at 1:00 P.M., he found the village occupied by US Brigadier General Edward O. C. Ord's five Pennsylvania regiments, including the one that gained fame as flamboyant marksmen, the Bucktails, supported by four cannons deployed along the Georgetown Pike. The Confederates attacked and drove in the Union right be-

fore Ord stopped them. Stuart's forces retreated at about 3:00 P.M. after having secured their wagons and forage.

Estimated Casualties: 71 US, 230 CS

Blockade of the Potomac River: September 1861– March 1862

Cockpit Point, Virginia (VA100), Prince William County, January 3, 1862

After his victory at Manassas, CS General Joseph E. Johnston established a new defensive line, with the left anchored on Leesburg, the center on Centreville, and the right along the Occoquan River to the Potomac River. The Confederates built batteries along the Potomac south of the Occoquan on a series of points that jutted into the river. Freestone Point, Cockpit Point (Possum Nose), Shipping Point (now Quantico), and Evansport became a six-mile gauntlet of thirty-seven heavy guns positioned to close the river to Federal traffic. CS Brigadier General Samuel G. French commanded the batteries and was supported by CS Brigadier General W. H. C. Whiting's Brigade camped at Dumfries.

The Union's Potomac Flotilla discovered the guns on Freestone Point on September 23 and in a daring raid on October 11 by the crew of the *Resolute*, burned the *Martha Washington*, which was anchored in Quantico Creek. The Federals did not learn of the other batteries until October 15, when the Confederates fired on the *Seminole* and the *Pocahontas* commanded by USN Commander Percival Drayton. The ships that ran the gauntlet were rarely damaged because the river was wide and they moved at night close to the opposite shore. While the battery was an economic and military threat, it was also a political embarrassment, so the Lincoln administration routed all supplies headed for Washington, D.C., through Baltimore and over the B & O Railroad. On January 3 USN Commander R. H. Wyman ordered the gunboats *Anacostia* and *Yankee* to shell the guns on Cockpit Point. Return fire from two heavy guns damaged the *Yankee,* and Wyman withdrew.

In early March Johnston evacuated Centreville and retreated behind the Rappahannock River to oppose US Major General George B. McClellan's Peninsula campaign. The night of March 8–9 the Confederates abandoned their batteries and their attempt to close the Potomac River.

Estimated Casualties: none

Missouri: June–October 1861

Boonville, Missouri (MO001), Cooper County, June 17, 1861

Missouri was admitted as a slave state, balanced by the new free state of Maine, in the Missouri Compromise in 1820. The expansion of settlement west of the Mississippi had forced the decision on extending slavery into the territories. The compromise divided the enormous Louisiana Purchase along the 36°30' parallel, permitting slavery south of it but not north of it, except for Missouri.

The Northwest Ordinance had been the first national legislation to limit the expansion of slavery. It was enacted in 1787 under the Articles of Confederation and confirmed by the first U.S. Congress after the Constitution was ratified. The ordinance prohibited slavery in the Northwest Territory, the area north of the Ohio River between the Appalachian Mountains and the Mississippi River. Slavery was not prohibited in the territory south of the Ohio.

The Missouri Compromise was the first major compromise over slavery after those in the Constitution. Slavery had been structured into the legal system of the United States through the Constitution, ratified in 1788, although the document did not include the words *slave* or *slavery.* Article I provided that three fifths of the number of "all other Persons" (slaves) in a state were to be added to the number of "free Persons" to determine the number of members a state would be allocated in the House of Representatives. It also provided that Congress could not prohibit the importation of "such Persons" (slaves) before 1808. Article IV provided for the first fugitive slave law: a "Person held to Service or Labour" will be "delivered up on Claim" to the "Party to whom such Service or Labour may be due."

Missouri, like the three other border states (Kentucky, Maryland, and Delaware), permitted slavery but did not vote to secede in 1861 because citizen opinion was divided. The state was important to the Lincoln administration because of the three major rivers (the Ohio, the Missouri, and the Mississippi), rich natural resources, sizable population, and the trails to the West that began there. To encourage the pro-Unionists, US Captain Nathaniel Lyon, commander of the Federal arsenal in St. Louis, was promoted to brigadier general. Lyon was a Connecticut soldier, outstanding leader, and fiery opponent of slavery. The governor, Claiborne Fox Jackson, had led proslavery invaders from Missouri into Kansas. Jackson and his Democratic administration were for slavery and secession but were thwarted by the vote against secession in the state convention. Jackson appealed to the Confederacy for help, and President Jefferson Davis sent four cannons and ammunition in crates marked "marble." The governor installed them at "Camp Jackson" outside St. Louis where he was drilling his prosecessionist Missouri state militia.

On May 10 Lyon's troops, including army regulars and German-American Unionists, captured and disarmed 700 state militiamen at Camp Jackson without violence. However, when they marched their prisoners through St. Louis, secessionists rioted. The 28 killed or wounded included civilians.

On May 12, with the support of the legislature in Jefferson City, the governor named Sterling Price, former governor and general in the Mexican war, the commander of a new force called the Missouri State Guard (MSG). On June 11 Governor Jackson and Major General Price met with Lyon and Representative Francis P. Blair, Jr., of St. Louis at the Planter's House hotel to discuss their irreconcilable positions. Lyon ended the meeting, declaring, "This means war."

Lyon advanced on Jefferson City to evict the governor before the secessionists had fully assembled. He occupied the capital on June 15, and Jackson's government moved westward to Boonville on the Missouri River. Lyon moved 1,700 men to Boonville by steamboat two days later and routed a smaller, poorly armed and trained MSG force commanded by Colonel John S. Marma-

duke. The occupation of Boonville established Union control of the Missouri River — the richest corridor in the state — and dampened secession efforts. Jackson and Price retreated separately to the southwest corner of Missouri, closer to potential help from Arkansas Confederates.

Estimated Casualties: 12 US, 8–12 MSG

Carthage, Missouri (MO002), Jasper County, July 5, 1861

While advancing on Boonville, US General Lyon sent forces to southwestern Missouri to cut off the MSG's retreat. Price reached the area first, began raising forces, and appealed to CS Brigadier General Ben McCulloch in Arkansas for help. Meanwhile Governor Jackson gathered a large MSG force at Lamar and began moving south on July 4 to join Price. On July 5 Jackson learned of the approach of a column of Federals under US Colonel Franz Sigel and established a line of battle about six miles north of Carthage. Unaware that he was outnumbered more than four to one, Sigel attacked with 1,100 men and was driven back through Carthage in a running fight lasting several hours. Sigel then rejoined the main force at Springfield.

McCulloch had joined Price in a forced march to Carthage, but the battle ended before their arrival. The Confederates returned to Arkansas. Price established a Missouri State Guard camp on Cowskin Prairie to train his 7,000–8,000 recruits, while Jackson departed on a political mission to Memphis and Richmond. Lyon reached Springfield in mid-July, bringing the Union forces there to more than 5,000. Unionists from the earlier state convention that had rejected secession met in the state capital, Jefferson City, declared their government the provisional government of a state in the United States, and ruled the state until 1865.

Estimated Casualties: 44 US, 74 MSG

The Battle of Carthage State Historic Site is on Chestnut Street in Carthage and includes 7.4 acres of the historic battlefield.

Wilson's Creek, Missouri (MO004), Greene and Christian Counties, August 10, 1861

Richard W. Hatcher III

Missouri was strategically important to the western half of the nation because the major trails to the West Coast—the California, Oregon, Santa Fe, and Pony Express trails—all began on its western edge. In addition, the three major shipping rivers of the United States—the Mississippi, the Missouri, and the Ohio—flow through or next to Missouri.

On August 6 CS Brigadier General Ben McCulloch's 12,000- to 13,000-man army camped twelve miles southeast of Springfield where Telegraph Road crossed Wilson's Creek. On the night of the ninth McCulloch canceled his dawn attack on the Federals in Springfield when rain threatened to soak the paper cartridges his men carried in their pockets or in cloth bags, effectively disarming them. The regular Confederate troops under McCulloch were somewhat better equipped than Major General Sterling Price's pro-Confederate Missouri State Guard, but many who had firearms had only short-range 1812-style flintlocks and muzzle-loading fowling pieces. The troops settled back into camp, but the pickets did not return to their posts.

The Union soldiers in Springfield, commanded by US Brigadier General Nathaniel Lyon, were in a precarious situation. The newly appointed commander of the Western Department, US Major General John C. Frémont in St. Louis, had denied Lyon reinforcements. Lyon had additional concerns. Many of his men had not been paid, others were poorly clothed and fed, and a large proportion of them were ninety-day enlistees whose term of service would soon end.

Lyon decided to attack and divided his army into three units. One stayed in Springfield to guard the city and the army's supply wagons. The other two marched out on the night of August 9 for a dawn attack. US Colonel Franz Sigel led one column of 1,200 men of the 3rd and 5th Missouri Volunteer Infantry Regiments, and Lyon led the other with 4,200 men. At 5:00 A.M. on August 10 Lyon's column launched its surprise attack down the west side of Wilson's Creek, driving a small Confederate cavalry force back onto "Bloody Hill" and into a retreat down the hill's south slope. By 6:00 A.M. the Federals had reached the crest of the hill. As they moved across its north face, CS Captain William E. Woodruff's Pulaski Artillery, located on a ridge on the east side of the creek, roared into action. It enfiladed Lyon's line, slowing the Union advance and giving Price the time he needed to form his infantry into battle lines to counterattack.

On hearing Lyon's attack, Sigel, positioned on a ridge east of Wilson's Creek and about two miles south of the Confederate cavalry camps, opened fire on the main camp with four of his six cannons. Taken by surprise, the Confederates abandoned their camp and fled to the north and west. Sigel crossed the creek, turned north, and moved into position on a knoll, blocking Telegraph Road.

By 6:30 A.M. the battle lines on Bloody Hill had been established, and the level of fighting had increased dramatically. To guard the Union left flank, Lyon sent US Captain Joseph B. Plummer's infantry column to the east side of Wilson's Creek. This force witnessed the effect of the Pulaski Artillery on the main column and advanced toward the battery. McCulloch countered this attack by sending CS Colonel James McIntosh with two regiments against the Federals. After a brief fight in John Ray's cornfield, the Union column was defeated and retreated back across Wilson's Creek. This action secured the east side of the battlefield for the Confederates and permitted

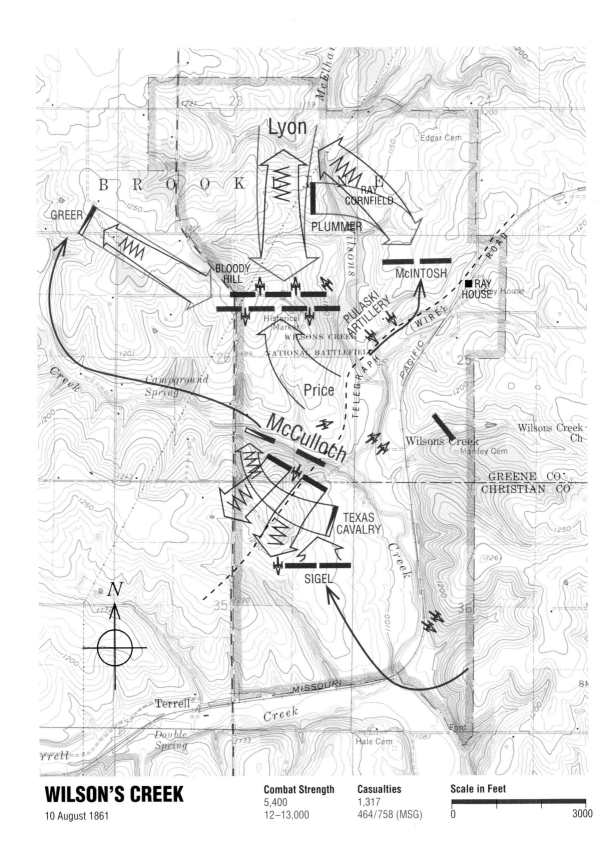

Lyon

BROOKE

GREER

RAY
CORNFIELD

PLUMMER

BLOODY
HILL

McINTOSH

RAY
HOUSE

PULASKI
ARTILLERY

Price

McCulloch

TEXAS
CAVALRY

SIGEL

Wilsons Creek

GREENE CO.
CHRISTIAN CO.

Wilsons Creek
Ch.

N

Terrell

Double
Spring

MISSOURI

Ford

WILSON'S CREEK
10 August 1861

Combat Strength
5,400
12–13,000

Casualties
1,317
464/758 (MSG)

Scale in Feet
0   3000

them to concentrate their forces against Lyon and Sigel.

McCulloch sent elements of three regiments to drive Sigel off the field. As the Confederates advanced in line of battle, Sigel, assuming that the advancing 3rd Louisiana troops were the gray-clad 1st Iowa Infantry sent by Lyon as reinforcements, ordered his men to hold their fire. At forty yards the Confederates stopped and fired a crashing volley into the Union position. Unprepared for this attack by what they thought were friendly forces, the Union troops broke into a rout and lost five of their six cannons. By 9:00 A.M. the Confederates had secured the southern end of the battlefield and began concentrating all their efforts on Bloody Hill.

At 7:30 A.M. 600 Missouri State Guardsmen launched an attack on Lyon's right flank — the first of three Confederate counterattacks on Bloody Hill. This assault was beaten off after a half hour of fighting. At 9:00 Price launched his second attack. The Union line was hard-pressed, but it held. An hour later CS Colonel Elkanah Greer's Texas cavalry regiment, attempting to go around the Union right flank and rear, launched the only mounted assault of the battle. This action diverted the Federals' attention, which gave Price time to disengage his men and regroup for another attack. Union artillery and musketry fire broke up the mounted assault, effectively ending the Confederates' second attack. During the fighting Lyon was slightly wounded by artillery. Later, while rallying his troops, he became the first Union general to die during combat, killed by a musket ball.

During a short lull the Confederates readied an estimated 6,000 men in battle lines a thousand yards long for the third and largest attack of the battle. As the Confederates began their advance, the Federals placed every available Union soldier except a small reserve force in the front line. The determined Confederates pressed their advance in spite of concentrated artillery and small-arms fire. In some areas they moved to within twenty feet of the Union line. The smoke of battle from both lines combined into one huge cloud that blanketed the south slope of Bloody Hill. The Confederates were unable to break the Union line and were forced back at all points.

At 11:00 A.M. the Confederates disengaged and regrouped down the hill. The Federals were exhausted and low on ammunition, their general was dead, and Sigel had been defeated. Bloody Hill had earned its name. They retreated to Springfield and then to Rolla, the nearest railhead. The Confederates were not able to follow up their victory. The battle of Wilson's Creek, the first major battle of the war west of the Mississippi River, was over. After six hours of fighting on a hot and humid August day in Missouri, 1,317 Union, 758 Missouri State Guard, and 464 Confederate soldiers were killed, wounded, or missing.

Estimated Casualties: 1,317 US, 464 CS, 758 MSG

Wilson's Creek National Battlefield, near Republic and ten miles southwest of Springfield, includes 1,750 acres of the historic battlefield.

Dry Wood Creek, Missouri (MO005), Vernon County, September 2, 1861

After the battle of Wilson's Creek, General Price and his MSG occupied Springfield. Price headed northwest with 6,000 poorly trained guardsmen to capture Fort Scott, Kansas. Pro-Union Kansas "Jayhawkers" commanded by US Senator James M. "Jim" Lane were using the fort as a base for raids into Missouri. On September 2 Lane's 600 men rode out to confirm the location of Price's force. Near Big Drywood Creek along the Kansas-Missouri border, they surprised the Confederates and skirmished with them for an hour through tall prairie grass. Price's numbers prevailed, and he forced Lane to retire. Lane withdrew to Fort Scott and, after providing for its security, headed north to guard the approaches to Kansas City. Price advanced north toward Lexington, recruiting more pro-Confederates.

Estimated Casualties: 14 US, unknown MSG

Lexington I, Missouri (MO006), Lafayette County, September 13–20, 1861

General Price's guardsmen marched on Lexington, a Union stronghold on the Missouri River, where US Colonel James A. Mulligan commanded 3,500 men and seven guns. On September 13 Price's cavalry encountered skirmishers south of town and drove them into Lexington, where Federal resistance stiffened. The cavalry withdrew to await the arrival of the infantry, artillery, and supplies. The Union forces entrenched north of town around the Masonic College, which was surrounded by open fields and overlooked the Missouri River. The Federals had the responsibility of protecting $900,000 and the Great Seal of Missouri. Their position was very strong, and Mulligan decided to hold out, though they had no water supply within the fortifications. After waiting four days for his ammunition train, Price attacked on September 18, bombarding the Federals with six batteries. The infantry stormed and captured the Anderson house, a strategic site 125 yards west of the Union lines being used as a hospital. Price lost the house to a counterattack, then recaptured it before darkness ended the fighting.

The next day Price kept the Federals under heavy artillery fire and prepared for the final attack on the fortifications. He also dispatched 3,000 men under M. M. Parsons, a Missouri State Guard brigadier general, to block a relief column of 1,000 men under US Brigadier General Samuel Sturgis en route from Mexico, Missouri. At 8:00 A.M. on September 20 Price's men advanced from around the Anderson house behind mobile breastworks made of dampened bales of hemp.

They forced Mulligan to surrender and paroled his command.

Estimated Casualties: 3,500 US, 100 MSG

The Battle of Lexington State Historic Site is in Lexington on 13th Street near Route 13 and includes 106 acres of the historic battlefield.

Liberty (Blue Mills Landing), Missouri (MO003), Clay County, September 17, 1861

On September 15 D. R. Atchison, a former U.S. senator and pro-Confederate leader, left Lexington with a partisan force to join the MSG forces at Liberty, northeast of Kansas City. At the same time US Lieutenant Colonel John Scott led 600 men, most of the 3rd Iowa Infantry, from Cameron toward Liberty. Atchison crossed to the north side of the Missouri River on the night of September 16–17 and prepared to battle Federal troops.

Early on September 17 Scott left Centreville for Liberty, preceded by his scouts. Skirmishing began in the late morning, and the fighting intensified in the afternoon when Scott approached Blue Mills Landing. After an hour of fighting the Union forces retreated and were unable to reinforce US Colonel Mulligan in the battle of Lexington.

Estimated Casualties: 56 US, 70 MSG

Fredericktown, Missouri (MO007), Madison County, October 21, 1861

Two columns commanded by US Colonels Joseph B. Plummer and William P. Carlin advanced on the Confederate partisan leader, MSG Brigadier General Meriwether "Jeff" Thompson, in Fredericktown. Thompson's forces headed south from Fredericktown on the morning of October 21 and hid their supply train twelve miles away. When they returned, the Federals had occupied the town. After unsuccessfully trying to assess enemy numbers, Thompson attacked at noon. Plummer led his column and a detachment of Carlin's forces against Thompson's outnumbered men in a two-hour battle outside the town. The partisans retreated, pursued by the Federal cavalry.

Estimated Casualties: unknown US, 62 MSG

Springfield I, Missouri (MO008), Greene County, October 25, 1861

When US Major General John C. Frémont was appointed commander of the Department of the West in St. Louis, he was well known as the "Pathfinder of the West," after his eleven years in the Army Corps of Topographical Engineers. He was also an important Republican: he had been the party's presidential nominee in its first national race in 1856 but had lost to the Democrat, James Buchanan.

Frémont did not become a successful Civil War general. The forces of his subordinates were defeated at Wilson's Creek and at Lexington. On August 30 he had issued a proclamation that included three startling declarations: martial law, death to guerrillas caught behind his lines, and freedom to slaves belonging to rebels. This resulted in a public rebuke from Lincoln, who was trying to keep the vital border states in the Union. Frémont then announced a plan for a military campaign that would, if successful, clear General Price's forces from the state, advance the war into northwest Arkansas and the Indian Territory, and save both his reputation and his command.

Frémont assembled 38,000 men and left the Tipton area on October 12 to move against Price, who retreated to Neosho, southwest of Springfield. The 5,000 Federal cavalrymen in-

cluded two intelligence-gathering units that scouted before the army: Frémont's Body Guard, commanded by US Major Charles Zagonyi, and US Major Frank J. White's Prairie Scouts, commanded by Zagonyi after White fell ill. As Frémont approached Springfield, Colonel Julian Frazier, the local state guard commander, requested additional troops from nearby forces. While Frémont camped on the Pomme de Terre River, about fifty miles from Springfield, Zagonyi's men continued on to meet Frazier's force of 1,000–1,500.

On October 25 Zagonyi thwarted an ambush led by Frazier, raced into Springfield, hailed Federal sympathizers, and released Union prisoners. Fearing a counterattack, he departed before nightfall. Frémont's army arrived in Springfield two days later and established a temporary stronghold. President Abraham Lincoln removed Frémont from command on November 2 and replaced him with US Major General David Hunter.

At Neosho Governor Jackson and the secessionist legislators passed an ordinance of secession on November 3 and joined the Confederacy, but remained a government in exile throughout the war. Missouri was tragically polarized and torn by local warfare, murder, and acts of terrorism.

Estimated Casualties: 85 US, 133 MSG

Grant on the Mississippi River: November 1861

Belmont, Missouri (MO009), Mississippi County, November 7, 1861

CS Major General Leonidas Polk held the Confederate bastion at Columbus, Kentucky, with 17,000 men and 148 guns. This stronghold on the east bank of the Mississippi effectively closed the river to all Union shipping. Polk's counterpart, US Brigadier General Ulysses S. Grant, held a thin line of strategic bases between Cape Girardeau, Missouri, Cairo, Illinois, and Paducah, Kentucky, with 20,000 men. Grant's orders were to cross into Missouri to cut off the escape of Meriwether "Jeff" Thompson, a brigadier general in the Missouri State Guard, through the "boot heel" area of Missouri.

Grant put his command in motion: two columns advanced from Cairo and Paducah to demonstrate on Columbus while another struck west to stop Thompson. On November 6 Grant embarked on transports at Cairo with the main body of 3,000 troops. His objective was to capture Belmont, Missouri, across the Mississippi River from Columbus. The next morning the Federals disembarked at the Hunter farm, marched two miles southeast, and prepared to attack the Confederate encampment. As they took their positions in thick woods, four regiments of reinforcements from Kentucky commanded by CS Brigadier General Gideon J. Pillow deployed opposite them along a low ridge protecting Camp Johnston. The Federals pressed through a cornfield, and Pillow countered with ineffective bayonet attacks. The Confederate line collapsed, and Grant captured their camp. His troops thought the battle was over and halted to loot the enemy encampment.

CS Brigadier General Frank Cheatham crossed the river from Columbus with two regiments and rallied the remnants of the Confederate force along the river bank north of the camp. The heavy guns from Columbus opened fire on the Union troops, catching them in a crossfire as Cheatham attacked their left flank. The Union line broke, and though briefly surrounded by the Confederates, the Federals fought their way through and retreated in disorder to the transports at the Hunter farm. The gunboats *Tyler* and *Lexington* fired on the pursuing Confederates as the Federals reboarded and returned to Cairo that night.

Grant's first major battle as a commanding officer was a limited, but welcome, success because it was fought at a time of little activity by Union forces. Grant was noted in Washington as a fighting commander and was slated for higher command.

Estimated Casualties: 607 US, 641 CS

The Belmont battlefield, eighteen miles east of East Prairie on Route 80, is marked by an information panel. The town of Belmont was washed away by the Mississippi River. The Columbus-Belmont State Park, across the river in Kentucky, includes earthworks.

Missouri: December 1861–January 1862

Mount Zion Church, Missouri (MO010), Boone County, December 28, 1861

US Brigadier General Benjamin M. Prentiss led five mounted companies and two companies of sharpshooters into Boone County to protect the North Missouri Railroad and to dampen secessionist sentiment there. He arrived in Sturgeon on December 26 and learned that Missouri State Guard forces were near Hallsville. The next day a Federal company battled MSG Colonel Caleb Dorsey's force there before fleeing to Sturgeon.

On December 28 Prentiss set out with his entire force, routed one MSG company on the road from Hallsville to Mount Zion, and advanced against the main force at Mount Zion Church. After a short battle at the church, the guardsmen retreated, abandoning their dead and wounded, supplies, weapons, and animals. After the battle, recruiting efforts to support the Confederacy slowed in central Missouri.

Estimated Casualties: 72 US, 210 MSG

Roan's Tan Yard, Missouri (MO011), Randolph County, January 8, 1862

To oppose Confederate recruiting and training, Federal cavalry from Missouri, Ohio, and Iowa units under the overall command of US Major W. M. G. Torrence rode for Silver Creek. On January 8 the Federals attacked MSG Colonel J. A. Poindexter's camp about fourteen miles northwest of Fayette, took prisoners, and destroyed the camp so the county could no longer be a base for recruiting and raiding.

Estimated Casualties: 11 US, 80 MSG

Florida: October 1861

Santa Rosa Island, Florida (FL001), Escambia County, October 9, 1861

On April 12 the Federals reinforced Fort Pickens, guarding Pensacola harbor. US Colonel Harvey Brown commanded about 1,800 men in positions extending east from Fort Pickens for one mile, anchored by the 600 men of US Colonel William Wilson's 6th Regiment, New York Volunteers, and protected by several U.S. warships blocking the harbor. CS Major General Braxton Bragg's 8,000-man Army of Pensacola held Forts McRee and Barrancas. Their sandbagged batteries joined and extended a four-mile line to the Pensacola Navy Yard. On September 14 sailors and marines from the USS *Colorado* made a successful night landing at the yard, spiked a cannon, and burned the *Judah,* which was being outfitted as a privateer.

In response Bragg ordered a raid on October 9 by CS Brigadier General Richard H. Anderson's 1,200 men. They landed on Santa Rosa Island four miles east of the fort and advanced in three columns, one on the south beach, one on the north beach, and the third following the north column with orders to wheel to the center to connect the other two units. They marched three miles across the soft sand, overran the Federal pickets, and routed the New Yorkers from their camp. The Confederates' advance slowed when they stopped to loot and burn the Federals' camp, giving Wilson's troops time to form two positions just to the west and return fire. The New Yorkers' gray uniforms added confusion to the battle. Troops in the third Confederate column became entangled in the alligator-infested marsh in the center of the island. Alerted by the gunfire and directed by the flames of the burning tents, Federal regulars from the fort launched a counterattack as Anderson began withdrawing his forces in a running battle. The Confederates re-embarked under a hail of musketry from Federals hidden behind sand dunes.

The Confederates evacuated Pensacola on May 9, 1862.

Estimated Casualties: 67 US, 87 CS

The Santa Rosa Island battlefield is in Gulf Island National Seashore. Fort Pickens is on Santa Rosa Island, south of Gulf Breeze, Florida, via Route 399.

Kentucky: September–December 1861

Barbourville, Kentucky (KY001), Knox County, September 19, 1861

Kentucky was one of the four border states (along with Missouri, Maryland, and Delaware) that permitted slavery. Kentucky was particularly important because of its large secessionist minority and its four rivers: the Ohio, the Cumberland, the Tennessee, and the Mississippi. Both Union and Confederate forces massed on the western border, each waiting for the other to move first. The Confederate seizure of Columbus near the confluence of the Ohio and Mississippi Rivers by CS Brigadier General Gideon Pillow was seen as an invasion. However, Kentucky stayed in the Union, and there was no opposition when US Brigadier General Ulysses S. Grant occupied Paducah at the mouth of the Tennessee River and a short distance down the Ohio from Smithland, at the confluence of the Cumberland and the Ohio Rivers. During the summer of 1861 Kentucky and Tennessee Union sympathizers trained recruits at Camp Andrew Johnson in Barbourville. CS Brigadier General Felix K. Zollicoffer arrived in Kentucky in mid-September with troops to strengthen the Confederate presence at Cumberland Gap and to support CS General Albert Sidney Johnston.

Zollicoffer sent 800 men under CS Colonel Joel A. Battle to disrupt the training activities in Barbourville. When Battle arrived at dawn on September 19 he found that the Union recruits had gone to Camp Dick Robinson and had left only a small home guard led by US Captain Isaac J. Black. In the first encounter of the war in Kentucky, the Confederates dispersed the home guard after a skirmish, destroyed the camp, and seized the remaining arms.

Estimated Casualties: 15 US, 5 CS

Camp Wildcat, Kentucky (KY002), Laurel County, October 21, 1861

Both the United States and the Confederacy needed to control the access into Kentucky from Tennessee through Cumberland Gap, along the Wilderness Road, and north across Wildcat Mountain. In mid-September 1861 CS General Zollicoffer occupied Cumberland Gap and Cumberland Ford where he awaited supplies and reinforcements. He planned to occupy the Bluegrass region and cut Union supply lines. US Brigadier General George H. Thomas sent US Colonel T. T. Garrard's 7th Kentucky Volunteers to establish a camp at Wildcat Mountain and block the Wilderness Road. US Brigadier General Albin F. Schoepf arrived with his brigade and took command.

On October 21 Zollicoffer moved his 7,500 men against the 5,400 Federals. The Union troops used natural and constructed fortifications to repel the Confederate attacks, primarily against the 33rd Indiana. Zollicoffer's men retreated during the night of October 21–22 and reached Cumberland Ford on the twenty-sixth.

Estimated Casualties: 43 US, 53 CS

Camp Wildcat battlefield is north of London off Interstate 75 at Exit 49. At U.S. 25 near Hazel Patch, historic markers provide directions to the area of the battlefield protected in the Daniel Boone National Forest.

Ivy Mountain, Kentucky (KY003), Floyd County, November 8–9, 1861

CS Colonel John S. Williams assembled 1,010 recruits at Pikeville in eastern Kentucky. US Brigadier General William Nelson advanced against them from Prestonsburg with a larger force in two columns. Williams sent about 40 cavalry pickets to meet Nelson eight miles from Pikeville. They engaged the Union vanguard on November 8 but retreated before superior numbers. Although he was poorly armed, Williams decided to fight to buy time until he could retreat to Pound Gap, Virginia.

The Confederates ambushed Nelson between Ivy Mountain and Ivy Creek north of Pikeville, but the fighting ebbed when neither side could gain the advantage. As the Confederates retreated, they burned bridges and felled trees to slow Nelson's pursuit and were able to reach Pound Gap the next day. The second Union column from Louisa under US Colonel Joshua W. Sill arrived in time to skirmish with the remnants of the retreating Confederates before occupying Pikeville on November 9. The Federals' victory consolidated their gains in the eastern Kentucky mountains.

Estimated Casualties: 30 US, 263 CS

Rowlett's Station, Kentucky (KY004), Hart County, December 17, 1861

After taking command of the Department of the Ohio in early November 1861, US Brigadier General Don Carlos Buell ordered US Brigadier General Alexander McD. McCook's Second Division to Nolin, Kentucky. On December 10 McCook attacked the Confederates' defensive line along the Green River near Munfordville. During the attack the Confederates partially destroyed the Louisville & Nashville Railroad bridge. Two companies of the 32nd Indiana Volunteer Infantry Regiment crossed the river to protect the engineers who were bridging the river.

When the engineers completed a pontoon bridge on December 17, eight more 32nd Indiana companies crossed the river, and the combined force advanced to a hill south of Woodsonville near Rowlett's Station. The Confederate cavalry attacked two Union companies in the woods, and a battle began between US Colonel August Willich's regiment and CS Brigadier General Thomas C. Hindman's larger force. Willich withdrew to a stronger position to await reinforcements. The Confederates disengaged and withdrew because of the approach of McCook's main body. Union forces occupied the area and ensured their continued use of the Louisville & Nashville Railroad south to Munfordville.

Estimated Casualties: 40 US, 91 CS

Kentucky: January 1862

Middle Creek, Kentucky (KY005), Floyd County, January 10, 1862

After the Confederate defeat at Ivy Mountain in December 1861, CS Brigadier General Humphrey Marshall led a force to Paintsville, north of Prestonsburg, to resume recruiting. By early January 1862 he had 2,200 volunteers but could not equip them adequately. US Brigadier General Don Carlos Buell, commander of the Army of the Ohio, ordered US Colonel James A. Garfield to lead the 18th Brigade south from Louisa to force the Confederates to retreat into Virginia. On January 6–9 the Federals pushed them south over the difficult terrain toward Prestonsburg.

On January 10 the brigade marched south to the mouth of Middle Creek and hit the Confederates near the forks of the creek. After several hours of fighting, Union reinforcements arrived. The Confederates retired south into Virginia on January 24.

Estimated Casualties: 27 US, 65 CS

Mill Springs, Kentucky (KY006), Pulaski and Wayne Counties, January 19, 1862

Kent Masterson Brown

Although relatively small in size, the battle of Mill Springs had enormous strategic importance. It broke a Confederate defense line through southern Kentucky that extended from the Mississippi River to Cumberland Gap. Never, after Mill Springs, would Kentucky form the western and northern frontier of the Confederacy.

After the battle at Wildcat Mountain in October 1861, CS Brigadier General Felix Zollicoffer moved his troops west from Cumberland Gap to Mill Springs, not far from Monticello, on the Cumberland River. They crossed the river and prepared entrenchments on the north bank near Beech Grove.

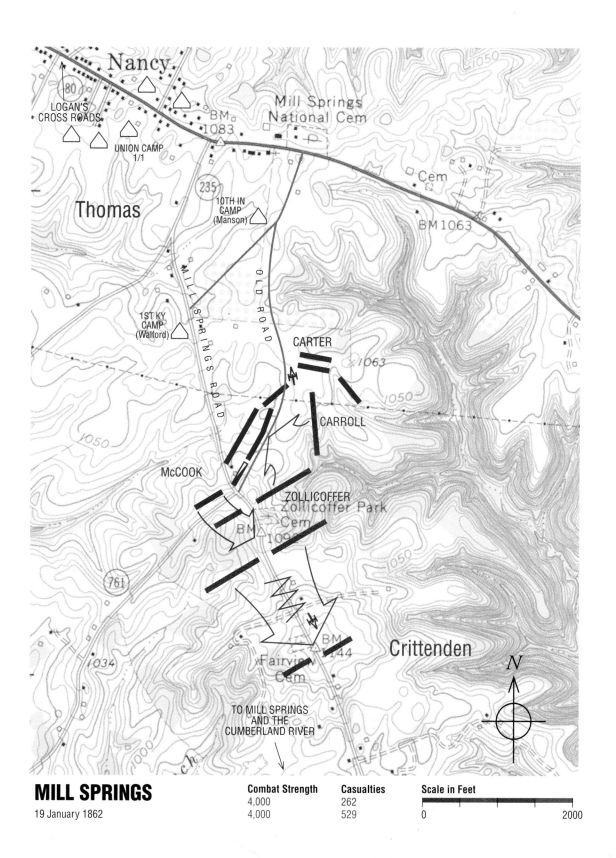

MILL SPRINGS

19 January 1862

Combat Strength	Casualties
4,000	262
4,000	529

Scale in Feet

0   2000

When CS Major General George B. Crittenden assumed command of the Military District of Cumberland Gap in late November, he ordered Zollicoffer to withdraw to the south bank of the Cumberland. Zollicoffer failed to move, and when Crittenden arrived to take personal command in January, he found the river at his rear and the enemy advancing. The river was swollen, and Crittenden resolved to give the enemy battle on the north bank rather than risk a river crossing.

Although US Brigadier General Don Carlos Buell was initially reluctant to order all of US Brigadier General George H. Thomas's division forward to support US Brigadier General Albin Schoepf due to the presence of CS Brigadier General Thomas Hindman's command at Columbia, Kentucky, he finally directed Thomas to join Schoepf at Somerset and march against Zollicoffer. Thomas's troops marched from Lebanon, Kentucky, on muddy roads in bad weather for eighteen days to reach Logan's Cross Roads (now Nancy), only forty miles away, on January 17. Schoepf remained near Somerset, expecting Thomas to join him there.

Crittenden took the offensive in the face of the Union threat. Moving out in a driving rainstorm at midnight, he ran into Thomas's cavalry screen, composed of the 1st Kentucky, commanded by US Colonel Frank Wolford, on January 19. US Colonel Mahlon D. Manson then ordered his 10th Indiana and the 4th Kentucky forward, but Crittenden's attack, spearheaded by Zollicoffer, pushed the Union regiments back. The fighting became close and confused due to the rain, fog, and smoke. During a lull, US Colonel Speed S. Fry of the 4th Kentucky rode to his flank to reconnoiter. At the same time Zollicoffer rode out to stop what he thought was Confederate fire against fellow Confederates. When the two officers met near the Union line, each thinking he was speaking to an officer on his own side, Zollicoffer ordered Fry to cease fire. As Fry turned to execute the order, one of Zollicoffer's aides rode up screaming, "General, these are the enemy," and fired at Fry, hitting his horse. Fry and nearby Union troops returned fire and killed Zollicoffer and his aide.

Zollicoffer's regiments became disorganized by the loss of their commander, but they were rallied by Crittenden, who then ordered a general advance with both Zollicoffer's brigade and that of CS Brigadier General William H. Carroll. Meanwhile Thomas arrived on the field and threw in US Brigadier General S. D. Carter's brigade to check Crittenden's assault. US Colonel Robert L. McCook brought up two more regiments to relieve the 10th Indiana and the 4th Kentucky. For the next half hour the two sides fought bitterly in the rain and fog until Carter gained the Confederate right and McCook the Confederate left. The Confederate left finally broke, leaving Thomas's force in command of the field. One of the many difficulties facing Crittenden in the battle was the fact that large numbers of his troops were armed with outdated flintlock muskets, which easily fouled in the rain. Crittenden, abandoning most of his equipment, horses, and mules, withdrew his army across the Cumberland River using a commandeered sternwheeler and two flatboats.

The loss was demoralizing for the Confederates, and it signaled the abandonment of a Confederate western frontier that, at the beginning of the war, extended from Columbus, Kentucky, on the Mississippi River, all across southern Kentucky to the Cumberland Gap.

Estimated Casualties: 262 US, 529 CS

The Mill Springs Battlefield is at Nancy on Route 80 eight miles west of Somerset, Kentucky. There are fifty-nine acres of the historic battlefield protected by the Mill Springs Battlefield Association, including the Zollicoffer Confederate Cemetery.

Indian Territory: November–December 1861

Round Mountain, Oklahoma (OK001), county unknown, November 19, 1861

The Confederacy recognized the strategic importance of Indian Territory and sent Albert Pike, a colorful journalist and frontier lawyer who worked well with the tribes, to secure treaties with the "Five Civilized Tribes" — Cherokee, Creek, Chickasaw, Choctaw, and Seminole — who had been removed from their homelands in the Southeast in the 1830s. The bitter strife between the Indians who had signed the removal treaties and those who had refused to sign was subsiding when the Civil War renewed it. Pike was initially unsuccessful with John Ross, the seventy-year-old Principal Chief of the Cherokees, who had become a successful, slave-owning planter. He was the leader of the traditional Cherokees who had opposed removal and were abolitionists. Ross stated that the tribe would remain neutral in the Civil War. Opposing him were the Cherokees who had supported removal, led by Ross's enemy, Stand Watie. They were pro-slavery and responded to the Confederate warnings about the North's invasion of the South by siding with the Confederacy and raising a regiment.

The Creeks were similarly split. Those who had opposed removal were led by the wealthy, eighty-year-old Chief Opothleyahola. Their opponents were led by Principal Chief Motey Kennard, Daniel N. McIntosh, and Chilly McIntosh. The Chickasaws and Choctaws, who lived near the Red River, were united in their support of the Confederacy, but the Seminoles, who had been forced to leave their homeland in Florida, were divided between the traditionalists and those led by John Jumper.

Pike's treaties with other Indian leaders, Watie's regiment, and the Confederate victory at Wilson's Creek led Ross to conclude that it was in the Cherokee Nation's best interest to sign also, and to offer a Cherokee regiment that would be led by a Ross supporter, CS Colonel John Drew. Pike's treaties with the five tribes assured them that they would not have to fight unless their lands were invaded, and that if the Federals did invade, the Confederacy's white troops would protect them. The Confederacy rewarded Pike by giving him command of the Department of Indian Territory with the rank of brigadier general.

Even though the tribes had signed treaties, splits continued within tribes, causing an Indian civil war. Many Unionist Indians began moving to Union areas of Kansas, seeking a leader. More than 3,500 fled to the plantation of Chief Opothleyahola. As the chief led them to better grasslands and toward the protection of Union forces, CS Colonel Douglas H. Cooper's 1,400-man force attacked them on November 19 at their camp near Round Mountain. Cooper's command included Choctaw, Chickasaw, Creek, and Seminole Indians, and 500 whites of the 9th Texas Cavalry. The short fight ended when the Indians set a prairie fire that threatened Cooper's wagon train. After dark the Unionist Indians retreated to their camp, which Cooper found abandoned the next morning. The Confederates claimed victory because Chief Opothleyahola had moved his camp.

Because of insufficient data, authorities are not certain of the location of the battle.

Estimated Casualties: unknown Unionist Indians, 10 CS

Chusto-Talasah, Oklahoma (OK002), Tulsa County, December 9, 1861

In search of safety after the battle at Round Mountain, Chief Opothleyahola and his 3,000 Unionist Indians, including about 2,300 women and children, camped at Chusto-Talasah (Caving Banks) on Bird Creek. At about 2:00 P.M. on December 9 CS Colonel Cooper's men attacked. The chief, strongly positioned at Horseshoe Bend, fought hard for almost four hours. Cooper had lost about 460 men before the battle when CS Colonel Drew's Cherokees refused to fight Unionist Indians and either left or joined Opothleyahola. The Confederates claimed victory, but the chief and his forces eluded them and camped at Shoal Creek.

Estimated Casualties: 412 Unionist Indians, 52 CS

Chustenahlah, Oklahoma (OK003), Osage County, December 26, 1861

After the battle at Chusto-Talasah, CS Colonel Cooper feared more defection of the Indians in his force and called for help from CS Colonel James McQueen McIntosh (no relation to the two Creek brothers) and his 1,400 Texas and Arkansas cavalrymen. They attacked the day after Christmas. The chief's men attempted to make a stand at their camp but were routed in bitter hand-to-hand fighting. Stand Watie and about 300 of his regiment joined the fight toward the end and continued the pursuit the next day. Several thousand of the Indians who were not killed or captured had to endure winter on the prairie without adequate clothes or food as they fled to Kansas. Many more died of exposure as they waited for help near the Federal military camps. Chief Opothleyahola's defeat allowed the Confederates to consolidate their hold on Indian Territory.

Estimated Casualties: 211 Unionist Indians, 40 CS

Pea Ridge, Arkansas: March 1862

Pea Ridge, Arkansas (AR001), Benton County, March 6–8, 1862

William L. Shea and Earl J. Hess

The battle of Pea Ridge resulted from Federal efforts to secure control of the border state of Missouri. US Brigadier General Nathaniel Lyon had seized control of St. Louis and the Missouri River but was killed at Wilson's Creek in his unsuccessful effort to eliminate Major General Sterling Price's pro-Confederate State Guard. In September 1861 Price pushed north, captured Lexington on the Missouri River, and then retired in the face of converging Union forces. He took refuge in the southwestern corner of the state, where he menaced Federal control of Missouri and threatened to disrupt the logistical support for a planned Federal invasion of the Confederacy down the Mississippi River.

In late December US Brigadier General Samuel R. Curtis was appointed commander of the Army of the Southwest and was instructed to drive Price out of Missouri. Curtis launched his campaign on February 11, chasing Price down Telegraph Road into northwestern Arkansas. Price joined Confederate troops under CS Brigadier General Benjamin McCulloch in the rugged Boston Mountains. Curtis halted near Pea Ridge, forty miles north of these mountains, and assumed a defensive position to shield Missouri.

On March 2 CS Major General Earl Van Dorn, newly appointed commander of Confederate troops west of the Mississippi, joined Price and McCulloch. He named their combined force the Army of the West and immediately began preparations for an invasion of Missouri. His offensive began on March 4 in the midst of a blizzard.

Learning of Van Dorn's approach, Curtis consolidated his 10,250 troops where the Telegraph Road crossed Little Sugar Creek, three miles south of Pea Ridge and the nearby hostelry called Elkhorn Tavern. The Federals fortified their naturally strong position along the creek. On

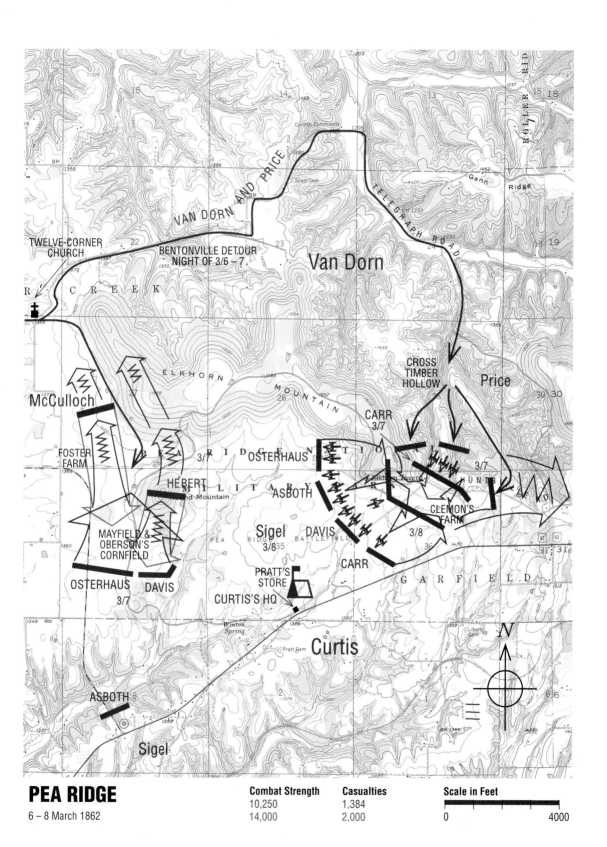

TWELVE-CORNER
CHURCH

BENTONVILLE DETOUR
NIGHT OF 3/6 – 7

Van Dorn

VAN DORN AND PRICE

Corinth Community

TELEGRAPH ROAD

ROLLER R.D.

Gann Ridge

CROSS
TIMBER
HOLLOW

Price

ELKHORN

MOUNTAIN

CREEK

McCulloch

FOSTER
FARM

HEBERT

MILITARY

Pratt Mountain

CARR
3/7

OSTERHAUS 3/7

OSTERHAUS

Elkhorn Tavern

ASBOTH

3/7

CLEMON'S
FARM

MAYFIELD &
OBERSON'S
CORNFIELD

Sigel
3/8

PEA

RIDGE

DAVIS

BATTLEFIELD

DAVIS

3/8

OSTERHAUS
3/7

DAVIS

CARR

PRATT'S
STORE

CURTIS'S HQ

GARFIELD

Winton
Spring

Liberty
Cem

Pratt Cem

Curtis

ASBOTH

Sigel

N

PEA RIDGE

6 – 8 March 1862

Combat Strength
10,250
14,000

Casualties
1,384
2,000

Scale in Feet

0   4000

March 6 Van Dorn managed to move fast enough to catch a small rear guard led by Curtis's second-in-command, US Brigadier General Franz Sigel, as it retreated from Bentonville toward the creek position. Sigel escaped from the pursuing Confederates with minor casualties.

That evening Van Dorn's army of 16,500 men, divided into two divisions led by Price and McCulloch, reached Little Sugar Creek. Rather than attack Curtis in his fortifications, Van Dorn decided to envelop the Federals by moving his army around to their rear. During the night of March 6–7, the weary Confederates marched along the Bentonville Detour, a local road that passed around the right flank of the Federal position. Price's Division reached the Telegraph Road by midmorning on March 7 and turned south toward Elkhorn Tavern, but McCulloch's Division fell so far behind that Van Dorn ordered it to leave the detour and move by a shorter route to rejoin Price's Division at Elkhorn Tavern. This decision divided the Confederate army and meant that the battle of Pea Ridge actually involved two separate engagements, at Leetown and at Elkhorn Tavern.

Curtis, who learned of the Confederate maneuver on the morning of March 7, was ready. He turned much of his army to the rear, so that his troops were facing north instead of south — one of the most extraordinary changes of front in the Civil War. He then launched sharp attacks against both Confederate divisions. McCulloch's Division was intercepted a mile north of the hamlet of Leetown by the First and Third Divisions, commanded by US Colonels Peter J. Osterhaus and Jefferson C. Davis. Price's troops were blocked by Colonel Eugene A. Carr's Fourth Division. Curtis held the remaining troops in reserve.

The fighting at Leetown was divided into three sectors by the vegetation, cultivated fields, and the road system. The first sector was the Foster farm, where McCulloch first encountered the enemy. The farm was a partially cleared swale from which a Federal battery, supported by a small cavalry force, fired on his division. McCulloch's cavalry, supported by two regiments of Cherokee Indians, easily captured the battery and scattered the cavalry.

The second sector was the cornfields of the Oberson and Mayfield farms. Osterhaus and Davis established a solid line of infantry and artillery in these fields, which were separated from the Foster farm by a belt of timber. As McCulloch led the advance, he was killed by a volley from two companies of Federal skirmishers posted in the woods. His successor, CS Brigadier General James McIntosh, ordered a general infantry attack. He personally led one regiment through the timber, and he too was killed by the Federal skirmishers. McIntosh's death ended the fighting in the Oberson and Mayfield fields as fighting began in the third sector.

This was an area of thick scrub timber and densely tangled brush east of the cornfields, separated from them by the road that ran north from Leetown. CS Colonel Louis Hébert led 2,000 infantry troops through this thicket. They were opposed by half as many Federals in two regiments of Davis's Third Division in an hour-long fight during which the brush reduced visibility to seventy-five yards. Hébert's men pushed these regiments back toward Leetown and captured two Federal cannons in the southeast corner of the cornfield.

This Confederate advance was repulsed as two Indiana regiments of Davis's other brigade outflanked Hébert's left and Osterhaus's division struck his right. Exhausted and unsupported, the remnants of Hébert's command retreated to the Bentonville Detour in midafternoon, along with the rest of McCulloch's Division. Hébert was captured by the Federals. Just then Sigel arrived at Leetown with heavy reinforcements, helped to secure the battlefield, and marched toward the ongoing fight at Elkhorn Tavern.

Price's Division, with Van Dorn at its head, had encountered Carr's Fourth Division at the tavern. The Confederates were at the bottom of a deep canyon known as Cross Timber Hollow; the Federals occupied a superb defensive position on top of the Pea Ridge plateau. For several hours Van Dorn engaged the Federals with artillery before ordering Price to attack. The Confederates ascended the steep hill, pushed back both of Carr's flanks, and gained a foothold on the plateau. The most intense fighting of the entire battle of Pea Ridge occurred around Elkhorn Tavern and just to the east at the Clemon farm. Carr's men were forced back nearly a mile before reinforcements arrived. Darkness halted the fighting.

During the night of March 7–8 Curtis concentrated his remaining 9,500 troops on the Telegraph Road in order to drive the Confederates away from Elkhorn Tavern in the morning. Van Dorn ordered the remnants of McCulloch's Division to the tavern. With only about half of his troops in any condition to fight because of exhaustion and lack of food, Van Dorn formed his men into a V-shaped defensive line running along the edge of the woods south and west of the tavern.

At dawn on March 8 Curtis deployed the First, Second, Third, and Fourth Divisions in numerical order from left to right, facing north. It was one of the few times in the war that an entire army from flank to flank was out in the open for all to see. Sigel directed the First and Second Divisions west of the Telegraph Road, while Curtis directed the Third and Fourth Divisions east of the road and retained overall command. During the next two hours Sigel gradually advanced and wheeled his troops around until they faced northeast. In this fashion the Federal line soon roughly corresponded to the V-shaped Confederate line.

To cover this movement the Federals hammered the Confederates with twenty-one cannons, most of them directed personally by Sigel. This unusually well-coordinated fire compelled the Confederates to fall back to safer positions. Van Dorn's ordnance trains had been separated from the army as a result of negligent staff work, so the Confederates did not have enough ammunition for their artillery. The Federal army then advanced. After a brief fight the Confederate rear guard disengaged, and the rout began. Van Dorn retreated southeast, leading the main body of his battered army entirely around the enemy army, a maneuver unique in the Civil War. Other Con-

federate units scattered north and west via their approach route, rejoining Van Dorn several days later in Van Buren. However, hundreds of Confederate soldiers left the colors to return home. Curtis did not know until the next day which route Van Dorn and the main column had taken, and by that time pursuit was futile.

The Confederates began the campaign with approximately 16,500 soldiers, including 800 Cherokees, but because the advance was so rapid, only about 14,000 were present at Pea Ridge and even fewer were actually engaged. About 2,000 Confederates were lost in the battle. The Federals had 10,250 soldiers at Pea Ridge and suffered 1,384 casualties. Half of the Federal losses were incurred by Carr's Fourth Division during the fighting at Elkhorn Tavern on March 7.

Despite being outnumbered three to two, the Federals achieved a decisive tactical and strategic victory at Pea Ridge. The outcome of the battle ended any serious Confederate threat to Missouri and led to the conquest of Arkansas. Van Dorn's impulsiveness, his obsession with speed and surprise, and his unconcern for logistics and staff work gravely weakened the Confederate effort. Conversely, Curtis's coolness and tactical boldness were major factors in the Federal victory.

Estimated Casualties: 1,384 US, 2,000 CS

Pea Ridge National Military Park, on Route 62 thirty miles north of Fayetteville, includes 4,300 acres of the historic battlefield.

Arkansas: June–July 1862

St. Charles, Arkansas (AR002), Arkansas County, June 17, 1862

After the defeat of the Army of the West under CS Major General Earl Van Dorn at Pea Ridge in March 1862, most of the army was ordered to the east side of the Mississippi River to oppose US Major General Ulysses S. Grant's advance up the Tennessee River. CS Major General Thomas C. Hindman, who had been rushed in late May from Corinth to Little Rock, was responsible for defending Arkansas. He created a 20,000-man army through both conscription and hard work. His immediate challenge was to cut the Federal supply line up the White River. It supported US Major General Samuel R. Curtis and his Army of the Southwest as they advanced from Pea Ridge across the Ozark Plateau to Batesville in north central Arkansas and toward Jacksonport at the confluence of the White and Black Rivers.

On the morning of June 17 the *Mound City* and the *St. Louis,* the timberclads *Lexington* and *Conestoga,* and several transports moved up the White River and were hit by fire from CSN Captain Joseph Fry's two heavy guns on the St. Charles bluffs. A shell ruptured the *Mound City*'s steam drum and filled the ship with scalding steam. Of the 175 men aboard, 105 were killed and 44 injured. US Colonel Graham N. Fitch's 46th Indiana Infantry disembarked a few miles below St. Charles and marched upriver. Their successful attack on the Confederate flank enabled them to storm the batteries and occupy St. Charles. The Federal vessels were unable to supply Curtis at Batesville because the river was not deep enough for them to ascend beyond De-Valls Bluff. Curtis's forces had to live off the countryside while they marched south to reach their supplies.

Estimated Casualties: 160 US, 40 CS

Hill's Plantation, Arkansas (AR003), Woodruff County, July 7, 1862

The Confederates skirmished with the Federals as US General Curtis marched south along the White River toward the supply flotilla waiting at Clarendon. On July 7 CS General Hindman ordered CS Brigadier General Albert Rust to stop them at the Cache River. Rust moved too slowly, so the forward elements of his force did not strike until four miles south of the river on Parley Hill's plantation near Cotton Plant. The outnumbered Illinois and Wisconsin infantry commanded by US Colonel Charles E. Hovey repulsed repeated, poorly organized attacks by CS Colonel William H. Parsons's two Texas cavalry regiments. The Confederates fled when Federal reinforcements arrived.

Curtis proceeded to Clarendon only to find that the flotilla had departed the previous day. He turned east toward Helena and occupied it on July 12. Federal forces controlled it for the duration of the war.

Estimated Casualties: 63 US, 250 CS

Sibley's New Mexico Campaign: February–March 1862

Valverde, New Mexico (NM001), Socorro County, February 20–21, 1862

New Mexico had become a U.S. territory as a part of the 1850 compromise proposed by Henry Clay to deal with slavery in the new Southwest Territory acquired from Mexico after the 1846–47 war. In the Senate debates on the compromise, William H. Seward, a Whig senator from New York, led those who wanted the area to be forever free of slavery, declaring that "there is a higher law than the Constitution": the law of God before which all people are equal. John C. Calhoun, a Democratic senator from South Carolina, held that Congress had no right to exclude slaves — they were like any other property — from the territories. The legislation provided for: a $10 million payment from the federal government to Texas — the amount of its public debt — in exchange for the settlement of its border dispute with New Mexico; the new territories of Utah and New Mexico without prohibiting slavery (Utah legalized slavery in 1852, and New Mexico approved it in 1859); the admission of California as a free state; the abolition of slave trading — but not slavery — in the District of Columbia; and a strong, new fugitive slave law. This law provided for federal action to secure the return of escaped slaves from anywhere in the nation, and for criminal penalties for anyone who helped fugitives.

In February 1862 CS Brigadier General Henry Hopkins Sibley led 2,500 Texans of the Army of New Mexico up the Rio Grande toward Santa Fe and Fort Union via Fort Craig on the west bank of the river. The fort was stocked with supplies that his men needed, and the 3,800-man garrison was too strong to leave in his rear as he headed northeast. US Colonel Edward R. S. Canby's command included the 1st New Mexico Volunteers under US Colonel Christopher "Kit" Carson. On February 19 Sibley camped on the sandhills east of the fort. His objectives were to cut the Federals' communications with their military headquarters in Santa Fe and to lure them out of the fort to battle on ground of his choosing. When the Federals marched forward on February 20, they were hit by Confederate artillery that forced the 2nd New Mexico Volunteers to fall back.

The next day the Confederates marched to Valverde Ford, six miles north of the fort. Canby's force crossed the Rio Grande and drove the Confederates out of the old riverbed and up into the sandhills. When Sibley became incapacitated, CS Colonel Thomas Green took command. An aggressive fighter, Green attacked a Union battery positioned on the left. Most of the Union center had shifted to the right to repel CS Major Henry W. Raguet's attack on their right, opening a dangerous gap. Green then launched his Texans in a vicious frontal attack that captured six artillery pieces and broke the Union line. Canby ordered a retreat to Fort Craig. Before the Confederates could cross the river in pursuit, Canby raised a flag of truce to remove his dead and wounded. Green assented to the request.

The Confederates controlled the battlefield but suffered heavy casualties in the hand-to-hand fighting for the battery. Still capable of effective resistance, Canby refused to surrender Fort Craig, and Sibley marched on toward Santa Fe. The Federals evacuated their storehouses in Albuquerque on March 1, and the Confederates occupied Santa Fe on March 10.

Estimated Casualties: 263 US, 187 CS

Glorieta Pass, New Mexico (NM002), Santa Fe and San Miguel Counties, March 26–28, 1862

Don E. Alberts

During March 1862 Union and Confederate troops fought the key battle of the Civil War in the Far West, the battle of Glorieta Pass, in the Territory of New Mexico. The Confederates were Texans of CS Brigadier General Henry Hopkins Sibley's Army of New Mexico. After an advance

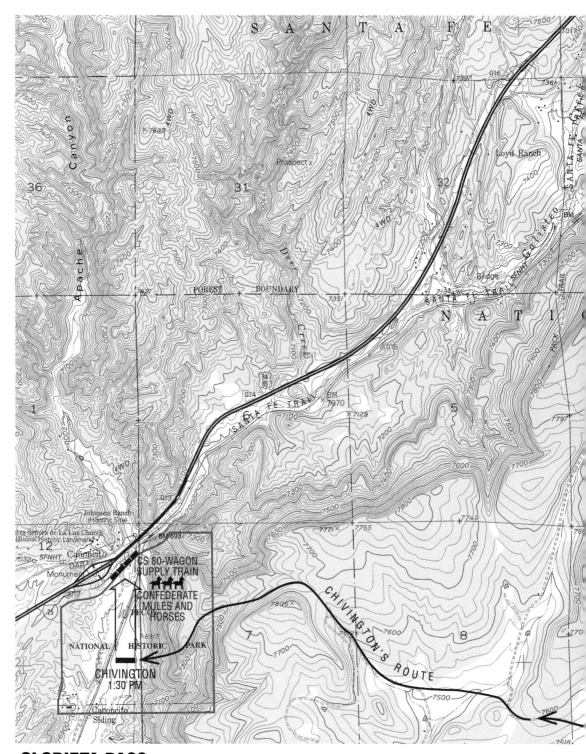

GLORIETA PASS
28 March 1862

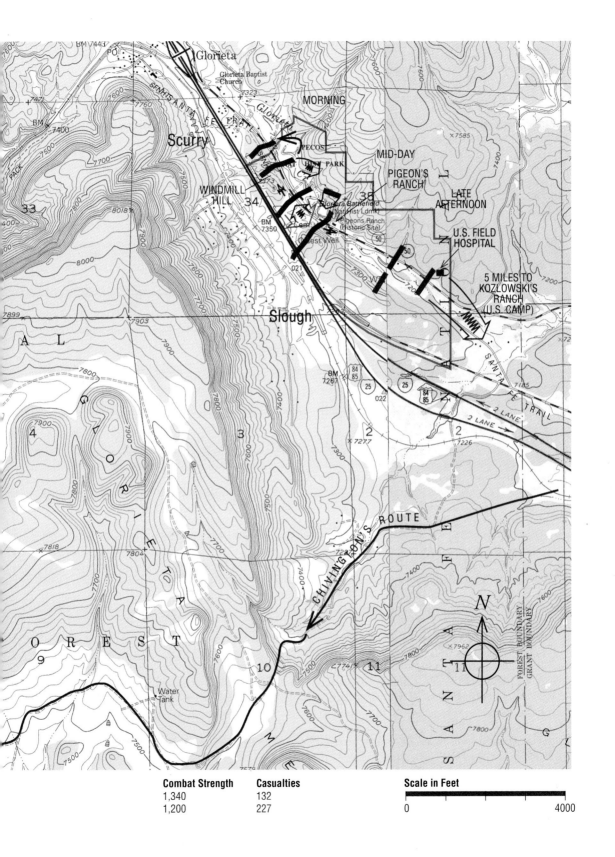

Glorieta

Glorieta Baptist
Church

MORNING

Scurry

PECOS

MID-DAY

PIGEON'S
RANCH

WINDMILL
HILL 34

Glorieta Battlefield
(Nat'l Hist Ldmk)

Pigeons Ranch
(Historic Site)

LATE
AFTERNOON

U.S. FIELD
HOSPITAL

5 MILES TO
KOZLOWSKI'S
RANCH
(U.S. CAMP)

Slough

SANTA FE TRAIL

2 LANE

2 LANE

CHIVINGTON'S ROUTE

Water
Tank

N

FOREST BOUNDARY
GRANT BOUNDARY

Combat Strength	Casualties
1,340	132
1,200	227

Scale in Feet

0   4000

party took the southernmost Federal post in the territory, Fort Fillmore near Mesilla, Sibley's Brigade moved northward, fighting and winning the battle of Valverde on February 21. Leaving the defeated but intact Union forces behind in nearby Fort Craig, the Texans continued northward along the Rio Grande, occupying the towns of Albuquerque and Santa Fe during early March. There they delayed to gather provisions for a further advance on Sibley's primary objective, Fort Union, the Federal supply center about a hundred miles northeast of Santa Fe on the Santa Fe Trail and on the route to the gold mines around Denver City, Colorado Territory.

The Union force was a regiment of frontiersmen from the mining districts around Denver City, the 1st Colorado Volunteers, commanded by US Colonel John P. Slough, a Denver lawyer. These "Pikes Peakers" were augmented by detachments of cavalry and infantry from the regular garrison of Fort Union. On March 22 Slough led his field column of 1,340 men out of Fort Union toward the Texans known to be in the vicinity of Santa Fe.

Sibley remained at his headquarters and supply depot in Albuquerque and sent his main field column through the mountains toward Fort Union. A smaller vanguard under CS Major Charles L. Pyron, 2nd Texas Mounted Rifles, occupied Santa Fe. On March 25 Pyron led his troops eastward along the Santa Fe Trail to find the enemy. His 400-man force included his own battalion, four companies of the 5th Texas Mounted Volunteers, several locally recruited units, including the "Company of Santa Fe Gamblers," artillerymen, and two cannons.

On the morning of March 26 Pyron's Texans left their camp at Cañoncito and again rode eastward along the Santa Fe Trail. Slough's advance guard, approximately 420 men under the command of US Major John M. Chivington, 1st Colorado Volunteers, marched westward toward them on the same road. The Union troops surprised and captured Pyron's advance party, then attacked his main body of troops. Forming in line of battle across the road approximately two miles

west of Glorieta Pass, the Texans unlimbered their artillery and opened fire. The Federals outflanked Pyron's line by climbing the hillsides bordering the Santa Fe Trail. The Confederates then withdrew westward toward Apache Canyon, a small valley of cultivated fields, and established a second battle line and then a third. Chivington repeated his outflanking tactic, and in addition sent a furious cavalry charge against the Texans' positions. Pyron managed to extract his two cannons, but the Union horsemen were among his men just as Chivington's flanking parties reached his rear. Seventy Confederates were captured during the battle of Apache Canyon, 4 Texans died, and approximately 20 were wounded. Pyron retreated to his camp at nearby Cañoncito and sent an urgent request for assistance to the main Texas column, camped fifteen miles away.

Chivington, with 5 men killed and 14 wounded, broke off the action and retired to the Union camp at Kozlowski's Ranch, a Santa Fe Trail station twelve miles away from the Texans. The following day both Chivington and Pyron awaited attacks that never came.

Leaving their supply wagon train behind at Cañoncito, guarded by a handful of noncombatants with a single cannon, the Confederates again marched eastward on the morning of March 28, seeking the enemy who barred their way to Fort Union and its necessary supplies. CS Lieutenant Colonel William R. Scurry of the 4th Texas Mounted Volunteers commanded approximately 1,200 men with three cannons. The forces advanced toward one another along the same road. The Texans encountered Slough's main Union force resting and filling canteens at Pigeon's Ranch, a hostelry one mile east of Glorieta Pass. At about 11:00 A.M. scattered shots opened the battle of Glorieta Pass. Slough had approximately 850 men available, supported by two artillery batteries of four guns each. The balance of Slough's troops, approximately 430 men led by Chivington, had left the main force earlier to act as a flanking force in attacking the Texans' camp at Cañoncito. As the battle opened, Chivington was pushing his men across a heavily wooded mesa south of the trail, unaware that the main columns had already met near Glorieta.

Both forces unlimbered their artillery and formed battle lines across the Santa Fe Trail a half mile west of Pigeon's Ranch. They exchanged fire until about 2:00 P.M., when, slightly outnumbering the foe, Scurry's troops outflanked the Union line, forcing Slough to withdraw to a second defensive line near the ranch buildings and corrals. Scurry then attempted a three-pronged attack, which failed on the right and center but was successful north of the road. Gaining the heights above the Union troops, the Texans forced Slough to withdraw to a third position another half mile east of Pigeon's Ranch. The Confederates followed, and both sides exchanged desultory cannon and small-arms fire. This effort died out in mutual exhaustion at dusk, and Slough decided to withdraw to his camp at Kozlowski's Ranch, about five miles to the rear. Scurry was left in possession of the battlefield. His triumph was immediately dashed, however, by word of disaster in his rear.

As the battle raged around Pigeon's Ranch, Chivington's party reached a point two hundred feet directly above the Texans' wagon park and camp at Cañoncito. They drove off the weak guard, descended the steep slopes, disabled the cannons left at the site, and burned and destroyed the eighty-wagon supply train. It contained virtually everything Scurry's force owned — reserve ammunition, baggage, food, forage, and medicines. The Federals retraced their route and rejoined Slough's main force at Kozlowski's Ranch after dark. That phase of the battle of Glorieta Pass, more successful than could have been expected, sealed the fate of the Confederate invasion of New Mexico.

The key battle ended in the darkness around Pigeon's Ranch. Texan casualties numbered about 48 killed and 60 wounded, along with 25 men lost as prisoners, while the Union forces had 38 killed, 55 wounded, and 20 captured. Both sides felt they were victorious, the Confederates since they remained on the field of battle, and the

Federals since they believed they had been unjustly kept from renewing the battle. The fight around the ranch saw neither side defeated, so it was considered a drawn battle, especially since the foe still stood between the Texans and their objective, Fort Union. When the undoubted Union victory at Cañoncito is considered, however, the battle of Glorieta Pass becomes a significant Federal victory, since it turned back the Confederate thrust into New Mexico and saved the Far West for the Union.

Slough's men returned to Fort Union after the battle, but Scurry remained at Pigeon's Ranch for another day, treating his wounded in the main building and burying his dead in a mass grave across the Santa Fe Trail. The Texans returned to Santa Fe in an unsuccessful attempt to recoup their fortunes and continue the campaign northward. Forced to evacuate the territorial capital, they joined Sibley's final retreat southward and out of New Mexico. They had fought bravely and well at Glorieta Pass, but had been turned back by chance and a determined enemy.

After Glorieta, Slough received orders from Canby to fall back to Fort Union immediately. Worried that he might have violated previous orders in leaving that post in the first place, Slough resigned his commission. Canby subsequently promoted Chivington to command the 1st Colorado Volunteers. Slough returned to New Mexico after the Civil War as the territory's chief justice. He was shot to death in Santa Fe's hotel, La Fonda, by a political rival. Chivington led the 1st Colorado and the 3rd Colorado in the infamous Sand Creek Massacre during 1864. As a volunteer officer he was mustered out of the army before criticism of his actions could result in any military or congressional actions against him. Sibley was court-martialed for drunkenness and cowardice following the 1863 battle of Franklin, Louisiana, and although he was acquitted, he never again held a command during the Civil War. After the war he was dismissed from the khedive of Egypt's army for similar offenses. Scurry became a brigadier general and led Texas troops at Galveston and in the Louisiana Red River campaigns during 1863 and 1864. He was killed on April 30, 1864, at the battle of Jenkins' Ferry, Arkansas.

Estimated Casualties: 132 US, 227 CS

The Pigeon's Ranch and Cañoncito units of the Pecos National Historical Park include 678 acres of the Glorieta Pass battlefield; 479 of these acres are privately owned. The park is east of Santa Fe off I-25.

Cumberland and Tennessee Rivers: February–June 1862

Fort Henry, Tennessee (TN001), Stewart County, February 6, 1862

Cairo, Illinois, at the confluence of the Ohio and the Mississippi Rivers, was vital to the United States because of its location and the operations base established there. The Mississippi Flotilla had nine new ironclad gunboats, seven of which were the creation of James B. Eads, a boat builder in St. Louis. Each of the seven had thirteen guns, a flat bottom, and shallow draft. Protection was provided by a sloping casemate covered with iron armor 2.5 inches thick designed by Samuel Pook. The most famous of "Pook's Turtles" was the USS *Carondelet*. The first test of three of these new warships was against Fort Henry, an earthen Confederate fort guarding the Tennessee River.

In a joint army-navy operation a fleet of seven gunboats — four ironclads and three wooden ones — under USN Flag Officer Andrew H. Foote steamed out of Cairo on February 2, leading the transports carrying US Brigadier General Ulysses S. Grant's force. Grant landed one division on the Tennessee side of the river and another on high ground on the Kentucky side. When CS Brigadier General Lloyd Tilghman realized that he could not hold Fort Henry, he ordered his barbette-mounted cannons to hold off the Union fleet while he sent most of his men to Fort Donelson, eleven miles away.

On February 6 the Union gunboats steamed to within 200 yards of Fort Henry and knocked out thirteen of the seventeen heavy guns. Confederate fire exploded the boiler of the *Essex*, a converted ironclad, causing 38 casualties. Tilghman surrendered after seventy minutes of bombardment, enabling the Federals' wooden gunboats to ascend the Tennessee River south to Muscle Shoals, Alabama.

Estimated Casualties: 47 US, 99 CS

Fort Donelson, Tennessee (TN002), Stewart County, February 12–16, 1862

John Y. Simon

Fort Donelson, Tennessee, guarding the Cumberland River, became the site of the first major Confederate defeat in the Civil War. Victory at Donelson started US Brigadier General Ulysses S. Grant on his road to Appomattox and the White House. His cool judgment under pressure saved the day after the Confederates threatened to break his lines, yet errors by his opponents handed him a victory that he did not fully earn.

Possession of the better part of two states vital to the South depended on the outcome of the battle at Fort Donelson. When war began in April 1861, Kentucky declared its neutrality in response to deep cleavages of opinion among its citizens. Considering neutrality impossible to maintain, North and South maneuvered for position once Kentucky was opened to military operations. The Confederates constructed fortifications on both the Tennessee and Cumberland Rivers just south of the Kentucky line. They built Fort Henry on the Tennessee River, on ground susceptible to flooding, but chose higher ground for Fort Donelson on the Cumberland.

Both sides coveted Kentucky but recognized that the first to cross its borders risked losing popular support. CS Brigadier General Gideon J. Pillow rashly seized Columbus, Kentucky, on the Mississippi River bluffs, a move that appalled President Jefferson Davis, who first ordered Pillow to withdraw, then allowed him to stay when he realized that the deed could not be undone. Grant, commanding at Cairo, Illinois, then occupied Paducah at the mouth of the Tennessee and Smithland at the mouth of the Cumberland, strategic points neglected by Pillow.

In November Grant tested Confederate strength at Columbus by landing troops across the Mississippi River at Belmont, Missouri. The drawn battle that followed sent him back to Cairo still eager to advance but not necessarily along the Mississippi. Knowing of the poor location of Fort Henry, he wanted to use Union gunboats to advantage and foresaw that the fall of Henry would open the Tennessee River as far as northern Alabama. Winning reluctant permission from his superior, US Major General Henry W. Halleck, Grant moved south in early February. The flooded Fort Henry fell to the gunboats on February 6, and most of the garrison fled to Fort Donelson, eleven miles away. Grant followed, after sending the gunboats back down the Tennessee and over to the Cumberland. In St. Louis, Halleck, a military bureaucrat par excellence, took no official cognizance of Grant's plans. If Grant captured Fort Donelson, Halleck would assume credit; if Grant failed, he would avoid responsibility.

CS General Albert Sidney Johnston, overall commander in the West, concentrated his troops at Fort Donelson, anticipating the loss of Nashville if Donelson fell. Torn between defending and abandoning the fort, Johnston took a middle course that led to disaster. He was criticized later for sending so many troops to Donelson without sending his whole force and taking command himself. By the time Grant arrived with approximately 15,000 men, Donelson held nearly 21,000, including at least two generals too many. CS Brigadier General John B. Floyd, who was commanding Donelson, had been a former secretary of war in the cabinet of President James Buchanan and was widely suspected by northerners of having transferred arms and munitions southward before the rebellion broke out. Pillow, the second-in-command, had little respect from his own men and contempt from Grant. Third in line but first in ability was CS Brigadier General Simon B. Buckner, the only professional soldier of the three.

Fort Donelson consisted of earthworks surrounding about fifteen acres, where the garrison lived in huts. Two batteries outside the fort commanded the river, and about two miles of fortifications, protecting both the artillery encampment and the nearby hamlet of Dover, stretched from Hickman Creek on the right to Lick Creek on the left. The creeks, flooded in February, protected both flanks. Confederate officers and engineers had complained continuously of shortages

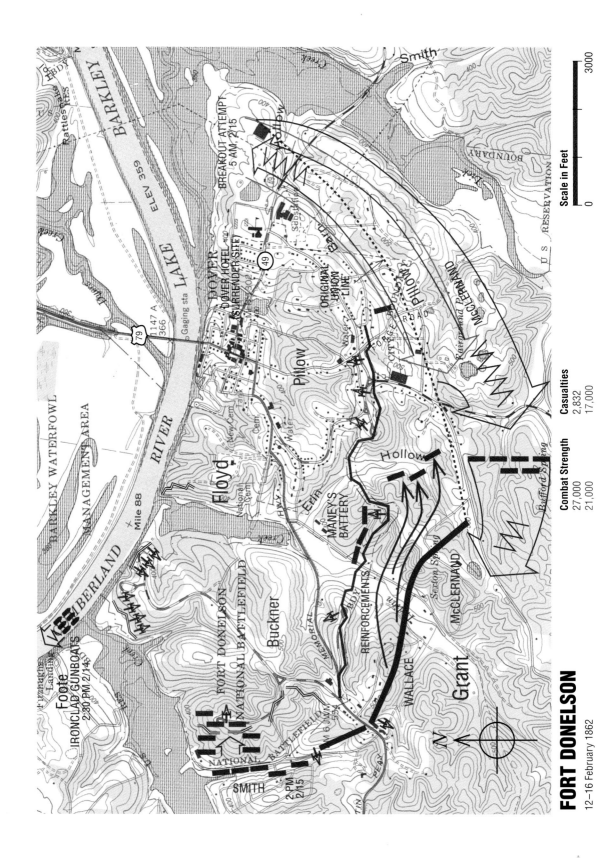

FORT DONELSON

12–16 February 1862

	Combat Strength	Casualties
	27,000	2,832
	21,000	17,000

Scale in Feet

0   3000

of men and supplies to complete the fortifications, but Federal forces encountered formidable earthworks fronted by trees felled, tangled, and sharpened to impede attack.

Grant advanced on February 12 and began to encircle Fort Donelson the next day, ordering US Brigadier General Charles F. Smith's division to probe the Confederate right, commanded by Buckner, and US Brigadier General John A. McClernand's division to probe the Confederate left, under US Brigadier General Bushrod R. Johnson. Grant found the Confederate lines too strong and well positioned for assault. Relying on this strength, however, the Confederates permitted Union troops to complete a virtual encirclement, leaving only a small gap on their right, and to select high ground for their base. If Grant's boldness had been matched by his opponents, they might have struck Union troops as they marched on two separate roads to Donelson, or the Confederates might have counterattacked at Donelson while they had superior numbers and Grant lacked naval support. However, they did not. USN Flag Officer Andrew H. Foote's gunboat fleet arrived late at night, carrying fresh troops, and a brigade commanded by US Brigadier General Lewis Wallace marched from Fort Henry. Ultimately, Grant's army numbered 27,000.

Both armies froze when overnight temperatures unexpectedly fell to twelve degrees. On February 14 Foote tested the water batteries with six warships, four of them ironclads, and the batteries prevailed, inflicting heavy damage on the flotilla. Although heavily outgunned, artillerists found the range when the gunboats came too close, and the fleet suffered too much to resume the assault.

The next morning Grant consulted Foote on his flagship, where he lay immobilized by a wound inflicted by the Confederate batteries. While they discussed their next move, Pillow struck the Union right with devastating force. Buckner's line was denuded as the Confederates massed troops to break free of encirclement. McClernand's right began to roll back on the center until reinforcements from Wallace halted the victo-

rious Confederates. When the fighting slackened, Pillow held the Forge Road, leading to Nashville.

Pillow had two sound choices: to press the attack to consolidate victory or to break free of Grant's grip by evacuating Fort Donelson. Inexplicably, he rejected both and withdrew to his original line. Stung by the morning offensive, the Union troops were confused and demoralized until Grant returned. Inspecting the haversacks of fallen Confederates, which contained rations for three days, Grant concluded that the assault represented a desperate effort to escape and ordered his troops to press the enemy. Smith's division was successful against Buckner's weakened line, which put U.S. troops inside the Confederate fortifications and threatened the redoubt.

Otherwise, the three days of fighting had left the armies close to their initial positions. Grant's reinforcements, however, were much exaggerated in the Confederate imagination, and Floyd and Pillow had squandered their only opportunity to evacuate. During the evening of February 15, the Confederate commanders planned the surrender. Floyd relinquished command to Pillow and Pillow to Buckner. The top brass slipped away by water with about 2,000 men. CS Colonel Nathan Bedford Forrest led his cavalry and a few infantry safely by land to Nashville.

When Buckner asked Grant to appoint commissioners to negotiate the terms of capitulation, Grant responded succinctly that "no terms except an unconditional and immediate surrender can be accepted." Denouncing this response as "ungenerous and unchivalrous," Buckner surrendered anyway. Meeting later at the Dover Hotel, Buckner told his old friend and military academy schoolmate that if he had held command, Union forces would not have encircled Donelson so easily. Grant answered that if Buckner had been in command, he (Grant) would have chosen different tactics.

Grant lost 2,832 killed or wounded, and Floyd lost about 2,000. But Grant took about 15,000 prisoners, 48 artillery pieces, and other war matériel the South could not afford to lose. The Confederates fell back from Kentucky and from much of middle Tennessee, abandoning Nashville. Grant won fame and promotion, while both Floyd and Pillow lost command. Robert E. Lee's later successes in Virginia obscured the significance of Fort Donelson as the first step toward the Confederate loss of the West, which spelled doom for the new nation.

Estimated Casualties: 2,832 US, 17,000 CS

Fort Donelson National Battlefield, on Route 79 at Dover, includes fifty-two acres of the historic battlefield; twelve of these acres are privately owned.

Shiloh, Tennessee (TN003), Hardin County, April 6–7, 1862

Stacy Allen

In February US Major General Henry W. Halleck ordered simultaneous offensives to destroy Confederate rail communications and recover the Mississippi Valley: the Army of the District of West Tennessee, commanded by US Major General Ulysses S. Grant, ascended the Tennessee River on a vast flotilla of steamboats and disembarked at Crump's and Pittsburg Landings; US Major General Don Carlos Buell's Army of the Ohio marched southwest from Nashville; US Brigadier General John Pope's Army of the Mississippi and USN Flag Officer Andrew H. Foote's Western Naval Flotilla, converged on Confederate defenses at New Madrid, Missouri, and Island No. 10 in the Mississippi; and US Brigadier General Samuel R. Curtis's Army of the Southwest invaded northwest Arkansas.

With orders from Halleck not to engage the Confederates until Buell arrived, Grant made Savannah, nine river miles north of Pittsburg Landing, his headquarters, positioned five of his divisions (49,000 troops) on the plateau above

Pittsburg Landing, twenty-two miles northeast of Corinth, and a sixth (8,500 men) at Crump's Landing, six miles farther north across Snake Creek.

CS General Albert Sidney Johnston, the Confederate commander in the West, concentrated his forces in Corinth to protect the vital railroad junction. He organized his 44,000-man Army of the Mississippi, many of whom were green volunteers, into four corps commanded by CS Major Generals Leonidas Polk, Braxton Bragg, and William J. Hardee, and by CS Brigadier General John C. Breckinridge. CS General P. G. T. Beauregard was second-in-command. Johnston advanced his army on April 3 to attack Pittsburg Landing and defeat Grant before Buell arrived. His plan was to turn Grant's left, cut his line of retreat to the Tennessee River, and drive the Union army back into Owl Creek to the west and north.

The Confederate approach was slowed by the weather and bad roads so Johnston did not attack until Sunday, April 6. He placed Hardee's Corps forward between Owl and Lick Creeks, reinforced by one of Bragg's brigades, while the rest of his corps deployed behind Hardee. Polk's and Breckinridge's Corps were the reserve, and cavalry picketed both flanks and their front.

Just before 5:00 A.M. a Federal patrol discovered the Confederates one mile south of Shiloh Church. Musket fire broke the morning stillness. Storming forward, the Confederates found that the Federals had not entrenched their position. Johnston had surprised Grant and outnumbered him. Sickness and noncombatants had reduced Union strength to under 40,000 men at Pittsburg Landing. After four hours of bitter fighting, Johnston seemed within reach of a smashing victory. Maneuvering half of his army under Hardee and Bragg to the right, Johnston attacked along the Eastern Corinth Road and overran US Brigadier General Benjamin M. Prentiss's inexperienced division. Most of Prentiss's survivors fled to the landing, the first of thousands of Federals forced back to the river during the day.

At about 7:15 A.M. Grant heard heavy firing upriver from his Savannah headquarters. He dictated a message for Buell and sent US Brigadier General William Nelson's division of Buell's army, which had arrived at Savannah, to the river opposite Pittsburg Landing. Grant arrived at Pittsburg Landing by steamer at 8:30 A.M. and found his army desperately engaged in resisting a massive attack. He directed US Major General Lewis Wallace's division to march from Crump's Landing to Pittsburg Landing, ordered ammunition wagons forward, and rode inland to join his embattled army.

While Johnston's right hammered Prentiss, his unsupervised left slammed into US Brigadier General William Tecumseh Sherman's division. When five Confederate brigades plunged across Shiloh Branch, they met savage resistance at Shiloh Church. Confederate ranks intermingled, and the lines of authority at the division and the corps levels disappeared in the dense battle smoke and heavy forest. Casualties mounted, crippling regiments and batteries on both sides. Despite support from a brigade from US Major General John A. McClernand's division, Sherman's position became untenable. From Prentiss's captured camp, Johnston sent Hardee and Bragg northwest with five brigades. They turned Sherman's left, broke his division apart, and forced him to withdraw at 10:00 A.M. to join McClernand on the Hamburg-Purdy Road.

Following Sherman's retreat, Bragg, Polk, and Hardee hastily reorganized their eleven intermingled brigades, with Hardee commanding the left near Owl Creek, Polk in the center, and Bragg on the right near the Eastern Corinth Road. Under Beauregard's direction, this avalanche hit Sherman and McClernand at 11:00 A.M., and for the next four hours both sides grappled for possession of the western third of the battlefield. When Grant's right, weakened by casualties, grudgingly gave way, the Confederates on the left steadily advanced northward and outdistanced their comrades on their right.

Johnston ordered CS Brigadier General Jones Withers's Division of Bragg's Corps to redeploy a mile east and attack the Federals holding the Hamburg Road near the river. They stormed across Locust Grove Branch at 11:00 A.M. and drove US Colonel David Stuart's brigade north-

east into a new position defended by US Brigadier General Stephen A. Hurlbut's division, supported by elements from US Brigadier General William H. L. Wallace's division. Johnston arrived with Breckinridge's Corps at noon to reinforce Withers, and they continued to press frontal attacks up the Hamburg-Savannah Road. Their advance stalled at Sarah Bell's cotton field and blossoming peach orchard.

Meanwhile, in the center, Confederate fragments under Bragg tangled with parts of the divisions of W. H. L. Wallace, Prentiss, and Hurlbut. The Federals held a low ridge, concealed within a dense oak thicket, astride the Eastern Corinth Road. Unsupported and isolated Confederate brigades crashed piecemeal into the thick underbrush where they "endured a murderous fire until endurance ceased to be a virtue." The survivors from CS Colonel Randall Lee Gibson's Louisiana and Arkansas brigade named the deadly thicket the "hornets' nest."

By late afternoon formal armies had disappeared and most brigades and regiments were disorganized. Johnston was struck by a stray bullet and bled to death at 2:30 P.M. Beauregard then assumed command.

When Grant's weakened flanks retired north after 4:00 P.M., Southern forces brought up eleven field batteries and massed more than fifty cannons to crush the "hornets' nest," while their infantry swept forward and surrounded the thicket. The Federal stronghold collapsed. W. H. L. Wallace was mortally wounded, and Prentiss and 2,250 Union soldiers surrendered at 5:30 P.M. In spite of this success, Johnston's plan to turn Grant's left flank had not succeeded. Instead, the Confederates had forced back the Union right. Grant was determined to hold the critical river landing and positioned his army for a final defense. US Colonel Joseph D. Webster, Grant's chief of staff, deployed fifty guns on the heights above the landing, while 25,000 Federals formed a defensive line along the Pittsburg Landing Road west to Owl Creek. This line protected the landing for Buell's arrival and the Hamburg-Savannah Road for Lewis Wallace's division.

In the late afternoon the vanguard of Nelson's

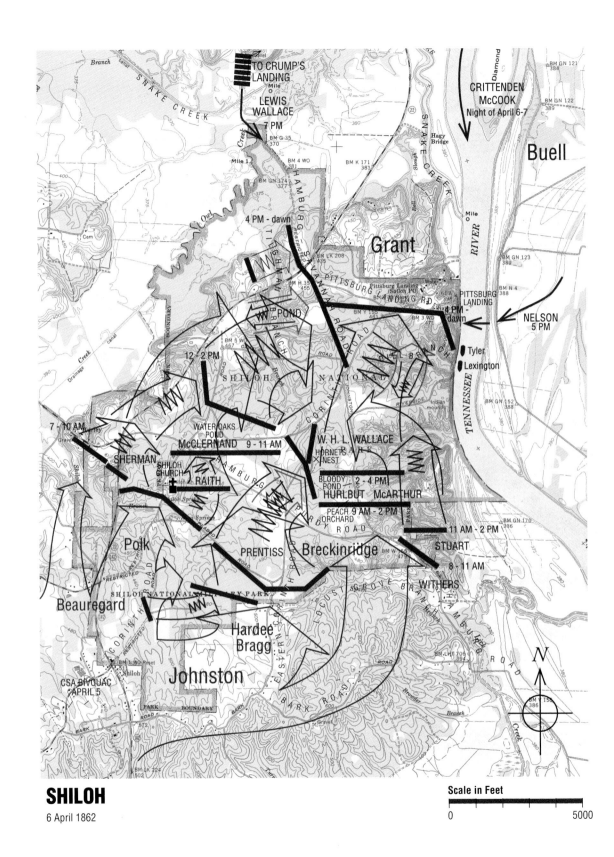

TO CRUMP'S
LANDING

LEWIS
WALLACE
7 PM

CRITTENDEN
McCOOK
Night of April 6-7

Buell

4 PM - dawn

Grant

PITTSBURG
LANDING
4 PM -
dawn

NELSON
5 PM

Tyler

Lexington

12 - 2 PM

7 - 10 AM

WATER OAKS
POND
McCLERNAND   9 - 11 AM

W. H. L. WALLACE

HORNET'S
NEST

SHERMAN

SHILOH
CHURCH   RAITH

BLOODY
POND   2 - 4 PM
HURLBUT   McARTHUR

PEACH   9 AM - 2 PM
ORCHARD

11 AM - 2 PM

STUART

Polk

PRENTISS   Breckinridge

8 - 11 AM

WITHERS

Beauregard

Hardee
Bragg

Johnston

CSA BIVOUAC
APRIL 5

SHILOH

6 April 1862

Scale in Feet

0   5000

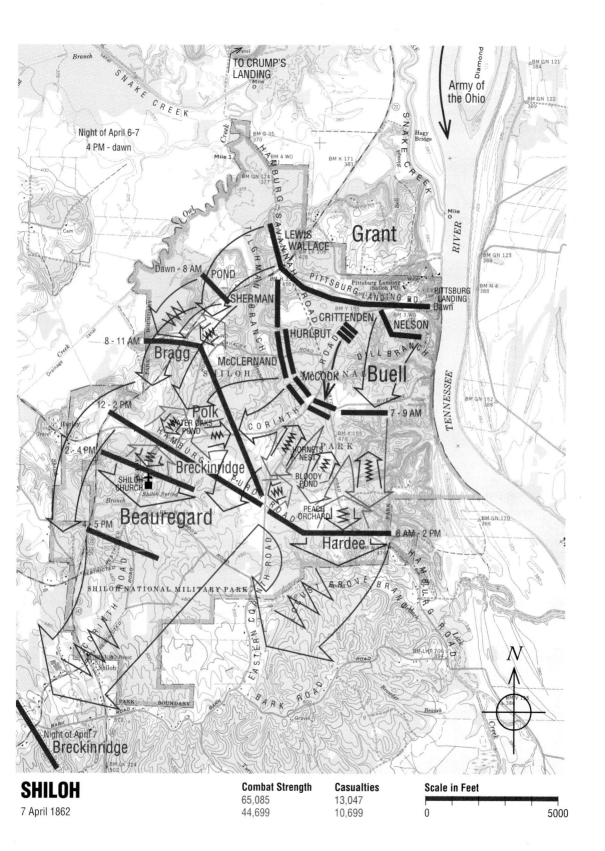

TO CRUMP'S
LANDING

Army of
the Ohio

SNAKE CREEK

Night of April 6-7
4 PM - dawn

LEWIS
WALLACE

Grant

RIVER

Dawn - 8 AM   POND

SHERMAN

PITTSBURG LANDING RD

Pittsburg Landing
(Shiloh P.O.)

PITTSBURG
LANDING
Dawn

8 - 11 AM

CRITTENDEN

HURLBUT

NELSON

Bragg

McCLERNAND

SHILOH

McCOOK

Buell

TENNESSEE

12 - 2 PM

Polk

WATER OAKS
POND

CORINTH

PARK

7 - 9 AM

2 - 4 PM

Breckinridge

HORNETS
NEST

BLOODY
POND

SHILOH
CHURCH

Shiloh Spring

Branch

Beauregard

PEACH
ORCHARD

4 - 5 PM

Hardee

8 AM - 2 PM

SHILOH NATIONAL MILITARY PARK

LOCUST GROVE BRANCH

HAMBURG ROAD

EASTERN CORINTH ROAD

BARK ROAD

N

Night of April 7
Breckinridge

SHILOH

7 April 1862

Combat Strength	Casualties
65,085	13,047
44,699	10,699

Scale in Feet

0   5000

division of Buell's army joined Grant's defenders above the landing. At sunset 6,000 Confederates scrambled into the rugged Dill Branch to assault Grant's left. They splashed across the flooded ravine and advanced through a hailstorm of musketry, field artillery, and gunboat fire. Although many reached the steep northern slope, their ranks were shattered and the attack failed. The fighting ceased, and night ended further carnage.

Beauregard's disorganized army retired to the southern half of the battlefield to seek shelter, food, and sleep. To harass them, Union gunboats *Lexington* and *Tyler* fired salvos into their lines at fifteen-minute intervals. While rain soaked the field, Buell's troops continued to arrive aboard steamboats from Savannah and deploy on Grant's left. Lewis Wallace's division finally slogged in, and by dawn on April 7 nearly 50,000 Federals were present for duty. Beauregard, unaware that Buell's army had arrived, planned to continue the attack, but it was Grant who hit at dawn.

Grant's counterattack caught the disorganized southerners unprepared. It was not until 10:00 A.M. that Beauregard had 30,000 men deployed to contest Grant's advance. The tenacious Confederates inflicted heavy casualties and repulsed Buell's initial thrusts down the Hamburg-Savannah and Eastern Corinth Roads. Toward the west the aggressive Federals drove Beauregard back to Shiloh Church. Southern morale began to falter. Gathering together several fractured regiments, Beauregard led counterattacks northward from the church. At Water Oaks Pond Beauregard stopped the Federal advance but was too outnumbered to continue. To avoid the destruction of his defeated army, he ordered a retreat and began the weary march back to Corinth. The exhausted Federals were satisfied with having recovered the field and did not pursue them.

The battle was over. The tragic carnage of 23,746 men killed, wounded, and missing was a grim warning to the United States and the Confederacy that they faced a long and desperate war.

Estimated Casualties: 13,047 US, 10,699 CS

Shiloh National Military Park, on Route 22 in Shiloh, includes 3,973 acres of the historic battlefield; four of these acres are privately owned.

Siege of Corinth, Mississippi (MS016), Alcorn County and Corinth, April 29–May 30, 1862

T. Michael Parrish

The siege of Corinth involved the confrontation of two huge armies headed by commanders intent on avoiding bloodshed. US Major General Henry W. Halleck and CS General P. G. T. Beauregard were so sobered by the carnage sustained at the battle of Shiloh in southwestern Tennessee in early April 1862 that they pressed for strategic advantage rather than for another large battle.

With control of the Mississippi valley the ultimate prize, Halleck, the commander of Union forces in the West, was so outraged at Grant's initial lapses and awful casualties at Shiloh that he assumed field command and put US Major General George H. Thomas in command of Grant's army. He made Grant second-in-command overall, a vague position of no real authority. Halleck gathered a massive army group at Pittsburg Landing and Hamburg Landing in Tennessee: the Army of the Tennessee under Thomas, the Army of the Ohio commanded by US Major General Don Carlos Buell, and US Major General John Pope's Army of the Mississippi. In his first and only performance as a field commander, Halleck, an expert in military theory and history, meant to capture Corinth, a small but pivotal town, by carefully husbanding his army's numerical superiority.

Corinth's strategic asset was the junction of two railroads, the Memphis & Charleston — the only substantial east-west line in the Confederacy —

and the Mobile & Ohio. Its importance compelled Beauregard to proclaim, with minimal exaggeration, "If defeated here we lose the whole Mississippi Valley and probably our cause." Food, weapons, ammunition, equipment, and soldiers — the immense resources necessary to prosecute war on a large scale — required rapid movement that only railroads such as these could provide over long distances.

Halleck spread out his forces, advanced cautiously, and ordered elaborate entrenchments constructed to protect his men. By May 3 the left under Pope was within four miles of Corinth's eastern approaches near Farmington. Bad weather quickly derailed the center under Buell. Faced with impassable roads, Buell's columns quickly fell behind schedule, and it was not until mid-May that his mud-covered army caught up with Pope's forces north of Farmington.

By May 3 the Union right had moved to within ten miles of Corinth and was threatened by the possibility of the Confederates' using the north-south Mobile & Ohio Railroad to transport troops northward — and turn the exposed Union right wing. Halleck had Thomas's army construct entrenchments following each general advance. They built seven complete lines and advanced only about eight miles between May 4 and May 28 when they were finally close enough to prepare for a massive bombardment of Corinth's defensive perimeter, an impressive line of formidable earthworks that protected the town's northern and eastern approaches.

Beauregard's reinforcements included CS Major General Earl Van Dorn's Army of the West, but Beauregard had no more than 70,000 men to hold off the 120,000 Federals. He slowed the Federals with heavy skirmishes and strong outposts stationed in advance of Corinth's defenses. Twice he maneuvered to mass his forces outside of their entrenchments in an attempt to isolate and crush portions of Halleck's command. Particularly inviting were Pope's unsupported advanced forces at Farmington which Beauregard sent Van Dorn to cut off and defeat. On May 22 Beauregard had CS Major General Leonidas

Polk's Corps, supported by CS Major General John C. Breckinridge, massed along the Mobile & Ohio north of Corinth, positioned to strike Thomas's right and roll it up. However, Van Dorn's inability to strike the Federal left at Farmington forced the Confederates to abandon the operation. The estimated casualties were about 1,000 killed and wounded for each side.

Beauregard concluded that he had to abandon Corinth for both military and health reasons. His commanders were also worried that Halleck would detach large columns to move around Corinth and cut their communications and lines of supply. The polluted water supply was a problem for both sides, and illness reached epidemic levels. In April and May nearly as many Confederates died of disease in Corinth as had been killed at Shiloh, and many thousands more were too ill to fight. Halleck had more than 150,000 men on the rolls, but he had only 95,000 effectives by the end of May. More than half of the Federal high command, including Halleck, had dysentery by the end of the campaign.

On May 25 Beauregard's generals advised him that Corinth would have to be evacuated to save his army. To avoid an attack, Beauregard had to keep the movement secret. Throughout the night of May 29–30 Beauregard orchestrated a perfect deception by running a succession of empty trains back and forth through the town while whistles blew and troops cheered as if massive reinforcements were arriving. By morning the Confederates had left Corinth, with Halleck suspecting nothing but an attack. Only when the Federals saw smoke from burning supplies abandoned by the Confederates did they realize they had been duped. The Confederates continued southward and reached relative safety at Tupelo on June 9.

"The retreat was conducted with great order and precision," Beauregard reported, "and must be looked upon, in every respect, by the country as equivalent to a brilliant victory." Northern newspaper reporters as well as Federal authorities agreed with him and saw a lost opportunity to crush the enemy army. Later there was some

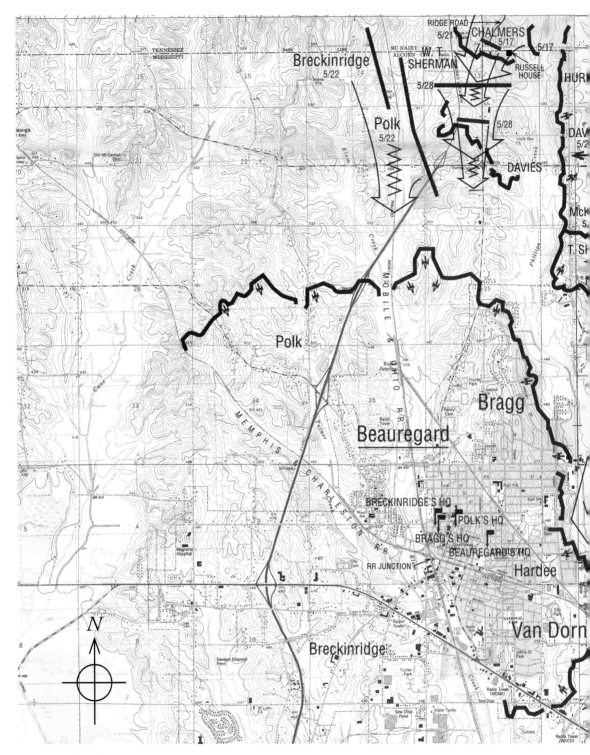

SIEGE OF CORINTH

29 April – 30 May 1862

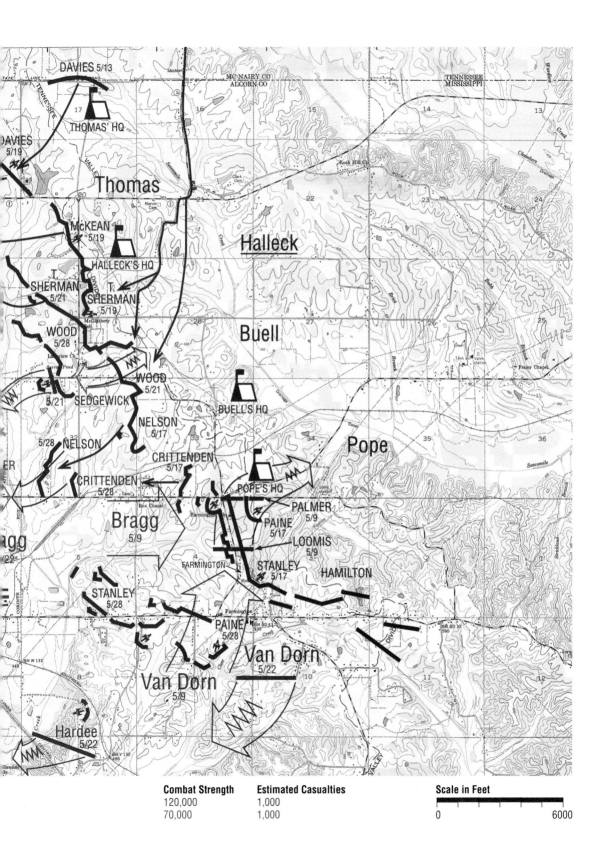

DAVIES 5/13

THOMAS' HQ
17

MC NAIRY CO
ALCORN CO

TENNESSEE
MISSISSIPPI

DAVIES
5/19

Thomas

McKEAN
5/19

HALLECK'S HQ

Halleck

SHERMAN
5/21

SHERMAN
5/19

WOOD
5/28

Buell

WOOD
5/21

5/21 SEDGEWICK

NELSON
5/17

BUELL'S HQ

5/28 NELSON

CRITTENDEN
5/17

Pope

CRITTENDEN
5/28

POPE'S HQ

PALMER
5/9

Bragg

PAINE
5/17

gg

Bragg
5/9

LOOMIS
5/9

FARMINGTON

STANLEY
5/17

HAMILTON

STANLEY
5/28

PAINE
5/28

Van Dorn
5/22

Van Dorn

Van Dorn
5/9

Hardee
5/22

Combat Strength	Estimated Casualties	Scale in Feet
120,000	1,000	0 6000
70,000	1,000	

appreciation of Halleck's plodding, unspectacular, cautious movements.

Beauregard's many critics, including President Jefferson Davis, saw greater truth in his earlier assertion that losing Corinth would result in losing the Mississippi Valley. Fort Pillow and Memphis soon fell, opening the river down to the Confederate bastion of Vicksburg.

Estimated Casualties: 1,000 US, 1,000 CS

Corinth battlefield is at Corinth near Routes 45 and 72. Historic areas open to the public include: ten acres including Battery Robinett at Fulton Drive and Linden Street; five acres including Battery F at Smithbridge Road (Linden Street extended) and Bitner Street; and the Civil War Visitors Center at Jackson and Childs Streets.

Middle Mississippi River: February–June 1862

New Madrid/Island No. 10, Missouri (MO012), New Madrid, Missouri, and Lake County, Tennessee, February 28–April 8, 1862

In February 1862 the Confederates lost Fort Henry and Fort Donelson in Tennessee, and in early March they evacuated Columbus, Kentucky, on the Mississippi River. CS General P. G. T. Beauregard, commander of the Confederate forces defending the Mississippi River, had only 7,000 Confederates at New Madrid and Island No. 10 — just north and west of the Tennessee border near the Missouri, Tennessee, and Kentucky state lines — to defend the river and prevent a Union thrust deep into West Tennessee. Both strongholds were located in hairpin turns of the river, about fifty miles downstream from Columbus, that created the New Madrid Bend, a peninsula that controlled long reaches of the river.

On February 28 US Brigadier General John Pope, commander of the Army of the Mississippi, set out with 18,000 men from Commerce, Missouri, to attack New Madrid and begin to open the river for the Federal advance on Fort Pillow and Memphis. The force slogged through swamps with their supplies and artillery, reached the outskirts of New Madrid on March 3, and invested it. On March 13 the garrison commander, CS Brigadier General John P. McCown, bombarded Pope's forces with heavy artillery but Federal strength forced him to evacuate New Madrid that evening. Pope's army occupied the town the next day.

The strong Confederate position on Island No. 10, upriver from New Madrid, and the land batteries on the Tennessee shore blocked Pope's access to the U.S. fleet, which was above Island No. 10. USN Flag Officer Andrew H. Foote's six ironclads and ten mortar scows unsuccessfully shelled the island. For three weeks Pope's regiment of engineers, assisted by contrabands, dug a canal that connected the bends in the Mississippi

River through two bayous. On April 4 the Federals sent light-draft steamboats from above Island No. 10 through the canal to New Madrid, avoiding the Confederate batteries.

During storms on the nights of April 4 and 6–7, the *Carondelet* and the *Pittsburg* slipped past the guns on Island No. 10. The ironclads protected Pope's troops as they crossed the river at Tiptonville on April 7 and blocked the base of the Reelfoot peninsula, the Confederate escape route. CS Brigadier General William W. Mackall, McCown's replacement, surrendered on April 7, and the formalities were completed the next day. The Mississippi River was open to the Federals down to Fort Pillow, Tennessee. Pope was a success, and US Major General Henry W. Halleck soon ordered him to Hamburg Landing, upstream from Pittsburg Landing, for the Federal march on Corinth.

Estimated Casualties: 51 US, 7,000 surrendered CS

Memphis I, Tennessee (TN004), Memphis, June 6, 1862

The Federal Mississippi Flotilla began bombarding Fort Pillow, the last obstacle between Union forces and Memphis, on April 14. On May 10 the eight rams of the Confederate River Defense Fleet commanded by CSN Captain James E. Montgomery attacked the Union fleet at Plum Run Bend. After sinking the *Cincinnati* and the *Mound City*, the Confederates retired behind Fort Pillow. Both Union ships were soon raised and repaired. After the evacuation of Corinth, CS General Beauregard ordered his troops out of Fort Pillow and Memphis. Their withdrawal left Montgomery's fleet as the only force available to defend Memphis against the impending naval threat that included eight river rams designed by US Colonel Charles Ellet, a civil engineer from Pennsylvania, and staffed by eight members of the Ellet family.

On June 6 the rams and USN Flag Officer Charles H. Davis's five ironclads set out for Memphis from Island No. 45, two miles to the north. They arrived off Memphis at 5:30 A.M. and by 7:00 A.M. had sunk or captured all the Confederate vessels except the *General Van Dorn*. Charles Ellet was mortally wounded, the only Union casualty of the battle, when the *Queen of the West* was rammed. His son, US Medical Cadet Charles Ellet, Jr., met the mayor of Memphis and raised the United States flag over the courthouse. He became the army's youngest colonel at age nineteen. The mayor officially surrendered the city to Davis, and US Colonel G. N. Fitch's Indiana brigade occupied it. The capture of Memphis, an important Confederate commercial and economic center, opened another section of the Mississippi River to Union shipping.

Estimated Casualties: 1 US, 180 CS

New Orleans: April–May 1862

Fort Jackson and Fort St. Philip, Louisiana (LA001), Plaquemines Parish, April 16–28, 1862

The Union's "Anaconda Plan" for isolating the Confederacy from its European markets included gaining control of the Mississippi River from Cairo, Illinois, to the Gulf of Mexico. The key to the river was New Orleans, the South's largest port, greatest industrial center, and only city with a prewar population of more than 170,000 people. The Confederacy needed to sell its cotton to British mills to sustain its economy and assumed that Great Britain would give its official recognition of the Confederacy as a new nation in order to ensure that southern cotton would reach its mills. The Union blockade of its ports gave the South a ready excuse to stockpile cotton until the British agreed to recognize the Confederacy, but the plan to secure recognition failed. Not only was there strong British opposition to slavery in the Confederacy, but British textile mills were overstocked in 1861. Although there was a brief cotton shortage, it was followed by higher international cotton prices. In response India and Egypt planted more cotton so that they, not the Confederacy, supplied most of the cotton to Europe from 1862 to 1865. Trade between the United States and Europe increased because crop failures on the Continent resulted in the purchase of U.S. farm products.

When Union armies advanced through West and Middle Tennessee under US Major Generals Ulysses S. Grant and Don Carlos Buell, the Confederates stripped New Orleans of defenders. They expected the main threat to the city to come from the north rather than from the Gulf of Mexico. The Federals, however, were preparing to seize New Orleans with an amphibious force. USN Flag Officer David G. Farragut's Western Gulf Blockading Squadron entered the Mississippi in March from the Gulf of Mexico. At Head of Passes he assembled seventeen steam-pow-ered warships and USN Commander David D. Porter's twenty-one mortar schooners and six gunboats. US Major General Benjamin F. Butler concentrated 15,000 men on Ship Island, preparing to occupy the city. The Confederates had obstructed the river about seventy miles below New Orleans with sunken hulks and a chain stretched across the river. Fort Jackson on the west bank protected the area. Fort St. Philip, across the river, was supported by CSN Flag Officer John K. Mitchell's River Defense Fleet and the ironclad *Louisiana*, which had no motor power. Together these two forts mounted more than one hundred heavy guns.

On April 18 Porter's mortar schooners began shelling Fort Jackson, the closer and more powerful of the two forts. The next day Confederate fire sank one of the schooners, but Porter repositioned some of his boats and continued to pulverize the fort. Two of Farragut's gunboats forced a break in the obstructions on the night of April 20. Porter continued the bombardment for three days but was unable to silence Fort Jackson's guns. On April 24 at 3:30 A.M. Farragut's warships began to steam through the breach. The *Hartford*, Farragut's flagship, ran aground in front of Fort St. Philip and was set ablaze by a fire raft, but the crew quickly put the fire out. Under heavy fire fourteen warships steamed past the masonry forts and engaged the Confederate flotilla. The Federals sank or captured thirteen enemy vessels, including the armored ram *Manassas*, while losing only the *Varuna*. This battle, followed by the destruction of the fleet at Memphis on June 6, ended the Confederate naval threat on the Mississippi River, except for the ironclad ram *Arkansas*.

After Farragut's fleet passed the forts, Butler landed his troops at Quarantine, five miles north of Fort St. Philip. On the night of April 27 the demoralized garrison of Fort Jackson mutinied, and half of the troops abandoned the fort. The next day the Confederates blew up the *Louisiana*, and CS Brigadier General Johnson K. Duncan surrendered the two forts to Porter.

Estimated Casualties: 229 US, 782 CS

Fort Jackson, a Plaquemines Parish historic site, is six miles south of Buras on Route 23.

New Orleans, Louisiana (LA002), St. Bernard and Orleans Parishes, April 25–May 1, 1862

The fall of New Orleans was inevitable after USN Flag Officer Farragut passed Fort Jackson and Fort St. Philip. CS Major General Mansfield Lovell ordered the city evacuated and withdrew all troops, guns, and supplies. The Confederates burned the stockpiled cotton on the wharves, destroyed the uncompleted ironclad the *Mississippi*, and sank dozens of vessels.

The fourteen warships of the Western Gulf Blockading Squadron reached New Orleans on April 25, silenced the batteries at Slaughter House Point, and dropped anchor. Farragut and the local authorities wrangled over the city's surrender, pending the arrival of the army. Four days later the mayor surrendered, and 250 marines guarded City Hall against an angry mob while the state flag was hauled down. US General Butler's troops occupied New Orleans on May 1. Farragut was promoted to rear admiral on July 16, the first officer to hold that rank in the U.S. Navy.

Union occupation of the Confederacy's largest city, combined with the effective blockade of southern ports (all significant harbors were Union controlled or blockaded except Charleston, South Carolina, and Wilmington, North Carolina), had international significance in decreasing cotton exports and the likelihood of European recognition of the Confederacy. When New Orleans fell, the South also lost the city's vital industrial capacity. The Confederacy's other major shipbuilding center, Norfolk, Virginia, fell on May 10.

Estimated Casualties: none

North Carolina: August 1861; February–December 1862

Hatteras Inlet Forts, North Carolina (NC001), Dare County, August 28–29, 1861

During the summer of 1861 the U.S. Navy bought or chartered merchant ships, so that by the end of the year, it had more than 260 warships and 100 more under construction. In August a joint army-navy operation began to extend the blockade from the major harbors such as Norfolk, Charleston, and New Orleans to the coast of North Carolina, where the Outer Banks shielded the small inlets and sounds capable of supporting blockade runners and commerce raiders. Hatteras Inlet at the southern end of Hatteras Island was one of North Carolina's busiest ports, a haven for commerce raiders, and the main inlet for Pamlico Sound. It was protected by two earthworks, Fort Hatteras and Fort Clark, manned by 350 Confederates.

USN Flag Officer Silas H. Stringham's squadron sailed out of Hampton Roads on August 26 on a joint operation with US Major General Benjamin F. Butler. It included five warships, a tug, and two transports carrying an 880-man force, mostly New York Volunteers. Two more warships joined them, and they bombarded the two forts on August 28. The Confederates soon abandoned the smaller Fort Clark. Despite the heavy surf, Butler ordered 318 men commanded by US Colonel Max Weber to land on the beach. When the storm drove their ships out to sea that night, Weber's force was at the mercy of the Confederates, but their more immediate threats were hunger and thirst.

During the night Confederate reinforcements arrived, including CSN Flag Officer Samuel Barron, the chief of the coastal defenses in Virginia and North Carolina. The next morning the Federals bombarded Fort Hatteras for more than three hours, until Barron surrendered his 670 troops. Butler left a garrison and a four-ship naval force and returned to Fort Monroe. The first major Federal army-navy operation of the war had been a success. It closed a major supply route for the Confederacy and opened North Carolina's inland seas to Federal ships. Hatteras Inlet became a major coaling station for the blockaders.

Estimated Casualties: 3 US, 670 CS

Areas of the battlefield are in Cape Hatteras National Seashore, near Hatteras. Fort Hatteras and most of Fort Clark have eroded into the sea.

Roanoke Island, North Carolina (NC002), Dare County, February 7–8, 1862

USN Flag Officer Louis M. Goldsborough, commander of the North Atlantic Blockading Squadron, and US Brigadier General Ambrose E. Burnside led a major amphibious expedition out of Fort Monroe on January 2 that included 15,000 men on eighty transports with twenty-six warships and gunboats. Their objective was to secure eastern North Carolina by taking Roanoke Island, New Bern, and Beaufort Harbor/Fort Macon.

Roanoke Island, the site of England's first attempt to settle North America, linked the Outer Banks to the North Carolina mainland and enabled the Confederates to control access to both Pamlico Sound and Albemarle Sound. The defenses of Roanoke Island were concentrated on its west side. Four forts—Huger, Forrest, Blanchard, and Bartow—guarded the narrow Croatan Sound where sunken ships and pilings slowed attacking ships. A large earthwork on Suple's Hill controlled the only north-south road.

The Federals set out to capture the island with nineteen warships, forty-eight transports, and 13,000 troops, leaving the rest of the forces at Hatteras Inlet. The fleet bombarded Fort Bartow on February 7, staying out of range of the other two forts, and skirmished with the seven vessels of

CSN Flag Officer W. F. Lynch's "mosquito fleet." Burnside landed 4,000 men that afternoon at Ashby's Harbor, three miles south of Fort Bartow and by midnight had 10,000 men ashore. The Confederates guarding the shore retired to the Suple's Hill earthwork without opposing the Federals. In Burnside's attack the next morning US Brigadier General John G. Foster's brigade assaulted the works but were pinned down under heavy fire. US Brigadier General Jesse L. Reno's brigade slogged through a swamp on the Confederate right and charged the fort. The Confederates abandoned the redoubt, retreated north up the causeway, and CS Colonel Henry M. Shaw and 2,500 troops surrendered.

Only one week after they had begun their expedition, Goldsborough and Burnside had successfully invaded North Carolina, captured Roanoke Island and two towns on the coast, sealed one of the state's primary canals, and destroyed the "mosquito fleet."

CS Brigadier General Henry A. Wise, who commanded the district from Norfolk to Roanoke Island, had requested reinforcements of CS Major General Benjamin Huger, commander of the Department of Norfolk, but received none. Wise later reported to an investigating committee: "I intend to accuse General Huger of nothing! nothing! nothing!!! This was the disease which brought disaster at Roanoke Island."

Estimated Casualties: 264 US, 2,643 CS

New Bern, North Carolina (NC003), Craven County, March 14, 1862

On March 11 US General Burnside left Roanoke Island with 11,000 troops on transports to join USN Commander Stephen C. Rowan's thirteen warships at Hatteras Inlet for an advance up the Neuse River. Union infantry disembarked on the west bank of the river on March 13 to approach CS Brigadier General Lawrence O'B. Branch's defenses at New Bern, the second largest town in the state. The main defensive line was anchored on Fort Thompson, six miles below New Bern, and stretched westward for one mile to the Atlantic & North Carolina Railroad, with rifle pits extending farther west to Brice's Creek. The Confederates expected attacks to come by water and had five forts (Thompson was the largest) and batteries along the Neuse, mounting about thirty heavy guns. The Federals landed on the thirteenth and camped in the rain.

On March 14 three Federal brigades attacked at 8:00 A.M. While US General Foster's brigade attacked on the right, US General Reno attacked the center of the Confederate line at the railroad and found a gap at a brick kiln. His attack broke through, but enemy reinforcements counterattacked and sealed the breach. US Brigadier General John G. Parke's brigade charged the weakened center, and the Confederates broke. They retreated across the Trent River into New Bern and burned the bridge behind them as Rowan's warships steamed up to the wharf. Branch retreated up the railroad to Kinston, leaving the town in Federal hands.

The loss of New Bern gave the Federals an opportunity to push into the interior. To prevent such a movement, the Confederacy rushed troops in and made CS Major General Theophilus H. Holmes commander of the Department of North Carolina. The successful Federal amphibious operation resulted in the promotion of Burnside to major general and in the resignation of the Confederacy's secretary of war, Judah P. Benjamin.

Estimated Casualties: 476 US, 609 CS

Fort Macon, North Carolina (NC004), Carteret County, March 23–April 26, 1862

Fort Macon guarded Beaufort Harbor and commanded the channel to Beaufort Inlet, the only major opening through the Outer Banks not under Union control. US General Parke's brigade marched south from New Bern down the Atlantic & North Carolina Railroad, occupied Beaufort and Morehead City, and worked for a month to invest and capture Fort Macon. Parke established a beachhead four miles from Fort Macon on March 29 and began digging siege lines on

April 12. His batteries opened fire on April 25. USN Commander Samuel Lockwood's blockading squadron fired at the fort from the sea until the Confederate fire drove off the warships. Federal land batteries, with the range corrections directed by US Lieutenant W. S. Andrews of the U.S. Signal Corps, disabled seventeen Confederate guns. The masonry fort was vulnerable to rifled artillery — just as Fort Pulaski was on April 10–11 — and began to crumble, threatening one of the magazines. CS Lieutenant Colonel Moses J. White's 439-man garrison surrendered the next morning, giving the Union control of the Outer Banks of North Carolina.

Wilmington remained the only major harbor in North Carolina open to the Confederacy. The Federal blockade tightened, decreasing the Confederacy's ability to sustain the war effort.

Estimated Casualties: 3 US, 439 CS

Fort Macon is in Fort Macon State Park, near Atlantic Beach, five miles southeast of Morehead City on Route 58.

South Mills, North Carolina (NC005), Camden County, April 19, 1862

On April 18 US General Burnside sent US General Reno from Roanoke Island to destroy the South Mills lock of the Dismal Swamp Canal, which connected New Bern via Norfolk to Elizabeth City. If successful Reno would prevent the rumored transfer of Confederate ironclad warships from Norfolk to Albemarle Sound. Reno's 3,000 troops disembarked from their transports near Elizabeth City that night and advanced the following morning on an exhausting march toward South Mills. CS Colonel Ambrose R. Wright posted his 900 men to command the road to the town. Reno encountered Wright's position at noon. The Confederates' determined fighting continued for four hours until their artillery commander, CS Captain W. W. McComas, was killed. To avoid being flanked, Wright retired behind Joy's Creek, two miles away. Reno did not pursue them because of his losses and his troops' exhaustion. That evening he heard a rumor that Confederate reinforcements were arriving from Norfolk and ordered a silent march back to the transports near Elizabeth City. They reached New Bern on April 22, mission defeated.

Estimated Casualties: 114 US, 25 CS

Tranter's Creek, North Carolina (NC006), Pitt County, June 5, 1862

On March 20 the Federals had briefly occupied Washington, North Carolina, at the mouth of the Tar River. Federal troops returned to Washington in early May to encourage the citizens who supported the Union.

When US Colonel E. E. Potter, the garrison commander, learned that CS Colonel George B. Singletary's 44th North Carolina was at Pactolus, twelve miles away, he ordered a reconnaissance toward the town by US Lieutenant Colonel F. A. Osborne's 24th Massachusetts. On June 5 at Tranter's Creek, three miles from Pactolus, Osborne's men encountered 400 Confederates positioned behind the creek and among three mill buildings, effectively blocking the bridge across the creek. The Confederate fire pinned down the Federals until Osborne's artillery shelled the mill buildings. Singletary was killed, and his troops fled. The Union soldiers returned to Washington.

Estimated Casualties: 40 total

Kinston, North Carolina (NC007), Lenoir County, December 14, 1862

US General Foster, named commander of the Department of North Carolina when US General Burnside was ordered to Virginia in July, led an expedition in December to destroy a major railroad bridge over the Neuse River at Goldsboro. On December 11 his 10,000 infantrymen and 640 cavalrymen headed out of New Bern toward the intersection at Goldsboro of the Atlantic & North Carolina Railroad with the Wilmington & Weldon Railroad. CS Brigadier General Nathan G. "Shanks" Evans's Brigade of 2,014 men attempted to stop the Union advance at Kinston, on the north bank of the Neuse River. On December 13 the Confederates were outflanked at Southwest Creek and fell back to woodlands two miles from the Kinston bridge across the Neuse River where they dug rifle pits.

On December 14 Evans let the Federals advance to within seventy-five yards of his line and then fired. In the confusion Foster's batteries fired on Federal troops. Foster finally turned the Confederate left, forcing Evans to retreat across the bridge to the north side of the Neuse River and west toward Goldsboro. The Confederates burned the bridge before all their troops had crossed, leaving 400 who became Federal prisoners. When Foster's force got across the river, they captured and looted Kinston.

Estimated Casualties: 160 US, 525 CS

White Hall, North Carolina (NC008), Wayne County, December 16, 1862

US General Foster's force left Kinston on December 15, recrossed the Neuse River, and marched along the river road toward Goldsboro. As Foster's cavalry approached White Hall (later renamed Seven Springs), eighteen miles southeast of Goldsboro, the Confederates torched the bridge over the Neuse. The Federals occupied White Hall the next day. CS Brigadier General Beverly H. Robertson's Brigade held the north bank of the river. Foster pounded the Confederates with his artillery from the hills near the town while his main column continued westward along the railroad.

Estimated Casualties: 150 total

Goldsboro Bridge, North Carolina (NC009), Wayne County, December 17, 1862

The Goldsboro Bridge across the Neuse River south of the town was critical to the Confederacy because it carried the Wilmington & Weldon Railroad, which supplied CS General Robert E. Lee's army and Richmond. US General Foster's objective was to destroy it. On December 17 he attacked, and CS Brigadier General Thomas L. Clingman's forces broke and fled to the north bank of the river, leaving the vital bridge in Federal hands. Foster burned it and sent his cavalry to destroy the railroad between Dudley Station and Everettsville to the south. His mission accomplished, Foster returned to New Bern. His success was, however, short-lived. The Confederates repaired and reopened the bridge later in the month.

Estimated Casualties: 220 total

Fort Pulaski: April 1862

Fort Pulaski, Georgia (GA001), Chatham County, April 10–11, 1862

Daniel A. Brown

Cockspur Island is typical of the low marshy islands along the Georgia coast. It sits at the mouth of the Savannah River, astride the two navigable channels, washed by the Atlantic Ocean on the east. It is approximately eighteen miles from Savannah, in a natural defensive position for guarding the seaward approaches to the port city. The tiny island's strategic advantages were evident to the early settlers of the Georgia Colony. The British constructed Fort George there in 1761 and abandoned it in 1776.

After the War of 1812 Congress authorized the army to improve the coastal defenses of the nation. In 1816 Brigadier General Simon Bernard, a distinguished French military engineer, was engaged. The fortifications devised by the Bernard Commission are known as the third-system forts. Twenty-six of these were constructed along the American coastline.

The fort constructed on Cockspur Island was named after Count Casimir Pulaski, the hero of the Revolution who was mortally wounded during the siege of Savannah in 1779. A young engineering officer who had graduated second in his class at West Point, Second Lieutenant Robert E. Lee, surveyed the fort site in 1829 and designed the dike system necessary for draining and protecting the construction area. Lee left Savannah in 1830, and construction began in 1831, when a more experienced engineer, First Lieutenant Joseph K. F. Mansfield, was assigned to the fort.

By 1847 the basic structure of Fort Pulaski was completed. The fort enclosed approximately five acres and was capable of mounting 146 guns. The brick walls were built seven and a half feet thick and thirty-five feet high, and were surrounded by a moat seven feet deep and thirty-five feet wide. The landward (west) side was protected by a triangular "demilune," or earthwork, also surrounded by a moat twenty-five feet wide. During the crisis with Great Britain in 1839, twenty 32-pounder cannons were mounted in the casemates. The rest of the armament was never completed.

On the eve of the Civil War, the fort was under the care of an ordnance sergeant and a caretaker, posted there to maintain the guns and other minimal military stores. On January 3, 1861, volunteer militia from Savannah, acting under orders from Governor Joseph E. Brown, landed on Cockspur Island and raised the flag of the State of Georgia over Fort Pulaski. State and Confederate forces began repairs on the fort and upgraded the armament. Twenty-eight guns were added, including several 8-inch and 10-inch columbiads manufactured at Tredegar Iron Works in Richmond, Virginia. The Confederates got two 4.5-inch Blakely rifled cannons through the Federal blockade from Britain.

Fort Pulaski's isolated location made it a vulnerable and tempting prize to the Union command, but to invest the fort, the Federals needed a foothold on the Georgia–South Carolina coast. Hilton Head Island, halfway between Savannah and Charleston, was an ideal place for this foothold. In addition, the northern tip of the island lay on Port Royal Sound, a large natural waterway that could serve as a coaling station for the Atlantic blockading squadrons. However, the Confederates had fortified both sides of the sound with two earthwork forts that held forty-one guns: Fort Walker on Hilton Head, and Fort Beauregard on Bay Point to the north.

On October 29, 1861, a combined Federal expedition set sail from Hampton Roads, Virginia. USN Flag Officer Samuel F. Du Pont commanded the fleet of seventy-seven ships, while US Brigadier General Thomas W. Sherman commanded the 12,000 troops of the South Carolina Expeditionary Corps. On November 7 Du Pont's squadron steamed straight into Port Royal Sound between the Confederate forts. The Union warships maneuvered into a circular formation and delivered a broadside as each passed the fortifications.

The Union fire was both heavy and accurate. After a five-hour bombardment the inexperi-

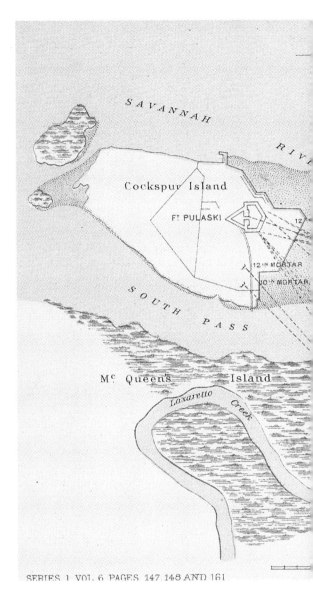

SERIES 1 VOL. 6 PAGES 147, 148 AND 161

enced Confederate defenders, low on ammunition and demoralized when several guns dismounted on the first discharge, abandoned the forts. The Federal force landed and occupied Fort Walker. Two days later Du Pont sailed south and captured Beaufort, South Carolina. Sherman and

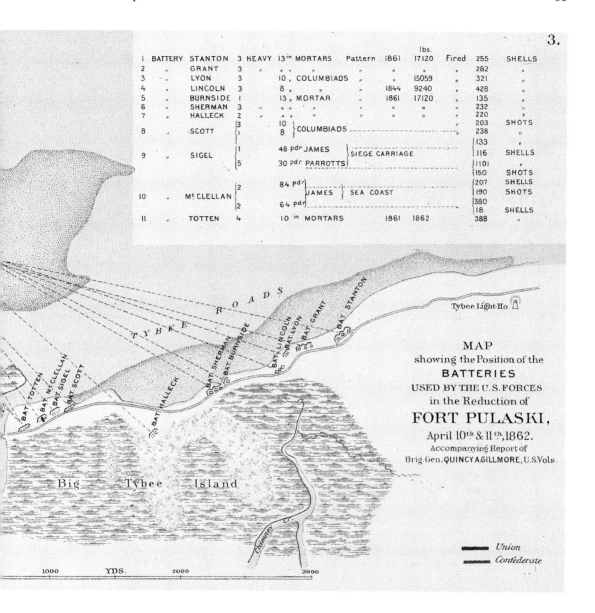

3.

No.	BATTERY	Name	No.	Type	Guns	Pattern	lbs. (year)	17120	Fired	Rounds	
1	BATTERY	STANTON	3	HEAVY	13 in MORTARS	Pattern	1861	17120	Fired	255	SHELLS
2	"	GRANT	3	"	" " "	"	"	"	"	282	"
3	"	LYON	3	"	10 " COLUMBIADS	"	"	15059	"	321	"
4	"	LINCOLN	3	"	8 " "	"	1844	9240	"	428	"
5	"	BURNSIDE	1	"	13 " MORTAR	"	1861	17120	"	135	"
6	"	SHERMAN	3	"	" " "	"	"	"	"	232	"
7	"	HALLECK	2	"	" " "	"	"	"	"	220	"
8	"	SCOTT	3 / 1		10 / 8 COLUMBIADS ----				"	203 / 238	SHOTS / "
9	"	SIGEL	1 / 5		48 pdr JAMES / 30 pdr PARROTTS	SIEGE CARRIAGE				133 / 116 / 1101 / 150	" / SHELLS / SHOTS
10	"	McCLELLAN	2 / 2 / 2		84 pdr / 64 pdr JAMES	SEA COAST				207 / 190 / 380 / 18	SHELLS / SHOTS / SHELLS
11	"	TOTTEN	4		10 in MORTARS	1861	1862			388	"

Tybee Light-Ho.

MAP
showing the Position of the
BATTERIES
USED BY THE U.S. FORCES
in the Reduction of
FORT PULASKI,
April 10th & 11th, 1862.
Accompanying Report of
Brig. Gen. QUINCY A. GILLMORE, U.S. Vols.

—— Union
—— Confederate

1000   YDS.   2000   3000

The map of the siege of Fort Pulaski, Georgia, by Union forces on April 10 and 11, 1862, prepared to accompany the report of the event by Brigadier General Quincy A. Gillmore. This copy is from *The Atlas to Accompany the Official Records of the Union and Confederate Armies,* the most detailed atlas of the Civil War, published by the Government Printing Office in thirty-seven parts between 1891 and 1895. (Civil War map no. 99, Geography and Map Division, Library of Congress)

Du Pont next laid out their plans for the siege and capture of Fort Pulaski. On November 10 the Confederates retreated from Tybee Island. US Engineer Captain Quincy Adams Gillmore's troops landed and occupied Tybee, only one mile from Fort Pulaski.

Gillmore was an outstanding engineering officer and a staunch proponent of the power and accuracy of rifled cannon, but rifled cannon had never been used successfully beyond six hundred yards, and it was more than a mile from Tybee Island to Fort Pulaski. The history of fortification supported the opinion of CS General Robert E. Lee, who told CS Colonel Charles H. Olmstead, the Confederate commander at the fort, that Union guns on Tybee Island could "make it pretty warm for you here with shells, but they cannot breach your walls at that distance." Military history had demonstrated that cannon and mortar could not break through heavy masonry walls at ranges beyond a thousand yards.

Sherman was committed to a siege operation, and he requested the heavy ordnance. By February 21, when the cannons began to arrive, Gillmore had decided to locate the batteries on the northwestern tip of Tybee Island. Union forces began the backbreaking task of moving the heavy guns. Working parties landed thirty-six smoothbores, mortars, and rifled guns in a heavy surf and built a two-and-a-half-mile road, firm enough to support the weight of the artillery, across the sand and marsh. To avoid detection by the Confederates at Fort Pulaski, Gillmore's men had to work on the last mile at night and in virtual silence. Within the month, eleven siege batteries, mounting thirty-six pieces, were in place less than two miles from the fort. Included in this formidable array were nine rifled cannons in batteries Sigel and McClellan, about one mile from the fort and bearing on its southeast angle. Unlike smoothbore cannons, rifled guns have spiraled grooves inside the barrel which cause the projectile to spin as it emerges, making it more accurate and giving it increased range and penetration power.

The Confederate garrison under Olmstead consisted of five Georgia infantry companies, totaling 385 men. It had forty-eight guns, twenty of which could be brought to bear on Gillmore's siege batteries: six 8-inch columbiads, four 10-inch columbiads, four 32-pounder guns, three 10-inch seacoast mortars, two 12-inch seacoast mortars, and one 4.5-inch Blakely rifled. One 10-inch and the two 12-inch mortars were located in advance batteries outside the fort but were abandoned.

At 8:10 A.M. on April 10, 1862, a single 13-inch mortar in Battery Halleck lofted its 218-pound shell in a graceful arc over Fort Pulaski. The fire of the Union columbiads and rifled cannons concentrated on the southeast angle of the fort. The rifles aimed first at the guns on the parapet, then shifted to the walls, literally picking away at the brickwork. The great columbiads shattered the brick loosened by the rifled projectiles. Confederate fire, at first brisk, diminished as gun after gun was dismounted or rendered unserviceable by the accurate fire of the Union artillerymen. By nightfall Olmstead's position was precarious. An inspection of the southeast angle revealed the enormous destruction wrought by the rifled cannons. Two embrasures had been enlarged and the surface of the wall had been reduced to half its thickness.

On April 11 Gillmore's gunners commenced firing at dawn. Confederate guns remounted during the night were quickly put out of action. The Union bombardment concentrated on enlarging the breech. By twelve o'clock shells were passing through the opening and exploding against the northwest powder magazine, which housed forty thousand pounds of powder. Olmstead knew the situation was hopeless. At 2:30 P.M. a white sheet replaced the Stars and Bars on the rampart wall. Fort Pulaski had fallen.

The cost in life and matériel was minor: the Union lost one man; one Confederate man was mortally wounded; all other wounds were not serious. The Union army expended 5,275 rounds from the thirty-six pieces in the thirty-hour bombardment. The rifled guns had done the real work while firing fewer than half the total rounds. The victory was as stunning as it was complete. An entire defense system, which had taken nearly fifty years to perfect, was made obsolete in less than two days. Today the fort serves not only as a memorial to the valor and dedication of those connected with its construction, bombardment, and defense but, in a larger sense, as a history lesson on the elusiveness of invincibility.

Estimated Casualties: 1 US, 1 CS

Fort Pulaski National Monument is on McQueens and Cockspur Islands near Savannah. There are 5,623 acres in the monument.

Charleston: June 1862

Secessionville, South Carolina (SC002), Charleston County, June 16, 1862

Stephen R. Wise

By the spring of 1862 Federal forces operating out of Port Royal Sound, South Carolina, had seized nearly all of their major objectives, yet the greatest prize — Charleston — eluded their grasp. The city was home to a government arsenal, industrial plants, a railroad hub, and the Confederacy's most active port. By 1862 powerful fortifications guarded the harbor, but the city's vulnerable land side was guarded by isolated batteries at the mouth of the Stono River on Cole's Island and by a rambling defense line across James Island.

On May 14 the Federals learned from Robert Smalls that CS Major General John C. Pemberton's forces had abandoned Cole's Island. Smalls, the pilot for the Confederate steamer *Planter*, had sailed the ship with his fellow slave crewmen out of Charleston harbor and turned it over to the Union navy while the white officers were ashore. Within a week US Flag Officer Captain Samuel Francis Du Pont's warships entered the Stono River and secured landing sites on James Island.

On June 2 the department commander, US Major General David Hunter, landed a 10,000-man strike force under US Brigadier General Henry W. Benham on James Island. US Brigadier General Horatio G. Wright's division and US Colonel Robert Williams's brigade of US Brigadier General Isaac Stevens's division encamped at the landing place, Thomas Grimball's plantation. The remainder of Stevens's division took up positions to the south on Sol Legare and Battery Islands. Hunter concluded that the Confederates were too strong and postponed any attack. He applied for reinforcements and left James Island on June 12 after ordering Benham not to advance on Charleston without reinforcements or specific instructions.

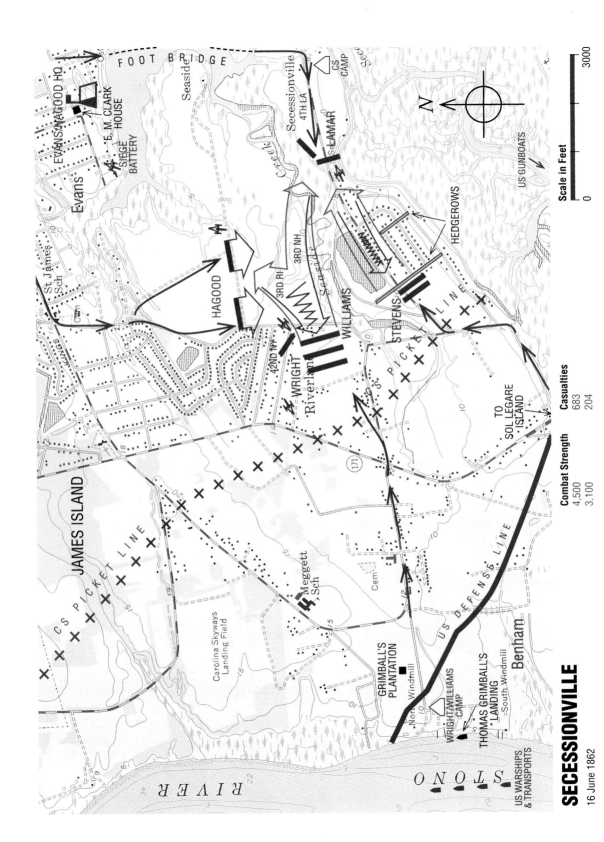

SECESSIONVILLE

16 June 1862

JAMES ISLAND

STONO RIVER

US WARSHIPS & TRANSPORTS

Benham

US DEFENSE LINE

GRIMBALL'S PLANTATION

North Windmill

WRIGHT/WILLIAMS CAMP

THOMAS GRIMBALL'S LANDING

South Windmill

Cem

Meggett Sch

Carolina Skyways Landing Field

CS PICKET LINE

TO SOL LEGARE ISLAND

PICKET LINE

STEVENS

WILLIAMS

WRIGHT

42ND NY

3RD RI

3RD NH

Riverland

Seaside

HAGOOD

HEDGEROWS

US GUNBOATS

St LAMAR

CS CAMP

4TH LA

Secessionville

Seaside

Creek

Seaside

FOOT BRIDGE

EVANS/HAGOOD HQ

Evans

E. M. CLARK HOUSE

SIEGE BATTERY

St James Sch

Cem

KINGS

	Combat Strength	Casualties
	4,500	683
	3,100	204

Scale in Feet

0   3000

N

Pemberton's 6,500 men on James Island were commanded by CS Brigadier General Nathan G. Evans, who concentrated 4,400 men along the island's southern defense line. Southwest of this line near the summer village of Secessionville stood an uncompleted and unnamed earthen battery that faced the Stono River and stretched across a narrow peninsula bordered by tidal creeks. Commanded by CS Colonel Thomas Lamar, the work mounted four seacoast and siege guns and was garrisoned by 100 artillerymen and 500 infantrymen.

Northwest of Secessionville, CS Colonel Johnson Hagood's 2,500 men skirmished with the Federals at Grimball's while Lamar's artillery dueled with gunboats and a three-gun siege battery located on Sol Legare Island. This activity had little effect except to convince Benham that he had to capture the Secessionville battery to maintain his position.

At about 4:00 A.M. on June 16, under indirect covering fire from US gunboats, Benham launched a dawn assault with 3,500 men in Stevens's two brigades against Secessionville while the 3,100 men of Wright's division and Williams's brigade provided support. Stevens's lead brigade overran Confederate pickets three quarters of a mile from Secessionville and soon came under fire from Lamar's garrison. Undaunted, the Federals continued up the peninsula through a hedgerow and into a cotton field. Four hundred yards from the battery they passed a second hedgerow. Under covering fire from a section of field guns, elements of the 8th Michigan swept into the battery's ditch and up its wall. The 79th New York joined the Michigan regiment, and both briefly clung to the parapet before being forced back. Using the hedgerows for cover, Stevens reformed his units and prepared to launch a second assault once Wright's division began its advance.

Shortly after 5:00 A.M. Williams moved his brigade along the southern edge of the marsh that separated Secessionville from the rest of James Island to a position that enfiladed the battery. Federal rifle fire crashed into the battery, cut-

ting down its defenders and wounding Lamar.

Before Stevens could renew his attack, Confederate reinforcements reached the field. The 4th Louisiana Battalion arrived at Secessionville opposite Williams's brigade and began exchanging volleys with the Federals across the marsh while units of Hagood's command attacked Williams's brigade from the rear. At the same time Confederate siege guns opened on the Union soldiers. Caught between three fires, Williams pulled his men back, forcing Stevens to cancel his second assault. Benham then ordered a general withdrawal, and by 10:00 A.M. the battle was over.

For the Federals the engagement had been a fiasco. Of the 4,500 men engaged, there were 683 casualties. The Confederates suffered 204 casualties of about 3,100 men engaged.

Hunter recalled Benham for disobeying orders and had him arrested and sent north for trial. With no prospect of reinforcements, Hunter evacuated James Island the first week of July. The Confederates completed the battery at Secessionville and named it Fort Lamar. Later Federal operations were primarily directed against Charleston's harbor defenses, which held until the city was evacuated on February 17, 1865.

Estimated Casualties: 683 US, 204 CS

The Secessionville battlefield, east of Route 171 and north of Folly Beach, is privately owned.

Simmons' Bluff, South Carolina (SC003), Charleston County, June 21, 1862

On June 21 during an expedition to cut the Charleston & Savannah Railroad, USN Lieutenant A. C. Rhind landed a force from the gunboat *Crusader* and the transport *Planter* near Simmons' Bluff. Robert Smalls piloted both ships up the Wadmalaw River south of Charleston. A detachment of Pennsylvania infantry surprised CS Colonel James McCullough's 16th South Carolina Infantry, burned their camp, and returned to their ships. There were many similar raids along the South Carolina coastline during the war.

Estimated Casualties: none

Mapping the Civil War

Richard W. Stephenson

◑

On the eve of the Civil War, few detailed maps existed of areas in which fighting was likely to occur. Uniform, large-scale topographic maps, such as those produced today by the United States Geological Survey, did not exist and would not become a reality for another generation.

The most detailed maps available in the 1850s were of selected counties. Published at about the scale of one inch to a mile or larger, these commercially produced wall maps showed roads, railroads, towns and villages, rivers and streams, mills, forges, taverns, dwellings, and the names of residents. The few maps of counties in Virginia, Maryland, and southern Pennsylvania that were available were eagerly sought by military commanders on both sides.

Federal military authorities were keenly aware that any significant campaign into the seceding states could be carried out successfully only after good maps, based on reliable data from the field, had been prepared. Existing mapping units, such as the U.S. Army's Corps of Topographical Engineers, the Treasury Department's Coast Survey, and the U.S. Navy's Hydrographic Office, were considered of immense importance to the war effort. In this the Union had one great advantage over the Confederacy: it was able to build on existing organizational structure, equipment, and trained personnel.

Federal authorities used every means at their disposal to gather accurate information on the location, number, movement, and intent of Confederate armed forces. Army cavalry patrols were constantly probing the countryside in search of the enemy's picket lines; travelers and peddlers

were interrogated; southerners sympathetic to the Union were contacted and questioned; and spies were dispatched to the interior. The army also turned to a new device for gathering information, the stationary observation balloon. Early in the war a balloon corps was established under the direction of Thaddeus S. C. Lowe and was attached to the Army of the Potomac. Although used chiefly for observing the enemy's position in the field, balloons were also successfully employed in making maps and sketches.

Field and harbor surveys, topographic and hydrographic surveys, reconnaissances, and road traverses by Federal mappers led to the preparation of countless thousands of manuscript maps and their publication in unprecedented numbers. The superintendent of the Coast Survey in his annual report for 1862 noted that "upwards of forty-four thousand copies of printed maps, charts and sketches have been sent from the office since the date of my last report — a number more than double the distribution in the year 1861, and upwards of five times the average annual distribution of former years." Large numbers of maps were also compiled and printed by the Army Corps of Engineers. The chief engineer reported that in 1865, 24,591 map sheets were furnished to the armies in the field.

The development and growing sophistication of the Union mapping effort was apparent in 1864, when it became possible for Coast Survey officials to compile a uniform, ten-mile-to-the-inch base map described by the superintendent as "the area of all the states in rebellion east of the Mississippi River, excepting the back districts of

North and South Carolina, and the neutral part of Tennessee and to southern Florida, in which no military movements have taken place." Moreover, as the superintendent noted, the map was placed on lithographic stones so that "any limits for a special map may be chosen at pleasure, and a sheet issued promptly when needed in prospective military movements."

Armies in the field also found it useful to have printing and mapmaking facilities so that multiple copies of maps could be produced quickly. On the eve of the Atlanta campaign, for example, the Army of the Cumberland's Topographical Department included draftsmen and assistants and was equipped with a printing press and two lithographic presses; it could also photograph and mount maps. To prepare for the campaign, the department worked night and day to compile, draw, edit, and lithograph an accurate campaign map of northern Georgia. "Before the commanding generals left Chattanooga," one participant wrote, "each had received a bound copy of the map, and before we struck the enemy, every brigade, division, and corps commander in the three armies had a copy." In addition to producing a standard edition of the campaign map lithographed on paper, the department printed the map directly on muslin and issued it in three parts, mainly for the convenience of the cavalry, which needed a map that was sturdy, of a manageable size, and washable.

The Confederacy had difficulty throughout the war in supplying its field officers with adequate maps, because of the lack of established government mapping agencies and the inadequacy of printing facilities. The situation was further complicated by the almost total absence of surveying and drafting equipment and by the lack of trained military engineers and mapmakers to use the equipment that was available.

In early June 1861, shortly after he was made head of the army in Virginia, Robert E. Lee took prompt action to improve the Confederate mapping situation. He assigned Captain Albert H. Campbell to head the Topographical Department. Survey parties were organized and dispatched

into the countryside around Richmond and into other Virginia counties in which fighting was likely to occur in order to collect the data for accurate maps. Based on the new information, Confederate engineers under the direction of Campbell and Major General Jeremy F. Gilmer, chief of engineers, prepared detailed maps of most counties in eastern and central Virginia. These were drawn in ink on tracing linen and filed in the Topographical Department in Richmond. Prepared most often on a scale of 1:80,000, with a few at 1:40,000, each county map generally indicated boundaries, villages, roads, railroads, relief (by hachures), mountain passes, woodland, drainage, fords, ferries, bridges, mills, houses, and names of residents.

Initially, when the Topographical Department received a request for maps of a particular area, a draftsman was assigned to make a tracing of the file copy. But "so great was the demand for maps occasioned by frequent changes in the situation of the armies," Campbell noted,

> that it became impossible by the usual method of tracings to supply them. I conceived the plan of doing this work by photography, though expert photographers pronounced it impracticable, in fact impossible. . . . Traced copies were prepared on common tracing-paper in very black India ink, and from these sharp negatives by sun-printing were obtained, and from these negatives copies were multiplied by exposure to the sun in frames made for the purpose. The several sections, properly toned, were pasted together in their order, and formed the general map, or such portions of it as were desired; it being the policy as a matter of prudence against capture to furnish no one but the commanding general and corps commanders with the entire map of a given region.

Perhaps the finest topographical engineer to serve during the Civil War was Jedediah Hotchkiss, a schoolmaster from Staunton, Virginia. He began his military service on July 2, 1861, when he joined the Confederate forces at Rich Mountain, where he made his first official maps. Because of his demonstrated skill in mapmaking, he was assigned to Major General Thomas J. "Stonewall" Jackson as topographical engineer of the Valley District, Department of Virginia. Shortly after his arrival, Hotchkiss was called before the great commander and told "to make me a map of the valley, from Harpers Ferry to Lexington, showing all the points of offense and defense in those places." The resulting comprehensive map, drawn on tracing linen and measuring seven and a half by three feet, was of significant value to Jackson and his staff in planning and executing the Valley campaign in May and June 1862. Hotchkiss went on to prepare hundreds of sketch maps, reconnaissance maps, battle maps, and reports, many of which are now preserved in the Library of Congress.

Throughout the Civil War, commercial publishers in the North and to a lesser extent in the South produced countless maps for a public in need of up-to-date geographical information. Maps of places in the news, particularly those perceived to be the sites of victories, guaranteed the publisher a quick profit. To give authenticity to their products, publishers based their maps on "reliable" eyewitness accounts, including those of active participants. Compared with publishers in the North, those in the South produced few maps for the general public, issuing those that did appear in small numbers. Printing presses and paper, as well as lithographers and wood engravers, were in short supply in the Confederacy. The few maps published for sale to the public were invariably simple in construction, relatively small, and usually devoid of color.

Cartography changed during the Civil War. Field survey methods were improved; the gathering of data became more sophisticated; faster, more adaptable printing techniques were developed; and photoreproduction processes became an important means of duplicating maps. The result was that thousands of manuscript, printed, and photoreproduced maps of unprecedented quality were prepared of areas where fighting erupted or was likely to occur.

It was not until 1879 that Congress created the U.S. Geological Survey, establishing the beginnings of a national topographic mapping program. Many years passed, therefore, before modern topographic maps became available to replace those created by war's necessity. The maps of the Civil War are splendid testimony to the skill and resourcefulness of Union and Confederate mapmakers and commercial publishers in fulfilling their responsibilities.

Jackson Against the B & O Railroad: January 1862

Hancock, Maryland (MD001),
Washington County, Maryland,
and Morgan County, West Virginia,
January 5–6, 1862

On January 1 CS Major General Thomas J. Jackson marched his command north from Winchester, Virginia, to disrupt the Baltimore & Ohio Railroad and drive Union forces from the three counties that in 1863 became the panhandle of the new state of West Virginia. He occupied Bath on January 4 after the Federals withdrew north of the Potomac River. The next day one of Jackson's brigades marched to Orrick's Hill on the south bank of the Potomac and bombarded Hancock, Maryland, on the opposite side. In two days of sporadic firing the Confederate artillery did little damage, and US Brigadier General Frederick W. Lander refused demands to surrender. The Confederates then burned the B & O bridge over the Big Cacapon River west of Bath.

On January 7 Jackson marched his troops southwest toward Romney, (now West) Virginia, during severe weather. They were ice-bound at Unger's Store from January 8 to 13, when they resumed their advance. The Federal garrison evacuated Romney, and Jackson occupied it on January 15. CS Brigadier General William W. Loring, a division commander in Jackson's army, reported to Richmond authorities that Jackson mistreated his troops by campaigning during the winter and by leaving Loring and his command isolated at Romney when he returned to Winchester with the Stonewall Brigade. CS Secretary of War Judah P. Benjamin ordered Romney abandoned on January 30, and Jackson resigned the next day. Virginia Governor John Letcher personally intervened with Jackson, and the general agreed to stay on. Loring was promoted and sent to another department.

Estimated Casualties: 25 total

Jackson's Shenandoah Valley Campaign: March–June 1862

First Kernstown, Virginia (VA101),
Frederick County and Winchester,
March 23, 1862

Thomas A. Lewis

As the advent of spring made possible the resumption of large-scale hostilities in 1862, the Confederate armies in Virginia were outnumbered, outgunned, short of supplies, and hard pressed. On March 17 US Major General George B. McClellan began a massive advance on Richmond by way of Fort Monroe, Yorktown, and the Peninsula between the James and York Rivers. CS General Robert E. Lee, acting as military adviser to the Confederate president, prepared the defenses of Richmond.

At the same time both he and the Federal authorities in Washington kept a wary eye on the Shenandoah Valley. This broad, fertile valley, angling northeast 150 miles from Lexington to Harpers Ferry and the Potomac, offered not only abundant supplies of food — it became known as the breadbasket of the Confederacy — but also a sheltered highway to the rear of the defenses of Washington City. Thus in March US Major General Nathaniel P. Banks advanced his 38,000-man V Corps into the northern Shenandoah in concert with McClellan's advance on Richmond. Banks met no resistance from the Confederate defenders, a ragtag lot under a general who had never held independent command before. CS Major General Thomas Jonathan Jackson was a Presbyterian deacon, a hypochondriac, and a thoroughgoing eccentric who had been known to his students at the Virginia Military Institute as "Fool Tom." More recently, however, both he and his brigade had won the sobriquet of "Stonewall" at the first battle of Manassas.

This was not the time for a stone wall. Jackson could not repulse Banks's overwhelming

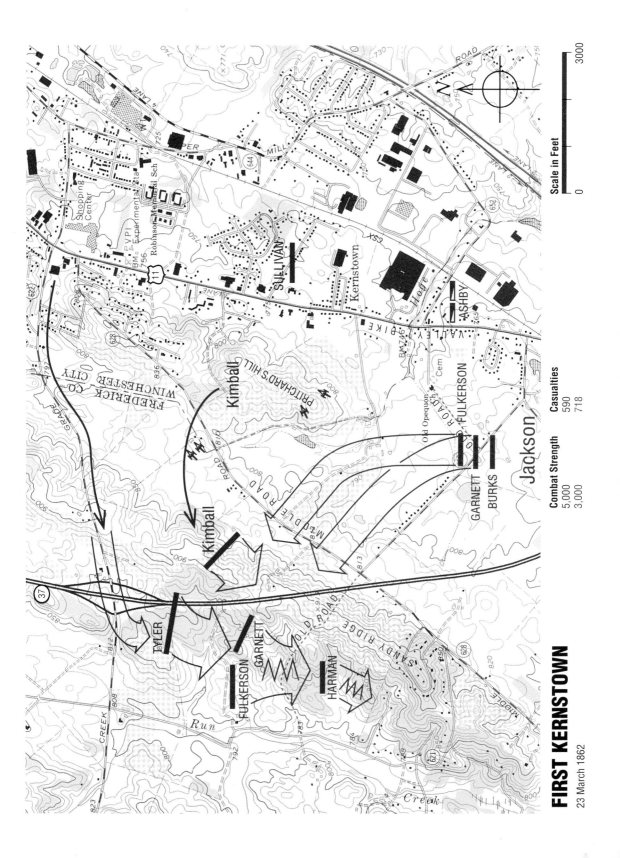

FIRST KERNSTOWN

23 March 1862

Combat Strength	Casualties
5,000	590
3,000	718

Scale in Feet

0   3000

numbers, but Lee ordered him to try to keep Banks from reinforcing McClellan. By March 21 the Federal command was so confident of its hold on the Valley that it decided to do just that, sending two of Banks's three divisions east and retaining only one — US Brigadier General James Shields's — to seal the north end of the Valley.

On Friday, March 21, Jackson's cavalry commander, CS Colonel Turner Ashby, reported that Shields was moving out of his camps at Strasburg and heading north to Winchester. Perhaps he too was leaving the Valley. After a forced march of forty-two miles in two days, Jackson and his main force reached Kernstown — a village just four miles south of Winchester — on the afternoon of March 23, a Sunday. Ashby relayed the erroneous reports from residents of the town that Shields had departed, leaving only four regiments behind. Jackson could see a force of about that size in a wheatfield just north of Kernstown and east of the Valley Pike, covered by two Federal batteries on Pritchard's Hill west of the pike.

He sent most of his infantry — CS Colonel Samuel Fulkerson's brigade along with Jackson's former command, the Stonewall Brigade (less the 5th Virginia) now under CS Brigadier General Richard Garnett — to attack the guns on the Federal right, or western, flank. Meanwhile Ashby's cavalry and a small infantry brigade under CS Colonel Jesse Burks would feint toward the Federal line to hold it in place. The 5th Virginia Regiment under CS Colonel William Harman was to remain in reserve. Fulkerson, followed by Garnett, gained the ridge and moved along it toward a clearing bisected by a stone wall, just as Federals appeared at the other end of

Right: Jedediah Hotchkiss, one of the outstanding topographical engineers and mapmakers of the war, began mapping the Valley with General Jackson in 1862. This map is included in the "maps & sketches" prepared to accompany the unpublished "Report of the Camps, Marches and Engagements, of the Second Corps, A.N.V. . . . during the Campaign of 1864." (Hotchkiss map collection no. 8, Geography and Map Division, Library of Congress)

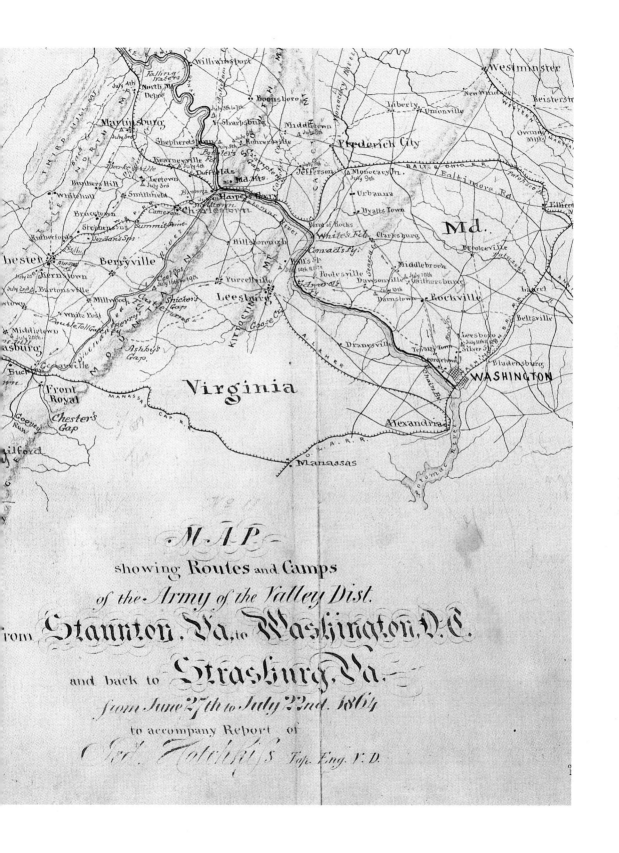

MAP

showing Routes and Camps

of the Army of the Valley Dist.

from Staunton, Va. to Washington, D.C.

and back to Strasburg, Va.

from June 27th to July 22nd 1864

to accompany Report of

Jed. Hotchkiss Top. Eng. V.D.

the clearing. The Confederates won the race for the wall and leveled a deadly fire, repulsing one Federal regiment, then another. But the enemy kept on coming.

Watching from a distance, a worried Jackson sent an aide to do what he might well have done earlier — estimate the size of the Federal forces. His guess: 10,000 men. "Say nothing about it," said Jackson. "We are in for it."

Indeed they were. Far from withdrawing, US Colonel Nathan Kimball, who had replaced the wounded Shields, had executed a deft maneuver. Of his three brigades, Kimball had let Jackson see only one — US Colonel Jeremiah C. Sullivan's along the Valley Pike. Meanwhile US Colonel Erastus B. Tyler's brigade had made a flanking movement of its own, during which it encountered Jackson's men at the stone wall. And Kimball's own brigade was concealed in reserve. Kimball moved first to support Sullivan, then shifted his men to the stone wall.

For two hours the Federals assaulted the stone wall. They could not break the Confederate resistance, but Garnett was running out of ammunition. Receiving no orders, he decided to retreat. The movement exposed Fulkerson's right flank, forcing him to follow suit. Jackson, on the way to the front with the 5th Virginia, was enraged at the sight of retreating men. "Halt and rally!" he bellowed at Garnett when he found him. But it was too late. Harman managed to hold the Federals at bay until Jackson's men collected their wounded and retreated. Furious, Jackson relieved Garnett and preferred charges against him.

Jackson's army camped that night at Newtown (now Stephens City), four and a half miles south of the battlefield. The Confederates had suffered a tactical defeat, taking 718 casualties while inflicting 590, yet events later showed them to have been the strategic victors. The Federals, startled by Jackson's aggressiveness, not only returned Banks's other two divisions to the Valley, but sent another to safeguard western Virginia and held a full corps at Manassas to cover the capital. McClellan was thus deprived of nearly 60,000 troops for his drive on Richmond. "I think I may say," Jackson gritted to an inquiring soldier

on the night of his defeat at Kernstown, "I am satisfied, sir."

Estimated Casualties: 590 US, 718 CS

The Kernstown battlefield is south of Winchester and west of Interstate 81. The battlefield is privately owned.

McDowell, Virginia (VA102), Highland County, May 8, 1862

Robert G. Tanner

On May 8 a small Confederate army under CS Major General Thomas J. "Stonewall" Jackson fought a battle in the mountains of western Virginia near the village of McDowell, thirty-two miles west of Staunton. A year later, on May 10, 1863, when he died of wounds received at Chancellorsville, Stonewall Jackson was a legend to his countrymen. His "foot cavalry" had become one of the finest fighting forces in the history of war. The year that spanned those two May days was one of triumph, a success that began with the battle of McDowell.

Yet at the beginning of May 1862 there seemed scant hope for the Confederacy. The war had not gone well for its troops for many months. They had been defeated at Pea Ridge and Shiloh. A huge Union army was advancing on Richmond, and Federal armies were on the attack across the South. The great port of New Orleans had recently fallen to the Union navy. US Major General Nathaniel P. Banks controlled much of the Shenandoah Valley. Another Union army, under US Major General John C. Frémont (the famous "Pathfinder of the West" in the 1840s and Republican presidential candidate in 1856), was closing in on Jackson from the Alleghenies, west of the Shenandoah. By early May Jackson knew that Frémont's 3,500-man advance guard under US Brigadier General Robert H. Milroy was

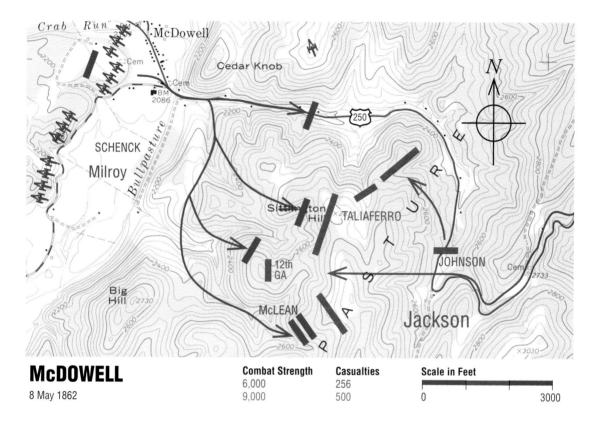

McDOWELL

8 May 1862

Combat Strength	Casualties	Scale in Feet
6,000	256	
9,000	500	0 3000

in the area of McDowell. On May 8 Milroy was reinforced by US Brigadier General Robert C. Schenck's brigade of 2,500 men.

Jackson had rebuilt his army since the battle of Kernstown and began moving his 9,000 soldiers into the Alleghenies. These were tough marches, the first of many that the foot cavalry would endure. They hustled through the windy passes and gorges west of Staunton, and by the morning of May 8 they were within sight of McDowell. There were 6,000 Federals around the village. Although heavily outnumbered, the Union forces took the offensive, led by US Colonel Nathaniel McLean's Ohio regiments.

The battle that erupted was influenced by features of the terrain that can still be seen today, because the battlefield is largely undisturbed. The jagged high ground surrounding McDowell was so rough that it was almost impossible to bring

cannons to the summits. Cannons situated on the lower ground were unable to reach the heights. McDowell was destined to be an infantryman's fight.

The battle occurred on a ridge running generally north and south along the eastern side of the Bull Pasture River, five hundred feet below. The flat area in the center of that ridge, Sitlington's Hill, is topped by an open field perhaps a mile in length surrounded by precipitous and densely forested slopes. Jackson moved quickly by way of a ravine that left the main turnpike about a mile and a half east of McDowell and seized Sitlington's Hill. From its top he surveyed the terrain to find a way to outflank the Union forces on the far side of the river. He was joined by his second-in-command, CS Brigadier General Edward "Allegheny" Johnson.

Before Confederate plans could unfold, however, Milroy launched his assault. Fighting their way up through tangled forest, the Union columns became ragged and somewhat disordered; nonetheless, they attacked with courage, taking advantage of depressions in the ground to find cover. With the sun to their backs, they were hidden by the ground and the shadows of the surrounding trees. The Confederates at the top of the hill were silhouetted against the brighter sky, making them easy targets. They suffered alarming casualties, including Johnson, who was severely wounded.

The Union firing was so intense that Jackson ordered reinforcements — CS Brigadier General William B. Taliaferro's men — to the Confederate right. Moving down the ridge into the woods along the right side of the hill, Taliaferro's troops stopped the Union thrust up the slope.

The fighting was increasingly intense, and heavy casualties were inflicted on Confederate troops in the center of Sitlington's Hill. That post was held by the 12th Georgia, which had entered the fray with 540 men. By the end of the day, 40 had been killed and 140 wounded, losses three times greater than those of any other regiment engaged. Nonetheless, the regimental commander was unable to make his men move back even a short distance to a better-protected position. Refusing such a retreat, one Georgia private blurted out: "We did not come all this way to Virginia to run before Yankees."

In the end no Federal attack gained the crest, given the number of Confederates and their firepower. By nightfall Milroy withdrew his troops across the Bull Pasture River and retreated to Monterey. He could have the satisfaction of knowing that his casualties, 256 men, were about half those of the Confederates, 500 men. An army attacking uphill against heavy odds could not expect to maintain a battle for this length of time, much less inflict greater casualties. The ratio of losses reflected shrewd use of the terrain by Union forces.

The next day, May 9, Jackson's foot cavalry entered McDowell and found that the enemy had withdrawn. The battle had been so rough that even Jackson did not launch an immediate pur-

suit. He spent the day resting and refitting his forces, and then paused briefly to write a famous message. Ever laconic, he gave his superiors in Richmond a one-sentence report: "God blessed our arms with victory at McDowell yesterday." Jackson began his pursuit of Milroy and Schenck the following day, continuing his great Valley campaign.

Estimated Casualties: 256 US, 500 CS

McDowell battlefield is on Route 250, one mile east of McDowell, thirty-five miles west of Staunton. One hundred twenty-six acres of the historic battlefield are owned by the Association for the Preservation of Civil War Sites and are open to the public.

Princeton Courthouse, West Virginia (WV009), Mercer County, May 15–17, 1862

US Brigadier General Jacob D. Cox's District of Kanawha forces were preparing to attack the East Tennessee & Virginia Railroad when CS Brigadier General Humphrey Marshall's Army of East Kentucky from Abingdon, Virginia, attacked them. In a three-day running battle from May 15–17 at Princeton Courthouse, Marshall defeated the Federals, and Cox withdrew to Camp Flat Top, twenty miles away.

Estimated Casualties: 129 US, 16 CS

Front Royal, Virginia (VA103), Warren County, May 23, 1862

After the battle of Kernstown and the return of all three of US General Banks's divisions to the Valley, one division was redeployed, leaving those of US General Shields and US Brigadier General

Alpheus S. Williams. In May the Federals ordered Shields's division to join US Brigadier General Irvin McDowell at Fredericksburg, preparatory to moving on Richmond. On May 21 CS General Jackson succeeded, with CS General Robert E. Lee's intervention, in adding CS Major General Richard S. Ewell's Division to his command. With the cavalry Jackson had 17,000 men. Their objectives were to threaten Washington so that President Abraham Lincoln would send Shields back to the Valley, decreasing the number of Federals advancing against Richmond from the north, and to keep Banks in the Valley. Banks deployed the main body of his remaining division at Strasburg, where 6,500 men dug in to stop any Confederate movement down the Valley Pike. A smaller 1,500-man force was in Front Royal, at the confluence of the North Fork and the South Fork of the Shenandoah River where the vital Manassas Gap Railroad ran across a long railroad bridge over the South Fork as it headed for Alexandria. Another 1,000 were in Winchester to guard the Federals' main supply base.

Jackson headed north to attack Banks but swung east at the gap at New Market and then north again, sheltered from Federal eyes by the long ridge down the Shenandoah Valley, known as Massanutten Mountain. Only CS Brigadier General Turner Ashby's cavalry continued north on the Valley Pike to feint against Banks.

On the afternoon of May 23, in a surprise attack on Front Royal, Jackson quickly defeated the Federals. The CS 1st Maryland and CS Major R. C. Wheat's Louisiana Tigers surprised the US 1st Maryland and two companies of the 29th Pennsylvania under US Colonel John R. Kenly and drove them through the town. The Federals made a stand on Camp Hill and again at Guard Hill after attempting to fire the bridges north of Front Royal. Outnumbered and outflanked, Kenly continued to retreat to Cedarville, where two Confederate cavalry charges routed his line. They took nearly 900 Union prisoners and two cannons.

At the same time Jackson sent Ashby to attack Buckton Station to the west and cut the rail and telegraph lines, further isolating Kenly's com-

mand. The victory at Front Royal threatened Banks's line of retreat to Winchester, so he evacuated Strasburg the next morning and raced along the Valley Pike to his supply base. Jackson sent Ewell north up the Front Royal–Winchester Road while he struck the Valley Pike at Middletown. His troops were slowed by rain, hail, and muddy roads as well as by their interest in plundering abandoned supply wagons.

When President Lincoln heard of the Confederate victory at Front Royal, he suspended McDowell's march south from Fredericksburg to rendezvous with US General McClellan's Army of the Potomac near Hanover Court House, and ordered three divisions — Shields's, US Major General Edward O. C. Ord's, and US Brigadier General Rufus King's — to the Valley. Jackson had spared Richmond from an attack from the north and had prevented McDowell from reinforcing McClellan. Lincoln ordered US General Frémont, who was just thirty miles west of Harrisonburg, to move against Jackson as he headed up the Valley.

Estimated Casualties: 904 US, 56 CS

First Winchester, Virginia (VA104), Frederick County and Winchester, May 25, 1862

US General Banks's forces reached Winchester before those of CS General Jackson but could not hold it. On the night of May 24–25 Jackson gave his troops a few hours of rest and then attacked the Federals on Bowers Hill, with 16,000 Confederates coming from three directions. CS Brigadier General Richard Taylor's Louisiana Brigade swept forward in a classic gray line on the left and crushed the Federal right flank. Ewell's men advanced on the Confederate right as Taylor's flank attack succeeded. The Federals panicked and fled through Winchester.

Soundly defeated, US Brigadier General Alpheus S. Williams's division of Banks's command retreated north across the Potomac. Jackson's men, exhausted by days of hard marching, threatened the Federals not by their pursuit but by their proximity to Washington.

Estimated Casualties: 2,019 US, 400 CS

Cross Keys, Virginia (VA105), Rockingham County, June 8, 1862

Donald C. Pfanz

The battle of Cross Keys is perhaps the least famous of the many battles fought by CS Major General Thomas J. "Stonewall" Jackson's troops in the 1862 Shenandoah Valley campaign. However, the victory secured by Confederate troops there on June 8 was important because it set the stage for Jackson's victory at Port Republic one day later. Taken together, Cross Keys and Port Republic marked the climax of a campaign that is considered a military masterpiece.

Cross Keys was among the last of a series of victories won by Jackson in the Valley that spring. With an army of just 17,000 men he had defeated Union detachments at McDowell, Front Royal, and Winchester and pushed his confounded opponents back to the Potomac River. Though substantially outnumbered by the Union armies that all but surrounded him, Jackson skillfully used the Valley's terrain to keep his opponents apart and struck the scattered components of the Union army before they could unite against him.

Such was the strategy he used at Cross Keys. After his victory at Winchester on May 25, Jackson advanced his army to Harpers Ferry on the Potomac River, while Federal troops led by US Major General John C. Frémont and US Brigadier General James Shields converged on the town of Strasburg in an attempt to cut Jackson off and destroy his small army. Jackson's "foot cavalry" marched more than forty miles in thirty-six hours to elude their trap. The Confederates then retreated up the Shenandoah Valley toward Harrisonburg, pursued by Frémont, while Shields moved by a parallel route up the Luray (or Page) Valley, which lies a few miles to the east. In a skirmish near Harrisonburg on June 6, Jack-

son's cavalry commander, CS Brigadier General Turner Ashby, was killed.

Jackson ordered CS Major General Richard S. Ewell to hold back Frémont. Ewell was a career soldier who had previously served at posts on the Plains and in the Southwest desert, where, he claimed, he "had learned all about commanding fifty United States dragoons and forgotten everything else." The Virginian proved he could handle a division as well as he did a company. On the day of the battle he had about 5,000 men, divided into three infantry brigades commanded by CS Brigadier Generals Arnold Elzey, George H. Steuart, and Isaac R. Trimble, and four batteries of artillery.

Ewell decided to block Frémont's progress at Cross Keys, a rural tavern located seven miles southeast of Harrisonburg. He placed his division in line of battle astride the Port Republic Road on a high, wooded ridge one mile south of the tavern. A shallow stream rippled across his front. In the center of the line, facing open fields, he massed his artillery, supported by Elzey's Brigade. He posted Steuart's and Trimble's Brigades in the woods to his left and right, with Trimble's Brigade, on the right, slightly advanced.

The battle opened at 9:00 A.M. when Frémont, pushing down the Port Republic Road, collided with Confederate pickets at Union Church near the tavern. The skirmishers fell back stubbornly, allowing Ewell time to complete his defensive arrangements. Finding the Confederates in force, Frémont brought forward his artillery to the hills opposite Ewell's position and engaged the Confederates in an artillery duel, at the same time deploying his infantry in line of battle southeast of the Keezletown Road. Altogether he had about 10,500 men, divided into six brigades of infantry, one brigade of cavalry, and ten batteries of artillery. Commanding his infantry brigades were US Brigadier Generals Julius Stahel, Henry Bohlen, Robert H. Milroy, Robert C. Schenck, and US Colonels John A. Koltes and Gustave P. Cluseret.

Frémont made a cursory reconnaissance of the battlefield and judged Ewell's right to be the strategic flank. If he could successfully assail that

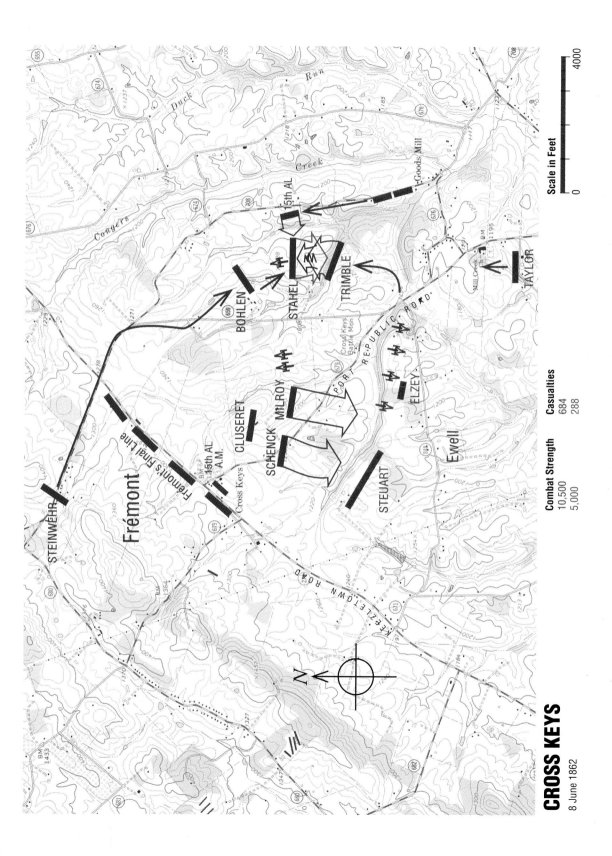

CROSS KEYS

8 June 1862

Scale in Feet

0   4000

Combat Strength	Casualties
10,500	684
5,000	288

flank, he could block Ewell's line of retreat and perhaps destroy the Confederate force. He accordingly ordered Stahel's brigade forward into the woods east of the Port Republic Road at 11:00 A.M., supported by Bohlen. Stahel soon encountered a line of Confederate skirmishers which he pursued through the woods and across a wheatfield toward the main Confederate line. Trimble's Brigade lay concealed behind a fence at the far edge of that field. Trimble allowed Stahel's men to approach within fifty yards of his line, then unleashed a savage volley.

Stahel's men fell back across the field in confusion. When they failed to renew the advance, Trimble seized the initiative and ordered his troops forward. Leaving two regiments in line behind the fence to hold the Union soldiers' attention, he led the 15th Alabama Volunteers up a nearby ravine to a position opposite Stahel's left flank. At Trimble's command, the Alabamians fell upon their unsuspecting foes and forced them back on Bohlen's brigade, which was advancing to their relief. Reinforced by two regiments from Elzey's Brigade, Trimble continued the attack, driving the Union troops back toward the Keezletown Road.

While Stahel and Bohlen were giving ground in the face of Trimble's spirited attacks on the left, Union brigades on the center and right moved forward. Cluseret and Milroy advanced through the woods west of the Port Republic Road and made feeble attacks against Ewell's center. Schenck's brigade meanwhile moved up on Milroy's right in an attempt to turn the left flank of the Confederate line. Ewell took steps to meet this threat. Early in the afternoon Jackson had reinforced him with the brigades of CS Colonel John M. Patton and CS Brigadier General Richard Taylor, and Ewell now hurried portions of these commands to support Steuart's brigade on his left. They were not needed. Before Schenck could launch his attack, Frémont, shaken by Stahel's repulse, ordered the Union army to withdraw to a new defensive line along the Keezletown Road. Ewell then advanced the wings of his army to occupy the ground held by Frémont during the battle. Trimble, feisty as ever, implored Ewell to attack the new Union position, but his commander wisely chose to break off the action.

The Union army lost 684 men in the contest; the Confederates, 288. That night Ewell quietly withdrew most of his men from Frémont's front and marched to Port Republic, where he arrived in time to turn the tide of battle in Jackson's favor the next day. Frémont took up pursuit early the next morning, marching over the ridge held by Ewell in the previous day's fight. As his troops tramped over the crest and down the opposite slope, they passed a Confederate field hospital located in a white frame church. By then Jackson and Ewell were engaged in battle with Shields at Port Republic. The sound of the fighting swelled on the wind as Frémont's men passed the church. In the distance they saw a column of black smoke, where Ewell's rear guard had set the North River bridge aflame. Unable to cross the river, Frémont's men looked on helplessly as Jackson and Ewell pursued Shields's defeated force toward Conrad's Store.

Estimated Casualties: 684 US, 288 CS

Cross Keys battlefield is southeast of Harrisonburg on Route 276, 2.5 miles south of Route 33. Seventy acres of the historic battlefield are owned by the Lee-Jackson Foundation and are open to the public with prior permission (P.O. Box 8121, Charlottesville, VA 22906).

Port Republic, Virginia (VA106), Rockingham County, June 9, 1862

Donald C. Pfanz

Port Republic was the final, climactic battle of CS Major General Thomas J. "Stonewall" Jackson's 1862 Shenandoah Valley campaign. In early June 1862 Jackson retreated up the Valley, pursued by two forces commanded by US Major General John C. Frémont and US Brigadier General James Shields. Frémont followed Jackson directly up the main valley, while Shields paralleled the Confederate march on the east, up the Luray Valley. By dividing their forces, the Union commanders gave Jackson the offensive opportunity he sought.

The Massanutten Mountain separates the Shenandoah and Luray Valleys. Through the Luray Valley, running between the Blue Ridge Mountains on the east and the Massanutten on the west, is the South Fork of the Shenandoah River, which in June 1862 was spanned by three bridges upstream from Front Royal: two near Luray and one at Conrad's Store (now Elkton). Jackson's cavalry destroyed each of these bridges, thus separating Frémont's and Shields's forces. The next closest point of crossing was at Port Republic, where the North and South Rivers meet to form the South Fork. Two fords crossed the South River there, and a bridge arched the rain-swollen North River at the northern end of town.

Jackson led his army, now reduced by casualties and straggling to perhaps 12,000 men, to Port Republic where he confidently turned to meet his pursuers. Fighting began on June 8 with Frémont attacking CS Major General Richard S. Ewell's Division at Cross Keys, four miles northeast of Port Republic, an attack that Ewell handily repulsed.

While Ewell battled Frémont at Cross Keys, Shields's cavalry dashed into Port Republic, nearly capturing Jackson and his wagon train, which was parked just outside the town. The Federals unlimbered a gun at the foot of the North River bridge and another on the plain east of Port Republic. Jackson engaged these guns with three of his own batteries, then sent CS Colonel Samuel Fulkerson's 37th Virginia Infantry Regiment charging across the bridge. The Union cavalry scattered in the face of Fulkerson's attack, abandoning their cannons as they escaped by way of the lower ford. A Union attack on Jackson's wagon train at the other end of the town was repulsed by the heroic efforts of Jackson's chief-of-staff, CS Major Robert L. Dabney. The Union cav-

alrymen retreated to a point approximately two miles east of the town, where they were reinforced later in the day by US Brigadier General Erastus B. Tyler, commanding the vanguard of Shields's division.

Jackson decided to attack Tyler at first light on June 9. Before dawn he ordered CS Brigadier General Charles Winder's Brigade to cross the South River and attack Tyler, whose troops held a position on the plain between the South Fork and the Blue Ridge Mountains. Tyler had chosen his position well. His two brigades of 3,000 infantrymen occupied a line a half mile long. Their right flank was on the river, and their left flank was anchored on a commanding knoll known as the Lewiston Coaling, where a local family had recently produced charcoal. Tyler had posted seven guns on the knoll, and as Winder's Brigade approached, they ripped into its right flank. At the same time Tyler's infantry opened a withering fire from their position in the field below. The Confederate advance slowed, then came to a halt altogether, as Winder's dazed men sought some form of shelter on the exposed plain.

Because of a snarl at the South River crossing, Winder's Brigade initially found itself without support. When CS Brigadier General Richard Taylor's Louisiana Brigade finally reached the field, Jackson sent one regiment to Winder's relief, while the rest of the brigade struggled through the tangled woods on the right to attack the smoking guns at the coaling. Winder resumed his stalled offensive. Finding himself outnumbered and pinned down both in front and on his flank, the Marylander ordered his men forward in a desperate attempt to forestall a Union attack on his position — an attack that he had every reason to believe would succeed. Supported by Confederate artillery, he charged to within two hundred yards of the enemy line before being halted by hostile fire. For an hour his men held on, taking heavy losses in an effort to buy Jackson time. Finally, with their ammunition nearly exhausted, the Confederates gave way and rushed in panic to the rear, chased by their opponents.

But once again Confederate reinforcements saved the day. As the Federals streamed forward

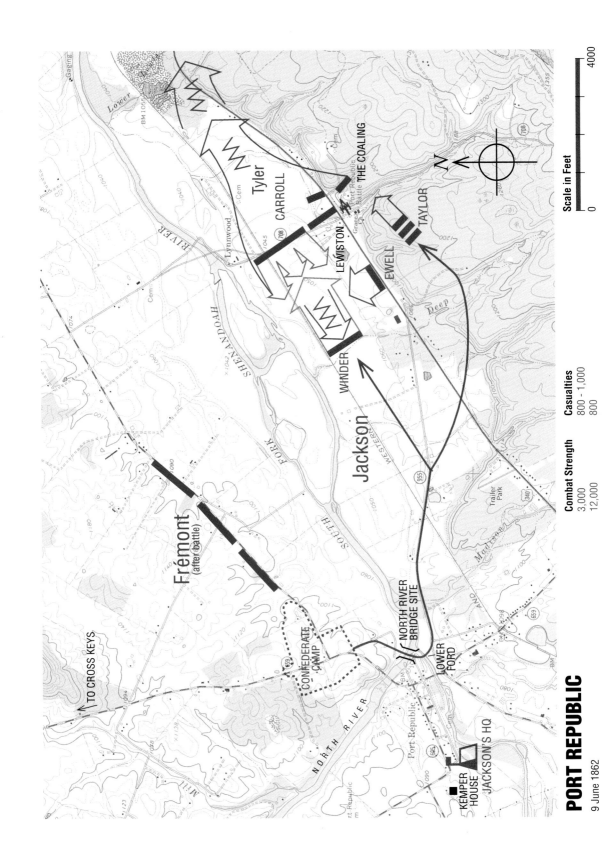

PORT REPUBLIC

9 June 1862

Scale in Feet

0   4000

Combat Strength
3,000
12,000

Casualties
800 – 1,000
800

across the plain in pursuit of Winder, Ewell arrived and struck the Union left flank with two regiments of infantry. At about the same time, the guns located at the coaling fell silent. Taylor had successfully stormed the position by struggling through a jungle of thick mountain laurel for more than an hour. Without pausing to form a proper line, the impetuous Louisianian had charged the guns. He was thrown back, but twice more he led his men forward, and in bloody hand-to-hand fighting they finally captured six of the guns. Tyler, seeing that the battery had been captured, wheeled his line to the left to charge the hill. To Taylor, the advancing blue masses seemed like a solid wall. "There seemed nothing left but to set our backs to the mountain and die hard," he later recalled. Just when all seemed lost, the sounds of artillery and musketry erupted once more on the plain below. Jackson had rallied Winder's men and with the help of reinforcements once more moved out to attack the foe.

For the Federals it was too much. Like Winder's men an hour before, they found themselves outnumbered and attacked on two sides. When the Confederate troops at the coaling added their fire to the melee, the Union line lost all cohesion, and its men broke for the rear. The Confederates pursued them for five miles.

For Jackson the hard-fought battle was won. In the four-hour fight he had lost 800 men while inflicting 500 casualties on the Union army and capturing as many more. Because of the length and severity of the battle, he was unable to recross the river and attack Frémont. His troops were in no condition to fight another battle that day. Realizing this, Jackson burned the North River bridge to prevent its capture by Frémont and withdrew his army to Brown's Gap, a short distance southeast, to rest and refit his men for future battles.

Jackson's victory at Port Republic capped a campaign in which he had defeated portions of three Union armies and tied up as many as 60,000 Union soldiers who might have been employed more profitably elsewhere. His success in the Valley changed the military outlook in Virginia and gave the struggling Confederacy new life. Jackson's army was soon on the move again, toward Richmond.

Estimated Casualties: 800–1,000 US, 800 CS

Port Republic battlefield is located on Route 340 near Port Republic, fifteen miles north of Waynesboro. Nine acres of the historic battlefield are owned by the Association for the Preservation of Civil War Sites and are open to the public.

Peninsula Campaign: March–August 1862

Hampton Roads, Virginia (VA008), Hampton Roads, March 8–9, 1862

The Confederates used the former U.S. Navy facilities at Norfolk to convert the hulk of the USS *Merrimack* into the ironclad ram *Virginia* (which the Federals continued to call the *Merrimack*). On March 8 CSN Captain Franklin Buchanan steamed into Hampton Roads, the main U.S. blockade base, to lift the blockade of the James River. The *Virginia* rammed and sank the *Cumberland* and then shelled the *Congress* until it surrendered. While supervising the removal of wounded prisoners from the *Congress* in the James River, Buchanan was wounded by fire from Federals on Newport News Point who had not surrendered. The *Congress* later blew up. The *Minnesota*, a fifty-gun steam frigate, ran aground, but the *Virginia*'s armor added so much weight that its twenty-two-foot draft prevented it from closing in on the mighty frigate before darkness fell. While broadsides bounced off the *Virginia*, some hits damaged the ship and took out two of its guns. The ironclad had, however, in one day, made obsolete both the powerful U.S. steam frigates and the older sailing ships.

On March 9 the arrival of the first U.S. ironclad, the *Monitor*, surprised the Confederates. Its new design included a revolving turret, a shallow eleven-foot draft, and an eight-knot speed, enabling it to out maneuver the *Virginia*. The powerful shelling in the battle between them did not seriously damage either ship, but when a shot hit the *Monitor*'s pilot house and injured the captain, USN Lieutenant John L. Worden, the *Virginia* used the lull to head back to Norfolk. While neither ship won, together they changed naval warfare forever.

Estimated Casualties: 409 US, 24 CS

Siege of Yorktown, Virginia (VA009), York County and Newport News, April 5–May 4, 1862

President Abraham Lincoln did not share other Republicans' doubts about the loyalty to the Union of US Major General George B. McClellan, a Democrat, but he did doubt the general's plan to attack Richmond via the Virginia Peninsula instead of moving south from Washington against the Confederate army. Lincoln demoted McClellan from general-in-chief, leaving him as commander of the Army of the Potomac, and withheld 35,000 troops to defend Washington. In March and early April McClellan moved the Army of the Potomac — about 146,000 men, as well as wagons, animals, supplies, and artillery batteries — on 389 vessels from Annapolis and Alexandria to Fort Monroe, the largest coastal fort in America, and to Newport News.

On April 5 CS Major General John B. Magruder's 11,000 men behind entrenchments at Lee's Mill stopped McClellan's army in its slow march on narrow and muddy roads up the Peninsula to attack Richmond. The Confederate works extended across the Peninsula from the York River at Yorktown, behind the Warwick River, to Mulberry Point on the James River. They incorporated earthworks built at Yorktown during the American Revolution.

"Prince John" Magruder marched his infantry and moved his artillery in such effective theatrics that he convinced McClellan that the Confederates were too strong for a successful Federal at-

Opposite: During and after the Civil War, commercial publishers, especially in the North, printed for the general public maps showing the theaters of war, major campaigns, and battles. This is a portion of "Johnson's Map of the Vicinity of Richmond, and Peninsular Campaign in Virginia," published in 1863 in Richard S. Fisher's *A Chronological History of the Civil War in America* and in editions of *Johnson's New Illustrated Family Atlas of the World*. It is from the 1870 edition of the *Family Atlas*. (Civil War map no. 602.65, Geography and Map Division, Library of Congress)

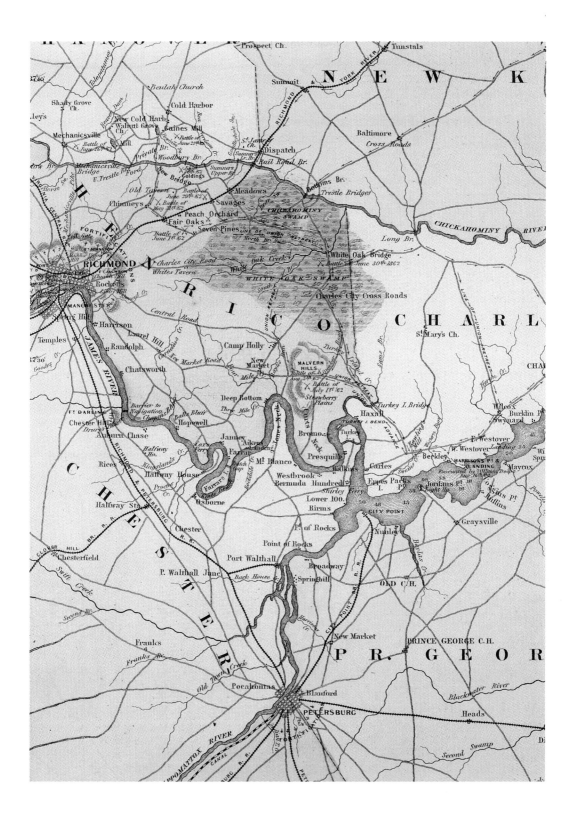

tack. CS Lieutenant Robert Miller said that his 14th Louisiana marched from Yorktown to the James and back six times during Magruder's show of strength. McClellan initiated siege operations and ordered heavy guns to the Yorktown front. In the meantime CS General Joseph E. Johnston, who had taken command of the Confederate army on April 12, reinforced Magruder so that by mid-April he had 35,000 men.

On April 16 McClellan ordered action: US Brigadier General William F. Smith was to stop the Confederates from strengthening their works at Dam No. 1 on the Warwick River, three miles from Lee's Mill. The attack was unsuccessful, due in part to McClellan's orders to "confine the operation to forcing the enemy to discontinue work" on their defenses and because Smith was thrown from his horse twice.

McClellan continued siege operations for the next two weeks and planned a massive bombardment to precede his May 6 attack. During the night of May 3–4 the 55,000 Confederates slipped away toward Williamsburg, leaving McClellan so unprepared to pursue that it took him twelve hours to get his 118,000 soldiers under way. McClellan opened his Peninsula campaign with a month-long siege against an enemy that was not penned in, that could, and did, slip away. The month gave the Confederates time to prepare Richmond's defenses.

Estimated Casualties: 182 US, 300 CS

Areas of the Yorktown battlefield are in Colonial National Historical Park at Yorktown. Newport News Park, off I-64 at Exit 250, includes 5.5 miles of earthworks and the Dam No. 1 and Lee's Mill battlefields. Fort Monroe is open to the public.

Williamsburg, Virginia (VA010), York County and Williamsburg, May 5, 1862

On May 5, 18,500 Federals — and all three corps commanders — caught up with the rear guard of the Confederate army slowed by the rain east of Williamsburg. CS Major General James Longstreet deployed his forces around Fort Magruder. The Confederates repulsed US Brigadier General Joseph Hooker's attack on Fort Magruder and counterattacked against the Federal left flank until US Brigadier General Philip Kearny's division arrived at about 3:00 P.M. US Brigadier General Winfield Scott Hancock's brigade threatened the Confederate left flank and occupied two abandoned redoubts. Longstreet called forward a portion of CS Major General Daniel Harvey Hill's command. Hancock's men repulsed an attack by CS Brigadier General Jubal A. Early's Brigade. Led by Early and Hill, the attack became a disaster in which Early was wounded. McClellan claimed a "brilliant victory," but he did not prevent the Confederates from continuing the methodical retreat to Richmond planned by CS General Johnston.

While McClellan moved on Richmond from the Peninsula, US Major General Irvin McDowell threatened the Confederate capital from Fredericksburg. The Federals had reinforcements available in the Shenandoah Valley — US Major General Nathaniel P. Banks's two divisions — and in the mountains west of the Shenandoah — US Major General John C. Frémont's Mountain Department. CS General Robert E. Lee, an adviser to the president of the Confederacy, Jefferson Davis, saw that an offensive by CS Major General Thomas J. "Stonewall" Jackson could divert Federal reinforcements away from McClellan and toward Washington, D.C. On May 8 Jackson attacked Frémont's advance columns at McDowell, Virginia.

Estimated Casualties: 2,283 US, 1,560 CS

Areas of the Williamsburg battlefield are within the boundaries of Colonial National Historic Park at Yorktown.

Eltham's Landing, Virginia (VA011), New Kent County, May 7, 1862

The Confederate withdrawal from Yorktown and Williamsburg opened the York River to the Federals. US General McClellan sent a flanking force to strike the Confederates before they could reach Richmond. US Brigadier General William B. Franklin steamed up the York River with 11,000 men and began going ashore at Eltham's Landing near West Point on May 6 and fortifying the landing. He was too late to cut CS General Johnston off from Richmond.

Johnston, who was with his army about five miles away in the Barhamsville area, ordered CS Brigadier General John Bell Hood to avoid a battle but hold off the Federals until the entire Confederate force was between Franklin and Richmond. Fighting in the dense woods on May 7, Hood's Texans pushed the Federals back until they broke for the rear. When the Union line was reinforced near the landing, Hood pulled back. The Confederates continued their retreat toward Richmond.

Estimated Casualties: 186 US, 48 CS

Drewry's Bluff, Virginia (VA012), Chesterfield County, May 15, 1862

The James River was virtually undefended after the Confederates evacuated Norfolk and blew up the *Virginia* in early May. A Union naval advance on Richmond was blocked only by the defenses at Drewry's Bluff, sited ninety feet above a turn in the river on the west bank, eight miles below the capital. This fort, known to the Federals as Fort Darling, was built on the land of Augustus

Drewry. The garrison, commanded by CS Commander Ebenezer Farrand, included the former crew of the *Virginia*, the Southside Heavy Artillery (led by CS Captain Augustus Drewry), and other units manning the big guns. The Confederates had sunk several boats in the bed of the river to block access to Richmond.

On May 15 five warships of the James River Flotilla under USN Commander John Rodgers steamed up the James River where they were hit by accurate fire from Drewry's Bluff. The shells did little damage to the *Monitor*, but it was ineffective because the crew could not elevate the ship's guns enough to hit the battery on the bluff. The ironclad *Galena* was hammered by forty-five hits during the four-hour battle. Confederate sharpshooters along the banks successfully sniped at the sailors and wounded one ship's captain. The effective fire forced Rodgers to take his squadron back downriver, and the U.S. Navy abandoned its attempt to approach Richmond from the river.

Estimated Casualties: 24 US, 15 CS

The Drewry's Bluff unit of the Richmond National Battlefield Park includes forty-two acres of this historic land.

Hanover Court House, Virginia (VA013), Hanover County, May 27, 1862

On May 23 CS General Jackson routed the Federals at Front Royal, Virginia, and on the twenty-fifth at Winchester, prompting President Lincoln to order US General McDowell, in command of the three divisions of US Brigadier Generals James Shields, Edward O. C. Ord, and Rufus King, to march from northern Virginia to the Shenandoah Valley to defend Washington and defeat Jackson.

US General McClellan ordered US Brigadier General Fitz John Porter, with one of his V Corps divisions and cavalry, to Hanover Court House on May 27 to stop a Confederate force that could threaten his flank. CS Brigadier General Lawrence O'B. Branch was guarding the Virginia Central Railroad at Peake's Crossing, four miles southwest of Hanover Court House, with his brigade of 4,000 men. The Confederates hit the Federal advance — the cavalry and the 25th New York — in heavy skirmishing east of Peake's. When most of the Confederates retreated up the road, Porter assumed they were headed toward the main force and pursued them, leaving the 25th and two other regiments to guard the crossroads near Peake's. Branch made the mistake of attacking them. Porter quickly turned his command around, counterattacked with his 12,000 men, drove the Confederates from the field, and occupied Peake's Crossing.

Estimated Casualties: 355 US, 746 CS

Seven Pines, Virginia (VA014), Henrico County, May 31–June 1, 1862

More than two months after landing at Fort Monroe and Newport News, US General McClellan's army approached the defenses of Richmond. McClellan positioned US Brigadier General Samuel P. Heintzelman's III Corps and US Brigadier General Erasmus D. Keyes's IV Corps south of the Chickahominy River, with Heintzelman in overall command of the 34,000 men. McClellan had maneuvered the other three corps to the north to protect his supply line and facilitate a rendezvous with US General McDowell, who, until recalled by President Lincoln's May 24 letter, had advanced south from Fredericksburg to reinforce McClellan.

When CS General Johnston learned that these two Federal corps were south of the wide, swampy Chickahominy River, isolated from the rest of the army, he saw the opportunity for a successful attack. He ordered CS General Longstreet to command the opening of the May 31 attack by the Confederate right wing on McClellan's left

wing with 39,000 of his 63,000 men. They were to march eastward in three columns and converge on Seven Pines: CS General Hill in the center, Longstreet on the left, and CS Major General Benjamin Huger on the right. Johnston's verbal orders to Longstreet were to attack by 8:00 A.M., and when he did not, Johnston sent an aide to look for Longstreet. The aide rode so far out in his search that he was captured. Johnston finally learned that Longstreet was not on the Nine Mile Road, his line of advance. He had changed the march route, which put both his and Huger's divisions on the Williamsburg Road and, as a result, put them five hours behind schedule. Longstreet never ordered Huger into battle.

Hill attacked at 1:00 P.M. across land flooded by torrential rains during the night. He broke the Federals' first line of defense, US Brigadier General Silas Casey's 6,000-man IV Corps division, the smallest and least experienced Union division, and drove on to the second at the Seven Pines intersection, just nine miles from Richmond. Heintzelman ordered US Brigadier General Philip Kearny's III Corps reinforcements forward. After a successful flank attack by CS Colonel Micah Jenkins with 1,900 men, the Federals established a new line east of Seven Pines. At about 4:00 P.M., when he learned of the action, Johnston rode out with three brigades commanded by CS Brigadier General W. H. Chase Whiting to launch an attack to protect his left wing. Near Fair Oaks Station, Whiting hit US Brigadier General John Sedgwick's II Corps division, which had been able to cross the rain-swollen Chickahominy River on the rickety Grapevine Bridge because the weight of the columns had stabilized it. The Confederates' casualties were three times those of the Federals and included Johnston, who was seriously wounded. In the separate battle along the Williamsburg Road, the Federals' third line east of Seven Pines held.

CS Major General Gustavus W. Smith temporarily assumed command and attacked again on June 1. The Federals had extended their line from the Chickahominy and Fair Oaks, and had bent their left back along the Richmond & York River Railroad. Divisions from the II and III Corps repulsed the Confederate attacks, and the fighting halted before noon with both armies in their May 31 locations.

President Jefferson Davis named CS General Robert E. Lee commander of the army, effective June 1, and Lee renamed it the Army of Northern Virginia. McClellan had learned of McDowell's withdrawal to Fredericksburg and his redeployment to the Shenandoah Valley after the battle of Hanover Court House. In mid-June McClellan shifted all but the V Corps south of the Chickahominy in preparation for the siege of Richmond.

Estimated Casualties: 5,000 US, 6,100 CS

Oak Grove, Virginia (VA015), Henrico County, June 25, 1862

On June 12 CS General Lee sent his audacious cavalry commander, CS Brigadier General J. E. B. Stuart, with 1,200 men to reconnoiter McClellan's 115,000-man army. Stuart rode northward from Richmond, then eastward past the isolated V Corps, and confirmed that McClellan's right flank, which guarded his railroad supply line, was unprotected. He continued toward the James River and circled around the Federals to get an accurate picture of their dispositions. Stuart turned west at Charles City Court House and rode back into Richmond on June 15. Stuart's three-day "Ride Around McClellan" resulted in the death of one Confederate trooper.

On the sixteenth Lee ordered CS General Jackson from the Shenandoah Valley to Richmond to move against McClellan's right. On June 25 a day-long battle south of the Chickahominy opened the Seven Days battles. McClellan's goal was to gain the high ground on the Nine Mile Road at Old Tavern so his siege guns could fire on the enemy's defenses. Troops of the III Corps advancing north and south of the Williamsburg Road clashed with the Confederates. US General Hooker's division, supported by US General Kearny's division, attacked across the headwaters of White Oak Swamp. They were repulsed by CS General Huger's Division. When the Confederates pulled back to their main line, the

Federals had gained only six hundred yards. It was McClellan's first and last offensive against Richmond.

Estimated Casualties: 626 US, 441 CS

Beaver Dam Creek (Mechanicsville/ Ellerson's Mill), Virginia (VA016), Hanover County, June 26, 1862

On June 26 CS General Lee launched his offensive against US General McClellan in the second of the Seven Days battles. He concentrated most of his army south of the Chickahominy River, ready to cross to attack US General Porter's isolated V Corps dug in behind Beaver Dam Creek near Mechanicsville. Lee's plan was to cut McClellan's supply line from the Pamunkey River by having CS General Jackson's 18,500 men turn the northern flank of Porter's position, while the divisions of CS Generals D. H. Hill and Longstreet and CS Major General Ambrose Powell Hill crossed to the north bank of the river unopposed. This was a serious gamble. Once in place the plan would leave only four small divisions north of the James River and south of the Chickahominy River to defend the entrenchments around Richmond. Lee was fortunate that McClellan believed the faulty intelligence reports that doubled the size of Lee's forces.

The three Confederate divisions maneuvered into position and waited for Jackson's signal. It never came. Jackson was running at least four hours behind schedule as a result of a late start and being slowed by the Federals' road obstructions. Powell Hill launched the attack on his own initiative with a frontal assault at 3:00 P.M. with 11,000 troops. He drove the Federals from Mechanicsville and into the Beaver Dam Creek defenses. There, Porter's 14,000 well-entrenched soldiers, protected by thirty-two guns in six batteries, repelled every Confederate attack and inflicted substantial casualties.

Jackson arrived near the Union right but went into camp not into battle. There was a general breakdown in communications. Even though

Jackson did not attack, his position beyond Porter's flank caused McClellan to order Porter to withdraw eastward after dark behind Boatswain's Swamp five miles away. McClellan concluded that the Confederate buildup on his right flank so threatened the Federal rail supply line, the Richmond & York River Railroad north of the Chickahominy River, that he had to shift his supply base to the James River. The results of this decision were critical for the campaign and for him as commander. Since there was no railroad to the James, and the railroad was critical in supplying his enormous army, his decision meant that he had to abandon his plan to take Richmond by siege. That night McClellan began the retreat of the Army of the Potomac from Richmond after having prepared for months for the full-scale attack that he never launched.

Estimated Casualties: 361 US, 1,484 CS

Beaver Dam Creek, a unit of Richmond National Battlefield Park, is northeast of Richmond off Route 156 and includes twelve acres of the historic battlefield. Nearby is the Chickahominy Bluffs unit, which includes thirty-nine acres significant to the Seven Days battles.

Gaines' Mill, Virginia (VA017), Hanover County, June 27, 1862

Michael J. Andrus

The Seven Days campaign ended a three-month Union effort to capture Richmond. For a week the armies of CS General Robert E. Lee and US Major General George B. McClellan fought, marched, and maneuvered from the Chickahominy swamps to the James River. These battles engaged more men and produced more casualties than any previous campaign in American military history. Gaines' Mill was that week's largest and most costly engagement.

Although Lee had been in command of the newly organized Army of Northern Virginia for less than a month, he had clearly seized the initiative from his adversary. While McClellan complained about lack of support from Washington, Lee consolidated his forces for the relief of Richmond. He had six Confederate divisions to confront US Brigadier General Fitz John Porter's huge V Corps — 30,000 men, who were separated from the other four corps of the Union Army of the Potomac by the swollen Chickahominy River.

On June 26 an impetuous assault failed to drive Porter from his entrenched position along Beaver Dam Creek. With CS Major General Thomas J. "Stonewall" Jackson's command pressing his right flank, Porter withdrew closer to the military bridges over the Chickahominy. That night and the following day both army commanders were busy planning the fate of the Union army; McClellan wanted to preserve his command while Lee hoped to destroy it. On June 27 Lee's plans were continually frustrated by inaccurate maps, poor staff work, and piecemeal attacks. Even Lee's assumption that McClellan would move to protect his supply base on the Pamunkey River proved wrong. Most threatening of all, a nearly impregnable Union position loomed before any Confederate advance.

Union engineers had chosen Porter's defensive line carefully. It lay atop a partially wooded plateau just beyond a marshy creek known locally as Boatswain's Swamp. US Brigadier General George W. Morell's three brigades secured the left, their line running north, then swinging east along the creek's wooded slope. US Brigadier General George Sykes's division extended Morell's right across the plateau. Artillery batteries unlimbered opposite the openings in the woods. US Brigadier General George McCall's Pennsylvania division plus two regiments of cavalry acted as a reserve. The front stretched for two miles, with the left anchored on the Chickahominy and the right protecting the main road to Grapevine Bridge. If disaster struck, three

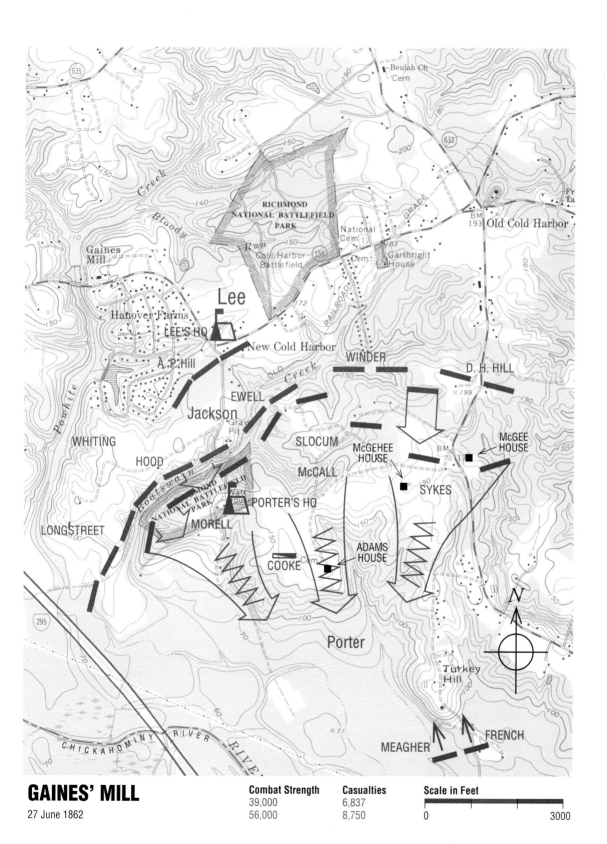

GAINES' MILL

27 June 1862

Combat Strength	Casualties
39,000	6,837
56,000	8,750

Scale in Feet

0   3000

military bridges linked Porter to McClellan's main force and the headquarters south of the Chickahominy.

"The morning of Friday, the 27th day of June, 1862," recalled one Federal veteran, "broke hot and sultry." On a day more suited for napping than fighting, the Union infantry hastily prepared for the anticipated attacks. Just beyond the Watt house, Porter's headquarters, Morell's front line formed along the swamp's brush-tangled bottom. A second line hugged the ravine's crest. Breastworks of knapsacks, logs, and dirt were quickly thrown up. Artillery commanders positioned their guns to contest any enemy advance across the open fields beyond the ravine. It was here that Lee opened the battle.

CS Brigadier General Maxcy Gregg's South Carolina Brigade, part of CS Major General Ambrose Powell Hill's Division, led the first assaults. Just after 2:30 P.M. Gregg's men sprang with a roar from the pine woods surrounding New Cold Harbor. The advance led across several hundred yards of cultivated fields and immediately caught the attention of the Union artillerists. The shelling, said one observer, turned the field into "one living sheet of flame." Once across, the Confederates swept down the wooded slopes before struggling through Boatswain's Swamp. When they reached the top of the opposite crest, they received orders to lie down and rest.

Gregg's attack came against the very center of the Union line, held by US Colonel Gouverneur K. Warren's brigade. One of his two regiments, the 5th New York, was dressed in the gaudy but somewhat tattered Zouave uniform of crimson breeches, short blue jacket, and red fez with a yellow tassel. The men had a fighting spirit to match. As Gregg's troops appeared against the distant woodline, the Zouaves steadied themselves.

"Charge bayonets!" screamed CS Colonel J. Foster Marshall, of the 1st South Carolina Rifles. And with that 500 men surged from the woods, aiming straight for the Union artillery. Spotting the advance, the Zouaves launched an attack of their own. They stormed into the 1st Rifles' flank. For a few minutes it was a hand-to-hand struggle with rifle butt and bayonet. Nearly half the thou-

sand men engaged were killed or wounded before the Confederates fell back into the woods.

Gregg's attack typified the Confederate effort that afternoon. Porter's artillery devastated A. P. Hill's movements across open ground, while his infantry denied every attempt to break the line. On the Confederate left, near Old Cold Harbor, CS Major General Daniel Harvey Hill focused on three of Sykes's batteries. A spirited charge by the 20th North Carolina succeeded in capturing several guns, but a counterattack led by the 16th New York recaptured the pieces. On the right, Lee held CS Major General James Longstreet's Division in reserve while he awaited the arrival of Stonewall Jackson.

For the second day in a row Jackson was late reaching the field. A civilian guide, misunderstanding the general's destination, led the command down a wrong road. Felled trees blocked the route, causing further delay. It was 5:00 P.M. before Jackson's three divisions arrived, commanded by CS Brigadier General Charles S. Winder, CS Major General Richard S. Ewell, and CS Brigadier General W. H. C. Whiting. Lee finally had his entire command of 56,000 men on the battlefield.

After four hours of what many felt had been the heaviest fighting of the war, both sides paused. Exhausted men collapsed from the oppressive heat and humidity. Rifles fouled by constant use were cleaned or discarded. Cartridges were gathered from the dead and wounded. Counting the 15,000 reinforcements sent to Porter from the commands of US Brigadier Generals Henry W. Slocum, William Henry French, and Thomas F. Meagher, 100,000 soldiers now faced each other across Boatswain's Swamp.

The "ominous silence" Porter remembered finally broke at about 7:00 P.M. Lee, hoping to end matters decisively, ordered an all-out assault to break the Union defense. The main effort focused against Morell's division, over much of the same ground A. P. Hill's six brigades had failed to carry. This time the brigades of CS Brigadier General John Bell Hood and CS Colonel Evander Law spearheaded the attack. As the Confederate columns formed, Lee stopped Hood for a last word.

"Can you break his line?" Lee asked. "I will try," Hood replied, and started forward.

Advancing on Law's left, Hood soon noticed a gap in the Confederate line. He personally led the 4th Texas and 18th Georgia behind Law and into the opening. Both the dead and the living of A. P. Hill's Division covered the ground. Survivors grabbed at the legs of the assaulting soldiers to try to prevent what they considered a suicidal act. All the while Union artillery tore through the ranks. But on the Confederates went, screaming the Rebel yell, under orders not to fire until they reached the enemy line. The wave never faltered, streaming down the wooded slope and across the shallow creek.

Elements of Morell's division, reinforced by US Brigadier General Henry Slocum's division, met the attack but could not check its concentrated fury. For the first time Confederate soldiers pierced the Union lines. Broken regiments scrambled up the slope, preventing a return fire and carrying away a second line. The sudden breach forced a general retreat along the entire front.

With darkness rapidly approaching, Porter's reinforced corps began its withdrawal toward the Chickahominy. One last incident caused years of controversy. Hoping to stem the enemy's pursuit, US Brigadier General Philip St. George Cooke ordered a desperate charge by the 5th and 2nd U.S. Cavalry. The charge soon turned into a rout as Confederate musketry fire killed or wounded many of the cavalry. In the resulting confusion, Hood and others captured fourteen guns. Porter never forgave Cooke for the loss.

Nightfall brought an end to the fighting. Lee's exhausted soldiers dropped to the ground atop the plateau, and many fell instantly asleep. Many others, however, took up the task of searching the battlefield for friends. In one day Lee's army had suffered nearly 9,000 casualties. Nevertheless, Gaines' Mill was the first major victory of Lee's celebrated career.

McClellan's military fate moved in a different direction. On June 26 two events provoked his decision to abandon the position along the Chickahominy. Not only had Lee boldly taken the offensive, but prisoners also confirmed "Stonewall" Jackson's presence. The Union commander believed his army outnumbered and outflanked, his supply line to the Pamunkey exposed and vulnerable. On June 27 Porter's corps and its reinforcements fought desperately, buying time while evacuation plans went forward. That evening McClellan issued orders for the army's withdrawal to the James River.

Estimated Casualties: 6,837 US, 8,750 CS

Gaines' Mill Battlefield, a unit of Richmond National Battlefield Park, northeast of Richmond off Route 156, includes sixty acres of the historic battlefield.

Garnett's and Golding's Farms, Virginia (VA018), Henrico County, June 27–28, 1862

While the battle raged at Gaines' Mill to the north, CS General Lee left the divisions of CS General Huger and CS Major Generals John B. Magruder, Lafayette McLaws, and Brigadier General D. R. Jones to guard Richmond. On June 27 CS Brigadier General Robert Toombs, a Georgia politician who was contemptuous of professional soldiers, was ordered "to feel the enemy" at Garnett's Farm, less than a mile from Old Tavern and the river. He attacked US General Smith's front where US General Hancock's brigade easily repulsed him and inflicted 271 casualties. The next morning Toombs was ordered to make a reconnaissance-in-force to determine whether the Federals were pulling back. He attacked Smith's forces unsuccessfully at Golding's Farm. As a result, the Confederates suffered more than twice as many casualties as the Federals.

Estimated Casualties: 189 US, 438 CS

Savage's Station, Virginia (VA019), Henrico County, June 29, 1862

The Federals continued their withdrawal, marching in intense heat and choking dust from the Chickahominy south to the James River. There were so many men and wagons, as well as 2,500 head of cattle — and so few roads — that it took three days to move fifteen miles, giving CS General Lee the opportunity to attack. Having lifted the siege of Richmond, his first goal, Lee moved on his second, to destroy the Army of the Potomac.

CS General Magruder's divisions moved along the Richmond & York River Railroad and the Williamsburg Road with orders from Lee to find and pursue the Federals and force them to fight while they retreated. CS General Jackson did not arrive on the field. There were misunderstandings of orders and delays in getting his command across the Chickahominy River. Lee ordered CS General Huger to leave Magruder and continue along the Charles City Road.

CS General McClellan had ordered the rear guard to retreat toward the James River but had put no one in command. US General Heintzelman concluded that US Major General Edwin V. Sumner's forces were adequate to protect the withdrawal, which included moving a field hospital and a wagon train, as well as destroying quantities of supplies too great to haul away. He followed McClellan's retreat orders and marched his III Corps toward the White Oak Swamp crossings, but he did not inform anyone.

The fourth of the Seven Days battles opened on the afternoon of June 29 when Magruder hit Sumner's II Corps, the army's rear guard, near Savage's Station, which had been the Federal supply depot since late May. Although Sumner had 26,000 troops against 14,000 Confederates, US General Sedgwick was outnumbered when CS Major General Lafayette McLaws's South Carolinians attacked in the afternoon. Sumner brought in reinforcements, and the fight, much of which was at close range, was intense. Lee used the "Land Merrimack," the first iron-clad armored railroad battery. Designed by the navy, it was a 32-pounder Brooke naval rifle protected by an iron casemate. The battle ended at about 9:00 P.M. in a stalemate. Magruder's losses were 444, nearly 300 of whom were South Carolinians from one brigade, while the Federals' were 919, including four of five brothers from Vermont, in addition to the 2,500 previously wounded men who were taken prisoner when the Confederates captured the field hospital.

Estimated Casualties: 919 US, 444 CS

Glendale, Virginia (VA020a), Henrico County, June 30, 1862

White Oak Swamp, Virginia (VA020b), Henrico County, June 30, 1862

Herman Hattaway and Ethan S. Rafuse

While a heavy rain fell, US Major General George B. McClellan's retreating Army of the Potomac withdrew from the vicinity of Savage's Station during the night of June 29–30 and concentrated behind White Oak Swamp. Hoping to catch the Federals before they could pass Glendale, near the critical crossroads that stood between Savage's Station and sanctuary on the James River, CS General Robert E. Lee directed CS Major General Thomas J. "Stonewall" Jackson's four divisions to pursue the Federal rear guard as it retreated on the White Oak Bridge Road, and to cross the White Oak Swamp. Lee rode with CS Major General James Longstreet's column for the attack from the west on the Federals along their line of march to the James. But once again — and typical of the Seven Days battles — Lee's plans miscarried, stymieing his plans for a coordinated offensive. The convoluted battle is now known by several names: Glendale (the name of the R. H. Nelson farm), White Oak Swamp, Frayser's Farm, Nelson's Farm, Charles City Crossroads, New Market Crossroads, and Turkey Bridge.

Jackson advanced his 20,000 men down the road to the bridge across the White Oak Swamp Creek. Shortly before 11:00 A.M. his lead force found the bridge destroyed. Even though there

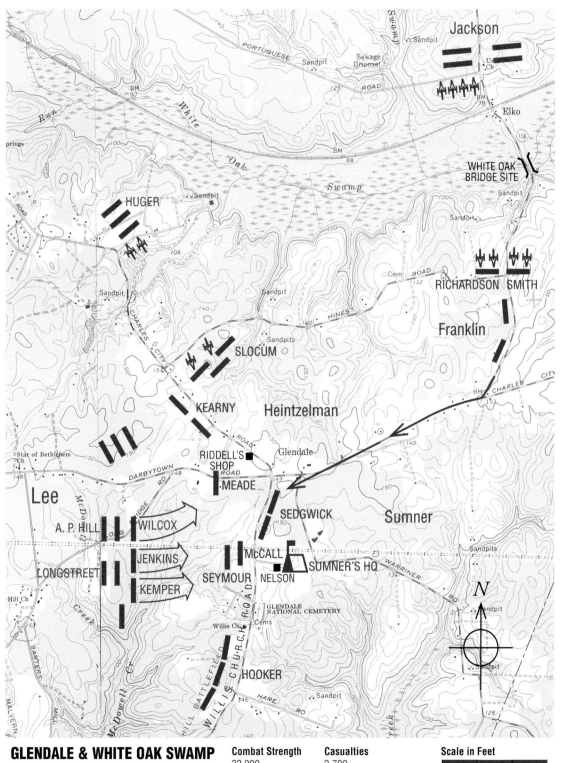

Jackson

Elko

WHITE OAK
BRIDGE SITE

HUGER

RICHARDSON SMITH

Franklin

SLOCUM

KEARNY

Heintzelman

RIDDELL'S
SHOP

Glendale

MEADE

Lee

SEDGWICK

Sumner

A. P. HILL

WILCOX

JENKINS

McCALL

SUMNER'S HQ

LONGSTREET

SEYMOUR

NELSON

KEMPER

GLENDALE
NATIONAL CEMETERY

HOOKER

GLENDALE & WHITE OAK SWAMP

30 June 1862

Combat Strength	Casualties
32,000	2,700
29,000	3,600

Scale in Feet

0   3000

were fords where Jackson perhaps could have forced a crossing, he chose instead to stop and hurl artillery shells across the creek. The extended artillery duel was between Jackson's divisions and the strongly positioned Union rear guard, US Major General William B. Franklin's 17,000-man command. It included US Brigadier General William F. Smith's VI Corps division and US Brigadier General Israel B. Richardson's II Corps division. Concluding that the Union rear guard was too strong to attack with any success, and ruling out any notion of seeking an alternative route to the Union rear, Jackson exchanged artillery fire with the Federals. His infantry was not involved in the battle.

Meanwhile CS Major General John B. Magruder and his three divisions were to support the attack of Longstreet's column under Lee's direct command. Magruder, however, was delayed by changes in his orders and in his route, and his 13,000 men missed the fighting. CS Major General Benjamin Huger's 9,000-man division was to open the Confederate offensive by marching toward Glendale on the Charles City Road and attacking US Brigadier General Henry W. Slocum. Huger's advance was slowed by felled trees across the road, and instead of a major infantry assault, he ordered "moderate" artillery fire.

By 11:00 A.M. Longstreet and CS Major General Ambrose Powell Hill had their 20,000 men in position, and they awaited Huger's firing, which would indicate the beginning of the concerted action. At 2:30 P.M. Longstreet heard artillery firing on his left and assumed it was Huger's attack. Longstreet passed the word for his batteries to open fire, signaling his cooperation with the expected advance.

President Jefferson Davis, Lee, their respective staffs, and a number of followers were with Longstreet in a field near the rear of Longstreet's right flank. Their conversations were interrupted by Federal artillery fire. One shell burst in the midst of the group, killing two or three horses and wounding one or two men. In response to Hill's "orders," Davis, Lee, and their entourage rode to safety while Longstreet took action to try to silence the twenty-four guns in the six Federal bat-

teries that were firing at his cannons. Long-range artillery fire proved inadequate, and Longstreet ordered CS Colonel Micah Jenkins to charge the offending batteries. That brought on a general fight between Longstreet's command and the Federals in their front.

Thus were Longstreet's and Hill's divisions hurled in piecemeal assault, belatedly beginning at 4:00 P.M., at the Federal position. The brunt of the attacks fell upon the position held by US Brigadier General George A. McCall's 6,000-man division of Pennsylvania Reserves of the V Corps. While the entire main Confederate force was concentrated within a three-mile radius and should have been able to hear the battle as it developed, Longstreet and Hill received no help from the other divisions. When a report arrived that Federals had reached Malvern Hill and the protection of Union gunboats on the James, Lee — mistakenly assuming that Jackson and Huger would be joining the attack at Glendale — ordered Magruder's Division south to support CS Major General Theophilus Holmes's efforts to prevent the head of the retreating Federals from establishing a position on Malvern Hill. Holmes was stopped by Federal fire from artillery on Malvern Cliff and from two gunboats. Holmes retired before Magruder approached.

Nevertheless, the attacking Rebels achieved some initial success. The Union line of 40,000 men positioned in an arc from north to south of the Glendale intersection was not continuous because there was no overall commander on the field to organize it. The fact that McClellan spent much of the battle on the gunboat *Galena* scouting positions along the James River led many of his critics to claim later that he had lost his courage to command. McCall's line broke in the course of vicious contests in the dense and tangled undergrowth, particularly where CS Brigadier General James Kemper's Virginians, supporting Jenkins, followed several hours later by CS Brigadier General Cadmus M. Wilcox and his Alabamians, achieved the breakthrough. The fighting grew even more intense when Wilcox's men hit US Brigadier General George Gordon Meade's Pennsylvanians, captured the six-gun battery of US Lieutenant Alanson Randol, and wounded Meade. McCall was captured when he rode into a Rebel picket post just after dark while determining the placement of reinforcements. However, the Confederate attack had been launched near the Union army's center, so ample reinforcements from the Union II Corps and III Corps were available to close the gap. US Brigadier General Philip Kearny's division suffered the greatest losses.

By the time the fighting ended at about 9:00 P.M. it was clear that Lee's effort to destroy the Union army had failed. The Federals had held, preserving their line of march to the James. That evening a disappointed Robert E. Lee reconcentrated his forces to follow the enemy toward Malvern Hill.

Estimated Casualties: 2,700 US, 3,600 CS

The Glendale National Cemetery is on Route 156 south of the crossroads of the Charles City and Darbytown Roads. Two hundred and eight acres of the historic battlefield are owned by the Association for the Preservation of Civil War Sites and are open to the public.

Malvern Hill, Virginia (VA021), Henrico County, July 1, 1862

Michael D. Litterst

On July 1, fifteen miles southeast of Richmond, two mighty armies numbering 160,000 men prepared to do battle for the sixth time in a week. In those seven days the Army of the Potomac, commanded by US Major General George B. McClellan, had been driven from the gates of Richmond by CS General Robert E. Lee and the Army of Northern Virginia. At Malvern Hill, a sharp rise seven miles from their new base at Harrison's Landing, McClellan's forces made a final stand before reaching safety under cover of the U.S. Navy's guns on the James River.

The Union position was a formidable one. Malvern Hill — more a plateau than a hill — rises about a hundred feet at its crest and forms a mile-and-a-half-long crescent, bordered on the east by Western Run and on the west by Crewes Run. The creeks and high ground formed a natural defensive position that made a flank attack difficult. Beyond the crest an open, gently falling slope dotted with shocks of wheat stretched north for a quarter of a mile. The Union had massed 80,000 infantry, consisting of US Brigadier General Edwin Sumner's II Corps, US Brigadier General Samuel Heintzelman's III Corps, one division of US Brigadier General Erasmus D. Keyes's IV Corps, and US Brigadier General Fitz John Porter's V Corps. In addition, more than 100 pieces of artillery rimmed the slope, and 150 more were in reserve near the Malvern house. Despite a warning by CS Major General Daniel Harvey Hill against attacking this strong position, Lee continued to bring his troops up and prepare for battle.

Throughout the Seven Days campaign, Lee had been plagued by costly troop movement delays, and Malvern Hill was no exception. It was noon on July 1 before the bulk of his army, 80,000 troops, began forming along a mile-long front at the base of the hill. Still missing, however, was CS Major General John B. Magruder, whose six brigades had mistakenly been sent down a road that led *away* from the gathering Confederate army. His arrival hours late hurt the Confederates in the battle.

During a reconnaissance of the area, CS Major General James Longstreet found a plateau on the Confederate right that was suitable for massing artillery against the Union line. Longstreet felt that with sixty guns on this plateau and an accompanying fire from CS Major General Thomas J. "Stonewall" Jackson's cannons on the left, Union troops would be caught in a crossfire that would allow Lee's infantry to assault their lines. D. H. Hill's, Magruder's, and CS Major General Benjamin Huger's commands would

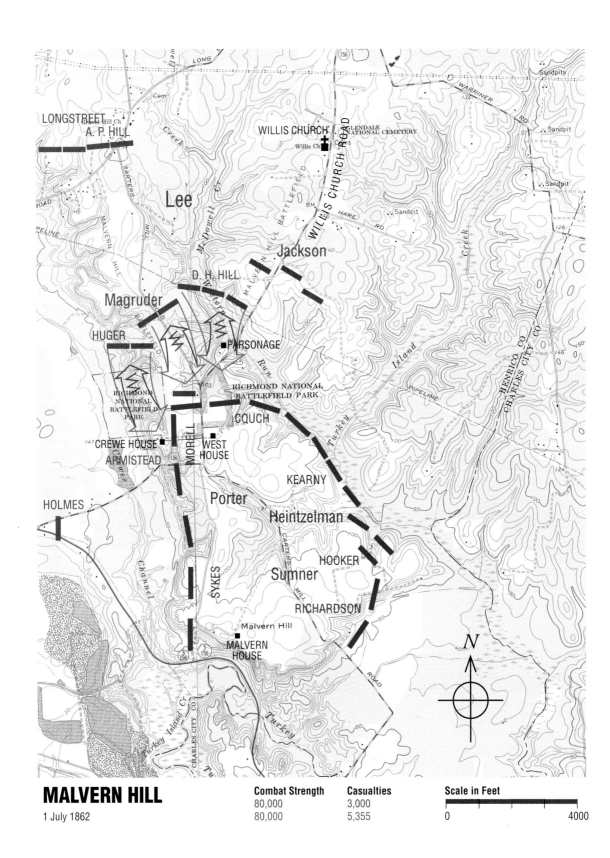

MALVERN HILL

1 July 1862

Combat Strength	Casualties
80,000	3,000
80,000	5,355

Scale in Feet

0　　　　　　　　　　　4000

bear the brunt of the fighting. Two of Jackson's divisions, under CS Major General Richard S. Ewell and CS Brigadier General W. H. C. Whiting, were in reserve. Longstreet's and CS Major General Ambrose Powell Hill's forces were to be withheld from the action because they had been severely engaged the day before at the battle of Glendale.

Lee thought that this plan had the greatest chance of success, and at about 1:30 P.M. he told his commanders: "Batteries have been established to rake the enemies' line. If broken, as is probable, [CS Brigadier General Lewis A.] Armistead, who can witness the effect of the fire, has been ordered to charge with a yell. Do the same." It soon became apparent, though, that it was far from "probable" that the Confederate artillery would succeed. Swampy ground and heavily wooded terrain blocked access to Longstreet's firing positions. The Confederate reserve artillery was not brought up, so only 20 guns out of Longstreet's planned 140 were deployed. Those that did manage to get in position were quickly silenced by the massed Union artillery. Lee soon realized that his plan would not succeed, and he began looking for another avenue of attack. Unfortunately, he failed to notify his commanders of the change in plans, and they continued operating on the assumption that the original order was still in effect.

While the Confederate artillery tried unsuccessfully to get into position, Armistead's men began coming under heavy fire from Union skirmishers. In an effort to protect themselves, they charged forward to drive back the enemy. Magruder finally appeared, arriving just in time to hear Armistead's troops rush onto the field. Remembering Lee's orders that "Armistead will charge with a yell," Magruder excitedly sent word to Lee that the Confederate attack was under way.

Hoping that the attack could succeed after all and not realizing that Armistead's men had not launched a full-scale assault, Lee sent Magruder orders to "advance rapidly . . . and follow up Armistead's success." Perhaps because of a rebuke by Lee a few days earlier, Magruder felt de-

termined not to give his commander any opportunity for criticism. Though his troops had not yet arrived, he was so determined to follow orders that he ordered the advance of two brigades not under his command. At 4:45 P.M. troops of Huger pressed forward through the hail of Union shot and shell and soon were joined by Armistead's men, who had been pinned down between the lines.

To the left of this attack, D. H. Hill heard the commotion. Believing that this was the signal referred to in Lee's orders, he quickly ordered his five brigades to enter battle, shortly before 6:00 P.M. When Hill's half-mile-wide battle line reached the base of Malvern Hill, four hundred yards from the Union line, the Union artillery switched from solid shot to canister, turning the cannons into giant shotguns. At this point Hill's advance across the wheatfield began to sputter, as the men desperately tried to find cover. The 3rd Alabama Infantry advanced to within two hundred yards of the Union line manned by US Brigadier General Darius Couch's division, only to find they were now within range of the infantry's muskets. The pressure eventually became too much for Hill's men, and at about 7:00 P.M. they began to fall back.

To Hill's right the brigades originally sent in by Magruder had battled to within seventy-five yards of the Union line held by US Brigadier General George W. Morell, where they remained, hugging the ground, unable to advance any farther. At the right of the Confederate line, CS Brigadier General Robert Ransom's Brigade managed to reach a point only twenty yards from the Union position before being driven off by "a fire the intensity of which is beyond description."

All along the battle line the situation was the same. The Union artillery and infantry prevented the Confederates from mounting a serious threat. A Union soldier wrote home after the battle that an artillerist told him "it made him heartsick to see how [firing the guns] cut roads through [the Confederates], some places ten feet wide." The infantry was firing so rapidly that their gun barrels overheated and "the men held their guns by the sling strap."

Despite their rapidly mounting casualties, the Confederates kept coming. Magruder's lagging command finally arrived, and he committed them to the battle. But with 7,000 Union troops in reserve and darkness rapidly falling, there would be no last-minute victory for the Confederates, as there had been at Gaines' Mill a few days earlier. Their failure to organize their forces and coordinate their attacks had doomed any chance of success. In a letter to Longstreet after the war, D. H. Hill recognized these critical mistakes: "We attacked," he aptly summed up, "in the most desultory, harum-scarum way."

As the rattle of musketry died away and the booming of the Union artillery ceased, the terrifying sights and sounds of battle slowly gave way to war's horrifying aftermath. The next day a summer storm added to the grisly scene of dead and wounded: "The howling of the storm, the cry of the wounded and groans of the dying . . . the ground slippery with a mixture of mud and blood, all in the dark, hopeless, starless night; surely it was a picture of war in its most horrid shape."

The following day the Army of the Potomac completed its withdrawal to Harrison's Landing. It had suffered more than 3,000 casualties defending Malvern Hill. For the Confederacy, 5,355 men fell advancing against the Federal bulwark. As D. H. Hill, who had seen his division cut to pieces there in a few short hours, wrote afterward, "It was not war, it was murder."

Nightfall ended the slaughter on Malvern Hill, marking the end of the Seven Days campaign. The cost of driving the Federals from the gates of Richmond was high for the Army of Northern Virginia. More than 20,000 Confederates had fallen between the banks of Beaver Dam Creek and the slopes of Malvern Hill, and yet the Army of the Potomac had slipped through the Confederates' grasp. "Under ordinary circumstances," reported Lee, "the Federal Army should have been destroyed."

Despite having lost 15,849 men, the Federal army had escaped. However, despite McClellan's claims that they had "not yielded an inch of ground unnecessarily," many of the rank and file saw the "change of base" for what it was. "We retreated," said one soldier, "like a parcel of sheep."

Estimated Casualties: 3,000 US, 5,355 CS

Malvern Hill Battlefield, a unit of the Richmond National Battlefield Park on Route 156 near Route 5 southeast of Richmond, includes 131 acres of the historic battlefield. The Association for the Preservation of Civil War Sites owns 508 acres, which are open to the public.

Northern Virginia Campaign: August–September 1862

Cedar Mountain, Virginia (VA022), Culpeper County, August 9, 1862

Robert K. Krick

On August 9 CS Major General Thomas J. "Stonewall" Jackson came close to suffering a thorough trouncing at the hands of a much smaller Union force that surprised him with a sharp attack launched across rolling farmland below the shoulder of Cedar Mountain in Culpeper County. He salvaged an important victory by personally rallying his men under intense hostile fire. The fight at Cedar Mountain — where Jackson drew his sword for the only time during the war — was his last independent battle. He won further fame as CS General Robert E. Lee's strong right arm, but he never again led a campaign as an independent commander.

Jackson's dazzling success in the Shenandoah Valley during the spring of 1862 had made his name a household word in both the North and the South. In late June he hurried to Richmond to help Lee drive Union troops away from the Confederacy's capital. Jackson fumbled in the unfamiliar swampy country below Richmond during the costly but successful campaign there. When a new Union threat loomed in northern Virginia, Lee sent Jackson with three divisions to suppress it.

The Union army operating west of Fredericksburg in the vicinity of Culpeper was commanded by US Major General John Pope, who had achieved some success in the West. More important, he was allied with the radical politicians then holding sway in Washington. Pope, who issued bombastic orders that his troops laughed at, announced draconian measures against southern civilians, adding an ugly new aspect to the conflict. In response, the Confederate government declared him, and by extension his officers,

outlaws whose demeanor put them outside the boundaries of civilized warfare.

Jackson faced Pope across the Rapidan River in early August, from encampments around Gordonsville and Orange Court House. On August 7 he thought he saw an opportunity to assail part of Pope's army near Culpeper Court House without having to face the rest of the Union strength. The effort to hurl his divisions, totaling 22,000 troops, at the 12,000 Union soldiers sputtered badly because of dreadful weather and poor country roads, combined with confused marching orders that resulted from Jackson's habitual reticence to share his plans with his principal subordinates. Troops who had won fame as Jackson's "foot cavalry" because of their hardy marching stood in the dust for hours without moving. Many units covered less than a mile. The Confederates crossed the Rapidan on August 8 and pushed into Culpeper County, but without engaging the enemy force or advancing with any real vigor. Early on August 9, a disgruntled Jackson wired Lee: "I am not making much progress."

By the time he sent that message, though, his forward elements were approaching a Union position near the northwest corner of Cedar Mountain. Men of both armies fell out of ranks because of the high temperature, some of them suffering fatal heat stroke. CS Brigadier General Jubal A. Early, commanding the first Confederate brigade on the field, found Union cavalry spread across the farmland just above Cedar Run. He could see hostile artillery positioned behind them and assumed that infantry supported the guns. Confederate artillery was moved to the front into strong positions all across a line perpendicular to the main road. Some of Jackson's cannons clustered under the protection of a wooded knoll that came to be known as the Cedars; more struggled up the steep slope of Cedar Mountain and found an artillery aerie on the mountain's shoulder, elevated above the infantry arena. During the fighting that ensued, that rock-solid position on the mountainside anchored the Confederate right.

A third cluster of Confederate guns gathered around a bottleneck where the main road

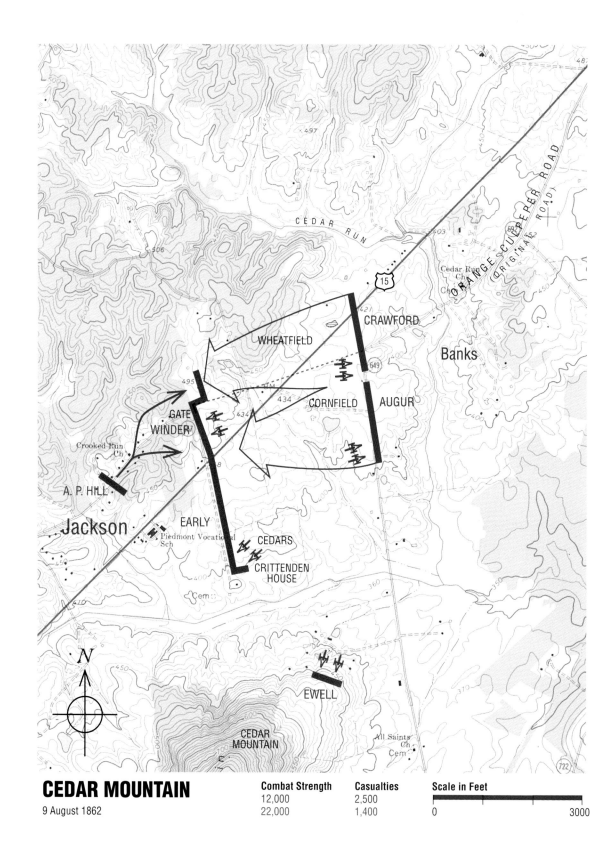

CEDAR RUN

ORANGE CULPEPER ROAD
(ORIGINAL ROAD)

15

Cedar Run Ch

CRAWFORD

Banks

WHEATFIELD

649

GATE
WINDER

CORNFIELD

AUGUR

Crooked Run
Ch

A. P. HILL

Jackson

EARLY

Piedmont Vocational
Sch

CEDARS

CRITTENDEN
HOUSE

Cem

EWELL

N

CEDAR
MOUNTAIN

All Saints
Cem

722

CEDAR MOUNTAIN

9 August 1862

Combat Strength	Casualties
12,000	2,500
22,000	1,400

Scale in Feet

0   3000

emerged from woods at the gate to a long lane leading to the Crittenden house. While artillery dueled all across the front, Confederate infantry maneuvered into position along a woodline facing a wheatfield and along the thousand-yard-long Crittenden Lane.

During the inconclusive artillery duel, the Union commander on the field, US Major General Nathaniel P. Banks, launched some of his force against the Confederate guns near the Crittenden gate and the rest of his men through a cornfield toward Crittenden Lane. US Brigadier General Samuel W. Crawford's brigade of men from Connecticut, Maine, Wisconsin, Pennsylvania, and New York moved into the wheatfield and headed for the Confederate woodline without knowing that they faced an enemy who heavily outnumbered them, but fortune smiled on the brave Union soldiers. Jackson concentrated his attention on the artillery duel, perhaps because of the interest he had developed during his Mexican War service. The Confederate infantry line was therefore poorly situated. CS Brigadier General Charles S. Winder of Maryland, commanding Jackson's old division, also focused on artillery matters, but a Union round shattered his side, mortally wounding him, just as the Union onslaught crashed through the wheatfield.

Crawford's men fell on a seam between Jackson's units and unraveled the entire left of his army, shattering regiment after regiment in the process. At the same time, US Brigadier General Christopher C. Augur's division boiled out of the rows of a cornfield and up against the Confederates near Crittenden Lane. Confederate artillery at the Cedars and the Crittenden gate limbered up and dashed away just in time.

At the crisis Jackson waded into the melee, waving his sheathed sword in one hand and a battle flag in the other while Union bullets flew past from three directions. The fleeing troops rallied at the sight of their fabled leader, but they probably could not have held on without CS Major General Ambrose Powell Hill's substantial reinforcements. As darkness fell, fresh brigades cleared the field and forced the Federals back toward Culpeper. The 22,000 Confederates de-feated 12,000 Federals, at a cost of about 2,500 casualties for the Federals and 1,400 for the Confederates.

Jackson subsequently declared that Cedar Mountain was "the most successful of his exploits," a judgment surely based on the excitement of an adrenaline-laced personal involvement rather than any sense of tactical or strategic prowess. Two days later Jackson fell back south of the Rapidan to await Lee's arrival from Richmond with the rest of the Army of Northern Virginia, to begin a campaign that ended three weeks later in the battle of Second Manassas.

Estimated Casualties: 2,500 US, 1,400 CS

Cedar Mountain battlefield, on Route 15 between Orange and Culpeper, is privately owned.

Rappahannock River, Virginia (VA023), Culpeper and Fauquier Counties, August 22–25, 1862

By mid-August CS General Lee knew that US Major General George B. McClellan was redeploying his army from the Peninsula to unite it with US General Pope's Army of Virginia on the Rapidan. Lee sent CS Major General James Longstreet from Richmond to reinforce CS General Jackson near Gordonsville. Lee arrived on August 15 to assume command. Pope withdrew to the Rappahannock River on August 20–21.

On August 22–23, in a daring raid on Pope's headquarters at Catlett Station, CS Major General J. E. B. Stuart's cavalry captured Pope's headquarters train, including his dispatch book. It gave Lee the timetable and the destinations of the Federal forces, including the major elements of the Army of the Potomac that were en route to reinforce Pope.

Lee acted decisively. While the two armies engaged in a series of minor battles along the Rappahannock at Freeman's Ford, Warrenton, Beverly's Ford, Sulphur Springs, and Waterloo Bridge from August 22 to 25 which fixed Pope's position along the river, Lee ordered Jackson's wing on a wide swing around Pope and through Thoroughfare Gap.

Estimated Casualties: 225 total

Manassas Station/Junction, Virginia (VA024), Prince William County, August 26–27, 1862

On the evening of August 26 CS General Jackson struck the Orange & Alexandria Railroad at Bristoe Station after a fifty-four-mile forced march in thirty-six hours through Thoroughfare Gap. He surprised the Federal commanders and shocked Washington by capturing the huge Union supply depot at Manassas Junction, well in the rear of US General Pope's army. On the twenty-seventh Jackson turned his troops loose to pillage the depot and then burn what they could not carry away.

Jackson's march forced Pope to abandon his defensive line along the Rappahannock River. CS General Longstreet advanced north, then east from behind the Rappahannock, and followed Jackson's route through Thoroughfare Gap to link up with him.

On August 27 Jackson routed a reinforced Federal brigade near Union Mills, inflicting several hundred casualties and mortally wounding US Brigadier General George W. Taylor. CS Major General Richard S. Ewell's Division fought a brisk rear-guard action against US Major General Joseph Hooker's division at Kettle Run and held the Union forces south of Broad Run until dusk.

That night Jackson marched his corps north toward the first Manassas battlefield.

Estimated Casualties: unknown

Thoroughfare Gap, Virginia (VA025), Prince William and Fauquier Counties, August 28, 1862

On August 28, in a skirmish near Chapman's Mill in Thoroughfare Gap, the Confederates seized the commanding ground north and south of the gap, outflanking US Brigadier General James Ricketts's division, while CS Brigadier General Cadmus M. Wilcox's Division headed for Hopewell Gap five miles north.

Ricketts retired to Manassas Junction via Bristoe Station, leaving Thoroughfare Gap open for CS General Longstreet to march through and join CS General Jackson. This minor action had major consequences. By focusing on Jackson and not on Longstreet, Pope permitted Lee to unite the two wings of his army on the Manassas battlefield.

Estimated Casualties: 100 total

Second Manassas, Virginia (VA026), Prince William County, August 28–30, 1862

John J. Hennessy

The warm winds of the late summer of 1862 blew across a hopeful and ambitious Confederacy. Union offensives of the spring and summer were, as one southerner joyously described it, "played out," and victory-starved northerners were grumbling with discontent. European recognition of the nascent Confederacy seemed a real possibility; so did independence. Confederate forces from Richmond to the Mississippi wanted to strike the blow that would bring the war to a triumphant close.

In Virginia, on which the eyes of most observers were firmly fixed, the job of striking such a blow fell to CS General Robert E. Lee. After dispatching US Major General George B. McClellan's Army of the Potomac during the Seven Days campaign, Lee turned his eyes northward to a

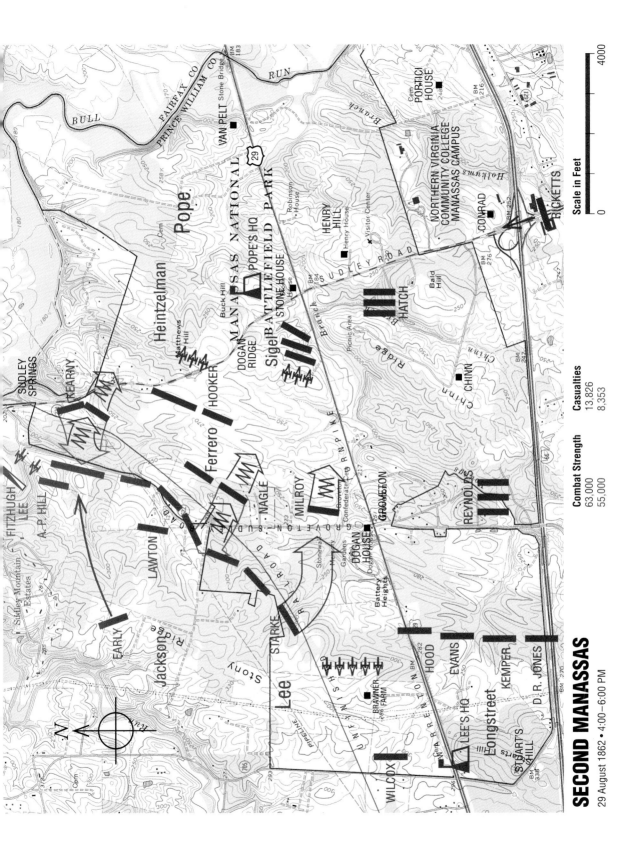

SECOND MANASSAS

29 August 1862 • 4:00—6:00 PM

	Combat Strength	Casualties
	63,000	13,826
	55,000	8,353

Scale in Feet

0   4000

second Union threat: US Major General John Pope's new Army of Virginia. Lee knew that if he allowed McClellan's 120,000 men, now on the move northward, to join Pope's 63,000 in northern Virginia, the Confederates would be outnumbered more than two to one. No strategic or tactical magic could overcome those numbers. Lee knew he must beat Pope before McClellan joined him.

In mid-July Lee ordered CS Major General Thomas J. "Stonewall" Jackson away from Richmond to confront Pope with 24,000 men. After Jackson's mismanaged and dearly bought victory over part of Pope's army at the battle of Cedar Mountain, Lee marched with the rest of his army — CS Major General James Longstreet's wing (31,000 men) — to join Jackson and defeat Pope's entire force. Pope and Lee sparred inconclusively for two weeks, first along the Rapidan River and then along the Rappahannock.

Finally, on August 25, Lee found his opening. Jackson and his "foot cavalry" marched fifty-four miles in thirty-six hours around Pope's right flank to cut the Federal army's supply line to Alexandria at Manassas Junction. Pope groped for Jackson, boasting he would "bag" the famous Confederate, only to have Jackson elude him. Jackson torched the Federal supplies at Manassas Junction and marched five miles north to familiar ground near the scene of the war's opening battle. There he secreted his men behind woods and ridges along an old unfinished railroad bed, north of the Warrenton Turnpike (now Route 29). He waited not just for Lee and the rest of the Confederate army (marching about thirty-six hours behind) but for Pope as well.

At 5:30 P.M. on August 28 one of Pope's columns appeared in Jackson's front, tramping unwarily eastward along the Warrenton Turnpike. Jackson quickly roused himself from a nap and rode out alone to watch the Union troops. On the ridge not far from farmer John Brawner's house, within musket range of the Federal column, Jackson paced his horse nervously, watching the Federals for perhaps three minutes. Suddenly he wheeled his horse and galloped toward his men in the dis-

tant woods. "Here he comes, by God," exclaimed one of his officers. Jackson neared and reined his horse to a stop. As if conversing with a next-door neighbor, he said quietly, "Gentlemen, bring up your men." The second battle of Manassas was about to begin.

Within minutes Jackson's artillery appeared, and shells began screaming over and through the Union column, sending the men scrambling for roadside cover. These men from Wisconsin and Indiana, later to be known as the Iron Brigade (US Major General Irvin McDowell's corps), formed expertly into lines of battle and swept across the fields and woods toward the Confederates. Near the Brawner house the two lines collided in a tumult of smoke and death. At a range of less than a hundred yards, with little cover other than splintered rail fences, Jackson's men and the Union forces battered each other. After two hours of bloody stalemate, darkness brought an end to the day's fighting. Thirty-three percent of those engaged were casualties.

Believing that he did indeed have Jackson "bagged," Pope ordered his army to converge on the Confederates. The next morning Jackson's men awoke to the distant boom of Union artillery as the Federals prepared to attack. Jackson hastily deployed the divisions of CS Brigadier General William E. Starke, CS Brigadier General Alexander R. Lawton, and CS Major General Ambrose Powell Hill along the cuts and fills of the unfinished railroad at the base of Stony Ridge. His left rested near the hamlet of Sudley Springs on Bull Run, and his right amid the wreckage at the Brawner farm. Stony Ridge rose behind Jackson's line, its lower reaches studded with his artillery. The ground undulated gently, marked here and there with woods, cornfields, and small farms as it sloped toward the Warrenton Turnpike.

Despite his loud proclamations that he would dispose of Jackson, Pope launched only a series of small, disjointed attacks against the Confederates on August 29. He struck Jackson's center with US Brigadier General Robert H. Milroy's two regiments, then his left with US Brigadier General Joseph Hooker's five, and at about 4:00 P.M. the center again, with US Colonel James Nagle's three regiments. Each of these attacks briefly broke Jackson's line, but each time Pope gave Jackson the opportunity to patch the breech and drive the unsupported Federals back. Only late in the day did he seriously threaten Jackson.

At 5:00 P.M. US Major General Philip Kearny, the pugnacious one-armed Mexican War veteran, led his division against Jackson's left. His men crossed the unfinished railroad and drove Hill's men beyond the Groveton-Sudley Road (now Route 622) to the lower slopes of Stony Ridge. There the Confederates stiffened, aided by CS Brigadier General Jubal A. Early's Brigade. Once again Pope failed to send reinforcements, and for the fourth time that day Union success turned into inglorious retreat.

While Pope focused single-mindedly on Jackson, Lee and Longstreet arrived on the field to complete the Confederate assemblage. Unknown to Pope, Lee placed Longstreet on Jackson's right, extending the Confederate line more than a mile southward and wrapping it around Pope's exposed left. Shaped like a huge pair of gaping jaws with Pope between them, Lee's line was ready to snap shut.

Pope's mild successes on August 29 were enough to encourage him to resume the attacks on August 30. After a morning of light skirmishing and cannon fire, Pope massed 10,000 men to attack Jackson's line at what was later called the Deep Cut. At 3:00 P.M. these troops swept forward. Jackson's men, protected by the unfinished railroad, cut them down in huge numbers. "What a slaughter! What a slaughter of men that was!" remembered one Georgian. "They were so thick it was just impossible to miss them." After thirty minutes of the battle's most intense fighting, the Federals, lashed also by Confederate artillery to their left, broke and fell back. Pope's biggest attack of the battle had failed.

At his headquarters on what came to be known as Stuart's Hill, Lee saw his opportunity and ordered Longstreet forward in a massive counterattack against the exposed Union left. Thirty thousand Confederates surged ahead, barreling over all Union opposition until they reached Chinn Ridge. Pope, facing disaster, patched together a makeshift defense, trying to buy enough time to get his army safely off the field. For more than an hour the fighting raged on the ridge, each side throwing in regiments and brigades as fast as they arrived. Finally, at about 6:00 P.M., the Federals gave way, but Pope had gained enough time to put together another line on Henry Hill (site of the climax of the first battle of Manassas thirteen months before). Longstreet hurled his men against this line, but darkness brought an end to the fighting. That night Pope led his badly beaten men back toward Washington. On their retreat they met troops from McClellan's army marching to assist them.

In less than a week Pope, who had come to symbolize the ills that affected the Union war effort during 1862, was ordered to Minnesota to fight Indians.

The second battle of Manassas brought Robert E. Lee and the Confederacy to the height of their power and opened the way for Lee's first invasion of the North. But his victory came with horrid losses to both sides: 3,300 dead and 15,000 wounded (Union, 9,931; Confederate, 8,353; the Union listed another 3,895 as missing). For years the land bore the scars: mangled trees, rows of depressions from disinterred graves, the bleached bones of dead horses. As one of the soldiers at Manassas said, "War has been designated as Hell, and I assure you that this was the very vortex of Hell."

Estimated Casualties: 13,826 US, 8,353 CS

Manassas National Battlefield Park, on Route 29 and Interstate 66 near Manassas, includes 5,072 acres of the historic battlefield; 715 of these acres are privately owned.

Chantilly, Virginia (VA027), Fairfax County, September 1, 1862

After the second battle of Manassas, US General Pope retreated across Bull Run and established a defensive position at Centreville. On August 31 CS General Lee sent CS General Jackson on a wide flanking march to intercept the Federal retreat toward Washington. Jackson's 20,000 men marched north, then east along the Little River Turnpike to cut the Warrenton Turnpike. Meanwhile CS General Longstreet's Corps was to hold Pope in place. Rain slowed Jackson's march, and Pope anticipated the turning movement. He fell back to Germantown to cover the intersection of the two turnpikes.

On September 1 Jackson occupied Ox Hill southeast of Chantilly Plantation and then halted his march after learning that most of the Federals blocked his route to the east. US Major General Jesse L. Reno's IX Corps surprised Jackson with a late afternoon attack through a raging thunderstorm. US Brigadier General Isaac Stevens's division led the attack. In severe fighting the Federals were repulsed, and Stevens was killed. US General Kearny's division arrived and continued the bloody assaults. Kearny mistakenly rode into the Confederate lines and was shot. The battle ended at about 6:30 P.M., and the Federal retreat to Washington continued. With Pope's army no longer a threat, Lee turned his army west and north to invade the North.

Dissatisfaction with Pope was so great that President Lincoln sent him west to fight the Indians as commander of the new Military Department of the Northwest. The president put Pope's army under US General McClellan and named him commander of the forces around Washington, creating a larger Army of the Potomac. Lincoln took this political risk — McClellan had failed on the Peninsula and was distrusted by the radicals in the Republican Party — to avoid another great risk — a demoralized army.

Estimated Casualties: 1,300 US, 800 CS

The Ox Hill Battlefield, a Fairfax County park at 4134 West Ox Road, includes 4.6 acres of the historic battlefield and the monuments to General Philip Kearny and General Isaac Stevens dedicated in October 1915 by veterans of the New Jersey Brigade.

Maryland Campaign: September 1862

Harpers Ferry, West Virginia (WV010), Jefferson County, September 12–15, 1862

Dennis E. Frye

CS General Robert E. Lee marched north after his victory at Second Manassas for several reasons. War-weary Virginia could not sustain Lee's army much longer, the rich farms of Maryland and Pennsylvania could feed both soldiers and horses, and Virginia farmers required time to reap the fall harvest. In addition, the U.S. congressional elections were approaching in November, and Lee hoped to embarrass President Abraham Lincoln as well as encourage European recognition of the Confederacy.

Lee's Army of Northern Virginia crossed the Potomac River at White's Ford on September 4–7. When the army reached Frederick, and before continuing the invasion, Lee had to open a lifeline back into Virginia through the Shenandoah Valley. This line of communication and supply was threatened, however, by the continuing presence of Federal troops guarding the Baltimore & Ohio Railroad in the Valley. Lee had expected the advance of his army to force the withdrawal of the 14,000 Union troops garrisoning Harpers Ferry and Martinsburg, but instead the Federal high command instructed US Colonel Dixon S. Miles "to hold Harpers Ferry to the last extremity."

Lee's solution was to divide his army into four parts and send three to Harpers Ferry to eliminate the problem. The fourth column would march to Boonsboro, fifteen miles north of Harpers Ferry, and await the return of the campaigners at South Mountain. Lee put CS Major General Thomas J. "Stonewall" Jackson, a native of Clarksburg, in command because Jackson had been commander of the Confederate units at Harpers Ferry in the spring of 1861 and knew the topography of the region. Jackson responded favorably to the task, observing that he had lately neglected his "friends" in the Valley.

At sunrise on September 10 three converging columns of Confederates methodically began driving toward Harpers Ferry. CS Major General John G. Walker's Division of 2,000 swung south across the Potomac River and then east toward Loudoun Heights. The 8,000 men of CS Major General Lafayette McLaws veered west and south toward Maryland Heights. Jackson, with three divisions — 14,000 veterans — raced west toward Martinsburg and then east toward Bolivar Heights.

Miles knew the Confederates were coming. Outnumbered almost two to one and further handicapped by his inexperienced troops — more than two thirds of them had been in the army for less than three weeks — he weakened his overall defense by dividing his forces to cover Maryland and Bolivar Heights. On September 13 the Confederates took up their positions near his garrison. Loudoun Heights fell quickly to Walker's men, and after a six-hour battle McLaws seized Maryland Heights. Jackson then drove in from the west, deploying his forces along School House Ridge, one half mile west of Bolivar Heights.

Later that night Confederate cannoneers dragged artillery to the ridgetops. At about 2:00 P.M. on September 14 the hills erupted in smoke and flame, and the bombardment continued until dark. Jackson's gunners zeroed in on Bolivar Heights, the main position of the trapped Federals. One Union lieutenant recalled the horror of the bombardment: "The infernal screech owls came hissing and singing, then bursting, plowing great holes in the earth, filling our eyes with dust, and tearing many giant trees to atoms." Darkness finally ended the firestorm, with the Stars and Stripes still flying over Harpers Ferry.

Jackson was becoming impatient. Word had arrived from Lee that the situation in Maryland had deteriorated. The Union army had advanced unexpectedly, aided by the discovery of Lee's original orders, and the Confederates had been forced to abandon South Mountain. Lee informed Jackson that he would have to cancel the invasion

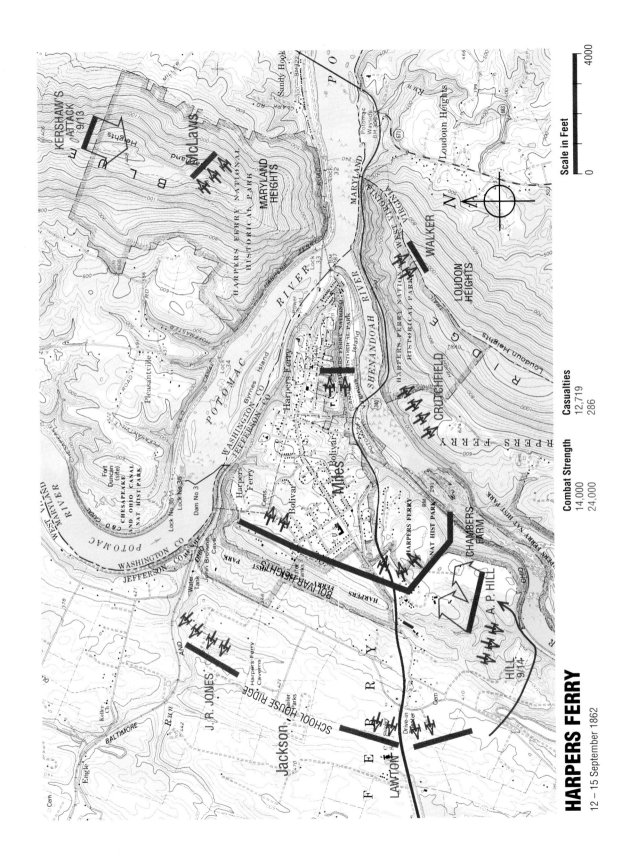

HARPERS FERRY

12 – 15 September 1862

	Combat Strength	Casualties
	14,000	12,719
	24,000	286

Scale in Feet

0   4000

of the North if Harpers Ferry did not fall in the morning.

To ensure success Jackson ordered CS Major General Ambrose Powell Hill to take his 5,000 men from the south end of School House Ridge and flank the Union left on Bolivar Heights. Jackson felt certain that this move, in conjunction with additional artillery on Loudoun Heights, would end the Union resistance. During the night of September 14 Hill's Confederates quietly snaked along the banks of the Shenandoah River until they discovered ravines leading up to the Chambers farm. In the darkness Hill deployed his men and artillery in open pastures behind the Union left. The fate of Harpers Ferry was sealed.

A thick fog blanketed the valley on the morning of September 15. As the rising sun burned away the mist, Confederate shells from the mountains again filled the sky. One Vermont soldier declared, "We [were] as helpless as rats in a cage." At about 8:00 A.M., with his artillery ammunition exhausted and his troops surrounded, Miles ordered white flags raised. Jackson received the formal Union surrender on School House Ridge, where he had coordinated the siege. He captured 73 pieces of artillery, 11,000 small arms, and 200 wagons, with a loss of only 286 men. In addition to the 219 Union men killed and wounded, 12,500 Federals were taken prisoner — the largest surrender of U.S. troops during the Civil War.

Lee greeted the news with enthusiasm. The fall of Harpers Ferry allowed him to make a stand in Maryland. However, the resulting battle of Antietam — America's bloodiest single-day battle — changed the course of the war in favor of the Union.

Estimated Casualties: 12,719 US, 286 CS

Harpers Ferry National Historical Park is at Harpers Ferry, the confluence of the Potomac and Shenandoah Rivers. The park includes 2,287 acres, 64 of which are privately owned.

South Mountain, Maryland (MD002), Washington and Frederick Counties, September 14, 1862

Dennis E. Frye

The inadvertent discovery of CS General Robert E. Lee's campaign plans, Special Orders, No. 191, presented the Union commander, US Major General George B. McClellan, with one of the best opportunities to destroy an enemy during the Civil War.

With one sudden strike through the gaps of South Mountain, McClellan could interpose the Army of the Potomac between the scattered wings of Lee's army, save the besieged garrison at Harpers Ferry, hurl the southern invaders from Union soil, and possibly precipitate an early end to the war in the East. "I think Lee has made a gross mistake," a jubilant McClellan wired President Lincoln. "I have all the plans of the rebels and will catch them in their own trap."

McClellan devised a scheme to "cut the enemy in two and beat him in detail." A successful strike at Crampton's Gap would relieve the besieged garrison at Harpers Ferry. At Fox's and Turner's Gaps, decisive blows would slice Lee's line of retreat and doom nearly half of the Confederate army at Boonsboro. With his plans articulated in orders to his subordinates, McClellan rashly proclaimed, "If I cannot whip Bobbie Lee, I will be willing to go home."

The battle of South Mountain was actually three battles, each contested separately on September 14. The most important was at Crampton's Gap, where McClellan ordered US Major General William B. Franklin's VI Corps to "cut off, destroy, or capture" the 8,000 Confederates in Pleasant Valley and relieve the surrounded garrison at Harpers Ferry.

Franklin advanced toward South Mountain at dawn on September 14. CS Major General Lafayette McLaws — unaware that his rear was threatened by the approach of 12,000 bluecoats — had only a rear guard of 500 defenders under CS Colonel William A. Parham thinly deployed behind a three-quarter-mile-long stone wall at the

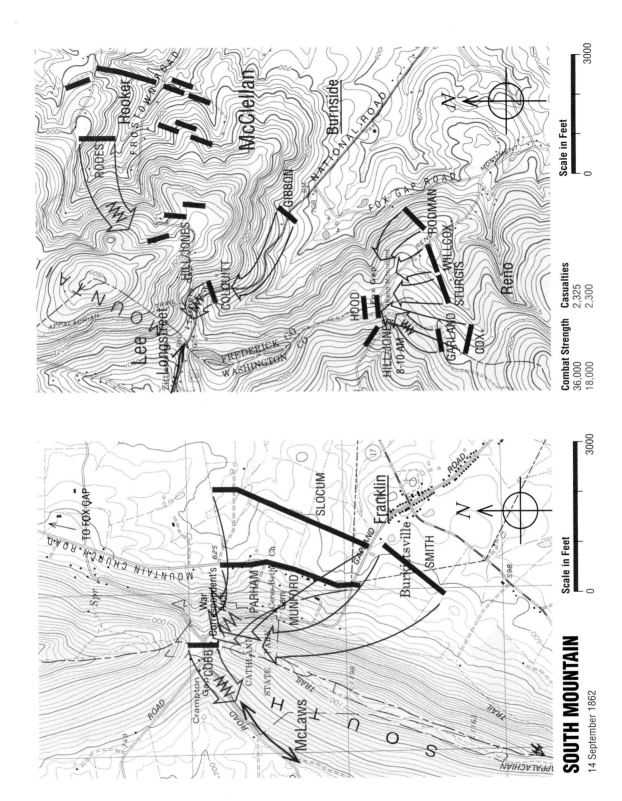

SOUTH MOUNTAIN

14 September 1862

Scale in Feet

0   3000

Combat Strength	Casualties
36,000	2,325
18,000	2,300

eastern base of Crampton's Gap. Franklin spent three hours deploying his force, reminding one southerner of a "lion making exceedingly careful preparations to spring on a plucky little mouse."

At 3:00 P.M., Franklin's force, with the division of US Major General Henry W. Slocum on the right and that of US Major General William F. Smith on the left, lurched forward. Franklin seized the gap and captured 400 prisoners, most of whom were from CS Brigadier General Howell Cobb's Brigade, which had arrived too late to reinforce Parham. Franklin refused to press on. He informed McClellan he was outnumbered "two to one" and that he could not advance "without reinforcements." Franklin's delusion ended the fighting at Crampton's Gap. He had failed to relieve the Union garrison at Harpers Ferry.

McClellan ordered the rest of his army to move west via the National Road toward Boonsboro to get between Lee and his reinforcements and to slice his line of retreat to Virginia. McClellan's plan was to drive through Turner's Gap. When the Federals discovered Confederates defending Turner's Gap, they decided to turn the Rebel flanks. US Major General Jesse L. Reno's IX Corps marched one mile south to Fox's Gap to pierce the Confederate right. US Major General Joseph Hooker's I Corps focused on the Rebel left, one mile north of Turner's Gap.

CS Major General Daniel Harvey Hill's Division defended the flanks with only 5,000 men stretched over more than two miles, forcing him to remark, "I do not remember ever to have experienced a feeling of greater loneliness."

US Brigadier General Jacob D. Cox's Kanawha Division of the IX Corps ascended the Old Sharpsburg Road and attacked at Fox's Gap at about 9:00 A.M. CS Brigadier General Samuel Garland, Jr.'s small brigade could not withstand the assaults against its extreme right, and following Garland's death, the line collapsed. A lull followed, while the rest of the IX Corps, including the divisions of US Brigadier Generals Samuel D. Sturgis, Orlando B. Willcox, and Isaac P. Rodman, ascended the mountain. This delay enabled Lee to reinforce the position with brigades from CS Brigadier General John Bell Hood's Division and

two from CS Major General David R. Jones's Division. As evening approached, the entire IX Corps attacked but failed to dislodge the stubborn Confederates. Fighting continued until dusk, when Reno was mortally wounded. Lee's forces held the gap until 10:00 P.M. when he ordered a retreat.

While the IX Corps concentrated on turning the Confederate right at Fox's Gap, the task of driving their left near Turner's Gap fell upon Hooker's I Corps. On the fourteenth Hooker positioned his three divisions opposite two peaks located one mile north of Turner's Gap. The Alabama Brigade of CS Brigadier General Robert Rodes defended the peaks on the extreme Confederate left, but with his men isolated and reinforcement impossible, Rodes steadily withdrew before the advancing Federals. Despite the arrival of Jones's three other brigades and CS Brigadier General Nathan G. Evans's Brigade, Hooker seized the peaks, but darkness and difficult terrain saved Lee's left from complete collapse. US Brigadier General John Gibbon threatened the Confederate center at Turner's Gap by advancing west along the National Pike, but CS Brigadier General Alfred H. Colquitt's Georgia Brigade refused to yield.

With Crampton's Gap lost and his position at Fox's and Turner's Gaps precarious, Lee ordered his beleaguered army to withdraw from South Mountain toward Sharpsburg on the night of September 14. The Confederates' spirited defense of the gaps had succeeding in keeping Lee's army intact, protected his line of retreat, and purchased time to ensure the capitulation of Harpers Ferry. McClellan's failure to accomplish his strategic aims at South Mountain set up the tragic collision at Antietam.

Estimated Casualties: 2,325 US, 2,300 CS

South Mountain battlefield is in Frederick and Washington Counties. Two areas are owned by the Central Maryland Heritage

League in Middletown and are open to the public: ten acres at Fox's Gap around the Reno Monument and an acre at Turner's Gap near the entrance to the Washington Monument State Park. About five hundred acres have been protected through easements purchased through Program Open Space and the Maryland Department of Transportation ISTEA program. Areas on top of South Mountain along the Appalachian National Scenic Trail are protected by the National Park Service. These are about four miles west of Middletown on Route 40-A. One hundred acres are protected in Crampton's Gap State Park, six miles south of Middletown off Route 17 in Burkittsville.

Antietam, Maryland (MD003), Washington County, September 17, 1862

Stephen W. Sears

CS General Robert E. Lee was driven by two ambitions in leading his Army of Northern Virginia across the Potomac River into Maryland early in September 1862. The first was to shift the contest from war-torn Virginia to what he called the Confederacy's northern frontier. The second was to force US Major General George B. McClellan's Army of the Potomac into a showdown battle that would be decisive for the South's independence.

That battle was fought along Antietam Creek at Sharpsburg, Maryland, but not in the setting Lee originally planned. Chance had intervened. Several days earlier a Confederate courier had lost a copy of his operational orders, which were found by a Union soldier and turned over to McClellan. Although McClellan moved too slowly on September 14 to break through the gaps in South

Mountain and cut off the scattered parts of the Confederate army, he did force Lee to decide to give battle sooner than he wanted and with fewer troops than he intended. Despite the odds against him, Lee deliberately chose to stand and fight at Sharpsburg, confident that he and his soldiers would win.

His confidence stemmed in part from the good defensive position he had chosen. He drew his line of battle on some four miles of rising ground behind Antietam Creek, taking advantage of the concealment offered by the rolling terrain, rocky outcroppings, scattered woodlots, and fields of corn standing tall and ready for harvest. He would have to fight defensively, for even when all his troops finally reached Sharpsburg from Harpers Ferry, where they had successfully besieged a Union garrison, he would have hardly 38,000 men of all arms. The Union commander, massing his troops and guns along the eastern bank of Antietam Creek, could put about 75,000 men on the firing line.

The terrain influenced McClellan's battle plan as well. South of Sharpsburg, where the right of Lee's line was posted, the ground was steep, broken, and difficult for maneuvering troops. Although his plan included a threat to that flank, McClellan intended the main weight of his assault to fall on the enemy's opposite flank, north of Sharpsburg, where the ground was more open. Antietam Creek itself was a major defensive feature, like a moat protecting a castle. Union troops crossing the creek to open an attack were supported by artillery batteries and ammunition trains that had to use one of the fords or one of the three stone bridges spanning the stream in the vicinity of Sharpsburg. As the battle lines were first drawn, two of these bridges were controlled by Union troops and one by the Confederates. All along the high ground east of the creek, McClellan massed his powerful long-range artillery to support his offensive. He regarded the creek as his own first line of defense should Lee attempt a counterstroke.

The battle opened at first light on September 17 as US Major General Joseph Hooker's I Corps struck hard against the Confederate left, under

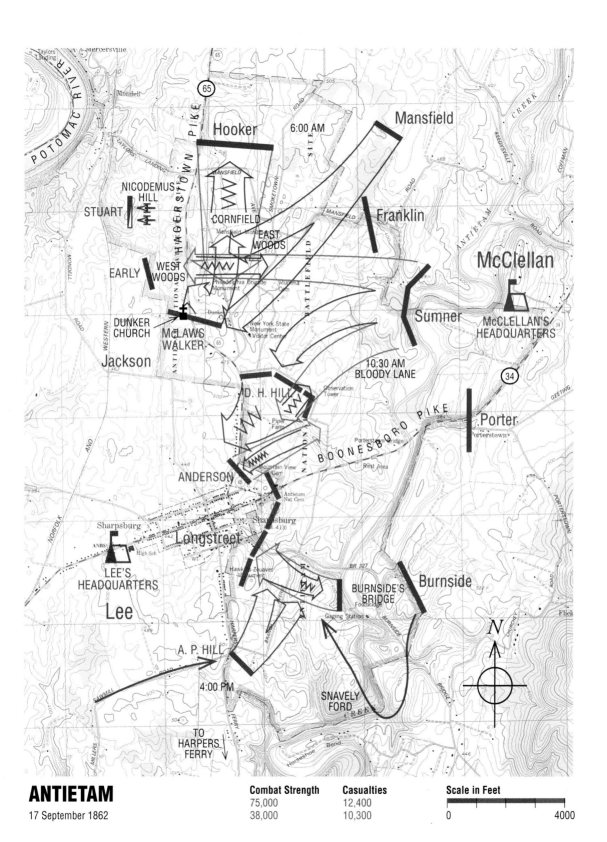

ANTIETAM

17 September 1862

Combat Strength	Casualties
75,000	12,400
38,000	10,300

Scale in Feet

0   4000

the command of CS Major General Thomas J. "Stonewall" Jackson. Hooker's objective was the open plateau in front of the little whitewashed Dunker church, where Confederate artillery batteries were massed. Off to the west on Nicodemus Hill, Confederate cavalryman CS Major General J. E. B. Stuart directed the fire of other batteries against the advancing Federals. The fighting surged back and forth through the East Woods and the West Woods and farmer David Miller's thirty-acre cornfield between them. In a series of charges and countercharges, both sides poured reinforcements into the struggle, but neither could gain a decisive advantage. In the first four hours of the battle that morning almost 13,000 men fell dead or wounded.

At midmorning, more by misdirection than by design, other Union troops ran up against the center of Lee's line, commanded by CS Major General D. H. Hill, posted in a farm lane so worn down over the years by erosion and travel that it was known locally as the Sunken Road. Before long it earned another name: Bloody Lane. Two of US Major General Edwin V. Sumner's divisions were hurled repeatedly against this strong position and were driven back. Then, through a mix-up in orders, the Confederates gave up Bloody Lane and retreated. For a critical moment it appeared that Lee's army would be cut in two. The cautious McClellan could not bring himself to renew the attack, however, and the thin Confederate line held.

One final act remained to be played in the drama. During the morning US Major General Ambrose E. Burnside's corps had been ordered by McClellan to make a diversionary attack against Lee's right flank while the main blow was struck against his left. But Burnside ran into great difficulty trying to force a crossing of Antietam Creek at the bridge on his front. A flanking column sent downstream to find a fording place lost its way and was three hours locating Snavely's Ford and making a crossing. Back at the bridge, meanwhile, storming parties launched headlong assaults that finally gained the span, which from then on was called Burnside's Bridge. By after-

noon Burnside had his corps across the creek and positioned to advance on Sharpsburg.

Throughout the day Lee had pulled men from this sector to reinforce the hard-pressed troops holding the rest of his line. Now the few remaining defenders under CS Major General James Longstreet were pushed back toward Sharpsburg by Burnside's relentless advance. Once again the Confederate army seemed on the brink of defeat. Then, at the last possible moment, the division of CS Major General A. P. Hill arrived on the field, after a hard march from Harpers Ferry, and smashed into Burnside's flank. The force of Hill's counterattack drove the Union forces back to the heights overlooking Burnside's Bridge as darkness ended the fighting.

September 18 found Lee holding his lines and defiantly inviting another attack, but McClellan refused the challenge. He was satisfied with the fact that his army had survived the battle, and he was unwilling to risk it further by renewing the fighting that day. During the night Lee led his army back across the Potomac into Virginia. He left behind a battlefield unique in American history. On no other field, in no other one-day battle, would so many Americans be killed, wounded, or missing: 22,700 — some 12,400 Federals and about 10,300 Confederates.

Antietam also proved to be one of the turning points of the Civil War. It ended Lee's invasion of the North and his hope of winning a decisive battle on northern soil in 1862. Although McClellan's cautious generalship prevented a decisive Union military victory, the battle's consequences were enough to convince Abraham Lincoln to issue the preliminary Emancipation Proclamation. What before Antietam had been a war waged solely for the Union now became a war against slavery as well, and that doomed the South's hope for foreign intervention. The course of the war, and the course of the nation, were forever changed as a result.

Estimated Casualties: 12,400 US, 10,300 CS

Antietam National Battlefield, near Sharpsburg, includes 3,256 acres of the historic battlefield; 840 of these acres are privately owned.

In a second the air was full of the hiss of bullets and the hurtle of grape-shot. The mental strain was so great that I saw at that moment the singular effect mentioned, I think, in the life of Goethe on a similar occasion — the whole landscape for an instant turned slightly red.

— Private David L. Thompson of the 9th New York
  Volunteers

Shepherdstown, West Virginia (WV016), Jefferson County, September 19–20, 1862

CS General Lee recrossed the Potomac River to Virginia during the night of September 18–19. He left behind a rear guard of two brigades and forty-five guns under the artillery chief, CS Brigadier General William N. Pendleton, to hold Boteler's Ford. On the nineteenth, US Major General Fitz John Porter's V Corps cannons engaged Pendleton's in an artillery duel across the river. After sundown a detachment of 2,000 Federals crossed the river at Boteler's Ford, surprised Pendleton's rear guard, and captured four guns. Pendleton raced to Lee with an exaggerated report of the number of his cannons that had been taken. In accordance with Lee's orders, CS General Jackson sent CS Major General A. P. Hill's Light Division to the river to counterattack.

Early the next morning Porter pushed elements of two divisions across the Potomac to establish a bridgehead. After a brief reconnaissance Porter ordered the withdrawal of the two divisions. During the retreat Hill arrived and at 9:00 A.M. launched a vicious counterattack against the Union rear. The Federals fled across the river in a chaotic retreat. The 118th Pennsylvania, known as the Corn Exchange Regiment, suffered 269 casualties. Lee's army retired to the Shenandoah Valley, unhindered by McClellan.

On November 5 President Abraham Lincoln relieved US General McClellan of the command of the Army of the Potomac for failing to pursue Lee's retreating army aggressively, and replaced him two days later with US General Burnside.

Estimated Casualties: 363 US, 291 CS

Confederate Heartland Offensive: June–October 1862

Chattanooga I, Tennessee (TN005), Hamilton County and Chattanooga, June 7–8, 1862

After US Major General Ormsby M. Mitchel's troops seized Huntsville, Alabama, in April, they were dispersed to repair and guard railroads. They soon occupied more than one hundred miles of the Memphis & Charleston Railroad. Mitchel ordered US Brigadier General James Scott Negley's small division to advance on Chattanooga from Fayetteville, Tennessee.

Negley emplaced two artillery batteries on Stringer's Ridge. On June 7 and 8 he bombarded Chattanooga as well as the Confederate defenses along the riverbanks and on Cameron Hill. The Confederate response was uncoordinated. Negley withdrew on June 10, but his attack warned of the gathering Union strength in southeastern Tennessee. On June 10 US Major General Don Carlos Buell's Army of the Ohio slowly advanced east from Corinth, Mississippi, toward Chattanooga.

CS Colonel Nathan Bedford Forrest was ordered to Chattanooga to reorganize and assume command of a cavalry brigade there that had failed in its efforts to oppose Negley's rapid advance.

Estimated Casualties: unknown US, 3 CS

Murfreesboro I, Tennessee (TN006), Rutherford County, July 13, 1862

In July CS Colonel Forrest and CS Colonel John Hunt Morgan launched cavalry raids into Middle Tennessee and Kentucky. Two of Forrest's regiments left Chattanooga for Murfreesboro on July 9 and joined other units on the way. The combined force of 1,400 planned a strike to gain control of Murfreesboro, the Union supply center on the Nashville & Chattanooga Railroad. US Brigadier General Thomas L. Crittenden arrived in Murfreesboro on June 12 to assume command of the garrison, camped in three locations in and about the town.

In a surprise attack at dawn on July 13 Forrest's cavalry overran a Federal hospital and the 9th Pennsylvania Cavalry Regiment's camp on Woodbury Pike. The Federals separated into two pockets of resistance. Forrest demanded their unconditional surrender. The Union troops gave up at one camp, but the other refused to surrender. Under a flag of truce Forrest led their commander, US Colonel Henry C. Lester, through the town, where he was shown the same Confederate troops over and over, giving him the impression of a larger force. Lester surrendered. The Confederates destroyed supplies and the rail lines through Murfreesboro. The raid diverted the Union army from Chattanooga and enabled CS General Braxton Bragg to concentrate forces there for his Kentucky offensive in September.

Estimated Casualties: 1,200 US, 150 CS

Richmond, Kentucky (KY007), Madison County, August 29–30, 1862

While CS General Robert E. Lee planned a decisive victory that would bring European recognition of the Confederacy and its independence from the United States, CS General Bragg, who had replaced CS General P. G. T. Beauregard in mid-June as commander of the Army of the Mississippi, prepared his army to invade Kentucky in conjunction with CS Major General E. Kirby Smith's forces of the Department of Kentucky. Bragg moved his army quickly by rail from Tupelo via Mobile and won the race for Chattanooga against US General Buell. Smith left Knoxville on August 14 with 10,000 men, spearheaded by CS Colonel John S. Scott's cavalry.

On August 29 Scott rode north from Big Hill toward Richmond and skirmished with Union troops. US Brigadier General Mahlon D. Manson's artillery and cavalry forced Scott back to Kingston, where he was joined by CS Brigadier General Patrick R. Cleburne's Division. Early the next morning Cleburne headed north through Kingston to confront Manson's line at the hamlet of Rogersville, a few miles from Richmond. The battle began with a two-hour artillery duel, thrusts, and counterattacks by both infantries. With the arrival of CS Major General Thomas J. Churchill's Division, and with Smith in command, the Confederates attacked, rolled up the Federals' right, and forced them to retreat north in a running battle for seven miles. Smith routed them from their third and final position on Cemetery Hill southeast of Richmond and took 4,300 prisoners. US Major General William Nelson, who had just arrived, escaped. The Confederates' victory cleared the way north toward Lexington and Frankfort.

Estimated Casualties: 5,625 US, 600 CS

Information on a driving tour with a brochure and a tape is available through the Richmond Tourism Commission.

Munfordville (Battle for the Bridge), Kentucky (KY008), Hart County, September 14–17, 1862

On August 28 CS General Bragg left Chattanooga with 30,000 men and headed toward Kentucky. Buell moved toward Nashville and then north in pursuit. US Colonel John T. Wilder commanded a small force strongly entrenched in Fort Craig, a stockade connected by entrenchments to earthworks, on the south bank of the Green River at Woodsonville, across from Munfordville. The fort protected the one-thousand-foot-long Louisville & Nashville Railroad bridge 115 feet above the Green River. The railroad brought critical sup-

plies to the Federal troops in Tennessee. When Wilder heard that Confederates were approaching, he wired the Union headquarters in Louisville for reinforcements.

On September 13 CS Colonel Scott rode into Munfordville to take the Union garrison. When Wilder rejected his demand to surrender, Scott called for assistance from CS Brigadier General James R. Chalmers's Brigade, fifteen miles away at Cave City. Early on September 14 Chalmers launched a poorly planned attack on Wilder, who repulsed him, inflicting heavy losses: 35 killed and 253 wounded. The Federals suffered 72 casualties. Chalmers, who had forces on both sides of the river, then demanded that Wilder surrender. Wilder responded: "Your note demanding the unconditional surrender of my forces has been received. If you wish to avoid further bloodshed keep out of the range of my guns."

US Colonel Cyrus L. Dunham arrived from Louisville with Indiana troops and took command on the fifteenth. More Federals, with artillery, reached the earthworks, increasing Dunham's strength to about 4,000. Bragg marched his army all night and arrived at the river the next day. After positioning CS Major General William J. Hardee's command in Munfordville and CS Major General Leonidas Polk's force upriver with artillery trained on the Union garrison, Bragg demanded Dunham's surrender. When Dunham informed headquarters of his intention to surrender, he was ordered to turn over his command to Wilder. Wilder entered the enemy lines under a flag of truce. CS Major General Simon B. Buckner showed him the strength of the Confederate forces, and he surrendered on September 17. Bragg paroled 155 officers and 3,921 soldiers and burned the bridge.

This victory in the battle known locally as the Battle for the Bridge disrupted the Union supply line, but Federal troopers reoccupied Munfordville after Bragg left. (Forts Willich and Terrill were constructed on the north bank of the Green River later in the war.)

Estimated Casualties: 4,148 US, 285 CS

Perryville, Kentucky (KY009), Boyle County, October 8, 1862

Paul Hawke

The importance of Kentucky in the Civil War was best stated by Abraham Lincoln: "I think to lose Kentucky is nearly the same as to lose the whole game." Without Kentucky, he said, the Union could not hold Missouri or Maryland. The battle that kept Kentucky in the United States was the largest and bloodiest fought in the state. It was tactically indecisive, but it ended the Confederate sweep across Middle Tennessee and deep into Kentucky, and as such it was a vital strategic victory for the Union.

Conditions in Kentucky were difficult in October 1862 for the armies because of the heat and a two-month drought that made water scarce. CS General Braxton Bragg spread his forces over a large area to forage and to locate the Union army. He had expected to be enthusiastically welcomed as his troops moved into Kentucky, but he was not. He was also disappointed in the enlistments in the state.

US Major General Don Carlos Buell was in trouble with his superiors in Washington because he had not pursued Bragg closely and had not engaged him during September. Buell took action in October against the Confederate threat by leading his main force southeast from Louisville toward Bragg's army at Bardstown while sending two divisions on a feint east toward Frankfort where Bragg was installing a provisional Confederate state government. Buell's deception succeeded. Bragg held about half of the Confederate forces in Kentucky near Frankfort, with the result that CS Major General Leonidas Polk had only 16,000 soldiers near Bardstown.

In 1862 Perryville had a population of several hundred residents. The rolling hills to the west and northwest were dotted with woods and farms, and the Chaplin River meandered northward from the center of town. Doctor's Creek ran from Walker's Bend toward the southwest, and Bull Run flowed into Doctor's Creek near the Mackville Pike crossing and the H. P. Bottom house. Because of the drought, none of the creeks had much water for the thirsty soldiers.

On October 7, as Buell's forces drew closer to Perryville, CS Colonel Joseph Wheeler's cavalry skirmished with them. US Major General Charles C. Gilbert's III Corps was on the Springfield Pike, US Major General Alexander McD. McCook's I Corps was on the Mackville Pike, and US Major General Thomas L. Crittenden's II Corps was on the Lebanon Pike. CS Major General William J. Hardee called up three brigades from CS Major General Simon B. Buckner's Division: CS Brigadier General Sterling A. M. Wood moved to the north of town, with CS Brigadier General Bushrod R. Johnson to his right east of the Chaplin River near the Harrodsburg Pike; CS Brigadier General St. John R. Liddell's Arkansas Brigade formed on the crest of a hill just east of Bull Run, north of the Springfield Pike, in anticipation of the soldiers' need for water, with one regiment thrown forward onto Peters Hill.

The first shots of the battle were fired in the early morning darkness of October 8 when Gilbert's skirmishers went forward to get water and encountered Liddell's pickets on Peters Hill. Near the Turpin house, US Colonel Daniel McCook's brigade of US Brigadier General Philip H. Sheridan's division pushed the 7th Arkansas back to Liddell's main line. The fighting along the Springfield Pike escalated as Sheridan — who had just earned his first star — pushed ahead and across Bull Run, only to be recalled to Peters Hill to assume a defensive stance by the faint-hearted Gilbert. By 9:30 A.M. the fighting had subsided. Sheridan positioned his men and made his headquarters at the Turpin house. Buell knew little about the action because he could not hear the fighting from his headquarters at the Dorsey house on the Springfield Pike, more than two miles west of Peters Hill.

Bragg had ordered Polk to Perryville to "attack the enemy immediately, rout him, and then move rapidly to join Major General [Kirby] Smith" near Versailles. The Confederates were in Perryville by 10:00 A.M., where Bragg made his headquarters at the Crawford house on the Harrodsburg

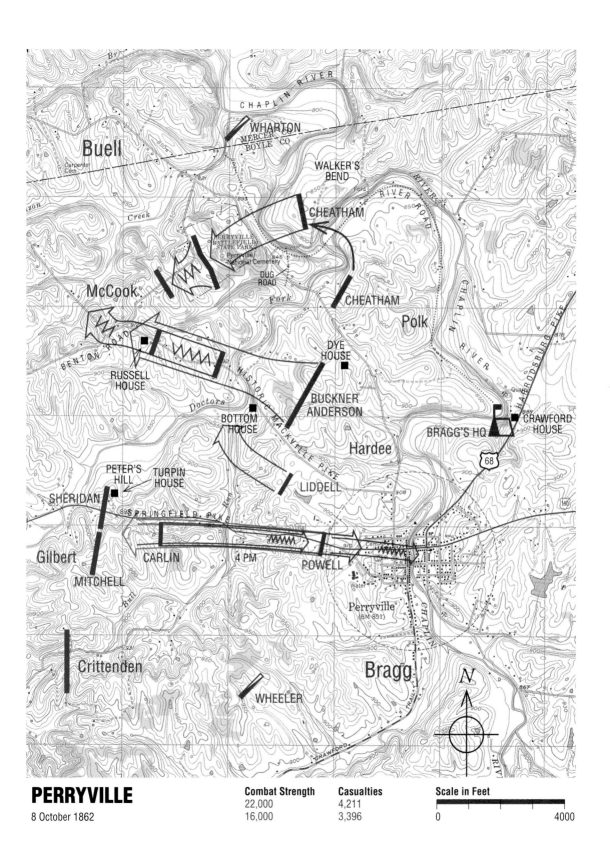

PERRYVILLE

8 October 1862

Combat Strength	Casualties
22,000	4,211
16,000	3,396

Scale in Feet

0   4000

Pike. He ordered Polk's right wing into position. CS Major General Benjamin Franklin Cheatham's Division was redeployed from the high ground west of Perryville to the Confederate right, south of Walker's Bend of the Chaplin River. Buckner's Division occupied the center, with CS Brigadier General James Patton Anderson's Division on the left. CS Colonel John A. Wharton's cavalry reported that the Union left was farther north than expected. Cheatham's Division moved into Walker's Bend, crossed the Chaplin River, and attacked at about 2:00 P.M.

The Confederate attack did not envelop the Union left flank as planned, but slammed into the front of McCook's 13,000-man corps. The fighting escalated as Buckner's and Anderson's Divisions became involved. As more Confederates joined the advance and the fighting raged, McCook's men slowly withdrew. US Brigadier Generals James S. Jackson and William R. Terrill were mortally wounded in the action. Cheatham's Tennesseans and Georgians, crushing Terrill's brigade, closed on US Brigadier General John Starkweather's soldiers from Wisconsin, Illinois, and Pennsylvania, supported by two batteries posted along the Benton Road. The fighting was savage as the Federals blunted the Confederate surge before pulling back to higher ground.

Some of the heaviest fighting was near the H. P. Bottom house on Doctor's Creek. As Johnson's men advanced over the creek, they came under heavy fire and took cover behind a stone fence. While Sheridan was hobbled by Gilbert's orders, CS Brigadier Generals Patrick R. Cleburne and Daniel W. Adams advanced in bitter fighting and drove two Union brigades from the high ground commanding the Mackville Road crossing of Doctor's Creek. Next, the Confederates encountered US Colonel George P. Webster's brigade of Jackson's division and pushed it back to the Russell house. Webster was mortally wounded while attempting to rally his men. The bitter resistance the Confederates encountered from Union regiments from three brigades and the eight cannons along the Russell house ridge bought time. It was 6:00 P.M. before the Confederates prevailed. Buell

finally realized that McCook's corps faced disaster and sent reinforcements from Gilbert's corps to shore up the Federal left. US Colonel Michael Gooding's brigade and six cannons were positioned to defend the vital intersection of the Benton and Mackville Roads as the Confederates called up reinforcements. First Wood's and then Liddell's Brigades hammered Gooding's men. In the interval between Wood's and Liddell's onslaughts, with daylight fading, CS General Polk narrowly escaped death or capture when he rode up to troops in battle line and ordered them to stop firing into a brigade of fellow Confederates. He discovered to his horror that the troops were in fact soldiers of the 22nd Indiana. Their colonel, however, did not think as quickly as Polk had earlier in the day when he took prisoner a Union officer who confused the portly and distinguished bishop-general with one of McCook's officers. Polk bluffed his way through and regained the Confederate lines.

At about 4:10 P.M. south of the old Springfield Road, the divisions of Sheridan and US Brigadier General Robert B. Mitchell repulsed the attack of CS Colonel Samuel Powell's Brigade. In a counterattack, US Colonel William P. Carlin's brigade chased Powell's men through the streets of Perryville and across the Chaplin River.

As darkness came, Liddell drove Gooding from the key intersection, but time had run out for the Confederates along McCook's front. Although they had gained ground, captured eleven cannons, and mauled five of McCook's brigades, night and the arrival of Union reinforcements stayed the Confederate tide.

That night Buell prepared to bring up the rest of his forces, including US Major General Thomas L. Crittenden's II Corps. Outnumbered, Bragg withdrew. Bragg joined Kirby Smith near Harrodsburg and withdrew through Cumberland Gap and into East Tennessee. In spite of telegrams from Washington urging him to follow Bragg and attack, Buell would not fight while living off the land. When Buell decided to return to Nashville to re-establish an offensive base again there, President Lincoln gave his command to US

Major General William S. Rosecrans and redesignated it the Army of the Cumberland.

For the numbers engaged, the battle was one of the bloodiest of the Civil War. Bragg lost about 20 percent of his 16,000 men, taking 3,396 casualties. Buell lost 4,211 of his 22,000 troops engaged in the battle.

Estimated Casualties: 4,211 US, 3,396 CS

Perryville battlefield is at Perryville near the intersection of Routes 68 and 150. There are 280 acres of the historic battlefield protected in the Perryville Battlefield State Historic Site and by the Perryville Battlefield Preservation Association.

A Civil War Legacy

William H. Webster

The battle that was fought outside the town of Perryville, Kentucky, on October 8, 1862, began as a squabble between Confederate and Union troops over access to the pools of water in a small creek. It ended with some question as to the victor. The North claimed that the battle kept Kentucky from joining the Confederacy. Southerners pointed to the high cost of this achievement, a loss by the Federals of more than 4,200 men. A small part of the field where this battle took place has been preserved as a state park. I attended the battlefield's dedication as the official delegate from Missouri, but I also attended to pay a personal tribute to an ancestor who gave his life in the battle.

Colonel George Penny Webster, my great-grandfather, was not a professional soldier. He was a loyal and patriotic American who left a law practice to serve his country in time of war. He had fought in the Mexican War with Zachary Taylor and volunteered again when the Civil War broke out. In the early stages of the conflict, Webster served as major of the 25th Ohio Volunteer Infantry. The unit fought against the Confederates in western Virginia (now West Virginia) and central Virginia in late 1861 and early 1862. It performed with exceptional distinction, fighting against Major General Thomas J. "Stonewall" Jackson during the battle of McDowell on May 8, 1862.

In late summer of that year George Webster was promoted to colonel and transferred to the western theater. He formed his own regiment and was then given command of the 34th Brigade of the Army of the Ohio's Tenth Division. Within two months Webster led the 34th in the battle of Perryville. In that battle the brigade lost 579 men, including Colonel Webster, who fell from his horse, mortally wounded. The men of the 34th mourned the loss of their leader, and after the war they gathered to dedicate a monument to him.

George Webster wrote to his wife every day from the camp and the battlefield. She saved his letters, and they have been passed on through the generations of our family. I keep them now, and I value them for helping me to appreciate the sacrifices and hardship he accepted in serving his country. Visiting the battlefield at Perryville reminds me that our nation's past embraces many acts of individual sacrifice, hardship, and heroism. Together, these acts form a heritage and a history in which all Americans can share, a history that is preserved for us at our Civil War battlefields.

Iuka and Corinth, Mississippi, Campaign: September–October 1862

Iuka, Mississippi (MS001), Tishomingo County, September 19, 1862

In the summer of 1862 President Abraham Lincoln named US Major General Henry W. Halleck general-in-chief. US Major General Ulysses S. Grant resumed command of the District of West Tennessee, and US Major General John Pope went to northern Virginia to command the newly constituted Army of Virginia. US Major General William S. Rosecrans took charge of Pope's Army of the Mississippi in the Corinth area.

CS General Braxton Bragg launched his plan to invade Kentucky and ordered CS Major General Sterling Price's 14,000-man Army of the West to advance on Nashville. Price occupied Iuka on September 14 while CS Major General Earl Van Dorn was a four-day march to the south, heading to Corinth to attack the Federals before he advanced into Tennessee. Grant saw an opportunity to stop the Confederate offensive and protect Kentucky — of central military and political importance to the United States — by trapping Price in Iuka, twenty miles southeast of Corinth, before the Army of the West could join Van Dorn.

Grant ordered 8,000 men commanded by US Major General Edward O. C. Ord to travel on the Memphis & Charleston Railroad to Burnsville, march toward Iuka, and attack Price from the northwest. At the same time Rosecrans was to lead 9,000 men from Corinth to Jacinto, advance on Iuka from the south and the west, trap Price, and cut off his escape route along the Fulton Road. Grant remained in Burnsville while Ord moved into position on September 18. Rosecrans was late in departing from Jacinto. Because of the support for the Confederacy among the population, Price learned of the Federals' movements and began to evacuate Iuka.

On the afternoon of the nineteenth, as Rosecrans approached from the southwest, Price attacked. A strong wind prevented Grant and Ord from hearing the guns, so Ord did not join the battle. CS Brigadier General Dabney H. Maury's Division barred Ord's advance, while CS Brigadier General Henry Little's brigades proved stronger than Rosecrans's divisions in a hard-fought battle one mile southwest of town. The outnumbered Confederates evacuated Iuka early the next morning along the Fulton Road to the south which Rosecrans had failed to guard. When Grant closed the trap, Price was gone.

Estimated Casualties: 790 US, 594 CS

Corinth, Mississippi (MS002), Alcorn County and Corinth, October 3–4, 1862

George A. Reaves III

After the occupation of Corinth in May, the Federal armies began to rebuild the railroads in the area. They felt their way toward Tupelo but did not force the Confederates to retreat farther south. US Major General Don Carlos Buell's Army of the Ohio headed eastward into the Tennessee Valley, rebuilding the Memphis & Charleston Railroad as it marched.

CS General P. G. T. Beauregard went on sick leave in mid-June, and President Jefferson Davis took advantage of the opportunity to replace him with CS General Braxton Bragg. In mid-July Bragg began to shift his Army of the Mississippi by rail to Chattanooga, where he intended to operate against the Union forces. He beat Buell to Chattanooga and then began a campaign in cooperation with CS Major General Edmund Kirby Smith, the Confederate commander in East Tennessee. Their armies were soon deep into Kentucky, threatening Louisville and Cincinnati. Bragg left soldiers in Mississippi, commanded by CS Major Generals Sterling Price and Earl Van Dorn. He expected them to advance into Middle Tennessee to support his thrust into Kentucky. After Price's Army of the West battered US Major General William S. Rosecrans at Iuka on September 19, Van Dorn, the senior of the two generals,

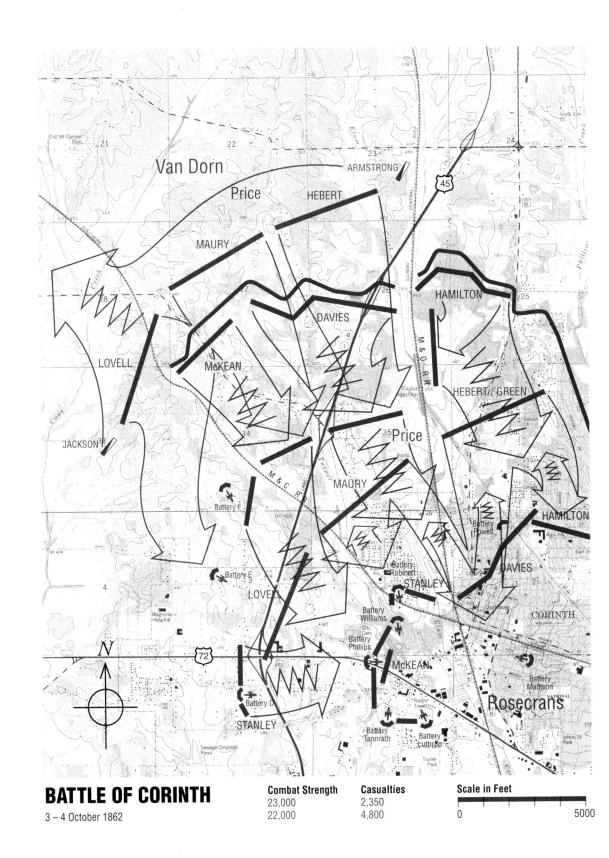

BATTLE OF CORINTH

3 – 4 October 1862

Combat Strength	Casualties
23,000	2,350
22,000	4,800

Scale in Feet

0   5000

decided to attack Corinth, the linchpin of Union defenses in northeastern Mississippi, and then advance into West or Middle Tennessee, as circumstances dictated. Using his seniority to control Price's movements, Van Dorn ordered an advance against Corinth.

Before leaving for Washington, US Major General Henry W. Halleck had ordered a defensive line constructed to protect Corinth against a Confederate force approaching from the west or south. Rosecrans considered these fortifications too extensive to be manned by the force available and questioned US Major General Ulysses S. Grant about them. Grant agreed to modify the line so that it protected the vital supply magazines in and around the junction of the two railroads. Several of the completed battery positions of the projected Halleck line, among them Battery F, lay between the old Confederate entrenchments and Corinth. When Rosecrans concentrated his 23,000 troops in and around Corinth on October 2, his line was much shorter than Beauregard's Confederate line had been during the previous spring.

These inner defenses consisted of batteries Robinett, Williams, Phillips, Tannrath, and Lothrop, in the College Hill area. Rosecrans gave orders to connect them by breastworks and to strengthen them, where possible, by *abatis*— logs sharpened and arranged in front for greater defense (the Civil War forerunner of barbed wire). The line was also extended to cover the northern approaches of the town. Battery Powell was not complete when the fighting started but was laid out for this purpose.

On October 2 Rosecrans discovered Van Dorn's Confederates advancing on Corinth from the northwest, which put Van Dorn between Rosecrans and any reinforcements that he might receive from Grant at Jackson and Bolivar, Tennessee. The Confederates deployed their army in an arc to the northwest of Corinth. CS Major General Mansfield Lovell's Division was on the right, and Price's two-division corps was on the left.

Rosecrans planned his defense to take advantage of all of the fortifications that had been built around Corinth. His skirmish line was posted along the old Confederate entrenchments, which were the outermost works. He planned to meet the Confederate attack with his main forces along the Halleck line, which was about a mile from the center of town. His final stand would be made in the battery positions in and around College Hill. This defense enabled him to sap the Confederates' strength as they advanced and to defend the supply depots in downtown Corinth and at the railroad intersection.

The attack started at about 10:00 A.M. on October 3, when units from three of Rosecrans's divisions advanced into old Confederate rifle pits north and northwest of town. US Brigadier General Thomas A. Davies was in the center of the Federal line, with US Brigadier General Thomas J. McKean on the left and US Brigadier General Charles S. Hamilton on the right. A fourth division, US Brigadier General David S. Stanley's, was held in reserve south of town. The Confederates attacked and applied pressure all along the line. By evening the Union soldiers had been forced two miles southward, back into the inner line of fortifications.

During the night Rosecrans positioned his troops in an arc-shaped line two miles long with redoubts at key points. Van Dorn put Lovell's Division on the right, south of the Memphis & Charleston Railroad, CS Brigadier General Dabney S. Maury's in the center, in front of Battery Robinett, and CS Brigadier General Louis Hébert's on the left. The next morning the Confederates stormed Battery Powell. Their charges were repulsed in savage fighting before Battery Robinett, where CS Colonel William P. Rogers, a Mexican War comrade of Jefferson Davis, was killed as he led the 2nd Texas. Union counterattacks soon drove the Confederates from Battery Powell and from the town.

By noon the Confederates had withdrawn, retreating toward the northwest. They had lost 4,800 of their 22,000 men. Rosecrans attempted to follow up, but because of his losses (2,350 of his 23,000 soldiers) and the exhaustion of his troops, his units were unable to mount an effective pursuit. The battle of Corinth was over. The

Union continued to hold Corinth until the winter of 1863–64, when they abandoned it as no longer having any strategic significance.

Estimated Casualties: 2,350 US, 4,800 CS

Corinth battlefield is at Corinth near Routes 45 and 72. Historic areas open to the public include: ten acres including Battery Robinett at Fulton Drive and Linden Street; five acres including Battery F at Smithbridge Road (Linden Street extended) and Bitner Street; and the Civil War Visitors Center at Jackson and Childs Streets.

Davis Bridge (Hatchie Bridge), Tennessee (TN007), Hardeman and McNairy Counties, October 6, 1862

After the battle of Corinth US General Grant ordered US General Ord and 8,000 men from the Army of West Tennessee to move down the west side of the Hatchie River, take the Davis Bridge, and trap the Confederate forces on the east side of the river. US General Rosecrans was to pursue them from Corinth into the trap and destroy them.

On October 5 Van Dorn's army, led by CS General Price's Corps, marched from Chewalla and reached the bridge over the Hatchie River— the Davis Bridge — before Ord arrived. Price deployed one brigade on the heights above the west bank to protect the bridge. The Federal vanguard struck the Confederates on the heights, captured four guns and 200 soldiers, took the bridge intact, advanced about five miles toward Chewalla, and trapped the Confederates east of the river as Grant had planned. Rosecrans, however, was too slow in pursuit. While Price's men resisted the Federals, commanded by US Major General

Stephen A. Hurlbut after Ord was wounded, Confederate scouts found another Hatchie River crossing to the south at Cram's Mill. By 1:00 A.M. Van Dorn's forces were across the river. They retreated west and reached Holly Springs on October 13. Because of Rosecrans's failure to move quickly to trap them, they remained a viable force to oppose Grant in his November advance on Holly Springs.

Estimated Casualties: 500 US, 400 CS

Missouri and Oklahoma: August–November 1862

Kirksville, Missouri (MO013), Adair County, August 6–9, 1862

James M. Lane, a U.S. senator from Kansas and fiery abolitionist, succeeded in getting US Brigadier General James G. Blunt named commander of the Department of Kansas in May 1862. The victory at Pea Ridge gave the U.S. government the opening it needed to respond to the overwhelming refugee problems of the Indians who had been forced off their lands. President Lincoln approved the "Indian Expedition" commanded by Blunt that would return Indians to their homeland, eliminate the threats to them posed by CS Colonel Stand Watie and his 1st Cherokee Mounted Rifles, and secure the area so the Federals could prepare to battle the army that CS Major General Thomas C. Hindman was forming in Arkansas. The 6,000-man expedition, including newly recruited Indians, left Baxter Springs, Kansas, in late June, commanded by US Colonel William Weer. The Federal soldiers won engagements and captured Cherokee Principal Chief John Ross before they mutinied against their alcoholic commander and returned the expedition to Fort Scott.

Chaos spread in Indian Territory as the Federal troops, both Indian and white, withdrew from the territory and into Kansas, leaving Watie and Cooper in control of the area. Cooper had succeeded Albert Pike as commander of the Indian Territory Confederates. The Union command permitted Cherokee Principal Chief John Ross to go to Washington to present his position to President Abraham Lincoln: that Federal withdrawal from Indian Territory had forced him to the Confederate side. (Ross died in Washington in 1866.) In Ross's absence, Watie became Principal Chief, and civil war among the Cherokees, Creeks, and Seminoles escalated.

Blunt was unable to return with the expedition because the increase in Confederate guerrilla attacks in Missouri required him to respond to US Brigadier General John M. Schofield's call for help against such daring leaders as CS Colonels Joseph C. Porter, John T. Hughes, Gideon W. Thompson, John T. Coffee, and Joseph O. Shelby. (The charismatic Shelby, who wore a black plume fastened to the brim of his hat, became one of the Confederacy's outstanding cavalry officers.)

In early August US Colonel John McNeil and his 1,000 troopers pursued CS Colonel Joseph C. Porter's 2,500-man Missouri Brigade for more than a week. They finally caught up with Porter at Kirksville and attacked on August 6. The Federals took prisoners and controlled the town within three hours. A second Union force arrived on the ninth and destroyed the rest of Porter's command. This victory strengthened Union control in northeastern Missouri.

Estimated Casualties: 88 US, 368 CS

Independence I, Missouri (MO014), Jackson County, August 11, 1862

At dawn on August 11 two columns of Missouri State Guardsmen commanded by Colonel J. T. Hughes, including the guerrilla leader Captain William C. Quantrill and his Confederate Partisan Rangers, attacked Independence from two directions. Hughes was killed, and Colonel G. W. Thompson assumed command. US Lieutenant Colonel James T. Buel, commander of the garrison, barricaded his command in his headquarters building until a fire in the adjacent building forced them to surrender. Buel and 150 of his men were paroled; the others escaped or were killed. Thompson's force headed toward Kansas City.

Estimated Casualties: 344 US, unknown MSG

Lone Jack, Missouri (MO015), Jackson County, August 15–16, 1862

US Major Emory S. Foster led an 800-man force from Lexington to Lone Jack and attacked CS Colonel J. T. Coffee's 1,600 Confederates at about

9:00 P.M. on August 15. Coffee's men fled from the area, but another Confederate force, 3,000-strong, attacked the next morning. Foster was among the casualties. After five hours of charges, counterattacks, and retreats, Coffee's force returned, forcing Foster's successor, US Captain M. H. Brawner, to order a retreat to Lexington.

Estimated Casualties: 272 US, unknown CS

Newtonia I, Missouri (MO016), Newton County, September 30, 1862

In mid-September two of US General Blunt's brigades commanded by US Brigadier General Frederick Salomon left Fort Scott for southwestern Missouri. On September 30 US Colonel Edward Lynde's 150 soldiers attacked 200 Confederates in Newtonia and drove them back into the town. CS Colonel Cooper arrived with a force including the 1st Choctaw and Chickasaw Regiment and drove Lynde back. When Salomon arrived with reinforcements, he halted the retreat and attacked their right flank but was repulsed. The Confederates massed for an attack, and the Missouri cavalry broke the Union left. Cooper's Indians attacked through the town at full gallop. The Union artillery posted in the roadway to discourage pursuit was hit. The Federals panicked and fled the town, some to Sarcoxie, more than ten miles away.

Most Confederates withdrew into northwest Arkansas in early October before the advance from Springfield of a formidable Union army led by US General Schofield.

Estimated Casualties: 245 US, 78 CS

Newtonia is six miles east of Route 71 on Route 86. The Newtonia Battlefield Association owns nine historic acres.

Old Fort Wayne, Oklahoma (OK004), Delaware County, October 22, 1862

After the defeat of US General Salomon, US General Schofield's Army of the Frontier advanced on Newtonia with US General Blunt's division in the lead and defeated the Confederates on October 4. Blunt and most of his division chased CS Colonel Cooper's 1st Choctaw and Chickasaw Regiment and CS Colonel Watie's Cherokees as they headed west into Indian Territory. At 7:00 A.M. on October 22 Blunt's troops attacked Cooper's command on Beattie's Prairie near Old Fort Wayne, two miles west of the Arkansas–Indian Territory border. The outnumbered Confederates resisted for half an hour, then retreated to the south side of the Arkansas River, leaving artillery and equipment behind.

Estimated Casualties: 14 US, 150 CS

Clark's Mill, Missouri (MO017), Douglas County, November 7, 1862

US Captain Hiram E. Barstow, the commander of Company C, 10th Illinois Cavalry, stationed at Clark's Mill, sent troops toward Gainesville on November 7 to engage the 1,750-man cavalry brigade under CS Colonel John Q. Burbridge. After skirmishing with the Confederate advance guard and driving it back, Barstow pulled his force into the blockhouse at the mill. The Confederates approached from the northeast and surrounded the fort. The Federals were forced to surrender after a five-hour fight. The Confederates paroled the Union troops, burned the blockhouse, and left.

Estimated Casualties: 119, including 113 prisoners, US, 34 CS

U.S.-Dakota Conflict of 1862: August–September 1862

Fort Ridgely, Minnesota (MN001), Nicollet County, August 20–22, 1862

The U.S.-Dakota conflict in Minnesota was not, as some believed, instigated by the Confederacy, even though it did occur during the Civil War. The approximately 6,500 Santee Dakotas (Sioux) were in four tribes, the Mdewakantons, Wahpekutes, Sissetons, and Wahpetons. In 1837, as wild game and opportunities for livelihood decreased, the Dakotas had agreed to sell to the federal government about 5 million acres of their land for $1 million. The government did not fulfill its obligations. In 1851 the Dakotas once again ceded land for money: 24 million acres in exchange for $3 million and life on a reservation 20 miles wide and 150 miles long on both sides of the Minnesota River. They were cheated out of much of their money, and the Senate cut the clause assuring them of the Minnesota reservation. Troubles mounted between the whites and the Dakotas, as well as between the Dakotas who maintained traditional ways and those who were living, dressing, and worshiping like the whites.

The Dakotas in Minnesota were facing starvation in the summer of 1862 and had not received their annuity payments. They lived on a reservation along the Minnesota River, extending from the unstockaded Fort Ridgely, just northwest of New Ulm, into Dakota Territory and including the Lower Agency and the Upper Agency. The agency warehouses were full of food, but the government agent refused to distribute it. The response of the leading trader at the agency, Andrew Myrick, was "So far as I am concerned, if they are hungry, let them eat grass."

The conflict began on August 18 when Little Crow, the hereditary chief of one of the Mdewakanton villages, led an attack on the Lower Agency. The body of the trader was later found, his mouth stuffed with grass. On August 23 about 350 warriors struck New Ulm, and by dark had killed or wounded 59 people. The uprising resulted in the deaths of more than 350 whites and

major property damage throughout the river valley. Those fleeing the Dakotas sought refuge at Fort Ridgely, thirteen miles east of the Lower Sioux Agency. US Captain John S. Marsh, the commander of the fort's 180-man garrison, set out for the agency with 46 men. A large force surprised the soldiers en route, killed half of them, including Marsh, and pursued the rest back to Fort Ridgely.

On August 20 Little Crow led 400 Mdewakantons in an unsuccessful attack on the fort. Two days later 400 Sissetons and Wahpetons joined the second attack on the fort. The fort's artillery, which included two 12-pounder mountain howitzers, a 6-pounder field gun, and a 24-pounder howitzer, stopped them.

Fort Ridgely remained a stronghold in the Minnesota River valley. On September 6 President Abraham Lincoln appointed US Major General John Pope (following his defeat at the second battle at Manassas) commander of the new Military Department of the Northwest to suppress the Indians, as the conflict spread north and west and involved more tribes and more Federal troops.

Estimated Casualties: 26 US, unknown Dakotas

Fort Ridgely State Park, seven miles south of Fairfax near Route 4, includes twenty acres of the historic battlefield.

Wood Lake, Minnesota (MN002), Yellow Medicine County, September 23, 1862

After the attack on Fort Ridgely, Little Crow's Mdewakantons led their families up the valley to avoid the soldiers. At Yellow Medicine Agency, the Dakotas who had not been involved in the conflict urged Little Crow to return their captives, but he refused. The talks ended in anger. The Mdewakantons moved on to the north, splitting the Santees into peace and war groups.

On September 19, Henry Hastings Sibley, a former governor of Minnesota who had been recently named a colonel of the state militia, set out from Fort Ridgely with about 1,600 men, including 270 Civil War veterans who had been captured and paroled. They headed up the Minnesota River valley in search of the Dakotas involved in the conflict. As Sibley approached their camps, 300 Dakotas declared their willingness to fight the soldiers while another 400 went along; others refused and stayed in camp. The Dakotas set up an ambush to trap Sibley's force, but it was foiled by a militia foraging party. The Minnesotans' coordinated charges and their 6-pounder gun helped to defeat the Dakotas near Wood Lake on the twenty-third. Little Crow and about 200 Mdewakanton and their families headed for what is now North Dakota.

Within a few weeks, Sibley held about 2,000 Dakotas who had been captured or had surrendered. With Pope's approval, Sibley set up a military commission that determined that 307 of the captives should be hanged. Lincoln intervened, ordered an investigation, and cut the number to thirty-eight, at least three of whom were determined later to have been innocent. Congress canceled all of the treaties with the Dakotas, including all payments, and ordered them out of the state. Sibley was promoted to brigadier general of the U.S. Volunteers and head of the Military District of Minnesota.

Estimated Casualties: 41 US, 25 Dakotas

Louisiana: August–October 1862

Baton Rouge, Louisiana (LA003), East Baton Rouge Parish, August 5, 1862

After the fall of New Orleans in April 1862, USN Flag Officer David G. Farragut's fleet steamed up the Mississippi River, passed the Vicksburg batteries in late June, and joined USN Flag Officer Charles H. Davis's Mississippi Squadron upstream. On July 15 the Confederate ironclad ram *Arkansas* headed down the Yazoo River and battled its way to Vicksburg through the combined Union squadrons. Though heavily damaged, the ram disabled the *Carondelet*. That night Farragut ran the gauntlet again in an unsuccessful attempt to destroy the *Arkansas*. A week later the *Essex* attacked the *Arkansas* at its anchorage before joining Farragut downstream. A few days later Farragut departed with his fleet for New Orleans, stopping to land US Brigadier General Thomas Williams and 3,200 soldiers at Baton Rouge, the former Confederate capital of Louisiana.

Farragut's departure led CS Major General Earl Van Dorn to seize control of a larger part of the Mississippi River. He sent the damaged *Arkansas* downriver toward Baton Rouge, but the engines failed. As the USS *Essex* prepared to attack the stranded ship, the crew blew it up. CS Major General John C. Breckinridge, formerly vice president of the United States, had headed down the railroad from Jackson, Mississippi, with 4,000 men from the Vicksburg garrison to recapture Baton Rouge. The Confederate land forces reached the eastern outskirts of Baton Rouge on August 5 and attacked at 4:30 A.M. Heavy fog, friendly fire, and unnecessary redeploying slowed their advance, but when one regiment on the Federal left broke, a rout followed. US Colonel Thomas W. Cahill assumed command when Williams was killed. His men continued to flee to the river, where shells from Union gunboats halted the pursuing Confederates. The Federals evacuated Baton Rouge on August 21. The Confederates occupied Port Hudson, twenty-five miles upriver, where they constructed a bastion nearly as strong as that of Vicksburg to control the Mississippi River between the two strongholds.

Estimated Casualties: 371 US, 478 CS

Donaldsonville I, Louisiana (LA004), Ascension Parish, August 9, 1862

David G. Farragut had been promoted to rear admiral rank as of July but did not learn of it until he reached New Orleans. In early August he decided to silence the Confederate sharpshooters at Donaldsonville, who were firing on Union shipping on the Mississippi. Farragut warned the town that the women and children should be evacuated. On August 9 he anchored in front of the town, bombarded it, and sent a detachment ashore to burn hotels, wharf buildings, houses, and buildings of the partisan leader, Phillippe Landry. The naval action temporarily stopped the firing on Federal shipping.

Estimated Casualties: unknown

Georgia Landing, Louisiana (LA005), Lafourche Parish, October 27, 1862

US Major General Benjamin F. Butler ordered 4,000 Department of the Gulf troops under US Brigadier General Godfrey Weitzel to the Lafourche region. They were to eliminate the Confederate threat there, seize sugar and cotton, and establish a base for future military operations. On October 25 Weitzel's men reached the confluence of Bayou Lafourche and the Mississippi River at Donaldsonville and advanced up the east bank of the bayou. CS Brigadier General Alfred Mouton ordered his forces to meet the threat. On the twenty-seventh the Confederates occupied positions on opposite banks of the bayou near Georgia Landing above Labadieville. Mouton could not unite his forces because the nearest bridge across the bayou was several miles away at Labadieville.

In a short skirmish the Federals drove back the Confederates on the east bank, then crossed on their pontoon bridge to the west bank and attacked Mouton's other force there. The Confederates stalled the Union advance until they ran out of ammunition. Mouton withdrew to Labadieville, abandoning control of much of the Lafourche region.

Estimated Casualties: 86 US, 229 CS

Blockade of the Texas Coast: September 1862– January 1863

Sabine Pass I, Texas (TX001), Jefferson County, September 24–25, 1862

On September 23 the steamer *Kensington*, the schooner *Rachel Seaman*, and the mortar schooner *Henry James* arrived off Sabine Pass on the Texas-Louisiana border. The next morning they opened fire on CS Major J. S. Irvine's shore battery and forced the Confederates to spike their guns and evacuate the defenses. The schooners destroyed the battery on the twenty-fifth. US Acting Master Frederick Crocker received the surrender of Sabine and captured eight small Confederate schooners and sloops in the port. Since there were no Federal troops to garrison the town, the Confederates reoccupied it in January 1863.

Estimated Casualties: unknown

Sabine Pass Battleground State Historic Park is 1.5 miles south of Sabine Pass on Route 3322 and fifteen miles south of Port Arthur via Route 87. There are about fifty-six acres of the historic battlefield in the park.

Galveston I, Texas (TX002), Galveston County, October 4, 1862

The U.S. Navy had begun the blockade of Galveston harbor in July 1861. Early on the morning of October 4, 1862, USN Commander William B. Renshaw ordered the *Harriet Lane* into Galveston Bay under a flag of truce to notify the Confederates to surrender or he would attack. CS Colonel Joseph J. Cook, the regional military

commander, did not respond, so the *Harriet Lane* returned to the fleet, and four Union steamers and a mortar schooner replaced it. The flotilla exchanged fire with the Confederates at Fort Point until 1:00 P.M. when Cook dispatched two officers to meet Renshaw on the *Westfield*. Renshaw demanded an unconditional surrender or the fleet would shell Galveston. The Confederate officers refused Renshaw's terms, placing the responsibility on Renshaw if he destroyed the town and killed women and children. Renshaw agreed to a four-day truce during which the noncombatants could evacuate Galveston. The terms stipulated that Renshaw could move closer to Galveston, and that Cook could not permit his men to strengthen existing works or construct any new defenses around the city. Renshaw agreed, but the two sides did not sign a written agreement. All of the Confederates evacuated Galveston during the truce, taking weapons and supplies with them.

Estimated Casualties: unknown

Galveston II, Texas (TX003), Galveston County, January 1, 1863

CS Major General John B. Magruder became commander of the Confederate forces in Texas in November 1862, and he launched plans to recapture Galveston with a combined land and sea attack. Early on the morning of January 1 two Confederate steamboats and two "cottonclads" under CS Colonel Thomas Green approached Galveston from the bay while the infantry attacked the Federals, three companies of the 42nd Massachusetts Volunteer Infantry Regiment under the command of US Colonel Isaac S. Burrell. During the battle the *Harriet Lane* and three supply ships were captured. The steamboat *Neptune* sank after it rammed the *Harriet Lane*. USN Commander Renshaw's flagship, the *Westfield*, ran aground, and Renshaw was killed while blowing it up to prevent capture. The Union squadron escaped from the harbor, abandoning the infantry on the wharf. Cut off from any assistance, the infantry surrendered to the Confederates, except for the regimental adjutant, who escaped. The Confederates once again controlled Galveston, but the Federals continued the partially effective blockade of the approaches to the harbor. Blockade runners continued to supply the Confederates through Galveston.

Estimated Casualties: 600 US, 50 CS

Florida: June–October 1862

Tampa, Florida (FL002), Tampa, June 30–July 1, 1862

On June 30 the gunboat USS *Sagamore* demanded that the Oklawaha Rangers, an independent Confederate company, surrender Tampa. When they refused, the Federals gave them until 6:00 P.M. to evacuate the civilians and then fired on the town for an hour. Three Confederate batteries returned fire but could not reach the ship. The next day the *Sagamore* bombarded Tampa again for two hours and withdrew after inflicting little damage.

Estimated Casualties: none

St. Johns Bluff, Florida (FL003), Duval County, October 1–3, 1862

The need to control the St. Johns River resulted in engagements between Confederate regulars and partisans on the land and Federals working from transports and strongholds along the river. One important battle was for St. John's Bluff, commanding the river between Jacksonville and the Atlantic Ocean. In early September 1862 CS Brigadier General Joseph Finegan established batteries on the bluff to prevent Union ships from moving up the river. On September 30 US Brigadier General John M. Brannan and 1,573 troops left Hilton Head, South Carolina, on four transports to destroy the batteries. USN Commander Charles Steedman's squadron of six gunboats joined them at the mouth of the river the next day. Brannan landed his troops at Mayport Mills and sent scouting parties in search of landing areas near the bluff.

On October 2 Union troops landed five miles from the Confederate position at the head of Mount Pleasant Creek. They pushed the Confederate pickets back, seized their hastily evacuated camp, and began the overland march to the bluff. CS Lieutenant Colonel Charles F. Hopkins overestimated the number of attackers, concluded that his position was about to be attacked by 5,000 troops, abandoned St. Johns Bluff, and evacuated the area during the night. The Confederate guns were silent when the Federals arrived. Finegan later described the withdrawal by Hopkins as a "gross military blunder."

Brannan's troops took Jacksonville unopposed on the fifth. Four days later they abandoned the town, the pro-Union citizens, and the contrabands to Confederate retribution.

Estimated Casualties: unknown

A portion of the site of the Confederate battery is in Fort Caroline National Memorial, thirteen miles from Jacksonville.

Arkansas: November– December 1862

Cane Hill, Arkansas (AR004), Washington County, November 28, 1862

In October 1862 US Brigadier General James G. Blunt's division of the Army of the Frontier advanced into northwest Arkansas and halted near Old Fort Wayne, on the border with the Indian Territory. CS Major General Thomas C. Hindman ordered a force of his First Corps cavalry, commanded by CS Brigadier General John S. Marmaduke, to gather food for the army and to prevent Blunt from uniting with the Federals in winter camps near Springfield, Missouri. Hindman started moving his corps to stop Blunt and the Federal threat to the Arkansas River valley. Marmaduke's cavalry, including CS Colonel Joseph O. "Jo" Shelby's 4th Missouri Cavalry Brigade (soon to be known as the Iron Brigade), rode toward the agricultural area of Cane Hill, a long, low ridge on the northern side of the Boston Mountains.

Blunt advanced thirty-five miles in less than two days and launched a surprise attack at Boonsboro, one of the three Cane Hill communities. In a nine-hour, twelve-mile running fight across difficult terrain, more than 5,000 Union soldiers steadily drove about 2,000 Confederates back into the Boston Mountains. Shelby had four horses shot out from under him while leading his successful rear-guard tactic of moving his cavalry back one group at a time — with the first dashing past the intervening ones and becoming the last — which meant constant fighting during the withdrawal. The next day Marmaduke continued to the Van Buren area, and Blunt remained at Cane Hill.

Estimated Casualties: 41 US, 45 CS

Prairie Grove, Arkansas (AR005), Washington County, December 7, 1862

William L. Shea

During the fall of 1862 the Union Army of the Frontier, commanded by US Brigadier General John M. Schofield, pushed several scattered Confederate detachments out of southwest Missouri and into Arkansas and Indian Territory. Schofield became ill toward the end of the campaign and departed for St. Louis, leaving the two wings of his small army widely separated. US Brigadier General James G. Blunt's division was operating in northwest Arkansas along the border of Indian Territory. Two other divisions led by US Brigadier General Francis J. Herron were camped more than seventy miles away near Springfield, Missouri. In Schofield's absence, overall command passed to Blunt, an aggressive campaigner. Late in November Blunt advanced deeper into Arkansas and defeated a Confederate cavalry force at Cane Hill, on the northern edge of the Boston Mountains. The two wings of the Army of the Frontier now were more than one hundred miles apart. Despite his isolated position far in advance of other Union forces, Blunt decided to stay at Cane Hill and await developments. He directed Herron to be ready to march to his support at a moment's notice.

On the opposite side of the Boston Mountains, only thirty miles south of Cane Hill, was CS Major General Thomas C. Hindman's Army of the Trans-Mississippi. Hindman's force consisted of about 11,000 men, many of them conscripts of dubious loyalty, and twenty-two cannons. Arms and ammunition were in short supply, food and forage were scarce, and wagons and draft animals were in decrepit condition. Hindman planned to invade Missouri in the spring, when his army would be ready for a major offensive, but when he learned of Blunt's proximity, he decided to strike at once. Hindman's plan was simple. While his cavalry moved directly north toward Cane Hill and fixed Blunt in place, his infantry would swing around to the east and strike Blunt in the rear before he could retreat or receive reinforcements from Herron. Success depended on speed, stealth, and surprise. On December 3 the Confederate army set out from Van Buren and entered the Boston Mountains. During the next three days men and animals inched their way across the rugged terrain on primitive roads.

Blunt knew that his advanced position was precarious, and he kept a close watch on Confederate activity around Van Buren. On December 2 he concluded that Hindman was up to something and ordered Herron to come at once. But instead of falling back toward Missouri, Blunt placed his 5,000 men in defensive positions around Cane Hill and prepared for a fight. Herron responded magnificently. He received Blunt's message on December 3 and put his 7,000 men on the road early the next morning. During the next three and one half days Herron's two divisions marched 110 miles across the Ozark Plateau — an average of thirty miles per day. Some units covered the final sixty-five miles in only thirty hours. It was the most extraordinary forced march of the Civil War. Not every soldier could maintain such a grueling pace, and the Union column dwindled as the hours passed, but by dawn on December 7 the vanguard of Herron's command was in Fayetteville, only eighteen miles from Cane Hill.

Late on the sixth Hindman learned of Herron's unexpectedly rapid approach. He scrapped his original plan to envelop Blunt and turned north to face Herron. Early the next morning the leading elements of each column collided near the Illinois River, about midway between Fayetteville and Cane Hill. The Confederates fell back to a wooded hill surrounded by an expanse of cultivated fields and natural grasslands. Atop the hill was the Prairie Grove Church. Hindman deployed his army along the crest in a curved line of battle facing north and awaited Herron's attack. The Confederates were directly between the two Union forces, but instead of attempting to defeat Blunt and Herron in detail, Hindman inexplicably assumed a passive defensive posture. This was a grave error, because it permitted

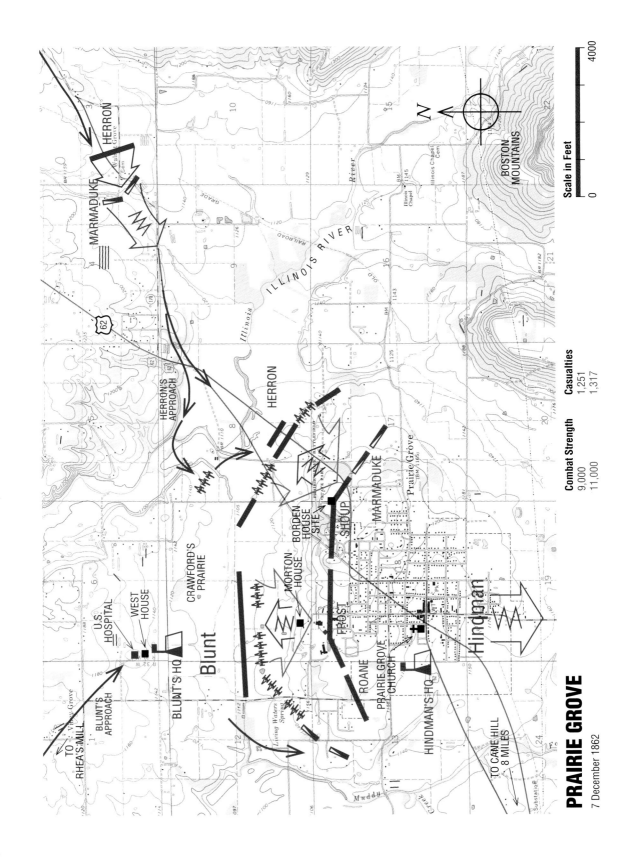

PRAIRIE GROVE

7 December 1862

	Combat Strength	Casualties
	9,000	1,251
	11,000	1,317

Scale in Feet

0   4000

BOSTON MOUNTAINS

ILLINOIS RIVER

HERRON
MARMADUKE

HERRON'S APPROACH

HERRON

MARMADUKE

SHOUP

Prairie Grove

Prairie Grove Church

HINDMAN'S HQ

Hindman

ROANE

FROST

MORTON HOUSE

BORDEN HOUSE SITE

CRAWFORD'S PRAIRIE

Blunt

BLUNT'S HQ

WEST HOUSE

U.S. HOSPITAL

BLUNT'S APPROACH

TO RHEA'S MILL

TO CANE HILL 8 MILES

the Union commanders to seize the initiative and join forces, the very thing Hindman needed to avoid.

Herron's two divisions forded the Illinois River and deployed on the north side of Crawford's Prairie, opposite the right wing of Hindman's line. The Union infantry was seriously depleted by the rigors of the march from Springfield and numbered fewer than 3,500 exhausted men. Nevertheless, Herron decided to attack at once. Intent on reaching Blunt at Cane Hill, which he still considered to be the point of danger, Herron thought he was opposed by a blocking force at Prairie Grove. He had no idea that he was facing the entire Confederate army. At 10:00 A.M. twenty-four Union rifled artillery opened a devastating two-hour bombardment that silenced the lighter Confederate batteries and forced many of Hindman's men to seek shelter on the lee side of the hill. Encouraged by this initial success, Herron sent his infantry forward to seize the high ground. About 2,000 Union troops swept across the prairie and up the slope past Archibald Borden's house, but near the crest they encountered two Confederate divisions led by CS Brigadier General John S. Marmaduke and CS Brigadier General Francis A. Shoup. The Union force was overwhelmed by vastly superior numbers and suffered heavy losses. Survivors fled down the hill to the shelter of the massed Union batteries on Crawford's Prairie. Pursuing Confederates fared no better; they were mowed down with canister when they emerged from the trees into the open grassland.

Hindman realized the relative weakness of Herron's force, at least in terms of infantry, and decided to wheel his unengaged left wing forward and push the two understrength Union divisions back across the Illinois River. The Confederates were slow to move, however, and by the time they advanced down the hill they were met by an unexpected barrage of artillery fire from the northwest, which drove them back to their original position. The guns were the advance element of Blunt's division.

All morning Blunt had waited at Cane Hill for Hindman's attack. Then he heard the roar of artillery to the northeast at Prairie Grove and realized what had happened. Blunt immediately marched toward the sound of the guns. By midafternoon most of his division was on the field, just west of Herron's beleaguered force, and opposite Hindman's left wing. Blunt opened fire with thirty guns and sent his infantry forward against CS Brigadier General Daniel M. Frost's Confederate division. For an hour fighting raged around William Morton's house at the top of the hill. At one point the Union troops fell back, and the Confederates again ventured out onto Crawford's Prairie in pursuit, but Blunt's artillery drove them off with heavy casualties. As darkness fell the battle sputtered out.

During the night Blunt called up 3,000 cavalrymen who had been guarding Union supply trains at Rhea's Mill. As many as 2,000 footsore stragglers from Herron's divisions dribbled in from the direction of Fayetteville. Hindman received no reinforcements, and hundreds of his Arkansas conscripts deserted, many going over to the Union side. The Confederates still held the hill, but their artillery was wrecked, and their ammunition was almost gone. Under cover of darkness the Army of the Trans-Mississippi slipped away toward the Boston Mountains. Desertion was rampant during the retreat, and Hindman returned to Van Buren with only a fraction of his original force. Prairie Grove was a costly tactical draw but a strategic victory for the Union. The Confederate attempt to destroy Blunt's isolated force and recover northwest Arkansas and southwest Missouri had failed.

"For the forces engaged, there was no more stubborn fight and no greater casualties in any battle of the war than at Prairie Grove, Arkansas," declared a Union officer. The Union Army of the Frontier went into battle with 9,000 men and suffered at least 1,251 casualties: 175 killed, 813 wounded, and 263 missing. The Confederate Army of the Trans-Mississippi had 11,000 men on the field and suffered a minimum of 1,317 casualties: 164 killed, 817 wounded, and 336 missing. These numbers almost certainly are low; the actual casualty rate probably was more than 15 percent for each army.

Estimated Casualties: 1,251 US, 1,317 CS

Prairie Grove Battlefield Historic State Park, at Prairie Grove, ten miles southwest of Fayetteville, includes 306 acres of the historic battlefield.

Fredericksburg: December 1862

Fredericksburg I, Virginia (VA028), Spotsylvania County and Fredericksburg, December 11–15, 1862

A. Wilson Greene

Catharinus Putnam Buckingham knocked gently on the pole of the commanding general's tent. With him stood a tall, handsome officer known best for his genial personality and distinctive whiskers. US Major General George B. McClellan welcomed his visitors to the headquarters of the Army of the Potomac and guessed the reason for their call. Buckingham carried President Abraham Lincoln's order to remove McClellan from his post and replace him with US Major General Ambrose E. Burnside, who watched uncomfortably as Little Mac digested the news of his professional demise. This quiet transfer of power led to one of the great battles of the Civil War.

Burnside's reputation later suffered because of his conduct of the Fredericksburg campaign in the autumn of 1862. However, his strategy when he assumed control of the Army of the Potomac had merit: use pontoon bridges to cross the Rappahannock River at Fredericksburg and move directly south against Richmond. To succeed, he would have to march quickly and get to Fredericksburg before CS General Robert E. Lee's two corps, led by Lieutenant Generals James Longstreet and Thomas J. "Stonewall" Jackson.

Burnside set his army in motion on November 15, 1862, organized into four grand divisions: the right, under US Major General Edwin V. Sumner; the center, under US Major General Joseph Hooker; the left, under US Major General William B. Franklin; and the reserve, under US Major General Franz Sigel (it did not participate in the battle). Some 115,000 Union soldiers were involved.

On November 17 Sumner's division appeared on Stafford Heights, overlooking Fredericksburg.

However, because of an inefficient bureaucracy and bad roads, the vital bridging equipment had not arrived. When the pontoons did appear, more than a week later, Lee had arrived too. By late November the basic premise of Burnside's campaign — an unopposed crossing of the Rappahannock — was no longer valid.

Lee positioned Longstreet's corps, consisting of divisions commanded by CS Major Generals Richard H. Anderson, Lafayette McLaws, George E. Pickett, and John Bell Hood, and Brigadier General Robert Ransom, Jr., on the high ground west of Fredericksburg, occupying a line anchored at Taylor's Hill near the Rappahannock on the left and at Hamilton's Crossing near marshy Massaponax Creek on the right. Jackson's four divisions, under CS Major Generals Daniel Harvey Hill and Ambrose Powell Hill and Brigadier Generals Jubal A. Early and William B. Taliaferro, ranged twenty miles downstream, guarding against any attempt to turn the far right flank. Lee's army numbered 78,000 men.

At 3:00 A.M. on December 11 Union engineers slipped their pontoons into the Rappahannock's icy waters and went to work. Their bridges progressed nicely until the first rays of dawn penetrated the foggy gloom that enveloped the river valley. Then minié balls whizzed through the mist, and the defenseless carpenters scrambled from their half-finished spans. The gunfire came from Mississippi and Florida troops commanded by CS Brigadier General William Barksdale who concealed themselves behind fences and in cellars near the water's edge. Burnside ordered a massive hour-long bombardment of Fredericksburg, in which 150 cannons rained 8,000 projectiles on the town. When the guns fell silent and the engineers warily returned to their spans, Barksdale's men met them with the familiar .58-caliber greeting.

Only one course remained. Union volunteers from Michigan, Massachusetts, and New York ferried themselves across the Rappahannock in the clumsy pontoon boats and battled the troops from Mississippi and Florida until the Confederates withdrew at darkness to their main line a mile in the rear, conceding the control of Fredericksburg to Burnside. Lee had never intended to prevent the Union forces from crossing the river; in fact he hoped Burnside would test his defenses behind the town. Barksdale's tenacity merely bought time for Lee to recall Jackson's corps from downstream and mass his army against Burnside's long-anticipated offensive.

On December 12 the Army of the Potomac crossed the Rappahannock en masse and squandered the day by looting the empty city in a shameful display of vandalism. Burnside had based his battle plan on the assumption that he faced only a portion of Lee's army, a circumstance that ceased to exist by December 13. Using tentative, ambiguous language, he ordered assaults for the thirteenth against Hamilton's Crossing on the Confederate right and Marye's Heights behind the town on Lee's left center.

The left grand division bore responsibility for the attack against Jackson. Even though he controlled almost 60,000 troops, Franklin placed the most literal and conservative interpretation on Burnside's orders and committed only 4,500 men to the offensive. US Major General George Gordon Meade's division of Pennsylvania Reserves prepared to advance, supported on each flank by divisions under US Brigadier Generals Abner Doubleday and John Gibbon.

Meade moved out at 8:30 A.M. His men, covered by a dissipating fog, crossed the Richmond Stage Road and began to march west toward Hamilton's Crossing. Suddenly Confederate artillery erupted behind them and to their left, halting the Union soldiers in their tracks. The guns belonged to a twenty-four-year-old Alabamian, CS Major John Pelham, commander of CS Major General James Ewell Brown Stuart's Confederate horse artillery. The young officer had recklessly advanced two pieces directly on Meade's flank and rear and boldly maintained his position, despite losing the use of one gun early in the action. Pelham defied orders to retreat and returned to his lines only after he had exhausted his ammunition.

Pelham's heroics not only delayed the Union

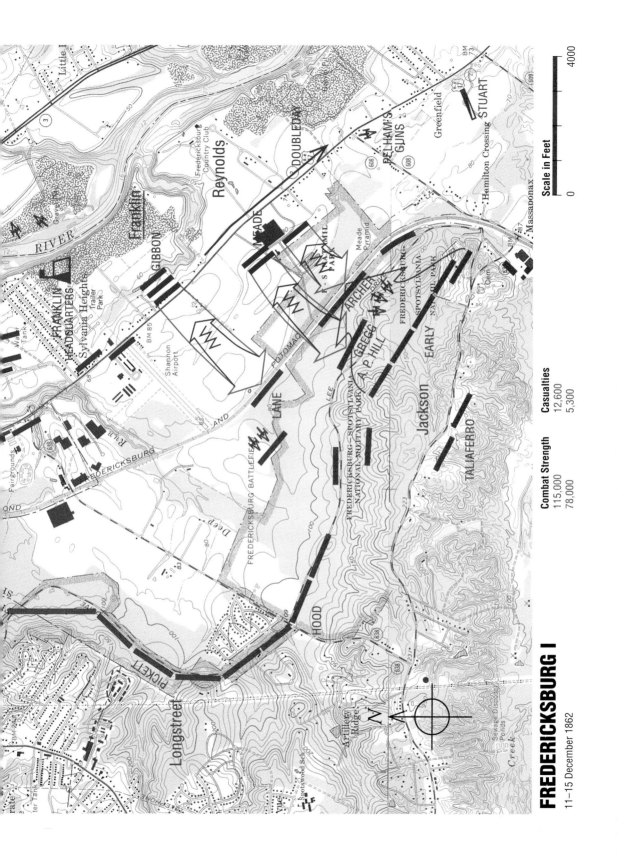

FREDERICKSBURG I

11–15 December 1862

	Combat Strength	Casualties
	115,000	12,600
	78,000	5,300

Scale in Feet

0   4000

advance but induced Meade's supports on the left to remain east of the Richmond Stage Road to meet other such unexpected attacks. Once Pelham withdrew, Meade's forces resumed their approach. When they were within eight hundred yards of Jackson's line, Confederate artillery, masked in the woods to their front, blasted them. The Union infantry found hasty cover in the fields, where they responded to the Confederate fire. During the extended artillery duel that followed, a Federal missile exploded a southern ammunition wagon. Meade's troops then dashed toward a triangular point of woods that extended across the railroad tracks at the base of Jackson's position. To their surprise, it was unoccupied. They had accidentally found the Achilles' heel of Jackson's defense — a six-hundred-yard gap in the front lines between the brigades of CS Brigadier Generals James J. Archer and James H. Lane.

The Federals quickly pressed through the woods and up to the high ground, upending CS Brigadier General Maxcy Gregg's South Carolina Brigade. Meade broke through but could see Confederates gathering in his front. Jackson's response to the emergency was to organize a devastating counterattack, so Meade's soldiers and a portion of Gibbon's division, which had surged forward on Meade's right, withdrew across the railroad, through the open fields, and back to the Richmond Stage Road. By this time Franklin's reserves had stemmed the Confederate rush, and Jackson stubbornly resumed his original position.

In Fredericksburg, Lee brilliantly crafted his defense so that artillery swept the open ground west of the city with a chilling efficiency. "A chicken could not live on that field when we open on it," boasted one Confederate cannoneer. Confederate infantry supported the guns and occupied the base of the hills as well. Immediately below Marye's Heights, soldiers from Georgia and North Carolina under CS Brigadier General Thomas R. R. Cobb crouched in a sunken road behind a stone wall and waited.

Burnside intended to begin his attack against Marye's Heights after Franklin had rolled up the Confederate right. When Meade's and Gibbon's attack bogged down in late morning, he unwisely opted to go forward with the second half of his offensive. This decision resulted in one of the great disasters of the Civil War. Wave after wave of Union troops from the corps of US Major Generals Darius N. Couch and Daniel Butterfield and US Brigadier General Orlando B. Willcox, and from US Brigadier General Amiel W. Whipple's division left the cover of the town. They crossed a canal ditch hidden in a small valley and moved west toward Marye's Heights, across four hundred yards of open terrain. The Federals staggered through the fire of massed artillery only to encounter a sheet of flame from the infantry 150 yards away, behind the stone wall. Men screamed as they moved forward, hunching their shoulders as if breasting a violent storm of wind and hail.

Tactics did not matter here. Lee poured reinforcements into the sunken road, where his riflemen stood six ranks deep on some portions of the line. Burnside ordered brigade after brigade — fifteen in all — to challenge the position, usually one or two at a time because the canal ditch valley could shelter only a few thousand men simultaneously. The attacks began at noon and continued until dark. When the firing ended, no Union soldier had laid a hand on the stone wall.

Burnside wanted to counter his losses by leading a new assault personally on December 14, but his lieutenants dissuaded him. The armies remained on the field for two more days. Many of the Union wounded froze to death in the no man's land between the lines. During a torrential downpour on the night of December 15 – 16, Burnside withdrew his men across the Rappahannock, and the battle concluded.

The battle of Fredericksburg cost Burnside 12,600 casualties, almost two thirds of which occurred on the few acres in front of the sunken road. Lee lost only 5,300. It appeared that the Army of Northern Virginia had won an overwhelming victory, but the Union army had not been destroyed, and Burnside quickly replaced his losses. Union morale dropped, but it never sagged enough to threaten the war effort. By the following spring Burnside's successor had re-fashioned the Army of the Potomac into a splendid fighting machine.

Lee regretted his opponent's escape across the Rappahannock, although in reality he could have done little to prevent it. His victory at Fredericksburg only postponed the next "On to Richmond" campaign by a few months.

Estimated Casualties: 12,600 US, 5,300 CS

Fredericksburg Battlefield, a unit of Fredericksburg and Spotsylvania National Military Park near Interstate 95 at Fredericksburg, includes 1,572 acres of the historic battlefield; 84 of these acres are privately owned.

Forrest's Raid into West Tennessee: December 1862

Jackson, Tennessee (TN009), Madison County, December 19, 1862

While CS Brigadier General John Hunt Morgan raided deep into Kentucky, CS Brigadier General Nathan Bedford Forrest led a cavalry expedition into West Tennessee. His goal was to destroy the Mobile & Ohio Railroad between Jackson, Tennessee, and Columbus, Kentucky, disrupting US Major General Ulysses S. Grant's supply line during his campaign down the Mississippi Central Railroad. Forrest's 2,500 cavalrymen crossed the Tennessee River at Clifton between December 15 and 17 and headed west. Grant concentrated 10,000 troops at Jackson under US Brigadier General Jeremiah C. Sullivan. He ordered 800 cavalrymen under US Colonel Robert G. Ingersoll ("the Great Agnostic") to stop Forrest. Forrest defeated the Union cavalry, captured Ingersoll at Lexington on the eighteenth, and continued his advance. Forrest's success prompted Sullivan to concentrate his forces in Jackson, leaving the countryside and the railroads undefended.

On December 19 Forrest attacked and drove the Federals a mile back into their fortifications in Jackson. It was a feint and show of force to hold the Federals' attention while two of his cavalry regiments destroyed the railroads north and south of town. CS Colonel George G. Dibrell's men destroyed Carroll Station and captured both soldiers and valuable rifles. CS Colonel A. A. Russell headed south and destroyed railroads that led to Corinth and Bolivar. The next morning they were gone.

Estimated Casualties: 6 US, unknown CS

Parker's Cross Roads, Tennessee (TN011), Henderson County, December 31, 1862

CS General Forrest tore up the Mobile & Ohio Railroad between Union City and Jackson and stopped traffic on it until the following March. He then rode southeast to cross the Tennessee River and end his raid. US General Sullivan tried to trap the hard-riding troopers before they could withdraw across the river. Federal gunboats waited at the river crossings to block Forrest's retreat while 10,000 Federals chased him.

On December 31 US Colonel Cyrus L. Dunham's brigade occupied Parker's Cross Roads to block Forrest's escape route to the south. The fight began one mile northwest of the crossroads at Hick's Field where Forrest used his cannons at close range so effectively that he forced Dunham to pull back and redeploy his brigade south of the crossroads. Forrest ordered his line to advance while two forces hit Dunham's rear, and victory was nearly his. As he was demanding Dunham's unconditional surrender, US Colonel John W. Fuller's brigade arrived from Huntingdon in a surprise attack on the Confederate rear. Forrest may or may not have ordered his men to "charge them both ways," but they moved quickly to attack Dunham's force while Forrest charged Fuller's artillery and infantry. Forrest rode past Dunham's scattered and demoralized men, saved much of his command, and crossed the Tennessee River on January 1, 1863.

Although both sides claimed victory, the Federals failed to stop Forrest. His cavalry had succeeded in disrupting US General Grant's supply and communications lines while CS Major General Earl Van Dorn destroyed the Union supply depot at Holly Springs. These successes forced Grant to abandon his effort to engage and hold Confederate troops in northern Mississippi while US Major General William Tecumseh Sherman's amphibious force advanced down the Mississippi River toward Vicksburg.

Estimated Casualties: 237 US, 500 CS

Brochures for a self-guided driving tour of the battlefield on public roads are available at Parker's Crossroads, off I-40 at Exit 108, Route 22.

Stones River Campaign: December 1862– January 1863

Hartsville, Tennessee (TN008), Trousdale County, December 7, 1862

A Federal force of about 2,400 soldiers, including the 39th Brigade of the Army of the Cumberland, commanded by US Colonel Absalom B. Moore guarded the Cumberland River crossing east of Nashville at Hartsville. On December 6 the charismatic raider CS Colonel John Hunt Morgan led 2,100 cavalry and infantrymen on an all-day march in sleet and snow from Baird's Mill. They began crossing the cold river late that night. (Moore's afteraction report stated that Morgan's vanguard got across because they wore U.S. uniforms.) The force included two regiments of the Orphan Brigade of Kentucky, so named because they were Confederates from a state that did not secede.

Pressing to surprise the Federals under cover of darkness, Morgan had to attack with only the 1,300 men who had made the difficult river crossing. Before dawn Morgan surprised the Federals in their camp. Pickets sounded the alarm and held them off until the brigade was in battle line. One of Moore's units fled during the battle. In less than two hours the Confederates had surrounded the Union soldiers and forced them to surrender. Time was critical because Morgan knew that Federal reinforcements were on the way. He crossed the river once again, this time with prisoners and supplies and returned to Murfreesboro.

The battle of Hartsville demonstrated Morgan's ability to combine infantry and cavalry into an effective strike force. He was promoted to brigadier general four days later. Morgan next launched his Third Kentucky ("Christmas") Raid, during which he severed US Major General William S. Rosecrans's lifeline to Louisville, wrecked Union railroads supplying the army in Tennessee, and hindered offensive operations.

Estimated Casualties: 2,096 US, 139 CS

Brochures are available in Hartsville for a driving tour of the battlefield, which is in private ownership.

Stones River, Tennessee (TN010), Rutherford County, December 31, 1862– January 2, 1863

Grady McWhiney

Just after Christmas in 1862, US Major General William S. Rosecrans moved the Army of the Cumberland south from Nashville toward Murfreesboro, Tennessee, to drive CS General Braxton Bragg's Army of Tennessee out of the state. "Press them, hard! Drive them!" Rosecrans urged his subordinates. "Make them fight or run!"

Bragg refused to run, even though an entire division had just been transferred from his army to Vicksburg by President Jefferson Davis, who advised Bragg to "fight if you can, and [then] fall back beyond the Tennessee [River]." Bragg deployed his forces on both sides of Stones River, north of Murfreesboro, in mostly open country without strong natural defenses, where trees grew in thick patches that could conceal the enemy and hamper Confederate cavalry and artillery movements. If Stones River rose — a likely event after the heavy rains earlier in December — he might be in trouble. But he disregarded these disadvantages in picking his battle line, because it was the only place he could concentrate the army and still cover the roads leading to his supply depot in Murfreesboro. He also feared that a retreat farther southward would expose East Tennessee to invasion.

Even though Bragg's defensive position was the best he could find for his purposes, he committed the serious tactical error of failing to have his left and right wings entrench. He missed the most obvious lesson he should have learned from earlier battles: defenders in strong positions generally lose fewer men than the attackers do. Per-

haps Bragg believed his men did not have time to use their spades to good advantage, but he also underestimated the value of fieldworks.

In the last days of December the two armies skirmished and groped into closer contact. As Rosecrans's forces moved toward Murfreesboro, Bragg sent CS Brigadier General Joseph Wheeler's cavalry around the Federal army to destroy supply trains and disrupt communications. The Confederates captured hundreds of prisoners, horses, wagons, and enough weapons to arm a brigade. But the cavalry raid was only the preliminary to what Bragg had in mind.

When Rosecrans failed to attack on December 30, Bragg decided to outflank the Federal right, cut the enemy's line of retreat, and fold Rosecrans's army back on itself like a closing jackknife. Near dawn on December 31, four fifths of the Confederate army began a wheeling movement from left to right on the west side of Stones River. Bragg's actions surprised the Federals. Rosecrans had planned to attack the Confederate right flank that same morning with the corps of US Major General Thomas L. Crittenden and US Major General George H. Thomas, but Bragg's men moved first, led by CS Lieutenant General William J. Hardee's Corps and followed by CS Lieutenant General Leonidas Polk's Corps. Their initial assault hit US Major General Alexander McD. McCook's corps, whose only assignment for the day had been to protect the Federal right. The strong resistance put up by US Brigadier General Philip H. Sheridan's men in the right center saved the Union from disaster by protecting the pike, the Federal supply line. Outflanked and overwhelmed by the Confederates, however, McCook's men retreated.

With the Federals forced back toward the Murfreesboro-Nashville Pike, Rosecrans called off his offensive and struggled to construct a defense line to save his only escape route. A Union general recalled that Rosecrans's "usually florid face had lost its ruddy color, and his anxious eyes told that the disasters of the morning were testing his powers to the very verge of endurance." Attacks against the Union right continued, but gradually the Federals rallied; their deadly rifle and artil-

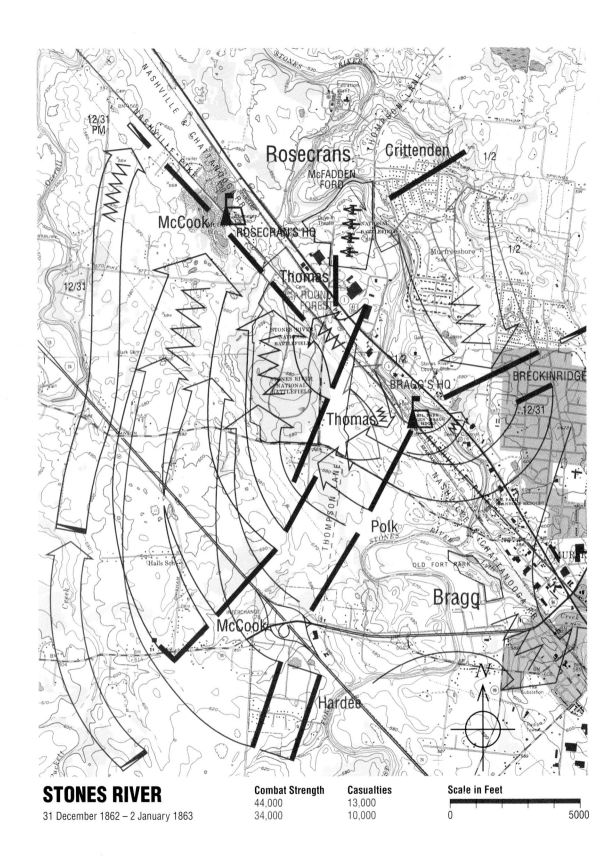

STONES RIVER

31 December 1862 – 2 January 1863

Combat Strength	Casualties
44,000	13,000
34,000	10,000

Scale in Feet

0   5000

lery fire slowed and then checked the Confederate advance. The movement Bragg had expected his army to perform was more suited to an open parade field than to the rough terrain dotted with cedar thickets over which the Confederates advanced. Officers soon found it impossible to keep their lines unbroken, as Bragg's orders required, or even to maintain contact with units on their flanks. As losses multiplied, more men straggled.

By noon the sharpest action was in the Round Forest, near the Union center, where the Federal line formed an acute angle. The Confederates struck this strong natural position repeatedly but unsuccessfully; half the men in CS Brigadier General James R. Chalmers's 44th Mississippi Regiment charged the Federal position armed only with sticks, and most of his 9th Mississippi attacked with their rifles too wet to fire, because of the previous night's rain. As the Mississippians faltered, CS Brigadier General Daniel S. Donelson's Tennessee Brigade rushed forward and was nearly destroyed: one regiment lost half its officers and 68 percent of its men; another lost 42 percent of its officers and more than half its men.

Unable to break the Federal line with Polk's troops, Bragg ordered four fresh brigades from CS Major General John C. Breckinridge's Division on his right flank across the river. He could not have picked a worse spot to make this major attack, and Polk compounded the error by sending these reinforcements, which arrived shortly before 2:00 P.M., into battle piecemeal. They were slaughtered. "The Federals," as one general reported, "were strongly posted in two lines of battle, supported by numerous batteries. One of [the lines formed] an excellent breastwork. We had no artillery, the nature of the ground forbidding its use. It was deemed reckless to [continue the] attack."

Action continued sporadically until dark, but the Confederates could not break the Federal line, now defended by units of McCook's, Thomas's, and Crittenden's corps. To Hardee's final appeal for reinforcements sometime after 4:00 P.M., Bragg replied that he had no men to send. Hardee refused to order another assault. "The enemy," he recalled, "lay beyond the range of our guns, se-

curely sheltered behind the strong defense of the railroad embankment, with wide open fields intervening, which were swept by their superior artillery. It would have been folly, not valor, to assail them in this position."

No further major action took place until January 2, when Bragg decided to dislodge a Union force, led by US Colonel Samuel Beatty of Crittenden's Third Division, which had crossed Stones River and occupied a position on the east bank, "from which . . . Polk's line was both commanded and enfiladed." Bragg ordered Breckinridge's Division, supported by artillery and cavalry, to drive the Federals back across the river. To divert attention from Breckinridge's assault, Bragg opened an artillery barrage along Polk's front at 3:30 P.M. About thirty minutes later Breckinridge's men advanced in two lines. "The front line had bayonets fixed," reported Breckinridge, "with orders to deliver one volley, and then use the bayonet." A member of Bragg's staff left the best brief account of what happened. "The division moved beautifully across an open field," he observed.

> A murderous fire was opened upon them. The enemy had concentrated a large force . . . and had combined a concentric fire from his artillery. . . . Our troops nevertheless marched up bravely and drove the enemy from the hill. The left of the division improvidently crossed the river contrary to orders: it was driven back in confusion. In [the] meantime, the enemy in large force assailed the right of the division, and it was compelled to retire. The [Confederate] cavalry[men] on the right were ordered to cooperate, but they were mere spectators. It was a terrible affair, although short.

An hour and twenty minutes of combat had gained the Confederates nothing but casualties.

Bragg's position was now precarious. Soldiers who had fought and waited in the rain and cold for five days without sufficient rest were exhausted. Straggling had increased significantly. Stones River, which had risen rapidly after several more days of heavy rain, might soon become unfordable, which would isolate part of the army. Furthermore, Bragg had just seen captured documents that indicated that Rosecrans had received reinforcements.

The Confederate retreat from Murfreesboro, which began at 11:00 P.M. on January 3 in drenching rain, was made without mishap. Supply trains led the way south, followed by the infantry. A cavalry screen protected their movements. Rosecrans did not pursue, but nearly 2,000 wounded Confederates and their medical attendants were left behind.

Stones River was one of the bloodiest battles of the Civil War. Of the approximately 44,000 Federals and 34,000 Confederates engaged in action near Murfreesboro, 13,000 Federals and 10,000 Confederates became casualties.

To many people the end of the war seemed no nearer after Stones River. A Confederate who admitted that he was "sick and tired" of fighting could "see no prospects of having peace for a long time to come. I don't think it ever will be stopped by fighting," he reasoned. "The Yankees can't whip us and we can never whip them, and I see no prospect of peace unless the Yankees themselves rebel and throw down their arms, and refuse to fight any longer." Northern leaders, in contrast, regarded Stones River as an important victory. It cost the Confederates not only a little more of Tennessee but a lot of what they could ill afford to lose — men. The Federals, who had more manpower, gained little additional territory, yet after the battle President Lincoln thanked Rosecrans for his "hard-earned victory" and confessed that had Stones River "been a defeat instead, the nation could scarcely have lived over [it]."

Estimated Casualties: 13,000 US, 10,000 CS

Stones River National Battlefield, on Route 41 near Interstate 24 at Murfreesboro, twenty-five miles southeast of Nashville, includes 708 acres of the historic battlefield; 213 of these acres are in private ownership.

Vicksburg Campaign and Siege: December 1862– July 1863

Chickasaw Bayou, Mississippi (MS003), Warren County, December 26–29, 1862

Terrence J. Winschel

After the battles of Iuka on September 19 and Corinth on October 3–4 in north Mississippi, US Major General Ulysses S. Grant launched a campaign aimed at Vicksburg. He split his force in two. He commanded one 40,000-man wing and marched south along the line of the Mississippi Central Railroad from Grand Junction, Tennessee, into Mississippi. The objective was to draw Confederate troops into northern Mississippi and keep them there while his other wing, 32,000 soldiers under US Major General William Tecumseh Sherman, made an amphibious thrust down the Mississippi River to capture Vicksburg.

Grant's column started on November 26 and marched through Holly Springs and Oxford toward Grenada where CS Lieutenant General John C. Pemberton was entrenched on the south bank of the Yalobusha River. On December 20 raiding cavalry under CS Major General Earl Van Dorn destroyed the Union advance supply base at Holly Springs. Another raid into West Tennessee, conducted by CS Brigadier General Nathan Bedford Forrest, resulted in the destruction of sixty miles of railroad vital to Grant. These Confederate successes compelled Grant to abandon his operations and fall back on Memphis.

Also on December 20 Sherman's expeditionary force boarded transports at Memphis, picked up additional troops at Helena, and headed downriver toward Vicksburg. The flotilla, seven gunboats and fifty-nine transports, arrived at Milliken's Bend, Louisiana, just above Vicksburg on Christmas Eve and tied up for the night.

The Federals moved up the Yazoo, came ashore on December 26–27, and advanced cautiously inland. (Before the landing, U.S. naval forces had conducted torpedo clearing operations on the

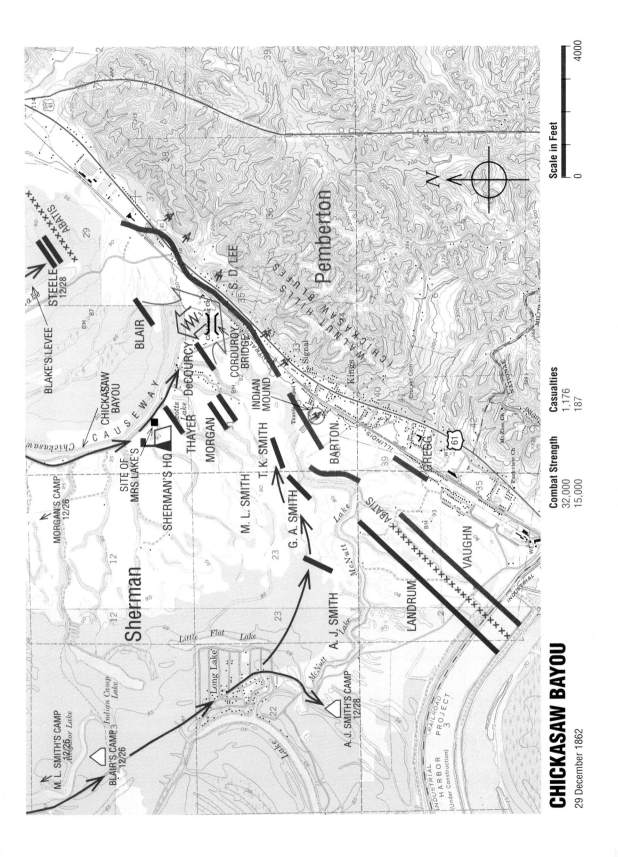

CHICKASAW BAYOU

29 December 1862

Combat Strength	Casualties
32,000	1,176
15,000	187

Scale in Feet

0   4000

Yazoo River, during which the "City Series" iron-clad *Cairo* was sunk.) The field of battle fronted the Walnut Hills north of the city. Along the base of the hills the Confederates had established a formidable defense line, which, throughout most of its length, was shielded by water barriers. The most formidable of these was Chickasaw Bayou, a sluggish, tree-choked stream approximately fifty yards wide and chest-deep which ran across most of the Union front before turning sharply to the north, bisecting the line of advance. The Confederates had also felled large numbers of trees in front of their works which formed a dense *abatis* to obstruct the Union advance.

Fighting escalated on December 27–28 as the Federals probed for a weakness in the Confederate defenses. On the twenty-eighth Sherman attempted to turn the Confederate right flank, but US Brigadier General Frederick Steele's division, advancing on a narrow front flanked by water barriers, was unable to reach the bluffs in the face of Confederate artillery fire. Although the Confederates were greatly outnumbered, their fortifications proved strong, and reinforcements were on the way from north Mississippi. (Grant's retrograde to Memphis enabled Pemberton and a large portion of his force, using interior rail lines, to move from Grenada to Vicksburg and arrive in time to meet Sherman's attack.)

Sherman launched his main attack on December 29. At 7:30 A.M. Union artillery roared into action. Confederate guns responded and for several hours an artillery duel raged but did little damage. At 11:00 A.M. Union officers deployed their troops in line of battle. Before them was a formidable task, and the chances of success were slim. Sherman said, "We will lose 5,000 men before we take Vicksburg, and may as well lose them here as anywhere else."

At noon Federal artillery fired a volley signaling the attack. US Brigadier General Francis P. Blair Jr.'s brigade advanced on the left, while US Colonel John DeCourcy's brigade in the center, supported by US Brigadier General John M. Thayer's brigade, advanced down the road from Mrs. Lake's. Blueclad soldiers surged forward with a cheer. Under a storm of shells and minié

balls, the men worked their way through the dense *abatis*, crossed the water barriers, and carried the advance Confederate rifle pits. As the Federals closed on the main Confederate defense line, they were checked by a murderous fire and driven back. The remnants of the two brigades and one regiment of Thayer's fell back across the bayou via a corduroy bridge. CS Brigadier General Stephen D. Lee's troops checked the assault and launched a counterattack that netted 332 prisoners, four battle flags, and five hundred stands of arms. The Confederates had dealt a decisive repulse that was repeated elsewhere along the line.

US Brigadier General A. J. Smith, advancing on the right with two divisions (his own and that of US Brigadier General Morgan L. Smith, who had been wounded the day before), attempted to cross Chickasaw Bayou and carry the Confederate position at the Indian mound in the center of the line held by CS Brigadier Generals Seth Barton and John Gregg. Several regiments of US Colonel Giles A. Smith's brigade, supported by US Colonel Thomas Kilby Smith's brigade, were posted along the edge of the bayou and deployed as skirmishers to cover the crossing. Soldiers of G. A. Smith's 6th Missouri splashed into the stream and waded across. Accompanied by twenty pioneers, the Missourians attempted to cut a road up the opposite bank. Although the Federals were within point-blank range of the Indian mound, they boldly made five unsuccessful attempts to carry the position. A. J. Smith also launched a feeble attack with US Colonel William J. Landrum's brigade against the southern end of the line, which was easily checked by CS Brigadier General John Vaughn.

Convinced that the position north of Vicksburg could not be taken, no further attacks were ordered. On January 1, 1863, the Federals boarded their transports and departed the area. The battle cost Sherman 1,176 men killed, wounded, or missing, compared with only 187 Confederates. "I reached Vicksburg at the time appointed," he reported, "landed, assaulted and failed."

Estimated Casualties: 1,176 US, 187 CS

The Chickasaw Bayou battlefield, two miles north of Vicksburg off Route 61, is privately owned.

Arkansas Post, Arkansas (AR006), Arkansas County, January 9–11, 1863

By late 1862 midwesterners were voicing increasing discontent with the war because they could not ship their goods down the Mississippi River. Their concerns increased the pressure on US Major General Ulysses S. Grant to capture Vicksburg. US Major General John A. McClernand, a prominent Democrat from Illinois, gained President Lincoln's approval to raise troops from the Midwest to attack Vicksburg. His plans for a command independent of Grant, who was the commander of the Department of West Tennessee, were frustrated by the general-in-chief, US Major General Henry W. Halleck. In the fall of 1862 the Confederates had built Fort Hindman and supporting earthworks at Arkansas Post, fifty miles up the Arkansas River from its confluence with the Mississippi, to block Federal access to Little Rock and to provide a base from which Confederate gunboats could attack Federal shipping on the Mississippi River. The fort contained three heavy guns emplaced in armored casemates and eight light guns. In January 1863 CS Brigadier General Thomas J. Churchill commanded the garrison of 5,000 Arkansas, Louisiana, and Texas troops.

McClernand and USN Rear Admiral David D. Porter led a powerful army-navy expedition against Arkansas Post as a prelude to the Federal operations against Vicksburg. Their force included three ironclad gunboats, several timber-clad gunboats, and sixty transports carrying 33,000 men. US General Sherman's corps and other troops landed downriver from the Confederate position on January 9 and approached overland while the gunboats bombarded the fort, stripping away the iron plating and silencing several guns. On January 11 the Federal infantry attacked. They gained a foothold on the Confederate earthworks, despite suffering heavy casualties. When several Confederate units stopped fighting and allowed the Federals inside their works, Churchill surrendered.

Estimated Casualties: 1,092 US, 5,004 CS

Areas of the battlefield are in Arkansas Post National Memorial at Gillett, Arkansas.

Grand Gulf, Mississippi (MS004), Claiborne County, April 29, 1863

By the spring of 1863 US General Grant had been unsuccessful in his efforts to capture Vicksburg and take control of the Mississippi River. One of these efforts involved digging a canal across De Soto Point, opposite the town and west of the river. In March he considered three alternatives: first, attack Vicksburg from across the river; second, move north to Memphis and proceed south by land; third, head south through Louisiana, cross the river and either attack Vicksburg from the south or continue downriver to attack Port Hudson. Grant concluded that the first was too costly to his army and the second too costly to him — it might be viewed in Washington as a retreat, and he could lose his command. On March 29 he ordered US General McClernand to march south to New Carthage, and US Major General James B. McPherson to follow by boat from Lake Providence to Milliken's Bend and then along McClernand's route.

Grant created several diversions to confuse the Confederates. He ordered US Major General Frederick Steele's division to destroy the Confederate food supplies along Deer Creek while US General Sherman threatened Snyder's Bluff. He also launched US Colonel Benjamin H. Grierson on a brilliant raid from La Grange, Tennessee, through Mississippi. Grierson tore up miles of railroads and diverted CS General Pemberton's cavalry and an infantry division sent to pursue him on his sixteen-day, 475-mile ride through enemy territory. US Colonel Abel D. Streight's raid across northern Alabama, in which he attempted to destroy the Confederate supply line, the Western & Atlantic Railroad, diverted CS General Forrest from Grierson.

On the nights of April 16 and 22, USN Admiral Porter's fleet of eight gunboats and nine transports ran the gauntlet past Vicksburg, losing two of the transports. The fleet continued downriver to prepare to ferry the corps of McPherson and McClernand across the river. By the end of the month Grant was ready. At 8:00 A.M. on April 29 Porter's seven ironclads attacked CS Brigadier General John S. Bowen's fortifications and batteries at Grand Gulf, thirty miles south of Vicksburg. This action was intended to silence the Confederate guns and cover the disembarkation of McClernand's XIII Corps waiting aboard steamboats and invasion barges. The ironclads moved within one hundred yards of the Confederate guns during the five-and-one-half-hour battle and silenced the lower batteries at Fort Wade but were unable to knock out the upper battery, Fort Cobun, because of its elevation. The *Tuscumbia* was put out of action, and the fleet withdrew. Porter declared that "Grand Gulf is the strongest place on the Mississippi." The ironclads returned at dusk to engage the Confederate guns while the steamboats and barges ran the gauntlet.

Confederate strength prevented Grant from crossing at Grand Gulf but did not stop him. Grant ordered his forces to continue to march south. In one of America's largest amphibious operations prior to World War II, the 24,000 men boarded transports, barges, and gunboats at Disharoon's Plantation and landed on the Mississippi side of the river at Bruinsburg Landing, guided by a contraband. The Confederates won at Grand Gulf but succeeded only in making Grant slightly alter his offensive against Vicksburg.

Estimated Casualties: 80 US, unknown CS

Grand Gulf Military Monument Park, on the Mississippi River about eight miles northwest of Port Gibson, west of Route 61, includes 150 acres of the historic battlefield.

Snyder's Bluff, Mississippi (MS005), Warren County, April 29–May 1, 1863

One of US General Grant's diversions was US General Sherman's combined army-navy force, which attacked Drumgould's Bluffs and Snyder's Bluffs to prevent Confederates from reinforcing Grand Gulf. On April 29 USN Lieutenant Commander K. Randolph Breese, with eight gunboats and ten transports carrying US General Blair's division, steamed slowly up the Yazoo River to the mouth of Chickasaw Bayou. The next morning they continued upriver to Drumgould's Bluffs and engaged the Confederate batteries. Artillery fire and feints by Union infantry continued for two days before Grant ordered Sherman to return his troops to Milliken's Bend. The gunboats returned to their anchorage at the mouth of the Yazoo.

Estimated Casualties: unknown

Port Gibson, Mississippi (MS006), Claiborne County, May 1, 1863

Edwin C. Bearss

On May 1, four miles west of Port Gibson, the first shots were fired in a bitter fight between 8,000 Confederates led by CS Brigadier General John S. Bowen and 24,000 Federals commanded by US Major General Ulysses S. Grant. US Major General John A. McClernand's corps and one division of US Major General James B. McPherson's corps had quickly headed east from Bruinsburg Landing toward the high bluffs several miles back

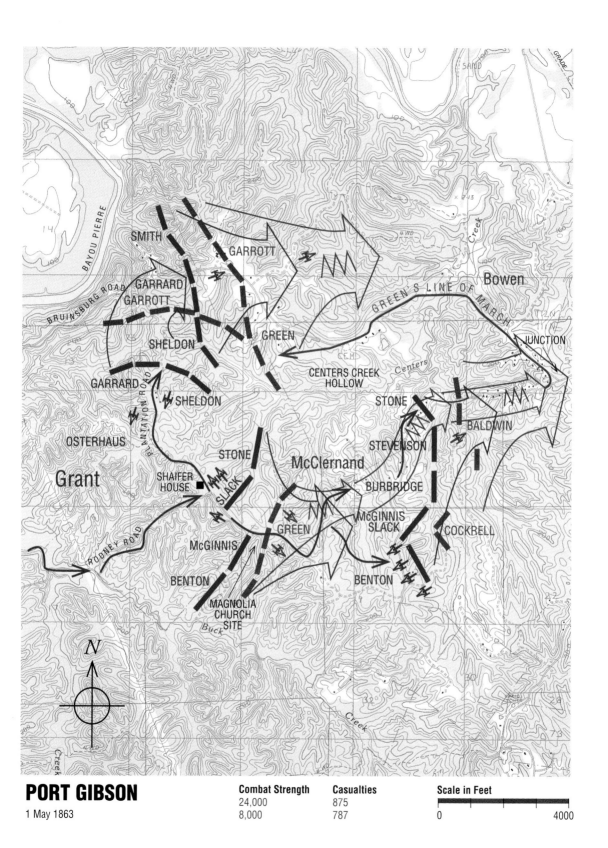

PORT GIBSON

1 May 1863

Combat Strength	Casualties
24,000	875
8,000	787

Scale in Feet

0   4000

from the river. Rapid marches were essential if they were to attack before the Confederates could bring in reinforcements. McPherson stayed at the river to supervise the crossing of his other division.

Bowen, the commander at Grand Gulf, had warned CS Lieutenant General John C. Pemberton about the Union march south and the troops, invasion barges, and steamboats preparing to cross the Mississippi. Pemberton, however, gave higher priority to coping with Union incursions into the Delta north of Vicksburg and to the threat to his railroad communications from US Colonel B. H. Grierson's cavalry, raiding the heart of Mississippi. If Bowen had been properly reinforced by troops from Vicksburg, the battle of Port Gibson might have had a different outcome.

The battle was hard fought. The Confederates, although outnumbered more than three to one and outgunned in artillery by five to one, held their own for nearly eighteen hours. Bowen and his senior officers gave the Federals a bitter lesson in how to exploit the topography, and Bowen's application of offensive-defensive tactics kept them off balance. No one has better described the ground and the problems confronting the Federals than Grant, who wrote: "The country in this part of Mississippi stands on edge, the roads running along the ridges except when they occasionally pass from one ridge to another. Where there are no clearings the sides of the hills are covered with a very heavy growth of timber and with undergrowth, and the ravines are filled with vines and canebrakes, almost impenetrable. This makes it easy for an inferior force to delay, if not defeat, a far superior one."

Pages 160–163: The battles of Port Gibson, Raymond, and Champion Hill, Mississippi, from Lieutenant Colonel James H. Wilson's "Map of the Country between Milliken's Bend, La. and Jackson, Miss. shewing the Routes followed by the Army of the Tennessee . . . in April and May 1863," one of several battlefield maps published in the 1870s by the U.S. Army Office of the Chief of Engineers. (Civil War map no. 261, Geography and Map Division, Library of Congress)

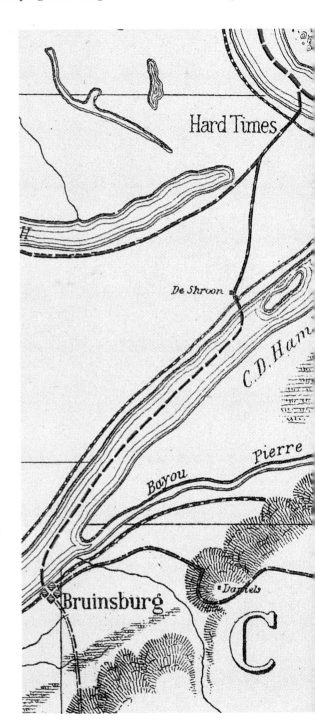

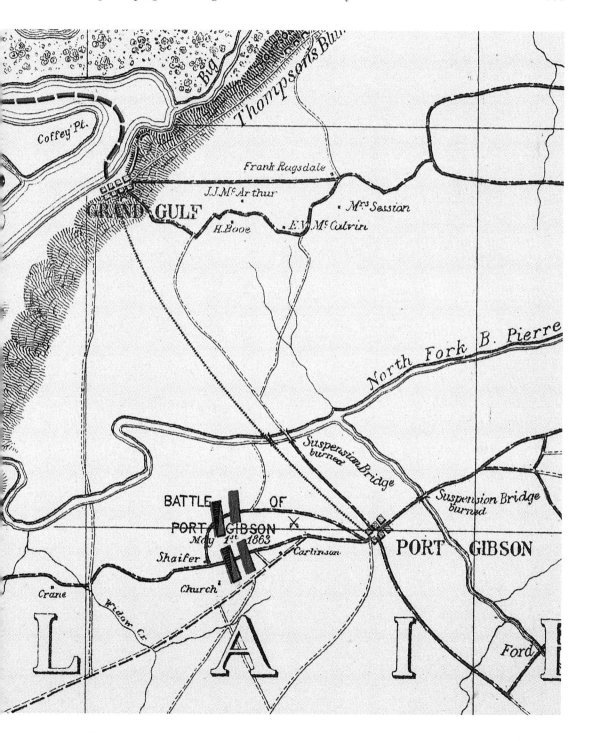

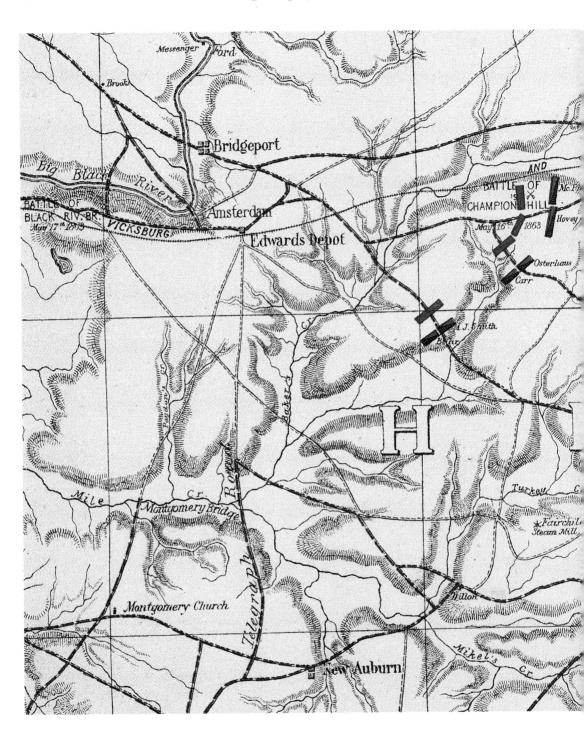

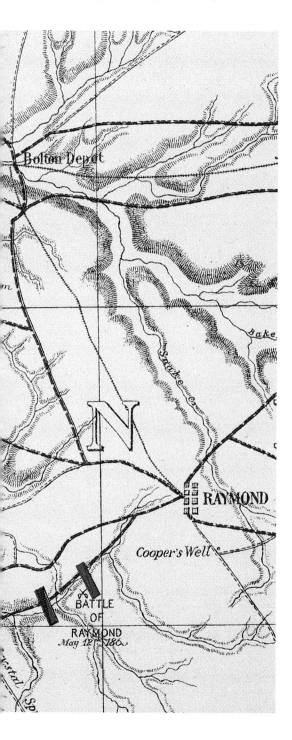

The battle was a desperate struggle that focused on the ridges and the hollows crossed by the Rodney and Bruinsburg Roads. East of the Shaifer farm road, connecting the Rodney and Bruinsburg Roads, was the deep and forbidding Centers Creek Hollow, which separated the troops battling on the Rodney Road from those fighting for the Bruinsburg Road as effectively as if they were many miles apart rather than two. The roads converged about two miles west of Port Gibson.

Two Confederate brigades led by CS Brigadier Generals Edward D. Tracy and William E. Baldwin marched forty-four miles from Vicksburg to reinforce Bowen but arrived exhausted from the twenty-seven-hour forced march. Grant had already gained his beachhead and was moving rapidly inland. Bowen posted CS Brigadier General Martin E. Green's Brigade, which had arrived after a short march from Grand Gulf, along a north-south ridge across the road that ran from Port Gibson to Rodney by way of the A. K. Shaifer house and Magnolia Church. Tracy's Brigade guarded the Bruinsburg Road approximately a thousand yards north of and parallel to the Rodney Road.

Shortly after midnight on May 1, Green rode forward from Magnolia Church to the Shaifer house to warn his pickets to be alert. He assured the women of the Shaifer household, who were hurriedly loading a wagon, that their haste was unnecessary, because the Union forces could not possibly advance to that point before daylight. As they spoke, Confederate pickets suddenly began firing. As minié balls from the Union vanguard struck the house, the Shaifer women whipped their team frantically down the road to Port Gibson.

The next several hours saw skirmishing and artillery fire as more and more Union troops arrived on the field. To delay the Union army until CS Major General William W. Loring's reinforcements arrived from Jackson, the Confederates set up roadblocks on the Bruinsburg and Rodney Roads.

North of the Shaifer house and just south of the Bruinsburg Road, US Brigadier General Peter J.

Osterhaus's division clashed with Tracy's Alabama Brigade. Tracy was killed, and CS Colonel Isham Garrott took command. On the Rodney Road the brigades of US Brigadier General William Benton and US Colonel William M. Stone, supported by US Brigadier General Alvin P. Hovey's division, fought the determined but much weaker Confederates of Green's Brigade. Green held his line until around 10:00 A.M., when he was forced back across Arnolds Creek and into the Irwin Branch hollow. Baldwin took over the defense of the Irwin Branch position while Green reorganized, and Bowen then sent Green to the Bruinsburg Road to assist Garrott.

CS Colonel Francis M. Cockrell's Brigade arrived from Grand Gulf at about noon and was placed in line behind Baldwin. Hovey's and US Brigadier General Eugene A. Carr's troops came under Baldwin's fire in a severe ninety-minute fight, then Bowen sent two of Cockrell's regiments to turn McClernand's right flank as his soldiers worked their way through canebrakes near the head of White Branch. Cockrell's Missourians overran US Colonel James R. Slack's brigade, but they in turn encountered a Union brigade and the fire of thirty cannons. Their ranks thinned by the savage fighting, Cockrell's men gave ground.

By now Grant was sending brigade after brigade into the Union lines. The right wing of the Confederate defenses posted on the Bruinsburg Road gave way, and Bowen, fearful that Union columns would outflank and cut off his troops, ordered retreat. The Confederates retired in good order, resisting until dark, when the pursuit ended. Accompanied by three brigades, Bowen crossed Bayou Pierre. Baldwin's Brigade withdrew through Port Gibson and across Little Bayou Pierre. The Confederate rear guard burned the suspension bridges over these streams as well as the Bayou Pierre railroad bridge.

The Confederates reported their Port Gibson losses as 60 dead, 340 wounded, and 387 missing, most of whom had been captured. Grant listed his casualties as 131 dead, 719 wounded, and 25 missing. The Confederates were forced to evacuate Grand Gulf, and Grant converted it into his supply base for the campaign against Vicksburg while he awaited the arrival of Sherman's corps.

Estimated Casualties: 875 US, 787 CS

Port Gibson battlefield is near Port Gibson and Route 61, twenty-five miles south of Vicksburg. There are fifteen acres of the historic battlefield within the Grand Gulf Military Monument Park.

Raymond, Mississippi (MS007), Hinds County, May 12, 1863

Edwin C. Bearss

On May 2 US Major General Ulysses S. Grant's columns occupied Port Gibson and drove northeastward. The Confederates evacuated Grand Gulf and retired across the Big Black River. Having secured his beachhead with the battle of Port Gibson, Grant halted his army and awaited US Major General William T. Sherman's corps, which was en route down the Louisiana side of the Mississippi from Milliken's Bend and Young's Point.

Grant had two options for his next move. He could move against Vicksburg from the south, using his bridgehead across the Big Black at Hankinson's Ferry. Such an advance would lead to the capture of the city, but CS Lieutenant General John C. Pemberton's army would be able to escape northeast up the Benton Road. Or he could march by way of Cayuga and Auburn and strike the Southern Railroad of Mississippi between Edwards and Bolton. Then, pivoting to the west, he could close in on Vicksburg from the east. An approach from this direction could cost Pemberton his army as well as the city. Grant, a great captain, had no trouble making his decision.

Grant put Sherman's corps in motion. Sherman

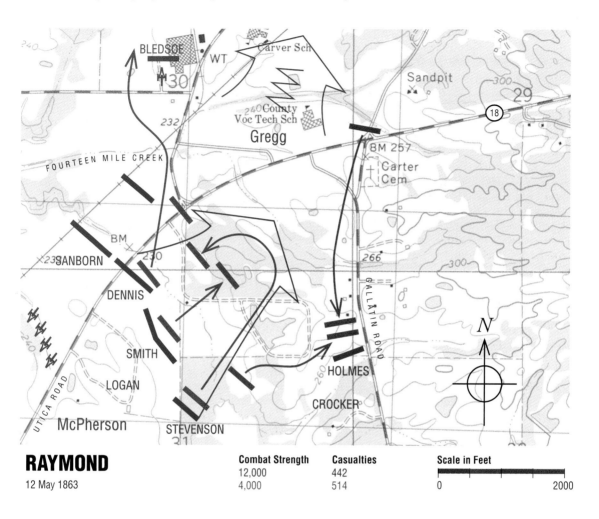

RAYMOND

12 May 1863

Combat Strength	Casualties
12,000	442
4,000	514

Scale in Feet

0   2000

crossed the Mississippi at Grand Gulf, and the Army of the Tennessee resumed its advance on May 8, supplied by large, heavily guarded wagon trains. Grant sent US Major General James B. McPherson's corps, which was to constitute his right, through Utica toward Raymond. US Major General John A. McClernand's corps, to be Grant's left, screened the Big Black crossings. Sherman's corps, to be the center, closed in on Auburn.

The battle of Raymond was McPherson's first as the commander of a major unit. It was not a success. He fought his troops piecemeal during

the six-hour struggle, and he did not undertake a coordinated attack on the enemy, although he outnumbered them three to one and outgunned them in artillery seven to one.

CS Brigadier General John Gregg's aggressive tactics, coupled with the failure of his scouts and patrols to assess the enemy's strength correctly, should have been his undoing, but against the cautious and hesitant McPherson he was successful — until there were just too many Union soldiers. His ability to put the fire of battle in his men marked Gregg as an invaluable brigade commander. In the winter of 1863–64 he was to assume command of one of the war's best-known fighting units, the Army of Northern Virginia's Texas-Arkansas Brigade.

The significance of the Raymond fight, however, has nothing to do with either the body count or the merits and demerits of McPherson and Gregg as battle commanders. The battle is important because of its effect on Grant's campaign plans. It forced Grant into a new estimate of the situation. First, he now knew that the Confederate forces assembling near Jackson were stronger than he had supposed. Second, he heard reports that Confederate reinforcements were pouring into Jackson, including CS General Joseph E. Johnston, the Confederate commander of the Department of the West. If these reports were correct, the proposed crossing of the Big Black River near Edwards Station would be exceedingly dangerous because it would leave a powerful army commanded by an able general in Grant's rear.

Grant changed his orders: instead of concentrating forces at Edwards and Bolton Stations, he ordered a march on Jackson. He realized that McPherson's corps at Raymond, which was closest to the capital city, would probably be inadequate to capture it, especially since Jackson was reported to be strongly fortified. Grant was determined to strike with his entire army, so he ordered McPherson to thrust northeast from Raymond to Clinton and then drive down the Jackson-Clinton Road to Jackson. Sherman's corps was ordered to march on Jackson from the southwest, via Raymond and Mississippi Springs. McClernand was to march three divisions of his corps along the road north of Fourteenmile Creek to Raymond. His fourth division, under US Brigadier General A. J. Smith, was to march to Old Auburn and await the arrival of US Major General Francis P. Blair Jr.'s division from the Grand Gulf enclave. The corps commanders had misgivings — such audacity was unheard of in modern military annals. Generals do not usually split their armies and send them into unfamiliar territory against a strong enemy who presumably knows the terrain.

On May 11 Gregg and his brigade, having reached Jackson from Port Hudson, Louisiana, marched to Raymond. Gregg was alerted by Pemberton at Vicksburg to look out for the advance of a Union column from the southwest up the Utica Road. This force was composed of two divisions of McPherson's corps, 12,000 strong. McPherson had his column on the road before daylight on May 12, and by 10:00 A.M. his vanguard had ascended a ridge three miles southwest of Raymond.

Alerted to the Union army's approach by scouts, Gregg posted three infantry units north of Fourteenmile Creek to dispute the nearby Utica Road crossing. Cannoneers of CS Captain H. M. Bledsoe's Missouri battery unlimbered their three guns while Gregg's other regiments marched out the Gallatin Road, taking a position from which they could sweep cross-country and envelop the Union army's right.

As McPherson's skirmishers came down the far slope, Bledsoe's gunners opened fire. One Union brigade, US Brigadier General Elias Dennis's, followed by a second, US Brigadier General John E. Smith's, deployed into line of battle, descended the grade, and entered the woods bounding the creek. Smoke and dust kept Gregg from seeing that he was outnumbered, and he hurled his troops against the Union soldiers. Some Union troops broke, but US Major General John A. Logan rallied them and forced two of Gregg's regiments that had forded the creek to withdraw.

By 1:30 P.M. US Colonel John Sanborn's brigade of US Brigadier General Marcellus M. Crocker's division had arrived and filed into position on Logan's left. Supported by the fire of twenty-two cannons, McPherson ordered a counterattack and seized the initiative. For the next several hours McPherson's and Gregg's regiments generally acted on their own, in confused fighting in which smoke and undergrowth kept the senior officers from knowing where their units were and what they were accomplishing.

After the collapse of his left wing, Gregg ordered the fight abandoned. The Confederates disengaged, retreated through Raymond, and took the road to Jackson. They halted for the evening on a ridge a mile east of Snake Creek, where they were reinforced by 1,000 men led by CS Brigadier

General W. H. T. Walker. On May 13 the Confederates withdrew into the Jackson defenses. The Federals occupied Raymond and camped there. Union losses in the battle were 66 killed, 339 wounded, and 37 missing. Gregg listed 72 killed, 252 wounded, and 190 missing.

Estimated Casualties: 442 US, 514 CS

Raymond battlefield, near Route 18, two miles southwest of Raymond, is privately owned.

Jackson, Mississippi (MS008), Hinds County and Jackson, May 14, 1863

After the battle at Raymond, US General Grant changed his plan and moved toward Jackson instead of toward Edwards and Bolton. When CS General Johnston arrived in Jackson on the evening of May 13 to take command of Confederate forces in the field, he learned that US General Sherman's XV Corps and US General McPherson's XVII Corps of the Army of the Tennessee were advancing on the state capital to break up the railroads that entered it from four directions. Since he had only 6,000 troops available to defend the town, he telegraphed Richmond, "I am too late." Although Jackson was strongly fortified and could withstand a siege, Johnston ordered the local commander, CS General Gregg, to begin the evacuation.

On May 14 the Federal forces attacked in rain, which slowed the fighting, and pushed the Confederates back into their fortifications. Johnston ordered Gregg to disengage and retreat up the Canton Road, and by 3:00 P.M. the Federals had occupied Jackson. They burned part of the town and cut the rail lines, isolating Vicksburg from the east. Grant, traveling with Sherman's corps, spent the night in the Bowman House, Johnston's old headquarters. Johnston's decision to abandon Jackson separated the Confederate forces. Grant

was between Johnston and CS General Pemberton at Vicksburg; a Confederate brigade from Port Hudson had reached Crystal Springs but was sent to Brookhaven; two brigades from Tennessee were at Meridian, east of Jackson; and a brigade from South Carolina that had arrived at Brandon was sent to Morton.

Estimated Casualties: 286 US, 850 CS

My son [age twelve] accompanied me throughout the campaign and siege, and caused no anxiety either to me or to his mother, who was at home. He looked out for himself and was in every battle of the campaign.

— General Ulysses S. Grant

Champion Hill, Mississippi (MS009), Hinds County, May 16, 1863

Edwin C. Bearss

On the evening of May 14 US Major General Ulysses S. Grant and his generals met in a Jackson hotel and decided to counter the threat posed by CS General Joseph E. Johnston. Johnston had ordered his outnumbered troops to retreat from Jackson northward up the Canton Road. He had also commanded CS Lieutenant General John C. Pemberton to march east with the 22,000 soldiers he had assembled at Edwards Station and attack the Union army near Clinton. The next day Grant positioned seven divisions (about 32,000 soldiers) along a five-mile front passing through Raymond and Bolton.

Pemberton conferred with his generals at Edwards Station and concluded that Johnston's May 13 order for the converging attack was "extremely hazardous," so he marched instead to the southeast, to intercept and destroy the Union supply trains en route from Grand Gulf to Raymond. At dusk on May 15 his army bivouacked along nearly four miles of roadway, with the advance guard at Mrs. Sarah Ellison's house. His supply train brought up the rear, at the crossroads where

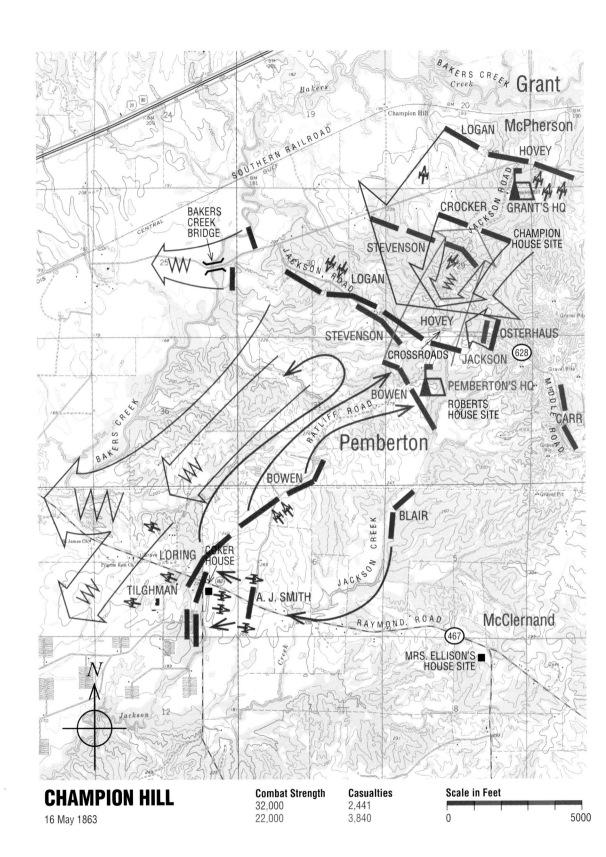

CHAMPION HILL

16 May 1863

Combat Strength	Casualties
32,000	2,441
22,000	3,840

Scale in Feet

0   5000

the Jackson Road turned to the left and passed over the crest of Champion Hill, one quarter mile to the north.

The next morning a courier reached Pemberton's command with a message from Johnston dated May 14, reiterating his May 13 orders. Although Pemberton had previously rejected them as "suicidal" and had wasted many hours marching in a different direction, he ordered the countermarch. The rear brigade with the trains became the vanguard as the Confederate army returned to Edwards via the Jackson-Vicksburg Road. To protect the army from a reported Union force approaching the crossroads, CS Brigadier General Stephen Dill Lee moved up the Jackson Road to Champion Hill and deployed his Alabama brigade on the ridge overlooking the Bakers Creek bottom.

From the hill Lee spotted the Union column, which consisted of US Major General James B. McPherson's corps, spearheaded by US Brigadier General Hovey's division of the XIII Corps. When Hovey reached the Champion house, about a half mile northeast of the crest of Champion Hill, he sighted Lee's soldiers and deployed his division to the left and right of the Jackson-Vicksburg Road. Grant and McPherson arrived with US Major General John A. Logan's division, which formed for battle on Hovey's right.

Lee realized that the two Union divisions could overwhelm his brigade, despite his commanding position on Champion Hill. His division commander, CS Major General Carter L. Stevenson, rushed reinforcements to him: three regiments of Georgians led by CS Brigadier General Alfred Cumming. They formed a salient angle at the crest of the hill, with Lee's soldiers in line along the ridge to the northwest. CS Brigadier General Seth Barton's Georgia Brigade came to Lee's assistance and took up a position on the left, with its supporting batteries on the ridge on the soldiers' left.

The Confederate line thus formed nearly a right angle, with Cumming, Lee, and Barton on the left. Pemberton's right, anchored on the Raymond-Edwards Road, was held by two Confederate divisions — CS Brigadier General John S.

Bowen's and CS Major General William W. Loring's — which were deployed by Pemberton on the high ground overlooking Jackson Creek. At the center were two of Cumming's regiments, positioned at the crossroads with a four-gun Alabama battery to support CS Colonel J. F. B. Jackson's roadblock. Their mission was to cover the Ratliff Road and maintain contact with the right. To Loring's front the divisions of US Brigadier General A. J. Smith and US Major General Francis P. Blair, Jr., cautiously felt their way forward. The divisions of US Brigadier Generals Eugene A. Carr and Peter J. Osterhaus were on the Middle Road opposite the Confederate center.

At 11:30 A.M. Logan's and Hovey's battle lines assailed the Confederate left. They shattered Barton's Brigade and then the three regiments of Cumming's Brigade, on the left and right of Lee's soldiers. Large numbers of Georgians were captured, along with twelve cannons. The Confederate soldiers were outflanked and forced back to the Jackson-Vicksburg Road. Hovey's left flank brigade, under US Colonel James R. Slack, drove for the crossroads, where they overpowered two Georgia regiments and the Alabama battery. From their position occupying the crossroads, the Federals could either swing to the right and crush Lee's forces or advance down the Ratliff Road to take Bowen's division in the flank. They could also destroy Jackson's men, who were blocking the Union advance on the Middle Road.

Pemberton's situation was desperate. He ordered Bowen to support Stevenson's mauled brigades. Bowen's vanguard marched up the Ratliff Road, reaching Pemberton's headquarters at the Roberts house just as Cumming's men at the crossroads were routed. The fate of Pemberton's army was in the balance, and Bowen responded with alacrity. CS Colonel Francis M. Cockrell's Missouri Brigade deployed to the left, CS Brigadier General Martin E. Green's Arkansas-Missouri Brigade moved to the right, and both advanced to the attack with savage vigor. Cockrell's Brigade showed once again why it was one of the war's most respected combat units. Bowen's men drove Slack's from the crossroads and recovered the four guns captured by the Federals.

Pressing on, the Confederates routed Hovey's other brigade, commanded by US Brigadier General George F. McGinnis, from the crest of Champion Hill and captured two Union cannons.

Bowen's men continued their advance. Less than a half mile to their front was the Champion house, Grant's headquarters. US Brigadier General Marcellus M. Crocker reached the field and deployed two brigades, sending one to reinforce Logan on the right and the other to plug the hole torn in the Union front by the defeat of Hovey's division. Cannoneers then unlimbered sixteen guns southeast of the Champion house and enfiladed the onrushing Confederate battle lines.

Pemberton lacked reserves to capitalize on Bowen's earlier success. He had called on Loring to come to the left, but Loring had refused, citing the strong Union columns to his front on the Raymond-Edwards Road. After the order was repeated, Loring marched for the battle's cockpit with two of his three brigades, leaving the third under CS Brigadier General Lloyd Tilghman to guard the Raymond-Edwards Road. However, Loring marched too late and by a roundabout route.

Meanwhile Bowen engaged US Colonel George B. Boomer's fresh brigade of Crocker's division. After a desperate struggle the Federals regained the upper hand. Bowen's men grudgingly gave ground until the crest of Champion Hill, and the crossroads were recovered by McPherson's troops. This was the third and final time that this terrain changed hands.

Loring covered the defeated Confederate army's retreat along the Raymond-Edwards Road. Carr's and Osterhaus's troops smashed Jackson's roadblock and reached the crossroads soon after Bowen's retreat. Carr's division continued west along the Jackson-Vicksburg Road and secured the Bakers Creek bridge. Tilghman, whose brigade remained to guard the Raymond-Edwards Road, was killed by artillery fire from the ridge near the Coker house. At about midnight Loring saw the glare of fires to the north and, realizing that Edwards had been abandoned, gave up his efforts to rejoin the army. He turned his division to the southeast and marched by way of Crystal Springs to report to Jackson, which had been reoccupied by the Confederates upon the May 16 evacuation by US Major General William T. Sherman's XV Corps. From Jackson, Loring reported by telegraph to Johnston, who had set up temporary headquarters at Vernon.

Grant's troops bivouacked on the field. They spent the late afternoon and evening tending the wounded, burying the dead, and counting the prisoners and spoils of war. Although Pemberton's army had escaped destruction, it was terribly mauled. Incomplete returns filed by Confederate officers listed their losses as 381 killed, 1,018 wounded, and 2,441 missing. Twenty-seven of their cannons had been left on the field. Union casualties totaled 410 killed, 1,844 wounded, and 187 missing.

The Union victory at Champion Hill was decisive. It prevented Pemberton and Johnston from uniting their armies and forced Pemberton back into Vicksburg.

Estimated Casualties: 2,441 US, 3,840 CS

Champion Hill battlefield is between Bolton and Edwards, about halfway between Vicksburg and Jackson, south of Interstate 20 between the Edwards and Bolton exits. The Jackson Civil War Round Table owns the Coker house and five acres on Route 467. (Not open to the public.) The Mississippi Department of Archives and History owns 825 acres of the historic battlefield. (Not open to the public.)

Big Black River Bridge, Mississippi (MS010), Hinds and Warren Counties, May 17, 1863

Reeling from their defeat at Champion Hill, the Confederates reached the Big Black River Bridge on the night of May 16. CS General Pemberton posted CS General Bowen's Division and CS Brigadier General John Vaughn's Brigade on the east bank of the river to hold the bridges so that CS General Loring could cross, not knowing that Loring could not get through to Edwards.

US General McClernand's XIII Corps advanced west from Edwards Station on the morning of May 17. They encountered 5,000 Confederates with their backs to the river, behind a line of breastworks made of cotton bales fronted by a bayou and *abatis* extending from the river to Gin Lake. The Federals opened fire with their artillery. US Brigadier General Michael K. Lawler massed his regiments into column by battalion on the Union right in a meander scar. In an extraordinary bayonet charge that lasted only three minutes, Lawler's 1,500 troops raced across the open ground through waist-deep water in the bayou and into the Confederate breastworks. The Confederates abandoned eighteen cannons and ran toward the bridges. Many of them drowned trying to escape across the river, and nearly 1,700 were captured.

To hinder the Federal pursuit, Pemberton's men burned the railroad bridge and the steamboat, *Dot,* used as a bridge. Fewer than half of the Confederates who had fought at Champion Hill made it into the defenses at Vicksburg.

Estimated Casualties: 276 US, 1,751 CS

Battle and Siege of Vicksburg, Mississippi (MS011), Warren County and Vicksburg, May 18–July 4, 1863

Edwin C. Bearss

The Army of the Tennessee crossed the Big Black River on the night of May 17 and closed in on Vicksburg the next day. On May 19 US Major General Ulysses S. Grant re-established contact with USN Rear Admiral David D. Porter's fleet on the Yazoo River above Vicksburg. The Federals established supply depots at Chickasaw Bayou and Snyder's Bluff and opened roads to supply the

confident, aggressive Union army. Grant, who thought that the victory at Champion Hill and the rout at the Big Black had shattered CS Lieutenant General John C. Pemberton's army, did not know that Pemberton had left two divisions in and around Vicksburg. These fresh units held the earthworks guarding the Graveyard, Jackson, and Baldwin's Ferry Roads — the routes over which the three Union corps approached. CS Major General Carter L. Stevenson's mauled division occupied the rifle pits extending south of the railroad to the Mississippi, while CS Brigadier General John S. Bowen's constituted Pemberton's reserve.

At 2:00 P.M. on the nineteenth, US Major General William Tecumseh Sherman's corps advanced against the defenses covering the Graveyard Road. Rugged terrain and felled timber threw the battle lines into disorder. Crashing volleys from Mississippi and Louisiana regiments savaged the Union ranks, and their surge was checked. However, US Major General James B. McPherson's and US Major General John A. McClernand's corps eventually drove in the Confederate pickets and seized ground within a quarter mile of the Vicksburg perimeter. After dark Sherman withdrew the soldiers who had been pinned down in front of Stockade Redan.

Thus Grant learned that Pemberton's army had not been shattered. He spent the next seventy-two hours regrouping his army, emplacing artillery, and preparing for an all-out attack. On the morning of May 22 massed cannons hammered the Confederate works. Porter steamed up the Mississippi with his ironclads and bombarded the river forts south of the city. At 10:00 A.M. the artillery fell silent, and massed brigades from the three corps charged. Sherman's and McPherson's rushes were blunted with ease, but McClernand's troops at the Second Texas Lunette gained the ditch fronting the work as they stormed Railroad Redoubt. Lack of a ready reserve prevented McClernand from exploiting his success, but, learning of his gains, Grant ordered the assaults renewed. Sherman hammered in vain at the Mississippi, Missouri, and Louisiana units posted in the works covering Graveyard Road; McPherson made a feeble effort to storm the Third Louisiana Redan. Pemberton's reserves, counterattacking savagely, cleared the ditch at the Texas Lunette and drove the Union soldiers from Railroad Redoubt before support troops could intervene. When he was satisfied that his men could not storm the Vicksburg defenses, Grant ordered the attack suspended. In the day's fighting, the Union side had suffered 3,199 casualties and the Confederates fewer than 500.

On May 25 Grant issued instructions for his engineers to begin siege operations, cutting off ammunition, food, and reinforcements to the city. Porter's fleet controlled the Mississippi above and below the city, and Union soldiers occupied the Louisiana shore. Along the siege lines, Union engineers pushed thirteen approach trenches toward the Confederate defenses. Advance breaching batteries were established. To conserve ammunition, Pemberton was compelled to restrict his cannoneers, and the Union artillery quickly established its ascendancy, hurling thousands of shells into the city. To escape the horrors of the bombardment, citizens dug caves in the hillsides. On June 25 and again on July 1, mines were exploded under the Third Louisiana Redan. An attack followed the detonation of the first mine, but the defenders from Louisiana and Missouri repulsed it.

Grant called for reinforcements to ensure the siege's success. Soldiers from as far away as Kentucky and Missouri were rushed to Mississippi, and by the third week of June Grant had more than 77,000 troops. President Jefferson Davis provided CS General Joseph E. Johnston with reinforcements and urged the Confederates of the Trans-Mississippi Department (west of the Mississippi) to take extreme measures to help hold Vicksburg and save Pemberton's army. Johnston, however, was overly cautious, and attacks by CS Major General Richard Taylor's troops on Union enclaves west of the river were repulsed.

Rations were in short supply by the fourth week of June, and the soldiers defending Vicksburg subsisted principally on pea bread. Mules and horses were slaughtered, and the meat was issued to the troops in lieu of beef and pork. There was no rationing or price controls. Citizens with the wherewithal were able to get plenty to eat, while those lacking the means suffered more than the soldiers. The long, hot days and nights in the rifle pits sapped the men's vigor. Morale sagged as it became clear that Johnston was not coming to their relief.

By July 2 Pemberton had only two options — to cut his way through the investing army or surrender. He argued for the first, but the majority of his generals explained that their men were in no condition to attack or make the necessary marches once the Union lines ruptured. Accordingly, Pemberton met with Grant on the afternoon of July 3 to discuss terms for the possible surrender of his army. Grant demanded unconditional surrender. Pemberton refused. That evening Grant modified his terms, after discussing the subject with his principal subordinates. The Confederates would surrender and sign paroles not to fight again until exchanged.

After some discussion with his division and brigade commanders, Pemberton accepted these terms. At 10:00 A.M. on July 4, the Confederate army, 29,495 strong, marched out in front of the works and stacked arms. Selected units from Grant's army marched in, took possession of Vicksburg, and raised the Stars and Stripes over the Warren County Court House.

The Vicksburg campaign and siege, culminating in the surrender of the city and its defending army, was a milestone on the road that led to the final success of the Union army and the reunification of the nation. The campaign, particularly the twenty days from April 30 to May 19, was critical to Grant's career and ensured his reputation as one of the great generals in military history. The capture of Vicksburg and the destruction of Pemberton's large and formidable army was a great Union victory, and many commentators second Grant's assertion that "the fate of the Confederacy was sealed when Vicksburg fell."

In the days following their Bruinsburg landing, his troops marched more than two hundred miles, won five battles, inflicted more than 8,000 Confederate casualties, and captured eighty-eight cannons. Although Generals Pemberton and

Johnston between them had more soldiers and presumably were more familiar with the area, Grant so maneuvered his columns that he had a decisive superiority in numbers and artillery at each battle. From Vicksburg, Grant's career took him to Chattanooga, then — as commander of all the Union armies — to the Wilderness, Petersburg, and Appomattox, and finally to Washington and the presidency.

On July 4, a thousand miles to the northeast of Vicksburg, CS General Robert E. Lee's Army of Northern Virginia was about to begin its retreat from Gettysburg. Although the war continued for another twenty months, these twin disasters blunted southern morale and hopes. News that Vicksburg had fallen caused the Confederate force invested at Port Hudson to surrender. With the capture of these two bastions, the Union regained control of the Mississippi River from Cairo to the Gulf, and President Abraham Lincoln wrote, "The Father of Waters again goes unvexed to the sea."

The Confederacy was now divided. In the weeks between March 29 and July 4 Grant had destroyed a Confederate army of 40,000 at a cost of 10,000 battle casualties. He had captured 260 cannons, 60,000 stand-of-arms, and more than 2 million rounds of ammunition. The Confederacy could not afford such a loss of men and matériel.

Estimated Casualties: 4,835 US, 32,697 (29,495 surrendered) CS

Vicksburg National Military Park in Vicksburg includes 1,736 acres of the historic battlefield; two of these acres are privately owned.

Milliken's Bend, Louisiana (LA011), Madison Parish, June 7, 1863

Throughout the winter of 1863, Milliken's Bend served as a staging area for US General Grant's operations against Vicksburg. In the flood-plagued camps, thousands of soldiers fell victim to dysentery, diarrhea, typhoid, malaria, and various fevers. The army established hospitals for them as well as for Grant's army during the siege of Vicksburg. The nurses of the U.S. Sanitary Commission helped the army doctors and eased the suffering of the sick and wounded. The commission also furnished supplies of pillows, blankets, clothing, medicine, fresh fruits and vegetables, candles, lanterns, ice, and other needed supplies. Relief efforts were also extended to the thousands of escaped slaves who fled to freedom behind Union lines in Louisiana. Black males were encouraged to enlist in the Union army, and training facilities for them were established at Milliken's Bend, at Goodrich's Landing, and at Lake Providence. These troops were vital in protecting Union supply lines and bases in Louisiana.

On June 6 US Colonel Hermann Lieb led his 9th Louisiana (Colored) Infantry and elements of the 10th Illinois Cavalry on a forced reconnaissance toward Richmond, Louisiana. Lieb encountered Confederate troops near the Tallulah railroad depot three miles north of Richmond and turned back toward Milliken's Bend. Halfway to the post Illinois troopers dashed up behind them, pursued by Confederate cavalry. A well-directed volley by the black soldiers drove the Confederates off, and Lieb's force retired to Milliken's Bend. Lieb prepared for an attack by requesting reinforcements. The 23rd Iowa Infantry arrived from Young's Point, and USN Rear Admiral David D. Porter sent the gunboat *Choctaw*.

CS Major General John G. Walker and his Texas division left Richmond at 6:00 P.M. on June 6. When they arrived at Oak Grove plantation, Walker sent CS Brigadier General Henry E. McCulloch's Brigade toward Milliken's Bend and CS Brigadier General James M. Hawes's Brigade toward Young's Point. At 3:00 A.M. on June 7 McCulloch's men drove in the Federal pickets and advanced toward the Union left flank. McCulloch's line paused briefly amid volleys from Federal guns, then charged in bloody hand-to-hand combat. During the intense battle the Confeder-

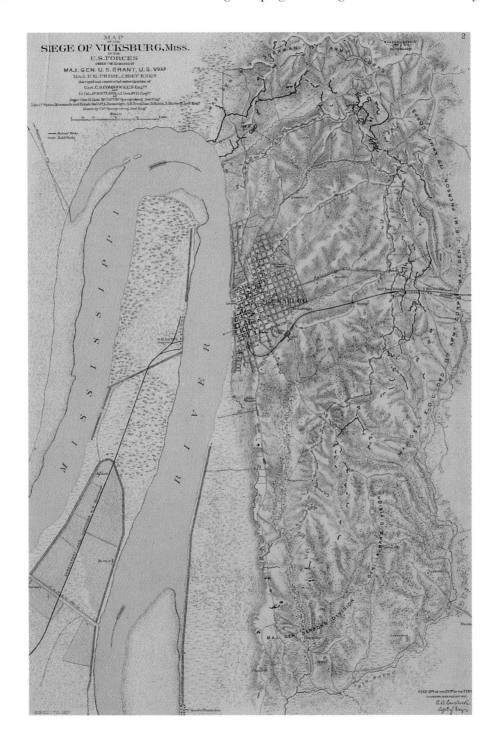

ates flanked the Union force and inflicted heavy casualties in a crossfire. As the U.S. troops withdrew behind the levee along the riverbank, the gunboat *Choctaw* fired on McCulloch. When the gunboat *Lexington* arrived at 9:00 A.M., he withdrew. In the fierce engagement 35 percent of the black troops were casualties. US Brigadier General Elias S. Dennis described their bravery: "It is impossible for men to show greater gallantry than the Negro Troops in this fight."

After the Federals stopped the Confederates at Milliken's Bend, Vicksburg's only potential source of help was CS General Johnston, with 32,000 men to the northeast. Grant had 70,000 penning Pemberton in Vicksburg. Seven of these divisions, commanded by US General Sherman, guarded the army's rear. After Vicksburg surrendered, Sherman headed after Johnston, who retreated into Jackson and then across the Pearl River.

Estimated Casualties: 652 US, 185 CS

Goodrich's Landing, Louisiana (LA014), East Carroll Parish, June 29–30, 1863

As escaped slaves fled to the shelter of the U.S. Army, the Federal government leased plantations in Louisiana on which the freedmen grew cotton. The government also established facilities to train black troops who could be assigned to protect the plantations, releasing veteran white troops to fight. CS Colonel William H. Parsons led a force from Gaines' Landing, Arkansas, to Lake Providence, Louisiana, to capture freedmen and

Opposite: Lieutenant Charles L. Spangenberg, an assistant engineer working under the direction of Captain Cyrus B. Comstock and Lieutenant Colonel James H. Wilson, drew this detailed map in 1863 of the Federal and Confederate works in front of Vicksburg, Mississippi. It is from the *Atlas to Accompany the Official Records of the Union and Confederate Armies* (Washington: 1891–95), plate XXXVI-2. (Civil War map no. 99, Geography and Map Division, Library of Congress)

destroy their crops. On June 29 the Confederates prepared to attack the Federal fortification on an Indian mound five miles northwest of Goodrich's Landing. Manned by two companies of the 1st Arkansas Infantry (African Descent), the fortification protected the plantations. When CS Brigadier General James C. Tappan's Brigade arrived, Parsons, rather than attack, demanded an unconditional surrender of the Union force. The white officers agreed to surrender on condition of being afforded their rights as prisoners of war while the blacks were to be surrendered unconditionally. After taking the 113 blacks and 3 white officers prisoner, the Confederates destroyed the surrounding plantations.

While Parsons fought companies of the 1st Kansas Mounted Infantry near Lake Providence on June 30, warships landed US Brigadier General Alfred W. Ellet's Mississippi Marine Brigade at Goodrich's Landing. His force and US Colonel William F. Wood's black units pursued Parsons. Parsons retreated, having disrupted Union operations, destroyed property, and captured men, weapons, and supplies. Confederate raids such as this were destructive but only temporary setbacks to Union control over the region.

Estimated Casualties: 150 US, 6 CS

Helena, Arkansas (AR008), Phillips County, July 4, 1863

At dawn on July 4, in a belated attempt to relieve Federal pressure on Vicksburg, CS Lieutenant General Theophilus H. Holmes launched his 7,600 troops in a four-pronged attack against US Major General Benjamin M. Prentiss in his fortifications at Helena on the Mississippi River. The 4,100 Federals were protecting an important supply depot for US General Grant's siege of Vicksburg.

The main effort was launched southwest of town by three brigades of CS Major General Sterling Price's Division against Union batteries atop the steep slopes of Hindman Hill and Graveyard Hill. CS Brigadier General James F. Fagan commanded a brigade that captured several lines of rifle pits at Battery D on Hindman Hill, but the Federals successfully defended the battery. Price led two brigades that overran the cannons in Battery C on Graveyard Hill until fire from Fort Curtis and from the gunboat *Tyler* stopped them. The Federals in Fort Curtis repulsed a frontal assault, and at 10:30 A.M. Holmes ordered a retreat. The Federals reoccupied Graveyard Hill.

Estimated Casualties: 239 US, 1,636 CS

Streight's Raid Through Alabama: April–May 1863

Day's Gap, Alabama (AL001), Cullman County, April 30, 1863

In April 1863 US Major General Ulysses S. Grant launched several diversions to confuse the Confederates while he prepared his Vicksburg campaign. One of these was US Colonel Benjamin H. Grierson's sixteen-day, 475-mile cavalry raid through Mississippi, one of the most successful and daring of the war. It was entirely through enemy territory. Grierson split his force so effectively that his ruse led CS Lieutenant General John C. Pemberton to send his cavalry and an infantry division to pursue him — effectively occupying Pemberton while Grant moved his forces down the Mississippi River. Before they rode into the Federal lines at Baton Rouge, Grierson's troopers had destroyed the track of three railroads that hauled supplies to Pemberton and his depots.

US Major General William S. Rosecrans, in coordination with Grant, sent US Colonel Abel D. Streight and his 1,500-man brigade on a cavalry raid to destroy the Western & Atlantic Railroad in western Georgia and to divert CS Brigadier General Nathan Bedford Forrest and his cavalry from interfering with Grierson's raid. Streight disembarked with his men and mules from steamboats on the Tennessee River and set out on April 21 from Eastport, Mississippi. They were reinforced at Tuscumbia, Alabama, and left at 11:00 P.M. on April 26. Since they rode mules, they moved slowly as they headed southeast toward the hills of northern Alabama. Forrest caught up with Streight on April 30 at Day's Gap on Sand Mountain. Forrest tried to surround the Federals, but Streight ambushed one of his columns, wounded Forrest's brother, and captured two guns.

The Federals rode east toward Rome, Georgia, pursued by Forrest. Streight planned to escape Forrest by crossing and then destroying the bridge over the Oostanaula River at Rome. On May 3 at Cedar Bluff near the Georgia border,

Forrest, with only 600 men, bluffed the 1,466 exhausted Federals into surrendering. Streight's raid, though costly and unsuccessful in destroying the railroad, pulled Forrest out of the crucial area just as Grant landed on the east bank of the Mississippi River below Grand Gulf to launch his campaign against Vicksburg.

Estimated Casualties: 23 US, 65 CS

Missouri and Arkansas: January–May 1863

Springfield II, Missouri (MO018), Greene County, January 8, 1863

Following the Confederate defeat at Prairie Grove on December 7, 1862, CS Major General Thomas C. Hindman ordered CS Brigadier General John S. Marmaduke, a West Pointer born in Missouri, to lead his troopers on a raid into Missouri. While one column rode toward Hartville, Marmaduke, with 2,000 veteran cavalrymen, headed toward Springfield, an important supply base. Springfield was not strongly defended because most of the soldiers were still away, having fought at Prairie Grove. US Brigadier General Egbert B. Brown assembled all available troops, as well as civilians and convalescents from the military hospital.

Marmaduke attacked on the morning of the eighth and was repulsed by the defenders, who were protected by earthen fortifications and a few artillery pieces. Brown was wounded in the day-long battle, but his forces succeeded in defending the supply base. The Confederates withdrew the next day, before Brown could be reinforced.

Estimated Casualties: 163 US, 240 CS

Hartville, Missouri (MO019), Wright County, January 9–11, 1863

On January 9 CS Colonel Joseph C. Porter's Missouri Cavalry Brigade left Pocahontas, Arkansas, attacked the Union garrison near Hartville, Missouri, and captured it. Porter rode on toward Marshfield where he joined CS General Marmaduke's column east of Marshfield to prepare for battle against US Colonel Samuel Merrill's 700-man force.

To protect his retreat route to Arkansas, Marmaduke attacked and drove Merrill's men back to Hartville on January 11. The Federals' defense was strong, and they inflicted casualties in the four-hour battle, but they did not capture the raiders. Marmaduke's force abandoned the raid and Missouri.

Estimated Casualties: 78 US, 329 CS

Cape Girardeau, Missouri (MO020), Cape Girardeau, April 26, 1863

In April CS General Marmaduke rode into Missouri to disrupt Federal operations. He pursued US Brigadier General John McNeil in his retreat from Bloomfield to the Federal defenses at Cape Girardeau. The town was an important port and supply depot on the Mississippi River, protected by four forts. On April 26 McNeil refused the Confederate demand to surrender, so Marmaduke ordered CS Colonel Joseph O. "Jo" Shelby's 4th Missouri Cavalry Brigade, the Iron Brigade, to demonstrate in order to determine Federal strength. This action escalated into an attack in which the Federals repulsed Marmaduke.

The Confederates withdrew the next morning when they received reports of Federal reinforcements en route. They rode hard across the boot heel of Missouri and toward Arkansas to escape the superior Union forces.

Estimated Casualties: 12 US, 325 CS

Chalk Bluff, Arkansas (AR007), Clay County, May 1–2, 1863

After CS General Marmaduke's unsuccessful raid into southeast Missouri in April, US Brigadier General William Vandever and US General McNeil pursued the retreating Confederates toward northeast Arkansas. On May 1–2 at Chalk Bluff, the Confederates constructed a crude floating bridge across the flooded St. Francis River and entrenched on the commanding heights while a rear guard skirmished with the approaching Federals. Marmaduke's main force crossed the river and escaped, but 250 Texas cavalrymen were trapped on the Missouri side when

the bridge supports were cut. They swam with their horses across the river into Arkansas.

Estimated Casualties: fewer than 100

The town of Chalk Bluff no longer exists. Historic plaques in Chalk Bluff Park, two miles north of St. Francis, Arkansas, tell of the battle.

West Louisiana: April 1863

Fort Bisland, Louisiana (LA006), St. Mary Parish, April 12–13, 1863

In April 1863, while US Major General Ulysses S. Grant was preparing his Vicksburg campaign, US Major General Nathaniel P. Banks concluded that Port Hudson was too strong for him to take by assault. He decided instead to defeat CS Major General Richard Taylor, capture Alexandria, and cut Port Hudson's supply line via the Red River. Banks launched an expedition with 16,000 men of the XIX Corps up Bayou Teche. Two divisions crossed Berwick Bay from Brashear City (now Morgan City) to the west side at Berwick, while a third, under US Brigadier General Cuvier Grover, steamed up Grand Lake to cut Taylor's retreat route.

On April 12 Taylor's command at Fort Bisland hit the approaching Federals with fire from the fort and the captured gunboat *Diana.* Banks's artillery returned fire and the following morning disabled the *Diana.* Banks deployed his troops and waited for Grover to land. Skirmishing began at 11:00 A.M. and continued until nightfall. Taylor learned that Grover's division was on the west bank of Bayou Teche and evacuated the fort that night. The Federals took control of the only fortification that could have impeded their offensive.

Estimated Casualties: 224 US, 450 CS

Irish Bend, Louisiana (LA007), St. Mary Parish, April 14, 1863

To protect his supply trains moving away from Fort Bisland, CS General Taylor deployed 1,000 men at Irish Bend. US General Grover's 5,000-man division crossed Bayou Teche on April 13. The Confederates attacked at dawn on April 14 and forced Grover to fall back under intense fire. The repaired gunboat *Diana* arrived to anchor the Confederate right flank on the river. As Grover prepared to attack, the outnumbered Con-federates blew up the *Diana* and retreated up the bayou.

Estimated Casualties: 353 US, unknown CS

Vermillion Bayou, Louisiana (LA008), Lafayette Parish, April 17, 1863

On April 17 the Confederates reached Vermillion-ville (now Lafayette), crossed Vermillion Bayou, destroyed the bridge over the bayou, and halted to rest. One of US General Banks's columns reached the bayou while the bridge was burning, advanced, and began skirmishing. Confederate artillery, strategically placed, forced the Federal troops to fall back. After an artillery duel, the Confederates retreated to Opelousas. Banks followed, seizing control of Bayou Teche, the Atchafalaya River, and the Red River up to Alexandria. His expedition was successful in severing Port Hudson's lifeline to the west.

Estimated Casualties: unknown

Louisiana: June– September 1863

Lafourche Crossing, Louisiana (LA012), Lafourche Parish, June 20–21, 1863

CS Major General Richard Taylor failed to overwhelm the Union enclaves at Milliken's Bend, Young's Point, and Lake Providence on the Louisiana side of the Mississippi River near Vicksburg in early June. He headed south to the Teche country to threaten New Orleans while US Major General Nathaniel P. Banks besieged Port Hudson. Taylor sent CS Colonel James P. Major to raid along Bayou Lafourche, the area west of the Mississippi River between New Orleans and Baton Rouge. US Brigadier General William H. Emory, commander of the Defenses of New Orleans, assigned US Lieutenant Colonel Albert Stickney to Brashear City and ordered him to stop the Confederates.

Stickney arrived at Lafourche Crossing early on June 20. Federal scouts exchanged fire with the rapidly advancing Confederates while Union reinforcements arrived from Terre Bonne. More troops came up during the night, taking up positions behind earthworks, a levee, and a railroad embankment. The Confederates attacked, but after a few hours of combat they disengaged and retired toward Thibodaux. Despite the defeat Major's raiders continued on to Brashear City.

Estimated Casualties: 49 US, 219 CS

Donaldsonville II, Louisiana (LA013), Ascension Parish, June 28, 1863

CS General Taylor sent CS Brigadier Generals Alfred Mouton and Thomas Green to attack Brashear City, US General Banks's supply base. On June 23, the 325 Confederates surprised the garrison, captured the town, took 700 prisoners and all of Banks's supplies.

Taylor tried to cut Banks's communications with New Orleans. He ordered three columns to attack the Federals at Donaldsonville, at the confluence of Bayou Lafourche and the Mississippi. CS General Green surrounded Fort Butler after midnight on June 28, but a wide ditch stopped the Confederate advance. The Federal gunboat *Princess Royal* shelled the attackers, repulsed the Confederate assaults, and inflicted heavy losses. Taylor blocked the Mississippi River to force Banks to lift his siege of Port Hudson, but his action came too late.

Estimated Casualties: 23 US, 301 CS

Kock's Plantation, Louisiana (LA015), Ascension Parish, July 12–13, 1863

After Port Hudson fell on July 9, the divisions of US Brigadier Generals Godfrey Weitzel and Cuvier Grover were shifted to Donaldsonville by transport to drive off CS General Taylor's batteries, which were blocking the Mississippi River. They marched up Bayou Lafourche, one division on each bank, until confronted by CS General Green. A Union foraging detachment skirmished on July 12 and reached Kock's Plantation (Saint Emma Plantation) about six miles from Fort Butler on July 13. A much smaller Confederate force routed the Federal troops, who eventually fell back to the protection of Fort Butler. The U.S. expedition failed, allowing Taylor to evacuate his captured supplies at Brashear City without interference.

Estimated Casualties: 465 US, 33 CS

Stirling's Plantation, Louisiana (LA016), Pointe Coupee Parish, September 29, 1863

Despite the Union defeat at Sabine Pass on September 8, US General Banks continued his efforts to occupy strategic locations in Texas. He dispatched troops up Bayou Teche, an alternate route into Texas. His men disembarked on the plains and marched overland. Elements of US Major General Napoleon J. T. Dana's division were sent to garrison Morganza and prevent Confederate troops from operating on the Atchafalaya River. US Lieutenant Colonel J. B. Leake's 100-man detachment was posted at Stirling's Plantation to guard the road to the river.

CS General Mouton decided to attack the Union forces near Fordoche Bridge. CS General Green crossed the river on September 25, and on the morning of September 29 Confederate cavalry skirmished with Federal pickets at the bridge. Green's other troops hit the Union force and took prisoners, but most of the cavalry escaped. Rain slowed Dana's reinforcements, enabling Green to get away. He won the engagement but did not stop Banks.

Estimated Casualties: 515 US, 121 CS

Siege of Port Hudson: May–July 1863

Plains Store, Louisiana (LA009), East Baton Rouge Parish, May 21, 1863

The Confederate strongholds at Vicksburg and Port Hudson protected the vital stretch of the Mississippi River that carried reinforcements and supplies between the trans-Mississippi region and the eastern Confederacy. On May 14 an army of three divisions under US Major General Nathaniel P. Banks, formerly the Republican speaker of the U.S. House of Representatives and governor of Massachusetts, moved on Port Hudson from the north down the Red and Mississippi Rivers. Simultaneously, US Major General Christopher C. Augur's division advanced north from Baton Rouge toward the intersection of the Plains Store and Bayou Sara Roads to secure a landing on the Mississippi below Port Hudson. If these two forces were to unite — Banks from the north and Augur from the south — Port Hudson would be surrounded. CS Colonel Frank P. Powers was dispatched with 600 troops to defend the vital crossroads at Plains Store.

US Colonel N. A. M. Dudley's brigade led Augur's division and skirmished with Powers at 10:00 A.M. on May 21. Powers was low on ammunition and withdrew before the Federals could outflank him. When 400 men under CS Colonel W. R. Miles arrived late in the day, they attacked, routed the 48th Massachusetts Infantry, and captured a cannon. Augur counterattacked with the 116th New York, recaptured the gun, and forced the Confederates back into Port Hudson.

During the Plains Store engagement CS Major General Franklin Gardner, the commander of Port Hudson, received orders from CS General Joseph E. Johnston to evacuate. Responding instead to the instructions of President Jefferson Davis, Gardner requested reinforcements. When Johnston repeated his order on May 23, it was too late. Banks had landed at Bayou Sara at 2:00 A.M.

on May 22 and by that evening had effectively blocked Gardner's escape.

Estimated Casualties: 150 US, 100 CS

Siege of Port Hudson, Louisiana (LA010), East Baton Rouge and East Feliciana Parishes, May 22–July 9, 1863

Lawrence Lee Hewitt

Control of the Mississippi River was one of the key objectives of the Union strategists at the beginning of the Civil War. In August 1862 forces under CS Major General John C. Breckinridge, a former vice president of the United States, occupied Port Hudson and began constructing a bastion as formidable as that at Vicksburg.

The terrain immediately surrounding Port Hudson is varied. The Mississippi River, which has eroded the Citadel — a three-sided redoubt that anchored the Confederates' downriver defenses — skirts the southwestern corner of the battlefield. A broad alluvial plain, where the river flowed in 1863, extends westward from the bluff. On the north and northeast the terrain is virtually impassable. Canyonlike ravines, sixty- to eighty-foot bluffs, and dense woods stretch to Foster Creek and beyond. The plateau on the east is grazing land. A mile and a half below Port Hudson, a massive ravine bounds the plateau on the south.

In the spring of 1863 USN Rear Admiral David Glasgow Farragut attempted to force the evacuation of Port Hudson by cutting off the food supplies it received down the Red and Mississippi Rivers. Of his seven vessels that attempted to pass the batteries on the night of March 14, only two, including the flagship *Hartford,* succeeded. These two vessels proved insufficient to halt the flow of supplies to Port Hudson.

In late March US Major General Nathaniel P. Banks had concentrated his troops west of the Mississippi. His XIX Corps moved up Bayou Teche and seized Alexandria on the Red River. This severed Port Hudson's supply line with the Confederate Trans-Mississippi Department west of the Mississippi, but the Confederates continued to garrison Port Hudson.

In mid-May Banks moved down the Red River to attack Port Hudson from the north. Additional Union columns moved north from Baton Rouge and New Orleans to attack from the south and east. When Banks closed the noose on Port Hudson on May 22, his 30,000 soldiers, supported by U.S. Navy vessels both upstream and downstream from the town, faced 7,500 Confederates behind four and a half miles of earthworks.

On the morning of May 27 Banks ordered a simultaneous assault all along the line, but the difficult terrain, vague orders, and uncooperative subordinates prevented a coordinated effort. The Confederates on the north side of Port Hudson, aided by reinforcements drawn from other portions of their line, managed to repulse several assaults against Commissary Hill, Fort Desperate, and along the Telegraph Road. Except for scattered musketry and artillery fire, the fighting along the north front ended before the remainder of Banks's army advanced from the east. The delay allowed the Confederates to redeploy men to repulse the Federal assaults across Slaughter's Field and against the Priest Cap.

That evening the Confederate lines remained unbreached. The terrain contributed to this unexpected turn of events because the thickly wooded ravines on the Union right separated enlisted men from their regimental officers and prevented any organized Federal effort. A withering fire covered the fields in front of the Confederate center and right so that Union soldiers were unable to reach the earthworks. Union losses were 2,000 killed or wounded; Confederate casualties were fewer than 500.

Several hundred of the Federal casualties were black soldiers. These included men of the 1st and 3rd Louisiana Native Guards. The 1st Louisiana Native Guards and a majority of its line officers consisted almost entirely of free blacks from New Orleans. Because of their education, wealth, and status in the community, these men were able to field an all-black unit in the antebellum Louisiana state militia. In the spring of 1862, when the

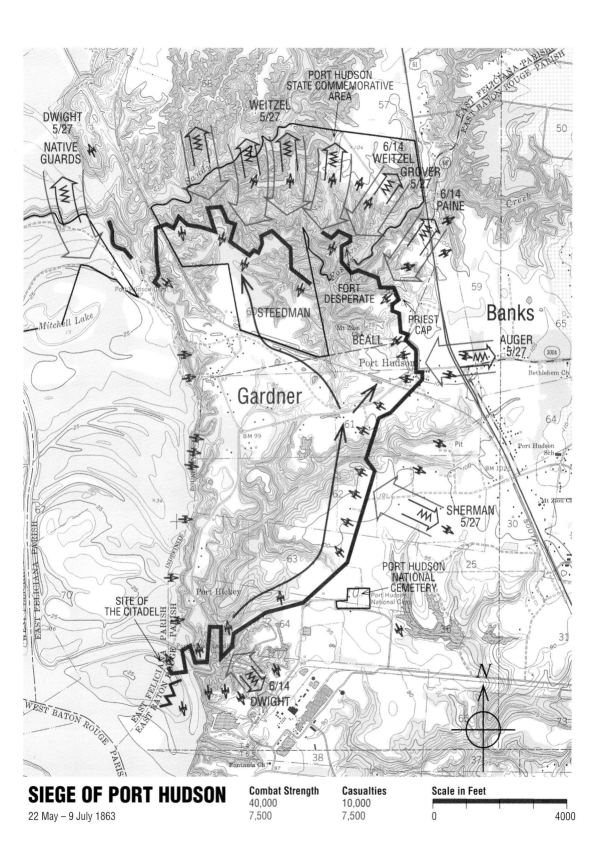

SIEGE OF PORT HUDSON

22 May – 9 July 1863

Combat Strength	Casualties
40,000	10,000
7,500	7,500

Scale in Feet

0   4000

Confederate government refused to arm the regiment, its members offered to fight for the United States.

During the siege of Port Hudson, the Native Guards units were redesignated. The 1st became the First Corps de Afrique; this designation was changed again in April 1864, when it became the 73rd United States Colored Troops. The 3rd Louisiana Native Guards, organized by the government in 1862, was composed of former slaves commanded by white officers. It too was twice redesignated during the war.

In the May 27 assault the 1st and 3rd Louisiana Native Guards advanced across open ground against the strongly fortified position of the 39th Mississippi. US Captain André Cailloux, a free black from New Orleans, led the advance, shouting orders in both English and French until a shell struck him dead. Other black troops waded through the backwater of the Mississippi to engage the enemy. Although repulsed with heavy casualties, the soldiers demonstrated both their willingness and their ability to fight for the Union and for abolition.

Having committed himself, Banks commenced siege operations and ordered sharpshooters and round-the-clock artillery fire. On June 13, after receiving reinforcements and additional cannons, Union gunners opened a tremendous one-hour bombardment. Banks then demanded that the garrison surrender. New York–born CS Major General Franklin Gardner replied, "My duty requires me to defend this position, and therefore I decline to surrender." Banks resumed the bombardment and ordered a full-scale assault the next day.

An entire division, commanded by US Brigadier General Halbert E. Paine and supported by diversionary attacks on the right by US Brigadier General Godfrey Weitzel and on the left by US Brigadier General William Dwight, advanced toward the Priest Cap at about 4:00 A.M. on June 14. A few of the Federals managed to enter the works,

but the breach was quickly sealed. By 10:00 A.M. the assault had failed and the Union had suffered 1,805 more casualties.

Banks spent the remainder of June and early July digging approach saps (trenches) and advancing his artillery. Although reduced to eating rats and mules, the Confederates were still holding out on July 7, after forty-six days of siege. When Gardner received word that Vicksburg had surrendered on July 4, however, he negotiated surrender terms. Without its counterpart up the Mississippi, Port Hudson lacked strategic significance.

On July 9 the Confederate garrison grounded arms. The longest true siege in American military history had ended. At Port Hudson about 7,500 Confederates had tied up more than 40,000 Union soldiers for nearly two months. Confederate casualties included 750 killed and wounded and 250 dead of disease. The Federals took 6,500 prisoners, but their own losses were nearly 10,000, almost evenly divided between battle casualties and disease, including sunstroke.

Estimated Casualties: 10,000 US, 7,500 CS

Port Hudson State Commemorative Area, near Zachary on Route 61, fifteen miles north of Baton Rouge, includes 909 acres of the historic battlefield.

Once let the black man get upon his person the brass letters, U.S.; let him get an eagle on his button, and a musket on his shoulder and bullets in his pocket, and there is no power on earth which can deny that he has earned the right to citizenship.

— Frederick Douglass

"Making Free"

African Americans and the Civil War

James Oliver Horton

◑

The abolition of slavery, for which black Americans worked and prayed so long, entered the political arena in the late 1830s with the formation of the Liberty Party. In the 1840s the Free Soil Party diluted the abolitionist message with the politically popular appeal to "keep the western territories free of slavery and open for the settlement of free labor." The aim of isolating slavery in the South attracted many white workers who were anxious to exclude African Americans from the frontier lands. In 1854 the Republican Party, an amalgamation of the politically disaffected, entered the field with the motto "Free Labor, Free Soil, Free Men."

The Republican candidate in 1860, Abraham Lincoln, had long refused to advocate federal action to abolish slavery and would not publicly condemn Illinois laws forbidding blacks to testify in state and local court cases involving whites. "If a white man happens to owe me anything," one black leader explained, "unless I can prove it by testimony of (another) white man, I cannot collect the debt." Nor did Lincoln oppose Illinois regulations that barred the children of tax-paying black property owners from attending public schools. Lincoln's record led many blacks to join antislavery whites in forming the Radical Abolitionist Party, backing Gerrit Smith, a white abolitionist from New York State, who stood no chance to win but whose candidacy would raise the antislavery issue. "Ten thousand votes for Gerrit Smith . . . ," Frederick Douglass contended,

"would do more for the ultimate abolition of slavery in this country than two million for Abraham Lincoln."

Although Lincoln's inaugural address made clear his intention not to interfere with slavery where it existed, the blacks of Philadelphia, for example, took consolation in the election of "if not an Abolitionist, at least an antislavery reputation to the Presidency." His antislavery reputation was a bit exaggerated, but Lincoln was committed to containing the spread of that evil institution. Shortly after his election, he wrote to his friend Alexander Stephens, who would that winter become the vice president of the Confederacy, putting into words what both men understood. "You think slavery is right and ought to be extended," Lincoln wrote, "while we think it is wrong and ought to be restricted. That I suppose is the rub." As the South declared itself separated from the United States, blacks understood this distinction as well, and many welcomed the secession. "Go at once," urged one black spokesman from Illinois. "There can be no union between freedom and slavery." With slavery isolated in the South and no longer protected by the military might of the United States, many abolitionists believed successful slave uprisings were inevitable.

Although abolition was not yet official U.S. policy, an *Anglo-African* editorial expressed the common belief: "The colored Americans cannot be indifferent. . . . Out of this strife will come freedom." African Americans knew very well that slavery was the central cause of this war. Initially, the United States was not willing to fight to abolish it, but the South was consumed by the need to defend it. Confederate leaders readily acknowledged that the preservation of slavery was the issue to which their cause was committed. Even before Lincoln's election, southern radicals argued that a Republican victory would be disastrous for the South because it would endanger slavery. Should the Republicans come to power, "abolitionism will grow up in every border Southern State," warned the *Richmond Enquirer.* The *Charleston Mercury* confirmed the importance of slavery, especially in the Deep South. While in the border states slavery might be a matter of convenience or "expediency," read one editorial, "to us the institution is vital and indispensable." The Confederate president, Jefferson Davis, agreed, arguing that the defense of slavery justified secession, for should the Republicans take office, he believed, their policies would render "property in slaves so insecure as to be comparatively worthless." Alexander Stephens declared that the Confederacy was founded on the principle of white supremacy and slavery, and that the "subordination to the superior race [was the black man's] natural and normal condition." He further claimed that the Confederacy was the "first [nation] in the history of the world, based on this great physical, philosophical, and moral truth." There was general agreement among white southerners that, as a lieutenant from Mississippi put it, "if the negroes are freed the country . . . is not worth fighting for. . . . We can only live & exist by that species of labor."

Under these circumstances, blacks were right to see the war as one against slavery, and they were anxious to strike a blow for freedom. All over the North blacks organized military units and offered their services to the United States. New York City units drilled in hired halls, African Americans in Boston petitioned their state for permission to serve, Pittsburgh blacks sent a letter to the state militia declaring their readiness, blacks in Washington, D.C., petitioned the

War Department directly. In all cases they were turned down. The War Department's position was clear: "This Department has no intention at present to call into service of the Government any colored soldiers." But after a year of fighting, U.S. forces needed men. This costly war forced a rethinking of recruitment policy. In July 1862 Congress provided for the enlistment of black troops into segregated units under white officers. The successes of these troops in combat created a more positive northern public opinion of black soldiers. The *New York Tribune* asserted, "Facts are beginning to dispel prejudices." Lincoln, quick to grasp the impact of Confederate defeats at the hands of black troops, urged white commanders to take advantage of every opportunity to use them.

By the summer of 1863 the Bureau of Colored Troops was in operation within the War Department. As the war ground on, the growing reluctance of white men to join the military increased the need for African American troops, but discriminatory policies made it more difficult to recruit black soldiers; they were paid less than whites and received inferior equipment and food. Another deterrent to serving in the military was the Confederates' announcement, in the spring of 1863, that captured black troops would be executed or enslaved and their white officers executed. A year later, reports confirmed that the Confederates had murdered several dozen black soldiers at Fort Pillow, Tennessee, after they had surrendered. At Memphis black troops knelt, taking an oath to avenge this barbarism. "Remember Fort Pillow" became their rallying cry for the duration of the war.

The booming northern economy also made military service less attractive to blacks. At the same time, white resentment of the blacks newly employed in industry was aggravated by whites' perception of the war as being for the benefit of blacks. Whites protesting the military draft attacked black communities, destroying property and killing black men, women, and children. African Americans had always been vulnerable to insults and sporadic violence, but during the war they were especially targeted. Black soldiers

This composite of photographs of recipients of the Medal of Honor is in the Christian A. Fleetwood files in the Library of Congress. Most of these men served in the U.S. Army during the Civil War. They are identified as follows in *Men of Color*, by William A. Gladstone. *Top row:* Robert A. Pinn, Milton N. Holland, John W. Lawson. *Second row:* John Denny, Isaiah Mays, Powhatan Beaty, Brent Woods. *Third row:* William H. Carney, Thomas R. Hawkins, Dennis Bell, James H. Harris. *Fourth row:* Thomas Shaw, Alexander Kelly, James Gardiner, Christian A. Fleetwood. (Christian A. Fleetwood files, Library of Congress, Box #2)

were attacked on the streets of Washington, New York, Boston, and other cities, sometimes in the presence of the police, who provided no protection. In spite of these deterrents, the recruitment efforts of black leaders such as Frederick Douglass, Williams Wells Brown, and John Mercer Langston maintained a steady enlistment.

At the same time, abolition was gradually becoming a U.S. war aim. Congress passed a series of confiscation acts to deprive the Confederacy of its human property, and Lincoln issued the dramatic Emancipation Proclamation. A military measure, the proclamation applied only to slaves who remained under Confederate control, but blacks and many white abolitionists treated it as a proclamation of general abolition. For them, New Year's Day, 1863, began the "Year of Jubilee."

More than 185,000 blacks served officially in the U.S. Army, and countless others served unofficially as scouts, spies, and laborers, building military fortifications. Blacks had served in the navy since 1812. Although insufficiently supplied and ill equipped, blacks were often employed as shock troops in the most dangerous missions. They made up less than 10 percent of the U.S. Army, but their casualty rate was disproportionately high. More than 30,000 were killed or died during the war, nearly 3,000 in combat. Sixteen black soldiers and four black sailors were recipients of the Medal of Honor. By the war's end just under one hundred blacks had been promoted to officer ranks, the highest ranking being a surgeon, Lieutenant Colonel Alexander T. Augustana.

The bravery of blacks in the war was the subject of many news reports. Although such reports did not eradicate prejudice, they did have some short-term effect on racial attitudes in the North. One black Philadelphian stated that "public sentiment has undergone a great change in the past month or two, and more especially since the brilliant exploits of several colored regiments."

This change in sentiment had legislative effect when the U.S. Congress repealed the prohibition against blacks carrying the U.S. mail, struck down the exclusion of blacks as witnesses in fed-

eral courts, and included African American males as eligible voters in the District of Columbia. In Illinois blacks successfully lobbied against laws prohibiting their immigration to the state; in Illinois and California they won the right to testify in trials involving whites.

By the end of the war most restrictive laws had been abolished in the North, but racially restrictive traditions and customs continued. Job discrimination ensured the perpetuation of black poverty. Although formal policies discriminating against blacks on public conveyances and in public schools were abolished in some northern cities after the war, discrimination in public accommodations continued. The fourteenth and fifteenth constitutional amendments, ratified in 1868 and 1870, granted citizenship to blacks and encouraged (but did not ensure) black suffrage.

The South was also changed, at least momentarily, by the terrible human cost of the war. By 1865 the Confederacy was so badly battered that several Confederate commanders strongly suggested, and Robert E. Lee supported, a proposal that slaves be recruited into the southern military and promised freedom in return for service. This was a bitter pill to swallow for a society founded on slavery and wedded to the argument that slaves did not desire freedom. Yet these desperate times required desperate admissions, and in March a bill authorizing the recruitment of slaves passed the Confederate congress. The war was over before slave recruits could see action, but the South's acceptance of such a measure challenged its deepest and most strongly held beliefs. The end of war brought a moment of social and political revolution in the South, as Reconstruction governments democratized voting and office holding, and brought public schools, health institutions, public housing, and other social services that southern poor whites and blacks had never known but sorely needed. Yet these changes did not last, and within a generation the old southern order returned with new forms of racial control asserted through restrictive legislation and political terrorism. Most southern African Americans remained economically dependent and politically mute. Although the freedom that the Emancipation Proclamation symbolized was generations away, progress toward racial equality through the next century was built on

the foundation laid by black and white abolitionists and soldiers and sailors fighting for the expansion of that vision of liberty that had called the nation into existence almost a hundred years before its Civil War.

Middle Tennessee: February–April 1863

Dover, Tennessee (TN012), Stewart County, February 3, 1863

After the battle of Stones River, CS General Braxton Bragg sent CS Major General Joseph Wheeler to raid along the Cumberland River and disrupt Union shipping. On January 26 Bragg sent CS Brigadier General Nathan Bedford Forrest to join the raid. Wheeler positioned two cavalry brigades on the river, but was unsuccessful because the Federals learned of the Confederate plan and halted all shipping.

Although Forrest opposed the attack on the fortified post at Dover, near Fort Donelson, Wheeler ordered it to begin on February 3 with an artillery bombardment. Wheeler planned to follow with a general attack by dismounted cavalry, but Forrest led his own mounted attack. Not only was Forrest repulsed by the 800-man garrison under US Colonel A. C. Harding, but he ruined the possibility of success for Wheeler's general attack, which followed.

The Confederate failure caused dissention between the two cavalrymen. Forrest declared his personal friendship for Wheeler, and then announced, "I will be in my coffin before I will fight again under your command." Wheeler responded, "As the commanding officer I take all the blame and responsibility for this failure."

Estimated Casualties: 110 US, 855 CS

Thompson's Station, Tennessee (TN013), Williamson County, March 4–5, 1863

On March 4 US Colonel John Coburn led a reinforced infantry brigade south from Franklin toward Columbia. The next day they confronted CS Brigadier General William H. "Red" Jackson's troops four miles north of Spring Hill. After a two-hour artillery duel, the Federals pushed the Confederates back, but Jackson established a new line. Coburn's attack on the Confederate center failed. CS Major General Earl Van Dorn, who had arrived to assume command of the Confederate forces, seized the initiative. He launched a frontal attack with Jackson's men, while CS General Forrest's Brigade swept around Coburn's left flank and into his rear. After three hard-fought attempts, Jackson carried the Union hilltop position while Forrest captured Coburn's wagon train and blocked the road to Columbia. Coburn, surrounded and out of ammunition, surrendered.

Estimated Casualties: 1,600 US, 357 CS

Vaught's Hill, Tennessee (TN014), Rutherford County, March 20, 1863

On March 18 US Colonel Albert Hall's brigade rode northeast out of Murfreesboro on a raid. CS Brigadier General John Hunt Morgan pursued them as they returned to Murfreesboro. On the twentieth he caught up with Hall's rear guard a mile west of Milton. Hall positioned his men in a perimeter defense on Vaught's Hill, a steep hill covered with rock outcroppings. When Morgan's men attacked the strong Federal position, they were hit by artillery fire. Morgan continued his attacks until late afternoon when he learned that Union reinforcements were en route from Murfreesboro. This defeat dimmed Morgan's reputation, and Federal forces continued to strengthen their positions in Middle Tennessee.

Estimated Casualties: 38 US, 150 CS

Brentwood, Tennessee (TN015), Williamson County, March 25, 1863

On March 15 CS General Forrest headed a cavalry division to capture the garrison at Brentwood, a station on the Nashville & Decatur Railroad held by US Lieutenant Colonel Edward Bloodgood. On March 24 Forrest ordered CS Colonel James W. Starnes to cut the telegraph, tear up railroad track, attack the stockade, and cut off any possible retreat for the Union forces there. The next day Forrest positioned his artillery and surrounded the town. Before shots were fired, Bloodgood surrendered.

Forrest rode on to Franklin and forced the 230-man garrison there to surrender.

Estimated Casualties: 529 US, 3 CS

Franklin I, Tennessee (TN016), Williamson County and Franklin, April 10, 1863

On April 10 CS General Van Dorn advanced northward from Spring Hill to determine whether Franklin had been reoccupied by Union troops. As CS General Forrest's command rode along the Lewisburg Turnpike, they began pushing back Union pickets. CS Colonel Starnes was surprised by a flank attack by Federal cavalry. US Brigadier General David S. Stanley's cavalry brigade had crossed the Big Harpeth River at Hughes' Ford behind the Confederate right rear. His force captured CS Captain Samuel L. Freeman and his Tennessee Battery. In the counterat-

tack, when the Confederates recaptured their artillery, a Federal cavalryman shot Forrest's popular artillery chief.

Van Dorn concluded that the Federals were in Franklin and withdrew to Spring Hill. The Federals rode back across the Big Harpeth River and continued to control the area.

Estimated Casualties: 100 US, 137 CS

Union Naval Attacks on Fort McAllister: January–March 1863

Fort McAllister I, Georgia (GA002), Bryan County, January 27–March 3, 1863

Fort McAllister, a sand and marsh mud-block fort on the south bank of the Great Ogeechee River south of Savannah, had seven gun emplacements separated by large traverses and ten additional cannons. USN Rear Admiral Samuel F. Du Pont decided to use the fort as a test range for the new monitors before they attacked Charleston harbor. On January 27 the monitor *Montauk*, several gunboats, and a mortar schooner ascended the river and bombarded the fort. The monitor was struck repeatedly during the four-hour engagement but not damaged. In the *Montauk*'s assault on February 1, the garrison commander, CS Major John B. Gallie, was killed.

On March 3 Du Pont ordered the ironclad monitors *Patapsco, Passaic,* and *Nahant* and six gunboats and mortar boats to conduct target practice on Fort McAllister. The squadron bombarded the fort for seven hours. The barrage did little damage. The tests provided information, including that the ironclads' big guns could damage but not destroy an earthen fort, and that manpower could move the earth back in place.

Estimated Casualties: 0 US, 1 CS

Fort McAllister Historic State Park, nine miles southeast of Richmond Hill off I-95 at Exit 15, includes five acres of the historic battlefield.

Charleston: April–September 1863

Charleston Harbor I, South Carolina (SC004), Charleston County, April 7, 1863

In the spring of 1863 Charleston was a strongly fortified city under the command of CS General P. G. T. Beauregard. A series of earthen and masonry fortifications armed with seventy-seven heavy guns ringed the inner harbor, mined obstructions blocked the ship channels, and three ironclads and several torpedo boats, the *Davids,* defended the city.

In April the Federals launched a joint army-navy operation to capture Charleston, control the harbor, shut down blockade running there, invade the Carolinas, and deliver a blow to southern morale. US Major General David Hunter, the commander of the Department of the South, prepared his 10,000 men, while the South Atlantic Blockading Squadron under USN Rear Admiral Samuel F. Du Pont assembled off North Edisto Island to bombard Fort Sumter. The squadron included seven monitors and two ironclads, the *Keokuk* and *New Ironsides.* Du Pont intended to attack Fort Sumter from the northeast and then swing around to the south to hit Morris Island. He described the challenge: "The Charleston defenses are like a porcupine hide with the quills turned outside in."

At noon on April 7 Du Pont's squadron steamed into Charleston harbor, but the heavy current and mined obstructions fouled his plan. The current slowed the monitors, making them easy targets for the Confederate guns in Fort Sumter and Fort Moultrie. Every ship took dozens of hits. The *Keokuk* bombarded Sumter point-blank for thirty minutes, then withdrew after being struck by more than ninety shots. It sank the next day. The rest of the squadron was damaged, and Du Pont retreated at dusk. Although several of Hunter's units embarked on transports, only one brigade landed on Folly Island. After the failed attempt,

USN Rear Admiral John A. Dahlgren replaced Du Pont, and US Brigadier General Quincy A. Gillmore took over Hunter's department.

Estimated Casualties: 22 US, 14 CS

Fort Wagner I, Morris Island, South Carolina (SC005), Charleston County, July 10–11, 1863

US General Gillmore's objective was to capture Morris Island, which controlled the southern approaches to the harbor. Gillmore was one of the army's best engineers and was chosen for this command because of his success against Fort Pulaski in April 1862. His command of 21,000 men included four black regiments. On July 10 Gillmore's artillery on Folly Island and US Admiral Dahlgren's four ironclads opened fire on the Confederate defenses protecting the southern end of Morris Island. The bombardment provided cover for US Brigadier General George C. Strong's brigade of 2,500 men to cross Lighthouse Inlet and land on the southern end of the island. Some of the Federals landed among the Confederate rifle pits, while others landed beside the ocean and flanked the batteries farther inland, capturing 300 prisoners and eleven guns. The Federals then advanced three miles to Fort Wagner (also known as Battery Wagner), which barred the approach to the northern third of the island.

Since the attack was just a week after the twin disasters of Gettysburg and Vicksburg, the Confederates could not afford another crushing defeat. They rushed several brigades to Charleston and reinforced Fort Wagner overnight. On July 11 CS Colonel Robert F. Graham's 1,770-man force repelled a dawn attack by the 7th Connecticut. The Federals advanced through a thick fog and overran a line of rifle pits before being repelled at the moat. Fort Wagner's artillery fire prevented supporting units from approaching and forced the attackers to fall back.

Estimated Casualties: 339 US, 12 CS

Grimball's Landing, South Carolina (SC006), Charleston County, James Island, July 16, 1863

US General Gillmore ordered two feints to divert Confederate reinforcements from his main attack against Fort Wagner. An amphibious force ascended the Stono River to threaten the Charleston & Savannah Railroad, while US Brigadier General Alfred H. Terry's division of 5,200 men landed on Sol Legare and James Islands on July 8 to demonstrate against the Confederate defenses. On July 16 the commander on James Island, CS Brigadier General Johnson Hagood, moved to attack the isolated camp of the 10th Connecticut at Grimball's Landing with 3,200 men. CS Brigadier General Alfred Colquitt's Brigade was to hit the main Union camp on Sol Legare and block Terry while Hagood destroyed the Federals at Grimball's. Colquitt attacked across River's Causeway. The pickets, the African American 54th Massachusetts, countered with determined volleys from across the causeway but were forced back by superior numbers. The rest of Terry's division came up in support. Union warships in the river fired on the Confederate right flank, forcing them back across Grimball's Causeway. The Confederates moved north of the causeway to attack the 10th Connecticut, but the regiment had escaped.

Their diversion accomplished, Federal troops withdrew on July 17 from James Island to Cole's Island. Many of these soldiers were transferred to Morris Island for the attack on Fort Wagner.

Estimated Casualties: 46 US, 18 CS

Fort Wagner II, Morris Island, South Carolina (SC007), Charleston County, July 18, 1863

After the failed assault on July 11, US General Gillmore reinforced his beachhead on Morris Island and brought up siege guns and mortars to bombard Fort Wagner, defended by 1,620 men with fifteen guns and a mortar. On July 18 Gillmore's batteries opened fire and were soon joined by six monitors, which approached to within three hundred yards of the fort. The bombardment continued for eight hours and sent the Confederate gunners into their bombproofs. However, the sandy walls absorbed much of the cannon shot, and the garrison survived unscathed.

US Brigadier General Truman A. Seymour drew up his 5,100-man division. The 650 men of the 54th Massachusetts spearheaded the attack of the lead brigade. They charged at dusk along the narrow open beach through heavy artillery and small arms fire. Some scaled the parapet, but the Confederates drove them back in brutal hand-to-hand combat. The unit's commander, US Colonel Robert Gould Shaw, was killed in the attack. The nine regiments that followed also reached Wagner's parapet but were thrown back with severe losses, including US General Strong, the brigade commander. US Colonel Haldiman S. Putnam's brigade overran Wagner's seaward salient, but in the resulting melee Putnam was killed, and the survivors were forced to withdraw. With two brigades wrecked and Seymour wounded, Gillmore called off the attack. The Confederates continued to strengthen their defenses in the inner harbor.

At Fort Wagner black soldiers made courageous assaults and demonstrated their fighting abilities, as they had at Port Hudson the previous May.

Estimated Casualties: 1,515 US, 222 CS

Peace does not appear so distant as it did. I hope it will come soon, and come to stay; and so come as to be worth the keeping in all future time. It will then have been proved that, among free men, there can be no successful appeal from the ballot to the bullet; and that they who take such appeal are sure to lose their case, and pay the cost. And then, there will be some black men who can remember that, with silent tongue, and clenched teeth, and steady eye, and well-poised bayonet, they have helped mankind on to this great consummation; while, I fear, there will be some

white ones, unable to forget that, with malignant heart, and deceitful speech, they have strove to hinder it.

— President Abraham Lincoln in his August 26, 1863, letter to James C. Conkling

Charleston Harbor II, South Carolina (SC009), Charleston County, September 5–8, 1863

US General Gillmore methodically advanced his lines, emplaced heavy artillery to hit Fort Wagner and Fort Sumter, and began a formal siege of Wagner. Using calcium lights to illuminate the fort at night, the artillery and the warships bombarded the battery while the infantry slowly dug approaching trenches. The Confederates countered by sniping at them during the day and by using small boats at night to replace and resupply the garrison.

On September 5 USN Admiral Dahlgren's ironclads and Gillmore's land batteries began a thirty-six-hour bombardment of Fort Wagner and killed 100 of the 1,200-man garrison. The Federals finally seized the Confederate rifle pits outside the fort and brought their lines to the moat. On September 6 CS General Beauregard ordered Morris Island evacuated. During the siege Beauregard had strengthened the harbor fortifications on Sullivan's Island and at Fort Johnson so that he no longer needed Morris Island. That night two Confederate ironclads guarded the evacuation of CS Colonel Laurence M. Keitt's troops on Morris, and Gillmore's soldiers occupied the entire island.

Estimated Casualties: 117 US, 100 CS

Fort Sumter II, South Carolina (SC008), Charleston County, August 17–September 8, 1863

On August 17 the Federals renewed the bombardment of Fort Sumter with batteries erected on Morris Island and with USN Admiral Dahlgren's squadron. On the night of September 1–2, after a day of bombardment, the ironclads steamed to within five hundred yards of the fort, fired for more than five hours, and reduced the masonry fort to rubble. The garrison continued to hold the fort.

The capture of Morris Island by US General Gillmore's troops failed to open Charleston harbor to the navy because the Confederates still held Fort Sumter, and it anchored a line of deadly obstructions and torpedoes. On the night of September 8, 400 marines and sailors assaulted the fort. Forewarned, the Confederates were waiting. They had withdrawn most of their artillery and had replaced the gunners with 300 men of the Charleston Battalion under CS Major Stephen Elliott. Their ironclad *Chicora* opened fire from one side while the guns of Fort Moultrie caught the Federals in a crossfire. The garrison captured 120 Federals and wounded many others as they escaped to their boats.

This attack ended the army-navy campaign in 1863 to seize Charleston. The army was severely weakened by the hot sun and unhealthy conditions on Morris Island, and the navy would not steam into the harbor until the obstructions and torpedoes were removed. By the end of the siege Charleston's defenses on James Island were stronger, and the Federals were on the outskirts of the harbor. They temporarily closed Charleston to blockade runners until March 1864. The runners then resumed their actions and continued them until the Confederates evacuated Fort Sumter and Charleston on February 17, 1865 — when US Major General William Tecumseh Sherman marched north.

Estimated Casualties: unknown

Fort Sumter National Monument, in Charleston harbor, includes 195 acres of the historic land.

Longstreet's Tidewater Campaign: March– April 1863

Fort Anderson, North Carolina (NC010), Craven County, March 13–15, 1863

In February 1863 CS General Robert E. Lee named CS Lieutenant General James Longstreet commander of the 45,000 troops in the Department of Virginia and North Carolina. Longstreet established his headquarters in Petersburg and took command of the First Corps divisions of CS Major Generals John Bell Hood and George E. Pickett, which Lee had detached from the Army of Northern Virginia to defend Richmond, and CS Major General Daniel Harvey Hill's Division in North Carolina.

This was Longstreet's first independent command, and it was challenging. President Jefferson Davis ordered him to protect Richmond, Lee needed to have Hood and Pickett ready to rejoin his army if the Federals launched an offensive along the Rappahannock River, and the Confederate secretary of war, James Seddon, urged Longstreet to gather supplies for Lee's army while keeping the Federals penned in their East Coast enclaves: New Bern/Fort Anderson and Washington in North Carolina, and Suffolk in Virginia. Lee's men were so low on food that the men were on half rations and suffering from scurvy. Their horses were dying of starvation. Longstreet responded to Davis and Lee by ordering Hood to the area of the railroad just south of Richmond and Pickett to Petersburg. Longstreet directed Hill to begin the supply operation.

Hill hit the Union stronghold of New Bern on the Neuse River with a three-pronged attack. While one column cut the Atlantic & North Carolina Railroad and communications south of New Bern, CS Brigadier General Junius Daniel's Brigade advanced from Kinston along the lower Trent Road. The Confederates encountered Union pickets ten miles from New Bern on March 13, pushed them back to Deep Gully, and stormed their position. The Federals retreated to their works around New Bern the next morning.

Hill directed CS Brigadier General James Johnston Pettigrew's Brigade to take Fort Anderson on the side of the Neuse River opposite the town. Since the only attack route was across a single causeway, Pettigrew demanded that the garrison surrender. The commander, US Lieutenant Colonel Hiram Anderson, refused, and Pettigrew shelled the earthworks for two days. Union gunboats steamed up, returned fire, and forced the Confederates to withdraw. Hill did not take the fort but was successful in filling wagons with hams, salted fish, flour, and cornmeal from counties not occupied by armies. During March and April wagon trains creaked their way to new supply dumps in the direction of Petersburg and Richmond.

Estimated Casualties: 7 total

Washington, North Carolina (NC011), Beaufort County, March 30–April 20, 1863

CS General Hill turned northward from New Bern to attack the 1,200-man Union garrison at Washington. By March 30 the Confederates occupied strategic points on both banks of the Tar River and blocked it. Hill positioned two brigades on the south side to watch out for a relief column from the New Bern garrison, while CS Brigadier General Richard B. Garnett's Brigade besieged the town, keeping the Federals penned in while Confederate foraging continued in the countryside. Even though the Confederates ringed the town with earthworks, and their siege artillery dueled with the enemy guns and warships, they were unable to prevent the Federals from being resupplied. US Major General John G. Foster ran the blockade and brought reinforcements by steamer from New Bern on April 19. Hill abandoned the siege and withdrew to Goldsboro.

Estimated Casualties: 100 total

Suffolk I, Virginia (VA030), Suffolk, April 13–15, 1863

US Major General John J. Peck had overseen the construction of eight forts and fourteen miles of entrenchments at Suffolk to protect his 17,000 men and the southern approaches to the shipbuilding center at Norfolk, sixteen miles to the east. The Federals were a threat to Longstreet's foraging efforts, but their works were too strong to assault. CS General Longstreet informed Lee that "I do not propose to do anything more than draw out the supplies from that country, unless something very favorable should offer." On April 8 Longstreet sent the forces of CS Major Generals Hood, Pickett, and Samuel G. French from Petersburg to hold the Federals inside their works while the Confederate commissary wagons gathered food and supplies under the direction of CS Major Raphael Moses, the First Corps commissary chief.

On April 13 the Confederates pushed their left flank to the Nansemond River and constructed a battery on Hill's Point to hinder Union shipping. The next day the Confederates crippled the *Mount Washington* when Federal gunboats tried to run past the batteries at Norfleet House farther upstream. On April 15 the Federals opened fire from batteries they had secretly constructed and drove the Confederates out of Norfleet House.

Suffolk II (Hill's Point), Virginia (VA031), Suffolk, April 19, 1863

On April 19 at 6:00 P.M., 270 Federals stormed off transports and surprised the Confederates in their earthworks at Hill's Point on the Nansemond River. In ten minutes they captured all five guns of CS Captain Robert M. Stribling's Fauquier Artillery, took 130 prisoners, and reopened the river to Union shipping.

US Brigadier General Michael Corcoran led a force from Fort Dix against CS General Pickett's extreme right on April 24, but the Federals' cautious approach was repulsed.

On April 30 CS General Lee wired Richmond for CS General Longstreet to disengage his First Corps divisions from Suffolk and rejoin the Army of Northern Virginia at Fredericksburg. On the same day US Major General Joseph Hooker outflanked Lee and arrived at Chancellorsville but lost the initiative when Lee chose to fight. On the night of May 3, when his supply wagons were safely near or across the Blackwater River, Longstreet lifted the siege of Suffolk. His troops marched northwest to the railroad. The First Corps boarded trains to rejoin the Army of Northern Virginia, the day after CS Lieutenant General Stonewall Jackson was mortally wounded in the brilliant Confederate victory at Chancellorsville.

Estimated Casualties: 1,160 total for the entire siege of Suffolk, from April 11 to May 4; 260 US, 900 CS

Cavalry Along the Rappahannock: March 1863

Kelly's Ford, Virginia (VA029), Culpeper County, March 17, 1863

After the battle of Fredericksburg in December 1862 the Confederate Army of Northern Virginia went into winter quarters along the south bank of the Rappahannock River. On March 17 US Brigadier General William W. Averell's 2,100-man cavalry division crossed the river at Kelly's Ford. They scattered Confederate pickets and captured more than 20 before they encountered CS Brigadier General Fitzhugh Lee's 800-man brigade a half mile from the ford. Averell immediately assumed a defensive posture, with his right flank resting on the river near the Wheatley house. Lee sent the 3rd Virginia Cavalry to charge the Union right. The Federals repulsed the attack and killed CS Major John Pelham, the twenty-three-year-old chief of CS Major General J. E. B. Stuart's horse artillery. The death of the "gallant Pelham," an outstanding artillery commander, was a blow to the Confederate cavalry and to Stuart.

Averell attacked Lee's right and broke the Confederate line. The outnumbered Confederates fell back behind Carter's Run to the Brandy Station Road. Lee ordered a charge with his entire force across the open field to their front. The Union right broke, but the left held, supported by four guns. When Averell learned of the approach of Confederate reinforcements, he ordered a retreat across the Rappahannock.

In the spring of 1863 areas of the Confederacy were particularly short of food, and the Army of Northern Virginia was reduced to half rations. There were bread riots during which desperate women took food for their families, particularly from the government warehouses and the stores of "speculators." The largest riot was in Richmond. In March CS General Robert E. Lee suffered the first of the heart attacks that would cause his death seven years later.

Estimated Casualties: 99 US, 80 CS

Chancellorsville Campaign: April–May 1863

Chancellorsville, Virginia (VA032),

Spotsylvania County,

April 30–May 6, 1863

Robert K. Krick

During the first week of May 1863, CS General Robert E. Lee and CS Lieutenant General Thomas J. "Stonewall" Jackson led a dramatically outnumbered Army of Northern Virginia to victory in the battle of Chancellorsville. That battle has been aptly called Lee's greatest victory and was one of the Confederacy's brightest moments.

The crushing Union defeat at the battle of Fredericksburg in December had left the Army of the Potomac in disarray during the winter of 1862–63. Officers and men alike doubted (with good cause) the capacity for command of the army's leader, US Major General Ambrose E. Burnside. As the two contending armies settled into camps facing one another across the icy Rappahannock River that winter, the northern cause was apparently at its nadir. Burnside compounded his troops' unhappiness when he led them out of their wintry camps in mid-January on a disastrous venture that came to bear the derisive name "the Mud March." Almost at once he was replaced by a general known for his political machinations and aggressiveness, US Major General Joseph "Fighting Joe" Hooker. Burnside slipped into relative oblivion and is best remembered today not for his military exploits but for his eponymous whiskers.

As soon as springtime made Virginia's roads passable, Hooker moved part of his army up and across the Rappahannock above Fredericksburg. His plan to fall on the rear of Lee's army was a daring one, and it was crisply executed. Placed at a disadvantage as great as any he faced during the war, Lee rushed his men west of Fredericksburg toward the tiny country crossroads of Chancellorsville, where there was only a single house. Dense, wiry underbrush covered more than half

the battlefield in an area known since the earliest settlement as the Wilderness of Spotsylvania. For an outnumbered army thrown on the defensive, such terrain offered tremendous advantages. The confusing sea of impenetrable thickets served as a sort of ready-made barbed wire behind which Lee could maneuver his slender military resources.

Hooker arrived at Chancellorsville late on the last day of April. The next morning he turned east, in the direction of Fredericksburg, and moved toward the rear of the Confederate position he had so thoroughly outflanked — and toward the eastern edge of the Wilderness. During the morning his advance reached the foot of a commanding ridge on which stood the small wooden Baptist sanctuary called Zoan Church. This ridge was the highest ground for miles; equally important, it was beyond the edge of the entangling Wilderness.

Lee and Jackson meanwhile conceived a remarkable plan for dealing with Hooker. Although the Federals outnumbered them more than two to one — about 130,000 to 60,000, the largest imbalance of any major battle in Virginia during the war — the Confederate commanders determined to divide their forces, leaving a rear guard at Fredericksburg. Jackson arrived at Zoan Church just as the Union advance was on the verge of capturing that crucial ridge. He attacked immediately and drove a suddenly pliant Hooker back toward Chancellorsville on two parallel roads. May 1 ended with the Union army digging in around and west of the crossroads, its right flank stretched somewhat aimlessly westward beyond Wilderness Church.

Through the dark hours of that night Lee and Jackson reviewed their alternatives and selected the most daring of the lot. In complete contravention of most of the established rules of warfare, they further divided their small force. Starting early on May 2 Jackson displayed the enormous energy and determination that were his dominant military traits as he hurried most of the available infantry on a twelve-mile march all the way around Hooker's army. While Jackson surged far out on a limb, Lee remained behind

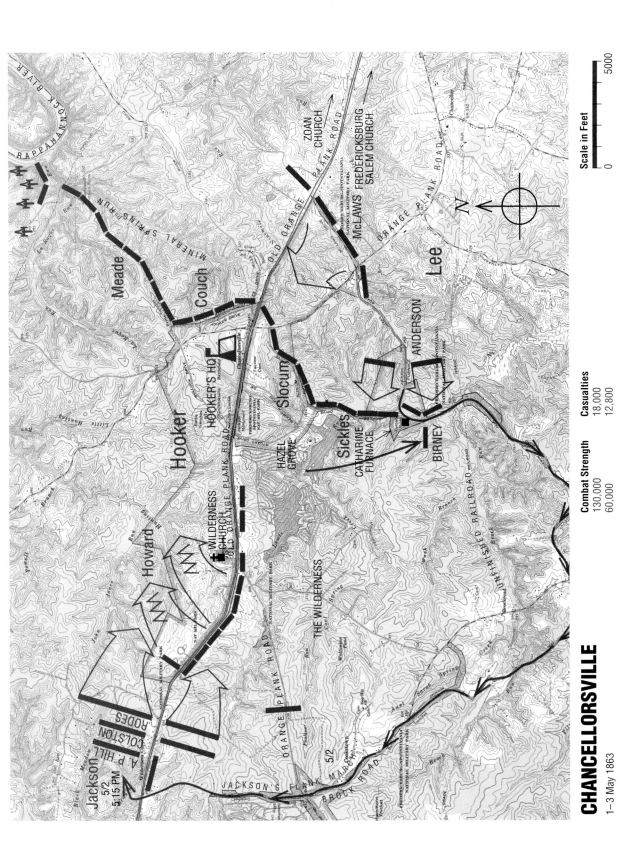

CHANCELLORSVILLE

1–3 May 1863

Combat Strength	Casualties
130,000	18,000
60,000	12,800

Scale in Feet

0   5000

with a relative handful of men from the divisions of CS Major Generals Richard H. Anderson and Lafayette McLaws and did his best to bemuse Hooker into assuming that he faced dire danger in his front.

Late in the afternoon of May 2 Jackson had his 30,000 men aligned behind the unsuspecting Union troops, the division of CS Brigadier General Robert E. Rodes in front, followed by those of CS Brigadier General Raleigh E. Colston and CS Major General Ambrose Powell Hill. When Jackson said to CS Major Eugene Blackford, commanding the skirmishers, "You can go forward then," the Confederate cause was at its highest tide. The hordes of ragged Confederates who came loping out of the Wilderness, screaming their spine-chilling Rebel yell, had little difficulty rolling over their opponents, destroying the corps of US Major General Oliver O. Howard and isolating that of US Major General Daniel E. Sickles.

After darkness halted the advance, Jackson rode in front of his disorganized men in quest of a route that would offer new opportunities. When he came back toward his troops, a North Carolina regiment fired blindly at the noise and mortally wounded him. Jackson died eight days later, in the office building of the Chandler plantation, south of Fredericksburg.

The most intense fighting during the battle of Chancellorsville developed on the morning of May 3 across the densely wooded Wilderness near where Jackson had fallen. The pivotal advantage finally came from Confederate artillery crowded onto a small, high clearing known as Hazel Grove. The guns at Hazel Grove supplied momentum to weary infantrymen who surged across the fields around Chancellorsville crossroads in midmorning to seal a southern victory that cost the Union 18,000 casualties.

The campaign wound down during the next three days, as static lines waited for Hooker's decision to admit defeat and recross the river. The battle of Chancellorsville gave the Army of Northern Virginia momentum that Lee turned into an aggressive campaign a few weeks later. That campaign led to Gettysburg. Chancellorsville cost the Confederacy 12,800 casualties.

The Confederacy suffered no greater loss as the result of direct battlefield action than the death of Stonewall Jackson. The general's spectacular achievements while operating independently in the Shenandoah Valley during the spring of 1862, at a time when southern fortunes stood at their nadir, served as a springboard for operations that saved his country from destruction. Soon thereafter Jackson joined Lee's army around Richmond and began a collaboration that developed into one of the most successful in all of American military history. Stonewall Jackson's tactical arrangements frequently fell far short of genius. His operational stratagems, however, applied with a tenacity and determination unequaled in either army, almost always yielded victories — often of dazzling proportions. His loss was an irreparable blow to Confederate hopes.

Estimated Casualties: 18,000 US, 12,800 CS, including the engagements at Fredericksburg and Salem Church

---

Chancellorsville Battlefield, a unit of Fredericksburg and Spotsylvania National Military Park, near Route 3 west of Fredericksburg off Interstate 95, includes 2,396 acres of the historic battlefield, 576 of which are privately owned.

Fredericksburg II, Virginia (VA034), Fredericksburg, May 3, 1863

While CS General Lee and US General Hooker waged the battle of Chancellorsville, their subordinates struggled for possession of Fredericksburg a dozen miles to the east. On the morning of May 3, US Major General John Sedgwick's VI Corps, reinforced by US Brigadier General John Gibbon's division of the II Corps, assaulted CS Major General Jubal A. Early's reinforced division, which held the same line that had proved impregnable during the December 1862 battle of Fredericksburg. The Federals successfully stormed Marye's Heights, driving off about 600 Mississippians. Early regrouped southwest of Fredericksburg while Sedgwick pushed west toward Chancellorsville, only to be stymied at Salem Church.

Estimated Casualties: included in the Chancellorsville total

Salem Church, Virginia (VA033), Spotsylvania County, May 3–4, 1863

On May 3, while the Confederates triumphed at Chancellorsville, US General Sedgwick's force broke out of Fredericksburg and headed west toward CS General Lee's rear. CS Brigadier General Cadmus M. Wilcox's Brigade fought a successful delaying action at Salem Church while Lee sent reinforcements. The little brick country church was a fort for Wilcox's Alabama troops during the battle and a hospital afterward.

The next day the Confederates formed an immense V-shaped line around Sedgwick's men and drove them back to the river at Banks' Ford. The VI Corps escaped across two pontoon bridges at Scott's Dam after dark. On the night of May 5–6 Hooker also recrossed to the north bank of the Rappahannock and abandoned the campaign.

Faced with the loss of Stonewall Jackson, Lee reorganized the Army of Northern Virginia into three corps, each with three divisions. CS Lieutenant General Richard S. Ewell assumed command of Jackson's old Second Corps, and CS Lieutenant General Ambrose Powell Hill took over the newly formed Third Corps. CS Lieutenant General James Longstreet continued in command of the First Corps.

Estimated Casualties: included in the Chancellorsville total

Salem Church is in the Fredericksburg and Spotsylvania National Military Park.

Preserving Civil War Battlefields

John Heinz

○

History with its flickering lamp stumbles along the trail of the past, trying to reconstruct its scenes to revive its echoes, and kindle with pale gleams the passion of former days.

— Winston Churchill

It is often said that we learn the lessons of history so that we might not fall victim once more to the mistakes of the past. But it is more important to note that history often provides examples of virtue, discipline, courage, and honor to which we individually aspire. To study history is to understand humanity. Nonetheless, Winston Churchill was quite correct in describing the light that history sheds on the "passion of former days" as most often like a "flickering lamp."

The value of history is undisputed, but the value of historic preservation is perhaps less clear. Yet if history comes to us only through academic discourse, the light that shines on the past may indeed "flicker." Recognizing this, we can soon see the importance of historic preservation. Undisturbed pieces of the past provide the individual with an undisturbed historical perspective. To appreciate history, we must evoke our imaginations, and this is best achieved through direct contact with the things that remain from past days.

Civil War history illustrates my meaning. Fort Sumter, the Gettysburg address, Stonewall Jackson, and Robert E. Lee are standard chapters in American history classes, supplemented by Civil War photography. (My favorite is the famous picture of Abraham Lincoln, who seems to exude some tangible moral confidence, towering above his generals in conference outside an army tent.) But we have only to look at the faces of schoolchildren visiting the Gettysburg battlefield to understand how intensely the field commands their attention and imaginations.

The battlefield at Antietam offers another opportunity to honor the heroes of the Civil War. Richard Halloran wrote, "It should be said that walking the battlefield at Antietam is a somber experience. It takes but little imagination to hear the thunder of cannon and the rattle of musketry, to listen to the cries of mangled young men, to see the rows of dead and to recall the carnage of that day." There were nearly 23,000 casualties on September 17, 1862, at Antietam; more American men died there than in any one-day battle in World War II, Korea, or Vietnam. Preservation of this and other Civil War battlefields is an important part of the vital task of preserving the memory of sacrifices made to ensure the survival of this nation and of freedom and justice for all.

In this light, we must consider the practical question of responsibility for the preservation of Civil War battlefields. These are areas of national historic importance, and the duty for their preservation should and does fall primarily on the federal government. But the national effort cannot succeed without a comparable, if not greater, commitment of resources and effort by the private sector, by individual volunteers, and by state and local governments. Many states and localities are home to invaluable battlefield sites that are not likely to be incorporated into the National Park System. These governments can and should take steps to preserve these sites and to provide for their historic interpretation. Community and national organizations can help. This process has already begun as individuals organize to purchase and preserve historic property.

National efforts to protect and restore historic sites, particularly battlefields, have generated controversy and a renewed emphasis on policies that govern such sites. The efforts of private groups like The Conservation Fund are appropriate to ensure a tangible history for our own and future generations and to prevent the irreversible loss of our national heritage. The federal government cannot possibly acquire and manage every battlefield or every historical site. Given this truth, I laud the efforts of The Conservation Fund, and of all private individuals and groups involved in preservation. Without their continuing efforts, the goals of historic preservation cannot possibly succeed.

Gettysburg Campaign: June–July 1863

Brandy Station, Virginia (VA035), Culpeper County, June 9, 1863

Clark B. Hall

In the early morning of June 9, a large Union cavalry column under US Brigadier General John Buford positioned itself along the Rappahannock River for a peremptory rush across Beverly's Ford. Buford's horsemen, as well as a wing of equal strength headed by US Brigadier General David McMurtrie Gregg six miles below at Kelly's Ford, had arrived in Culpeper County, Virginia, looking for a fight. US Colonel Benjamin F. "Grimes" Davis's New York Cavalry led the Union column thundering across the ford, thus opening the battle of Brandy Station, the most hotly contested cavalry engagement of the Civil War. It was the largest single mounted battle ever fought on the American continent: of the 20,500 troops who were engaged, 17,000 were cavalrymen.

In early June US Major General Joseph Hooker was informed of a growing Confederate cavalry presence near the town of Culpeper. His scouts were partially correct. Most of the Confederate cavalry were in fact in Culpeper County, but they were at Brandy Station, not Culpeper. "Fighting Joe" Hooker did not know that two full corps of Confederate infantry, under CS Lieutenant Generals James Longstreet and Richard S. Ewell, were preparing for the march north that would lead them to Gettysburg. The Confederate cavalry was positioned to screen this infantry from discovery and to protect the army's flank as it proceeded north across the Blue Ridge. The Confederates included CS Brigadier Generals Wade Hampton, W. H. F. "Rooney" Lee, Beverly Robertson, and William E. "Grumble" Jones, CS Colonel Thomas T. Munford, CS Major Robert F. Beckham of the horse artillery, and 9,500 troopers, all commanded by the bold CS Major General J. E. B. Stuart.

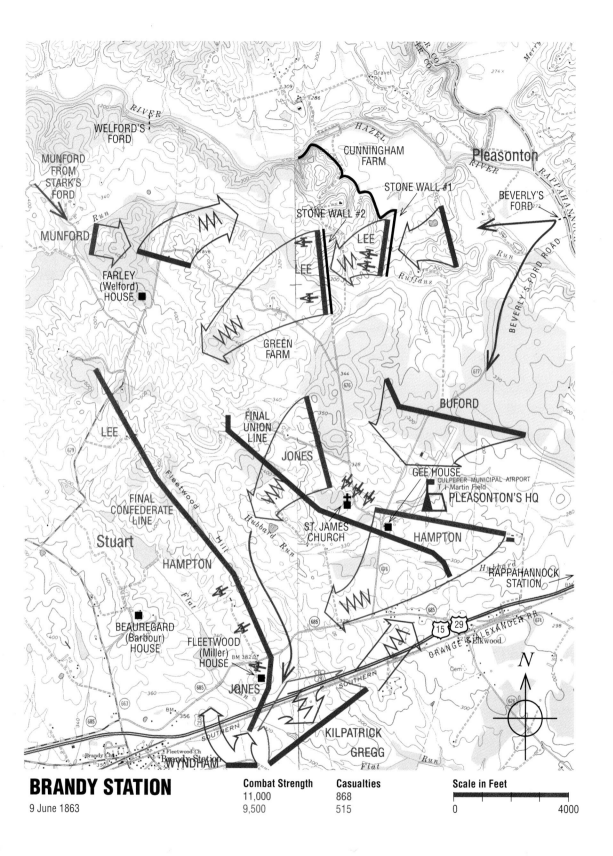

BRANDY STATION

9 June 1863

Combat Strength	Casualties
11,000	868
9,500	515

Scale in Feet

0   4000

Map labels:

WELFORD'S FORD

MUNFORD FROM STARK'S FORD

MUNFORD

FARLEY (Welford) HOUSE

CUNNINGHAM FARM

STONE WALL #1

STONE WALL #2

LEE

LEE

LEE

Pleasonton

BEVERLY'S FORD

BEVERLY'S FORD ROAD

RAPPAHANNOCK

HAZEL RIVER

GREEN FARM

BUFORD

FINAL UNION LINE

JONES

GEE HOUSE

CULPEPER MUNICIPAL AIRPORT
T. I. Martin Field

PLEASONTON'S HQ

FINAL CONFEDERATE LINE

Stuart

LEE

ST. JAMES CHURCH

HAMPTON

HAMPTON

BEAUREGARD (Barbour) HOUSE

FLEETWOOD (Miller) HOUSE

JONES

RAPPAHANNOCK STATION

ORANGE & ALEXANDER RR

Elkwood

SOUTHERN

KILPATRICK

GREGG

WYNDHAM

ORANGE & ALEXANDER RR

15 29

N

In addition to Davis, the Union cavalry commanders included US Colonels H. Judson Kilpatrick and Percy Wyndham, and US Captains Wesley Merritt, George Armstrong Custer, and Elon J. Farnsworth. Hooker ordered most of his cavalry and two brigades of infantry — about 11,000 men in all, commanded by US Brigadier General Alfred Pleasonton — to "disperse and destroy" the Confederates. When Buford stormed across Beverly's Ford, he was not expecting to find the enemy in immediate force. The Confederates were also taken by surprise: the cavalry was asleep. Buford's orders directed him to Brandy Station, four miles to the front, where he was to link up with Gregg, but his attack stalled when the gallant Davis fell to the dirt on Beverly's Ford Road, a saber in his hand and a bullet in his head, killed by CS Lieutenant Robert O. Allen of the 6th Virginia Cavalry.

Taking heavy losses but regrouping effectively, the Confederates quickly established a strong position anchored near a little brick church on a slight ridge above Beverly's Ford Road. Their horse artillery was centered at Saint James's Church. Hampton's Brigade was east of the cannons, Jones was to the west of the church, and Rooney Lee's Brigade faced east along a north-south ridge of the Yew Hills. Lee positioned artillery at Dr. Daniel Green's house and ordered dismounted troopers to a low stone wall several hundred yards beneath and east of the Green house plateau.

In hand-to-hand combat men fought for control of the thick woods across from the church. The 6th Pennsylvania Cavalry emerged in perfect order from the woods and pounded directly for the spewing cannons at the church, sabers drawn, guidons flying high in the morning sun. Several astonished Confederates later recorded this assault as the most "brilliant and glorious" cavalry charge of the war. In spite of such superlatives, many brave men of Pennsylvania never arose again from the broad plain beneath the church.

Continuing his attempts to turn the Confederate left, Buford shifted most of his Union cavalry to the Cunningham farm, where they stubbornly assaulted the stone wall below the Green house.

Having a clear terrain advantage, Rooney Lee's line continued to hold firm. Startling developments at the Confederate rear, however, created timely opportunities for Buford and potential disaster for the Confederate cavalry. As Buford's emphasis shifted to the Confederate left, Gregg arrived from Kelly's Ford with his 2,200-man division. They entered the village of Brandy Station from the south near Fleetwood Hill. Whoever controlled this elevation would dominate the battlefield.

Gregg's arrival caused Stuart hurriedly to abandon his Saint James line. He dispatched Jones's and Hampton's brigades to save the hill and his recent headquarters near the Fleetwood house. Rooney Lee's right was dangerously unsupported, so he pulled back through the Yew Hills toward yet higher ground on Fleetwood. Buford followed, fighting all the way against Lee's rear guard.

On the southern flanks of the two-and-a-half-mile-long Fleetwood Hill, opposing regiments collided. As a participant wrote, "Thousands of flashing sabers steamed in the sunlight; the rattle of carbines and pistols mingled with the roar of cannon; armed men wearing the blue and the gray became mixed in promiscuous confusion; the surging ranks swayed up and down the sides of Fleetwood Hill, and dense clouds of smoke and dust rose as a curtain to cover the tumultuous and bloody scene."

Stuart later wrote that "the contest for the hill was long and spirited." CS General Robert E. Lee observed part of the battle from the James Barbour house, now Beauregard, and praised the gallantry on both sides. After desperate charges by Hampton, the Confederates finally won Fleetwood Hill and the ground south of the railroad and east of Brandy Station — and saved their chief's headquarters. A division of 1,900 men under US Colonel Alfred Duffié sent via Stevensburg was delayed there by two Confederate regiments in a valiant stand. Duffié could have made a difference in the fight, but he arrived too late to be put into action.

Realizing an opportunity on his far left, Stuart ordered Rooney Lee to counterattack Buford's forces. In this charge, which Major Heros von Borcke later asserted "decided the fate of the day," Rooney Lee went down with a severe wound, but the Virginians and North Carolinians slammed into Buford, who then received orders to disengage and retrograde across Beverly's Ford.

The day-long battle of Brandy Station was over, resulting in 868 Union and 515 Confederate casualties. The Union cavalry had begun its rapid rise to power over the proud but dwindling Confederate cavalry.

Estimated Casualties: 868 US, 515 CS

Brandy Station battlefield, near Routes 29 and 15 at Brandy Station, is privately owned.

Second Winchester, Virginia (VA107), Frederick County and Winchester, June 13–15, 1863

After the battle of Brandy Station on June 9, CS General Robert E. Lee completed his plans to invade the North for the second time. He sent CS General Ewell's Second Corps across the Blue Ridge Mountains to clear the lower Shenandoah Valley of Union troops and open a supply line to the Valley before the army crossed into Maryland. Ewell's columns converged on US Major General Robert H. Milroy's 6,900-man garrison at Winchester. The divisions of CS Major General Edward "Allegheny" Johnson and CS Major General Jubal A. Early approached the town from the south, while CS Major General Robert Rodes's Division marched to Martinsburg by way of Berryville to hit the B & O Railroad.

The battle began on June 13, and the Louisiana Brigade captured the West Fort on the fourteenth. Milroy abandoned his entrenchments at 1:00 A.M. to escape a Confederate trap and attempted to retreat toward Charles Town. Johnson's night

flanking march cut off Milroy's retreat four miles north of Winchester at Stephenson's Depot. Almost 4,000 Federals surrendered after a desperate fight on June 15. Ewell's first victory as a corps commander demonstrated his tactical proficiency and also cleared the way for Lee's invasion of Pennsylvania.

Estimated Casualties: 4,443 US, 266 CS

Aldie, Virginia (VA036), Loudoun County, June 17, 1863

On June 17 US General Hooker dispatched his Army of the Potomac cavalry under US General Pleasonton to find CS General Lee. The Confederates had vanished after crossing the Blue Ridge into the Shenandoah Valley. Pleasonton headed toward Aldie, in a gap in the Bull Run Mountains, a ridgeline east of the Blue Ridge. Meanwhile CS General Stuart screened the army as it prepared to cross the Potomac. Stuart sent a brigade under CS Colonel Munford to Aldie to cover the gap. Farther south he positioned a brigade commanded by CS Colonel John R. Chambliss near Thoroughfare Gap, while he held a third brigade under CS General Robertson in reserve at Rectortown.

US Brigadier General H. Judson Kilpatrick's brigade of the Second Cavalry Division encountered Munford's troops near Aldie. Elements of the 1st, 2nd, 4th, and 5th Virginia Cavalry Regiments held off Kilpatrick while Munford brought up the remainder of his brigade. Munford held out under four hours of heavy Federal attacks before Stuart ordered him to retire westward to counter the Federal attack on Middleburg. This was the first of the cavalry engagements in which Pleasonton tried to pierce the Confederate cavalry screen to find Lee's infantry.

Middleburg, Virginia (VA037), Loudoun and Fauquier Counties, June 17–19, 1863

While CS Colonel Munford battled US General Kilpatrick at Aldie, US Colonel Duffié's 1st Rhode

Island Cavalry Regiment slipped past CS Colonel Chambliss's Brigade and through Thoroughfare Gap in the early hours of June 17. Duffié's mission was to reconnoiter the Blue Ridge Mountains, a bold and dangerous operation deep into enemy-held territory.

Duffié skirmished with the 9th Virginia Cavalry just west of the gap and arrived at Middleburg, CS General Stuart's headquarters, at 4:00 P.M. Stuart had no information about the strength of the Federal force, so he evacuated the town and ordered CS General Robertson's Brigade to contest the threat. That evening Robertson attacked and drove Duffié's cavalry out of Middleburg. The next morning Chambliss's Brigade cut off the Federal escape route. The 1st Rhode Island scattered, and the Confederates took about 200 prisoners. Duffié escaped into the woods and reformed the rest of his regiment at Centreville.

On June 19 US General Gregg's division attacked Stuart's two brigades commanded by Robertson and Chambliss, along Mount Defiance west of Middleburg. Fighting both on foot and on horseback along a line that stretched for more than a mile, Gregg slowly pushed Stuart back beyond Kirk's Branch stream. At the same time US General Buford tried to flank Stuart's line with his division. This led to fighting at Pot House as well as a skirmish south of Millville in the early evening.

Upperville, Virginia (VA038), Loudoun and Fauquier Counties, June 21, 1863

The Federal cavalry made a determined effort to pierce CS General Stuart's cavalry screen along the Blue Ridge on June 21. US General Buford's division rode north from Middleburg and turned west to flank Stuart's position. US General Gregg's division rode west along the Little River Turnpike with one infantry brigade from the V Corps in support. When Gregg encountered the brigades of CS Generals Hampton and Robertson, they fell back behind Goose Creek, but two other brigades blocked Buford's advance. Stuart began to pull his four brigades back to Upperville. Be-

fore the Confederates could disengage, Gregg pressed on along the turnpike and in desperate fighting pushed Stuart's troopers 4.5 miles beyond Upperville. CS General Longstreet sent infantry and artillery across the Shenandoah River to hold Ashby's Gap and support the cavalry.

Estimated Casualties: for Aldie, Middleburg, and Upperville, 827 US, 510 CS

Hanover, Pennsylvania (PA001), York County, June 30, 1863

CS General Lee ordered CS General Stuart to cross the Potomac River east of the infantry's crossing, delay the Federals, and take a position on CS General Ewell's right, guard it, and stay in contact with him in Pennsylvania. Although Stuart's orders were discretionary, his cavalry was to cover the right flank of the Army of Northern Virginia and stay between Lee and US General Hooker. Stuart rode to the east on June 25 with three brigades. After encountering US Major General Winfield Scott Hancock's II Corps, he decided to ride around the Union army and cross the Potomac at Rowser's Ford near Dranesville. This violated Lee's intent since Stuart could no longer stay in communication with Lee. Stuart crossed the Potomac on the night of June 27–28 and captured a large supply train at Rockville, Maryland, which slowed his progress to Hanover.

On June 30 Stuart attacked the 18th Pennsylvania Cavalry and drove it through the streets of Hanover. US Brigadier General Elon J. Farnsworth's brigade of US General Kilpatrick's division countermarched and counterattacked, routing the 2nd North Carolina Cavalry and nearly capturing Stuart. Reinforced by US Brigadier General George A. Custer's brigade, Farnsworth held his ground, resulting in a stalemate. Stuart continued north and east, slipped around the Union cavalry, and shelled Carlisle Barracks. This further delayed him in rejoining Lee's army, which was concentrating at Cashtown Gap west of Gettysburg. Stuart's ride denied Lee his eyes as the Army of Northern Virginia invaded the North.

At the same time U.S. intelligence operations provided critical information about the Confederate forces converging on Gettysburg.

Estimated Casualties: 154 US, 74 CS

Gettysburg, Pennsylvania (PA002), Adams County, July 1–3, 1863

Harry W. Pfanz

The battle of Gettysburg was the great three-day battle of the Civil War and a crucial event in American history. It involved approximately 170,000 soldiers of the U.S. Army of the Potomac and the C.S. Army of Northern Virginia, and there were about 51,000 casualties. The following November 19, President Abraham Lincoln delivered his Gettysburg address at the dedication of the cemetery for Union dead.

In 1863 Gettysburg had a population of about 2,400 and was the meeting place of ten roads leading to towns in Maryland and Pennsylvania. It was surrounded by gently rolling terrain dominated by low north-south ridges and scattered hills, and was set amid farms with grain fields, orchards, and woodlots that concealed outcroppings of dark granite boulders.

The battle was the culmination of CS General Robert E. Lee's Pennsylvania campaign. Lee led his army north to ease the burden of war in Virginia, to disrupt the Union's 1863 operations, and, if a major battle were fought, to win a victory that, unlike his victories in Virginia, would be decisive. The march began on June 3, and CS Lieutenant General Richard S. Ewell's 22,000 troops were in the lead. By the end of June, Lee's 75,000-man army was in Pennsylvania, spread from Chambersburg to Carlisle and York. As Lee marched north, the Army of the Potomac also moved, staying between the Confederates and Washington. Lee was unaware that CS Major General James E. B. Stuart and his three cavalry brigades, who were to screen Lee's march and provide him with information on the enemy's movements, were separated from him by the Federals and could not contact him.

Not until June 28 did Lee learn from a spy that the 95,000 Federals, led by their new commander, US Major General George Gordon Meade, had crossed the Potomac and were moving north from Frederick, Maryland. Since Meade could soon strike his scattered forces, Lee ordered his army to concentrate east of South Mountain in the Gettysburg-Cashtown area to give battle.

On July 1, as most of the Confederate army marched east through Cashtown Pass, CS Lieutenant General Ambrose Powell Hill sent two 7,000-man divisions, those of CS Major Generals Henry Heth and William D. Pender, toward Gettysburg to investigate the Union forces reported there. At midmorning they met Union cavalry pickets west of the town. The 2,900 men in two brigades of Heth's Division deployed on Herr Ridge and advanced, driving the cavalry and striking the arriving US I Corps infantry on McPherson Ridge. In the sharp fight that followed, the Federals repulsed the Confederate attack, but the Union commander on the field, US Major General John F. Reynolds, was killed. Reinforcements for both sides arrived during a lull that lasted into the afternoon. By then the divisions of Heth and Pender faced the 12,000-man I Corps west of the town, while two divisions of Ewell's Corps approached from the north to confront the 5,500 men in two divisions of the arriving XI Corps forming north of the town.

The afternoon's fighting began when CS Major General Robert Rodes's Division advanced from Oak Hill, and Hill's troops again struck the I Corps troops on McPherson Ridge. CS Major General Jubal A. Early's Division arrived along the Harrisburg Road and smashed the XI Corps's right. Lee's men assaulted the outnumbered Union troops in front and on the flanks, and in hard fighting drove them through the town to Cemetery Hill. Lee reported that the Confederates had captured more than 5,000 Union soldiers in the July 1 battle. The remaining ones rallied at about 4:30 P.M. on the hill, where US Major General Oliver O. Howard, commander of the XI Corps, had posted his reserve. US Major General Winfield Scott Hancock of the II Corps, who had replaced Howard as commander of the Federal

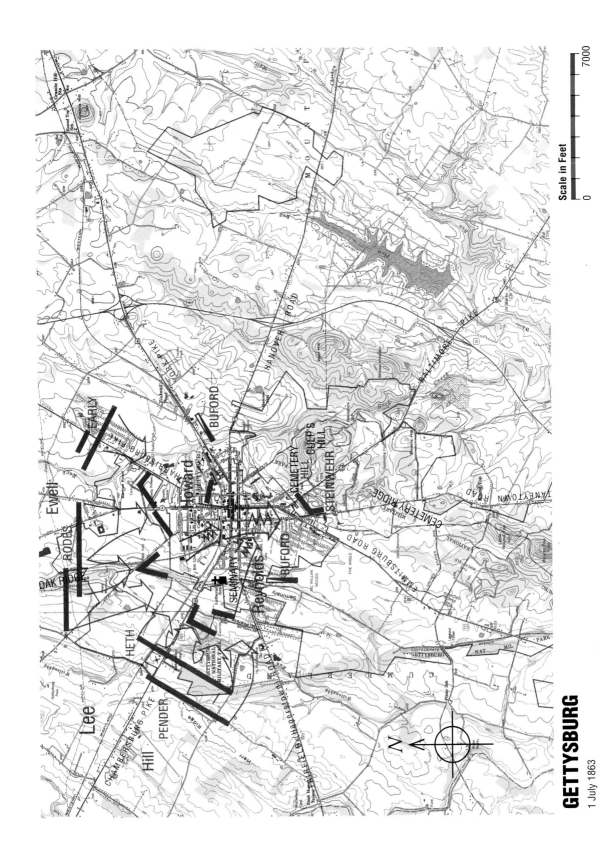

GETTYSBURG

1 July 1863

Scale in Feet

0   7000

N

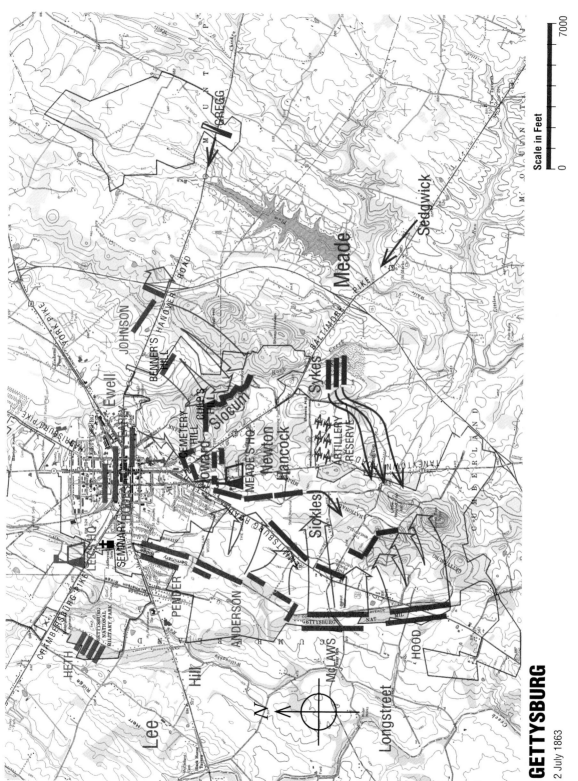

GETTYSBURG

2 July 1863

Scale in Feet

0 ⊢ 7000

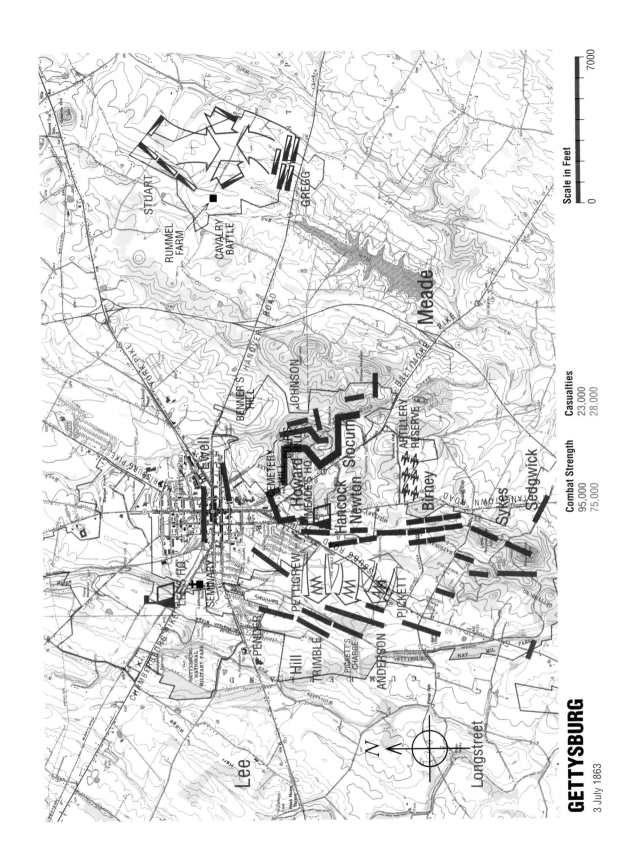

GETTYSBURG

3 July 1863

Combat Strength	Casualties
95,000	23,000
75,000	28,000

Scale in Feet

0   7000

STUART

RUMMEL FARM

CAVALRY BATTLE

GREGG

Meade

JOHNSON

BENNER'S HILL

EWELL

CEMETERY HILL

Howard HDQS.

MEADE'S HQ.

Hancock

Newton

Slocum

ARTILLERY RESERVE

Birney

Sykes

Sedgwick

Lee

Hill

SEMINARY

PENDER

TRIMBLE

PETTIGREW

PICKETT'S CHARGE

ANDERSON

PICKETT

Longstreet

N

YORK PIKE

CHAMBERSBURG PIKE

HARRISBURG PIKE

HANOVER ROAD

BALTIMORE PIKE

TANEYTOWN ROAD

forces as they rallied on Cemetery Hill, sent a brigade of I Corps troops to occupy a portion of Culp's Hill to the east. Since the Confederates were exhausted, and Lee, Ewell, and Hill had no information on Federal troop strength, they did not order attacks against this Union position. The day's fighting ended.

During the night and the morning of July 2, both armies reached the Gettysburg area and prepared for battle. Meade established a hook-shaped line that embraced Culp's Hill on its right and Cemetery Hill, and extended south along Cemetery Ridge two miles to two hills, the Round Tops. Lee's positions faced Meade's line, extending along the Hanover Road east of Gettysburg, into the town, and south on Seminary Ridge about a mile west of Cemetery Ridge. At noon US Major General Daniel E. Sickles, commander of the III Corps, made a dangerous move: he advanced the two divisions of his corps from their assigned position to high ground along the Emmitsburg Road between the ridges. His line ran back from the Peach Orchard to the Wheatfield and to Devil's Den, a massive boulder outcrop five hundred yards in front of the Round Tops.

During a day of misunderstandings and delays, CS Lieutenant General James Longstreet, commander of Lee's First Corps, extended the Confederate line south along Seminary Ridge beyond Sickles's salient. At 4:30 P.M. he launched Lee's attack with the divisions of CS Major Generals John Bell Hood and Lafayette McLaws against Sickles's salient. CS Major General Richard H. Anderson's Division of Hill's Corps attacked the Federals along the Emmitsburg Road north of the Peach Orchard and their center on Cemetery Ridge. Meade sent the V Corps and portions of the I, II, VI, and XII Corps to bolster Sickles's line and the Union center. There were attacks and counterattacks at Little Round Top, at Devil's Den, the Wheatfield, and along the road and ridge. Despite the efforts of Meade, Sickles (who lost a leg), Hancock, US Major General George Sykes, and others, the Confederates smashed the salient, and troops of Anderson's Division reached the ridge's crest at the Union center. By day's end Meade had repulsed the Confederate attack and re-established his position firmly on Cemetery Ridge. Both armies suffered heavy losses in the day's fight.

Lee ordered Ewell to create a diversion against the Union right on Culp's Hill and Cemetery Hill at the time of Longstreet's assault, and to convert his feint, if possible, into a "real attack." Ewell's artillery fire against the Union forces on Cemetery Hill was squelched by Federal batteries. At sunset, as Longstreet's attack was dying, CS Major General Edward Johnson's Division attacked Culp's Hill, the lower crest of which had been vacated by the XII Corps troops summoned to reinforce their comrades on Cemetery Ridge. At the same time, two brigades of Early's Division assaulted East Cemetery Hill. The Federals repulsed Early's attack, but Johnson's troops occupied the vacated lower crest of Culp's Hill and established a precarious hold on the main hill's east slope. The firing on Culp's Hill stopped before midnight. The portion of the XII Corps sent to Cemetery Ridge returned and sealed off the penetration on the lower crest. By dawn reinforcements sent by Ewell nearly doubled the size of the Confederate force.

On the night of July 2, Meade met with his corps commanders and determined to "stay and fight it out" but remain on the defensive. Lee's initial plan for July 3 was to order Longstreet and Ewell to attack the Federal left and right at daybreak. However, that morning Longstreet convinced Lee that an attack against the Union left was not feasible. Lee directed that it be made instead against the Union center. It took several hours to prepare this new attack, so it was delayed from daybreak until the afternoon.

Ewell, unaware of the delay, renewed his attack against the XII Corps on Culp's Hill at daybreak and fought alone for about six hours. Most of the Federals there fired from behind breastworks. They repelled three assaults against their position and drove the Confederates from the lower crest of Culp's Hill. By noon the battle for Culp's Hill was over. In the meantime Meade's troops on Cemetery Hill and Cemetery Ridge remained in their positions and awaited Lee's next attack.

Stuart and his three cavalry brigades (fewer than 6,000 troopers) had reached the Gettysburg area on the afternoon of July 2. The next morning, at Lee's order, they rode east beyond Ewell's position to cover the Confederate left. That afternoon Stuart attempted to move his fatigued force toward the Union rear. About three miles east of Gettysburg, near the Hanover Road, he met US Brigadier General David Gregg's smaller cavalry force guarding the Federal right. One of the largest cavalry battles of the Civil War opened, with dismounted skirmishing followed by slam-bang mounted charges across the Rummel farm. The Union forces held, and Stuart's efforts came to naught.

In the meantime Lee and Longstreet prepared the major assault against the Union center on Cemetery Ridge. Longstreet had 12,000 men in eleven brigades, including three fresh ones from CS Major General George E. Pickett's Division and eight bloodied ones from Hill's corps, led that day by CS Major General Isaac Trimble and CS Brigadier Generals J. Johnston Pettigrew and Cadmus M. Wilcox.

At 1:00 P.M. the Confederate artillery opened fire with approximately 180 guns, including those of Ewell's corps. The Union guns replied, shrouding the field in smoke. After two hours the artillery fire ceased. Lee's assault began with all the brigades except Wilcox's advancing in two lines on the right and three on the left across open fields toward the Union center on Cemetery Ridge. Union shot and shell began to decimate their formations. Canister and rifle fire riddled the gray ranks after they crossed the Emmitsburg Road, but they closed, and the lines pressed on. Union troops to the right and left swung forward to fire into the assault column's flanks, boxing it in with fire. A huge mass of men reached the Union line, and a few pushed into the Union position, but by this time formations, firepower, and momentum had been lost. Wilcox's two brigades advanced unsuccessfully to support the attackers' right. The Union center, commanded by Hancock, held and gave a bloody repulse to "Pickett's Charge." No one knows how many

casualties resulted from Pickett's Charge. The Confederates lost an estimated 5,600 men and the Federals more than 1,500. Losses in the three-day battle were about 23,000 Federals and 28,000 Confederates.

Lee's try for a decisive victory in Pennsylvania had failed. There were two years of war ahead, but Meade's army had won a decisive victory. After Gettysburg, Lee was never again able to launch a major offensive. His road from Gettysburg was long, bloody, and hard and ultimately led to Appomattox Court House and surrender.

Estimated Casualties: 23,000 US, 28,000 CS

Gettysburg National Military Park, near Route 15 at Gettysburg, includes 5,907 acres of the historic battlefield, 1,854 of which are privately owned.

Williamsport, Maryland (MD004), Washington County, July 6, 1863

After the battle of Gettysburg, the Army of Northern Virginia retreated toward Williamsport on the Potomac River, with the ambulance and supply trains on routes different from that of the infantry. Federal cavalrymen crossed South Mountain to Boonsboro so they were between Lee's army and his supply trains.

A Confederate force that included CS Brigadier General John D. Imboden's Brigade fought off US General Buford's attempt to hit the wagon trains at Williamsport. Meanwhile US General Kilpatrick's troopers pushed CS Colonel Chambliss's cavalry brigade through Hagerstown until they had to retreat when CS Brigadier General Alfred M. Iverson's infantry and CS General Jones's cavalry reinforced Chambliss. Kilpatrick sent two brigades to reinforce Buford and retained one south of Williamsport until CS Brigadier General

Fitzhugh Lee's Brigade arrived and attacked. The Federals disengaged and rode for Boonsboro.

Estimated Casualties: 400 US, 254 CS

Boonsboro–Funkstown–Falling Waters, Maryland (MD006), Washington County, July 8–14, 1863

The fighting continued between Boonsboro and Funkstown and along Beaver Creek while CS General Stuart's cavalry screened the Confederates entrenching along a high ridge nine miles long between Hagerstown and Downsville. They needed a strong defensive position to protect them while they built a makeshift pontoon bridge to replace the one at Falling Waters, three miles downstream from Williamsport, which the Federal cavalry had destroyed on July 4. By the time US General Meade advanced on the Confederate defenses, they were too strong to attack. On the night of July 13 the Potomac River was low enough for CS General Ewell's corps to cross at the Williamsport ford while the corps of CS Generals Longstreet and A. P. Hill crossed with the army's trains on the pontoon bridge. Stuart's cavalry occupied the evacuated Confederate works and covered the retreat before crossing at the ford. CS General Heth's Division protected the bridge at Falling Waters during the crossing. A detachment of the 26th North Carolina was the last to cross the river. Troopers from US General Kilpatrick's division attacked the Confederate rear guard at Falling Waters on July 14 and took more than 700 prisoners.

Estimated Casualties: 158 US, 920 CS

Areas of the Potomac River crossings are protected in the Chesapeake & Ohio Canal National Historical Park.

He [the enemy] was within your easy grasp, and to have closed upon him would, in connection with our other late successes, have ended the war.

— President Abraham Lincoln

This quotation is so well known and controversial that it requires elaboration. It is from a letter President Abraham Lincoln wrote but did not send to US Major General George Gordon Meade after the battle of Gettysburg, and it reveals the president's agitation. Historians disagree on the accuracy of Lincoln's conclusion. Some concur with Lincoln's assessment of Meade as a timid general. Some concur with US General Winfield Scott Hancock and CS General E. Porter Alexander that Meade failed to take advantage of his best opportunity to destroy the Army of Northern Virginia: in a determined counterattack after repulsing the Confederates at Cemetery Ridge on the afternoon of July 3. Some hold that Meade would have risked defeat if he had attacked Lee at the time Lincoln seems to suggest: in one of Lee's positions during his retreat to Virginia.

Manassas Gap, Virginia (VA108), Warren and Fauquier Counties, July 23, 1863

After the Confederates crossed the river, US General Gregg's cavalry approached Shepherdstown on July 16, where the brigades of CS General Fitzhugh Lee and CS Colonel Chambliss held the fords against the Federal infantry. The Confederates attacked Gregg, but he held his position until nightfall before withdrawing. US General Meade's infantry advanced along the east side of the Blue Ridge, trying to get between the retreating Confederates and Richmond.

On July 23 US Major General William H. French's III Corps attacked CS General Anderson's Division at Manassas Gap, forcing it back to high ground near the crest of the Blue Ridge. That afternoon a second Federal attack drove Anderson back again to a position where he was reinforced by artillery and by CS General Rodes's Division. By dusk the Federals abandoned their poorly coordinated attacks, and the Confederate forces withdrew into the Luray Valley. The Army of the Potomac occupied Front Royal on July 24, but Lee's army was safely beyond pursuit. Lee's army survived, but the defeat at Gettysburg and the surrenders of Vicksburg and Port Hudson ended all hope for European recognition of the Confederacy.

Estimated Casualties: 440 total

It is now conceded that all idea of [European] intervention is at an end.

— Henry Adams

It seems incredible that human power could effect such a change in so brief a space. Yesterday we rode on the pinnacle of success — today absolute ruin seems to be our portion. The Confederacy totters to its destruction.

— Josiah Gorgas, chief of ordnance for the Confederacy

The Gettysburg Address

November 19, 1863

Abraham Lincoln

●

Fourscore and seven years ago our fathers brought forth on this continent, a new nation, conceived in Liberty, and dedicated to the proposition that all men are created equal.

Now we are engaged in a great civil war, testing whether that nation or any nation so conceived and so dedicated, can long endure. We are met on a great battle-field of that war. We have come to dedicate a portion of that field, as a final resting place for those who here gave their lives that that nation might live. It is altogether fitting and proper that we should do this.

But, in a larger sense, we cannot dedicate — we cannot consecrate — we cannot hallow — this ground. The brave men, living and dead, who struggled here, have consecrated it, far above our poor power to add or detract. The world will little note, nor long remember what we say here, but it can never forget what they did here. It is for us, the living, rather, to be dedicated here to the unfinished work which they who fought here have thus far so nobly advanced. It is rather for us to be here dedicated to the great task remaining before us — that from these honored dead we take increased devotion to that cause for which they gave the last full measure of devotion — that we here highly resolve that these dead shall not have died in vain — that this nation, under God, shall have a new birth of freedom — and that government of the people, by the people, for the people, shall not perish from the earth.

Morgan's Indiana and Ohio Raid: July 1863

Corydon, Indiana (IN001), Harrison County, July 9, 1863

CS Brigadier General John Hunt Morgan had repeatedly raided into Kentucky, inflicting damage to Federal communications and to the Louisville & Nashville Railroad, which supplied US Major General William S. Rosecrans's Army of the Cumberland. In July 1863 he launched his most daring raid: across the Ohio River and into the North to upset the offensive timetable of two Union armies. Rosecrans's army was advancing on Chattanooga, and the Army of the Ohio under US Major General Ambrose E. Burnside was assembling at Cincinnati to march into East Tennessee.

Morgan crossed the Cumberland River at Burkesville, Kentucky, on July 2 with 2,500 cavalrymen, slipping around the 7,000-man cavalry division of US Brigadier General Henry M. Judah. They advanced to the Green River where a Federal regiment repelled them on July 4 at Tebbs Bend. Morgan rode north to Lebanon, Kentucky, burned it after his brother Tom was killed, and headed west. Against CS General Braxton Bragg's orders, Morgan ferried his command across the Ohio River on two captured steamboats and into Indiana from Brandenburg, downriver from Louisville, Kentucky. His bold move was briefly successful. State officials called out militiamen in Indiana and Ohio and organized their defenses.

On July 9, elements of Morgan's force led by his brother, Richard, rode north from Mauckport, Indiana. One mile south of Corydon, they battled 450 militiamen under Colonel Lewis Jordan and captured most of them. Morgan paroled the prisoners, raided stores, and collected ransom money from propertyowners. The Confederates continued north and east to Ohio, destroying bridges, railroads, and government stores. Burnside organized Federal columns to prevent Morgan's recrossing into Kentucky.

Estimated Casualties: 360 US, 51 CS

Battle of Corydon Memorial Park, south of Corydon on Route 135, is a Harrison County park and includes five acres of the historic battlefield.

Buffington Island, Ohio (OH001), Meigs County, July 19, 1863

On July 13–14, CS General Morgan's raiders passed north of Cincinnati, and as they rode east they found little support for their raid. They had to keep moving to prevent capture, and their horses frequently gave out. Their numbers dwindled as Union columns picked up the stragglers. On July 18 the exhausted cavalrymen reached Portland, a ford across the Ohio River at Buffington Island into West Virginia. Union infantrymen held the ford, so Morgan rested his men for a morning attack.

Two Federal cavalry columns that had been following Morgan caught up with him: that of US Brigadier General Edward H. Hobson on horseback, and that of US General Judah by steamboat. When the Confederates tried to ford the river on July 19, the guns of the USS *Moose* blocked the crossing. Hobson and Judah attacked from the west, but Morgan and 400 men escaped to the north through a ravine. The rest of the force surrendered, and their entire train was captured.

Estimated Casualties: 25 US, 900 CS

Salineville, Ohio (OH002), Columbiana County, July 26, 1863

After his narrow escape at Buffington Island, CS General Morgan continued north to find a safe crossing of the Ohio River. Pursued by US General Burnside's cavalry, Morgan rode through Salineville and down the railroad toward Smith's Ford. When the Union forces cut Morgan off at the New Lisbon Road on July 26, he surrendered. During this campaign Morgan and his men covered seven hundred miles in twenty-five days, one of the longest cavalry raids of the war. They captured and paroled thousands of soldiers and militiamen, destroyed bridges, disrupted railroads, and diverted militiamen and regular army troops from other duties.

While the damage to the overall Union war effort was minimal, Morgan had tied up Burnside's cavalry and prevented him from moving on Knoxville. In defeating Morgan the Union cavalry relieved pressure on the supply lines of the Federals operating in Tennessee. The following November Morgan escaped from prison and continued leading smaller raids until he was killed at Greeneville, Tennessee, in September 1864.

Estimated Casualties: 0 US, 364 CS

Arkansas, Idaho, and Oklahoma: January–September 1863; February 1864

Bear River, Idaho (ID001), Franklin County, January 29, 1863

Bear River was the first and the worst of the massacres of American Indians in the West. For fifteen years the Northwestern Shoshoni had been dispossessed of their traditional lands by the Church of Jesus Christ of Latter Day Saints pioneers, whose cattle herds were destroying the grass seeds that were their primary food. As the white hunters increased, the wild game decreased, taking another Shoshoni source of food. Without their lands the Shoshoni were starving, so they raided the farms on the lands that had been theirs. The policy of Brigham Young, the Church's leader, was that the settlers would provide food to the Shoshoni in exchange for the return of much of what they had taken.

The peace bought with food for the Shoshoni was an uneasy one. While the Shoshoni avoided the settlers' homesteads, the emigrants on trails and on the Overland Stage, with their supplies of food, were targets of their attacks. In one of their 1860 raids the Shoshoni along the Oregon Trail killed members of an emigrant family and captured three young children. In the search for the children, one man concluded that a young white boy in Bear Hunter's band of Shoshoni was his nephew. The Shoshoni said the boy was the son of a tribal woman and a French trapper. The uncle petitioned US Colonel Patrick Edward Connor to retrieve the boy. During the negotiations the soldiers killed four Shoshoni men. When a gold miner was killed by the Shoshoni on the Montana Trail, supposedly in retribution, a Salt Lake City judge issued a warrant for Bear Hunter's arrest.

The primary mission of Connor and his California Volunteers was to guard the overland mail, the vital connection between the East and the

West. Their orders permitted them to "hang on the spot" any Indians accused of hindering the mail. Connor used the warrant as his mandate to kill Shoshoni and discredit the Church of Jesus Christ of Latter Day Saints's policy of providing food for them.

Connor launched a surprise attack on the Shoshoni on January 21 by sending 69 men of the 3rd California Infantry with two 6-pounder mountain howitzers toward Bear River. Three days later he and US Major Edward McGarry left Fort Douglas near Salt Lake City with about 220 men of the 2nd California Cavalry. Traveling at night to avoid detection, they headed northward, suffering in the intense cold and snowstorms. The two columns united on January 27.

The Shoshoni were in a favorite winter camp, located near hot springs and protected from winter winds by willow trees. Their seventy-five lodges were along Beaver Creek (now known as Battle Creek) where the protected ravine widened. Their horse herd was farther south in the meadow. Bluffs that almost circled the ravine provided defense.

On January 29 McGarry crossed the Bear River with the cavalry and attacked. Bear Hunter's warriors easily repulsed the initial frontal attack. Connor then ferried his infantry across the river on cavalry horses and surrounded the camp. When the Californians broke through a ravine on the Shoshoni's left, the battle became a massacre and then a slaughter. There were no wounded on the field because the soldiers had bludgeoned them to death.

While there were about 200 men engaged on each side, the Shoshoni included old men. As a result of the four-hour fight in the bitter cold, there were 42 wounded and 23 killed in Connor's force. Connor reported a month later that 112 men were still incapacitated from frostbite and injuries. About 20 Shoshoni men escaped, but Bear Hunter was killed and his body mutilated by the soldiers. Connor left the surviving women and children with a small supply of grain, destroyed the rest of their provisions, and burned their tipi poles to warm his troops.

The massacre enraged the surviving Indians in the area, and for six months raids — that avoided Connor — continued, until Superintendent of Indian Affairs in Utah James J. Doty was successful in engaging them in talks and then treaties later in the year.

Connor was promoted two months later and became an adviser to US Colonel John Chivington, the commander in the massacre at Sand Creek in November 1864.

Estimated Casualties: 65 US, 250 Shoshoni

Cabin Creek, Oklahoma (OK006), Mayes County, July 1–2, 1863

US Major General James G. Blunt resumed preparations for his long-delayed Indian Expedition, which would return dislocated Unionist Indians to their homeland in Indian Territory. He ordered US Colonel William A. Phillips's 3,000-man Indian Brigade to escort about 1,000 Creek, Cherokee, and Seminole families back to what might be left of their homes. The Indians' own civil war had resulted in mass destruction of the formerly prosperous area. The Creeks and Seminoles had to stay with Phillips at Fort Gibson since their lands were still controlled by the pro-Confederate Indians.

US Colonel James M. Williams of the 1st Kansas Colored Infantry led a Federal supply train of three hundred wagons southward from Fort Scott, Kansas, to reinforce Fort Gibson. CS Colonel Stand Watie, commanding 2,000 pro-Confederate Cherokees and a force of Texans, tried to intercept the column at Cabin Creek, the fortified ford south of Baxter Springs, but he was outnumbered. He waited for CS Brigadier General William L. Cabell's 1,500 reinforcements from Arkansas, but they were unable to cross the flooded Grand River to reinforce him. In two days of intense fighting, the Federals drove off the Confederates with artillery fire and two cavalry charges. The wagon train continued to Fort Gibson at the junction of the Arkansas and Grand Rivers, where Williams delivered supplies that enabled Union forces to maintain their presence in Indian Territory.

At Cabin Creek in September 1864, Watie, in support of CS Major General Sterling Price's Missouri Expedition, captured 130 wagons bound from Fort Scott for Fort Gibson, carrying about $1.5 million in goods destined for 16,000 Unionist Indians.

Estimated Casualties: 21 US, 59 CS

Cabin Creek Historic Site, fifteen miles southeast of Vinita off Route 28, includes twelve acres of the historic battlefield.

Honey Springs, Oklahoma (OK007), Muskogee and McIntosh Counties, July 17, 1863

Bob L. Blackburn and LeRoy H. Fischer

By July 1863 Confederate and Union commanders in the trans-Mississippi West knew that the struggle for Indian Territory was rapidly approaching a climax. Both sides thought it was a contest they could win.

The objective of CS Brigadier General Douglas H. Cooper and his 5,700 troops at Honey Springs was to drive US Major General James G. Blunt and his 3,000 men out of Fort Gibson and regain control of that crossroads outpost. When Blunt learned that CS Brigadier General William L. Cabell and 3,000 men were marching west out of Arkansas to join Cooper at Honey Springs, a small Creek community located twenty-four miles south of Fort Gibson, he knew that he had to strike south and attack Cooper's Indian and Texas troops before Cabell reached them.

On July 15 and 16 the Federals drove off the Confederate pickets from the Arkansas River and started south. Blunt's troops were from Wisconsin, Colorado, Kansas, and the Indian Territory and included three regiments of Indian Home Guards and the 1st Kansas Colored Regiment, an

all-black unit. His force was strengthened by twelve pieces of artillery.

While Blunt's army made the twenty-four-mile forced march, Cooper deployed his troops north of Honey Springs on either side of the Texas Road, with the steep banks of Elk Creek at his back. He positioned the Texans with their artillery in the center protecting the only bridge across the creek. The Indian troops were placed on the flanks to protect the fords. Despite their numerical superiority, Cooper's poorly equipped troops had only four guns, inferior small arms, and defective powder.

Blunt's men marched all night, had a brief rest, then formed into a line of battle at about 10:00 A.M. on July 17. Their line extended about five hundred yards on either side of the Texas Road, with less than five hundred yards separating them from the Confederate breastworks in the timber. Artillery fire knocked out one gun on each side while the infantry exchanged steady fire. Blunt, thinking he saw an opportunity at one point, ordered the 1st Kansas Colored to fix bayonets and charge an artillery position. The Confederate line stood firm. Despite losing their colonel, the black troops maintained enough discipline to continue small arms fire against the Texans.

After two hours of smoke-obscured action, the 2nd Indian Home Guards (Creek, Seminole, Osage, Delaware, and Quapaw) fighting for the Union strayed into the no man's land between the opposing lines. When a Union officer yelled for them to get back, the always aggressive Texans thought they heard a Federal command to retreat. With a Rebel yell they jumped from their breastworks and charged the center of the Union line. Instead of finding a retreating enemy, however, they ran directly into the massed fire of the 1st Kansas Colored Regiment. At twenty-five yards the Confederate colors went down, but a Texan picked them up and led his men on. The black troops held firm once again and leveled a volley at point-blank range. When the colors fell again, the Confederate charge wavered, and the line began to crumble.

Cooper decided his only hope was a controlled

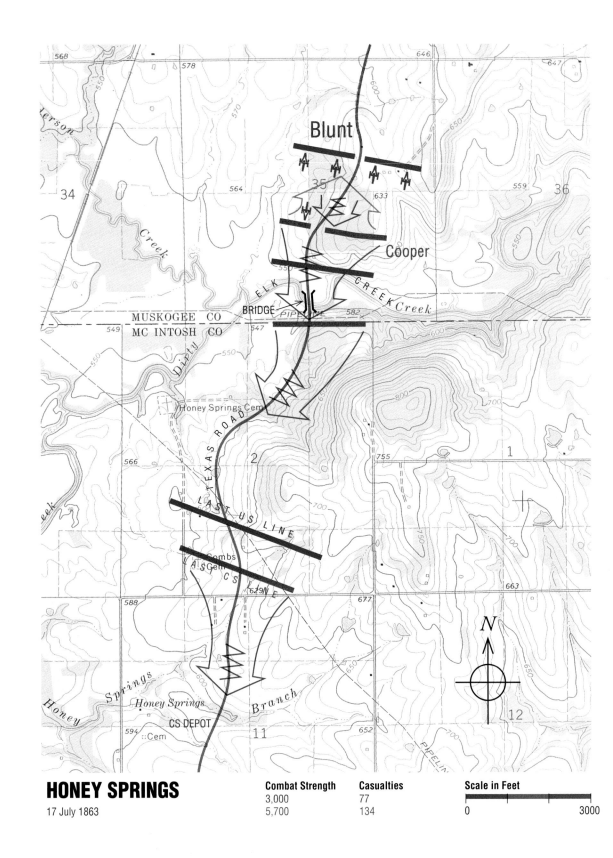

Blunt

Cooper

34

35

36

568
578
646
647
564
559
633

Creek

ELK

CREEK Creek

MUSKOGEE CO
BRIDGE
PIPE
582
MC INTOSH CO
549
547
550

Dirty

Honey Springs Cem.

T E X A S   R O A D

566

2

755

800
700

L A S T   U S   L I N E

700
750
700

Combs
Cem.
CS

L A S T   C S   L I N E
629
N E

663

588
677

N

12

Honey
Springs
Honey Springs

Branch

CS DEPOT

594
Cem.
11
652
700

PIPELINE

HONEY SPRINGS

17 July 1863

Combat Strength	Casualties
3,000	77
5,700	134

Scale in Feet

0   3000

retreat that would save his remaining forces and artillery. He could then join forces with Cabell, who was approaching from the east. Some of the bloodiest fighting of the day soon followed as Cooper's men guarded the bridge from the south bank while the artillery was limbered and hauled across. Union troops, firing from timber on the raised bank to the north, had the clear advantage but could not overwhelm the retreating Confederates.

Fighting continued as the two armies moved the mile and a half south to the Honey Springs depot. Cooper's reserve units stopped the Union advance momentarily, but Blunt's superior firepower soon broke the last line of defense. With his main forces dashing east to meet Cabell, Cooper set fire to the remaining stores and fled. Blunt's men, exhausted by the long fight and the forced march the night before, could not pursue. The Union forces went into camp and returned to Fort Gibson the next day.

Although the number of men engaged — about 9,000 — and the casualties — 134 Confederate and 77 Union — were small by comparison with other battles, the battle of Honey Springs was important. The Federals took control of Indian Territory and retained the loyalty of many Cherokee, Seminole, and Creek warriors. The battle also cleared the way for the Union march on Fort Smith, known as the Little Gibraltar, which fell on September 1. The battle of Honey Springs was unique in the composition of its units: Indian and black troops outnumbered the white troops in the battle. Today, Honey Springs Battlefield Park stands as a memorial to their courage.

Estimated Casualties: 77 US, 134 CS

Honey Springs Battlefield Park, four miles north of Checotah near Route 69, includes nearly one thousand acres of the historic battlefield.

Devil's Backbone, Arkansas (AR009), Sebastian County, September 1, 1863

US General Blunt occupied Fort Smith after the battle of Honey Springs, and on September 1 he sent US Colonel William F. Cloud in pursuit of the retreating Confederates. At the base of the Devil's Backbone, a ridge in the Ouachita Mountains sixteen miles south of Fort Smith, Cloud's 1,500 2nd Kansas cavalrymen and CS General Cabell's 1,200 Arkansas troopers clashed in a three-hour engagement. The Confederates then resumed their retreat, but without many of the conscripts who deserted both during and after the engagement.

Casualties: 14 US, 17 CS

Middle Boggy, Oklahoma (OK005), Atoka County, February 13, 1864

In February 1864 US Colonel William A. Phillips set out from Fort Gibson on the Arkansas River for the Texas border to force the Chickasaws and Choctaws to join the Unionists. During the month-long expedition, the Federals subsisted off the land and laid waste to the country. On February 13 US Major Charles Willette, in command of three companies of the 14th Kansas Cavalry Regiment, surprised a Confederate force at Middle Boggy: CS Major John Jumper's Seminole Battalion, Company A of the 1st Choctaw and Chickasaw Cavalry Regiment, and a detachment of the 20th Texas Regiment. In the 30-minute fight the Federals killed 47 poorly armed Confederates and routed their forces. When Willette received word that enemy reinforcements were en route from Boggy Depot, twelve miles away, he retreated.

Phillips's destructive expedition resulted in the deaths of about 250 Indians and failed to persuade the pro-Confederate Indians to become Unionists.

Estimated Casualties: 0 US, 47 CS

North Dakota: July–September 1863

Big Mound, North Dakota (ND001), Kidder County, July 24, 1863

In August 1862 Henry Hastings Sibley (unrelated to Henry Hopkins Sibley) accepted, at the urging of Governor Alexander Ramsey of Minnesota, the command of a force organized to respond to the U.S.-Dakota conflict. The attack on Fort Ridgely had been led by Little Crow and included warriors from three of the four Santee Dakota (Sioux) tribes: Mdewakanton, Sisseton, and Wahpeton. Many of the Dakotas opposed it and did not participate.

In the spring of 1863, US Major General John Pope, commander of the Military Department of the Northwest, launched a two-pronged campaign through Dakota Territory where many Dakotas had fled. This campaign did not involve the Confederacy, but it did divert U.S. troops from Civil War battles. US Brigadier General Henry Hastings Sibley led one prong with about 3,000 men from Camp Pope on the Minnesota River to capture Dakotas or drive them toward the Missouri River where they could be intercepted by the campaign's other prong: 1,200 soldiers advancing northward up the Missouri, led by US Brigadier General Alfred Sully.

On July 24 Sibley overtook a force of about 1,000 Dakotas, including Sissetons and Wahpetons led by Standing Buffalo who had not joined Little Crow's uprising. While Sibley's troops set up camp, scouts from each side met to talk. Dr. Josiah Weiser, a St. Paul physician who spoke the Dakota languages, joined the group. Suddenly one of the Dakotas shot Dr. Weiser, and in the panic the shooting spread. Sibley's artillery drove the Dakotas out of the wooded draws, and his troops began surrounding them as they headed back to camp to protect their families.

During the battle on Big Mound, US Colonel Samuel McPhail's cavalry rode to the western edge of the plateau and prevented the Dakotas' retreat to the west. The Dakotas then headed off the Big Mound plateau to their village and gathered the belongings they could carry. Fighting as they withdrew, the warriors fled across the plains with their families. The troops pursued them until dark and then returned to camp. Some Dakotas headed northwest and finally made it to Canada. Others fled to the southwest beyond Dead Buffalo Lake.

Estimated Casualties: 7 US, 80 Dakotas

The Big Mound Battlefield State Historic Site, nine miles north of Tappen near County Road 71, includes one tenth of an acre of the battlefield; access is difficult.

Dead Buffalo Lake, North Dakota (ND002), Kidder County, July 26, 1863

After taking a day to rest his force, US General Sibley continued his pursuit of the Dakotas, none of whom had been involved in the uprising. They included Sissetons and Yanktonais led by Inkpaduta, a Wahpekute chief, and Hunkpapa and Blackfeet tribes of the Teton Lakota (Sioux) who were hunting buffalo east of the Missouri River.

On July 26, as Sibley's men approached Dead Buffalo Lake, the Dakotas and Lakotas challenged them, but their combined numbers in several assaults were no match for Sibley's howitzers. The Dakotas and Lakotas tried to flank the troops but were driven off by two companies of cavalry that were resting out of sight. The Dakotas and Lakotas retreated, ending the battle.

Estimated Casualties: 1 US, 9 Dakotas and Lakotas

Stony Lake, North Dakota (ND003), Burleigh County, July 28, 1863

US General Sibley pursued the retreating Dakotas and Lakotas to Stony Lake, where he camped because his animals were exhausted. On July 28 Sibley and some of his headquarters staff, escorted by the 10th Minnesota Volunteer Infantry Regiment, were the first to leave camp. When they reached the crest of a hill west of the camp, there was a long line of mounted warriors preparing for battle. The warriors attacked, flanked the escort, and tried to surround the camp but were driven off by artillery and rifle fire.

The Dakotas and Lakotas retreated to the Missouri River, about thirty miles to the southwest, where they quickly fashioned boats of buffalo hides stretched across willow branches and escaped across the river throughout the night. Those who could not swim were ferried in the boats, and many who were still crossing at dawn, including women and children, drowned when the light revealed them to the soldiers' fire.

Sibley reported that Stony Lake was "the greatest conflict between our troops and the Indians, so far as the numbers were concerned." The Dakotas' and Lakotas' losses on July 29 at what is known as the battle of Sibley Island, included their equipment and their food for the winter. None of these battles included the Mdewakanton who had initiated the Minnesota uprising in 1862.

Estimated Casualties: 0 US, unknown Dakotas and Lakotas

Whitestone Hill, North Dakota (ND004), Dickey County, September 3–4, 1863

US General Sibley returned to Minnesota, and the Dakotas recrossed the Missouri River and resumed hunting east of the river. US General Sully, leading the second prong of US General Pope's campaign, missed his meeting with Sibley by a month. He assumed that the Indians east of the Missouri were the hostiles in the Minnesota uprising.

On September 3 Sully's scouting party, four companies of the 6th Iowa Volunteer Cavalry, rode into the large camp of several thousand Dakotas led by Inkpaduta near a small, shallow lake at the foot of a rocky landmark known as Whitestone Hill. The Dakotas surrounded the

soldiers but did not attack. US Major Albert E. House demanded that they surrender. They refused. The delay gave a courier time to ride to Sully, ten miles away. Sully rode with the 2nd Nebraska Cavalry to support the Iowans, while the Dakotas prepared to cover the escape of their families. Sully's troops charged into the camp and trapped them in the small basin until the Dakotas found a weak point in the soldiers' lines and broke through. They scattered during the night, and Sully captured their camp of more than four hundred lodges.

Sully made camp on the battlefield and sent out scouting parties while the main command destroyed the lodges and vast quantities of buffalo meat being prepared for the winter. The Iowans suffered about 70 casualties, killed about 300 Dakotas, and captured about 250, mostly women and children. The prisoners were marched across the prairie in blazing heat to Crow Creek on the Missouri where the Dakotas from Fort Snelling were being held. Those not taken prisoner joined other bands dispersed across the plains and had to face a cold winter with little food, lodging, or clothing.

While Pope's campaign stopped the warfare east of the Missouri River, it pushed conflict farther west and created more enemies among the Plains Indians.

Estimated Casualties: 70 US, 550 Dakotas

Whitestone Battlefield State Historic Site, six miles southwest of Merricourt near Route 56, includes sixty-six acres of the historic battlefield.

Kansas: August–October 1863

Lawrence, Kansas (KS001), Douglas County, August 21, 1863

In 1854 Senator Stephen A. Douglas led the Kansas-Nebraska Act through Congress. It organized two territories, Kansas and Nebraska, and repealed the ban in the Missouri Compromise on slavery in the Louisiana Purchase north of the 36°30′ parallel. The act left the decision on whether the territories would be slave or free to the voters in each territory, through "popular sovereignty." The act increased the sectional differences over slavery and altered the national political parties. The Whig Party had begun to lose out as a national party — in the South to the American (Know Nothing) Party and then to the Democratic Party, and in the North to the new Republican Party. The Republicans evolved in the North as a coalition of former Whigs, Free Soilers, Know Nothings opposed to slavery, various antislavery organizations, and splinter groups. In February 1856 the first Republican was elected speaker of the House of Representatives, Nathaniel P. Banks, who was later a U.S. general.

The act brought about such violence between those for and against slavery in the territory that it became known as "Bleeding Kansas." The most violent were the Kansas "Jayhawkers" and the Missouri-based "Border Ruffians." In 1858 President James Buchanan supported the admission of Kansas as a slave state, amid Southern threats to secede if it were not, despite the estimated two-to-one majority of Kansas Territory settlers who were in favor of statehood as a free state. Douglas opposed the president, widening the crack in the Democratic Party. The statehood measure passed the Senate but was defeated in the House. Kansas was finally admitted as a free state in 1861.

On August 21, 1863, William C. Quantrill, the guerrilla leader who held the rank of captain in the Confederate Partisan Rangers, led 450 raiders (who included Frank and Jesse James) in an attack on Lawrence, Kansas, a center of opposition to slavery. In three hours Quantrill's men shot and killed about 150 men and boys and destroyed many buildings before riding off when Federal troops approached the town. One of Quantrill's men was killed in Lawrence.

The "Lawrence Massacre" prompted US Brigadier General Thomas Ewing, Jr., to issue his General Order No. 11, which forced all civilians to evacuate four counties in Missouri that bordered Kansas and provided safe haven for border ruffians. Union soldiers then destroyed the farms in the region, creating a "burnt district."

Estimated Casualties: 150 US, unknown CS

Baxter Springs, Kansas (KS002), Cherokee County, October 6, 1863

On October 6 William C. Quantrill sent half of his force, commanded by David Poole, to attack the Union post at Baxter Springs. The Federals were holding off the raiders with the aid of a howitzer when US Major General James G. Blunt approached with 100 men on his way to his new field headquarters at Fort Smith, Arkansas. Quantrill's men were wearing Federal uniforms, so Blunt thought they were part of the garrison riding out to meet him. Quantrill quickly overwhelmed Blunt's smaller force. Although many of the Federals tried to surrender, Quantrill's men killed 70 of them, including US Major Henry Z. Curtis, the son of US Major General Samuel R. Curtis. Blunt and a few mounted men escaped from what came to be known as the "Baxter Springs Massacre."

Estimated Casualties: 103 US, 3 CS

*The doctrine of self-government is right—
absolutely and eternally right—but it has no
just application, as here attempted. Or perhaps
I should rather say that whether it has such just
application depends upon whether a negro is
not or is a man. If he is not a man, why in that
case he who is a man may, as a matter of self-
government, do just as he pleases with him. But
if the negro is a man, is it not to that extent a total destruction of self-government to say that he
too shall not govern himself? When the white
man governs himself, that is self-government; but
when he governs himself and also governs another man, that is more than self-government—
that is despotism. If the negro is a man, why then
my ancient faith teaches me that "all men are
created equal;" and that there can be no moral
right in connection with one man's making a
slave of another. . . .*

*Slavery is founded in the selfishness of man's
nature—opposition to it in his love of justice.
These principles are an eternal antagonism,
and when brought into collision so fiercely as
slavery extension brings them, shocks and
throes and convulsions must ceaselessly follow.
Repeal the Missouri compromise—repeal all
compromises—repeal the declaration of independence—repeal all past history, you still cannot repeal human nature. It still will be the abundance of man's heart that slavery extension is
wrong; and out of the abundance of his heart,
his mouth will continue to speak.*

—Abraham Lincoln on the Kansas-Nebraska Act,
   October 16, 1854

Tullahoma Campaign: June 1863

Hoover's Gap, Tennessee (TN017), Bedford and Rutherford Counties, June 24–26, 1863

The Army of the Cumberland, commanded by US Major General William S. Rosecrans, remained in the Murfreesboro area after the battle of Stones River. To counter the Federals, CS General Braxton Bragg's Army of Tennessee established a fortified line along the Duck River from Shelbyville to McMinnville. On the Confederate right, infantry and artillery detachments guarded three gaps—Liberty, Hoover's, and Guy's—through the small mountains known as knobs in the Cumberland foothills. Rosecrans's superiors learned that Bragg was detaching large numbers of men to break the siege of Vicksburg and urged Rosecrans to attack.

On June 23 Rosecrans feigned an attack against CS Lieutenant General Leonidas Polk at Shelbyville while concentrating three corps against the Confederates at Liberty and Hoover's Gaps. US Major General George H. Thomas massed against Hoover's, while US Major General Alexander M. McCook pushed against CS Lieutenant General William J. Hardee at Liberty Gap. On the extreme left US Major General Thomas L. Crittenden's XXV Corps moved southeast through Bradyville. Federal mounted infantry under US Colonel John T. Wilder occupied Hoover's Gap in a driving rainstorm on June 24 and held against a counterattack by a Confederate division. Thomas's men arrived the next day and drove off the Confederate forces. Only then did Bragg realize the extent of the turning movement. The fighting continued until noon on June 26, when the Confederates withdrew.

Rosecrans's careful planning and maneuvering forced Bragg to give up his defensive position and retreat from Middle Tennessee. Bragg retired behind the Tennessee River at Chattanooga, opening up East Tennessee and Chattanooga to an advance by Union forces.

The victory at Hoover's Gap was due in part to the new seven-shot Spencer repeating rifles that Wilder had purchased and sold to his soldiers. Rosecrans's frustration that his success at a cost of fewer than 600 Federal casualties was overshadowed by the U.S. victories at Vicksburg and Gettysburg is evident in his response to a message from Secretary of War Edwin M. Stanton: "You do not appear to observe the fact that this noble army has driven the rebels from Middle Tennessee."

Estimated Casualties: 583 US, unknown CS

Chickamauga Campaign: August–September 1863

Chattanooga II, Tennessee (TN018), Hamilton County and Chattanooga, August 21, 1863

On August 16 US Major General William S. Rosecrans launched the Army of the Cumberland in an offensive to take Chattanooga. He divided his army into three columns to move through the mountain gaps to take Chattanooga and create diversions to deceive CS General Braxton Bragg, commander of the Army of Tennessee. On the Federal left, US Major General Thomas L. Crittenden worked his way up onto the Cumberland plateau. On the right, US Major General Alexander M. McCook headed for Bellfonte and Stevenson, while US Major General George H. Thomas, in the center, marched by way of Cowan and Battle Creek. Timing was critical, and Rosecrans planned well.

On August 21 US Colonel John T. Wilder's Lightning Brigade with the 18th Indiana Artillery Battery shelled Chattanooga from a position on Stringer's Ridge — visible to Bragg — across the river from and west of Chattanooga while Crittenden demonstrated upstream. When Bragg learned that Rosecrans's army was also in force southwest of Chattanooga, he abandoned the town on September 8. The vital rail junction of the Nashville & Chattanooga, the East Tennessee & Georgia (which ran to Virginia via Knoxville), and the Western & Atlantic (which ran to Atlanta and by connections to the Atlantic and Gulf coasts) fell into Union hands.

The opposition to Bragg as commander of the Army of Tennessee intensified. The reasons included his poor health and the fact that many of his senior officers and troops had lost faith in him. Also, he often blamed his subordinates when his plans failed. Bragg's competence was in conceiving plans for battles, not in acting as a field commander.

Estimated Casualties: unknown

Davis' Cross Roads, Georgia (GA003), Dade and Walker Counties, September 10–11, 1863

When CS General Bragg evacuated Chattanooga, US General Rosecrans ordered his separate columns to continue to move over the rough terrain of north Georgia and pursue the withdrawing Confederates. When Bragg learned that the Federal forces were separated, he halted his march southward. Late on September 9 he ordered an attack on the vanguard of US General Thomas's XIV Corps, which had crossed Lookout Mountain by way of Stevens Gap.

The next day US Major General James Scott Negley's division was in McLemore's Cove on the Dug Gap Road, with Negley riding at the head of the column, when they were hit by Confederate fire. Negley advanced toward the gap but then withdrew to Davis' Cross Roads on the evening of September 10 to await US Brigadier General Absalom Baird's division. Poor coordination of the Confederates sent to attack Negley resulted in their inaction and a missed opportunity. Bragg ordered another unsuccessful assault the next morning. Negley, reinforced by Baird, retired to Bailey's Cross Roads, covered by a strong rear guard that took positions on Missionary Ridge between the valleys of West Chickamauga and Chattanooga Creeks. The rear guard skirmished with the Confederates as the Federal divisions made their way onto Lookout Mountain to hold Stevens Gap and await the arrival of the remainder of the XIV Corps.

Estimated Casualties: unknown

Chickamauga, Georgia (GA004), Catoosa and Walker Counties, September 18–20, 1863

William Glenn Robertson

When US Major General William S. Rosecrans brought the Army of the Cumberland to the Tennessee River in August 1863, his goal was to cap-ture Chattanooga, Tennessee. A town of only 2,500 people, Chattanooga was important because of its rail lines, its mineral resources, and its position astride a railroad pathway through the Appalachian Mountains into the South's heartland. Defending Chattanooga was the Confederate Army of Tennessee, commanded by CS General Braxton Bragg with 50,000 troops. Rosecrans's army numbered approximately 80,000 officers and men, but nearly one fifth remained in the rear, guarding Middle Tennessee and the army's long line of communications.

In early September, while four Union brigades executed a masterly deception upstream from Chattanooga, the bulk of Rosecrans's army crossed the Tennessee unopposed at four sites far south of the city. Rosecrans divided his army into three columns and then began a wide-front advance on Chattanooga while US Major General Ambrose E. Burnside took Knoxville, one hundred miles to the north. Outflanked and outnumbered, Bragg abandoned Chattanooga on September 8 without a battle. Rather than retreat toward Atlanta, however, Bragg concentrated his army near La Fayette, Georgia, and prepared for a counterstroke. When his subordinates failed in two attempts to destroy isolated elements of the Army of the Cumberland, Bragg suspended operations for several days. During this period reinforcements arrived from Mississippi and Virginia, swelling his army to approximately 65,000 men.

Finally recognizing his dangerous position, Rosecrans hastily began to concentrate his scattered units and move them north toward Chattanooga. After an epic march, US Major General Alexander McCook's XX Corps joined US Major General George H. Thomas's XIV Corps on September 17. Together the two corps then continued northward along the west bank of Chickamauga Creek toward US Major General Thomas L. Crittenden's XXI Corps at Lee and Gordon's Mill. On September 18, fearing that Bragg would attempt to cut him off from Chattanooga, Rosecrans ordered Thomas to occupy a new position beyond Crittenden's left flank. At the same time, believing that Crittenden's corps was Rosecrans's

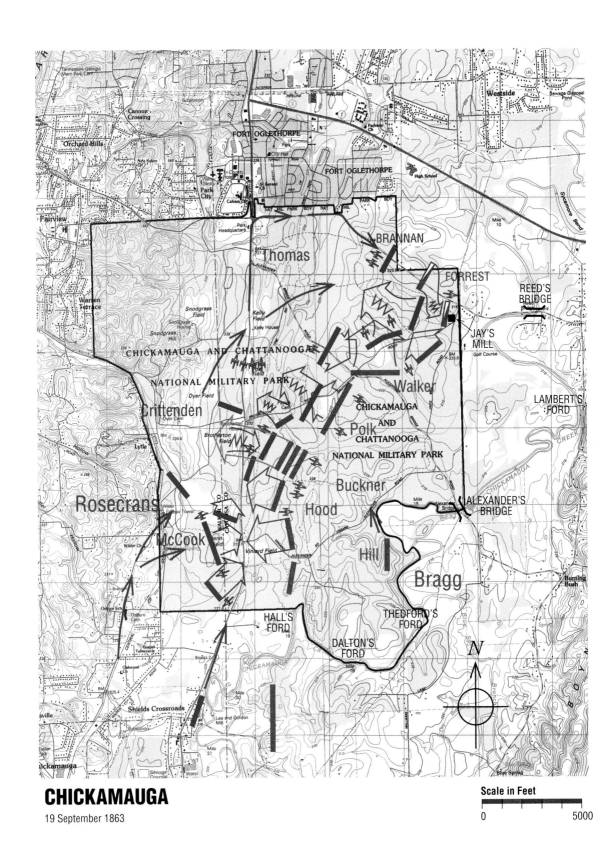

CHICKAMAUGA

19 September 1863

Scale in Feet

0   5000

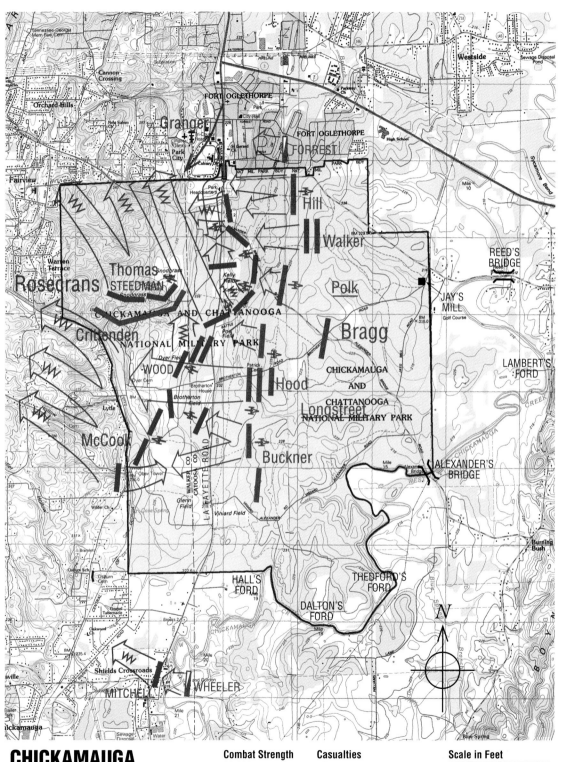

CHICKAMAUGA

20 September 1863

Combat Strength	Casualties
62,000	16,170
65,000	18,454

Scale in Feet

0   5000

northernmost unit, Bragg ordered most of his army to seize crossings over Chickamauga Creek downstream of the Federals, then drive Rosecrans's army south into McLemore's Cove and away from Chattanooga.

By the evening of September 18, CS Brigadier General Bushrod Johnson's provisional division had captured Reed's Bridge, crossed Chickamauga Creek, and advanced south toward the La Fayette Road. The corps of CS Major Generals William H. T. Walker and Simon B. Buckner had also gained the west bank of Chickamauga Creek and had bivouacked for the night in the woods east of the La Fayette Road. None of the Confederate units was aware of Thomas's XIV Corps as it marched northward through the night and took position on the La Fayette Road at the Kelly farm. The only night contact occurred when a brigade of US Major General Gordon Granger's reserve corps, attempting to destroy Reed's Bridge, bumped into rear-echelon elements of Johnson's Division at a road junction near Jay's Mill.

Believing that they had trapped a single Confederate brigade west of the creek, Granger's men withdrew to rejoin the reserve corps early on the morning of September 19. Thomas sent US Brigadier General John Brannan's division east into the forest to destroy that brigade. In the forest west of Jay's Mill, Brannan's men met a Confederate cavalry brigade covering Bragg's right rear, and the battle was joined. For the remainder of the day both Rosecrans and Bragg could do little more than feed reinforcements into the fight in order to stabilize the situation. Their efforts were hindered by the nature of the battlefield, which consisted of a thick forest occasionally broken by a few small farms. The woods limited maximum visibility to 150 yards, far less than rifle range, and made it almost impossible to control linear battle formations. Similarly, the terrain provided few fields of fire for the armies' artillerymen. Neither commander had wanted a battle in the thickets between Chickamauga Creek and the La Fayette Road, but the collision near Jay's Mill ensured that the battle would be fought there.

Bragg brought forward Walker's reserve corps to drive Brannan's men back. In turn, Thomas re-inforced Brannan with more of the XIV Corps. When Walker was supported by part of CS Lieutenant General Leonidas Polk's Corps, Rosecrans sent divisions from both McCook and Crittenden to assist Thomas. Next, a division of Buckner's Corps joined the fight. In a spirited effort it shattered one of Crittenden's divisions, gained the La Fayette Road, and threatened to split the Federal army. Federal reinforcements finally forced Buckner's men to withdraw eastward into the forest. CS Major General John Bell Hood's forces mounted the final threat of the day at the Viniard farm but were finally fought to a bloody standstill by elements of all three Federal corps. When darkness closed the fighting, the Federals still held the La Fayette Road, but Thomas's men had been forced back to a defensive position around the Kelly farm.

During the night Rosecrans strengthened his lines with log breastworks and prepared for a coordinated defense the following day. Meanwhile Bragg planned a coordinated attack, beginning on the Confederate right and rolling southward, which would again attempt to outflank the Federal army and drive it away from Chattanooga. The arrival during the night of CS Lieutenant General James Longstreet permitted Bragg to reorganize his five infantry corps into two wings, with Longstreet commanding the left wing of six divisions, and Polk the right wing of five divisions. CS Lieutenant General Daniel Harvey Hill's Corps was to begin the attack at sunrise on September 20, but because of poor staff work and lack of initiative, Hill did not learn of his critical mission until the day was well advanced.

When the Confederate attack finally began, four hours late, one of Hill's divisions actually passed beyond Thomas's flank and several hundred yards into the Federal rear before being ejected by Federal reinforcements. Elsewhere troops of the Confederate right wing futilely assaulted Thomas's unyielding defenses. One of Longstreet's divisions, attacking soon after Hill's men, also made no impression on the Federal line. Just to the south along the Brotherton Road, Hood's three divisions in column were withheld by Longstreet until just after 11:00 A.M., when they swept forward with the remainder of the left wing. Fortuitously, Hood's column struck a segment of the Federal line that was momentarily devoid of troops and crashed through.

The opening in the Federal line was the result of a complicated series of events that had been developing all morning. Even before the action began on the Federal left, Thomas had been calling for reinforcements, and he continued to do so in the face of the Confederate attacks. Both Rosecrans and Thomas ordered units from the army's center and right toward the left. As a result of these movements, Rosecrans came to believe that a gap existed in the Federal right-center, and he ordered US Brigadier General Thomas Wood's division, already in line, to move north to close it. In fact, there was no gap in the Federal line until Wood's departure created one. McCook agreed to occupy Wood's position, but Hood's Corps crashed through before he could act, and the Federal line was irreparably split.

As Longstreet's troops swept through the gap into the Dyer field, Federal units on both sides of the break crumbled and fled to the rear. Rosecrans, McCook, and Crittenden were all swept from the field. Two intact Federal brigades and fragments of several others rallied northwest of the break on a rugged, timber-clad height known as Horseshoe Ridge or Snodgrass Hill. Just as they were about to be outflanked by Bushrod Johnson's Confederates, they were reinforced by US Brigadier General James Steedman's division of Granger's reserve corps, which had just arrived from Rossville. Although Confederate units continued to attack Snodgrass Hill for the remainder of the afternoon, they were unable to drive the Federals from the commanding ridge. Finally, near sundown, Thomas received a message from Rosecrans to withdraw the surviving Federal units beyond Missionary Ridge. Although a few units were lost, Thomas successfully gathered most of the Army of the Cumberland at Rossville. One day later the Federals withdrew into Chattanooga, their original objective.

Both armies suffered heavily at Chickamauga for little tangible gain. Rosecrans lost 16,170 killed, wounded, and missing out of about 62,000

engaged, while Bragg suffered a total of 18,454 casualties out of approximately 65,000 engaged.

As the largest battle and last Confederate victory in the western theater, the battle of Chickamauga served mainly to buy a little more time for the southern cause. Federal troops in both Virginia and Mississippi were diverted from their primary missions to rescue the defeated Army of the Cumberland, thereby affecting the timetable for Federal victory in those areas. Otherwise the great expenditure of lives by both sides had little effect. Because they left the field while others stayed, Rosecrans, McCook, and Crittenden all had their military careers blighted. Nor did the victors, Bragg and Longstreet, gain much from their success. Only George Thomas, the "Rock of Chickamauga," left the dark woods bordering the "River of Death" with his reputation enhanced.

Estimated Casualties: 16,170 US, 18,454 CS

Chickamauga Battlefield, a unit of Chickamauga and Chattanooga National Military Park, is south of Chattanooga near Route 27 at Fort Oglethorpe, Georgia, south of Interstate 24 and west of Interstate 75. It includes 5,235 acres of the historic battlefield.

Blockade of the Texas Coast: September 1863

Sabine Pass II, Texas (TX006), Jefferson County, September 8, 1863

In June 1863 Emperor Napoleon III had ignored the Monroe Doctrine and sent troops to overthrow the Mexican government. They ousted President Benito Juárez and made Maximilian the emperor of Mexico. The Confederacy needed French support, including French-built ships, and offered to recognize the French-installed government in Mexico in exchange for help. This prompted Lincoln to order US Major General Nathaniel P. Banks's forces to Texas as a warning to the French, to stop the Confederacy from trading cotton for arms with Mexico across the Rio Grande, and to re-establish "the national authority in Western Texas as soon as possible."

US Major General Henry W. Halleck proposed a combined army-navy movement from the Mississippi River, up the Red River, and into Texas, but the water in the Red was too low. Instead Banks headed toward the Texas coast. Sabine Pass, the narrows at the mouth of the Sabine River, which formed the Louisiana-Texas border, was a haven for blockade runners. In September 1863 Banks launched a joint army-navy operation led by US Major General William B. Franklin, the veteran commander of the XIX Corps who had been sent to the trans-Mississippi following the Union defeat at Fredericksburg in December 1862.

Franklin was to silence the Confederate forts covering the pass and capture Sabine City. One of the forts was Fort Griffin, commanded by CS Lieutenant Richard W. "Dick" Dowling. Its defenses included six guns manned by the Jeff Davis Guards, 46 Irish American longshoremen of the 1st Texas Heavy Artillery Regiment. They were expert marksmen and had prepared for an attack by driving poles into the mud to guide their fire against Federal ships.

Early on September 8 four gunboats commanded by USN Lieutenant Frederick Crocker entered Sabine Pass to cover the landing of Franklin's 5,000 soldiers from eighteen transports. The Texans held their fire until Crocker had all four gunboats and seven transports up the river. The *Sachem* led the way up the far side of the channel. As it passed the first stakes in the river, the Texans opened fire with deadly accuracy. They shot the *Sachem* through the boiler and forced Crocker to surrender his flagship, the *Clifton*. The rest of the flotilla backed down the channel after losing two gunboats and 350 sailors. It was a resounding Confederate victory.

Banks ordered Franklin to head up the Teche while he took a force across the Gulf to the Texas coast. Napoleon's problems in Europe soon diminished his interest in Mexico and in the Confederacy.

Estimated Casualties: 350 US, 0 CS

Sabine Pass Battleground State Historic Park, 1.5 miles south of Sabine Pass on Route 3322 and fifteen miles south of Port Arthur via Route 87, includes fifty-six acres of the historic battlefield.

Arkansas: September–October 1863

Bayou Fourche (Little Rock), Arkansas (AR010), Pulaski County, September 10, 1863

In August 1863 US Major General Frederick Steele, commander of the Army of the Arkansas, had advanced west from Helena with 12,000 men to capture Little Rock, the state capital. The Arkansas River and the entrenchments along its banks provided some protection from the Federals, but CS Major General Sterling Price knew that his approximately 7,700 troops could not hold the capital if a large force attacked. While Price prepared to evacuate, the state government moved to Washington, southwest of Little Rock.

CS Brigadier General John S. Marmaduke was released from arrest to lead the cavalry. He had been arrested after he had mortally wounded CS Brigadier General Lucius M. Walker in a duel on September 6. Marmaduke had accused Walker of cowardice in battle, and Walker had challenged him to a duel.

On September 10 about 7,000 Federals approached Little Rock. Steele ordered US Brigadier General John W. Davidson's cavalry division to cross to the south bank of the river to outflank the Confederate defenses while he moved on the Confederate entrenchments on the north bank. At Bayou Fourche, a few miles east of Little Rock, Marmaduke's small cavalry force tried to stop Davidson while Price completed the evacuation.

A Federal battery on the north side of the river drove off the Confederates who fled back to Little Rock and then, with Price's entire command, retreated to Arkadelphia and Camden.

The fall of Little Rock, the fourth state capital taken by Federal forces, further isolated the trans-Mississippi area from the rest of the Confederacy.

Estimated Casualties: 72 US, 64 CS

Pine Bluff, Arkansas (AR011), Jefferson County, October 25, 1863

Federal forces occupied several towns along the Arkansas River after the capture of Little Rock. CS General Marmaduke decided to test their strength at Pine Bluff. He attacked the garrison, the 5th Kansas and 1st Indiana Cavalry commanded by US Colonel Powell Clayton.

On October 25 Marmaduke's 2,000 Arkansas and Missouri cavalrymen approached the town from three sides. The 550 Federals, actively supported by 300 recently liberated slaves, barricaded the courthouse square with cotton bales and positioned their nine cannons to command the adjacent streets. The Confederates made several direct attacks on the square, then attempted to set the courthouse on fire. They were unsuccessful and withdrew after damaging and looting the town.

Estimated Casualties: 56, including 17 freedmen, US, 40 CS

Photography
in the Civil War

David McCullough

○

These are extraordinary photographs from the Civil War. But let the viewer be warned. There is an accompanying risk here. It is our natural tendency to accept such photographs, because they are photographs, as faithful representations of the reality of a bygone time, and to assume that such people as we see here were like us.

We and they share that part of history that has transpired since the advent of photography, and so we feel a kinship of a kind we do not for those whose lives and world were never recorded by the camera. The soldiers of the Civil War are closer to us, much more "real" in our eyes, than are those, say, who fought in the Revolutionary War, for the very reason that we have their photographs. Yet the soldiers of the Civil War were closer in time to those of the Revolution than they are to us, and had far more in common.

We see them posed here, young, proud, a little awkward before the camera, and we know the feeling. We too have stood or sat dutifully attentive, turning this way or that, breath held, whatever was required of us by the photographer, trying as they do to look our best. And so we take them to be the same. They are people we know, we feel. Only the clothes are different, we are inclined to conclude, and we are quite mistaken.

They were not like us, be assured. Theirs was a vastly different world from ours, different in detail, different in atmosphere, and they were correspondingly different as a consequence. They did not live as we do, or think as we do. Their outlook was different, their adversities. Their food, whiskey, the everyday implements of their lives,

all were different, and crude by our standards. Such toil and hardship as they took to be natural we would consider unacceptable. Most of the young men you see in these pages have come to the army from the farm. They were accustomed to discomfort, to ten- and twelve-hour days of rough toil in all weather, accustomed to making do under nearly any circumstances, used to working with animals, used to the everyday reality of death. To say they knew nothing of indoor plumbing or central heat, let alone Freud or Einstein, or even Darwin, is only to begin to fathom the difference in their world, their outlook, from our own.

As for the black Americans in the photographs, nearly all were slaves but a short time earlier and had known no other life.

What we see are shards of time. These are incomplete messages of a kind, jumping-off points for the imagination, and only with imagination is the past ever recoverable. In the expression of our motion picture era, these are "stills." And still — motionless, silent — they are. There is no sound here of war, no stench of death, none of the fragrance of spring winds in Virginia after the rain.

And, of course, the world was in full color then, too. There was color in all these faces, save the dead, color in their eyes, color in the sky. The raw earth of Virginia is red, let us remember. Nor were any flesh-and-blood Americans ever so stiff or solemn or so funereal in real life as we have come to suppose from so many posed pictures from the time.

Yet with a little imagination, how vivid, how haunting these images become, and the more so the more time we give them. To dwell on even one, to close out the present and live within the photograph, is almost to bridge the divide, while the accumulative effect of one photograph after another, with such amazing clarity and detail, can be profoundly moving.

Scholars know how much may be found through close study of old photographs. What we feel from the experience of these pages can count still more, teach us more.

In May 1862 General McClellan's Army of the Potomac was poised for the advance on Richmond, the Confederate capital. Photographer James F. Gibson recorded this view of Union soldiers surveying their sprawling encampment at Cumberland Landing on the Pamunkey River. (Library of Congress)

Alexander Gardner photographed the Middle Bridge spanning Antietam Creek five days after the battle of Antietam, fought on September 17, 1862. During the battle, cavalry, horse artillery, and elements of the V Corps crossed the bridge and skirmished with the Confederates, but General McClellan failed to commit them to an assault on General Lee's embattled line. (Library of Congress)

East Tennessee: September–October 1863

Blountville, Tennessee (TN019), Sullivan County, September 22, 1863

Much of East Tennessee was settled by small farmers who had little in common with the slave-holding planters in the rest of the state. They were pro-Union even though Confederate forces occupied the region early in the war. President Abraham Lincoln wanted to strengthen Federal control in East Tennessee. In late August US Major

General Ambrose E. Burnside marched from Kentucky with 24,000 soldiers of the Army of the Ohio to secure the East Tennessee & Virginia Railroad from Knoxville to beyond Abingdon, Virginia. The Confederates retreated up the railroad to Zollicoffer Station on the South Fork of the Holston River. The citizens of Knoxville welcomed Burnside's vanguard on September 3. Federal troopers forced the surrender of Cumberland Gap on September 9. Burnside's rapidly moving columns followed the railroad to Carter's Depot where the Confederates held the crossing of the Watauga River. US Colonel John W. Foster led

In June 1863 General John Sedgwick's VI Corps crossed the Rappahannock River to test the Confederate lines south of Fredericksburg. During the operation Timothy O'Sullivan photographed cannoneers of Lieutenant Edward Williston's Battery D, 2nd U.S. Artillery, manning their guns in support of Sedgwick's infantry. (Library of Congress)

Alexander Gardner's photograph, one of the Civil War's most famous images, was taken during the October 3, 1862, meeting of President Lincoln and General McClellan at the headquarters of the V Corps commander, General Fitz John Porter, on the Grove farm one mile southwest of Sharpsburg. (Library of Congress)

his 1,500-man cavalry brigade on a roundabout ride to burn the railroad bridges above Bristol on September 19. Foster completed his mission, returned by way of Blountville, and tried to attack Zollicoffer Station from the rear. A Confederate brigade at Beaver Creek stopped him on September 20.

On September 22 Foster tried again and was hit by a force under CS Colonel James Carter. For several hours artillery dueled across the town and set fire to a dozen buildings. Foster's troopers pushed the Confederates out of Blountville but could not penetrate the gap to the south. Foster rode to rejoin Burnside's troops, who had been recalled to Knoxville following the news of the defeat of the Federal army at Chickamauga. The Confederates reoccupied the region as far as Blue Springs.

Estimated Casualties: 27 US, 165 CS

Resplendent in white gloves and polished brass, soldiers of the 1st South Carolina Volunteer Infantry — one of the Union's first regiments of black troops — assembled at dress parade in January 1863 in Beaufort, South Carolina, for a reading of President Lincoln's Emancipation Proclamation. (Library of Congress)

On April 10, 1865 — one day after General Lee surrendered to General Grant at Appomattox — a wagon train heads west out of Petersburg, bearing supplies to the victorious Union forces. This photograph was probably taken by John Reekie, one of Alexander Gardner's cameramen. (Library of Congress)

Blue Springs, Tennessee (TN020), Greene County, October 10, 1863

US General Burnside and the IX Corps arrived from Knoxville at Bull's Gap by railroad on October 9 and joined the XXIII Corps, which was already on the field at Blue Springs (present-day Mosheim). Against the 20,000 Federals, CS Brigadier General John S. "Cerro Gordo" Williams held a line across the wooded hills east of town with only three brigades and two batteries of artillery. His 3,200 men were to pin down the Federals while a second Confederate column recaptured Cumberland Gap. Williams made his force appear larger by shifting units and keeping up a spirited resistance against the Federal cavalry.

At dawn on October 10, Burnside ordered a methodical advance to give his troopers time to ride around to Williams's rear. Federal skirmishers pressed to within a hundred yards of Williams's line, probing for weaknesses. Williams extended his flanks along a one-and-one-half-mile front between the railroad and the Knoxville Road. At about 5:00 P.M. US Brigadier General Edward Ferrero's division deployed in a compact mass south of the road and stepped off. They overwhelmed the Confederates. Those not taken prisoner fell back half a mile to prepared entrenchments on a high ridge where they held out until dark. They were able to retreat toward Greeneville because Burnside's cavalry never reached their rear. Williams later learned that the diversion had been unnecessary because the Confederate advance on Cumberland Gap had been called off.

Estimated Casualties: 100 US, 216 CS

Virginia & Tennessee Railroad: November 1863

Droop Mountain, West Virginia (WV012), Pocahontas County, November 6, 1863

In June 1863 the state of West Virginia was admitted to the United States. On November 1 US Brigadier General William W. Averell's 4,000-man column marched southward from Beverly along the Staunton-Parkersburg Turnpike. US Brigadier General Alfred N. Duffié's 970 men set out from Charleston two days later. Their goal was to unite at Lewisburg and destroy the Virginia & Tennessee Railroad in southwest Virginia. Averell met CS Colonel William L. Jackson's 600 troops at Mill Point and drove them back to Droop Mountain. CS Brigadier General John Echols rushed from Lewisburg, bringing the Confederate strength to 1,700 men.

On November 6 the Federal cavalry feinted against Echols's front while Averell sent US Colonel Augustus Moor's two infantry regiments around the Confederate left. Averell launched his flank attack at 1:30 P.M. In a ninety-minute fight, he broke the enemy line and forced Echols to retreat to the south.

The two Union columns united at Lewisburg the following day but were in no condition to continue the raid against the railroad. This battle marked the near collapse of Confederate resistance in West Virginia, although Echols reoccupied Lewisburg after the Union forces retreated.

Estimated Casualties: 140 US, 275 CS

Droop Mountain Battlefield State Park, fourteen miles south of Marlinton on Route 219, includes 287 acres of the historic battlefield.

Memphis & Charleston Railroad: November 1863

Collierville, Tennessee (TN022), Shelby County, November 3, 1863

The battle at Collierville on November 3 was one of four there within three months. It began as a Confederate cavalry raid to break up the Memphis & Charleston Railroad behind US Major General William Tecumseh Sherman's troops while they redeployed from Vicksburg to Chattanooga by way of Memphis. CS Brigadier General James R. Chalmers knew of only two Union regiments defending Collierville, so he attacked from the south. US Colonel Edward Hatch was warned of Chalmers's approach, so he rode from Germantown with cavalry reinforcements. Chalmers, surprised by Hatch's presence on his flanks, concluded that he was outnumbered, called off the battle, and withdrew into Mississippi. The Federals continued to control the Memphis & Charleston Railroad to Tuscumbia, Alabama.

Estimated Casualties: 60 US, 95 CS

The Cracker Line: October 1863

Wauhatchie, Tennessee (TN021), Hamilton, Marion, and Dade Counties, October 28–29, 1863

After the battle of Chickamauga and the Federal retreat to Chattanooga, US Major General William S. Rosecrans had too few men in his Army of the Cumberland to protect his best supply lines into Chattanooga. President Abraham Lincoln approved reinforcements for Rosecrans from US Major General George G. Meade, who had not launched an offensive since his victory at Gettysburg. In the fourth week of September, US Major General Joseph Hooker and the XI and XII Corps of the Army of the Potomac left Warrenton, Virginia, and arrived in Bridgeport, Alabama, in eleven days, a record made possible by the cooperation of the presidents of the railroads.

On October 17 Lincoln created the Division of the Mississippi, with US Major General Ulysses S. Grant in command. It included the area between the Appalachian Mountains and the Mississippi River, as well as the state of Arkansas. Grant replaced Rosecrans with US Major General George H. Thomas and ordered him to hold Chattanooga.

When Grant reached Chattanooga on October 23, the Union garrison had been reduced to half rations because of Confederate control of the supply lines. Grant immediately approved the plan US Brigadier General William F. "Baldy" Smith, an engineer, had developed to open an effective supply line to Chattanooga from Bridgeport, Alabama, on the Tennessee River — the terminus of the Union railroad from Nashville (the Confederates had destroyed it between Bridgeport and Chattanooga). The plan involved troops' converging from three directions on the Confederates defending the crossing at Brown's Ferry. Hooker marched from Bridgeport through Lookout Valley while two Federal forces from Chattanooga converged on Brown's Ferry. One floated downstream on pontoon boats powered by the river's strong current, while the other marched west across the neck of Moccasin Bend to cross on the pontoons to the ferry. On the morning of October 27 the Federals from Chattanooga took Brown's Ferry in a thirty-minute surprise attack on the small Confederate force there.

The next day Hooker marched from Bridgeport into Lookout Valley with three divisions. He detached US Brigadier General John W. Geary's 1,500-man division at Wauhatchie Station on the Nashville & Chattanooga Railroad — less than two miles from the northern end of Lookout Mountain — to protect his communications line to the south and the road west to Kelley's Ferry. Hooker continued northward with US Major General Oliver O. Howard's two XI Corps divisions and joined the Federals at Brown's Ferry.

CS General Braxton Bragg ordered CS Lieutenant General James Longstreet to drive Hooker from the valley. Longstreet had three divisions, but did not use them to prevent the Federals from gaining control of the Tennessee River crossing nor did he direct them all against Hooker. Since the Federal artillery on Moccasin Bend controlled the roads over the northern end of Lookout Mountain, Longstreet had to attack at night. When preparations delayed his attack, he canceled it. However, his lead division commander, CS Brigadier General Micah Jenkins, decided to proceed with an attack on Geary's isolated division at Wauhatchie Station, three miles southwest of Brown's Ferry, while three of his brigades held the road to prevent Hooker from sending reinforcements from the ferry. On October 29 Jenkins hit the Federals with one brigade at 12:30 A.M. in one of the few night engagements in the Civil War. Forewarned, Geary, formerly the first mayor of San Francisco and territorial governor of Kansas, made effective use of his artillery, his V-shaped battle line, and the darkness to defend his force. Geary's son, an artillerist, was killed in the battle. US Brigadier General Carl Schurz's division from Brown's Ferry hit the Confederate roadblock on what was later named "Smith's Hill" and doomed the Confederates' attack. They withdrew at about 3:30 A.M. to Lookout Mountain.

During the battle, the Federals' mules broke loose and may — or may not — have stampeded into the Confederates. They did inspire a Federal soldier to recall Alfred Lord Tennyson's poem and compose a parody, the "Charge of the Mule Brigade." It concluded:

> Honor the charge they made,
> Honor the Mule Brigade,
> Long-eared two hundred.

The Federals' pontoon bridge across the river at the ankle of Moccasin Bend opened their new supply line — named the "Cracker Line" by hungry soldiers — into Chattanooga.

Estimated Casualties: 216 US, 356 CS

Chattanooga-Ringgold Campaign: November 1863

Chattanooga III, Tennessee (TN024), Hamilton County and Chattanooga, November 23–25, 1863

Charles P. Roland

The Union Army of the Cumberland, approximately 40,000 troops, which reeled back into Chattanooga after its defeat at Chickamauga on September 20, 1863, was disorganized and demoralized. The army commander, US Major General William S. Rosecrans, wired his superiors in Washington, "We have met with a serious disaster. . . . The enemy overwhelmed us, drove our right, pierced our center, and scattered the troops there." The following day he ended another gloomy telegram with the alarming statement, "We have no certainty of holding our position here."

President Abraham Lincoln was keenly aware of the strategic importance of Chattanooga, the gateway to the lower South. The city is situated just above the Tennessee-Georgia line on the Moccasin Bend of the Tennessee River — a shape resembling an Indian shoe — at the point where the river's westward flow cuts through the Cumberland plateau. The city lay on the Nashville & Chattanooga Railroad, which joined lines that ran to the Mississippi River, the south Atlantic coast, and northern Virginia.

The Confederate commander, CS General Braxton Bragg, chose to conduct a siege instead of an attack, and deployed the Army of Tennessee, initially between 40,000 and 50,000 troops, in an effort to cut off Union supplies and oblige the Federals either to surrender or to abandon Chattanooga. The terrain appeared to be suited to his purpose. Towering above the city on the southwest, and dominating both the river and the Nashville & Chattanooga Railroad, was the promontory of Lookout Mountain; overlooking the city on the east and extending south of it, controlling

the railroads to Knoxville and Atlanta, was a rugged escarpment known as Missionary Ridge.

Bragg's main body occupied this ridge with an advance line on Orchard Knob, a foothill three quarters of a mile to the front. On the shoulder of Lookout Mountain (around the Cravens house), between the peak and the Tennessee River, Bragg located a force of approximately 2,700. Their orders were to command the river and the railroad in an attempt to sever the Union army from its railhead at Bridgeport, Alabama, and from its primary base at Nashville. At Brown's Ferry, across the bend from the city and marking the head of safe navigation on the river, Bragg stationed a detachment of about 1,000 troops to prevent supplies from arriving by that route.

Lincoln wired messages of reassurance to his shaken general and ordered heavy reinforcements to Chattanooga: 20,000 troops from Mississippi under US Major General William Tecumseh Sherman, and a like number from northern Virginia under US Major General Joseph Hooker. Though Rosecrans gradually began to recover from the shock of Chickamauga, his messages for weeks remained vague and unpromising. He seemed unable to regain his poise and confidence; Lincoln came to the conclusion that he was acting "confused and stunned like a duck hit on the head." On October 17 the president appointed US Major General Ulysses S. Grant, fresh from the victorious Vicksburg campaign, to command all Union forces between the Appalachians and the Mississippi, as well as those in Arkansas. Grant immediately sent orders dismissing Rosecrans and replacing him with US Major General George H. Thomas — savior of the army at Chickamauga — with instructions to hold Chattanooga at all costs, to which the indomitable Thomas replied, "We will hold the town till we starve."

The Confederate force was insufficient to invest the city completely, and the Union army there was able to bring in a trickle of supplies from its railhead by a roundabout, sixty-mile trail through the mountains north and west of the city. But the Union situation soon became extremely

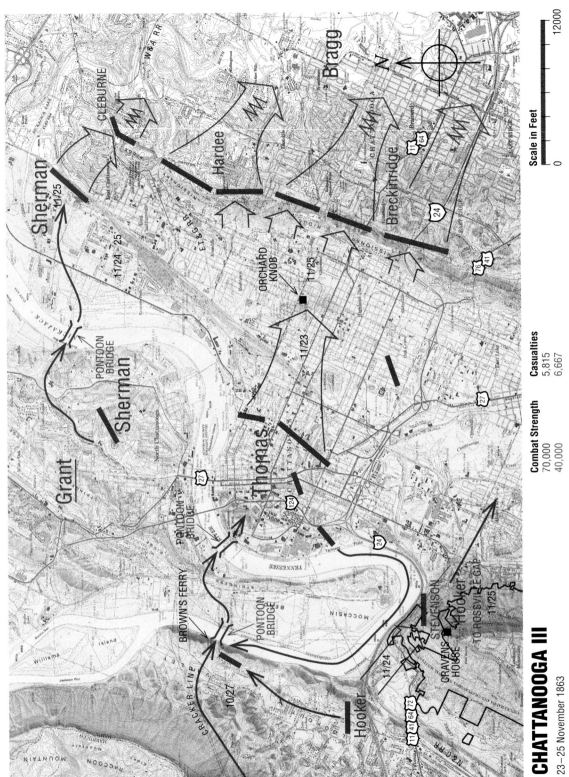

CHATTANOOGA III

23 – 25 November 1863

	Combat Strength	Casualties
	70,000	5,815
	40,000	6,667

Scale in Feet

0   12000

desperate; the troops eventually were reduced to eating only half of the usual daily ration. Grant reached Chattanooga on October 23 and within a week opened an effective supply line, known as the "Cracker Line." Grant awaited Sherman's arrival, when he would be strong enough to attempt to break the siege.

The Confederate command at Chattanooga was in serious disarray. Bragg's failure to press the Union army after Chickamauga had destroyed the corps commanders' last traces of confidence in his leadership, and immediately after the battle they asked President Jefferson Davis to remove him. CS Lieutenant General James Longstreet, hero of the Confederate victory at Chickamauga, put aside a previous disagreement with CS General Robert E. Lee at Gettysburg and wrote to the secretary of war, "I am convinced that nothing but the hand of God can save us or help as long as we have our present commander. . . . Can't you send us General Lee? The army in Virginia can operate defensively, while our operations here should be offensive — until we recover Tennessee at all events. We need some great mind as General Lee's (nothing more) to accomplish this." Of the Confederate siege of Chattanooga, Longstreet later wrote in derision, "We were trying to starve the enemy out by investing him on the only side from which he could not have gathered supplies."

Davis responded to these overtures by paying Bragg and his subordinates a visit in early October. He dealt with the criticisms by leaving Bragg in command and removing his severest critics. Davis ordered CS Lieutenant General Leonidas Polk to Mississippi, removed CS Lieutenant General Daniel Harvey Hill and left him without a command, and approved Bragg's plan to dispatch Longstreet with 15,000 troops to retake Knoxville, which had been captured earlier by a Union column marching from Kentucky under US Major General Ambrose E. Burnside. This left Bragg with only about 40,000 troops available for duty at Chattanooga to oppose a Union aggregation that would soon reach 70,000. The Union forces were being concentrated under their three most capable generals, while the Confederate forces were

being dispersed and led by the weakest of their field commanders.

Sherman arrived in mid-November, and Grant completed his plans for a coordinated attack. Sherman was to lead the main effort, crossing the river above the city to strike the northern end of the Confederate line on Missionary Ridge. Hooker was to drive off the Confederate force, now commanded by CS Major General Carter L. Stevenson, which was holding the slope between Lookout Mountain and the river, then move to the Rossville Gap and envelop the southern flank of the Confederate line on Missionary Ridge. Thomas was to seize Orchard Knob and demonstrate against the center of the Confederate line on Missionary Ridge to prevent Bragg from reinforcing his flanks. On November 23 Thomas's troops took their objective. The following day Hooker accomplished the first part of his mission. His troops also scaled the mountain, drove off the handful of Confederates there, and planted the Stars and Stripes amid the mists of Point Lookout. The entire Lookout Mountain operation soon became romanticized as "the battle above the clouds."

Sherman's repeated assaults on November 25 against the Confederate right (CS Lieutenant General William J. Hardee's Corps) were fierce, but the line held. The troops of Confederate division commander CS Major General Patrick Cleburne — known by his associates as the "Stonewall Jackson of the West" — fought with particular stubbornness. Hooker was slow in crossing Chattanooga Creek and approaching the Rossville Gap; his attack became more or less a mopping-up operation. The decisive action of the day, one of the most remarkable actions of the war, was carried out by Thomas's troops in the center against the corps of CS Major General John C. Breckinridge. In the late afternoon, after advancing and seizing the line of Confederate rifle pits along the base of Missionary Ridge, the Union troops charged, without orders but with invincible spirit, up the steep slope of the ridge while Grant and Thomas watched from below in alarm. Grant said somebody would "pay for" the blunder if the assault failed.

It did not fail. The Confederate position at the

center of the line was improperly located along the comb of the ridge instead of the "military crest" — that is, the line of the forward slope allowing the longest unobstructed field of observation and fire. But perhaps most damaging was the Confederates' pervasive demoralization and lack of faith in their commanding general. In a moment of panic at the climax of the Union charge, the Confederate center broke and the soldiers fled. The siege of Chattanooga ended with the Union "Miracle on Missionary Ridge."

With Cleburne's Division fighting a grim and effective rear-guard action, Bragg was able to concentrate his disorganized army in the vicinity of Dalton, Georgia, on the railroad twenty-five miles southeast of Chattanooga. Disheartened and disgraced, he asked to be relieved of command and confided to Davis, "The disaster [at Missionary Ridge] admits of no palliation, and is justly disparaging to me as a commander. . . . I fear we both erred in the conclusion for me to retain command here after the clamor raised against me." On Lee's advice, Davis recalled CS General Joseph E. Johnston from inactivity and placed him at the head of the Confederate army in Georgia.

The toll in casualties at Chattanooga was not heavy when compared with such other Civil War battles as Antietam, Gettysburg, or Chickamauga. Union losses: 5,815 overall, 752 killed, 4,713 wounded, 350 missing or captured. Confederate losses: 6,667 overall, 361 killed, 2,160 wounded, 4,146 missing or captured. But both the tactical and strategic results were immense. One of the two major Confederate armies had been utterly defeated. Southern morale, soaring after Chickamauga, now plummeted. Chattanooga was left firmly in Union hands; five months later it would be the staging point for Sherman's mission of havoc to the sea.

Estimated Casualties: 5,815 US, 6,667 CS

The Chattanooga Battlefields, units of Chickamauga and Chattanooga National

Military Park, include Wauhatchie, Orchard Knob, Lookout Mountain, Signal Point, and Missionary Ridge. They are off Interstate 24 in Chattanooga and include 2,884 acres of the historic battlefields.

Ringgold Gap, Georgia (GA005), Catoosa County, November 27, 1863

Keith S. Bohannon

The battle of Missionary Ridge on November 25 resulted in a precipitous retreat into northwest Georgia by the defeated Confederate Army of Tennessee. Hoping to delay the pursuing Federals and save his wagon trains and artillery, CS General Braxton Bragg ordered CS Major General Patrick R. Cleburne's Division to defend the mountain pass, Ringgold Gap. Bragg's choice for this critical assignment was fortuitous because Cleburne was one of the best officers in the luckless Army of Tennessee.

In the predawn darkness of November 27 Cleburne's 4,157 infantrymen forded the icy waters of East Chickamauga Creek. After marching through the town of Ringgold, they took up positions one half mile to the southeast in Ringgold Gap. Through this thousand-foot-wide gap between White Oak Mountain to the north and Taylor's Ridge to the south ran the Western & Atlantic Railroad, a wagon road, and East Chickamauga Creek. Cleburne carefully positioned his division in and around the gap, and hid his men and artillery in the woods, in a ravine, and behind brush screens. On the crest of Taylor's Ridge was a single regiment of CS Brigadier General Mark P. Lowrey's Brigade. Within the gap Cleburne placed two cannons and almost all of CS Brigadier General Daniel C. Govan's Brigade. The remainder of Lowrey's command and a portion of CS Brigadier General Lucius E. Polk's Brigade were held in reserve behind Govan. Cleburne placed CS Brigadier General Hiram B. Gran-

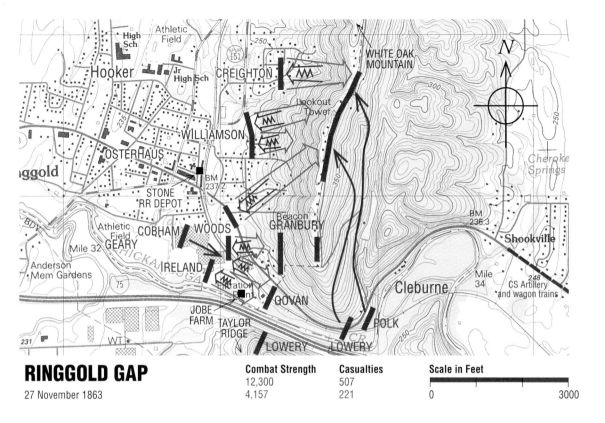

RINGGOLD GAP

27 November 1863

Combat Strength	Casualties	Scale in Feet
12,300	507	
4,157	221	0 3000

bury's Brigade along the base and eastern slope of White Oak Mountain.

At about 7:30 A.M. a Union column commanded by US Major General Joseph Hooker drove off the Confederate cavalrymen guarding a ford and a covered bridge over the creek. Flushed with success after victories at Lookout Mountain and Missionary Ridge, the blue-coated troops entered Ringgold. Unionist civilians and ex-slaves told Hooker about the demoralized state of the Confederates. Despite the absence that morning of his artillery, Hooker believed that attacking the Southern rear guard would result in the capture of Confederate wagons and artillery.

Shortly before 8:00 A.M. Federal soldiers from US Brigadier General Charles Woods's brigade of US Brigadier General Peter J. Osterhaus's division approached Cleburne's concealed position. Volleys from CS General Granbury's Texans stopped Woods's three center regiments. A fourth that marched into Ringgold Gap also suffered a costly repulse. Woods sent a fifth regiment up

White Oak Mountain in an attempt to turn the Confederate right flank. When the Confederates pinned this unit near the crest of the ridge, US Colonel James A. Williamson pushed several regiments from his brigade up the mountain in support. Cleburne reacted by ordering Polk and Lowrey to drive back the Federals. After intense fighting at close quarters, the Federals retreated down the slopes, having lost two flags and dozens of men killed, wounded, or captured.

Hooker then sent forward US Brigadier General John W. Geary's division to turn Cleburne's right flank. Geary ordered US Colonel William R. Creighton's brigade to ascend White Oak Mountain. Creighton's men, veterans of the Army of the Potomac, climbed past the prone lines of Williamson's Iowans. Vowing they would teach the Western troops a lesson, Creighton's men advanced up the steep slopes. Within minutes a fearful Confederate frontal and enfilade fire drove the easterners back down the mountain. Geary's other brigades under US Colonels George A. Cobham, Jr., and David Ireland advanced against the Confederate center and left. Cobham's men made it to a small rise in front of Cleburne's line before lying down to trade volleys with the enemy. Ireland's New Yorkers moved up as far as the buildings of the Isaac Jobe farm before they became pinned down by rifle and cannon fire coming from the gap.

US Major General Ulysses S. Grant arrived in Ringgold at about noon to confer with Hooker. Grant, preoccupied with the necessity of relieving US Major General Ambrose E. Burnside's besieged forces in Knoxville, discontinued the attacks against the Confederates in Ringgold. The four-hour battle of Ringgold Gap, which Grant called an "unfortunate" affair, cost the Federals about 507 casualties.

While Grant and Hooker conferred behind the stone railroad depot in Ringgold, Cleburne received a dispatch stating that the Confederate trains were safe, and he could withdraw his command. By 2:00 P.M. the Confederate rear guard had retreated one mile to the south. At a cost of 221 casualties Cleburne saved the wagon trains and much of the artillery of the Army of Tennessee and earned the thanks of the Confederate Congress.

Estimated Casualties: 507 US, 221 CS

The Ringgold Gap battlefield is at Ringgold, north of Interstate 75. The state of Georgia and the city of Ringgold own 5.76 acres of the battlefield.

Knoxville Campaign: November–December 1863

Campbell's Station, Tennessee (TN023), Knox County, November 16, 1863

On November 4, during the Confederate siege of Chattanooga, CS General Braxton Bragg detached CS Lieutenant General James Longstreet with two divisions of infantry and 5,000 cavalry to recapture Knoxville. This order was in the aftermath of President Jefferson Davis's visit to Bragg's headquarters to consider the corps commanders' complaints and their pleas that he remove Bragg from command. Instead Davis kept Bragg and authorized the transfer or removal of corps commanders.

US Major General Ambrose E. Burnside commanded elements of the IX Corps and XXIII Corps garrisoning the Knoxville area. US Major General Ulysses S. Grant's orders to Burnside were to avoid serious losses while keeping Longstreet occupied until Grant could get a Federal force between Longstreet and Bragg that would cut Longstreet's supply lines and force him to abandon his campaign against Burnside. One of Grant's many challenges was to allay President Abraham Lincoln's fears for Burnside's army and the East Tennessee Unionists while Grant prepared his attack on Bragg's right flank upstream from Chattanooga.

Following parallel routes, Longstreet and Burnside raced for Campbell's Station, a strategic hamlet seven miles southwest of Knoxville where the Concord Road from the south intersected the Kingston Road to Knoxville. If Longstreet reached Campbell's Station first, he would cut Burnside off from his Knoxville fortifications and compel him to fight unprotected by the earthworks. Burnside's advance reached the vital intersection by forced marches at about noon on a rainy November 16.

A few minutes later Longstreet's skirmishers approached, followed by troops of CS Major General Lafayette McLaws's Division. They struck with such force that they turned the Federal right but were soon thrown back by a counterattack. CS Brigadier General Micah Jenkins was unable to move a brigade through the woods along the southern ridge to get behind the Federal left flank. Burnside ordered his troops to withdraw under fire, supported by their artillery, to a tighter line three fourths of a mile to their rear. Longstreet ordered Jenkins to outflank the new position, but darkness halted the action. The Federals marched into their strong Knoxville defenses.

Estimated Casualties: 400 US, 570 CS

Fort Sanders, Tennessee (TN025), Knox County, November 29, 1863

CS General Longstreet conducted a siege of Knoxville while he determined the best place to assault the strong Federal works that extended from East Knoxville to College Hill. They included Fort Sanders, on a rise nearly 200 feet high, northwest of College Hill. It was manned by 440 soldiers with twelve cannons and protected by a ditch six to eight feet deep at the base of the steep parapet. Amidst conflicting opinions and information — Longstreet held that the ditch was three feet deep even though he had been informed that it was twice that — he decided to attack the fort.

On the morning of November 29, the brigades of CS Brigadier Generals Benjamin G. Humphreys, Goode Bryan, and William Wofford charged. Union wire entanglements, including telegraph wire stretched between tree stumps, slowed the Confederates. The fort's deep ditch halted them, and the Federals hit them with devastating fire. Since they did not have scaling ladders, they were trapped. In the twenty-minute attack about 800 were wounded, killed, or captured in the "death pit."

Immediately after the battle Longstreet received word of CS General Bragg's decisive defeat at Chattanooga and orders from President Jefferson Davis to rejoin Bragg in Georgia. After several days of consultations with his generals, Longstreet concluded that logistics precluded a march to Georgia. They voted to retreat toward Virginia and encamp for the winter.

Estimated Casualties: 15 US, 800 CS

Bean's Station, Tennessee (TN026), Grainger County, December 14, 1863

CS General Longstreet's First Corps began to retreat in a pouring rain on the night of December 4–5 and marched all night northeast toward Rogersville. When the US IV Corps arrived from Chattanooga, US General Burnside ordered US Major General John G. Parke's infantry and US Brigadier General James M. Shackelford's cavalry to pursue the Confederates. Longstreet turned on his pursuers at Bean's Station, an old stagecoach stop on the Holston River seventeen miles southwest of Rogersville, and maneuvered three columns to trap the 10,000 Federals.

The battle began early on December 14, but the Confederate trap failed to close. CS Major General William Martin did not get his cavalry into position behind Shackelford, nor did CS Brigadier General William "Grumble" Jones and his two brigades. The Federals barricaded themselves within the three-story hotel that dominated the center of their line. They withstood CS Brigadier General Bushrod Johnson's assaults and delivered heavy artillery fire until Confederate fire hit the building. They retired to Blain's Cross Roads.

On December 12 Burnside, at his own request, was relieved as commander of the Army of the Ohio for reasons of health and was replaced by US Major General John G. Foster. (Burnside returned to duty in March 1864.) On December 19 Longstreet headed east to winter quarters along the railroad near Russellville, Tennessee.

Estimated Casualties: 115 US, 222 CS

East Tennessee: December 1863– January 1864

Mossy Creek, Tennessee (TN027), Jefferson County, December 29, 1863

CS Lieutenant General James Longstreet, commander of the Department of East Tennessee, went into winter quarters along the East Tennessee & Virginia Railroad in northeast Tennessee after his failed Knoxville campaign. His request to be relieved of his command was refused. On December 28 US Brigadier General Samuel D. Sturgis responded to the report of Confederate cavalry near Dandridge on the French Broad River east of Knoxville by ordering most of his cavalrymen out from Mossy Creek to Dandridge on two different roads.

The next morning at Mossy Creek CS Major General William T. Martin's cavalry attacked the remainder of Sturgis's force, commanded by US Colonel Samuel R. Mott. The Confederates advanced, driving the Federals in front of them. When the Union troopers who had set out for Dandridge returned, they drove the Confederates back. Martin retreated from the area after dark, but Sturgis did not mount a pursuit.

Estimated Casualties: 151 US, unknown CS

Dandridge, Tennessee (TN028), Jefferson County, January 17, 1864

When US Major General Ulysses S. Grant visited Knoxville early in the year, he directed US Major General Gordon Granger, commander of the IV Corps of the Army of the Cumberland, to push the Confederates under CS General Longstreet back from their winter quarters and through Buck's Gap. US Major General John Parke advanced on Dandridge on January 14 and forced CS General Longstreet's troops to fall back. Long-

street brought up reinforcements the next day to threaten the Union base at New Market. On the sixteenth US General Sturgis rode out to occupy Kimbrough's Crossroads. Within three or four miles of the crossroads his cavalry met Confederate troops and pushed them back toward the crossroads. As the Union cavalry advanced, they were engaged by Confederate infantry and cavalry supported by artillery. Longstreet led one of CS General Martin's brigades in the attack that compelled the Federals to retire to Dandridge.

On January 17 at about 4:00 P.M. the Confederates attacked at Dandridge, and the battle continued until after dark with neither side gaining ground. That night the Union forces fell back to New Market and Strawberry Plains, pursued by the Confederates. The Federals were short on food and ammunition and were suffering in an unusually cold winter without adequate shelter, clothes, and supplies.

Estimated Casualties: 150 US, unknown CS

Fair Garden, Tennessee (TN029), Sevier County, January 27–28, 1864

After the battle of Dandridge, Federal cavalry crossed to the south side of the French Broad River to disrupt Confederate foraging and capture supply wagons. On January 26 US General Sturgis deployed his troops to watch the fords and roads in the area.

On the morning of January 27, in a heavy fog, Sturgis attacked the converging Confederate forces on Fair Garden Road with US Colonel Edward M. McCook's regiments. They drove back CS General Martin's forces, ending the battle late in the afternoon with a saber charge that routed the Confederates.

The next day Sturgis pursued them, inflicted additional casualties, and took prisoners. Although short of supplies and greatly outnumbered, Sturgis attacked CS Brigadier General Frank C. Armstrong's cavalry division, posted at Swan's Island in the river about three miles away, unaware that

Armstrong had strongly fortified his position and that three infantry regiments had reinforced him. The attack continued until dark when the Federal troopers retired from the area, exhausted and short on supplies and ammunition.

Estimated Casualties: 100 US, 165 CS

Bristoe Campaign: October–November 1863

Auburn I, Virginia (VA039), Fauquier County, October 13, 1863

After the Confederate defeat at Gettysburg, CS General Robert E. Lee's Army of Northern Virginia fell back south of the Rapidan River. US Major General George Gordon Meade slowly followed with the Army of the Potomac and occupied the area north of the Rappahannock River in September 1863. Since there had been little battle action in Virginia for about six weeks, the Confederacy decided in early September to stave off disaster in East Tennessee and northwest Georgia by rushing CS Lieutenant General James Longstreet, with two of Lee's infantry divisions, to reinforce CS General Braxton Bragg. The Lincoln administration prodded Meade to occupy the area between the Rappahannock and the Rapidan Rivers. After the Federal defeat in the battle of Chickamauga on September 18–20, US Major General Joseph Hooker was recalled to duty and ordered to Tennessee with two of Meade's corps, the XI and the XII.

Lee launched the Bristoe campaign when he saw Meade's reduced strength as an opportunity for an offensive action — a turning movement to get around Meade's right flank, and isolate and defeat the Army of the Potomac in detail before the Federals could get to their defenses east of Bull Run. Part of Lee's plan was to threaten Washington so that additional Union troops would not be sent to Tennessee.

CS Major General J. E. B. Stuart rode ahead of Lee's army, screening its movements, while Meade began to withdraw, first from the Rapidan and then from the Rappahannock. The Confederates concentrated at Warrenton. Lee sent Stuart on a reconnaissance to Catlett's Station, nine miles to the southeast. At Auburn, five miles from Warrenton, Stuart skirmished with elements of US Major General William H. French's III Corps. Their valuable wagon park tempted the Confederates to attack, but since it was strongly guarded, they hid in the woods and watched. French's corps moved on. Suddenly the Confederates were all but surrounded by the arrival of US Major General Gouverneur K. Warren's II Corps, but no Federals saw Stuart's troopers.

Estimated Casualties: 50 total

Auburn II, Virginia (VA041), Fauquier County, October 14, 1863

On the morning of October 14, the Confederate cavalry emerged from hiding and skirmished with two brigades from US General Warren's II Corps. CS General Stuart boldly bluffed and escaped disaster. Warren pushed on to Catlett's Station on the Orange & Alexandria Railroad. Stuart's information about the route of the Union retreat along the railroad determined the course of the battle of Bristoe Station later that day.

Estimated Casualties: 113 total

Bristoe Station, Virginia (VA040), Prince William County, October 14, 1863

Jan Townsend

US Major General George Gordon Meade, believing that CS General Robert E. Lee would attack the Union army at Centreville, issued orders on October 13 instructing his corps commanders to mass there the next day. Lee, however, had no intention of engaging Meade's army at Centreville. He planned to intercept it sooner, preferably along the Orange & Alexandria Railroad. Bristoe Station was on the railroad.

Early on October 14, Meade's I and VI corps, followed by the III and V corps, crossed Broad Run north of Bristoe, heading toward Manassas. Marching from Catlett's Station along the south side of the railroad, the rear of the Federal infantry — US Major General Gouverneur K. Warren's II Corps — arrived at Bristoe early in the afternoon. Lee ordered CS Lieutenant General Richard S. Ewell's Second Corps and CS Lieutenant General Ambrose Powell Hill's Third Corps to march to Bristoe via Greenwich on October 14. At Greenwich the Confederates encountered Union army stragglers. Ewell knew the countryside and decided to go cross-country and by back roads to Bristoe while Hill's troops followed the road.

Hill rode ahead, and from a high point he sighted troops of the V Corps crossing Broad Run. He ordered CS Major General Henry Heth to form a battle line anchored on Greenwich Road. North Carolinians commanded by CS Brigadier General John R. Cooke and CS Brigadier General William W. Kirkland deployed on the right and left of the road, with CS Brigadier General Henry H. Walker's Virginia Brigade behind Kirkland's Brigade. Before they were in place, the impatient Hill sent his troops forward and directed CS Major William T. Poague's artillery to fire into the Union troops.

Hill erred, and launched a tragedy. He focused on the Union troops near Broad Run and failed to see Warren's corps as it came up, its columns screened by the railroad cut to his right. He also neglected to note that Ewell's corps was too far away to reinforce him.

When Union skirmishers spotted the Confederates' advance toward Broad Run, they crossed to the north side of the tracks and shielded Warren's men as they hastened into position behind the two- to ten-foot-high railroad embankment. Warren ordered the concealed troops commanded by US Colonel Francis E. Heath, US Colonel James Mallon, and US Brigadier General Joshua T. Owen to hold their fire. Artillery under US Captain William Arnold and US Captain Robert Bruce Ricketts unlimbered on ridges behind them. Lieutenant T. F. Brown's artillery, positioned on a hill across Broad Run, later joined Arnold and Ricketts.

As the Confederates closed on Broad Run at 2:00 P.M., troop movements and musket fire behind the railroad drew their attention. Cooke's and Kirkland's brigades shifted to the right to face the attack. Then the hidden Union soldiers rose and fired directly into the charging Confederate soldiers. Despite the odds, the Confederates

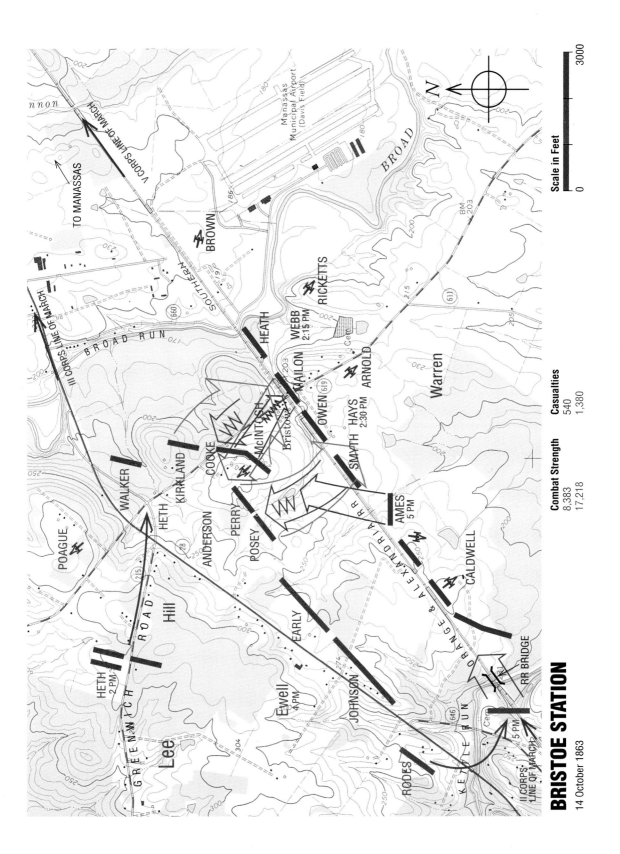

BRISTOE STATION

14 October 1863

Combat Strength	Casualties
8,383	540
17,218	1,380

Scale in Feet

0   3000

breached Mallon's line and mortally wounded Mallon. Point-blank Union fire and an artillery enfilade severely wounded Cooke and Kirkland and forced the Confederates to retreat in disarray.

CS Brigadier General Carnot Posey's Mississippians and CS Brigadier General Edward A. Perry's Floridians swarmed across the tracks and enveloped US Colonel Thomas Smyth's left flank. US Captain Nelson Ames's artillery roared into action and forced Perry and Posey back. When Cooke and Kirkland retreated, they left CS Major David G. McIntosh's artillery battery without infantry protection. Union soldiers rushed forward, captured five guns, and pulled them back to the south side of the tracks.

By 4:00 P.M. the Confederate battle lines had reformed about five hundred yards north of the railroad, and Ewell's corps and Lee had arrived. Union and Confederate artillery units began dueling, with the Union artillery having the advantage of stronger positions. At about 5:00 P.M. CS Major General Robert E. Rodes's Division of Ewell's Corps seized the Kettle Run railroad bridge one mile west of Bristoe. Darkness approached, and the battle of Bristoe Station was over.

Sporadic artillery fire continued during the evening. Confederate soldiers remained at their battle stations on the field, and it began raining. Throughout the night, the men listened to the cries of their wounded who lay near the railroad embankment and the Union line. The Federals carried their wounded off the battlefield, and by midnight they had quietly waded across Broad Run and resumed their march to Centreville.

Early the next morning Lee and Hill rode across the battlefield. Lee was displeased. He told Hill to "bury these poor men and let us say no more about it." Upon reading the battle reports, Jefferson Davis concluded, "There was a want of vigilance." Hill's misreading of the Federals' troop and position strength, his failure to determine the proximity of Confederate reinforcements, and his impatience, combined with Warren's patience and effective use of the battlefield terrain — including the railroad embankment — resulted in

the Confederate defeat. They lost about 1,380 men, and the Federals, about 540. The North Carolina brigades suffered the most. Cooke's casualties were 700, and Kirkland's 602.

Estimated Casualties: 540 US, 1,380 CS

The Bristoe Station battlefield, near the intersection of Routes 619 and 28 near Bristow, is privately owned.

Buckland Mills, Virginia (VA042), Fauquier County, October 19, 1863

CS General Lee followed the retreating Federals as far as Bull Run. Unable to sustain his army in that forward position, Lee withdrew from the plains of Manassas, shielded by CS General Stuart's cavalry. While Stuart covered the army at Buckland, he awaited the arrival of CS Major General Fitzhugh Lee's Division from Auburn. On October 19 US Brigadier General H. Judson Kilpatrick's cavalry, pursuing Stuart along the Warrenton Turnpike, crossed Broad Run to skirmish with the Confederates. Stuart fell back toward Warrenton and lured Kilpatrick into pursuit, knowing that Fitzhugh Lee was maneuvering around Kilpatrick's division to attack him from the rear.

US Brigadier General George A. Custer's brigade was guarding the ford at Broad Run when Lee attacked. The Union troopers halted the Confederate advance after heavy fighting. Meanwhile Stuart, in command of both Lee's cavalry and CS Major General Wade Hampton's Division, wheeled them around and charged the Union cavalry. (Hampton was recovering from the severe wound he had received at Gettysburg.) The Federals feared the enemy to their rear, and they broke, chased by Stuart for five miles in what became known to the victors as the "Buckland Races." Custer's brigade, still covering the ford, finally halted the pursuit and protected the Union cavalry while it crossed the stream. Stuart retired from Buckland the next day to join Lee's army behind the Rappahannock River.

Estimated Casualties: 230 total

Rappahannock Station, Virginia (VA043), Culpeper and Fauquier Counties, November 7, 1863

After the defeat at Bristoe Station, CS General Robert E. Lee retreated south of the Rappahannock River, with US General Meade in pursuit. Lee established a fortified bridgehead on the north bank of the river at Rappahannock Station. He planned to force the Federals to cross the river at Kelly's Ford farther to the southeast and then counterattack as the Federal army crossed. He concentrated his army near the ford, leaving Rappahannock Station protected only by the Louisiana Brigade under CS Brigadier General Harry T. Hays. The Army of the Potomac approached on November 7. CS Major General Jubal A. Early reinforced the bridgehead with CS Colonel Archibald C. Godwin's Brigade.

US Major General John Sedgwick's VI Corps surrounded the bridgehead, with the V Corps in support. Sedgwick designated two VI Corps brigades to lead the assault. After dark the 2,100 Federals used a railroad embankment to conceal their movement up to the earthworks. In their surprise attack they overran the Confederates, taking 1,673 prisoners there and another 300 when US Major General William H. French's III Corps stormed across Kelly's Ford. Because of the Union success at Rappahannock Station and Kelly's Ford, Lee abandoned his plan to winter in Culpeper County and retreated south of the Rapidan River.

Estimated Casualties: 461 US, 2,041 CS

Mine Run Campaign: November–December 1863

Mine Run, Virginia (VA044), Orange County, November 26–December 2, 1863

Richard Moe

Just a few miles east of Mine Run lies Chancellorsville, site of the great Union disaster of May 1863. A few miles farther east lies Fredericksburg, site of an even more tragic disaster five months earlier. At different points the Mine Run campaign of late 1863 appeared to have the makings of replicating for the Army of the Potomac both of these defeats — and at the hands of the same man who had caused them, Robert E. Lee. But it was not to be; Mine Run was the great battle of the Civil War that never happened.

With Thanksgiving approaching, US Major General George Gordon Meade and his Army of the Potomac were emboldened by their recent successes against the Confederate Army of Northern Virginia. Not only had they defeated Lee several months earlier at Gettysburg, but just weeks before they had prevented him from turning the Union flanks as the two armies raced toward Washington from their positions below the Rappahannock River. Meade's forces had mauled the southerners first at Bristoe Station and then at Rappahannock Station and Kelly's Ford, and Lee had been forced to return to the safety of his camps south of the Rapidan River. After US Major General Ulysses S. Grant had opened the Cracker Line and was positioning his troops to attack CS General Braxton Bragg at Chattanooga, the Lincoln administration pressured Meade to take the offensive before going into winter quarters. Believing he had a two-to-one advantage in manpower, Meade decided to seize the initiative from Lee by pursuing him across the Rapidan. He proposed to cross the river at fords far beyond the Confederate right and then swing swiftly to the west and hit Lee's unsuspecting flank. With the Confederates stretched along a

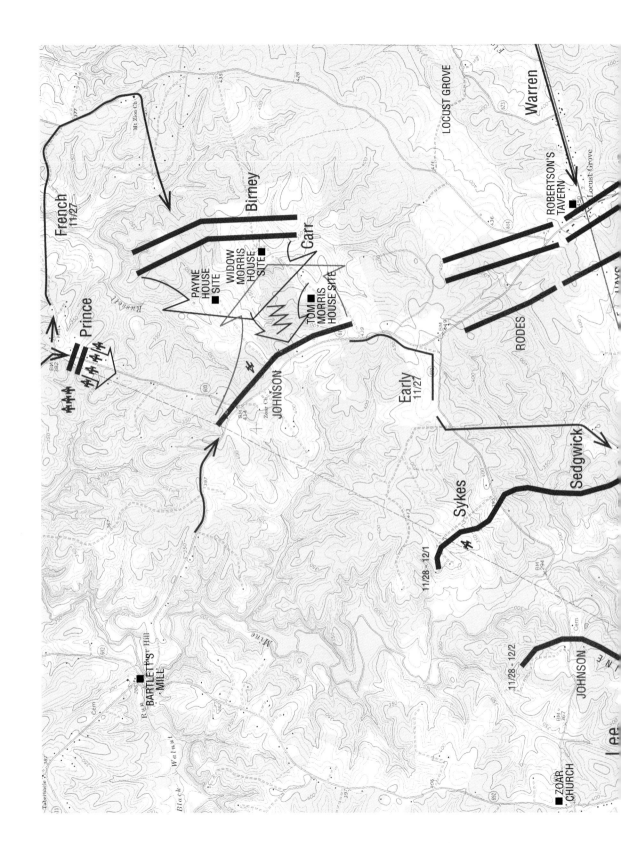

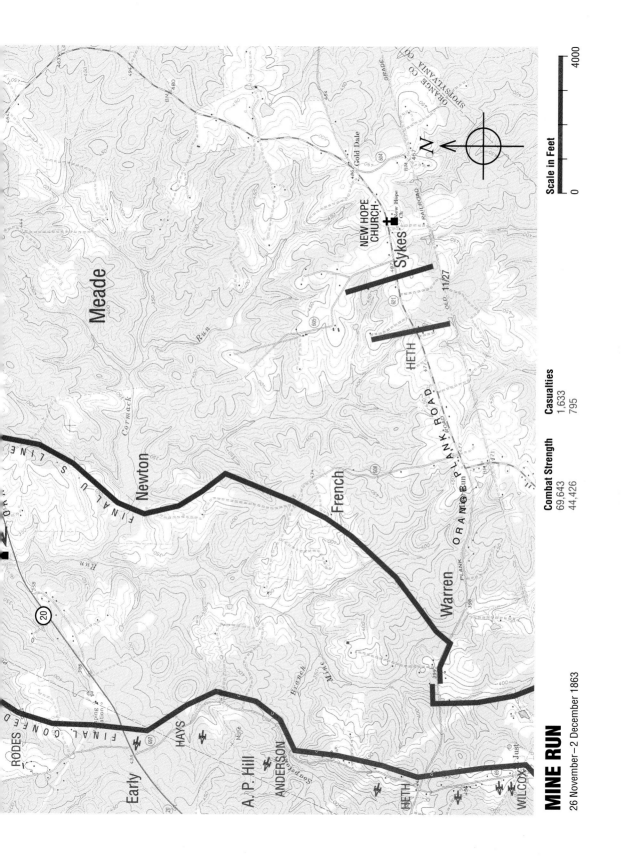

MINE RUN

26 November–2 December 1863

	Combat Strength	Casualties
	69,643	1,633
	44,426	795

Scale in Feet

0   4000

N

thirty-mile line on the south bank of the Rapidan, Meade intended to bring his full force to bear on only a part of Lee's. The plan was premised on stealth and speed, qualities not always associated with the Army of the Potomac, but Meade was determined to deal Lee the decisive blow he had failed to deliver at Gettysburg and since.

A series of Union delays caused the crossing on November 26 to go neither smoothly nor quickly. A scouting report enabled Lee to discover it sooner than Meade had wished, but the Confederate commander was uncertain whether the Union aim was to engage his army or head south toward Richmond. To meet either eventuality, he ordered the left wing of his army, CS Lieutenant General Ambrose Powell Hill's Third Corps, brought up to join the main force. On November 27 Lee directed CS Major General Jubal A. Early, temporarily in command of the Second Corps, to the east to intercept the Federals, and before long the Second Corps ran straight into the III Corps led by US Major General William H. French. Through a series of delays and misadventures caused largely by his own bad judgment, French was a full day behind schedule by the time he encountered Early.

Two of Early's divisions at Locust Grove blunted the advance of the II Corps along the Orange Turnpike. Farther to the north, CS Major General Edward Johnson's Division fought a delaying action at Payne's farm against most of the III Corps. These two engagements inflicted more than 500 casualties on each side, disrupted the Federal movement timetable, and bought Lee valuable time to establish a heavily fortified defensive line west of Mine Run, a creek flowing north into the Rapidan.

Lee ordered Early to withdraw behind Mine Run. By permitting his forward units to be pushed back to Mine Run while the rest of his army was coming up to it, Lee was able to deploy his forces behind seven miles of earthworks with an unobstructed slope that provided clear fields of fire. Precisely as Lee had in mind, this offered an opportunity for a massacre like the one that had devastated the Army of the Potomac at Fred-

ericksburg. Meade was nonetheless determined to go forward after entrenching for two days, and he ordered an artillery barrage on the morning of November 30, to be followed by infantry assaults against both flanks of the Confederate line.

Many of the men in the Army of the Potomac that night had been at Fredericksburg, and they had been spared, but when they saw the earthworks before them, they believed they would not be spared again. They had also been at Antietam, Gettysburg, and a dozen other bloody battles, and the growing ferocity of the war convinced them of that. But instead of the few fleeting seconds they had had in earlier engagements to grasp the danger they confronted, they now had all night to think about it. The soldiers knew that if they were wounded even slightly, enemy fire would prevent stretcher bearers from reaching them. They knew that if they lay disabled for long in the wintry cold that was already turning the water in their canteens to ice, they could easily freeze to death.

On picket duty in front of the II Corps and poised to lead the assault against the far right of the Confederate line was the 1st Minnesota, a regiment nearly decimated at Gettysburg in a heroic charge. The assistant adjutant general of the II Corps, concealing his rank under an overcoat, ventured out to learn what the men on the skirmish line were thinking. One of the Minnesota veterans declared it "a damned site worse than Fredericksburg," and added, "I am going as far as I can travel, but we can't get more two-thirds of the way up that hill." The eerie quiet before the storm, according to another veteran, was "one of the most sublime scenes I have witnessed," while yet another called the suspense "almost painful." So it was up and down the Union line.

Adding to the Union gloom was the sight of Confederate reinforcements arriving during the night. US Major General Gouverneur K. Warren, the hero of Little Round Top, who was commanding the II Corps that night of November 29–30, saw the reinforcements as well and assessed the situation anew. He concluded that an assault not only would fail but would be suicidal. He sent for Meade to come and make his own assessment. At the last moment Meade agreed, and he called off the attack on both ends of the line. The lesson of Fredericksburg had been learned after all: it was sheer folly to send men up an open slope against artillery and entrenched infantry. The lesson was obvious, but it almost had been lost. Because it wasn't, thousands were spared. Among them was a seventeen-year-old veteran named Charley Goddard who had just returned to the 1st Minnesota after being severely wounded at Gettysburg. He wrote his mother that he had seen "some fighting, been in some hot places, but never in my life did I think I was gone up the 'spout' until the order came to charge those works and I was shure as I set here writing to you that if I went up in that charge Chas. E. Goddard would be no more. . . . I thought it was the longest day of my life."

Lee, meanwhile, had learned of a weakness on the Union left and planned to exploit it with the kind of maneuver that had worked so brilliantly for him at Chancellorsville. But he was even more eager to have a repeat of Fredericksburg, and so he chose to wait behind his heavy earthworks for the assault he was sure would come. Uncharacteristically, he waited too long. Meade decided there was nothing to be gained by remaining below the Rapidan, and he ordered his army to withdraw after dark on December 1. Once Lee discovered the movement the next day, he pursued the Federals, but they had had too much of a head start, causing Lee to remark, "I am too old to command this army. We should never have permitted those people to get away." Just as Meade was denied his long-sought decisive victory over Lee, so was Lee denied a repeat of his two earlier successes a few miles to the east.

Meade was severely censured in Washington for canceling the attack, and his critics demanded his recall. After the decisive victories at Vicksburg and Chattanooga, Congress promoted Grant to the rank of lieutenant general in March 1864 and appointed him general-in-chief so it was clear that Grant outranked all other officers. He was the first officer to hold this rank in the U.S.

Army since George Washington. Grant decided to keep Meade in command of the Army of the Potomac and bumped US Major General Henry W. Halleck up to the position of chief-of-staff.

Mine Run was a case of missed opportunities on both sides, and after they returned to their earlier positions, both had little to show for their efforts except 1,633 casualties for the North and 795 for the South. Nothing else of consequence had been resolved, but lessons had, at last, been learned, including the folly of attacking an entrenched position.

Estimated Casualties: 1,633 US, 795 CS

The Mine Run battlefield, near Mine Run and Route 621, south of Route 20, is privately owned.

Gloom and unspoken despondency hang like a pall everywhere.

— Mary Chesnut, the Virginia diarist, December 1863

Rapidan River, Virginia: February 1864

Morton's Ford, Virginia (VA045),
Orange and Culpeper Counties,
February 6–7, 1864

While US Major General Benjamin F. Butler moved to attack Richmond to release Union prisoners, units of US Brigadier General Alexander Hays's division of the II Corps launched a diversion to draw Confederate troops northwest of the city. They crossed the Rapidan River at Morton's Ford on February 6 and were reinforced at dusk by US Brigadier General Alexander S. Webb's division. The I Corps demonstrated at Raccoon Ford, and their cavalry crossed at Robertson's Ford. CS Lieutenant General Richard Ewell's Second Corps of the Army of Northern Virginia arrived on February 7 to resist the crossing. Fighting was sporadic, the attacks stalled, and the Federals withdrew.

A Union deserter alerted the Confederates to the Federal advance from Williamsburg, so Butler abandoned his planned rescue and turned back at Bottom's Bridge.

Estimated Casualties: 723 total

Kilpatrick-Dahlgren Raid: February–March 1864

Walkerton, Virginia (VA125),
King and Queen County,
March 2, 1864

On February 28 US Brigadier General H. Judson Kilpatrick and US Colonel Ulric Dahlgren launched a raid on Richmond from the Union camps at Stevensburg. Kilpatrick had 3,500 men, and Dahlgren, the twenty-one-year-old son of USN Rear Admiral John Dahlgren, commanded an advance force of 460 men. While the main body rode along the Virginia Central Railroad tearing up track, Dahlgren struck south to cross the James River to penetrate Richmond's defenses and release the Union prisoners at Belle Isle. Kilpatrick reached Richmond on March 1 and skirmished before the city's defenses, waiting for Dahlgren, who was behind schedule, to rejoin the main column. When Kilpatrick finally withdrew, he was attacked by CS Major General Wade Hampton's cavalry near Mechanicsville. The Federals retreated to join parts of US Major General Benjamin F. Butler's Army of the James at New Kent Court House.

Dahlgren's command was unable to cross the James, so the troopers rode north of the capital to escape to the east. On March 2, elements of the 5th Virginia Cavalry and the 9th Virginia Cavalry and the King and Queen Home Guards ambushed Dahlgren and about 100 of his troopers near Walkerton. The Confederates killed Dahlgren and captured the others. Papers found on Dahlgren's body included instructions to burn Richmond and assassinate CS President Jefferson Davis and his cabinet. These papers caused a political furor. US Major General George Gordon Meade stated that neither the U.S. government nor any officer "authorized, sanctioned, or approved" such actions.

Estimated Casualties: 100 US, none CS

Deep South: January–February 1864

Athens, Alabama (AL002), Limestone County, January 26, 1864

On January 26 CS Lieutenant Colonel Moses W. Hannon's 600-man cavalry brigade attacked Athens, a town on the Nashville & Decatur Railroad, held by about 100 Union troops. In a two-hour battle US Captain Emil Adams's force, although outnumbered and without fortifications, repulsed the attackers. The Confederates retreated, having failed to take Athens.

They succeeded the following September when CS Major General Nathan Bedford Forrest captured the town and the garrison.

Estimated Casualties: 20 US, 30 CS

Meridian, Mississippi (MS012), Lauderdale County, February 14–20, 1864

US Major General William T. Sherman's Meridian expedition — essentially a raid — was an independent command. Sherman had been US Major General Ulysses S. Grant's favored lieutenant and, with US Brigadier General John A. Rawlins, Grant's chief-of-staff, his closest confidant. Sherman's objective was to destroy the supply center in Meridian and break up the railroads connecting it to two other major supply bases, Selma and Mobile. Sherman ordered US Brigadier General William Sooy Smith's cavalry force of 7,000 men to strike south from Memphis by February 1, wreck the Mobile & Ohio Railroad, and hit Meridian in advance of the infantry. Such destruction would slow the Confederacy's ability to send troops to the Mississippi River and to western Tennessee, enabling Sherman to pull more troops from those areas for his planned spring offensive south from Chattanooga, the Atlanta campaign. The Federals could then move on from Meridian to other supply centers, turn west, head up the Red River, and take Shreveport. Sherman left Vicksburg with 26,000 men on February 3, marched east, and launched the other part of his raid: destroying the Mississippi countryside so that the people would lose faith in their government's ability to protect them — and give up on the war.

CS Lieutenant General Leonidas Polk's scattered forces were inadequate to slow the Federals, but Polk was fortunate in that he had almost all of the region's trains at Meridian. By working around the clock, he had the last trainload of supplies on its way to Demopolis just before Sherman's soldiers arrived on February 14. When Sherman arrived that afternoon, the Confederates were gone, the warehouses were empty, and Smith had not arrived. He never did. His forces had been delayed in leaving Memphis by necessary preparations, and their advance was slow because they destroyed farms as they marched and because about 3,000 former slaves had joined the troopers, seeking help. On February 20 Sherman began his return to Vicksburg.

The Meridian expedition had mixed results. It did not succeed in freeing up soldiers to join the Federals in Chattanooga, and so it did not achieve its strategic objective. It did cause CS President Jefferson Davis to order three divisions of CS Lieutenant General William J. Hardee's Corps — led by CS Major Generals Benjamin Franklin Cheatham, Patrick R. Cleburne, and William H. T. Walker — to join Polk, thus weakening CS General Joseph E. Johnston's army in north Georgia. The destruction of the railroads did not have a lasting effect because equipment could straighten out the bent rails, known as "Sherman neckties." The public saw the expedition as a defeat because they assumed its purpose was to take Mobile.

Estimated Casualties: 170 US, unknown CS

Okolona, Mississippi (MS013), Chickasaw County, February 22, 1864

US General Smith needed reinforcements before starting for Meridian. He finally left Memphis on February 11, instead of February 1 as US General

Sherman had ordered. Smith's troopers met almost no opposition along the way as they rode slowly, only about fifteen miles a day, destroying farms and the track of the Mobile & Ohio Railroad. On February 18 Smith reached Okolona, the center of a rich agricultural area. Two days later, as he neared West Point, ninety miles north of Meridian, he fought 2,500 cavalrymen under CS Major General Nathan Bedford Forrest at Prairie Station and Aberdeen. On February 21 Smith skirmished with CS Colonel Jeffrey Forrest, General Forrest's youngest brother. Reinforcements brought the Confederate strength to 4,000, and the fighting intensified. Smith realized he was in a trap, so he ordered a retreat to the north. General Forrest arrived, ordered a pursuit, and routed the Union rear guard. The rest of Smith's force rallied just south of Okolona.

On February 22 Forrest attacked before dawn and pushed the Federals through the town. Smith established a new line two miles to the northwest, but Forrest maneuvered him out of this position and raced after the retreating Federals. In an eleven-mile running battle, both sides attacked and counterattacked. Smith rallied his men five miles north of Okolona, and Forrest led two brigades against them. Forrest's brother was killed, and his attack was repulsed. He then maneuvered around the Union right flank and forced the line to collapse. The Federals again rallied and counterattacked, but the intense fighting stopped them. They finally broke off the fighting and headed for Pontotoc at nightfall. Forrest did not order a pursuit because his men were exhausted and low on ammunition.

Smith arrived in Collierville near Memphis on February 26, having destroyed farms and railroad track. However, he had failed to reinforce Sherman and had been hammered hard by Bedford Forrest.

Estimated Casualties: 388 US, 144 CS

Dalton I, Georgia (GA006), Whitfield County and Dalton, February 22–27, 1864

While US General Sherman operated against Meridian, US General Grant ordered US Major General George H. Thomas's Army of the Cumberland to probe the Confederate lines around Dalton to determine whether CS General Johnston's Army of Tennessee was vulnerable to attack after President Davis ordered three of his divisions to Alabama to reinforce CS General Polk. Heavy rains delayed the Federal advance, but on February 22 Thomas's men advanced down the Western & Atlantic Railroad toward Mill Creek Gap, the opening in Rocky Face Ridge that shielded Dalton on the west.

Beginning on the twenty-fourth the Federals skirmished with the Confederates around Rocky Face Ridge, and discovered that the ridgeline was well entrenched and the gap was heavily defended. The Union troops almost turned the Confederate right flank after intense skirmishing in the Crow Valley on the twenty-fifth. That same day US Colonel Thomas J. Harrison's 39th Indiana Mounted Infantry stormed Dug Gap, south of Mill Creek Gap. The next day CS Brigadier General Hiram B. Granbury's Brigade drove them out.

The divisions sent to Polk returned in time to oppose Thomas, so the Federals were outnumbered. Thomas concluded that Johnston's lines were too strong to attack, and, having accomplished his mission, he withdrew toward Chattanooga on the twenty-seventh. He had also discovered Snake Creek Gap, through which Sherman sent US Major General James B. McPherson on May 9, 1864.

Estimated Casualties: 289 US, 140 CS

Florida: October 1863 and February 1864

Fort Brooke, Florida (FL004), Tampa, October 16–18, 1863

US Rear Admiral Theodorus Bailey learned that the blockade runners *Scottish Chief* and *Kate Dale* were loading cotton in the Hillsborough River, so he sent the *Tahoma* and the *Adela* to seize them. As a diversion, the warships bombarded Fort Brooke and Tampa on October 16. A landing party of 107 sailors under US Acting Master Thomas R. Harris disembarked at Ballast Point at 11:00 P.M. Guided by a local loyalist, Henry Crane, they marched fourteen miles to the Hillsborough River and burned the Confederate blockade runners at dawn. The Confederates destroyed the steamer *A. B. Noyes* to preclude its capture. A detachment of Tampa's garrison under CS Captain John Wescott attacked the Federals at the beach as they returned to their ship, killing or wounding 16 before the rest escaped.

Estimated Casualties: 16 US, unknown CS

Olustee, Florida (FL005), Baker County, February 20, 1864

While debate raged about secession, slavery, and the structure of the national community after the war, President Lincoln held that secession was illegal and that the Confederate states were still within the United States but out of their proper relationship with it. His position was that the rebels who had taken over the states must be replaced with leaders loyal to the United States, and that there were many people in the Confederacy who were opposed to secession. To encourage them to support the return of their states to the Union, Lincoln issued the Proclamation of Amnesty and Reconstruction on December 8, 1863. It offered amnesty and pardon to all (except Confederate government officials and high-ranking military officers) who would pledge their allegiance to the

United States and to its laws on slavery. When 10 percent of the number of people in a state who voted in the 1860 election so pledged, they could form a state government that the president would recognize. There was an effort in the U.S. House of Representatives to pass legislation that would create territorial governments for the secessionist states, but it was defeated.

One state in which Lincoln tried to encourage 10 percent to support the Union was Florida. In February 1864 he sent his personal secretary, John Hay, with US Major General Quincy A. Gillmore, commander of the Department of the South at Hilton Head, South Carolina, to northern Florida, an area of Unionist support.

The Federal force, US Brigadier General Truman A. Seymour's division, included the 54th Massachusetts Infantry, the African American unit that had fought courageously at Fort Wagner. They landed at Jacksonville on February 7 and pushed inland along the railroad. As the cavalry approached Olustee, the commander, US Colonel Guy V. Henry, was informed that Confederates were gathering in Lake City. He turned back to the main force and learned that Gillmore had left for Hilton Head, South Carolina, to handle logistical needs that had emerged. Gillmore's orders were for Seymour to protect Jacksonville by holding the town of Baldwin but not to extend the Federal occupation. Instead, Seymour decided to advance toward Lake City and continue on to destroy the railroad bridge over the Suwannee River. He assumed that his 5,500 soldiers could defeat the gathering Confederates. (Meanwhile a Federal diversion at Charleston did not prevent the Confederates from rushing reinforcements. They stopped the diversion and sent CS Brigadier General Alfred H. Colquitt's Brigade to Florida.)

Two Confederate brigades and a reserve, under CS Brigadier General Joseph Finegan, the commander of the District of East Florida, were along the railroad thirteen miles east of Lake City. Seymour advanced with his men and sixteen guns to engage them. On February 20 he encountered Finegan's 5,100 men in open pine woods north of the railroad near Ocean Pond. Colquitt advanced his brigade to meet Seymour on a field that limited Federal movement and artillery: a narrow stretch of land near Ocean Pond between two wetlands. The Federals attacked the Confederate center in the early afternoon but were repulsed and lost two guns. After several hours of heavy skirmishing, Colquitt was reinforced. He swept around the Union right and captured three more guns. The Federals fell back, and Seymour brought up the 54th Massachusetts to stabilize his crumbling line while he organized the retreat to Jacksonville.

The Union forces retreated at dusk. The Confederates took 150 prisoners but did not pursue Seymour. On February 23 the Federals reached Jacksonville and occupied it for the rest of the war.

Estimated Casualties: 1,861 US, 946 CS

Olustee Battlefield State Historic Site, fifteen miles east of Lake City and two miles east of Olustee on Route 90, includes 267 acres. Additional areas of the battlefield are protected in the Osceola National Forest.

There have been men who have proposed to me to return to slavery the black warriors of Port Hudson & Olustee. I should be damned in time & in eternity for so doing. The world shall know that I will keep my faith to friends & enemies, come what will.

— President Abraham Lincoln in August 1864

Military Strategy, Politics, and Economics

The Red River Campaign

Ludwell H. Johnson

○

The primary military objective of the Union invasion of northwestern Louisiana (March–May 1864) was the capture of Shreveport, headquarters of the Confederate Trans-Mississippi Department, and the consequent breakup of organized resistance in that theater of operations. US Major General Nathaniel Prentiss Banks, a Massachusetts politician devoid of military talent, led a force up the Red River accompanied by vessels from the Mississippi Squadron commanded by USN Rear Admiral David Dixon Porter, who was flamboyant, able, and sticky-fingered. A supporting column of 10,000 men under US Major General Frederick Steele was to march on Shreveport from Little Rock, Arkansas. CS General E. Kirby Smith, commander of the semiautonomous Trans-Mississippi Department, was responsible for meeting this formidable invasion by Banks, Porter, and Steele. Smith ordered CS Major General Richard Taylor, District of West Louisiana, to defend the Red River. Taylor was the son of former president Zachary Taylor, a skillful amateur soldier, and a veteran of CS Major General Thomas J. "Stonewall" Jackson's Shenandoah Valley campaign.

These military particulars give no hint of the real origins of the campaign. Years before the war began, some Americans, especially New Englanders and New Yorkers, had called for a migration of northerners to Texas. There Yankee civilization would replace southern barbarism, the new settlers would find rich farms, and the textile mills of the Northeast would have an alternative source of cotton. The coming of war seemed to make this dream realizable. The French invasion of Mexico and the fall of Mexico City in the summer of 1863 gave the Lincoln administration an additional reason to heed those who were lobbying for the occupation of Texas; a possible collaboration between Jefferson Davis and Napoleon III along the Rio Grande was not a comforting thought.

Furthermore, invading Texas by way of the Red River would open up more of Louisiana to the plan of political reconstruction Lincoln had set forth in his proclamation of December 8, 1863, and which he had ordered Banks to expedite. Finally, the valley of the Red River reportedly contained large quantities of baled cotton, the price of which had risen manyfold since 1861. This cotton could feed the mills of both England and New England and enrich the swarms of traders who planned to follow the armies, carrying Treasury Department or presidential permits to trade with the enemy. As for Porter and his jolly tars, they looked forward to a new opportunity for lining their pockets with the proceeds from cotton seized as "prize of war." This was the web of causality that drew the Federals up the Red River in the spring of 1864.

The campaign began on March 12 when 10,000 men under US Brigadier General Andrew J. Smith, sent from Vicksburg by US Major General William T. Sherman, landed at Simmesport, on the Red River near its confluence with the Mississippi, and proceeded to capture Fort DeRussy.

After brushing aside the outnumbered Confederates, Smith's soldiers and Porter's sailors went on to Alexandria. While waiting for Banks to come up from southern Louisiana, Porter's men fanned out through the countryside, commandeering wagons and teams, collecting "prize" cotton, and stuffing it into their gunboats. Ten days later Banks arrived with 20,000 infantry, artillery, and cavalry. After elections were held in the name of the "restored" government of Louisiana, the army and navy pressed on up the river. Taylor, with no more than 7,000 troops of all arms, fell back.

On April 3 Banks reached Grand Ecore. Thus far he had been keeping close to the river and to the comforting guns of the Mississippi Squadron. After holding more elections, Banks left the river, turned west, and began to follow the crest of the watershed between the Red and Sabine Rivers, where a few narrow roads ran over low hills and through dense pine woods. The road chosen led through Pleasant Hill and Mansfield, and then, turning back toward the river, to Shreveport.

Taylor, still looking for a chance to turn on the enemy, fell back until he reached Mansfield, where he made a stand east of the town. The result was a resounding Confederate victory. Neither side emerged as the decisive winner in the battle of Pleasant Hill the next day. After the battle, CS General Smith made the grave mistake of taking most of Taylor's infantry to Arkansas to meet Steele, who, harassed by Confederate cavalry and very short of food, had already begun to retreat. Taylor was outraged, for this decision eliminated any chance that he might cut Banks off and capture Porter's gunboats, which were experiencing great difficulties because of unusually low water in the Red.

Acting on the advice of several of his generals, Banks fell back from Pleasant Hill to Grand Ecore, and by the nineteenth had resumed his retreat to Alexandria: 25,000 Federals stalked by 5,000 Confederates. Banks's men burned everything that could not be stolen, leaving behind them a smoking wasteland. Taylor tried to trap Banks between the Red and Cane Rivers on April 23 and 24, but failed because the odds against him were too heavy. By the twenty-sixth, Banks was back in Alexandria, where reinforcements brought Federal strength up to 31,000. It was essential to make a stand here because the water on the falls was so shallow that Porter's flotilla was trapped. Time was needed to build a 750-foot-wide dam, which was to become famous in the history of military engineering: constructed in two weeks, it raised the water level sufficiently to allow the Mississippi Squadron to escape downstream, though not until the gunboats jettisoned their "prize of war" cotton.

Banks was then free to conclude one of the most wretched Union failures of the war. The army moved out of Alexandria on May 13, but not before the town was fired by soldiers belonging to the command of A. J. Smith, who rode amid the flames shouting, "Hurrah, boys, this looks like war!" At Mansura and at Yellow Bayou, Taylor tried again to disrupt the enemy's retreat. There was some brisk fighting at Yellow Bayou, but as usual the disparity in numbers was too great for the Confederates to prevail. By May 20 Banks had put the Atchafalaya Bayou between him and his pursuers, and the campaign was over.

The Red River expedition had important effects on the major campaigns east of the Mississippi. Sherman lost the services of A. J. Smith's 10,000 hard-fighting veterans, whom he had planned to use in his advance on Atlanta. Banks's fiasco also tied up troops intended for an attack on Mobile. That in turn released 15,000 Confederates from the Gulf states to join CS General Joseph E. Johnston in north Georgia. These changes in combat strength probably substantially postponed southern defeat in Georgia and may have lengthened the war by weeks or months. The Red River campaign is, however, most significant to history as an illustration of the way political and economic considerations shape military strategy.

Red River Campaign: March–May 1864

Fort DeRussy, Louisiana (LA017), Avoyelles Parish, March 14, 1864

In early March President Abraham Lincoln named Ulysses S. Grant general-in-chief and promoted him to the rank of lieutenant general. Grant's strategy was to press the Confederacy on all fronts so that its armies could not reinforce each other. His orders for US Major General George Gordon Meade, commander of the Army of the Potomac, were to go after CS General Robert E. Lee's army. US Major General William Tecumseh Sherman was to break up CS General Joseph E. Johnston's army and damage the Confederacy's war resources in Georgia. Grant brought US Major General Philip H. Sheridan east to lead Meade's cavalry. He ordered the navy to tighten the blockade while US Major General Benjamin F. Butler's Army of the James moved up the James, threatened Richmond from the south, and cut the railroad that supplied the capital. US Major General Nathaniel Prentiss Banks was to attack Mobile after driving up the Red River in Louisiana and capturing Shreveport while US Major General Franz Sigel took control of the Shenandoah Valley.

During the second week of March one of the largest amphibious forces ever assembled on the Mississippi River set out from Vicksburg against CS General E. Kirby Smith's Trans-Mississippi Department in Shreveport. The 30,000 men and sixty warships and transports were under the joint command of Banks and USN Rear Admiral David D. Porter. US Major General William B. Franklin's XIII and XIX Corps headed toward Shreveport via Berwick Bay and Bayou Teche; Porter's fleet and 10,000 men of the XVI and XVII Corps from the Army of the Tennessee under US Brigadier General A. J. Smith headed up the Red River. On March 23 another 8,500 men under US Major General Frederick Steele marched from Little Rock to link up with Banks at Shreveport.

Smith's forces disembarked at Simmesport on March 12. Thirty miles farther they approached Fort DeRussy, a fortification partially plated with iron to resist Federal fire from ironclads on the river. On the thirteenth, Smith's troops dispersed a Confederate brigade, clearing the way to the fort. When the Union forces arrived before Fort DeRussy the next day, the 350-man Confederate garrison opened fire. While Porter's gunboats bombarded the fort from the river, Smith sent US Brigadier General Joseph A. Mower's division to take the fort from the rear. Mower's troops scaled the walls that evening and forced the Confederates to surrender. The fall of Fort DeRussy opened the Red River to Alexandria, which the Federals occupied on March 16.

Estimated Casualties: 48 US, 269 CS

Mansfield, Louisiana (LA018), DeSoto Parish, April 8, 1864

Arthur W. Bergeron, Jr.

US Major General Nathaniel Prentiss Banks's main antagonist in the Red River campaign was CS Major General Richard Taylor, the son of former President Zachary Taylor. This was the second time in the war that the two men had opposed each other; the first was in CS Major General Stonewall Jackson's Shenandoah Valley campaign, when Banks commanded a Union army and Taylor the Louisiana Brigade. While Banks advanced up the west side of the Red River, USN Rear Admiral David Dixon Porter's sailors raided the countryside, collecting cotton for transport down the river. Taylor fell back toward Shreveport, watching for an opportunity to take on Banks.

Taylor decided that his army had retreated far enough when it reached the little town of Mansfield. The Union army, commanded by Banks, had left the protection of Porter's fleet on the Red River. The Federals had marched away from the river at Natchitoches and moved into northwestern Louisiana along the Old Stage

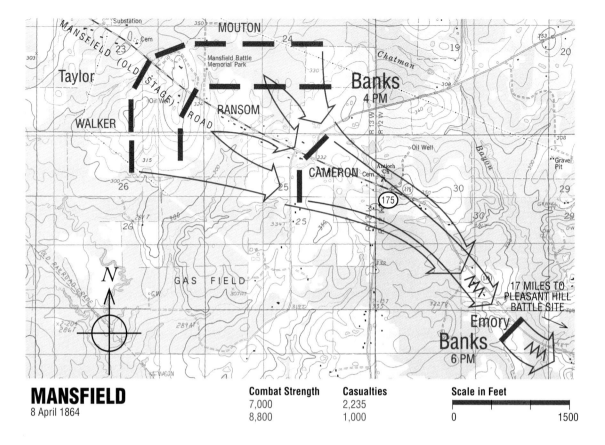

MANSFIELD
8 April 1864

Combat Strength	Casualties	Scale in Feet	
7,000	2,235	0	1500
8,800	1,000		

Road (now Route 175), a narrow track through dense pine forests and rolling hills. Once past Mansfield, Banks could put his men on any of three roads leading to Shreveport, and one of those roads would place the Federals back under the protection of their fleet. Taylor saw the strategic advantage in striking the Federals while the terrain forced them into a long line strung out along the Old Stage Road.

Taylor positioned his army about three miles southeast of Mansfield on the Moss Plantation along a road that intersected the Old Stage Road. This road led east toward Blair's Landing and the Red River and west toward the Sabine River. The 8,800 Confederates established their line just inside the woods between a cleared field and the crossroads, with the infantry division of CS Brigadier General Jean Jacques Alfred Alexander Mouton to the east of the main road and the infantry division of CS Major General John George Walker

to the west of it. Cavalrymen under the command of CS Brigadier General Thomas Green covered both flanks. Because of the dense forest, Taylor kept most of his artillery in reserve.

Shortly after noon on April 8 cavalrymen under US Brigadier General Albert Lindley Lee, supported by one brigade of US Colonel William Jennings Landrum's Fourth Division, XIII Corps, entered the clearing across from the Confederate positions. The Federal soldiers slowly crossed the field and drove the skirmishers stationed along the crest of Honeycutt Hill back to their main line. As the Union cavalrymen neared the hidden line of Mouton's infantry, they were hit by a heavy volley of musketry. Falling back to the crest of Honeycutt Hill east of the main road, the Federals took a position protected by a rail fence.

At about 3:30 P.M. Landrum's second brigade arrived on the field. The Union line soon formed a ninety-degree angle, one arm stretching south of the Old Stage Road and the other to the east. Lee placed one cavalry brigade on each flank of the infantry forces. Federal artillery batteries were interspersed at various points along the line. In all, about 5,700 Union soldiers were on the battlefield. US Brigadier General Thomas Edward Greenfield Ransom, who led the detachment of the XIII Corps in Banks's army, held command on the field during this first phase of action.

After the two sides had skirmished for a while, Taylor decided to attack the Federals before daylight ended. Mouton's Division opened the assault at about 4:00 P.M. The Confederates suffered heavy casualties, particularly in officers, as they crossed the open space under a heavy fire of musketry and artillery. Soon Walker's men and the cavalry joined in the attack and helped Mouton's depleted ranks rout the Federals. US Brigadier General Robert Alexander Cameron's Third Division of the XIII Corps had formed a second Union line about a half mile behind Ransom's force near Sabine Cross Roads. Placing his 1,300 men on either side of the Old Stage Road, Cameron ordered them forward. Some of the men from the first Union line joined Cameron's. This force held the Confederates back for about an hour, but, outflanked on both sides, they were soon routed. The Confederates overran the Union cavalry wagon train, which was stranded along the narrow road.

About three miles from the first Union line, US Brigadier General William Hemsley Emory's First Division of the XIX Corps formed a third line at Pleasant Grove along the edge of a clearing overlooking Chatman's Bayou and a small creek. Taylor's Confederates struck this position at about 6:00 P.M. and pushed the Federals back slightly from the two streams. During the night Emory's men retreated to Pleasant Hill.

In the battle of Mansfield the Confederates captured twenty artillery pieces, hundreds of small arms, around 150 wagons loaded with supplies, and nearly one thousand horses and mules. The price was about 1,000 men killed and wounded. Included among the dead was Mouton, who fell just as his men were throwing back the first Union line. Federal casualties numbered 113 men killed, 581 wounded, and 1,541 missing.

Estimated Casualties: 2,235 US, 1,000 CS

Mansfield State Commemorative Area, four miles south of Mansfield near Route 175, includes 177 acres of the historic battlefield.

Pleasant Hill, Louisiana (LA019), DeSoto and Sabine Parishes, April 9, 1864

Arthur W. Bergeron, Jr.

At Pleasant Hill US Major General Nathaniel Prentiss Banks ordered the supply train, the remnants of two cavalry brigades, and the men of the XIII Corps back to Natchitoches. On the field he had about 12,000 men in the two divisions of US Brigadier General Andrew Jackson Smith's XVI Corps, US Brigadier General William Hemsley Emory's division of the XIX Corps, and two cavalry brigades. On the morning of April 9 they took up positions near their camps, which were widely dispersed on a cleared plateau near the town of Pleasant Hill. There were wide gaps between the various Federal brigades. Banks, shaken by the defeat at Mansfield, failed to correct the faulty placement of his troops and failed to exercise command of his army during the battle.

In contrast, CS Major General Richard Taylor planned a masterful strategy on April 9 to keep the Federals demoralized and to force them to continue their retreat from Shreveport. With the addition of two infantry divisions of nearly 4,000 men from Arkansas and Missouri under CS Brigadier General Thomas James Churchill, Taylor had about 12,100 men, a slight numerical superiority over the Yankees. Taking advantage of the

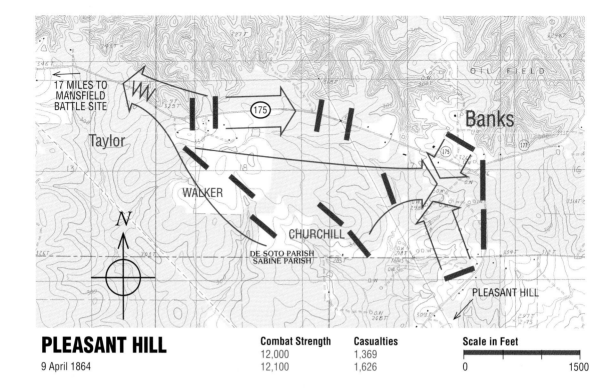

PLEASANT HILL

9 April 1864

Combat Strength	Casualties
12,000	1,369
12,100	1,626

Scale in Feet

0   1500

Federals' scattered positions, Taylor planned a flanking movement. Churchill's troops would march south of the road that ran from Pleasant Hill to the Sabine River, turn toward the northeast, and crush the Union left flank. CS Major General John George Walker's Division would move between the Mansfield and Sabine River Roads, charge the enemy when it heard Churchill's men making their attack, and connect its lines with Churchill's. Two cavalry brigades would attack the town once the Union flank was crushed, and two other cavalry brigades would then ride toward the north around the Federals' right to cut off their retreat toward Blair's Landing on the Red River.

The Confederates took most of the day to march the nearly twenty miles from Mansfield to Pleasant Hill. Churchill's men had marched about forty-five miles in the past two days, and the remainder of the army was still tired from the battle the afternoon before. Although the advance elements of Taylor's cavalry reached the vicinity of Pleasant Hill at about 9:00 A.M., the head of Churchill's column did not arrive at a point about

two miles west of the town until 1:00 P.M. Taylor allowed his men to rest for two hours before moving forward. Things began to go wrong from the first. Confused by the heavily wooded and hilly terrain, Churchill's men did not march far enough past the Sabine River Road and thus could not outflank the Union left. Their attack began at about 5:00 P.M. When Churchill's troops came out of the pine forest, they found themselves facing enemy troops in a deep ravine. The Arkansans and Missourians charged and drove the Federals back up the hill and almost into the town. Another Union force counterattacked. Soon this portion of the Confederate assault was repulsed with heavy losses. Once Churchill's flank movement failed, the other elements of Taylor's plan could not succeed. All of the Confederate assaults bogged down after some initial successes, and a number of the men fell back in confusion. Eventually night put an end to the fighting, and Taylor's men withdrew to look for water. The Federals did not attempt to follow them.

Controversy exists over the winner of the battle of Pleasant Hill. Most historians concede a tactical victory to Banks's men, while a few call the engagement a draw. The Union commander decided to order his army back toward Natchitoches during the night, and this retreat gave Taylor's men a strategic victory. Had Churchill's flank attack succeeded, Taylor would have won a second smashing victory on the battlefield. The Confederate army lost about 1,200 men killed and wounded and 426 captured. Casualties in Banks's army amounted to 150 men killed, 844 wounded, and 375 missing, a total of 1,369.

These two battles blunted Banks's Red River campaign; Mansfield was one of the last major field victories by a Confederate army. Though the Union army outnumbered his force, Taylor had succeeded in striking three enemy detachments and defeating them in detail. He aggressively pursued the Federals, and the Confederate attack at Pleasant Hill caused the Yankees to continue their retreat. Taylor demonstrated generalship of a high order in these battles.

US Lieutenant General Ulysses S. Grant ordered Banks to send Smith's men to assist in the Atlanta campaign and to move his other troops against Mobile, Alabama, ending Banks's march toward Shreveport and, once his army had reached the safety of the Mississippi River, ending his career as a field commander.

Estimated Casualties: 1,369 US, 1,626 CS

Pleasant Hill battlefield, south of Mansfield near Route 175 and Pleasant Hill, is privately owned.

Blair's Landing, Louisiana (LA020), Red River Parish, April 12, 1864

After the battle of Pleasant Hill, US General Banks retired to Grand Ecore and ordered his troops to dig in. USN Admiral Porter's fleet and the detachment of US General Smith's XVII Corps that was still in Louisiana had advanced farther up the

Red River. With Banks's defeat, they were isolated and had to fall back. Furthermore, the river level was dropping rapidly. On April 12 CS General Green's forces discovered a squadron of Federal transports and gunboats stalled at Blair's Landing. They dismounted, took cover behind available trees, and fired on the vessels. Hiding behind bales of cotton and sacks of oats, the men on the vessels repelled the attack and killed Green, Taylor's capable cavalry commander and hero of the 1862 battle of Valverde. The Confederates withdrew, and the fleet continued downriver.

Estimated Casualties: 60 US, 57 CS

Monett's Ferry, Louisiana (LA021), Natchitoches Parish, April 23, 1864

On April 19 US General Banks began the retreat of his force from Grand Ecore toward Alexandria on the narrow strip of land between the Red and Cane Rivers, his campaign a failure. The Confederates had defeated him in battle, the rapidly dropping Red River threatened to strand USN Admiral Porter's fleet, and US General Grant had ordered Smith's forces from Banks's command to reinforce US Major General William Tecumseh Sherman's Atlanta campaign. CS General E. Kirby Smith, commander of the Trans-Mississippi Department, concluded that Banks in retreat was less of a threat than US General Steele in Arkansas, so he headed toward Arkansas, leaving Taylor with only 5,000 men.

To trap Banks CS General Taylor sent CS Brigadier General Hamilton P. Bee with 1,600 cavalrymen and four batteries of artillery to seize Monett's Ferry, a major crossing over the Cane River. Bee occupied the bluffs overlooking the ferry and was ready when US Brigadier General Richard Arnold, the cavalry commander, approached the crossing. However, instead of hitting Bee head-on, Arnold found a ford upstream. On the morning of April 23 US Brigadier General William H. Emory's division crossed the upstream ford and hit Bee's flank while more Federals demonstrated against his other flank. Bee retreated, and Taylor later removed him from command. The Federals continued their rapid retreat to Alexandria.

By the time Porter reached Alexandria, the river level had fallen so much that his boats were trapped above the double falls. While Confederates sniped at the vessels from the shore, US Lieutenant Colonel Joseph Bailey, the chief engineer to US General Franklin, drew upon his lumbering experience and rescued the fleet. In less than two weeks he built two wing dams stretching from the banks toward the center of the river, with barges filled with rubble sunk to fill the gap between the dams. These dams — and another pair built upriver — raised the water level enough for the fleet to continue downriver. Bailey was promoted to brigadier general.

Estimated Casualties: 200 US, 400 CS

Mansura, Louisiana (LA022), Avoyelles Parish, May 16, 1864

US General Banks left Alexandria on May 13 after burning most of the town. CS General Taylor arrived before Banks at Mansura, on the Avoyelles prairie a few miles south of Marksville. On May 16, he massed his 5,000 men on either side of the town on the three-mile-wide prairie, so that he controlled three main roads and blocked the Union retreat route. It was a picture-book battle, and, as a Federal soldier described it, "miles of lines and columns . . . couriers riding swiftly from wing to wing; everywhere the beautiful silken flags." After a four-hour artillery duel, Banks brought troops forward, and the outnumbered Confederates fell back. The Federals continued on toward the relative safety of the opposite banks of the Atchafalaya River.

Estimated Casualties: unknown US, unknown CS

Yellow Bayou, Louisiana (LA023), Avoyelles Parish, May 18, 1864

On May 17 US General Banks's retreating troops reached the Atchafalaya River at Simmesport, but the river was too wide to bridge with pontoons. Once again US Colonel Bailey saved the Federals. He bolted all available boats together with timbers and planking, spanning the nearly half-mile river with a temporary bridge.

On May 18, while Bailey constructed his boat-bridge, the Union rear guard under US Brigadier General Joseph A. Mower attacked CS General Taylor's forces at Yellow Bayou to protect the Federals backed up against the river. They drove the Confederates back to their main line. A counter-attack forced the Federals to give ground, but the Union troops finally repulsed the Confederates. A brushfire forced both sides to retire. By May 20 Banks had crossed the Atchafalaya River, ending his ill-fated Red River campaign. The Confederates had not only won battles, but they had also prevented US General Smith's 10,000 men from reinforcing US General Sherman. Banks's failures prevented the Federals from moving against Mobile, enabling the Confederacy to transfer 15,000 reinforcements from Mississippi and Alabama to defend northwest Georgia.

Estimated Casualties: 360 US, 500 CS

Camden, Arkansas, Expedition: April–June 1864

Elkin's Ferry, Arkansas (AR012), Clark and Nevada Counties, April 3–4, 1864

US Lieutenant General Ulysses S. Grant ordered US Major General Frederick Steele to march from his base at Little Rock and link up with US Major General Nathaniel P. Banks and capture Shreveport, the headquarters of the Confederate Trans-Mississippi Department. Steele was opposed to the expedition, particularly because the area was "destitute of provision," but headed southwest from Little Rock on March 23 with 8,500 men toward Arkadelphia and Washington.

CS General E. Kirby Smith, the Confederate commander, had stripped most of the troops from Arkansas to oppose Banks, leaving CS Major General Sterling Price with only 7,500 men. Price's orders were to harass the Federals as they advanced, trading territory for time. Smith planned to defeat Banks, reinforce Price, and defeat Steele.

On April 3 CS Brigadier General Joseph O. "Jo" Shelby's cavalry struck the rear of the Federals near Okolona, but Shelby's men were routed by honeybees disturbed by artillery fire. On April 4 CS Brigadier General John S. Marmaduke's cavalry made a mounted attack against the Federals as they were crossing the Little Missouri River at Elkin's Ferry. The prolonged skirmish continued into the afternoon when the Confederates withdrew. US Brigadier General John M. Thayer's 5,000 men marched from Fort Smith and caught up with Steele at the ferry on the ninth. Price's delaying tactics and scorched-earth policy slowed the Federals and prevented them from foraging in the countryside.

Estimated Casualties: 26 US, 29 CS

Prairie D'Ane, Arkansas (AR013), Nevada County, April 10–13, 1864

To protect Washington, Arkansas, CS General Price evacuated his fortified base at Camden, marched northwest for two days, and arrived at Prairie D'Ane on April 7. His 5,000-man force quickly dug earthworks. The combined forces of US Generals Steele and Thayer continued their advance south into Arkansas. On April 10 they approached from the Cornelius farm and saw the Confederate line across the prairie. In the skirmishing, which lasted until about midnight, the Federals pushed the Confederates back to their entrenchments on the southern and western edges of the prairie. The next afternoon the Federals advanced and then withdrew. CS Generals Shelby and Marmaduke pulled their cavalry back to Prairie De Rohan (the site of today's Hope), while Price withdrew most of his force toward Washington, leaving only a small force on the western side of the prairie.

On April 12 Steele continued the push. While his cavalry shielded his movements, he surprised the Confederates by changing the direction of his march from Shreveport to Camden to the east because of the desperate shortage of food and forage. A small force attacked Thayer's rear guard on April 13. Thayer pursued the Confederates back across the prairie for about four miles, before joining Steele. The Federals occupied Camden on April 15, and Price fell back to Washington.

Estimated Casualties: 100 US, 50 CS

Poison Spring, Arkansas (AR014), Ouachita County, April 18, 1864

The Federals continued to suffer food shortages. They had had inadequate supplies when they started, they had depleted those they did have while US General Steele waited for US General Thayer, and there was little available food in the countryside. On April 17 Steele sent out a 1,100-man foraging party from Camden, commanded by US Colonel James M. Williams, which filled nearly two hundred wagons.

As the party returned the next day, CS Brigadier Generals Marmaduke and Samuel B. Maxey attacked Williams near Poison Spring, sixteen miles west of Camden and blocked the Camden Road. The 3,600 Confederate cavalrymen included the 700-man 1st Regiment of Choctaw and Chickasaw Mounted Rifles commanded by CS Colonel Tandy Walker, a Choctaw. Williams formed a defensive line, but the Confederates also attacked the Union rear. The Federals retreated, regrouped, and fell back to Camden, having lost their wagons and four guns. The 1st Kansas (Colored) Infantry suffered heavy casualties (117 killed and 65 wounded) because the Confederates killed wounded and captured soldiers. The loss of wagons and provisions was a serious blow to Steele's plans to remain in Camden.

Estimated Casualties: 301 US, 114 CS

Poison Spring Battlefield State Park, twelve miles northwest of Camden on Route 76, includes eighty-four acres of the historic battlefield.

Marks' Mills, Arkansas (AR015), Cleveland County, April 25, 1864

After the battle of Pleasant Hill in Louisiana, CS General Smith began to concentrate his forces to destroy US General Steele. He ordered three infantry divisions to travel north from the Red River on separate roads to ease the foraging problems en route. Smith arrived at Woodlawn on April 19 to assume command. He sent CS Brigadier General James F. Fagan and CS General Shelby with 4,000 cavalrymen to cut the supply routes from Pine Bluff to Steele's army at Camden. A Union force of 1,600 men commanded by US Lieutenant Colonel Francis M. Drake escorted 240 empty wagons from Camden toward Pine Bluff after

bringing supplies to Steele. Shelby learned about the column on April 24, and the Confederates rode forty-five miles that night.

They attacked the Federals at Marks' Mills at dawn, and the fighting was intense until Drake was wounded. Union resistance then crumbled. In the rout the Confederates captured 1,300 men and all of the wagons. Fagan continued northward on his raid. The Federals at Camden were almost out of food. When Steele learned of the disaster at Marks' Mills and of Banks's defeat on the Red River, he moved out of Camden during the night of April 26 and headed toward Little Rock to save his army.

Estimated Casualties: 1,500 US, 293 CS

Marks' Mills State Park, ten miles east of Fordyce on Route 8, includes six acres of the historic battlefield.

Jenkins' Ferry, Arkansas (AR016), Grant County, April 30, 1864

CS General Smith drove his men through heavy rains to catch the Federals as they headed north toward Little Rock. Smith's command included CS Brigadier General Thomas J. Churchill's Arkansans, CS Brigadier General Mosby M. Parsons's Missourians, and CS Major General John G. Walker's Texans. US General Steele's men were weakened by exhaustion and inadequate rations, but they were able to corduroy the muddy road to the crossing of the Saline River at Jenkins' Ferry. Union engineers laid a pontoon bridge over the river while 4,000 infantrymen built log breastworks. A thick swamp protected their left, and a creek their right.

On April 30 Smith attacked in the early morning fog. First the Arkansans, then the Missourians, and finally the Texans were thrown back. By early afternoon the Federals had crossed the river and dismantled the pontoon bridge. Smith's men were hungry and exhausted and had no bridge across the river. Steele arrived in Little Rock on May 2. The final Union strategic offensive in Arkansas was a failure.

Estimated Casualties: 700 US, 1,000 CS

Jenkins' Ferry State Park, four miles north of Leola, includes forty acres of the historic battlefield.

Ditch Bayou (Old River Lake), Arkansas (AR017), Chicot County, June 6, 1864

In May and June 1864 CS Colonel Colton Greene's cavalry brigade based in Lake Village in southeastern Arkansas interdicted traffic on the Mississippi River by firing at passing steamboats. After the Red River campaign, the 10,000 men of the XVI and XVII Corps under US Major General Andrew J. Smith returned to Vicksburg. On June 4 they headed north by boat for Tennessee to reinforce US Major General William Tecumseh Sherman's Atlanta campaign. Smith decided to capture Lake Village and landed a 3,000-man force at Sunnyside Landing on the evening of June 5.

The next morning the two brigades, commanded by US Brigadier General Joseph A. Mower, marched along the Old Lake Road south of Lake Chicot. As the 600 Confederates fell back five miles to Ditch Bayou, a natural moat, they skirmished with the Federals, who were never able to get into battle line because of the impassable bayou. Although they were outnumbered, Greene's men with their six cannons held off Mower's force until 2:30 P.M., when they ran out of ammunition. They withdrew to Parker's Landing on Bayou Mason, three miles west of Lake Village. The Union troops advanced to the town, sacked it, camped there overnight, and rejoined the flotilla on the Mississippi River at Columbia the next day.

Estimated Casualties: 133 US, 37 CS

Forrest's Raid on Paducah and Fort Pillow: March–April 1864

Paducah, Kentucky (KY010), McCracken County, March 25, 1864

After defeating US Brigadier General William S. Smith at Okolona, CS Major General Nathan Bedford Forrest led 3,000 cavalrymen from Columbus, Mississippi. He had two objectives: to recruit in West Tennessee and the Jackson Purchase area of Kentucky, and to prevent Union forces from reinforcing US Major General William Tecumseh Sherman at Chattanooga.

On March 25 the Confederates occupied Paducah and forced US Colonel Stephen G. Hicks and his 650 troops into Fort Anderson. Hicks had the support of two gunboats on the Ohio River and refused Forrest's demand to surrender. The troopers raided supplies and rounded up horses and mules. Hicks repulsed their assault on Fort Anderson. After holding Paducah for ten hours and destroying all property of military value, Forrest returned to Tennessee. When newspapers bragged that the Confederates had not found the 140 horses hidden during the raid, Forrest sent CS Brigadier General Abraham Buford back to Paducah, both to get the horses and to divert Federal attention from his attack on Fort Pillow. On April 14 Buford's men found the horses and galloped off with them to join Forrest.

Estimated Casualties: 90 US, 50 CS

Fort Pillow, Tennessee (TN030), Lauderdale County, April 12, 1864

On April 12 CS General Forrest and about 1,500 men attacked Fort Pillow, a U.S. military outpost on the Mississippi River about fifty miles north of Memphis. It was one of the fortifications that supplied Federal gunboats patrolling the Mississippi River. The fort included sutler facilities, civilians, and soldiers. The garrison of 585–605 men included two groups of about 300 each who were anathema to Forrest: southern white men who remained loyal to the United States, whom Forrest called "traitors," and former slaves serving as U.S. Colored Troops, whom Forrest considered to be property belonging to those who had held them in slavery.

Before Forrest arrived, CS Brigadier General James R. Chalmers had positioned sharpshooters on the high ground so their fire could cover most of the fort. When they killed US Major Lionel F. Booth, commander of the 6th U.S. Heavy Artillery (Colored), US Major William F. Bradford, commander of the 13th Tennessee Cavalry (Bradford's Battalion), took charge. Forrest arrived, and during his reconnaissance of the area, he was injured when several of his horses were shot out from under him. Bradford refused Forrest's demand to surrender. Forrest ordered the attack but stayed four hundred yards back and did not lead it, as he often did.

The Confederates quickly scaled the thick walls and began firing point-blank into the Federals. In the melee, while soldiers of both sides were shooting, some Federals tried to surrender while others attempted to escape, but they did not attempt to lower the U.S. flag as a symbol of surrender. Union troops ran for the protection of the gunboat *New Era* in the river, but it could not help them. The gunners were vulnerable to the Confederate sharpshooters and had taken the gunboat out of range.

Federal casualties were high, with 277 confirmed as dead: 32 percent of the white soldiers, the Tennessee Cavalry; and 64 percent of the black soldiers, the 6th U.S. Heavy Artillery (Colored) and the 2nd U.S. Light Artillery (Colored). The battle became known as the Fort Pillow Massacre.

The Confederates evacuated Fort Pillow that night and turned over the badly wounded prisoners of both races to the Federals the next day. Chalmers told a U.S. officer that he and Forrest "stopped the massacre as soon as they were able to do so" and that the Confederate soldiers "had such a hatred toward the armed negro that they could not be restrained from killing the negroes after they had captured them."

Three days later Forrest described Fort Pillow: "The river was dyed with the blood of the slaughtered for 200 yards. . . . It is hoped that these facts will demonstrate to the Northern people that negro soldiers cannot cope with Southerners." He also stated that his policy was to capture African American soldiers, not kill them. US Brigadier General James H. Wilson, the cavalry commander who defeated Forrest at Selma the following April, later wrote of Forrest: "He appears to have had a ruthless temper which impelled him upon every occasion where he had a clear advantage to push his success to a bloody end, and yet he always seemed not only to resent but to have a plausible excuse for the cruel excesses which were charged against him." Forrest's record in American history as a brilliant cavalry officer and unsurpassed leader of mounted infantry also includes his responsibility as commander at Fort Pillow and, after the war, as a leader of the Ku Klux Klan.

Estimated Casualties: 549 US, 100 CS

Fort Pillow State Historic Area, on Route 7 near the Mississippi River about eighteen miles west of Henning, includes an interpretive center, earthworks, and the restored fortification.

North Carolina: April–May 1864

Plymouth, North Carolina (NC012), Washington County, April 17–20, 1864

On April 17 the Confederates commissioned their new ironclad ram *Albemarle*, commanded by CSN Commander J. W. Cooke, and launched a joint operation with CS Brigadier General Robert F. Hoke's infantry against Plymouth, on the Roanoke River near Albemarle Sound. Their infantry and artillery attacks began on April 17. Early on April 19 the *Albemarle* attacked USN Commander Charles W. Flusser's Union gunboats, damaged the *Miami,* and rammed the *Southfield* and sank it. On April 20 Hoke ordered an infantry assault on Plymouth, defended by the garrison of Fort Williams commanded by US Brigadier General Henry W. Wessells. CS Brigadier General Matt W. Ransom's Brigade attacked the town from its unprotected east side while Hoke feinted from the west. The unrelenting artillery fire from land and from the *Albemarle* forced Wessells to surrender.

Estimated Casualties: 2,900 (including 2,834 prisoners) US, 300 CS

Albemarle Sound, North Carolina (NC013), Chowan and Washington Counties, May 5, 1864

After losing Plymouth the Federals evacuated Washington, North Carolina, on April 30. CS General Hoke next moved against New Bern with the *Albemarle*, the captured steamer *Bombshell,* and the *Cotton Plant,* which was loaded with assault troops. The Confederate flotilla steamed out of Plymouth on May 5. When the three ships reached the mouth of the Roanoke River at Albemarle Sound, they caught the wooden warship *Miami* and two other ships laying torpedoes (mines). To protect his assault troops, CSN Commander Cooke sent the *Cotton Plant* back to Ply-

mouth. At 4:40 P.M. the *Albemarle* engaged seven Union warships under USN Captain Melancton Smith. The more maneuverable Federal ships circled and rammed the unwieldy ironclad, but their shots bounced off its armored casemate. The battle continued until dark, when the Federals recaptured the *Bombshell.*

The *Albemarle*'s machinery and boilers were damaged in the fight, so Cooke had to return to Plymouth, having failed to take New Bern. Hoke's command returned to the Army of Northern Virginia to strengthen Petersburg against the Union forces landing at Bermuda Hundred. The following October, in a daring mission led by USN Lieutenant William B. Cushing, the Federals blew up the ironclad. Without its protection the Confederates could not hold Plymouth.

Estimated Casualties: 88 total

Bermuda Hundred Campaign: May 1864

Port Walthall Junction, Virginia (VA047), Chesterfield County, May 6–7, 1864

By May 1864 US Lieutenant General Ulysses S. Grant's coordinated strategy to defeat the Confederacy was under way. He had launched his campaign against CS General Robert E. Lee, and US Major General William Tecumseh Sherman had begun to press CS General Joseph E. Johnston in north Georgia.

On May 5, while Grant and Lee clashed in the Wilderness, US Major General Benjamin F. Butler's 39,000-man Army of the James disembarked from transports at Bermuda Hundred, a wide neck of land between the James and Appomattox Rivers. Butler was to sever the Richmond & Petersburg Railroad and cut off supplies to Richmond. He landed with two corps: US Major General William F. "Baldy" Smith's XVIII Corps and US Major General Quincy A. Gillmore's X Corps. On the way up the river Butler had dropped off garrisons — mostly U.S. Colored Troops — at vital supply points, including Wilson's Wharf and City Point.

CS General P. G. T. Beauregard commanded the Department of North Carolina and Southern Virginia, and his immediate subordinate in Petersburg was CS Major General George Pickett. The two immediately took defensive measures to protect Petersburg. The Federals were initially unopposed, but instead of advancing, Butler dug in along Ware Bottom at Cobb's Hill on May 6. He sent US Brigadier General Charles Heckman's brigade of Smith's corps southwest toward Port Walthall Junction, to threaten the railroad that ran north from Petersburg to Richmond. At 5:00 P.M. Heckman attacked the brigades of CS Brigadier Generals Johnson Hagood and Bushrod R. Johnson at the junction. When he came under heavy artillery fire from the railroad, Heckman concluded that there was a strong force to his front and retired.

The following day Butler sent a larger force to Port Walthall Junction under US Brigadier General William T. H. Brooks. Pickett was confronted with a dilemma: if he stripped Petersburg of defenders, the Union garrison at City Point might move into the city; but if he kept his meager garrison in Petersburg, Butler's army could sever the railroad to Richmond. Pickett decided to protect the supply line. Brooks advanced on the junction of the Richmond & Petersburg Railroad with the Port Walthall Railroad with his entire division, attacked Johnson's Brigade, and captured the junction. The Confederates retired behind Swift Creek to await reinforcements.

Estimated Casualties: 550 total

Swift Creek and Fort Clifton, Virginia (VA050), Chesterfield County, May 9, 1864

On May 9 US General Butler advanced against the Confederates' defensive line behind Swift Creek north of Petersburg. After skirmishing all morning CS General Pickett ordered CS General Johnson to attack the superior Union numbers and reopen the turnpike to Richmond. CS General Hagood's Brigade advanced across Swift Creek toward Arrowfield Church at 3:45 P.M., but point-blank volleys by US General Heckman's brigade shattered the attack. Butler did not press on to capture Petersburg but dispatched the X Corps to tear up the railroad tracks near Chester Station. At the same time five Union gunboats and a brigade of US General Brooks's division bombarded Fort Clifton, an earthwork protecting the mouth of the creek. US Brigadier General Edward W. Hincks brought 1,800 U.S. Colored Troops from City Point to fire at the fort from across the Appomattox River. The Confederates returned the fire, sank one gunboat, and drove off the other ones.

Estimated Casualties: 990 total

Chester Station, Virginia (VA051), Chesterfield County, May 10, 1864

CS General Beauregard arrived in Petersburg on May 9 with CS Major General Robert F. Hoke's Division from North Carolina. The following day two brigades under CS Brigadier General Robert Ransom advanced south from Richmond at 5:15 A.M. Ransom attacked US General Gillmore's X Corps at Chester Station, where the Federals were destroying the railroad tracks. Heavily outnumbered, the Confederates were forced to withdraw as Union reinforcements came up from Swift Creek. Gillmore headed his troops back to the Bermuda Hundred lines at about 4:30 P.M., followed by US General Smith's XVIII Corps. The Confederates reopened their communications between Petersburg and Richmond.

Estimated Casualties: 569 total

Proctor's Creek (Drewry's Bluff), Virginia (VA053), Chesterfield County, May 12–16, 1864

US General Butler withdrew the Army of the James into the entrenchments at Bermuda Hundred. CS General Beauregard cobbled together a force of 18,000 to confront Butler's 30,000. On May 12 at 4:00 A.M. Butler ordered US General Smith's corps out in a pouring rain to strike north along the Richmond and Petersburg Turnpike to attack the Confederate line at Drewry's Bluff on the James River. This action was designed to cover a cavalry raid by US Brigadier General August V. Kautz against the Richmond & Danville Railroad. Smith soon encountered CS General Hoke's Division deployed along the north bank of Proctor's Creek. The Federals halted to await reinforcements from US General Gillmore's X Corps.

On May 13 Gillmore circled to the west to outflank the Confederate line. Smith pushed across the creek to find that the Confederates had abandoned the works for a stronger fortified position to their rear. Gillmore flanked this line at Wooldridge Hill, and the Confederates retreated again. Beauregard arrived to take command of the Confederates the following day and constructed a new line extending westward from Drewry's Bluff. The Federals dug in before this new line. Butler's cautious advance gave Beauregard time to concentrate his forces. He summoned CS Major General W. H. C. Whiting's Division from Petersburg and planned a converging attack on the Union lines: Whiting would attack northward, hitting Butler's rear, while Hoke and CS General Ransom's Divisions, attacking *en echelon* from left to right, would drive the Federal right back from Drewry's Bluff.

Ransom, with his right anchored near Fort Stevens, attacked down the Old Stage Road through heavy fog on the morning of May 16. He rolled up the Union line from right to left until his offensive stalled — his troops could not see through the fog. Rather than counterattack, Smith ordered his troops to retreat to the turnpike. Whiting inched northward from Petersburg to Port Walthall Junction but missed the battle. Butler ordered his demoralized army back to Bermuda Hundred that afternoon, ending his offensive against Richmond.

Estimated Casualties: 3,004 US, 1,000 CS

Drewry's Bluff, a unit of Richmond National Battlefield Park south of Richmond off Interstate 95, includes forty-two acres of the historic battlefield. Fort Stevens, a Chesterfield County park, is at the intersection of Pams Avenue and Norcliff Road.

Ware Bottom Church and Howlett Line, Virginia (VA054), Chesterfield County, May 20, 1864

On May 20 Confederate forces advanced to Ware Bottom Church. US General Butler occupied a strong line of earthworks across Bermuda Hundred, with US General Gillmore's X Corps on the right and US General Smith's XVIII Corps on the left. The Confederates struck Gillmore's front, drove his pickets back almost a mile, and hit the main line of entrenchments. After being repulsed, the Confederates constructed the Howlett Line, effectively bottling up Butler between the James and Appomattox Rivers. The Confederate victories at Proctor's Creek and Ware Bottom Church enabled CS General Beauregard to release men to reinforce CS General Lee for the battles of North Anna and Cold Harbor. US General Grant pulled out the XVIII Corps to reinforce the Army of the Potomac before the battle of Cold Harbor.

Estimated Casualties: 1,500 total

Areas of the Ware Bottom Church and Howlett Line battlefield are in the Parkers Battery unit of the Richmond National Battlefield Park. Parkers Battery is on Route 617 south of Route 10 and east of Interstate 95.

Grant's Overland Campaign: May–June 1864

Wilderness, Virginia (VA046), Spotsylvania County, May 5–6, 1864

Noah Andre Trudeau

Though they made few efforts to memorialize it after the war, the soldiers who fought there never forgot the Wilderness. "Imagine," a North Carolina soldier, W. A. Smith, later wrote in his book, "a great, dismal forest containing . . . the worst kind of thicket of second-growth trees . . . so thick with small pines and scrub oak, cedar, dogwood and other growth common to the country . . . [that] one could see barely ten paces." It was, according to the Bostonian Charles Francis Adams, Jr., a "fearfully discouraging place." Civil War correspondent William Swinton argued that it was "impossible to conceive a field worse adapted to the movements of a grand army." Yet two grand armies not only moved through but fought across this area for two bloody days in early May 1864.

The region, which was known as the Wilderness long before the Civil War, lay ten miles west of Fredericksburg, a patch of natural entanglement some twelve miles wide and six miles deep along the south bank of the Rapidan River. German colonists brought over in the early eighteenth century by Virginia governor Alexander Spotswood had tried to tame the Wilderness and failed. Spotswood's and other entrepreneurs' attempts to establish mining in the area resulted in heavy cutting of timber to plank the roads and fuel iron-smelting operations, such as the one at Catharine Furnace. When the would-be industry was abandoned, the forest returned with a vengeance; by 1860 it had produced an almost impenetrable second-growth woodland.

The land shaped the strategies of the opposing forces that met there. For Union planners the Wilderness was something to be crossed with the least possible delay. For CS General Robert E. Lee the Wilderness was an ally that would negate the enemy's numerical advantage in artillery and men. From the moment on May 4 when he

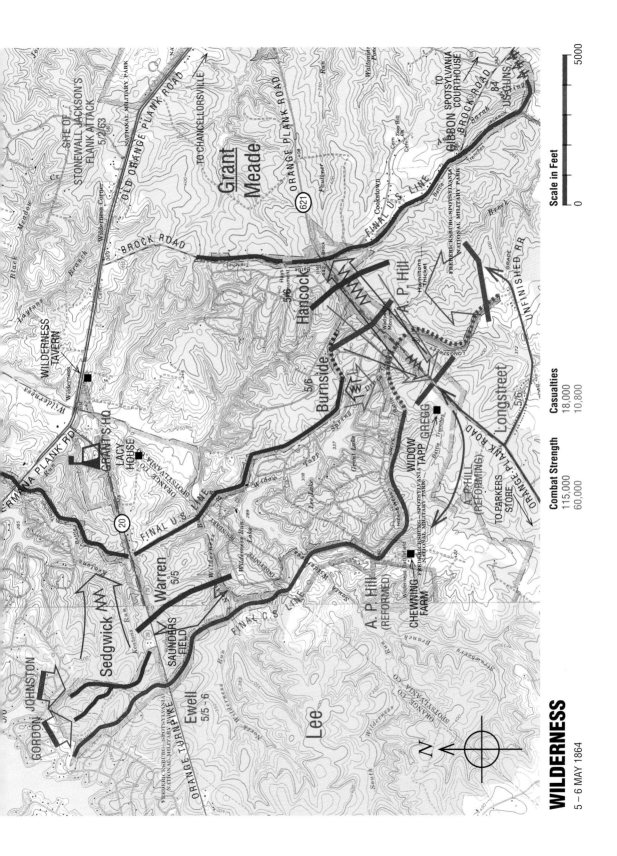

WILDERNESS

5 – 6 MAY 1864

Combat Strength

115,000

60,000

Casualties

18,000

10,800

Scale in Feet

0   5000

learned that the massive Union army was heading into the Wilderness, Lee planned to stop it there.

The Federal movement was one part of US Lieutenant General Ulysses S. Grant's grand strategy to squeeze the pressure points of the Confederacy. Simultaneously with this move, other Union forces were advancing aggressively against Atlanta and Petersburg and into the fertile Shenandoah Valley. The role given to the Army of the Potomac and its commander, US Major General George Gordon Meade, seemed simple: engage the Army of Northern Virginia in battle, defeat it if possible, and under no circumstances allow it enough freedom of action to upset Union plans elsewhere. To make certain Meade carried out this role, Grant made his headquarters in the field with the Army of the Potomac.

The Union army entered the Wilderness in two dusty, spiky columns totaling 115,000 men. The Union V, VI, and IX Corps marched in from the northwest via the Germanna Ford Road. Farther east the Union II Corps, most of the Yankee cavalry, and the long army supply train crossed the Rapidan at Ely's Ford to camp for the night on another Wilderness battlefield of unpleasant memory — Chancellorsville. Lee's 60,000-man army moved from its winter quarters west and south of the Wilderness. CS Lieutenant General Richard S. Ewell's Second Corps marched eastward along the Orange Turnpike (now Route 20), while CS Lieutenant General Ambrose Powell Hill's Third Corps moved on a parallel course farther south, on the Orange Plank Road (now Route 621). These two corps were a day closer to the Union army than CS Lieutenant General James Longstreet's.

Union plans to clear the Wilderness on May 5 were upset shortly after dawn when some of US Major General Gouverneur K. Warren's V Corps, screening the area to the west, spotted Ewell's men moving toward them. Soon afterward reports came to Union headquarters near the Lacy house of Hill's movement farther south, which threatened to sever connections between the two prongs of the Union advance.

Fighting began early in the afternoon alongside the Orange Turnpike and raged across a small clearing known as Saunders Field. The combat spread slowly southward as more units came into line. Initial Union gains were rolled back by savage Confederate counterattacks. Even the late-afternoon arrival of portions of US Major General John Sedgwick's VI Corps was unable to break the stalemate.

Farther south Hill's Corps was less successful. A small Union cavalry force managed to delay Hill's eastward advance long enough for a Union division to seize and hold the vital intersection of the Plank and Brock Roads. Later that afternoon troops from US Major General Winfield Scott Hancock's II Corps arrived on the scene and launched a poorly coordinated but fierce attack that was finally stopped through the use of every available Confederate reserve. By nightfall the northern half of the Confederate line was bloodied but solid. Its southern half, however, was scattered, exhausted, and ill prepared for what the morning would surely bring. Robert E. Lee, who had not wanted to fight a major battle with only two thirds of his army, downplayed the problem. Around midnight he refused a request from Hill to regroup, believing that Longstreet's Corps would arrive from Gordonsville in time to take the burden of the battle off Hill's men.

Dawn came but not Longstreet. At Grant's urging Union forces attacked at first light. The assaults along the axis of the Orange Turnpike stalled before effective Confederate defenses. To the south, attacking westward in a direction marked out by the Orange Plank Road, Union forces met significant success. Just when it seemed that Lee's right flank would be destroyed, Longstreet's men did arrive. Their vicious counterattack stunned the Federals, who came to a standstill. The drama of Longstreet's arrival was heightened when an emotionally charged Lee tried personally to lead the first counterattacking units across the open fields of the Tapp farm. CS Brigadier General John Gregg's Texans politely but firmly sent him back. The cries of "Lee to the rear" capped one of the most memorable episodes of the battle. Longstreet's men later went on an offensive of their own, flanked the advancing Union line, and sent it whirling back to a line of entrenchments thrown up earlier along the north-south Brock Road.

The confusing tangles of the Wilderness knew no allegiance. At the high point of the Confederate success that day, Longstreet, Lee's ablest corps commander, was seriously wounded by his own men. Early that evening an all-out Confederate offensive surged against both flanks of the Union line. The assault across the bloody ground along the Plank Road was stopped at the Brock Road line. To the north CS Brigadier General John B. Gordon led his men on a flanking swing against the Union right, which succeeded for a brief, intoxicating moment, but any substantial gains were nullified by darkness, the difficulty of maneuvering in the tangled woods, and the unwillingness of Gordon's superior, CS Major General Jubal A. Early, to press the matter.

In the May 5–6 fighting in the Wilderness nearly the full force of both armies was engaged. Union casualties tallied nearly 18,000, and the Confederate toll was estimated at 10,800. To the claustrophobic nature of the combat was added the terror of numerous flash fires that raged through the dry underbrush, incinerating soldiers too badly wounded to escape. A northern private wrote that "it was a blind and bloody hunt to the death, in bewildering thickets, rather than a battle." A southern officer declared, "I do not think I have ever seen a battlefield where there was more destruction and more horrors than that of the Wilderness."

Despite his heavy losses, Grant ordered the Army of the Potomac to continue its campaign by sliding past Lee's flank and moving south. For the first time in his Civil War experience, Robert E. Lee faced an adversary who had the determination to press on despite the cost. Grant's overland campaign moved along to other bloody battlefields, ending in the slow strangulation of Lee's army at Petersburg. The moment of truth came in the Wilderness. Once Grant decided to move forward and not retreat, it was just a question of time. The battle of the Wilderness marked the beginning of the end for the Army of Northern Virginia and for the Confederacy itself.

Estimated Casualties: 18,000 US, 10,800 CS

The Wilderness Battlefield, a unit of Fredericksburg and Spotsylvania National Military Park, is near Route 3, west of Fredericksburg. There are 3,303 acres of the historic battlefield in this unit, 1,008 acres of which are privately owned.

Spotsylvania Court House, Virginia (VA048), Spotsylvania County, May 8–21, 1864

William D. Matter

On May 7 at 6:30 A.M. US Lieutenant General Ulysses S. Grant issued a directive to the Army of the Potomac commander, US Major General George Gordon Meade. The order, one of the most important of Grant's military career, began, "General: Make all preparations during the day for a night march to take position at Spotsylvania Court-House."

On the night of May 7–8 the US V Corps and the CS First Corps, moving independently and unknown to each other, led the marches of their respective armies toward Spotsylvania Court House. In the morning the lead elements met on the Spindle farm along the Brock Road (now Route 613), and the fighting lasted throughout the day as more units from each army arrived. Elements of the VI Corps joined in the attack around midday, but the Union troops were unable to force their way through, and nightfall found two sets of parallel fieldworks across the Brock Road. What the Federals had thought would be a rapid march into open country had stalled behind these

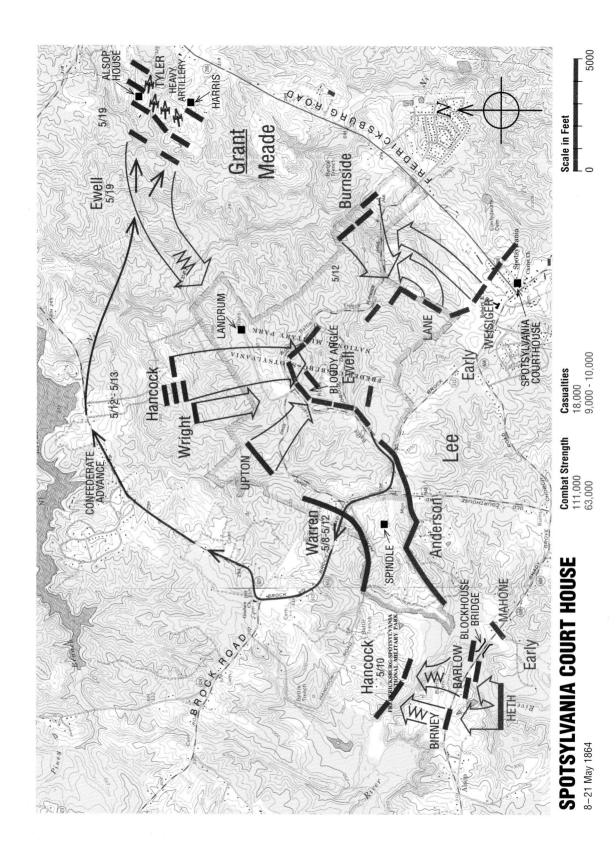

SPOTSYLVANIA COURT HOUSE

8–21 May 1864

Scale in Feet

0   5000

Combat Strength	Casualties
111,000	18,000
63,000	9,000 - 10,000

works. The battle of Spotsylvania Court House was under way.

More units of each army continued to arrive on May 9. The Third Corps marched along the Shady Grove Church Road (now Route 608) to the village of Spotsylvania Court House. The II Corps, commanded by US Major General Winfield Scott Hancock, moved from Todd's Tavern along the Brock Road, then moved off the road to take position to the right of the V Corps, overlooking the Po River. Late in the afternoon troops from Hancock's corps crossed the river and moved east on the Shady Grove Church Road as far as the Block House bridge over the Po before darkness halted them.

During the night CS General Robert E. Lee sent one brigade, commanded by CS Brigadier General William Mahone, to block and one division, led by CS Major General Henry Heth, to attack the Federal force the following day. On the morning of May 10, Hancock's three divisions south of the Po River were directed to return north of that stream to assault another segment of the Confederate line. While recrossing, US Major General Francis Barlow's division was attacked by Heth.

Elsewhere that day, the Federal commanders attempted to execute a combined attack all along the lines. A series of piecemeal assaults by elements of the V and II Corps at Laurel Hill proved unsuccessful. A bit farther east a charge by twelve Union regiments against the western face of a great salient in the Confederate line was far more carefully arranged. The British military historian C. F. Atkinson, writing in 1908 in *Grant's Campaigns of 1864 and 1865,* called it "one of the classic infantry attacks of military history." This dramatic action also failed, because of the failure of a supporting assault and because of strong Confederate counterstrokes.

Grant decided to attack the apex of the Confederate salient with Hancock's II Corps on May 12, while two divisions of US Major General Ambrose Burnside's IX Corps were to attack the east face of the Confederate position. The II Corps moved into position after dark.

At 4:35 A.M. on May 12 Hancock's corps moved forward from its position near the Brown house,

advanced across the Landrum farm clearing, and struck the apex of the salient. Continuing forward for about half a mile, the Federals captured approximately 3,000 soldiers of CS Lieutenant General Richard S. Ewell's Second Corps before being driven back to the outside of the works by Confederate reserve forces. Both sides forwarded reinforcements (the Federals added units of US Major General Horatio Wright's VI Corps to the assault), and the northern face of the salient became the focus of close fighting that lasted for twenty-three hours. In midafternoon a division of the IX Corps advanced, and a portion of it was struck by an advancing pair of brigades, CS Brigadier General James H. Lane's and CS Colonel David A. Weisiger's, in an area approximately three quarters of a mile north of the village of Spotsylvania Court House. The resulting engagement was a wild melee in dark woods, with every soldier trying to fight his way back to his own lines.

A US II Corps soldier, viewing the churned landscape around the "bloody angle" on the morning of May 13, wrote: "The trench on the Rebel side of the works was filled with their dead piled together in every way with their wounded. The sight was terrible and ghastly." Sometime before 2:00 A.M. on May 13 a large oak tree just behind the west face of the salient crashed to the ground. Its trunk, twenty-two inches in diameter, had been severed by Federal musket fire coming from one direction. (The shattered stump is in the Smithsonian's National Museum of American History in Washington, D.C.)

The Confederates successfully withdrew to a newly constructed line along the base of the salient just before dawn. On the night of May 13–14 the US V and VI Corps marched around to the Fredericksburg Road (now Route 208) and went into position south of that road on the left of the IX Corps. On May 15 the II Corps joined the other three Union corps so that the Federal lines, east of the village, now faced west and ran north and south. Three days later two Union corps returned to the salient and attacked the Confederates' final line but were unsuccessful.

On May 19 Ewell made a forced reconnaissance around to the Fredericksburg Road to attempt to locate the right flank of the Union line. There he ran into some newly arrived Federal troops who had formerly manned the forts surrounding Washington, D.C. These heavy artillerymen, most of whom were serving under US Brigadier General Robert O. Tyler, were acting as infantry for the first time. The resulting engagement on the Harris farm exacted a heavy toll on both sides: it cost the Confederates 900 casualties and the Federals slightly more than 1,500.

The battle of Spotsylvania Court House was over. If Grant's intention had been to defeat or even destroy the Army of Northern Virginia, he was unsuccessful at Spotsylvania. Assuming that Lee's primary objective was to hold the line of the Rapidan River and keep the enemy out of central Virginia, the battles of the Wilderness and Spotsylvania can be considered strategic defeats. However, by delaying Grant for two weeks at Spotsylvania, Lee permitted other Confederate forces to resist Union efforts in the vicinity of Richmond and in the Shenandoah Valley, unmolested by the Army of the Potomac.

Confederate casualties for the two-week-long battle were estimated at 9,000–10,000 (combat strength: 63,000), while Federal casualties were reported as slightly less than 18,000 (combat strength: 111,000). The most notable death was that of VI Corps commander US Major General John Sedgwick, killed by a sharpshooter's bullet as he prowled the front lines on May 9. Shortly before, Sedgwick had chided some infantrymen trying to dodge the occasional minié balls whistling past with the comment that the Confederates "couldn't hit an elephant at this distance."

Both armies departed Spotsylvania on May 20 and 21. Lee rode south, aware that he had to avoid a siege of Richmond or the Confederacy would be doomed. He would next meet Grant at the North Anna River.

Grant had sent a dispatch on May 11 declaring, "I propose to fight it out on this line if it takes all summer." It would take that long and more.

Estimated Casualties: 18,000 US, 9,000–10,000 CS

Spotsylvania Court House Battlefield, a unit of Fredericksburg and Spotsylvania National Military Park, is near Routes 613 and 208, southwest of Fredericksburg and north of Spotsylvania Court House. There are 1,573 acres of the historic battlefield in this unit; 105 of these acres are privately owned.

Yellow Tavern, Virginia (VA052), Henrico County, May 11, 1864

During the battle of Spotsylvania Court House, US Major General Philip H. Sheridan launched a major cavalry raid against Richmond. Since the Kilpatrick-Dahlgren raid on February 28–March 3, the Union cavalry had only provided flank protection for the Army of the Potomac, and Sheridan disputed the role that US General Meade had assigned to his horsemen. He won permission from US General Grant to cut loose from the army, disrupt CS General Lee's road and rail communications, and draw the Confederate cavalry into a fight. Grant also saw the raid as a means to separate the disputants.

Sheridan's three divisions, 12,000 troopers, set out on May 9. They circled to the east of the Confederate lines at Spotsylvania, rode southwest, severed the Virginia Central Railroad, and destroyed the depot at Beaver Dam Station. They continued southward toward Richmond, riding slowly enough to permit the Confederate cavalry to engage them in battle. CS Major General J. E. B. Stuart's 5,000 cavalrymen galloped for two days to intercept Sheridan north of the Richmond defenses.

They met at Yellow Tavern, six miles north of Richmond at noon on May 11 in a series of Federal frontal assaults that were repulsed with losses on both sides. At 4:00 P.M. US Brigadier General George A. Custer's brigade broke the Confederate center. Stuart rode up with part of the 1st Virginia Cavalry to repair the breach, and as his cavalry counterattacked, he was mortally wounded. Stuart died the next day in Richmond.

The Federals rode south to threaten the Richmond defenses and reached Haxall's Landing and Shirley Plantation on the James River on May 14. After communicating with US Major General Benjamin F. Butler at Bermuda Hundred and refitting his command, Sheridan rejoined the Army of the Potomac on the North Anna River on May 24.

Estimated Casualties: 800 total

North Anna, Virginia (VA055), Hanover and Caroline Counties, May 23–26, 1864

J. Michael Miller

"If I can get one more pull," wrote CS General Robert E. Lee, "I will defeat him." After two weeks of battle, first starting in the dense thickets of the Wilderness and then at Spotsylvania Court House, Lee knew that US Lieutenant General Ulysses S. Grant had an overwhelming superiority in numbers. He also knew that Grant's force could not be defeated in open battle. Lee's plan after Spotsylvania was to continue to fight Grant behind earthworks until the Confederates had an opportunity to crush a portion of the Union army. At some point during May 1864, Grant would make an error and leave himself open to attack. Until that time Lee would conserve his army and wait.

The opportunity came near the North Anna River. On May 21 Grant lured Lee from behind his earthworks at Spotsylvania by sending an army corps to Milford Station to threaten Hanover Junction, the intersection of two Confederate supply lines to Richmond. The separation of the Union infantry from the main body of the Army of the Potomac invited Lee to attack. The Army of Northern Virginia marched down the Telegraph Road and other back roads to protect the junction, its vanguard arriving at the North Anna River on

the morning of May 22. The Confederate troops relaxed in the shade and bathed off the grime of two long weeks of fighting.

Lee was confident that Grant would do as all his previous opponents had done: hold his army in check for several weeks to recuperate from the heavy fighting of the Wilderness and Spotsylvania and then continue to advance. Grant had no such intention. He knew that both armies had suffered heavy losses, and he concluded that since Lee had not attacked the exposed men at Milford Station on May 21, the Confederate army was too damaged for offensive operations. Early on the morning of May 23 the Union army marched south to the North Anna River, expecting easy progress.

The lead Union column reached the river along the Telegraph Road, surprising the Confederates, who had not entrenched. Faulty maps confused Grant's columns, but they deployed to cross the river and open the road to Richmond. US Major General Winfield Scott Hancock's II Corps moved against the Telegraph Road bridge, while the V Corps, commanded by US Major General Gouverneur K. Warren, marched upstream to cross the North Anna at a ford at Jericho Mill. Lee, believing the Union forces were only a reinforced scouting party, kept most of his men in camp. He left a single brigade on the north bank of the river to cover the Telegraph Road bridge and awaited further Union movements.

In the late afternoon of May 23, Union artillery signaled an assault on the Confederate brigade on the Telegraph Road. Lee, now alerted to the Union intention to attack, still believed the thrust to be a small one, so he left the single brigade on the north bank. At 6:00 P.M. two Union brigades attacked, charging across Long Creek into an open plain, where they were slowed by Confederate artillery fire. They continued their advance and drove the Confederates back across the river in confusion, capturing the bridge intact. The bridge provided Grant with the necessary access to the south side of the river for his advance on May 24. Lee's men tried to burn the bridge during the night but were unsuccessful. The Confederates did destroy a railway bridge downstream.

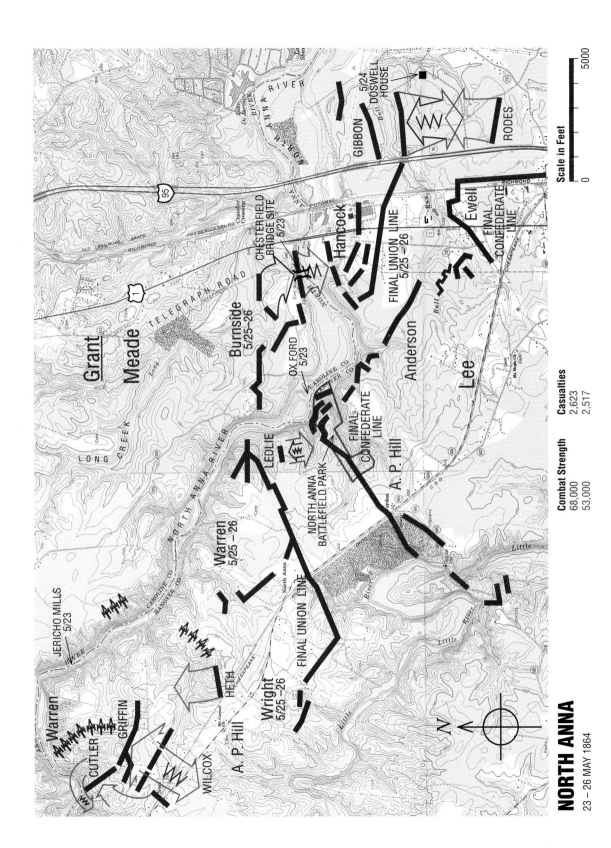

NORTH ANNA

23 – 26 MAY 1864

	Combat Strength	Casualties
	68,000	2,623
	53,000	2,517

Scale in Feet

0   5000

At Jericho Mills the Union V Corps crossed the river with little trouble and camped on the south bank. The supposedly formidable Confederate defense line on the North Anna River had been easily breached. The Federals met so little opposition that most began to cook their evening meal without entrenching. However, the Union crossing had been reported to CS Lieutenant General Ambrose Powell Hill, who ordered an attack before dark. He took the Union line by surprise, but the Federal forces rallied behind three batteries of artillery, which slowed the Confederate attack. Infantry reinforcements drove Hill's men back at nightfall. Additional Confederate troops arrived on the field in time to join in the fighting, but they were committed to the opposite side of the battlefield instead of bolstering the attack.

Under the cover of darkness Lee pondered his army's awkward position. Grant had pierced his defenses in two separate places, making a river defense line impossible. If Lee retreated any closer to Richmond, he would lose his most valuable tool, maneuverability. If Grant got too close to Richmond, Lee could prevent its capture only by keeping his army between Grant and the city. Lee had to defeat Grant on the North Anna River or lead the defense of Richmond.

Lee held a conference of his officers at Hanover Junction and devised a remarkable plan. He decided to form his army into a U-shaped line with the middle on the North Anna River at Ox Ford, a crossing that the Confederates still held. The end of the left arm, held by Hill's Third Corps, would rest on the Little River; the right arm, held by CS Major General Richard H. Anderson's First Corps and CS Lieutenant General Richard S. Ewell's Second Corps, would rest on a bend of the North Anna as it flowed to the Pamunkey River. The formation was intended to draw Grant over the river in two places separated by the U: Jericho Mill and the Telegraph Road bridge. Grant's army would be split into three pieces, one at Jericho Mill on the south bank of the North Anna, one on the north bank (unable to cross at Ox Ford), and one on the south bank on the Telegraph Road. Lee could hold one side of his U with a small force

and then concentrate his army against one of the three Federal sections and crush it.

Grant fell into the trap on May 24. Finding the Confederates gone from in front of his Jericho Mill and Telegraph Road bridgeheads, he assumed that Lee had given up the fight and retreated to the defense of Richmond. He ordered his army to pursue. US Major General Horatio G. Wright's VI Corps and Warren's V Corps faced the U on the Union right, while US Major General Ambrose E. Burnside's IX Corps held the center. Hancock's II Corps completed the concentration, facing the U on the Union left. Advancing formations of Federal infantry met bloody repulses in a driving rainstorm at Ox Ford and the Doswell house on the evening of May 24. A Union IX Corps brigade, led into hopeless combat by its drunken commander at Ox Ford, was butchered by the Confederates, who called out to their enemy, "Come on to Richmond." A II Corps division was mauled at the Doswell house by a reinforced Confederate skirmish line, often in hand-to-hand combat.

Not until evening did Grant realize that Lee had constructed overnight the strongest field fortifications the Union general had ever faced. Grant ordered his army to entrench, and by dawn of the following day the Union army was safely under cover of heavy earthworks. The two armies skirmished that day and on May 26. The battle involved 68,000 Union soldiers and 53,000 Confederates. Losses were about equal: Union 2,623, Confederate 2,517.

Grant withdrew, then moved to within a day's march of the Confederate capital. Why did Lee allow Grant to pass out of his trap? The Confederate leader became so ill on May 24 that he was confined to his tent and unable to lead his men. He repeated over and over, "We must strike them a blow, we must never allow them to pass us again." But he had no trusted lieutenant to lead the attack.

Grant and his army escaped, and it was on to Richmond.

Estimated Casualties: 2,623 US, 2,517 CS

North Anna Battlefield Park is three miles from Doswell near Route 684, fifteen miles north of Richmond off Interstate 95 at the Route 30 exit. It includes eighty acres of the Ox Ford area of the battlefield.

Wilson's Wharf, Virginia (VA056), Charles City County, May 24, 1864

When US General Butler moved up the James River for the Bermuda Hundred campaign, he had established Fort Pocahontas on the north side of the river at Wilson's Wharf. The fort was built and defended by 1,100 U.S. Colored Troops commanded by US Brigadier General Edward Wild. On May 24, with the help of the gunboat *Dawn*, the troops repulsed several determined attacks by 2,500 cavalrymen commanded by CS Major General Fitzhugh Lee. Lee withdrew toward Richmond during the night.

Estimated Casualties: 26 US, 140 CS

The Wilson's Wharf defenses, near Sherwood Forest, the estate of President John Tyler, are on Route 5 twenty miles west of Williamsburg and are open to tours.

Haw's Shop, Virginia (VA058), Hanover County, May 28, 1864

Two of US General Sheridan's cavalry divisions under US Brigadier General David M. Gregg and US Brigadier General Alfred T. A. Torbert screened the advance of the Army of the Potomac as it crossed the Pamunkey River. Fighting dismounted, Gregg and Torbert attacked the cavalry divisions of CS Major Generals Fitzhugh Lee and Wade Hampton entrenched along the line of woods at Enon Church, west of Haw's Shop. CS Brigadier General Calbraith Butler's Brigade checked the May 28 Union advance. US General Custer's Michigan Brigade arrived to reinforce Gregg. The Federal cavalry struck again at dusk and broke the line. They drove the Confederates away from Enon Church and secured the crucial intersection at Haw's Shop.

Estimated Casualties: 344 US, 400 CS

Totopotomoy Creek and Bethesda Church, Virginia (VA057), Hanover County, May 28–30, 1864

On May 29 US General Grant ordered three corps to uncover CS General Lee's positions: US General Wright's VI Corps to Hanover Court House, US General Hancock's II Corps toward Totopotomoy Creek, and US General Warren's V Corps along the Shady Grove Church Road. US General Burnside's IX Corps remained in reserve. The U.S. soldiers found that Lee had maneuvered his ten infantry divisions onto the low ridge along the headwaters of Totopotomoy Creek and was well entrenched. The Federals made several attempts to force their way across the creek but settled on a flanking maneuver. By noon on May 30 the V and IX corps had worked their way east and crossed to the south side of the creek. Lee decided to strike, stating to CS General Early, "We must destroy this army of Grant's before he gets to James River. If he gets there it will become a siege, and then it will be a mere question of time."

Lee sent Early, newly named commander of the Second Corps, to turn the Union left. Spearheaded by CS Major General Robert E. Rodes's Division, the Confederates hit Warren's V Corps near Bethesda Church. They pushed the U.S. infantry back to Shady Grove Road but were repulsed with heavy losses because the Confederates delayed in following up on Rodes's attack.

Estimated Casualties: 731 US, 1,159 CS

Matadequin Creek (Old Church), Virginia (VA059), Hanover County, May 30, 1864

CS General Lee's health had improved since the battle of North Anna, but the prospects for his army had not. US General Grant had a reinforced corps from US General Butler landing at White House, fifteen miles down the Pamunkey River from Hanovertown and close to the Confederate right flank. The cavalry was active in the area between Totopotomoy Creek and the Chickahominy River. On May 30 US General Torbert's cavalry division attacked CS General Hampton's cavalry at Matadequin Creek. After heavy fighting the Federals drove the Confederates back to within 1.5 miles of Old Cold Harbor, preparing the way for US General Sheridan to seize control of the vital crossroads the next day.

Estimated Casualties: 90 US, unknown CS

Cold Harbor, Virginia (VA062), Hanover County, May 31–June 12, 1864

Richard J. Sommers

The forces of US Lieutenant General Ulysses S. Grant and CS General Robert E. Lee had fought almost incessantly from May 5 to May 24. After the battle of the North Anna, Grant resumed his characteristic strategic advance around the Confederate right. Such advances assured him of uninterrupted supplies up Virginia's tidal rivers and, more important, allowed him to preserve the strategic initiative and forge farther into Virginia.

Grant began crossing the Pamunkey River on May 27, and during the rest of that month, he struck westward and southwestward through Hanover County. Fighting flared at Haw's Shop, Totopotomoy Creek, Bethesda Church, and Matadequin Creek. On May 31 US Major General Philip H. Sheridan's cavalry corps drove the southern horsemen, plus a feeble foot brigade, from the crucial Old Cold Harbor crossroads.

On the roads radiating from that point, Grant could threaten not only the Confederate army to the northwest but Richmond itself, just ten miles to the southwest beyond the Chickahominy. He could also cover his new depot at White House on the Pamunkey and prevent the interception of his reinforcements.

Those reinforcements, nine Army of the James brigades under US Major General William F. Smith of the XVIII Corps, sailed down the James from Bermuda Hundred, then up the York and Pamunkey to White House, where they landed on May 30 and 31. One brigade remained there, and the others, 10,000 strong, marched toward Grant. Misworded orders led them astray up the Pamunkey instead of directly to Sheridan. On discovering the error, they trudged south over narrow, dusty roads into Old Cold Harbor, exhausted by ten extra miles of marching. Still, by 3:00 P.M. on June 1 they began reaching the front.

Throughout May, Lee too had requested reinforcements. Seven of his own brigades and CS Major General John C. Breckinridge's two Shenandoah Valley brigades joined him in the middle of May. Now that he was near Richmond, he asked for more troops from CS General P. G. T. Beauregard's army blocking the Army of the James at Bermuda Hundred. Lee's appeals, initially unproductive, turned to demands as he learned of Smith's approach. Minutes before he was ordered by Richmond to act, Beauregard dispatched CS Major General Robert F. Hoke's Division to Lee.

Hoke's van reached Old Cold Harbor on May 31 but could not save it from the subsequent Federal attack. By the next day his division was massed to the west. To the northwest, CS Lieutenant General Jubal A. Early's small Second Corps on the right of Lee's main line exchanged places with CS Lieutenant General Richard H. Anderson's larger First Corps in the center. Once on the right, Anderson advanced southeastward and eastward against Old Cold Harbor with CS Major General Joseph B. Kershaw's and Hoke's divisions on June 1.

Intelligence reports of the danger led Sheridan to withdraw from Old Cold Harbor. However, US Major General George Gordon Meade, commanding the Union Army of the Potomac, or-

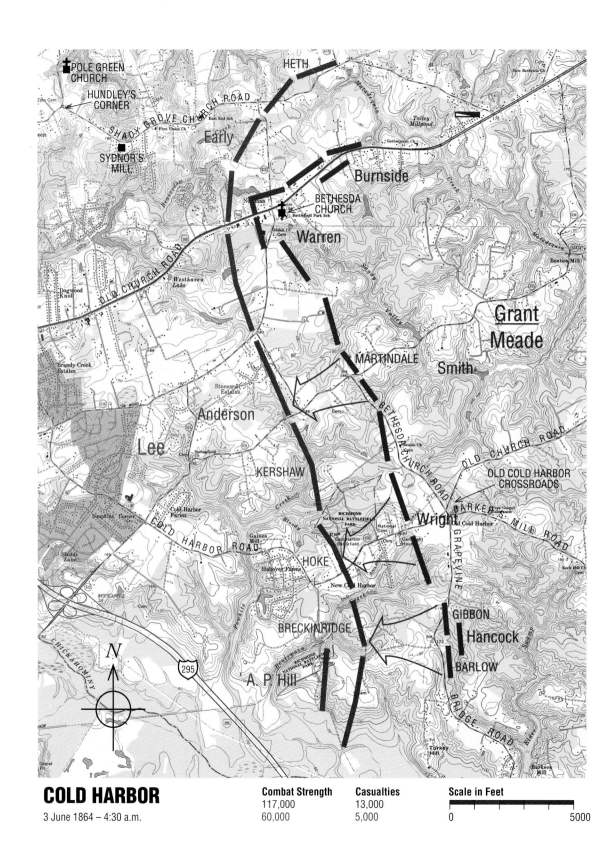

COLD HARBOR

3 June 1864 – 4:30 a.m.

Combat Strength	Casualties	Scale in Feet
117,000	13,000	0 5000
60,000	5,000	

dered him to return and hold the intersection at all costs. Sheridan's dismounted cavalry poured devastating fire from their repeating carbines into the Confederate attackers. Kershaw's inexperienced van broke and fled, sweeping his veterans off too. Even worse, the typically uncooperative Hoke remained inactive. Anderson's great counterattack failed totally, and he then withdrew onto a north-south ridge between Old and New Cold Harbor and hastily began fortifying.

The tactical initiative reverted to the Federals. At about 10:00 A.M. US Major General Horatio G. Wright's VI Corps from the Union far right replaced Sheridan's troopers at Old Cold Harbor. Six hours later Smith's arriving XVIII Corps deployed to Wright's right.

Although the hour was late, Meade attacked. Two divisions each from Wright's and Smith's corps struck west from Old Cold Harbor at 6:00 P.M. They drove skirmishers from a wood line, then continued over the broad open slope up to Anderson's breastworks. Heavy fire stopped the outer two divisions, but the two center divisions poured up a ravine and penetrated the line between Hoke's left and Kershaw's right, routing two Confederate brigades. Before the Federals could exploit the breakthrough, however, Anderson brought up three brigades and sealed the penetration.

On June 1 Grant thus secured Old Cold Harbor, bowed in Anderson's right, and captured 750 prisoners. But he lost 2,800 men and failed to turn or overrun Lee's right. Achieving those larger objectives would require further fighting.

Both commanders deemed it necessary to continue fighting. Lee might have retired across the Chickahominy, but with characteristic audacity he risked battle with that deep, swampy river behind him in order to cover his railroads. Accordingly, on June 2 he moved Breckinridge and two divisions of CS Lieutenant General Ambrose Powell Hill's Third Corps to connect Hoke's right to the Chickahominy Swamp. In taking this position, Breckinridge drove Union outposts off Turkey Hill, part of the 1862 battlefield of Gaines' Mill.

Those outposts belonged to US Major General Winfield Scott Hancock's II Corps, which had marched from Meade's right to the left overnight on June 1–2. Grant believed that massing three corps at Old Cold Harbor would provide enough punch to break Anderson's line. Once broken, the Confederates might well be driven into the Chickahominy.

However, Hancock's night march, like so many in the Civil War, went astray. The II Corps took ten hours to march twelve miles, and when it finally reached Old Cold Harbor, Hancock concluded that his men were too exhausted to attack. Meade and Grant reluctantly acquiesced.

Except for skirmishing at Turkey Hill, the only action on June 2 occurred to the north at Bethesda Church, where Early had failed to turn the Federal left, US Major General Gouverneur K. Warren's V Corps, on May 30. As the armies sidled southward, the Union right was resting there by June 2. It too withstood Early's assault. After initially overrunning part of US Major General Ambrose E. Burnside's IX Corps, Early was repulsed by Burnside's and Warren's main line.

Throughout that day and into the night the armies prepared to renew the battle. The Confederates continued to improve their field fortifications, which ran from Turkey Hill northwest along a low ridge, whose gentle, open, east-facing slope offered excellent fields of fire. The Federals also prepared: the generals deployed troops, and the soldiers pinned on name tags for identification if they were killed.

Many of the Union soldiers were killed when fighting resumed at 4:30 A.M. on June 3. Hancock, Wright, and Smith attacked simultaneously, but their advance was soon fragmented. From Hancock's left, US Brigadier General Francis C. Barlow's division drove the Confederate pickets from a wood line and penetrated a swampy, poorly defended portion of Breckinridge's sector. Barlow, however, lacked support, and Hill soon repelled him.

No other Federals fared even that well. To Barlow's right US Brigadier General John Gibbon's division became mired in a swamp and was bloodily repulsed. In the center Wright found that his June 1 penetration now exposed him to shattering crossfire. Farther north most of Smith's troops, under US Brigadier General John H. Martindale, were massed in a ravine leading into Anderson's line. The ravine proved a slaughter pen, raked by devastating crossfire.

Within barely half an hour all three Union corps were repulsed, with the staggering loss of 7,000 men. The survivors entrenched as near the front as they dared, often fifty yards or less from Lee's lines. Throughout the day sharpshooting and shelling took their toll.

However, the charge and the battle of Cold Harbor were over. For another nine days the armies remained in place, and many of the wounded remained between the lines unattended, suffering in the sweltering heat. When Grant, usually a humane commander, finally brought himself to request a truce on June 7, most of those wounded had died. Their war was over, but the Civil War continued. In mid-June both armies departed: the cavalry to Trevilian Station, Breckinridge and Early to Lynchburg and the Shenandoah Valley, and the main bodies to Petersburg.

Approximately 117,000 Federals and 60,000 Confederates participated in operations from May 31 to June 3. Some 13,000 Union troops and perhaps 5,000 southerners were casualties. More than half of the Union losses (versus 1,200 Confederates) occurred that final morning. However, thousands more soldiers fought and fell from Haw's Shop to Bethesda Church. The final onslaught was just one part of the overall operation in Hanover County, but it was not characteristic of those operations or of Grant's generalship. Grant did not usually fight battles that way. Even after the war he reflected, "I have always regretted that the last assault at Cold Harbor was ever made."

In a broader sense, the overall operations at this time carried the Federals more deeply into Virginia. When their southward strategic drive from Culpeper to the Chickahominy was finally checked at Cold Harbor, Grant, undaunted, sought a new route to Richmond: from the south via its rail center, Petersburg. By late June the

mobile war of spring would change to the stagnant siege of summer as Grant, who characteristically learned from experience, evolved new tactics to match his new strategy.

These Federal operations denied Lee the initiative and burdened him with the constricting strategic imperative of closely defending Richmond and Petersburg. Yet in this defense the masterful Virginian remained dangerous, as he had clearly demonstrated at Cold Harbor, his last great victory in the field.

Estimated Casualties: 13,000 US, 5,000 CS

Cold Harbor Battlefield, a unit of the Richmond National Battlefield Park, is northeast of Richmond near Route 156 and includes 149 acres of the historic battlefield.

Trevilian Station, Virginia (VA099), Louisa County, June 11–12, 1864

While the Army of the Potomac prepared to cross the James River to assault Petersburg, US General Grant sent most of US General Sheridan's cavalry to raid the Virginia Central Railroad northwest of Richmond and distract CS General Lee. If possible, Sheridan was to link up at Charlottesville with US Major General David Hunter, who was marching up the Shenandoah Valley, and threaten Richmond from the west.

Sheridan set out from the Cold Harbor lines on June 7 and headed westward on the north side of the North Anna River with the cavalry divisions of US Generals Torbert and Gregg. Lee sent the 5,000 cavalrymen from the divisions of CS Major Generals Wade Hampton and Fitzhugh Lee to oppose them, with Hampton in command. By June 10 Hampton was at Trevilian Station and Lee at Louisa Court House.

The Confederates attacked Sheridan the next

morning at Clayton's Store and pushed him back. Meanwhile US General Custer had infiltrated his brigade into the gap between the two Confederate divisions and captured Hampton's wagon train at Trevilian Station. Hampton broke off the fight to send CS Brigadier General Thomas L. Rosser's Laurel Brigade to attack Custer. With Confederates on three sides, Custer was in grave danger. Torbert's division finally broke through to him in a dramatic rescue. The Union forces camped at Trevilian Station that night.

Hampton established a strong new line with clear fields of fire along the railroad west of the station. Lee's Division joined his left at noon on June 12. Sheridan spent the morning tearing up five miles of railroad track, then rode west to attack Hampton's lines. The Confederates repulsed seven attacks in severe fighting. Lee finally attacked Sheridan's right flank and drove him back, nearly shattering the Union line. Sheridan broke off the fight at 10:00 P.M. He headed back to the Army of the Potomac the next day, abandoning the raid and any plan to fight his way through to Charlottesville and link up with Hunter.

Hampton had become an outstanding cavalry commander, particularly in understanding, as did Forrest and Sheridan, the use of mounted infantry: horses providing mobility for infantrymen.

Estimated Casualties: 1,007 US, 1,071 CS

Samaria Church (Saint Mary's Church), Virginia (VA112), Charles City County, June 24, 1864

CS Generals Hampton and Fitzhugh Lee harassed but could not intercept US General Sheridan's cavalry as they rode eastward from Trevilian Station. Lee unsuccessfully attacked the isolated depot at White House on June 20. Sheridan's arrival relieved that base. The next day Sheridan crossed southward over the Pamunkey River, penetrated the Confederate cordon at Saint Peter's Church, and began escorting nine hundred wagons toward the James River. They crossed the Chickahominy River at Jones's Bridge on June 22–23

and overcame stiff opposition south of there on June 23.

Sheridan headed southwest toward Bermuda Hundred via the new Deep Bottom bridgehead. The Confederates stalled US General Torbert's division near Westover Church. The next day US General Gregg's division, occupying covering positions to the north near Samaria Church (Saint Mary's Church), endured heavy attacks by Lee, Hampton, and two fresh brigades. After prolonged resistance, Gregg's defeated troopers retreated in disorder.

Blocked by Hampton's cavalry, Sheridan withdrew on June 25 into Wyanoke Neck where the Army of the Potomac had crossed in midmonth. His trains and then his troopers crossed the James on June 26–28. Hampton had succeeded in protecting the railroads and Richmond but had failed to trap Sheridan. He discontinued his pursuit and moved against a new threat, the Wilson-Kautz Raid.

Estimated Casualties: 350 US, 250 CS

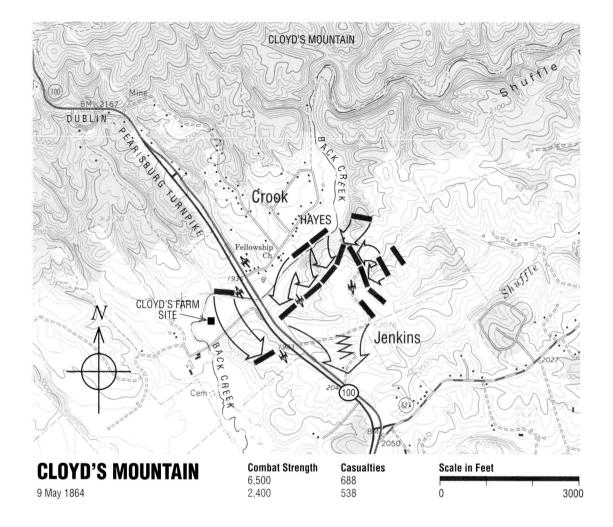

CLOYD'S MOUNTAIN

Shuffle

100

Mine

BM×2167

DUBLIN

PEARISBURG TURNPIKE

BACK CREEK

×2130

Crook

HAYES

Fellowship Ch

Shuffle

CLOYD'S FARM SITE

Jenkins

N

BACK CREEK

Cem

100

627

2050

CLOYD'S MOUNTAIN	Combat Strength	Casualties	Scale in Feet	
9 May 1864	6,500	688	0	3000
	2,400	538		

Southwest Virginia: May 1864

Cloyd's Mountain, Virginia (VA049), Pulaski County, May 9, 1864

James I. Robertson, Jr.

Cloyd's Mountain was the largest Civil War battle fought in southwestern Virginia. A future president of the United States was conspicuous on the field, and the engagement produced some of the most violent combat of the entire war. As a result of the action, the Confederacy lost for some time its only rail connection to East Tennessee.

The battle resulted from US Lieutenant General Ulysses S. Grant's 1864 grand offensive into Virginia. While two Union armies drove toward Richmond and a third advanced into the Shenandoah Valley, another Federal column began creeping through the gaps of the Appalachian Mountains. Its aim was to destroy the Virginia & Tennessee Railroad connecting Richmond with Tennessee. This force, under US Brigadier General George R. Crook, numbered 6,500 infantry and twelve artillery pieces. For ten days in late April and the beginning of May, Crook's troops struggled through rough country and foul weather to reach the New River railroad bridge and the nearby town of Dublin.

On May 5 CS Brigadier General Albert G. Jenkins received orders to take command of the meager and scattered Confederate forces in the southwestern part of the state. Jenkins, a heavily bearded cavalry brigadier then recovering from a serious wound received at Gettysburg, had been at his new duties less than a day when he learned of Crook's approach. The Confederate general frantically called in an infantry brigade about to embark by train for the Shenandoah Valley. He also rounded up an artillery battery plus several companies of home guards. Although woefully outnumbered, Jenkins was determined to make a contest of it.

Jenkins and his second-in-command, CS Brigadier General John McCausland, resolved to make a stand at the parallel wooded bluffs to the east of Cloyd's Mountain, long and imposing, running north to south. Between the two ridges lay a five-hundred-yard-wide open valley, with Back Creek meandering through its center. Bolstered by the last-minute arrival of 700 additional troops, Jenkins had 2,400 Confederates and ten guns stretched along a half-mile front.

The sun had barely risen on May 9, a clear day, when Crook's brigades arrived at Cloyd's Mountain. A quick survey of the Confederate position across the way convinced Crook that a frontal attack would be suicidal. He ordered his brigades to swerve around through underbrush and drive for the Confederate right flank.

Shortly before noon, following a brisk artillery duel, Federal infantry assailed the Confederate works. The West Virginia brigade, in its first battle, drove to within twenty yards of the Confederate line. The West Virginians could go no farther and, in an exposed position, steadily took casualties. On their left the Ohio brigades likewise became pinned down by musketry. Meanwhile the gunfire caused a thick carpet of leaves to burst into flames. Many wounded and helpless soldiers were cremated.

Jenkins was still desperately shifting troops to his endangered right flank when US Colonel Rutherford B. Hayes led his Ohio brigade in a concerted attack against the Confederate right center. Hand-to-hand combat raged in and around the crude earthworks. The battle area became what an Ohioan called "one living, flashing sheet of flame."

As the Union troops began falling back through the smoke and heat, Crook sent two fresh regiments into the action. Other Federals overran the Confederate cannons that had checked their advance. Jenkins fell wounded, his arm shattered. McCausland took command and maintained a spirited rear-guard action for a quarter hour before ordering his outflanked and outmanned soldiers from the field.

The battle lasted little more than an hour, yet the ferocity of the fighting was evident from the casualty lists. Union losses were 688, roughly 10 percent of those engaged. Confederate losses were 538, about 23 percent of their numbers. Jenkins was captured by the Federals and later died of complications following the amputation of his arm. Crook continued his advance and severed the Virginia & Tennessee Railroad, one of the Confederacy's last vital lifelines, at Dublin.

Estimated Casualties: 688 US, 538 CS

Cloyd's Mountain battlefield is north of Dublin on Route 100, forty-three miles southwest of Roanoke and five miles from Interstate 81. The battlefield is privately owned.

Cove Mountain, Virginia (VA109), Wythe County, May 10, 1864

On May 5 US Brigadier General William W. Averell set out with 2,000 men from Logan Court House, West Virginia, for Saltville, seventy miles away. His objective was to destroy the salt mines, unite with US General Crook, and join US Major General Franz Sigel at Staunton. Three days later Averell discovered that the Confederate raider CS Brigadier General John Hunt Morgan was defending Saltville. Averell immediately changed his objective to Wytheville and its lead works. He sent word to Crook that he would be delayed and would join him later. After his victory at Cloyd's Mountain, Crook returned to West Virginia.

Meanwhile Morgan assembled his cavalry to repel Averell at Saltville. When Morgan learned that Averell was headed toward Wytheville, he rode there. The town was held by the brigade of CS Brigadier General William E. "Grumble" Jones in a strong defensive position on Cove Mountain. Jones repelled Averell's attacks on May 10 until Morgan arrived. The two then counterattacked, forcing the Union troops to retreat toward Dublin to the east. Averell caught up with Crook at Union five days later.

Estimated Casualties: 300 total

Shenandoah Valley: May–June 1864

New Market, Virginia (VA110), Shenandoah County, May 15, 1864

Joseph W. A. Whitehorne

On May 15, while US Lieutenant General Ulysses S. Grant battled CS General Robert E. Lee at Spotsylvania Court House and US Major General William T. Sherman was pushing CS General Joseph E. Johnston toward Atlanta from Resaca, Georgia, the first battle of the 1864 Valley campaign occurred at New Market in Shenandoah County. The opposing forces had begun marching slowly toward the town on about May 1. The situation was so critical on the southern side that Lee had authorized CS Major General John C. Breckinridge, the local commander, to order out the Virginia Military Institute corps of cadets in his support. The participation of the 257 young men and their six officers gives the battle an added interest and poignancy. Breckinridge had massed his forces effectively at Staunton by May 12, while his opponent, US Major General Franz Sigel, had allowed his units to become badly strung out between New Market and Woodstock as he moved south toward Mount Jackson to gain control over the terminus of the Manassas Gap Railroad, and to New Market to control the only road across Massanutten Mountain.

Skirmishing between the two sides began in earnest on May 13 at the Mount Jackson bridge eight miles north of New Market. Growing Union forces pressed the Confederate cavalry screen south along the Valley Pike throughout May 14. By nightfall the Federals had established a line on the north side of the village and on the high ground to its west. The Confederate screen broke contact late in the night, and its commander, CS Brigadier General John D. Imboden, briefed Breckinridge, who was with his main force at Lacy's Springs, twelve miles to the south.

Breckinridge immediately decided to move north and confront the Union troops. His force of 5,335 men left Lacy's Springs at about 1:00 A.M.

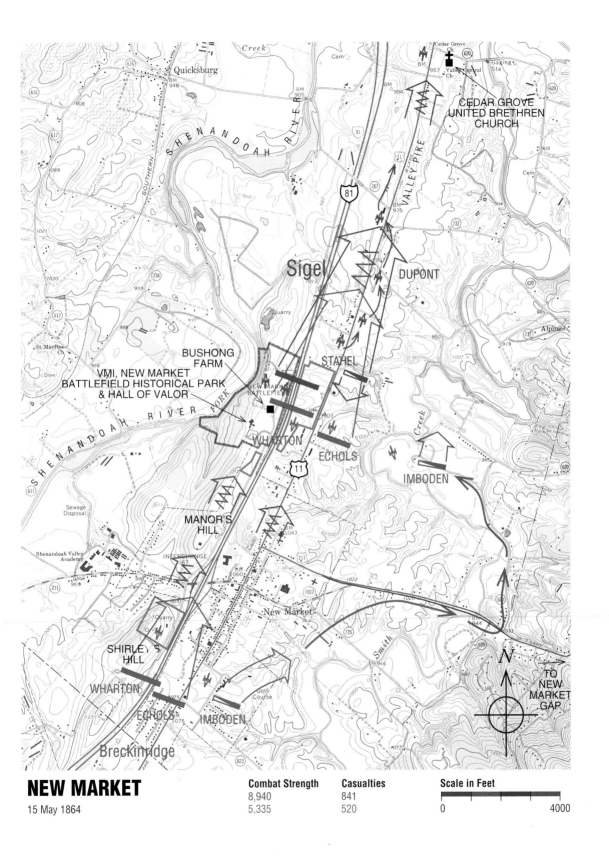

CEDAR GROVE
UNITED BRETHREN
CHURCH

Sigel

DUPONT

BUSHONG
FARM

VMI, NEW MARKET
BATTLEFIELD HISTORICAL PARK
& HALL OF VALOR

STAHEL

WHARTON

ECHOLS

IMBODEN

MANOR'S
HILL

SHIRLEY'S
HILL

WHARTON

ECHOLS   IMBODEN

Breckinridge

TO
NEW
MARKET
GAP

N

NEW MARKET

15 May 1864

Combat Strength	Casualties	Scale in Feet
8,940	841	0 4000
5,335	520	

on May 15 and reached the Shenandoah–Rockingham County line (the old Fairfax survey line) at about 6:00 A.M. Breckinridge moved his artillery forward to Shirley's Hill, just southwest of New Market, and deployed the rest of his force on the high ground farther south. In the meantime more Union units continued to arrive on the line established during the night. However, confusion persisted, and the Union command realized that the force of 8,940 men was too spread out. When Sigel arrived at about noon, he directed that a new line be formed on the high ground north of the Bushong farm, two miles below the village. By pulling farther north he hoped to combine his dispersed forces sufficiently to give battle.

When Breckinridge realized that the Union troops would not attack him, he decided to go on the offensive. By 11:00 A.M. he had deployed his infantry, under the command of CS Brigadier Generals Gabriel C. Wharton and John Echols, on Shirley's Hill and eastward in a line to Smith Creek. He also sent Imboden's cavalry across Smith Creek with a battery of four guns. Imboden was to take the Federals in flank and to burn the Mount Jackson bridge over the North Fork of the Shenandoah River, thus trapping Sigel. Shortly thereafter the Confederates swept over Shirley's Hill into the New Market valley. One unit moved up Indian Hollow, a small valley running to the north-northwest, while the rest pressed northward onto the ridge leading to the Bushong farm and beyond. The Union rear guard resisted briefly in the positions established the night before, then was forced back. The Federals held again briefly midway back to the line north of the farm, but soon were shattered by the Confederate advance. By 12:30 P.M. the village was cleared of Federal soldiers, and the Confederates were pressing toward the final Union position. Thunderstorms occurred throughout the battle and became increasingly violent.

Sigel had established a line on the ridge that now bears his name, about three hundred yards north of the Bushong farm. Its flanks were anchored on the west by the bluffs of the Shenandoah River and on the east by Smith Creek. The western part of the line was manned by three batteries of artillery and was then extended eastward by three infantry regiments with one more in reserve. It was a strong position, and the artillery fire was increasingly effective as the Confederates approached. By the time Breckinridge's advance reached the line of the Bushong farm, his units around the farm had suffered all they could take. When they began to waver, he put in the corps of Virginia Military Institute cadets to restore his line.

Sigel tried to direct a charge against the weakened Confederate lines west of the Valley Pike (now Route 11), but it was not well managed and soon sputtered to a halt. Sigel had been minister of war for some of the revolutionary forces in Germany during the unsuccessful revolution of 1848 and had come to America in 1852. According to his chief-of-staff, Sigel gave his orders in German during the New Market battle, which caused considerable confusion. On the opposite side of the pike, US Major General Julius Stahel led his cavalry in a charge against Echols's Brigade. The Confederate guns on a ridge just east of the pike opened up, taking the horsemen in a crossfire that soon forced them to retreat. As the Union faltered, Breckinridge saw his chance and directed a charge all along his line. Sigel ordered his artillery to withdraw and regroup around a church visible at the base of Rude's Hill, two miles to the north (now the Cedar Grove United Brethren Church). The loss of this firepower doomed the Union infantry line, and it was soon forced back in disorder by the charging Confederates. They swept on for about a quarter mile until confronted by a Union battery commanded by Captain Henry A. du Pont, at which point Breckinridge ordered a halt to reorganize. Du Pont then leapfrogged his guns by pairs back to Rude's Hill, buying time for the Union forces to retreat. By the time Breckinridge was ready to go again, Sigel had pulled all of his forces north of the river, and at 7:00 P.M. the rear guard under du Pont destroyed the Mount Jackson bridge to prevent pursuit. By the night of May 16, Union troops were back at Cedar Creek, having suffered

841 casualties. Confederate losses were about 520, including 57 of the cadets and officers.

Breckinridge's victory temporarily unhinged Union plans for the Valley, preserving its resources longer for the faltering Confederate war effort. The Union loss resulted in Sigel's replacement and an intensification of the Union war effort in the Valley.

Estimated Casualties: 841 US, 520 CS

Virginia Military Institute New Market Battlefield Historical Park and Hall of Valor is at New Market, twenty miles north of Harrisonburg off Interstate 81. It includes 280 acres of the historic battlefield.

Piedmont, Virginia (VA111), Augusta County, June 5, 1864

Joseph W. A. Whitehorne

The defeat of US Major General Franz Sigel at New Market on May 15 led CS General Robert E. Lee and CS Major General John C. Breckinridge to assume that once more the Union forces had been neutralized as a threat in the Shenandoah Valley. They did not take into account the persistence of the new Union leadership. Sigel was replaced by US Major General David Hunter, who made preparations for a move up the Valley with a larger, better-organized force than that of his predecessor. US Brigadier General Jeremiah C. Sullivan commanded the two brigades of infantry, while US Major General Julius Stahel led the two brigades of cavalry. Hunter also began a much harsher policy toward Confederate sympathizers, destroying enemy property and assets. Many of his units had been with Sigel and wanted to avenge their defeat at New Market.

On May 26 the 12,000-man Union army began moving from its base at Belle Grove on Cedar Creek and headed south to Fisher's Hill and then on to Woodstock, where Hunter paused for a few days to resupply and to complete his planning. He arranged to rendezvous with the forces of US Brigadier Generals George R. Crook and William Averell in the Staunton area. Crook was to bring his command from Meadow Bluff, West Virginia, having cut the Virginia & Tennessee Railroad at Dublin, Virginia, on May 10. US Lieutenant General Ulysses S. Grant directed both commanders to travel light and to live off the land. The advancing armies foraged and pillaged vigorously, motivated in part by the effects of partisan operations against their own supply lines.

Hunter's column marched to New Market on May 29, pausing to rest and rebury properly those who had fallen during the previous battle. Hunter pushed on south of Harrisonburg on June 2 where he encountered the first significant Confederate defense, CS Brigadier General John D. Imboden's cavalry, deployed at Mount Crawford. Imboden resisted desperately while requesting reinforcements from Richmond. Virtually every able-bodied Confederate was called into service in the emergency, including supply soldiers, miners, and elderly militia reserves. Even more important, CS Brigadier General William E. "Grumble" Jones's Brigade of infantry was rushed by rail from Bristol, Virginia, bringing the Confederate strength to about 5,600 men.

The Confederate position at Mount Crawford blocked the Valley Pike at a point where it crossed the North Fork of the Shenandoah. Imboden's preparations promised a hard fight. Consequently Hunter decided to sidestep the prepared Confederate defenses with a move east to Port Republic, then south on the East Road toward Staunton. His move surprised Imboden and Jones, who were in the process of organizing and integrating their commands at Mount Crawford. Hunter was delayed crossing the river near Port Republic because of the inefficiency of his engineers, and this gave Imboden time to hustle his cavalry eastward to confront the Union threat. Jones followed with the infantry and more cavalry under

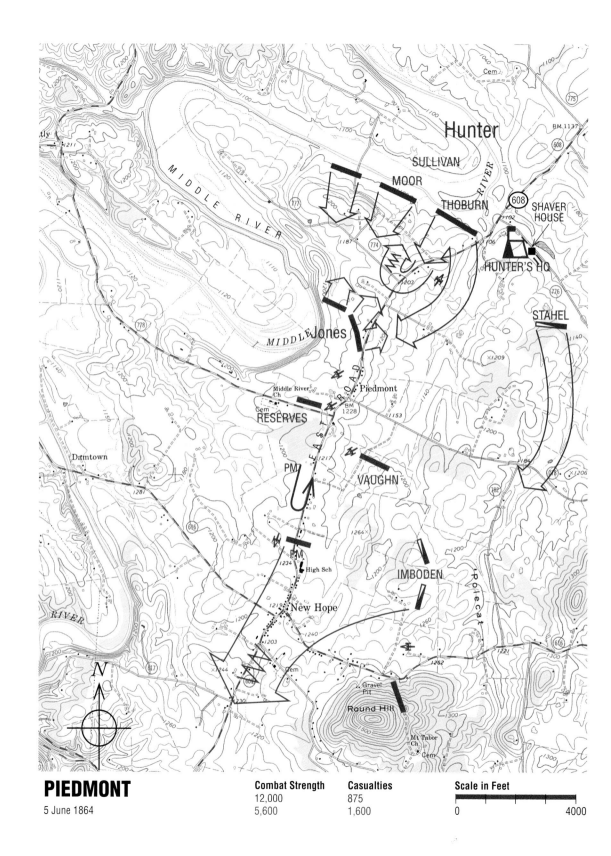

Hunter

SULLIVAN

MOOR

THOBURN

SHAVER
HOUSE

HUNTER'S HQ

STAHEL

Jones

Piedmont

Middle River
Ch

RESERVES

VAUGHN

Damtown

PM

PM

High Sch

IMBODEN

New Hope

RIVER

N

Round Hill

Mt Tabor
Ch
Cem

PIEDMONT

5 June 1864

Combat Strength	Casualties	Scale in Feet
12,000	875	0 4000
5,600	1,600	

CS Brigadier General John C. Vaughn, and these troops took up positions in the vicinity of Piedmont, located about seven miles south of Port Republic and one mile north of New Hope on the East Road to Staunton.

In 1864 the hamlet of Piedmont consisted of about ten houses nestled in rolling farmland interspersed with woods southeast of the steep banks of a looping curve of the Middle River. Jones deployed most of his infantry northwest of the town, with its flank anchored on the river. Jones concentrated his cavalry southeast of the intersection of the road west from the pike and the East Road, and gave specific orders to hold and block a Union move around the east flank. This placement inadvertently created a gap between the two wings of his force near the village.

Early on the morning of June 5 Hunter's cavalry, across the river near Port Republic, ran into some cavalry outposts set up by Imboden at the crossroads near Mount Meridian. A swirling cavalry "pile on" took place, soon joined by horse artillery, as the greater Union numbers pressed Imboden's men south a mile to the Crawford farmhouse, Bonnie Doon. The Confederates held there until Union artillery massed on the road to the north and forced them farther south to another delaying position at Crawford Run near the Shaver farm, later Hunter's headquarters. Again the preponderant Union artillery forced the Confederates back to the main positions that Jones had selected around Piedmont.

Jones positioned two infantry brigades behind barricades of rails and trees to form a large arc along the woods northwest of Piedmont, while less reliable infantry reserves were positioned along the crossroads in town. Most of the Confederate artillery supported the infantry. When Imboden's horsemen clattered back from delaying the Union advance, they joined Vaughn's cavalry southeast of the village. No one noted the large gap between the infantry and the cavalry.

At about noon the Union forces came up to this line just as the sun emerged after the morning rains. Hunter decided to concentrate on the Confederate infantry. Sullivan's two brigades, led by US Colonels Joseph Thoburn and Augustus

Moor, advanced in an attempt to flank the Confederate positions. One brigade made at least three desperate frontal attacks to fix Confederate attention, while the other took advantage of low ground to move around the right flank of Jones's infantry. This force was resisted fiercely by Confederate artillery. However, the Union attacks did reveal the gap in the Confederate lines. The flanking Union brigade tried another attack into this gap with heavy artillery support just as the Confederates were shifting some units. In the meantime the Union cavalry under Stahel rode eastward en masse, forcing the Confederate cavalry to remain southeast of the town to protect Jones's eastern flank.

The violent Union attack into the gap presaged thirty minutes of hand-to-hand struggle in the woods. Jones rushed from one imperiled point to another, encouraging the troops, until he was killed instantly by a bullet to the head. His death marked the collapse of his line and the precipitous withdrawal of the Confederate infantry, making the position of the cavalry untenable. Vaughn and Imboden withdrew southward down the East Road to Fishersville. The Confederate rear guard on the East Road between New Hope and Piedmont discouraged any Union pursuit.

The battle was a disaster for the Confederates. Hunter shattered their military force in the Valley and exposed the well-established depots and logistical facilities in Staunton and elsewhere. The upper Valley was opened to invasion for the first time in the war, with serious psychological and economic implications for the Confederacy. In the North the victory solidified President Lincoln's position at the Republican convention then in progress in Baltimore.

Estimated Casualties: 875 US, 1,600 CS

Piedmont battlefield, one mile north of New Hope and seven miles south of Port Republic on Route 608 off Interstate 81, is privately owned.

Lynchburg, Virginia (VA064), Lynchburg, June 17–18, 1864

US General Hunter's Federals raided the upper Shenandoah Valley after the battle of Piedmont. They occupied Staunton, wrecked the railroads and warehouses, and on June 10 continued south to Lexington. US General Crook, advancing after his victory at Cloyd's Mountain, joined Hunter, bringing the Union force to 18,500. On the eleventh, as Hunter's vanguard prepared to cross the Maury River, it was fired on by Confederates posted on the grounds of the Virginia Military Institute. Hunter called up artillery. Against the objection of many of his officers, including the chief of artillery, US Captain Henry A. du Pont, Hunter ordered the buildings to be burned in retaliation for the VMI cadets' role in the battle of New Market. The superintendent's quarters were excepted. (After the war, when du Pont was a U.S. senator, he sponsored legislation awarding $100,000 to VMI to repair the war damage.)

While Hunter was in Lexington, CS President Jefferson Davis urged CS General Lee to send more men to the Valley. Lee consented but noted the cost: "I think that is what the enemy would desire." Lee detached the 9,000 men of CS Lieutenant General Jubal A. Early's Second Corps from the Cold Harbor lines to drive Hunter out of the Valley, cross the Potomac, and threaten Washington, D.C. On June 17 Early's troops boarded trains for Lynchburg.

The Federals left Lexington and crossed the Blue Ridge by way of Peaks of Otter to threaten the Confederate rail depot at Lynchburg. Lynchburg housed thirty-two hospitals and served with Charlottesville as a recuperation point for wounded Confederate soldiers. CS General Breckinridge assembled two brigades and the VMI cadets to hold the fortifications around Lynchburg. They repulsed Hunter's first tentative attacks from the southwest and the south on June 17. Units of Early's Corps arrived that night, and by the following morning, 13,000 Confederates manned the defenses.

Although Hunter's forces outnumbered Early's, the Federals' attacks from the Liberty Turnpike against the strong Confederate earthworks were easily repelled, so they began to retreat after dark. Since Hunter feared the late CS Lieutenant General Stonewall Jackson's old corps, as well as a return march of one hundred miles through the Valley that his forces had devastated, he made a disastrous decision: he led his men westward along the railroad toward Salem and into West Virginia's Kanawha Valley, which was held by Union forces. This route back to the Potomac took his army to the Ohio River and out of the war for nearly a month. The Shenandoah Valley was open to a Confederate advance toward the Potomac River, Maryland, and Washington. Early pursued Hunter on June 19 and defeated the Union rear guard at Liberty (now Bedford) and at Hanging Rock near Salem on the twenty-first before breaking off the chase to advance north down the Valley. On July 4 the Confederates occupied Harpers Ferry on their march to Maryland, compelling the defenders to seek protection on the impregnable Maryland Heights.

Estimated Casualties: 700 US, 200 CS

Early in Maryland, Pennsylvania, and the Shenandoah Valley: July–August 1864

Monocacy, Maryland (MD007), Frederick County, July 9, 1864

Gary W. Gallagher

CS Lieutenant General Jubal A. Early and the 14,000 soldiers of his Army of the Valley (Early's name for the Second Corps of the Army of Northern Virginia plus other attached units) were on the move in the second week of July 1864. Early had received orders from CS General Robert E. Lee to clear the Shenandoah Valley of Union forces, menace Washington and Baltimore, and compel US Lieutenant General Ulysses S. Grant to counter his movements, thereby weakening the Army of the Potomac. Early drove Union troops from the Valley and then crossed the Potomac, swinging north and east from Shepherdstown to approach Washington from the rear.

On the morning of July 9 General Early's army was in the vicinity of Frederick, Maryland, with CS Major General Robert E. Rodes's Division in the lead on the National Road, moving east to threaten Union forces guarding the direct route to Baltimore. CS Major General Stephen Ramseur's Division edged southward on the Georgetown Pike connecting Frederick with Washington. The divisions of CS Major General John B. Gordon and CS Brigadier General Gabriel C. Wharton, under the command of CS Major General John C. Breckinridge, and the cavalry of CS Brigadier General John McCausland advanced down the Buckeystown Road. Two artillery battalions were with Ramseur and one with Breckinridge.

A force of about 5,800 soldiers under US Major General Lewis Wallace awaited the Confederates on the east bank of the Monocacy River just below Frederick. Uncertain whether Early's goal was Washington or Baltimore, Wallace had selected a position from which he could dispute

Confederate crossings of the Monocacy on both the National Road to Baltimore and the Georgetown Pike. Northern estimates placed Early's force at between 20,000 and 30,000 men — far too many for Wallace to defeat in a stand-up fight. The Union commander did hope to determine Early's destination, secure an accurate count of Confederate numbers, and detain the army long enough for Grant to "get a corps or two into Washington and make it safe." Wallace's command included home guards and other second-line troops consolidated as a brigade under US Brigadier General Erastus B. Tyler, as well as US Brigadier General James B. Ricketts's veteran VI Corps division from the Army of the Potomac. Sent away from the Petersburg lines in response to Early's campaign in Maryland, Ricketts's two brigades had joined Wallace at about 1:00 A.M. on July 9.

Wallace expected the Confederates to attack in the vicinity of Monocacy Junction — where the Georgetown Pike and the Baltimore & Ohio Railroad cross the river — or to seize fords farther downstream. Watching both of these critical points on the line were Ricketts's brigades, positioned on high ground running southwest from a covered wooden bridge that carried the Georgetown Pike across the river. Tyler's brigade held the Union right, guarding fords and bridges from the Baltimore & Ohio's iron bridge upstream to the National Road. Union defenders at the junction made use of two blockhouses, one on each side of the Monocacy, and rifle pits on the east bank of the river. A line of Union skirmishers crouched behind the railroad embankment west of the river. Six 3-inch rifled guns and a 24-pounder howitzer, the latter in an emplacement overlooking the bridges near the junction, supported the Union infantry.

The morning of July 9 was bright and warm, with a cooling breeze sweeping over the lush countryside south of Frederick. Skirmishing erupted at about 6:30 A.M. between Ramseur's Division and Union soldiers positioned astride the Georgetown Pike west of the river. The Confederates pushed the Union pickets back and moved into position in the fields of the Best farm, west of

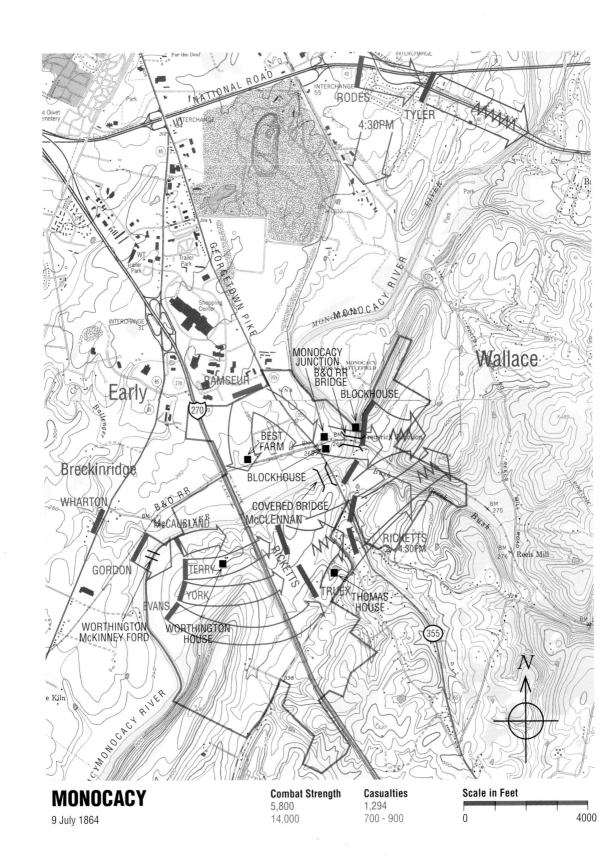

MONOCACY

9 July 1864

Combat Strength
5,800
14,000

Casualties
1,294
700 - 900

Scale in Feet
0   4000

the railroad and the pike. Soon three Confederate batteries were dueling with the Federal guns across the river. Convinced by the volume of Union fire that it would be costly to storm the covered bridge on the Georgetown Road, Ramseur asked Early if there were some other route across the Monocacy. To the north, meanwhile, Rodes's Division had engaged Tyler's troops in fitful fighting along the National Road.

The focus of the battle shifted to the southwest when McCausland's Confederate cavalry forced its way across the Monocacy a mile and a quarter below the junction at the Worthington-McKinney Ford. Ricketts reacted swiftly by moving across the Thomas farm toward the Worthington farm and placing some of his soldiers behind a fence that divided the two properties. Late in the morning McCausland's dismounted cavalrymen advanced through waist-high corn between the Worthington house and the river. Union infantry, partially hidden by the fence, easily stopped the surprised Confederate troopers. McCausland reformed his men and renewed the attack at about 2:00 P.M., this time striking the Union force farther to the right. After gaining ground in the direction of the Thomas farm, the Confederates fell back a second time in the face of superior Union firepower.

Both Wallace and Early realized the importance of McCausland's movements. Wallace sensed potential disaster on his left and decided to commit all of Ricketts's veterans on that end of the line. He ordered the covered bridge burned, thus releasing its defenders from their stations, and deployed all but one piece of artillery on Ricketts's front. As smoke billowed skyward from the blazing span shortly after noon, Early was at work on the west side of the Monocacy. Orders went to Breckinridge "to move rapidly with Gordon's and Wharton's divisions to McCausland's assistance . . . and strike the enemy on his left flank, and drive him from the position commanding the crossings in Ramseur's front, so as to enable the latter to cross."

The climactic phase of the battle began at about 3:30 P.M. Ramseur and Rodes continued to apply pressure at Monocacy Junction and the National Road, while Gordon's three brigades prepared to assault the Union left from positions on the Worthington farm. The Confederate attacks began with CS Brigadier General Clement A. Evans's Brigade of Georgians, which moved over Brooks Hill to strike US Colonel William S. Truex's brigade of Ricketts's division. Bitter fighting in the wheatfield on the Thomas farm brought a bloody stalemate. Evans received a serious wound, and a Georgia private wrote later that "it made our hearts ache to look over the battle field and see so many of our dear friends, comrades and beloved officers, killed and wounded."

Gordon's two other brigades rapidly added their power to the Confederate attacks. CS Brigadier General Zebulon York's regiments engaged Truex just to Evans's left, followed closely by CS Brigadier General William Terry's men, who collided with US Colonel Matthew R. McClennan's brigade near the river. Union defenders fought valiantly in the fields and among the buildings of the Thomas farm, yielding slowly to pressure from Gordon's infantry and the enfilading fire from Confederate artillery across the Monocacy. A final Union line took advantage of fences and cuts in the Georgetown Pike on the north side of the Thomas farm. Sheltered by that natural breastwork, men from New York, Pennsylvania, Vermont, and New Jersey sent a crippling fire into Confederates struggling up from a small creek bottom in their front. "In this ravine the fighting was desperate and at close quarters," Gordon recalled after the war. "Nearly one half of my men and large numbers of the Federals fell there."

It soon became clear that Union courage must give way to Confederate numbers. Wallace, fearing that prolonged resistance might bring the destruction of his small force, ordered a withdrawal to the National Road. At about 4:30 P.M. the Union army abandoned its position in front of Ramseur, enabling the Confederates to cross the railroad bridge. Gordon's exhausted troops watched as Ramseur's soldiers harried the retreating Union soldiers. Rodes subsequently joined Ramseur, but Early called off the pursuit and allowed Wallace to escape. Early's somewhat puzzling explanation after the war was that he did not wish to be encumbered by a large number of prisoners.

The battle of the Monocacy was a clear tactical victory for Jubal Early. At a cost of between 700 and 900 men killed and wounded, the Army of the Valley drove Wallace's troops from the field and inflicted heavy casualties. In Ricketts's division, which bore the brunt of the fighting on the northern side, 726 were killed and wounded and 568 listed as missing. Tyler's brigade lost 70 killed and wounded and 115 missing. Union losses totaled 1,294 of the 5,800 present for duty.

Despite suffering a clear tactical defeat, Wallace achieved his larger strategic goal. Early expended a precious twenty-four hours, which permitted reinforcements from the Army of the Potomac to reach Washington ahead of the Confederates. Had Wallace failed to intercept Early south of Frederick, the Army of the Valley might have fought its way into Washington on July 10. The political implications of such a victory for the Confederacy are interesting to contemplate but impossible to gauge with any certainty. It can be said with confidence that Wallace's troops spared the Lincoln government a potential disaster, and for that reason the battle of the Monocacy must be considered one of the more significant actions of the Civil War.

Estimated Casualties: 1,294 US, 700–900 CS

Monocacy National Battlefield, three miles south of Frederick near Interstate 270 and Route 355, includes 1,647 acres of the historic battlefield; 331 of these acres are privately owned.

Fort Stevens, District of Columbia (DC001), District of Columbia, July 11–12, 1864

In the spring of 1864 more than 48,000 men had been sent from the Military Defenses of Washington to reinforce the Army of the Potomac. The capital had only 9,000 Home Guards, one-hundred-day Ohio troops, clerks, and convalescents to man the sixty-eight forts protecting the city. One of the forts was Fort Stevens.

On July 10 CS General Early's exhausted Confederates marched from Monocacy toward Washington. The following morning dawned hot and humid as they arrived in what is today Silver Spring, Maryland, where Early established his headquarters on the Blair property. He pushed his skirmishers forward to scout the Federal defenses. The Union line on the north side of Washington straddled the Seventh Street Road (now Georgia Avenue). The northernmost earthwork, Fort Stevens, was located just west of the road near Rock Creek. The Confederates encountered Federal skirmishers near the fort, and the exchange of fire convinced Early that the works were strongly held, when in fact only a heavy artillery battery occupied the fort. Confederate sharpshooters fired from a tulip tree that is on the grounds of Walter Reed Hospital.

The Federal defense of Washington was quickly strengthened. Elements of US Major General Horatio G. Wright's veteran VI Corps began to arrive that day by transport from City Point, Virginia, raced through the capital, and by the evening had occupied the line of forts. The XIX Corps, en route from New Orleans to reinforce US General Grant at Petersburg, was also diverted to Washington for the Federal attack up the Seventh Street Road on July 12. Early did not have the strength to capture the city, so he demonstrated against Forts Stevens and DeRussy while he planned his retreat. President Lincoln was at Fort Stevens when the Union troops drove the Confederates back from their advanced position before the forts.

Early sent 1,500 cavalrymen under CS Brigadier General Bradley T. Johnson to raid toward

Baltimore and free 10,000–12,000 Confederate prisoners at Point Lookout, where the Potomac merges with the Chesapeake. This was to be a combined operation with two Confederate steamers from North Carolina: the ships were to land 1,800 soldiers on July 12 and join with Johnson to free the prisoners. However, the press learned of the operation, and Union gunboats took positions commanding the land and water approaches to the prison pier. CS Major Harry W. Gilmor raided the outskirts of Baltimore, cut the Philadelphia & Wilmington Railroad northeast of the city, and briefly captured US Major General William B. Franklin on a train. Johnson continued his raid, threatening the eastern defenses of Washington near Beltsville. Early recalled Johnson and Gilmor on July 12 for the retreat to Virginia. The Confederates reached White's Ford on the Potomac the next day and camped at Leesburg on July 14.

Estimated Casualties: 373 US, 500 CS

Fort Stevens Park, on 13th Street, N.W., off Military Road in Washington, includes a restored section of the fort. Fort DeRussy is in Rock Creek Park. Both parks are administered by the National Park Service.

Cool Spring, Virginia (VA114), Clarke County, July 17–18, 1864

A Union column of 10,500 men under US General Wright slowly pursued CS General Early's army as it withdrew from Washington. On July 17 fighting broke out when US Brigadier General Alfred N. Duffié's cavalry rode through Snickers Gap and tried to cross the Shenandoah River at Snickers Ford (Castleman's Ferry). The troopers included some of US Brigadier General George R. Crook's command, back from US Major General David Hunter's retreat through West Virginia af-

ter the battle of Lynchburg. They cleared the gap, and the next day US Colonel Joseph Thoburn led his division downstream to cross the river at Judge Richard Parker's ford to flank the Confederate position. Early's three nearby divisions intercepted his movement. CS General Rodes assembled his division at the Cool Spring farm on a ridge overlooking the ford. His attack shattered Thoburn's right flank of 1,000 dismounted cavalry. The Federals withstood three attacks at the river's edge before dusk enabled them to withdraw. Some of the soldiers drowned fleeing across the river.

Estimated Casualties: 422 US, 397 CS

Rutherford's Farm, Virginia (VA115), Frederick County and Winchester, July 20, 1864

A month after the defeat at Lynchburg, US General Hunter's Army of West Virginia emerged from the mountains at Martinsburg. To support US Generals Crook and Wright at Cool Spring, he sent US Brigadier General William W. Averell's cavalry division to threaten CS General Early, who was camped at Berryville. Early pulled back from the Shenandoah River and sent CS General Ramseur's Division ahead to stop Averell. The Federal cavalry advanced up the Valley Pike (now Route 11) and on July 20 attacked Ramseur three miles north of Winchester at Rutherford's Farm. This sudden assault hit the flank of CS Brigadier General W. Gaston Lewis's Brigade as it was deploying on the left. Ramseur withdrew toward Winchester in confusion, and Averell captured four guns and nearly 300 men.

Early withdrew his army to Fisher's Hill near Strasburg to reorganize his forces. Convinced that the Confederate threat to the North was alleviated, Wright started moving his VI Corps and elements of the XIX Corps to Washington in preparation for their return to the Petersburg front. He left Crook with three small infantry divisions and a cavalry division to guard the Valley.

Estimated Casualties: 242 US, 500 CS

Second Kernstown, Virginia (VA116), Frederick County and Winchester, July 24, 1864

Joseph W. A. Whitehorne

On July 22 US Brigadier General George R. Crook moved his force to Winchester, where he learned that CS Lieutenant General Jubal A. Early was in the vicinity of Strasburg. The Union cavalry was in contact with Confederate cavalry, and their skirmishing intensified throughout the day. Crook intended to remain in Winchester only a day or two to rest his troops before continuing north. However, on July 23 the fighting became so intense that he ordered the infantry divisions to march from Winchester and form a support line just north of Kernstown. When the cavalry was pressed north late in the afternoon, US Colonel Isaac H. Duval's infantry division, including a brigade commanded by US Colonel Rutherford B. Hayes (who became president of the United States in 1877), advanced and cleared Kernstown of Confederates. Crook then left a cavalry brigade to picket Kernstown and pulled the rest of his force back to Winchester.

Early learned from his cavalry that the Union pursuit was over and that his forces outnumbered the Union's, 14,000 to 9,500. At first light on July 24, Confederate forces headed by CS Major General John C. Breckinridge began to advance down the Valley Pike to attack Crook. The divisions of CS Major General John B. Gordon and CS Brigadier General Gabriel C. Wharton were to press the Union line in its center at Kernstown. Ramseur's Division left the pike at Bartonsville and headed west to the Middle Road to turn the Federals' right flank. CS Major General Robert E. Rodes's Division was ordered over to the Front Royal Road to make a similar move on the east. Confederate cavalry was placed on each flank to exploit the expected infantry victory.

The cavalry skirmishing intensified. When Crook learned from his scouts that a large infantry force was on the way, he moved his infantry back into position at Kernstown. US Colonel

James A. Mulligan's division set up behind some stone walls north of Hoge Run, west of the Valley Pike. Mulligan immediately sent out skirmishers to Opequon Church and southward to relieve the cavalry, which then deployed to the west to guard the Union flank. At midmorning Duval's two brigades each moved to one of Mulligan's flanks, and Hayes's brigade set up east of the pike. Crook's Third Division, led by US Colonel Joseph Thoburn, moved into trenches in the woods on Pritchard's Hill, northwest of the main line. US Captain Henry A. du Pont unlimbered Crook's artillery on the hill.

The infantry battle began at noon as elements of Gordon's Division chased back the Union skirmish line. Mulligan immediately ordered a counterattack supported by Hayes's brigade. The Union right advanced to the protection of the walls of Opequon Church and its cemetery; the Federals farther east fought in an open orchard next to the pike. Within half an hour they were compelled to fall back under the intense fire of Gordon's men, many of whom had fought in the same place under CS Lieutenant General Thomas J. "Stonewall" Jackson two years before. The Union soldiers in the churchyard were forced back as well, and the Confederates then pressed into the area.

The Union line underwent some changes during this adjustment. Duval's brigade on Mulligan's right (west) moved farther west, near the cavalry on Middle Road. The gap created was filled by Thoburn's division. The Confederate line was extended westward by another of Gordon's brigades, which arrived and swept across the open ground west of Opequon Church, forcing Thoburn's units from the protection of one stone wall to a second stone wall farther north. They were soon dislodged from this position and forced back to their original places on the northwest slope of Pritchard's Hill. By that time Thoburn was aware of Ramseur's approach on the west. This shift exposed Mulligan's division to vicious fire on its west flank as it desperately held on to the Hoge Run line.

A new Confederate threat then appeared on the east. Breckinridge had moved Wharton's Di-

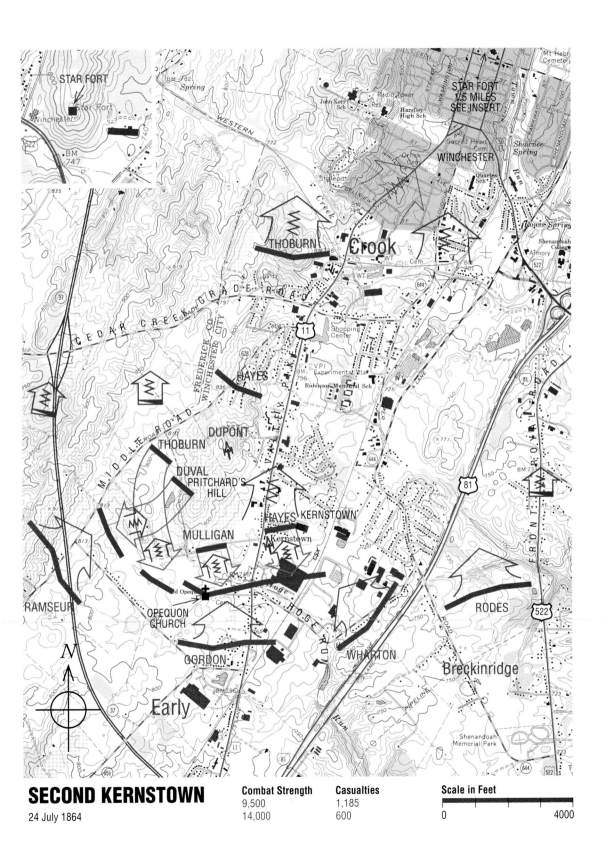

SECOND KERNSTOWN

24 July 1864

Combat Strength	Casualties
9,500	1,185
14,000	600

Scale in Feet

0   4000

vision to a ridge southeast of Kernstown, where it formed close to the Union left flank. Hayes had noted the movement as he tried to support Mulligan's increasingly desperate defense north of the church. Hayes's left flank, unprotected, began to crumple as soon as Wharton's men began their advance. Hayes rallied his men briefly behind a stone wall just east of the pike but soon was forced to pull back farther. Wharton's charge was a signal for Gordon's men to advance as well. This placed Confederate forces on both of Mulligan's flanks. Soon his line began to yield. Mulligan tried to rally his men but was mortally wounded. The collapse of the Union center forced Crook to withdraw his entire force.

The remnants of Hayes's brigade held the north part of Pritchard's Hill to enable du Pont's artillery to withdraw. The Union cavalry on the west charged into the advancing Confederates to buy time for Thoburn's division and the remainder of Duval's to pull back in good order. The Union cavalry on the Front Royal Road withdrew without making any contribution to the battle. One brigade of Thoburn's division blocked the Valley Pike briefly on the high ground at Cedar Creek Grade north of Pritchard's Hill, then retreated under pressure.

The Union troops quickly retreated through Winchester, in some disorder, to Bunker Hill, having suffered 1,185 casualties. On July 25 they continued their retrograde movement to the Potomac, eventually reaching Harpers Ferry on July 27. The victorious Confederates remained in the Winchester area and held Union prisoners at Star Fort, north of the town. (Star Fort had been lost one other time by the Federals in June 1863, when US Major General Robert H. Milroy was defeated at the battle of Second Winchester.) Once more the Valley was cleared of Union troops, and Jubal Early soon had his cavalry on the march. They destroyed the rail yards at Martinsburg and burned Chambersburg, Pennsylvania, a few days later.

News of the defeat and Early's actions once again raised concerns for the security of Washington. More significantly, it was the final straw for US Lieutenant General Ulysses S. Grant. He fired a number of inept Union commanders, returned the VI and XIX Corps to the Valley, and put his protégé, US Major General Philip H. Sheridan, in command. Sheridan had orders to neutralize the Valley once and for all and to end its economic value to the Confederacy. Second Kernstown marks the beginning of the Valley's most tragic wartime period.

Estimated Casualties: 1,185 US, 600 CS

Second Kernstown battlefield, near Route 11 and Interstate 81 south of Winchester, is privately owned.

Folck's Mill, Maryland (MD008), Allegany County, August 1, 1864

On July 29 five of CS General Early's cavalry brigades crossed the Potomac River into Maryland while CS General Breckinridge's two divisions wrecked the B & O rail yard at Martinsburg. Early sent two cavalry brigades, 4,000 men under CS Generals McCausland and Johnson, to ransom or burn Chambersburg, Pennsylvania, in retaliation for US General Hunter's raid on the Valley in June. The Confederates demanded $500,000 in cash or $100,000 in gold, and when the town could not raise the money, they burned the center of the town. They retreated toward Cumberland, Maryland, to disrupt the B & O Railroad, pursued by US General Averell's cavalry.

US Brigadier General Benjamin F. Kelley, the commander of the garrison defending Cumberland, deployed his men on a hill three miles from the town near Folck's Mill. On August 1 McCausland's cavalry attacked, and Kelley repulsed them. When US General Averell's cavalry approached, the Confederates broke off the fight and recrossed the Potomac at Oldtown into West Virginia.

Estimated Casualties: 30 US, 30 CS

Moorefield, West Virginia (WV013), Hardy County, August 7, 1864

After CS General McCausland burned Chambersburg, Pennsylvania, the Confederates went into camp at Moorefield, at the confluence of the South Fork and the South Branch of the Potomac River. US General Averell continued his pursuit and crossed the Potomac at Hancock with 1,600 men on August 1. On August 7 Averell's troops surprised the Confederate camp after capturing the pickets without firing a shot. One brigade attacked CS General Johnson's Brigade and drove it back across the South Branch into CS General McCausland's camp. Johnson's retreat shattered the Confederates, and they were repeatedly flanked. They abandoned four guns and their wagon train.

This Federal cavalry victory dealt a decisive blow to the morale and effectiveness of the Confederate cavalry in the Valley.

Estimated Casualties: 31 US, 500 CS

Sheridan's Shenandoah Valley Campaign: August 1864–March 1865

Guard Hill, Virginia (VA117), Warren County, August 16, 1864

After the battle of Second Kernstown and the Confederate raids in Maryland and Pennsylvania, US Lieutenant General Ulysses S. Grant focused upon the need to end Confederate control of the Shenandoah Valley and to destroy its capacity to provide food for CS General Robert E. Lee's army. Grant's instructions to US Major General Henry W. Halleck in July had been vivid but were as yet unfulfilled: pursue CS Lieutenant General Jubal A. Early and "eat out Virginia clean and clear as far as they go, so that crows flying over it for the balance of this season will have to carry their provender with them."

Grant needed a determined general. After US Major General David Hunter agreed to step aside, showing what Grant later described as "a patriotism none too common in the army," Grant appointed US Major General Philip H. Sheridan. On August 7 Grant created a new Middle Military Division covering West Virginia, western Maryland, and the Valley. It included elements of the VIII Corps (the former Army of West Virginia), the VI and the XIX Corps, and three cavalry divisions. Grant bluntly stated, "I want Sheridan put in command of all troops in the field, with instructions to put himself South of the enemy, and follow him to the death. Wherever the enemy goes, let our troops go also." Sheridan designated his 43,000-man force the Army of the Shenandoah.

Early had only about 16,000 men in his army, so on August 6 Lee dispatched CS Lieutenant General Richard H. Anderson with CS Major Wilfred E. Cutshaw's artillery battalion and two divisions from the Petersburg lines to reinforce Early: CS Major General Joseph B. Kershaw's infantry and CS Major General Fitzhugh Lee's cavalry. On August 10 Sheridan marched southward with his superior numbers from Harpers Ferry toward Berryville. This move threatened Early's position at Winchester, so on the twelfth the Confederates retreated to Fisher's Hill south of Strasburg. The Federals camped along Cedar Creek with cavalry outposts at Front Royal.

On August 16 Lee's troopers scattered the Federal pickets at the Shenandoah River crossings at Front Royal and galloped in pursuit of them down the Front Royal Pike (now Route 340). At Guard Hill, a prominent landmark, the Confederates were hit by US Brigadier General Thomas C. Devin's dismounted cavalry brigade firing their carbines from the scrub along the steep banks of Crooked Run. CS Brigadier General William Wofford's Brigade attempted a flanking movement by wading across the river downstream, but two of Devin's New York brigades attacked them and took 300 prisoners. US Brigadier General George A. Custer's brigade rode toward the gunfire and extended Devin's line along Crooked Run until Confederate artillery on Guard Hill forced the Federals to withdraw to Cedarville.

Uncertain of Early's strength and ordered by Grant not to risk a defeat, Sheridan pulled back to Charles Town to protect the B & O Railroad and his supply depot at Harpers Ferry.

Estimated Casualties: 71 US, 480 CS

Summit Point and Cameron's Depot, West Virginia (WV014), Jefferson County, August 21, 1864

CS General Early reoccupied Winchester while US General Sheridan concentrated his army at Charles Town. Early resumed his offensive by launching converging columns on August 21. He led one column on the Valley Pike to Bunker Hill and eastward through Smithfield toward Charles Town. CS General Anderson led another northward toward Summit Point and sent his cavalry to Berryville to close in on Charles Town from the south.

Early crossed Opequon Creek at Smithfield Crossing (near present Middleway) and drove a division of US General Wright's VI Corps back to Cameron's Depot, about three miles from Charles Town. US General Sheridan brought up his three infantry corps. Early expected Anderson to arrive and outflank Sheridan, but the Federal cavalry had slowed the Confederate troopers at Summit Point and north of Berryville.

During the night Sheridan fell back to prepared entrenchments at Halltown, where the Federal flanks were protected by the Potomac and Shenandoah Rivers. His cavalry blocked every ford to prevent Early's horsemen from crossing the Potomac into Maryland. The Confederates were in an area devastated by Federal troops, so they withdrew westward to Bunker Hill on August 26. Sheridan reoccupied Charles Town.

Estimated Casualties: 600 US, 400 CS

Smithfield Crossing, West Virginia (WV015), Jefferson and Berkeley Counties, August 28–29, 1864

On August 26 US General Sheridan pushed CS Generals Early and Anderson across to the west bank of Opequon Creek and brought his army back to Charles Town. On August 28 the cavalry skirmished heavily at Smithfield Crossing (near present Middleway), and the next morning US Brigadier General Wesley Merritt succeeded in pushing a brigade across the Opequon. Early ordered CS Generals Ramseur and Gordon to retake the crossing with their infantry, but they were hit by the fire of the troopers' seven-shot Spencer carbines. Gordon crossed a brigade upstream to attempt to get in their rear. The Federals retired fighting toward Charles Town. US Brigadier General James B. Ricketts's veteran VI Corps division deployed in the late afternoon three miles west of Charles Town and advanced, but the Confederates were recrossing the creek. The Federals took control of Smithfield Crossing at about sunset.

Estimated Casualties: 100 US, 200 CS

Berryville, Virginia (VA118), Clarke County, September 3–4, 1864

With a clearer understanding of CS General Early's strength, US General Sheridan marched south to Berryville on September 3 while Early sent CS General Kershaw's Division east on a reconnaissance from Winchester out the Berryville Pike. At about 5:00 P.M. Kershaw attacked US Colonel Joseph Thoburn's VIII Corps division while the men were going into camp about one half mile west of Berryville. Kershaw routed Thoburn's left flank before the rest of the corps came to the rescue. Darkness ended the fighting, and both sides brought up strong reinforcements during the night. The next morning, when Early saw the strength of the Union entrenched position, he withdrew once again behind Opequon Creek. Sheridan telegraphed US General Grant about the difficulty of attacking Early because the "Opequon is a very formidable barrier."

Sheridan was unwilling to risk a pitched battle since a defeat in the Valley would open an invasion route to the North again just two months before the U.S. presidential election. Neither army moved for two weeks. The soldiers called this sparring between Sheridan and Early the "Mimic War."

Estimated Casualties: 312 US, 195 CS

Opequon (Third Winchester), Virginia (VA119), Frederick and Clarke Counties and Winchester, September 19, 1864

After US Major General William Tecumseh Sherman captured Atlanta on September 2, US General Grant and President Lincoln agreed that US General Sheridan should move against CS General Early. When Grant came from Petersburg to Harpers Ferry to meet with Sheridan, he found that Sheridan was ready with a plan. Sheridan had just learned from Rebecca Wright, a Quaker schoolteacher in Winchester, that he had more than twice as many troops as Early. She reported that on September 15, in response to CS General

Robert E. Lee's orders, Early had started CS General Anderson back to Richmond with CS General Kershaw's Division and CS Major Wilfred E. Cutshaw's artillery battalion so that Lee could extend his Richmond-Petersburg line to protect his flanks. Grant had cut the railroad between Petersburg and Weldon, North Carolina, in the battle of Globe Tavern in mid-August. When Sheridan outlined to Grant his strategy to control the Shenandoah Valley, the general responded with the brief order "Go in." Early had further weakened his force by dispatching two infantry divisions to raid the B & O Railroad at Martinsburg and had only two divisions to hold Winchester.

On September 19 Sheridan launched his bold dash for Winchester with 37,000 men. The three Union infantry corps marched along the Berryville Pike, crossed Opequon Creek, and headed west into the two-mile-long Berryville Canyon. US Brigadier General James H. Wilson's cavalry division riding ahead surprised CS General Ramseur's Division at the western entrance to the canyon. While they battled, US Major General Horatio G. Wright's VI Corps moved slowly through the narrow canyon. The wagons and guns held back his infantry as well as that of US Major General William H. Emory's XIX Corps. This "stupid clutter" set Sheridan's timetable back four hours, and he lost the opportunity to strike Early while the Confederate forces were separated. Early had time to concentrate three of his divisions along a wooded ridgeline east of the town. His line extended from Abrams Creek north across the Berryville Pike to Red Bud Run, with artillery batteries on the high ground. CS Major General John C. Breckinridge covered the Valley Pike north of town with CS Brigadier General Gabriel C. Wharton's infantry and CS General Fitzhugh Lee's cavalry.

The Federals attacked just before noon. On their right US Brigadier General Cuvier Grover's XIX Corps division advanced through the woods and attacked across an open field (later known as Middle Field). CS General Gordon's Division hit them with a withering fire, then counterattacked, and inflicted nearly 1,500 Federal casualties in less than an hour. When Emory led his Second

Division forward, he was trapped for two hours in "that basin of Hell." On the left the VI Corps was successful against Ramseur until CS General Rodes saw a gap between the two Federal corps, sent his division in, and knocked out a Federal division. US Brigadier General David A. Russell's division counterattacked and halted the Confederate drive. Both Rodes and Russell were killed.

US General Merritt's cavalry division crossed Opequon Creek about two miles north of the Berryville Pike crossing but was slowed by fire from Wharton's infantry, deployed to block the Union advance by Breckinridge, commanding the army's left flank. Fitzhugh Lee's troopers were on the infantry's left. Sheridan extended the Federal line north of Red Bud Run with US General Crook's VIII Corps. While US Captain Henry A. du Pont's eighteen cannons fired from a hill opposite Gordon's flank, the infantry attacked across Redbud Run at the Hackwood house and drove the Confederates back toward Winchester.

Merritt and US Brigadier General William W. Averell attacked Early's compact L-shaped line, which covered the Valley and Berryville Pikes. In one of the largest mounted charges of the war, their five cavalry brigades thundered down the Valley Pike and crumpled the Confederate left. Early ordered a general retreat to Fisher's Hill with the Federals in close pursuit. Sheridan wired Washington that he had sent Early "whirling through Winchester." Early lost one fourth of his men, including 2,000 taken prisoner, in the first of the climactic battles in the Shenandoah Valley campaign.

Estimated Casualties: 5,020 US, 3,610 CS

Fisher's Hill, Virginia (VA120), Shenandoah County, September 21–22, 1864

Joseph W. A. Whitehorne

US Major General Philip H. Sheridan's victory at the third battle of Winchester on September 19

was incomplete. CS Lieutenant General Jubal A. Early's force, battered as it was, remained intact, and Early retreated twenty miles south to a strong position at Fisher's Hill, two miles from Strasburg. Massanutten Mountain rises just east of Fisher's Hill, narrowing the Shenandoah Valley to about five miles. Fisher's Hill itself is a high, rocky ridge fronted by a small stream, Tumbling Run. The hill and the stream block the Valley, creating a formidable barrier that stretches from the North Fork of the Shenandoah River near the base of Massanutten westward to Little North Mountain in the foothills of the Alleghenies. Early's position was enhanced further by prepared trenches. The Valley Pike emerged from Strasburg and penetrated the ridge somewhat farther west than it does today.

Early placed CS Brigadier General Gabriel C. Wharton's Division on his right, east of the pike. His remaining infantry divisions, commanded by CS Major Generals John B. Gordon, John Pegram, and Stephen D. Ramseur, extended his line farther westward. Unfortunately, he had insufficient manpower to occupy his whole line in strength, and the last mile of his front continued to Little North Mountain with a thin line of dismounted cavalry. Anticipating that the greatest threat to his line was in the eastern part, Early concentrated the bulk of his artillery there with Wharton's and Gordon's men. He sent the remainder of his cavalry into the Luray Valley to prevent any Union attack against his line of retreat through the more southerly Massanutten gaps.

The 20,000-man Union force reached the area on the afternoon of September 20. The VI Corps deployed midway between Strasburg and the Back Road, which runs along the base of Little North Mountain. US Major General William H. Emory's XIX Corps occupied a position closer to Strasburg on the high ground overlooking the pike and the Shenandoah. US Brigadier General George Crook's VIII Corps was positioned miles to the rear in the woods north of Cedar Creek near Belle Grove. Sheridan, very much aware of the Confederate lookout station at Signal Knob on the Massanutten, wanted the VIII Corps to remain concealed to deceive his opponent about his

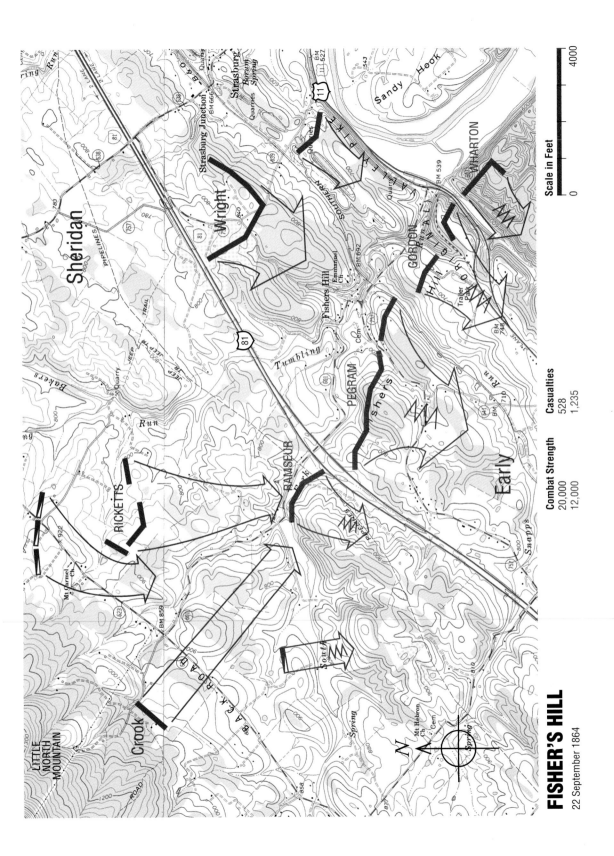

FISHER'S HILL

22 September 1864

	Combat Strength	Casualties
	20,000	528
	12,000	1,235

Scale in Feet

0   4000

strength and intentions. Sheridan sent most of his cavalry into the Luray Valley with orders to cut Early's line of retreat at New Market.

Late on the afternoon of September 21 US Brigadier General James B. Ricketts's division of US Major General Horatio G. Wright's VI Corps seized part of the high ground north of Tumbling Run within seven hundred yards of the Confederate positions. This provided a good view of a large part of the Confederate defenses and gave the Union artillery good firing positions. The VI Corps was also in a better position to support the main element of Sheridan's attack. Sheridan recognized that Early's strength on the east precluded any successful frontal assault straight up the pike, while his thin line to the west invited a movement against that flank. Sheridan placed his remaining cavalry on the Back Road in a position to exploit any infantry success on that side, and directed the VIII Corps to execute a flanking move to the west. The other two corps were to create as much distraction as possible.

Crook moved his VIII Corps, carefully screened from the Confederate observers on Signal Knob, from Cedar Creek to the north side of Hupp's Hill below Strasburg and on to the Back Road. Once he had his force in the protection of the forest along Little North Mountain, he hurried them southward to a point opposite Early's western flank. He was in position by 4:00 P.M. on September 22 and immediately threw both of his divisions into the attack. The Confederate line buckled, and the weak resistance from the 12,000 startled Confederates was the signal for the westernmost VI Corps division to attack, while its artillery provided support.

The Confederate line began to unravel from west to east as the triumphant Union troops advanced. The VI and XIX Corps joined in as the resistance diminished. Soon the entire Confederate line was in retreat, "at first stubborn and slow, then rapid, then — rout," in Gordon's words. The Confederate stampede was hastened by the Union cavalry coming in from the west behind Crook.

In the Luray Valley Confederate cavalry stymied Sheridan's horsemen in a series of sharp delaying engagements and kept Early's line of retreat open. Early pulled back to Narrow Passage north of Edinburg the day of the battle, to New Market the next day, and then, under Union pressure, all the way back to Rockfish Gap near Waynesboro. Although his force was relatively intact, Early had lost large amounts of equipment, and 240 of his men had been killed or wounded. One of the greatest losses to the army was the death of CS Major Sandie Pendleton, who had served as adjutant to Stonewall Jackson and Early. Most of the 995 missing straggled in over the next few weeks. Union losses totaled 528.

Sheridan assumed that the Confederate forces were no longer a threat after their second defeat in less than a week. The victory was acclaimed throughout the North as vindication of Grant's strategy and Lincoln's policy. Locally it presaged the other phase of that policy, the economic destruction of the Valley. Fisher's Hill marks the beginning of "Red October," the burning of the Valley, which was to leave its mark on the people, the terrain, and the economy for generations.

Estimated Casualties: 528 US, 1,235 CS

Fisher's Hill battlefield is near Routes 11 and 601, four miles southwest of Strasburg. One hundred ninety-four acres of the historic battlefield are owned by the Association for the Preservation of Civil War Sites and are open to the public.

Tom's Brook, Virginia (VA121), Shenandoah County, October 9, 1864

After his victory at Fisher's Hill, US General Sheridan pursued CS General Early's army up the Shenandoah Valley to Staunton. On October 6 Sheridan began to withdraw down the Valley after ordering US Brigadier General Alfred T. A. Torbert's three cavalry divisions to confiscate livestock and burn everything of "military significance," including barns and mills. The Federals destroyed a ninety-two-mile swath between Staunton and Strasburg between October 6 and 8 in what is known as "The Burning."

CS General Robert E. Lee reinforced Early with CS Brigadier General Thomas L. Rosser's Laurel Brigade from Petersburg, and ordered CS General Kershaw's Division and CS Major Cutshaw's artillery — which were en route to Richmond — to return to the Valley. "I have weakened myself very much," Lee wrote, "to strengthen you. It was done with the expectation of enabling you to gain such success that you could return the troops if not rejoin me yourself. I know you have endeavored to gain that success, and believe you have done all in your power to assure it. You must not be discouraged, but continue to try. I rely upon your judgment and ability, and the hearty cooperation of your officers and men still to secure it. With your united force it can be accomplished."

Rosser had been made commander of the two Confederate cavalry divisions after CS General Fitzhugh Lee was wounded in the battle of Opequon, and he began to follow the Union forces as they retreated down the Valley. On October 8 he camped at Tom's Brook just south of Strasburg but twenty-six miles north of Early's army at Rude's Hill. Sheridan grasped the opportunity and ordered Torbert's 4,000 cavalrymen to destroy Rosser's isolated command.

At dawn on October 9 two Union cavalry divisions advanced from Fisher's Hill and Round Hill to attack the Confederate camps at Tom's Brook. US General Merritt's division advanced up the Valley Pike, but artillery fire pinned down his troopers for two hours. US General Custer's division finally attacked up the Back Road on the west and broke the enemy line. The Confederates fled south, pursued by the Federal troopers along both the Back Road toward Columbia Furnace and the Valley Pike to beyond Woodstock in what became known as the "Woodstock Races." The Confederates lost eleven cannons and their entire baggage train. This action effectively demoralized Early's cavalry for the rest of the campaign.

Estimated Casualties: 57 US, 350 CS

Eight acres of the historic Tom's Brook battlefield are owned by the Association for the Preservation of Civil War Sites and are open to the public.

Cedar Creek, Virginia (VA122), Frederick, Shenandoah, and Warren Counties, October 19, 1864

Joseph W. A. Whitehorne

The last major battle of the 1864 Shenandoah Valley campaign took place at Cedar Creek on October 19. The battle area extended from Fisher's Hill, just south of Strasburg, north to a point about three miles below Middletown. A few days earlier, after burning the Valley as far south as Staunton, US Major General Philip H. Sheridan had established his lines along the high ground north of Cedar Creek. Sheridan and his men were confident that CS Lieutenant General Jubal A. Early's Army of the Valley was no longer a threat. As a result, at Cedar Creek the Union troops focused more on rest and recuperation than on a possible renewal of the struggle.

The aggressive Early, reinforced with CS Major General Joseph B. Kershaw's Division to offset his September losses, quickly pressed his 21,000 men northward. He occupied Fisher's Hill and probed the Union positions for weak points. A sharp fight at Hupp's Hill on October 13 signaled the cautious Sheridan that Early was on more than a scouting mission. The 32,000 Union soldiers were deployed in echelon from southeast to northwest, conforming to the flow of Cedar Creek. US Brigadier General George Crook's VIII Corps was east of the Valley Pike, its two divisions almost a mile apart. US Major General William H. Emory's XIX Corps was just west of the pike, occupying strong positions along Cedar Creek. US Major General Horatio G. Wright's VI Corps was farther north and west. This corps, en route to

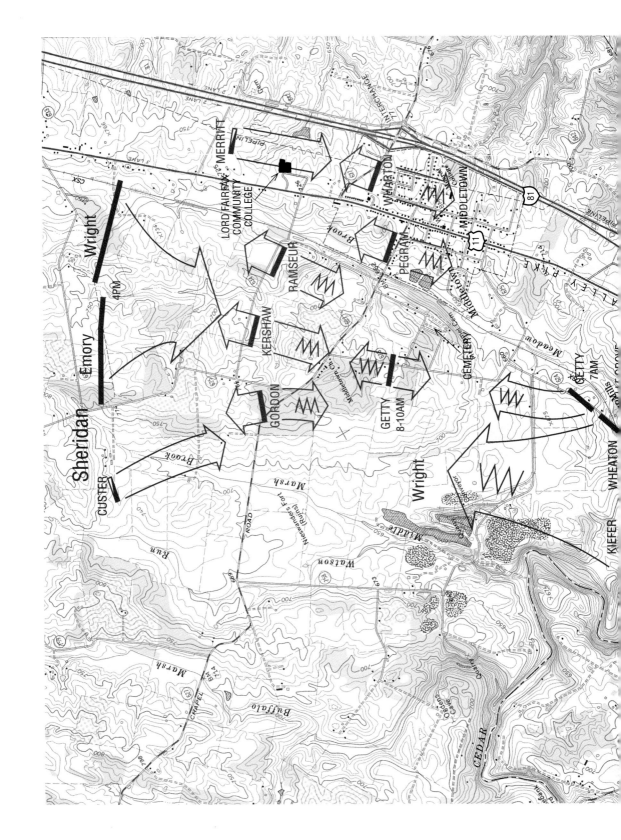

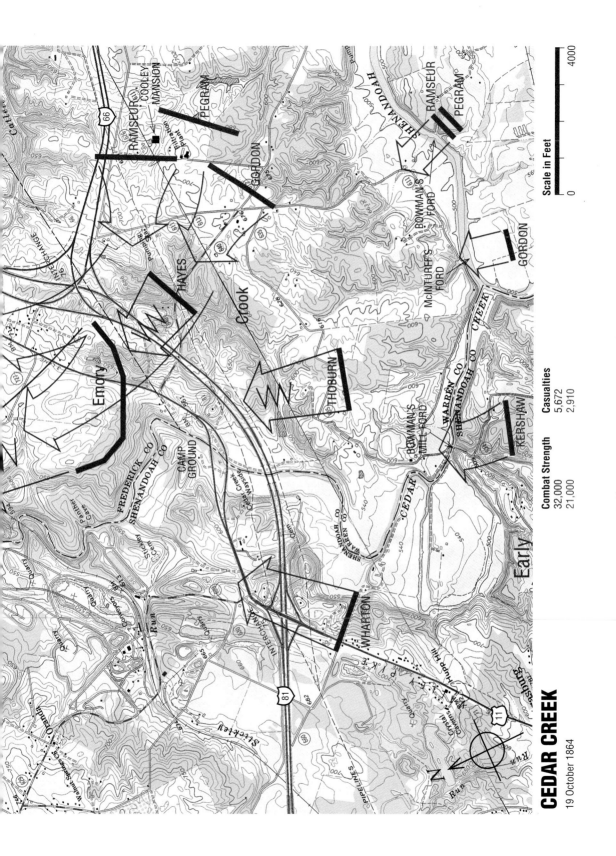

CEDAR CREEK

19 October 1864

	Combat Strength	Casualties
	32,000	5,672
	21,000	2,910

Scale in Feet

0   4000

Washington after the Hupp's Hill fight, had been recalled by Sheridan, and it returned just in time to set up camp but without any fortifications. On October 16 Sheridan went to a conference in Washington, leaving Wright in command. Wright placed the large cavalry corps to the west of the VI Corps.

The strong Union positions seemed to stymie Early, who, because of a shortage of supplies, would soon be forced to pull back unless he acted quickly. One of his division commanders, CS Major General John B. Gordon, and his corps cartographer, CS Captain Jedediah Hotchkiss, gave him a plan. The two men had climbed up to Signal Knob on Massanutten Mountain, where they had a full view of the Union positions. They noted the dispersal of the VIII Corps and the apparent reliance on the rough terrain along Cedar Creek and the North Fork of the Shenandoah to secure its eastern flank. A local resident told them of a trail that infantry could use to cross the tongue of Massanutten to reach fords on the river. They could then get to the Union flank east of the VIII Corps.

Early then approved a plan of great daring. It was in essence a three-column, converging night attack with cavalry support on each flank. Gordon took his division, along with CS Major General Stephen Ramseur's and CS Major General John Pegram's, over the trail to McInturff's and Bowman's Fords on the North Fork. From there they hustled northward until Ramseur's Division in the lead reached the Cooley mansion. At this point all they had to do was stop and face west; they were a half mile east of US Brigadier General Rutherford B. Hayes's division of the VIII Corps. Meanwhile Kershaw's Division marched from the Fisher's Hill assembly area up the pike through Strasburg to Bowman's Mill Ford across Cedar Creek. From there he confronted the other division of the Union VIII Corps. CS Brigadier General Gabriel C. Wharton's Division moved farther north up the pike to Hupp's Hill, from which it prepared to cross Cedar Creek at the Valley Pike bridge when conditions allowed.

The Confederate approach on October 18–19 was aided first by moonlight and then by an early morning fog. Kershaw's men opened the fight as scheduled at 5:00 A.M., quickly shattering the First Division, VIII Corps, commanded by US Colonel Joseph Thoburn. The only bright spot in the collapse of Crook's corps was the handling of the artillery by US Captain Henry A. du Pont, the acting corps chief of artillery. He was able to extricate most of the guns and wagons of all three of the corps' batteries while also keeping them in action. Their fire began the series of delays that eventually halted Early's attack. Du Pont later established an artillery position north of Middletown that served as the rallying point for the withdrawing Federals where they reformed and from which they launched their counterattack. Du Pont received a brevet promotion and the Medal of Honor for his exceptional bravery and leadership.

A few minutes after hitting Thoburn's division, Gordon's men smashed into Hayes's division, forcing it westward into the confused XIX Corps. That corps put up greater resistance, especially around the Belle Grove mansion, which was serving as corps and army headquarters. Finally, however, the XIX Corps was pressed westward through a line established by the VI Corps. The time bought by the VIII and XIX Corps had allowed the VI Corps to get well established on the high ground just west of Belle Grove. Each of its three divisions fought fiercely, although all were slowly pressed back. Finally, most of the Union forces broke contact and retreated to the north, eventually setting up a line perpendicular to the pike about three quarters of a mile north of today's Lord Fairfax Community College.

The Second Division of the VI Corps held on alone in a position around the Middletown Cemetery just northwest of the village. For more than one hour they resisted everything the Confederates threw at them, halting the Confederate momentum while buying time for the main Union force to reorganize. Early lost full vision of the battlefield and was unable to control all of his forces. Despite the entreaties of his senior commanders to bypass the problem, he decided to concentrate on this one division, which he finally forced back to the new Union position. The Confederates then established a line westward from the north edge of town. Later they edged half a mile farther north, waiting for the next Union move.

In the meantime Sheridan had returned to Winchester from Washington on October 18. On the morning of the nineteenth he was two miles south of town when he began to encounter numerous stragglers, each with his own tale of disaster. Sheridan rode quickly up the Valley Pike, inspiring the retreating ranks of men to turn and join him in saving the army. At Newtown (now Stephens City) he directed a young VIII Corps staff officer, US Captain William McKinley, to set up a straggler line to halt and channel the men southward to reinforce the Federal lines set up by Wright. Sheridan then rode along the new line, waving and bowing to the cheers of the Union soldiers. His presence, in the words of one, was like an "electric shock." Sheridan later said he had resolved to give his men a success or to suffer defeat with them.

The fiery army commander quickly re-established control and restored morale, then spent the afternoon carefully planning an assault on Early's lines. At about 4:00 P.M. he sent his massed cavalry in a counterattack that sent the Confederates into a retreat that turned into a rout. A bridge broke on the south side of Strasburg, forcing Early's troops to abandon all their rolling stock and all that they had captured. The infantry survivors rallied at Fisher's Hill and withdrew southward the next morning.

Early had helped Lee's defense of Richmond by tying down a large Union force for several months. However, at a moment of great opportunity, he made the fatal decision to pull back, allowing Sheridan to smash the Confederate military power in the Valley forever. The news of Sheridan's triumph assured a Republican victory in the upcoming November elections and the prosecution of the war to its end on President Abraham Lincoln's and Lieutenant General Ulysses S. Grant's terms.

Estimated Casualties: 5,672 US, 2,910 CS

Cedar Creek battlefield is near Route 11 and off Interstate 81 near Middletown and north of Strasburg. The battlefield is privately owned except for the 100-acre historic property Belle Grove, owned by the National Trust for Historic Preservation, the 101 acres of Lord Fairfax Community College, and 158 acres owned by the Cedar Creek Battlefield Foundation.

Sheridan has knocked down gold and G. B. McClellan together. The former is below 200 [while it rose to 3,000 against the Confederate dollar], and the latter [who was the Democratic Party's presidential candidate] is nowhere.

— George Templeton Strong, the New York diarist

Waynesboro, Virginia (VA123), Augusta County, March 2, 1865

After the Confederate defeat at Cedar Creek, CS General Robert E. Lee reinforced the lines at Petersburg with soldiers from CS General Early's command, leaving Early with fewer than 2,000 men to defend the Shenandoah Valley. Early's force settled into winter camps between Staunton and Rockfish Gap.

On February 27 US General Sheridan rode south from Winchester up the devastated Valley with two divisions of cavalry totaling 10,000 men. They reached Staunton on March 1 after a sharp skirmish at Mount Crawford. Early's command fell back to Waynesboro, twelve miles to the east, to cover Rockfish Gap in the Blue Ridge Mountains. Two brigades of CS General Wharton's Division — only 1,700 men and fourteen cannons — dug hasty entrenchments. Their line extended through the town on the right, while their left rested on high ground above the South River. There were not enough troops for the entire front, so there was a gap between the line and the river.

US General Custer's division led the Union advance. Custer discovered the small gap and at 3:30 P.M. ordered three dismounted regiments to attack the enemy's left flank. The rest of the division made a mounted frontal attack, and the Confederate line broke. In the wild charge through the town, Custer's division captured all of the Confederates except Early and his staff.

Sheridan's forces crossed the Blue Ridge, rode through Charlottesville, a major Confederate hospital center, and then eastward along the Virginia Central Railroad. Sheridan sent out columns to destroy the railroad tracks and wreck the locks of the James River and Kanawha Canal. Sheridan crossed the James and Appomattox Rivers and rode into City Point to lead Grant's spring offensive.

Estimated Casualties: 30 US, 1,600 prisoners CS

Hallowed Ground

Sam Nunn

The American Civil War, the most violent and traumatic chapter in our nation's history, shaped the course of American history more than any other event since the War of Independence. The war had its greatest impact on the American South in large part because it was waged almost entirely on southern soil. This may explain why southerners even today retain a depth of fascination with the conflict rarely found among their fellow citizens in other parts of the country.

The loss of life in the Civil War marred future generations. Some 365,000 Union and 260,000 Confederate soldiers and sailors lost their lives from 1861 to 1865, numbers all the more staggering when one considers that they were drawn from a population of only 31 million Americans. For every U.S. serviceman who died in Vietnam, almost eleven died in the Civil War.

Yet those who died at such places as Chancellorsville, Shiloh, Brandy Station, Cedar Creek, Vicksburg, Gettysburg, Fredericksburg, Antietam, Chickamauga, and the Wilderness did not sacrifice their lives in vain. The Civil War resolved forever two great issues that had sapped the health of the American Republic from Yorktown to Fort Sumter: the future of a cruel institution, slavery, and the political relationship of individual states to the Union. Though the Union did not enter the Civil War seeking to abolish slavery where it legally existed, the circumstances of the war itself made slavery's elimination possible and necessary. President Abraham Lincoln did not fail to take advantage of the war as an engine of fundamental social change.

Of equal importance for the future of our nation was the final defeat of a theory of constitutional government that threatened to produce a Disunited States of America — the claim that individual states, having voluntarily joined the Union, had a right to leave it. The surrender of the Confederate armies in the spring of 1865 put an end to the threat of weakness and division, of America's political balkanization.

The Civil War was also important from a military standpoint. It was the first truly modern war, for it saw the first widespread use of railroads for military movements and of the telegraph for strategic communications, the first mass employment of rifled firearms, the first use of machine guns, the first appearance of tinned rations, the first combat between ironclad warships, and the first use of rail-mounted artillery.

The war also produced American military leaders whose place in the lists of great captains is forever secure. Few armies in history have operated under military genius equal to that of the Army of Northern Virginia's General Robert E. Lee, Lieutenant General Thomas J. "Stonewall" Jackson, and Lieutenant General James Longstreet.

Though the Civil War was a human tragedy, we are a far better and more powerful country today because of the changes the war brought about. The war had a tremendous impact on what we stand for as Americans today.

For these reasons and many others, we must not allow the battlefields where so much American blood was so heroically spilled over such fundamental issues to become disposable property subject to commercial development.

Civil War battlefields are a historical legacy belonging to all Americans, a resource as precious as our national parks and forests and worthy of the same protection. To sell off bits and pieces of them is to sell off pieces of American history and to break faith with the hundreds of thousands of Americans who died on those battlefields.

Atlanta Campaign: May–September 1864

Rocky Face Ridge, Georgia (GA007), Whitfield County and Dalton, May 7–13, 1864

Jay Luvaas

US Major General William Tecumseh Sherman's Atlanta campaign was a vital part of US Lieutenant General Ulysses S. Grant's strategic plan launched in the spring of 1864. While Grant moved against CS General Robert E. Lee near Fredericksburg, Virginia, with US Major General Philip H. Sheridan commanding the Federal cavalry, the navy tightened the blockade. US Major General Benjamin F. Butler's forces attacked Richmond's supply lines in Chesterfield County, Virginia. US Major General Franz Sigel battled CS Major General John C. Breckinridge in the first battle of the 1864 Shenandoah campaign at New Market. US Major General Nathaniel P. Banks, whose orders were to expand Federal control of Louisiana, had lost the battle of Mansfield and had retreated back down the Red River.

Grant sent Sherman, the commander of the Military Division of the Mississippi, to break up CS General Joseph E. Johnston's army in north Georgia. Sherman was also to prevent Johnston from sending troops to reinforce Lee in Virginia, and "get into the interior of the enemy's country as far as you can, inflicting all the damage you can against their war resources." Atlanta was a Confederate logistical and industrial center with four major railroads.

US Major General George H. Thomas's Army of the Cumberland was the largest in Sherman's 110,100-man army group, with about 72,900. US Major General James B. McPherson had nearly 24,400 in his Army of the Tennessee, almost twice as many as US Major General John M. Schofield's Army of the Ohio with 12,800. The estimated strength of the Confederate forces under Johnston was 54,500, before CS Lieutenant General Leonidas Polk's Corps from the Army of Mississippi joined Johnston's Army of Tennessee in stages from Resaca to Cassville.

Johnston had taken command of the Army of Tennessee after the Confederate defeat at Chattanooga the previous November, and he began to address the army's problems: the condition of the horses, the infantry's lack of shoes, blankets, and small arms, and the morale and discipline of the troops. Sherman's overriding concern was logistics: he had sufficient men and equipment, but he had to accumulate vast quantities of food and forage in the Nashville and Chattanooga storehouses and then transport them to the armies in the field.

Confederate earthworks and gun positions lined the precipitous Rocky Face Ridge near Dalton. At Mill Creek Gap, known locally as Buzzard's Roost, there were more formidable earthworks. According to Sherman, batteries extended the "whole length from the spurs on either side, and more especially from a ridge at the farther end like a traverse directly across its debouch."

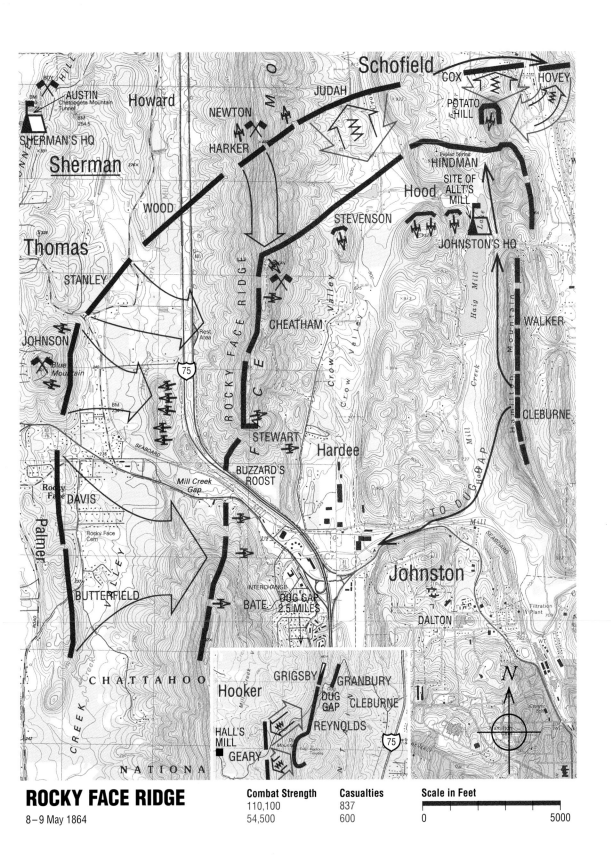

ROCKY FACE RIDGE

8–9 May 1864

Combat Strength	Casualties
110,100	837
54,500	600

Scale in Feet

0   5000

Johnston had fortified all approaches to Dalton from the north and west to protect the junction there of the East Tennessee & Georgia Railroad with the Western & Atlantic.

By May 7 Sherman's army group was in motion. He ordered McPherson's army on a turning movement through Snake Creek Gap to sever the railroad near Resaca. To keep Johnston distracted at Dalton, Sherman sent Thomas to move in force against Tunnel Hill, a lesser ridge west of Rocky Face, and Schofield to approach Dalton from the north. By late afternoon the Confederate outposts had fallen back to prepared positions on the slopes of Rocky Face.

On May 8 a regiment of the Union XIV Corps seized Blue Mountain, southeast of Tunnel Hill, and used it as a lookout and signal station. A brigade from US Major General Oliver O. Howard's IV Corps ascended the northern end of Rocky Face and moved south along the narrow crest. Sherman ordered Thomas to seize Dug Gap, four miles farther south, and to attack Confederate works along the northern half of Rocky Face Ridge. Schofield was to make a strong demonstration against the Confederate right flank in Crow Valley north of Dalton. In the afternoon two brigades from US Brigadier General John W. Geary's 4,500-man division of the XX Corps assaulted the Confederate position at Dug Gap, but they were thrown back by CS Colonel J. Warren Grigsby's cavalry, reinforced by CS Brigadier General Daniel H. Reynolds's infantry, later supported by CS Brigadier General Hiram B. Granbury's infantry brigade.

On May 9 Union infantry moved forward to probe for other weak points in the five-hundred-foot-high Rocky Face barrier. US Brigadier General Charles G. Harker's brigade reached the crest, but the terrain was so rough and narrow that in places the men could advance only in single file. Harker hit the angle where the right of CS Major General Benjamin F. Cheatham's Division joined the left of CS Major General Carter L. Stevenson's Division. The fight "was obstinate and bloody," Stevenson reported. The main Confederate position on the slope and crest

of Rocky Face Ridge could not be carried. The Union suffered 837 casualties, the Confederates 600.

Thomas convinced Sherman that his troops could not take Rocky Face Ridge and that any attempt to insert columns "into the jaws of Buzzard Roost would be fatal." Sherman called the gap "the door of death." On May 11 he left Howard's IV Corps and two cavalry divisions to "keep up the feint of a direct attack on Dalton" and marched with the rest of his forces to join McPherson at Snake Creek Gap. The following afternoon CS Major General Joseph Wheeler's cavalry division followed the trail of Schofield's army around the north end of Rocky Face. Wheeler learned from prisoners that Sherman was headed for Resaca. By 1:00 A.M. on May 13 the Confederates had withdrawn from their positions near Buzzard's Roost and marched to Resaca. Howard's IV Corps occupied Dalton.

Estimated Casualties: 837 US, 600 CS

Rocky Face Ridge battlefield, near Dalton off Interstate 75 and nineteen miles southeast of Chattanooga, Tennessee, is privately owned.

Dug Gap Battle Park is southwest of Dalton on Walnut Avenue/Dug Gap Battle Road 1.6 miles from Exit 136 off Interstate 75. The park, which includes nearly four acres of the historic battlefield, is owned by the Whitfield-Murray Historical Society.

Resaca, Georgia (GA008), Whitfield and Gordon Counties, May 13–15, 1864

Jay Luvaas

On May 9, while US Major General William T. Sherman was probing CS General Joseph E. Johnston's position at Rocky Face Ridge, US Major General James B. McPherson marched the Army of the Tennessee through the unprotected Snake Creek Gap and advanced toward Resaca with US Major General Grenville M. Dodge's XVI Corps and US Major General John A. Logan's XV Corps, about 23,000 men. Sherman's orders on May 5 were for a "bold and rapid movement on the enemy's flank or line of communications." McPherson was to cut through the gap, destroy the railroad at Resaca, then retreat to the gap. When Johnston retreated from Dalton, McPherson was to pounce on him.

Dodge encountered Confederate cavalry and then pressed forward to the old Calhoun and Dalton crossroads. While Dodge's Fourth Division secured the crossroads, US Brigadier General Thomas W. Sweeny's Second Division captured Bald Hill from CS Brigadier General James Canty's Brigade of infantry. The Confederates fell back across Camp Creek to the Resaca defenses. To protect the railroad bridge over the Oostanaula River near Resaca, they had only about 4,000 troops, composed of Canty's Brigade, part of CS Lieutenant General Leonidas Polk's Corps, which was joining Johnston from Alabama, and a brigade from the vicinity of Dalton.

McPherson was cautious, and he missed his opportunity for a major victory. However, he had received no word from Sherman all day and was concerned that if Johnston had concentrated his entire army against him, he would be annihilated. McPherson recalled Dodge to the mouth of Snake Creek Gap to entrench and bring forward supplies. McPherson later explained, "If I could have had a division of good cavalry, I could have broken the railroad at some point." For the next two days McPherson remained in his defensive stance on the Resaca side of the gap and dug in

his troops. On May 10 Sherman ordered US Major General Joseph Hooker's XX Corps to reinforce McPherson, to be followed the next day by the rest of the Army of the Cumberland, except for US Major General Oliver O. Howard's IV Corps, which continued to hold the Union position at Buzzard's Roost and defend the railroad. On the thirteenth US Major General John M. Schofield's army also moved into the gap.

Johnston used the time given him by McPherson to concentrate his forces at Resaca and to prepare the battlefield. The troops of Polk's Corps who had arrived from Alabama occupied the Confederate left, their flank anchored on the Oostanaula River. CS Lieutenant General William J. Hardee's Corps held the center along the high ridge overlooking Camp Creek. CS Lieutenant General John Bell Hood's Corps was posted on the right, his line running east to a hill near the Conasauga River.

On May 14 Sherman's army closed in, enveloping the Confederate lines from the north and west. Hooker's XX Corps supported McPherson's troops, while US Major General John M. Palmer's XIV Corps was on Hooker's left with orders to fight its way to the railroad. Palmer attacked at about noon, supported on his left by Schofield's troops and later by Howard's IV Corps on Schofield's left. The fighting was severe as Schofield and Howard drove the Confederates back into their prepared positions. Palmer's subordinates were unaware of these breastworks and took heavy losses in front of CS Major General Patrick R. Cleburne's position at the center of Hardee's line.

The heaviest fighting was near the headwaters of Camp Creek, where late in the afternoon US Major General Jacob D. Cox's division of Schofield's army drove the Confederate outposts over rough and wooded ground into their works. Two divisions of Howard's IV Corps later moved up to secure the position, opposite CS Major General Thomas C. Hindman's Division on the left of Hood's line.

At 6:00 P.M. Johnston launched a fierce counterattack from the Confederate right with two of

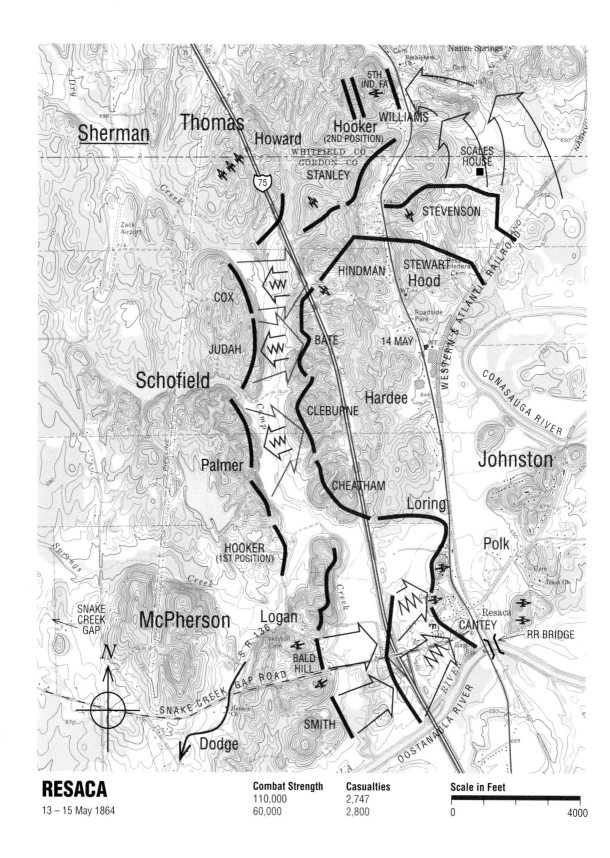

RESACA

13 – 15 May 1864

Combat Strength	Casualties	Scale in Feet
110,000	2,747	
60,000	2,800	0 4000

Hood's divisions, supported by two brigades from CS Major General William H. T. Walker's Division of Hardee's Corps. Holding with his left, Hood executed a swing movement that enabled his right to advance about two miles, overrunning a round-topped hill just east of the Dalton Road that anchored the Union flank. The lead division of the XX Corps under US Brigadier General Alpheus S. Williams rushed to the vicinity of Nancy Springs at dusk, just in time to repel Hood's assault.

The Union attacks succeeded on the right, led by a brigade of US Major General Morgan L. Smith's division of the XV Corps which stormed across Camp Creek. The fighting continued until dark, and McPherson's men held. Throughout the night the Federals dug entrenchments.

The attack on May 15 did not materialize as Sherman had planned. The rough, unknown terrain on the Union left slowed the deployment of the divisions of US Major General Daniel Butterfield and US Brigadier General John W. Geary. The configuration of the terrain gave the Confederates "unusual facilities for cross firing and enfilading," and the Union brigades were forced to attack in columns without adequate artillery support. The brunt of the Union attacks was borne by CS Major General Carter L. Stevenson's Division. In places the Federals advanced to within thirty paces of Stevenson's defenses. They briefly overran the "Cherokee Battery" of four 12-pounders, but the Confederate line held. A counterattack by CS Major General Alexander P. Stewart's Division later that afternoon against the Union left was bloodily repulsed.

During the day the Federals had laid Sherman's two pontoon bridges across the Oostanaula River at Lay's Ferry, about three miles below Resaca. US Brigadier General T. W. Sweeny's Second Division of the XVI Corps crossed the river and beat back an attack by a portion of Walker's Division. Once Sweeny's men had fortified the bridgehead, Johnston's position was turned. Johnston then concluded that he did not have enough troops to protect his rail line to Atlanta and at the same time hold his position and defeat Sherman. He crossed the Oostanaula that night, burned the

railroad bridge and damaged the wagon bridge, and headed for Calhoun.

At Resaca the Confederates lost about 2,800 of their 60,000 men, and the Federals, 2,747 of their 110,000.

Estimated Casualties: 2,747 US, 2,800 CS

Resaca battlefield is near Resaca off Interstate 75. The battlefield is privately owned except for a state of Georgia commemorative wayside near the entrance of Resaca Confederate cemetery on U.S. 41, six miles north of Calhoun.

Adairsville, Georgia (GA009), Bartow and Gordon Counties, May 17, 1864

In ten days US General Sherman had pushed CS General Johnston out of strong defensive positions and south of the Oostanaula River. Johnston rejected Calhoun as a place to battle Sherman and headed on southward seven miles to Adairsville. As US General Howard's IV Corps advanced north of Adairsville, the van, US Major Frank Sherman's brigade, was hit by heavy artillery and sniper fire from CS General Cheatham's entrenched division at the Saxon (Octagon) house. Three Union divisions prepared for battle, but US General Thomas halted them as darkness gathered.

Johnston had planned to deploy his men across the valley near Adairsville and anchor his flanks on the hills, but he concluded that the valley was too wide. That night he withdrew to a strong position at Cassville, eleven miles farther south. By May 19 CS General Polk's entire corps had joined Johnston: three infantry divisions and one cavalry division.

Estimated Casualties: 200 US, unknown CS

New Hope Church, Georgia (GA010),
Paulding County, May 25–26, 1864;
Pickett's Mill, Georgia (GA012),
Paulding County, May 27, 1864; and
Dallas, Georgia (GA011), Paulding
County, May 28, 1864

Jay Luvaas

When US Major General William Tecumseh Sherman's army crossed the Etowah River on May 23, the Atlanta campaign entered a new phase. Sherman's purpose had been to turn or outflank CS General Joseph E. Johnston's army by threatening the railroad in his rear. Sherman knew from a visit to the area twenty years earlier that Allatoona Pass was very strong. Instead of attacking Johnston there at the pass, where he was guarding the railroad, Sherman surprised the Confederates by leaving his railroad supply line and striking out cross-country south to Marietta via Dallas with more than 85,000 fighting men and twenty days' supplies in his wagons. Sherman's army group advanced in separate columns: US Major General James B. McPherson's Army of the Tennessee in the west near Van Wert, US Major General George H. Thomas's Army of the Cumberland in the center along the main road to Dallas, and US Major General John M. Schofield's Army of the Ohio to the left rear.

US Major General Joseph Hooker's XX Corps of the Army of the Cumberland took the lead. On May 25 his three divisions advanced on roughly parallel roads: US Major General Daniel Butterfield's division on the left, US Brigadier General John W. Geary's in the center, and US Brigadier General Alpheus S. Williams's on the right. Geary's division encountered Confederate cavalry near Owen's Mill on Pumpkinvine Creek. The lead brigade pushed ahead for three more miles and encountered Confederates who fought a delaying action for about a mile back to CS Lieutenant General John Bell Hood's main line centering on New Hope Church. CS Lieutenant

General Leonidas Polk's Corps was not far away in the direction of Dallas. The total Confederate strength was about 70,000. Geary halted on a ridge in the woods, entrenched, and waited for Butterfield and Williams to arrive.

The terrain was crisscrossed by small ravines and covered by dense woods with considerable underbrush, and as Williams's division advanced in three lines, the troops could scarcely see the main Confederate rifle pits. The massed Union formations were exposed to a continuous fire of canister and shrapnel. Hooker's troops were repulsed at all points, although the leading line advanced to within twenty-five or thirty paces of the Confederate defenses before the Confederates forced them to fall back and entrench. The Confederates lost 350 men, while Hooker reported losses of 1,665.

US Major General Oliver O. Howard's IV Corps moved into position on Hooker's left during the dark, rainy night, prolonging the line beyond Brown's Mill. The next morning the leading division of US Major General John M. Palmer's XIV Corps arrived and entrenched on Hooker's right. On May 26 Schofield's army came up to extend Howard's line to the left. To meet this threat, Hood moved CS Major General Thomas C. Hindman's Division to the right of his line. For four days the fighting in the area near New Hope Church was incessant. Visibility was poor in the dense woods, and the lines were so close that the troops were constantly under fire. The Confederates had the advantage of position, being entrenched on higher ground. Sherman's superior artillery and ability to maneuver were generally negated by the terrain. "We have been here now five days," a Union general wrote his wife, "and have not advanced an inch. . . . On some points the troops sent to relieve us did not hold, and some of our dead lie there unburied. . . . It is a very tedious and worrying life."

At first Sherman assumed that only Hood's Corps was in his front. He ordered McPherson to move into Dallas, link up with US Brigadier General Jefferson C. Davis's division of Palmer's XIV Corps, and then advance toward New Hope

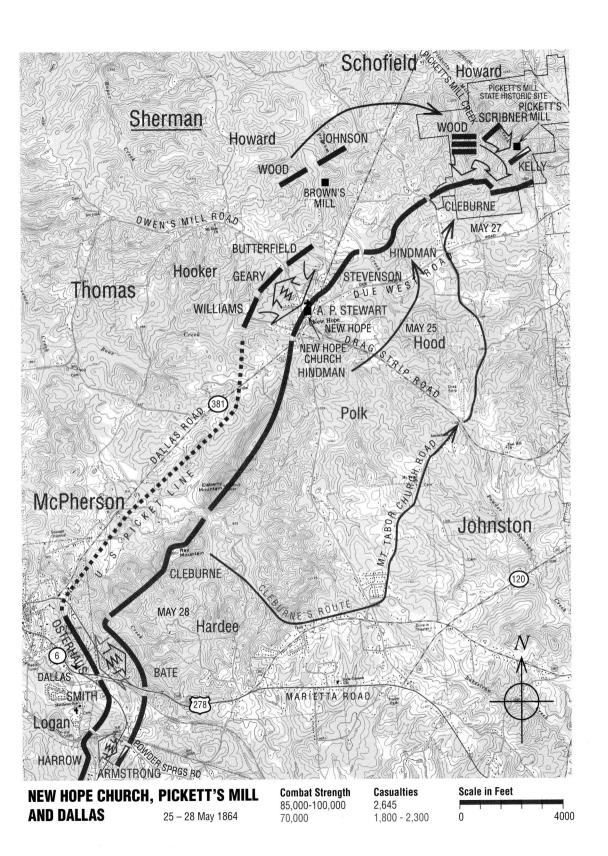

NEW HOPE CHURCH, PICKETT'S MILL AND DALLAS
25 – 28 May 1864

Combat Strength	Casualties	Scale in Feet
85,000-100,000	2,645	
70,000	1,800 - 2,300	0 4000

Church to hit Hood's left flank. On May 26 US Major General John A. Logan's XV Corps moved south through Dallas on the Powder Springs Road and ran into CS Lieutenant General William J. Hardee's Corps behind strong fieldworks that extended across the Powder Springs and Marietta Roads. McPherson's men threw up a line of works during the night. The next day, May 27, Sherman ordered McPherson to close in toward Hooker. McPherson would then be able to move his army to the left around Johnston's right flank and place it between the Confederates and the railroad.

On May 27 Howard led 14,000 Federals to the Union left to attack the Confederates on Hood's right, initiating the battle of Pickett's Mill. This was the bloodiest thus far in the campaign. After struggling through dense forests and deep ravines and over difficult ridges, US Brigadier General Thomas J. Wood's division of Howard's corps attacked the Confederate right flank at 4:30 P.M. However, CS Major General Patrick R. Cleburne's Division had been detached from Hardee's Corps and sent into position on Hood's right, and had just extended the line to Pickett's Mill. The next fifty minutes were terrible for US Brigadier General William B. Hazen's brigade, which began the assault. Everything went wrong. US Colonel William H. Gibson's brigade suffered heavier losses than Hazen's and was unable to provide support. Hazen's first line advanced a quarter mile across a ravine and was hit by CS Brigadier General Hiram B. Granbury's heavy fire. Hazen's men exhausted their ammunition supply, and CS Brigadier General Mark P. Lowrey's Brigade edged into a position from which it attacked Hazen's second line.

Several hundred yards to the east, US Colonel Benjamin F. Scribner's brigade of US Brigadier General Richard W. Johnson's division of the XIV Corps found its way blocked by CS Brigadier General John H. Kelly's dismounted cavalry, sheltered behind rude breastworks. Scribner was not close enough to align with Hazen, so Lowrey's Brigade was able to fire into Hazen's left rear.

The fighting lasted well into the night, but the Confederate flank held firm. The Union troops withdrew in the dark and entrenched on a ridge farther to the north. Wood's division alone suffered about 1,400 casualties in what one Union officer described as "the crime at Pickett's Mill." The Union forces, Cleburne reported, "displayed a courage worthy of an honorable cause. . . . The piles of his dead on this front [were] pronounced by the officers . . . who have seen most service to be greater than they had ever seen before." Cleburne lost about 450 men and the Federals about 1,600.

The final battle in the area was at Dallas on May 28. Because of faulty communications, CS Major General William B. Bate's Division, on the left of Hardee's Corps, mistakenly stormed out of its trenches late in the afternoon to assault McPherson's force in his front. "Fortunately," Sherman noted, "our men had erected good breastworks, and gave the enemy a terrible and bloody repulse." The Union troops held, and in about two hours Bate's men fell back, leaving more than 300 dead on the field. Federal losses were about 380, and Confederate between 1,000 and 1,500. On June 1 all three Union armies slid a few miles to the left. By June 4 Union cavalry occupied Allatoona Pass. With the great railroad bridge over the Etowah rebuilt, Sherman could sidestep Johnston, link up with the railroad, and push on toward Marietta and the Chattahoochee.

The fighting along the Dallas–New Hope Church–Pickett's Mill line represented a new phase in Civil War tactics, at least for the western armies. Although some units at Chickamauga and Chattanooga the previous fall had resorted to earthworks and log breastworks, not until the Atlanta campaign did both armies habitually entrench, and even then one side usually had to advance from its own lines to attack an enemy position. In the fighting around New Hope Church, however, both armies fought from behind breastworks in the near presence of the enemy and often under intense fire. According to Sherman, even the skirmishers "were in the habit of rolling logs together, or of making a lunette of rails, with dirt in front, to cover their bodies." This was characteristic of a siege but a new experience for armies in the field.

At New Hope Church, Johnston either anti-cipated Sherman's moves or reacted quickly enough to use the terrain and the defensive power of earthworks to offset Sherman's advan-tage in numbers. He used the Confederate cavalry effectively not only to provide timely information but also as mobile firepower. Without CS General Wheeler's dismounted troops to hold the right of the line at Pickett's Mill, Sherman's effort to turn Johnston's right flank might well have suc-ceeded. Eventually the fighting along the Dallas–New Hope Church–Pickett's Mill line convinced Sherman that the best way out of the impasse was to discontinue his efforts to outflank Johnston. He decided instead to shift to the east around Johnston's lines to the railroad, regain his line of communications, resupply his armies, and then advance upon Marietta and the Chattahoochee. The total losses for the three battles were Union, about 2,645, and Confederate, about 1,800–2,300.

Estimated casualties, New Hope Church: 665 US, 350 CS
Estimated casualties, Pickett's Mill: 1,600 US, 450 CS
Estimated casualties, Dallas: 380 US, 1,000–1,500 CS
Estimated casualties for New Hope Church, Pickett's Mill, and Dallas: 2,645 US, 1,800–2,300 CS

New Hope Church battlefield, at New Hope, twenty-five miles northwest of Atlanta off Interstate 75, is privately owned. Pickett's Mill Historic Site, northeast of New Hope off Interstate 75, includes 765 acres of the historic battlefield. Dallas battlefield, east of Dallas, is privately owned.

Lost Mountain–Brushy Mountain Line, Georgia (GA013), Paulding and Cobb Counties, June 9–18, 1864

On June 4 CS General Johnston pulled his troops back from the New Hope Church–Dallas line to ten miles of prepared positions to the east. These positions extended from Lost Mountain through Pine Mountain to Brushy Mountain and shielded Marietta and the railroad. US General Sherman halted the offensive while he resupplied his army and repaired the railroad from Kingston to Ac-worth. He shifted his army to the east, and his railroaders bridged the Etowah River in record time. After three weeks Sherman was again con-nected to his railroad supply line, and the veteran XVII Corps of US Major General Francis P. Blair Jr. arrived from Cairo, Illinois, to reinforce him. Sherman sent his troops forward on June 10.

On June 14, the first day of sun after eleven days of rain, Sherman made a personal recon-naissance of the Pine Mountain area to determine how to dislodge Johnston without attacking the Confederate fortified position on Pine Mountain, one mile in advance of the Confederate main line, occupied by CS General Bate's Division. When Sherman spotted a group of Confederates on the mountain, he commented, "How saucy they are." He ordered three volleys fired at the group, which included Johnston, CS General Hardee, and CS General Polk. The fire from the 5th Indiana Bat-tery killed Polk. That night Johnston abandoned Pine Mountain.

On June 15 the XX Corps attacked the Confed-erate center at Gilgal Church with the divisions of US Generals Butterfield and Geary. CS General Cleburne's Division repulsed the attack. That evening Federal artillery enfiladed Cleburne's position, and Hardee's Corps pulled back behind Mud Creek. Sherman sent US General Schofield's army to attack the Confederate extreme left flank at Lost Mountain the next day. At the same time McPherson's army pushed all the way to the base of Brushy Mountain on the Confederate right flank. Johnston withdrew his left that night from Lost Mountain. Hardee's Corps took up a new po-sition behind Mud Creek, creating a salient where his corps joined with Polk's Corps, under the temporary command of CS Major General William W. Loring. US General Thomas's artillery bombarded this salient on June 18.

Johnston withdrew after midnight to an arc-shaped position anchored on Big Kennesaw Mountain and Little Kennesaw Mountain, just twenty miles north of Atlanta.

Estimated Casualties: unknown

Kolb's Farm, Georgia (GA014), Cobb County, June 22, 1864

When US General Sherman encountered the entrenched Confederates at Kennesaw Mountain, he repeated his tactics of maneuvering around the enemy position. He extended his right wing, US General Schofield's army, to envelop CS General Johnston's left flank and menace the railroad to Atlanta. On June 21 Johnston countered by shifting the 11,000 men of CS General Hood's Corps from the right flank to Mount Zion Church on the left. CS General Wheeler's cavalry, along with soldiers commanded by CS General Loring who extended to the right, held the vacated entrenchments confronting US General McPherson's infantry. Hood deployed astride the Powder Springs Road near Kolb's Farm.

On June 22 US Generals Schofield and Hooker advanced up the Powder Springs Road where they encountered the Confederates. Schofield had been Hood's roommate at West Point and was confident that the impetuous general would attack. The Federals sent two infantry regiments forward to find Hood's forces, which were massing in the woods, while others built hasty defenses on high ground commanding the Kolb's Farm plateau. At 5:00 P.M. Hood launched a frontal attack north of the Powder Springs Road. CS General Stevenson's Division pushed back the two Union regiments. As the Confederates moved across the open ground, artillery caught them in a crossfire and sent them back to their lines with heavy casualties. CS General Hindman's Division advanced on Stevenson's right but ran into a swamp and

halted. The battle checked Sherman's effort to outflank the left of the Confederates' Kennesaw Mountain position.

Estimated Casualties: 350 US, 1,000 CS

Areas of the battlefield are protected within the Kolb's Farm unit of the Kennesaw Mountain National Battlefield Park at Marietta.

Kennesaw Mountain, Georgia (GA015), Cobb County, June 27, 1864

Jay Luvaas

From the top of the 691-foot Kennesaw Mountain, the Confederates could easily observe US Major General William T. Sherman's movements. Wagon trains, hospital encampments, quartermaster and commissary depots, and long lines of infantry were visible as far as the eye could see. Sherman reported to Washington, "The whole country is one vast fort, and Johnston must have at least fifty miles of connected trenches with abatis and finished batteries. We gain ground daily, fighting all the time. . . . Our lines are now in close contact and the fighting incessant, with a good deal of artillery. As fast as we gain one position the enemy has another all ready. . . . Kennesaw . . . is the key to the whole country."

Sherman decided to break the stalemate with an attack on June 27 intended to destroy the Confederate army. He had ordered US Major General John M. Schofield to extend his right to induce Johnston to lengthen his lines. US Major General James B. McPherson was to make a feint on his extreme left with his cavalry and a division of infantry and attack southwest of Kennesaw Mountain, while US Major General George H. Thomas assaulted the Confederate works near the center and Schofield exploited the toehold his troops

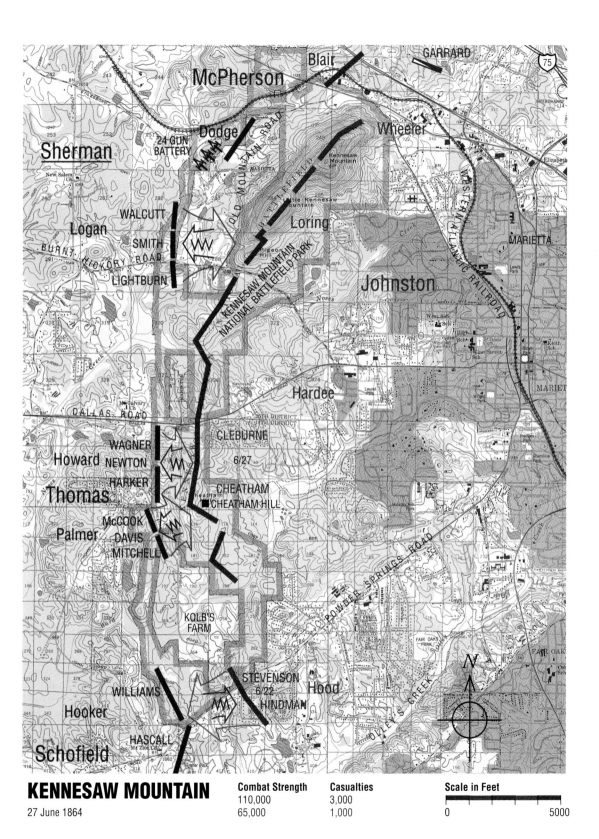

KENNESAW MOUNTAIN

27 June 1864

Combat Strength	Casualties
110,000	3,000
65,000	1,000

Scale in Feet

0   5000

had gained south of Olley's Creek on June 20. Sherman ordered each commander to keep all preparations as secret as possible, to determine the exact points of assault, then to be prepared to advance toward Marietta and the Western & Atlantic Railroad.

At 8:00 A.M., after a "furious cannonade" by about two hundred guns, the Federal soldiers advanced. At Pigeon Hill near the Burnt Hickory Road, three brigades of US Major General John A. Logan's XV Corps moved forward. The officers knew nothing of the terrain and very little of the Confederate position as the Federals struggled through dense thickets and a swampy creek. On the right US Brigadier General Joseph A. J. Lightburn's brigade attacked south of the hill and was stopped short of the Confederate breastworks by enfilading fire. US Brigadier General Giles A. Smith, commanding the center brigade, moved in two lines against Pigeon Hill. The terrain was rugged and the works were formidable. Farther to the left, US Colonel Charles C. Walcutt's brigade worked its way into a deep gorge between Little Kennesaw and Pigeon Hill. Although Lightburn's attacking troops overran the rifle pits fronting them, they failed to dent the main Confederate line. Before the men could get within thirty feet of the Confederates' principal defenses, they were driven to cover.

An hour later, behind schedule, and two miles to the south, two divisions from the Army of the Cumberland (9,000 men) assaulted entrenchments held by the divisions of CS Major Generals Benjamin F. Cheatham and Patrick R. Cleburne. At the report of two signal guns, US Brigadier General John Newton's division of the IV Corps and US Brigadier General Jefferson C. Davis's division of the XIV Corps advanced. Newton's division charged in two columns of "division closed in mass" — one regiment following another, each with a front of two companies, making a formation ten ranks deep and perhaps forty files across, preceded by a strong line of skirmishers. On the left, US Brigadier General George D. Wagner's brigade penetrated the dense undergrowth, timber slashing, and *abatis* to the foot of the Confederate works but was unable to break through. On

the Federal right, the Confederates repulsed the first charge of US Brigadier General Charles G. Harker's brigade. Harker was mortally wounded leading his men in a second charge.

Davis's division on Newton's right suffered a similar experience. Here the ground sloped down toward the marshy bed of a creek, beyond which the ground rose abruptly to the crest, where it jutted outward to form an angle on Cheatham Hill. At 9:00 A.M., when the Union bombardment ceased, US Colonel Daniel McCook's brigade in columns of regiments at intervals of ten paces swept down the slope to the creek. Their orders were to make the assault in silence, capture the works at Cheatham Hill, "and then cheer, as a signal for the reserves to go forward and beyond us, to secure the railroad and to cut Johnston's army in two." Crossing the stream and the wheatfield beyond, they advanced to the top of the hill. "The air seemed filled with bullets," one survivor recorded, "giving the sensation of moving swiftly against a heavy wind and sleet storm." When McCook's men came to within ten or fifteen feet of the Confederate works, "with one accord the line halted, crouched, and began firing." The brigade lost its momentum, as well as two commanders, nearly all of its field officers, and one third of its men. US Colonel John G. Mitchell's brigade, advancing on McCook's right, suffered a similar fate. After brutal hand-to-hand fighting, the Federals dug in. Both sides recalled this place as the "Dead Angle." By 10:45 A.M. the Federal assaults were over.

The assaults of June 27 cost Sherman about 3,000 casualties; the Confederates lost about 1,000. Although the survivors of the assaulting columns at Cheatham Hill spent the next five days in advanced works only thirty yards from the Confederate position, there was no more heavy fighting at Kennesaw. On July 2 when Sherman sent McPherson's Army of the Tennessee and US Major General George Stoneman's cavalry around the Confederate left, Johnston once again fell back to a previously prepared position, to Smyrna, where he could again block the railroad to Atlanta.

At Kennesaw Sherman learned again the cost

of assaulting an enemy behind earthworks. For Johnston the lesson learned had been evident since the beginning of the campaign: earthworks can delay but not defeat a determined enemy who can maneuver.

As the campaign moved on toward Atlanta, it became evident that it was a masterpiece of offensive and defensive maneuver. With greater numbers and mobility, Sherman managed to outflank or threaten the lines of communication of each of Johnston's positions. Johnston succeeded against formidable odds in keeping his army intact and positioned between Sherman and Atlanta. Sherman showed his genius for logistics as he moved reinforcements and supplies forward over great distances and hostile territory against a skilled opponent, even though his general objective was known and his line of advance was dependent upon a single railroad. Greater industrial and manpower resources were among the reasons the North won the war. Sherman's concepts, organization, and efficiency brought those resources together in the Atlanta campaign.

Estimated Casualties: 3,000 US, 1,000 CS

Kennesaw Mountain National Battlefield Park, north of Marietta, off I-75 at Exit 116, includes 2,884 acres of the historic battlefield.

No officer or soldier who ever served under me will question the generalship of Joseph E. Johnston. His retreats were timely, in good order, and he left nothing behind.

— US Major General William Tecumseh Sherman

Peachtree Creek, Georgia (GA016), Fulton County, July 20, 1864

On the evening of July 2 CS General Johnston's forces fell back six miles south of Kennesaw Mountain to a prepared position north of the Chattahoochee River at Smyrna. Once again, the Federal superiority in numbers enabled US General Sherman to outflank Johnston. The Federals crossed the river upstream from the Confederate position on July 8–9, forcing the Confederates to retire to a new line along Peachtree Creek, just five miles north of Atlanta. Sherman moved against the Confederate center with US General Thomas's Army of the Cumberland while sending his other two armies around the enemy right toward Decatur, six miles east of Atlanta. This movement isolated Thomas's army and created a gap of nearly three miles between it and US General Schofield's army. Johnston's plan was to attack over open ground while the Union forces were crossing Peachtree Creek and drive them in a counterclockwise direction back against an unfordable section of the Chattahoochee River.

In CS President Jefferson Davis's view, Johnston had too often fallen back instead of fighting and had permitted Sherman to maneuver the Confederates out of the mountains of north Georgia and position Federal forces at the gates of Atlanta. On July 17 Davis commissioned CS General Hood, who he knew would attack, to the temporary rank of full general and named him commander of the Army and Department of Tennessee. Several generals, including Hood, urged Davis to retain Johnston in command until after the big battle for Atlanta, but they were unsuccessful.

Hood concentrated the corps of CS General Hardee and CS Lieutenant General Alexander P. Stewart to assault the Army of the Cumberland. When Thomas crossed the creek on July 20, he did not know that most of the Confederate army was massing to his front. Hood was unaware that Sherman's left wing was advancing on Atlanta from Decatur until CS General Wheeler notified him at 10:00 A.M. that only his 2,500 cavalrymen stood between US General McPherson and

Atlanta. Hood delayed his attack three hours while he shifted his army to the right to meet Sherman's threat. When Hood finally launched his attack at 4:00 P.M., the Federals were already across the creek and on higher, more defensible ground. He attacked two miles west of Johnston's planned attack, crossing terrain so wooded and cut by deep ravines that his offensive was doomed to failure. It was also made in a clockwise movement that would have driven Thomas into, rather than away from, Schofield. Hood's lack of competence at this level of command was evident also in his management of the army. An Alabama soldier wrote, "The most perfect order and system in movements of the Army [under Johnston] suddenly changed into utter confusion. Cavalry were hurrying in one direction; artillery flying in another; infantry, double quicking in another; and everywhere confusion."

The Federals immediately switched to the defense as the Confederate right attempted to roll up their left flank. Thick undergrowth and sweltering heat impeded the attack. US General Newton's division of the IV Corps repulsed Hardee's Corps on the Union left, and Hood shifted his attack to the center. Fighting was bitter as the Confederates — long pent up behind trenches — eagerly drove forward, but their assaults were too uncoordinated or too weak to be successful. Thomas's men held off the Confederates and in two hours inflicted heavy casualties. Hood called off the battle at 6:00 P.M. when Wheeler called for help to try to stop McPherson, who had advanced up the Decatur Road to within three miles of Atlanta. Hood reinforced Wheeler with Cleburne's Division.

Estimated Casualties: 1,710 US, 4,796 CS

Atlanta, Georgia (GA017), Fulton and De Kalb Counties, July 22, 1864

US Brigadier General Mortimer D. Leggett's division drove CS General Cleburne from Bald Hill and began to terrify Atlantans by shelling the city from one and a half miles away. On the night of July 21 Hood withdrew two of his three infantry corps from the Atlanta line. He sent CS General Hardee's Corps on a fifteen-mile march to strike US General McPherson east of the city. He also ordered CS General Wheeler's cavalrymen to hit McPherson's supply train parked in Decatur while CS General Cheatham's Corps attacked the Union front.

After a night march that lasted much longer than expected, Hardee came into position opposite the Union left flank, rather than in their rear as planned. He finally attacked at noon on July 22, but McPherson was prepared. US General Dodge had arrived on the field with his XVI Corps and had positioned it in support of and en echelon to the right and rear of the right wing of US General Blair's XVII Corps. Dodge's troops repulsed Hardee's attack, and it foundered in a swamp. Cleburne's Division penetrated the gap between Dodge and Blair. In the midst of the battle McPherson rode into the Confederate line and was killed — the only U.S. Army commander to be killed during the war. Sherman then named US Major General John A. Logan commander of the Army of the Tennessee. Determined but disjointed Confederate attacks continued, but the Union forces held.

Later that afternoon two of Cheatham's brigades broke through the XV Corps line near the Troup Hurt house. From his headquarters at the Howard house (now the site of the Carter Presidential Center), US General Sherman massed twenty artillery pieces on a knoll, shelled the Confederates, and halted their drive. Logan then counterattacked, restored the Union line, and inflicted heavy casualties. Hardee pounded the Federal works with heavy artillery in his final attempt to take Bald Hill from the rear but was not successful. (After the war Logan commissioned a painting to commemorate the battle. The Atlanta Cyclorama is in Grant Park in Atlanta.)

Estimated Casualties: 3,641 US, 8,499 CS

Ezra Church, Georgia (GA018), Fulton County, July 28, 1864

The Confederates continued to hold Atlanta, so US General Sherman shifted the Army of the Tennessee, commanded by US General Howard, from the left to the right wing to threaten the Macon & Western Railroad at East Point, Hood's last railroad supply line west of Atlanta. US Major General Lovell H. Rousseau's 2,500 cavalrymen cut Hood's supply line from Alabama by wrecking thirty miles of railroad and arrived in Marietta on July 22.

Hood sent CS Lieutenant General Stephen D. Lee and CS General Stewart, each with two divisions, to intercept and destroy the Union movement against the railroad. He instructed the generals not to engage in a battle, just halt the Federals' advance down the Lick Skillet Road. He was preparing for a July 29 flank attack against Howard. Lee, however, violated orders. At 12:30 P.M. on July 28 his troops assaulted Howard at Ezra Church. Howard was prepared. The XV Corps was entrenched on the Federal right flank in the Confederate path and repulsed Lee's first attack. Stewart launched a series of frontal attacks over the same ground that Lee had earlier assaulted. The Federals repulsed the attacks and inflicted heavy losses, but Hood continued to hold the Lick Skillet Road and prevented Howard from cutting the railroad.

On July 30 CS Lieutenant General Jubal A. Early's cavalry shocked the North by riding into Pennsylvania and burning Chambersburg, while the Confederates in Virginia inflicted 4,000 casualties in the battle of the Crater in Petersburg. As the presidential campaign began, Republicans looked to Sherman rather than to US Lieutenant General Ulysses S. Grant and US Major General Philip H. Sheridan for a decisive victory to ensure President Lincoln's re-election.

Estimated Casualties: 700 US, 4,642 CS

Utoy Creek, Georgia (GA019), Fulton County, August 5–7, 1864

To cut the Confederate supply line between East Point and Atlanta, US General Sherman swung US General Schofield's army from east to west to aim for the railroad at East Point, where the Atlanta & West Point and the Macon & Western Railroads converged. Sherman put US General Palmer's XIV Corps of the Army of the Cumberland under Schofield, prompting Palmer to ask to be relieved of his command. Sherman granted the request after two days in which the XIV Corps had not moved into battle, giving the Confederates time to construct a strong line running to the west along the Sandtown Road, which shielded East Point. Schofield ordered US General Cox's division to attack the Confederate left at Utoy Creek, but CS General Bate's Division, protected by a wide swath of felled trees, easily repulsed them. Schofield tried again to flank Bate, and the 400 Confederates pulled back after dark to another line. The next day the Federals overran the abandoned works and approached the new line. It was too formidable to attack, so Schofield entrenched his army. Sherman had brought up siege artillery from Chattanooga and began to bombard Atlanta on August 9.

Estimated Casualties: 400 US, 225 CS

Dalton II, Georgia (GA020), Whitfield County and Dalton, August 14–15, 1864

In late July US General Sherman had sent 9,000 cavalrymen under US Brigadier General Kenner Garrard, US Major General George Stoneman, and US Brigadier General Edward McCook against CS General Hood's railroad supply lines. CS General Wheeler's troopers defeated them, rendering much of Sherman's cavalry in the Atlanta area combat ineffective.

Hood ordered Wheeler to ride north with most of the cavalry to destroy Sherman's railroad between Marietta and Chattanooga, ride into Tennessee, cut the railroads from Nashville that supplied the Federals, and return to Atlanta, leaving

1,200 men to continue against the railroads there. Wheeler's troopers rode north ninety miles to Dalton and on August 14 demanded that the small Union garrison surrender. The commander, US Colonel Bernard Laiboldt, refused, so Wheeler attacked. The outnumbered Federals fell back to a fortified hill outside Dalton, Mount Rachel, where they held on throughout the night. The next morning a relieving column of infantry and cavalry commanded by US Major General James B. Steedman pushed the Confederates out of Dalton.

Wheeler continued north destroying railroad tracks in East Tennessee, but the raid had no significant effect on Sherman's operations near Atlanta.

Estimated Casualties: unknown

Lovejoy's Station, Georgia (GA021), Clayton County, August 20, 1864

On August 16 US General Sherman ordered his army group to move against the Macon Railroad south of Atlanta. When his north Georgia commanders reported CS General Wheeler's cavalry in their area, Sherman suspended his orders and telegraphed US Major General Henry W. Halleck: "I will avail myself of his [Wheeler's] absence to reciprocate the compliment." He sent US Brigadier General H. Judson Kilpatrick's 4,700 cavalrymen to attack the railroad near Jonesboro so it could not supply Atlanta. The troopers tore up only one half mile of track at Jonesboro before a heavy rain began. Warned by an intercepted telegram that Confederates were approaching, Kilpatrick rode toward Lovejoy's Station late on August 19.

On the morning of August 20, Arkansans and Mississippians hit the Federal vanguard near the station while Texans attacked the rear. The Federals broke out of the pocket by riding stirrup to stirrup with sabers drawn. After fending off CS Brigadier General Frank Armstrong's cavalry brigade, Kilpatrick rode for Decatur in the rain. The Federal troopers had ridden around both armies

and had lost 237 men but were not successful in destroying the railroad. They had used most of their energy in avoiding their own destruction.

Estimated Casualties: 237 US, 240 CS

Jonesboro, Georgia (GA022), Clayton County, August 31–September 1, 1864

By late August the Federal armies had been within three miles of Atlanta for more than a month, and the Confederate lines stretched fifteen miles to protect the city. It was time for action. US General Sherman had only a week's supply of grain for the animals and three weeks' supply of rations for his men. The Republicans needed a Sherman victory to win the November election, particularly since US General Grant had had no dramatic summer victories resulting from his strategy of applying pressure simultaneously on the Confederacy's defenses north of the James River and on its supply lines out of Petersburg.

Sherman abandoned the formal siege of Atlanta and launched his earlier plan to force CS General Hood to retreat or attack. He ordered his supply wagons driven north of the Chattahoochee and guarded by the XX Corps positioned on the south bank. When the Confederates found the Federal fortifications abandoned on August 26, they occupied them and feasted on the food left behind. Atlanta welcomed the end of the bombardment. On August 28 the XV and XVII Corps reached the railroad at Fairburn, and the IV and XIV Corps hit it at Red Oak (today just southwest of the airport) and continued destroying it through the twenty-ninth.

With little cavalry, having sent CS General Wheeler to north Georgia to cut Sherman's supply line, Hood had no information on the Federal armies. He concluded that Sherman had retreated north, and the Confederates had celebrations in Atlanta. Hood continued to guard his rail connection to Macon. When Federal troops were reported near Jonesboro, Hood concluded that they were cavalry on a raid. In fact they were all of Sherman's forces except the XX Corps.

When US General Howard's army emerged west of Jonesboro on August 31, Hood finally acted. He ordered CS General Hardee with two corps (his own and CS General Lee's) to attack Howard's army west of Jonesboro. The Federals repulsed Hardee, and Hood pulled Lee's Corps back that night to cover the Atlanta defenses. Hardee entrenched along the railroad. On September 1 the Federals destroyed miles of the railroad track. At 5:00 P.M. one of Howard's corps and two of Thomas's assaulted and broke Hardee's line at Jonesboro.

The loss of the railroad forced Hood to evacuate Atlanta that night, and the XX Corps occupied the city the following morning. Sherman received no news about Atlanta while he pursued Hardee's 8,000–10,000 troops who had slipped out of Jonesboro and entrenched in a strong position one mile north of Lovejoy's Station. Sherman learned of the fall of Atlanta on September 3 and decided to end the Atlanta campaign. He wired Washington, "So Atlanta is ours and fairly won. I shall not push much farther on this raid, but in a day or so will march to Atlanta and give my men some rest. Since May 5, we have been in one constant battle or skirmish, and need rest." Sherman had launched the Atlanta campaign with 110,000 men. His armies suffered about 37,000 casualties. The Confederates' maximum numerical strength was nearly 70,000 men. Their losses were about 10,000 under CS General Johnston and about 20,000 under Hood.

The fall of Atlanta left little doubt that the Confederacy would be defeated in the Civil War. Republicans who, before the fall of Atlanta, had wanted to replace President Abraham Lincoln, saw him after Atlanta as a victorious leader. In the 1864 presidential election the peace plank of the Democratic Party platform called for ending the war — which was described as "four years of failure to restore the Union" — as well as an armistice, and a Union that guaranteed "the rights of the States unimpaired." Slavery would be protected. George B. McClellan, in accepting the Democratic Party's nomination for president, rejected one part of the platform, the peace plank, and stated, "The Union is the one condition of peace — we ask no more." Lincoln held firm to his position that peace required both union and emancipation. He was re-elected in November 1864, the first president to win two terms since Andrew Jackson in 1832.

Estimated Casualties: 1,149 US, 2,000 CS

Morgan's Last Kentucky Raid: June 1864

Cynthiana, Kentucky (KY011),
Harrison County, June 11–12, 1864

After repulsing US Brigadier General William A. Averell at Cove Mountain on May 10, CS Brigadier General John Hunt Morgan began his last Kentucky raid on May 30. His 2,700 cavalrymen foiled US Brigadier General Stephen G. Burbridge's planned raid into southwest Virginia and forced Burbridge to turn back to pursue them.

At dawn on June 11 Morgan attacked Cynthiana, a Federal supply center thirty miles northeast of Lexington, guarded by 500 men commanded by US Colonel Conrad Garis. Morgan launched his 1,400 men in three columns against the outnumbered Union infantry. The raiders drove the Union soldiers north along the railroad and set the town afire. As Burbridge's 5,200 men approached Cynthiana, Morgan decided to fight even though his troops were tired, low on ammunition, and heavily outnumbered. He established a defensive position two miles south of town which Burbridge attacked at 2:30 A.M. on June 12. The Confederates held him off until they ran out of ammunition and had to abandon the position. Confederate losses during the two days of battle were about 1,000 men but did not include the elusive Morgan. He escaped and arrived back in Abingdon, Virginia, eight days later.

Cynthiana was his last raid. Morgan was killed in September 1864 at Greeneville, Tennessee.

Estimated Casualties: 1,092 US, 1,000 CS

A brochure describing a driving tour of the battlefield is available from the Cynthiana Public Library.

Forrest's Defense of Mississippi: June–August 1864

Brices Cross Roads, Mississippi (MS014),
Union, Prentiss, and Lee Counties,
June 10, 1864

Edwin C. Bearss

In March 1864 President Abraham Lincoln placed US Lieutenant General Ulysses S. Grant, the victor at Vicksburg and Chattanooga, in command of all Union armies. Grant concluded that the only way to win the war was to employ the North's superior resources to destroy the two major Confederate armies. Grant maintained his headquarters with the Army of the Potomac and oversaw the campaign against CS General Robert E. Lee's Army of Northern Virginia. US Major General William Tecumseh Sherman, on his return from the Meridian expedition, took charge of the armies massed near Chattanooga. Sherman's mission was the destruction of CS General Joseph E. Johnston's Army of Tennessee, which was camped in and around Dalton, Georgia, and the capture of Atlanta. The Union armies began their advance in the first week of May. Johnston, a masterful defensive fighter, withdrew to Resaca, where he was reinforced by CS Lieutenant General Leonidas Polk's two infantry divisions. CS Major General Stephen Dill Lee commanded the Confederate forces in Mississippi and Alabama.

As Sherman drove toward Atlanta, he was concerned about the security of the single-track railroad over which he supplied his 110,000 men. CS Major General Nathan Bedford Forrest, the great Confederate cavalry leader, was then based in northeast Mississippi. To keep Forrest occupied and away from his supply line, Sherman proposed to employ the Union forces based at Memphis and Vicksburg. Early in May US Brigadier General Samuel D. Sturgis advanced from Memphis to Ripley and returned without seriously engaging Forrest, who was recruiting for his corps

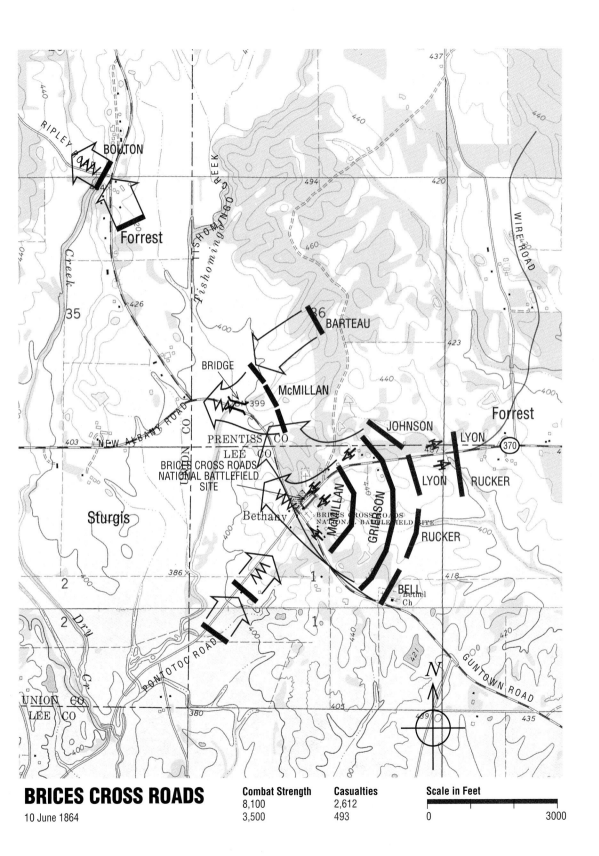

BRICES CROSS ROADS

10 June 1864

Combat Strength	Casualties
8,100	2,612
3,500	493

Scale in Feet

0   3000

at Tupelo following his raid into western Tennessee and Kentucky.

In late May, while facing Johnston in front of New Hope Church, Sherman ordered Sturgis to undertake another expedition to seek out and destroy Forrest's Corps. Sturgis left Memphis on June 2 with 8,100 infantry and cavalry and twenty-two cannons manned by 400 artillerists. One cavalry regiment was armed with seven-shot Spencer carbines. The march was methodical, and by June 7 the Union troops were at Ripley. Sturgis's advance came at an inopportune moment for the South because Forrest, in accordance with instructions from S. D. Lee, had left Tupelo en route to Middle Tennessee to raid the Nashville & Chattanooga Railroad, Sherman's lifeline. On June 3, before he crossed the Tennessee River, Forrest was recalled to meet Sturgis.

To counter Sturgis, Forrest deployed his brigades at Rienzi, Booneville, and Baldwyn on the Mobile & Ohio Railroad, with patrols thrown out toward New Albany. Before leaving Ripley, Sturgis started some 400 of his men who were not holding up well on the march back to Memphis as an escort to forty-one empty wagons and a number of broken-down horses and mules. On June 9 Sturgis advanced from Ripley and massed his army on the Stubbs plantation, nine miles northwest of Brices Cross Roads. Lee's plan was for Forrest to engage the Federals near Okolona. Forrest, however, ordered his three columns to meet the Union forces at Brices Cross Roads.

On June 10 Sturgis's 3,300 cavalry, led by US Brigadier General Benjamin H. Grierson, broke camp at 6:00 A.M. and started toward Brices. Sturgis's infantry and artillery followed an hour later. It had been raining for days and the roads were muddy. At daybreak the clouds cleared, and the day became hot and humid. Grierson's cavalry put to flight the Confederate patrol sent by Forrest to pinpoint the Union column, and the Federals reached Brices Cross Roads by 9:45 A.M. The Union vanguard hounded the Confederates down the Baldwyn Road for about a mile until they encountered one of Forrest's brigades fighting dismounted. Although outnumbered by more than

three to one, the Confederates held their own, awaiting the arrival from Booneville of CS Colonel Edward Rucker's Brigade. Forrest then boldly seized the initiative in slashing attacks in the wooded area, with each of his men armed with two six-shot Colt revolvers. His plan to beat Grierson's cavalry before Sturgis could bring up his infantry was successful.

By 1:00 P.M. Forrest had beaten Grierson, but the Federals, pending CS Colonel Tyree H. Bell's arrival, retained their three-to-one superiority in numbers. Sturgis marched his infantry forward on the double, and so his men's energy was sapped by the time they reached the crossroads. Bell's Brigade joined Forrest in a frontal attack, which, in conjunction with a dash at the Union force's left and right, compelled Sturgis's force to give ground, grudgingly at first. Forrest ordered his artillery forward, under CS Captain John Morton, to fire point-blank into the Union lines. He later told Morton, "Well, artillery is made to be captured, and I wanted to see them take yours." In bitter fighting, the Union soldiers were driven from the crossroads, and, with their flanks threatened, they fell back into the Tishomingo Creek bottoms. A wagon driven by a frightened teamster overturned and blocked the bridge. Most of the Federals broke and crossed the creek at fords upstream and downstream from the bridge. Forrest led his hard-hitting cavalry up the Ripley Road in an all-out pursuit of Sturgis's battered army. Roadblocks manned by black soldiers were broken as Forrest kept the "skeer" (scare) on Sturgis. As the Union troops straggled across the Hatchie Bottom on the night of June 10, what had been a disorganized retreat became a rout. Fourteen cannons and more than one hundred wagons were abandoned. Sturgis declared, "For God's sake, if Mr. Forrest will let me alone, I will let him alone."

The Confederates continued the relentless pursuit throughout the daylight hours on June 11 and captured hundreds of fleeing Federals. On the morning of the thirteenth, Sturgis and the disorganized and dismayed survivors of his once-proud army were back in Memphis. Union casualties in the battle of Brices Cross Roads were 2,612 killed, wounded, or missing, while Forrest's command had only 493 killed and wounded in the fight. Forrest captured 250 wagons and ambulances, 18 cannons, and 5,000 stands of small arms.

The battle of Brices Cross Roads was a bitter defeat for the Union troops. It is of national significance because of the leadership exhibited by Forrest, one of the few geniuses of the Civil War, and because of the repercussions it had for the Union's grand strategy. The key to the victory was Forrest's use of cavalry as mounted infantry. Horses and mules gave his men mobility, which, combined with their ability to dismount and fight as infantry, meant victory. Although the concept of mounted infantry did not originate with Forrest, British Field Marshal Viscount Garnet J. Wolseley wrote, "Forrest was the first general who in modern days taught us what Turenne and Montecuculli knew so well, namely the use of the true dragoon, the rifleman on horseback, who from being mounted, has all the mobility of the horse soldier." Forrest's men, along with US Major General Philip H. Sheridan's cavalry corps in the Army of the Potomac, were the precursors of World War II's panzer grenadiers and armored infantry.

Forrest's tactical employment of his heavily armed escort was well in advance of his day. Always at or near the point of danger, he employed his escort as a strategic reserve to exploit successes or to reinforce units struggling to contain an enemy breakthrough.

On June 15, Sherman, having learned of the Brices Cross Roads disaster, wrote to Secretary of War Edwin M. Stanton: "But Forrest is the very devil, and I think he has some of our troops under cower. I have two officers at Memphis that will fight all the time — A. J. Smith and Mower.... I will order them to make up a force and go out and follow Forrest to the death, if it cost 10,000 lives and breaks the Treasury. There never will be peace in Tennessee till Forrest is dead."

Estimated Casualties: 2,612 US, 493 CS

Brices Cross Roads National Battlefield Site, administered by the Natchez Trace Parkway, is seventeen miles north of Tupelo near Route 45 and includes one acre of the historic battlefield; 831 acres are owned by the Association for the Preservation of Civil War Sites and are open to the public.

Tupelo, Mississippi (MS015), Lee County and Tupelo, July 14–15, 1864

Frank Allen Dennis

CS Major General Nathan Bedford Forrest openly broke with CS General Braxton Bragg in October 1863 and obtained an essentially independent command from President Jefferson Davis. From late 1863 until the Franklin-Nashville campaign of November–December 1864, Forrest and his gray riders operated throughout West Tennessee and northern Mississippi, with a foray in the spring of 1864 north as far as Paducah, Kentucky, on the Ohio River. At Tupelo Forrest made one of his attempts to interdict the long supply line to US Major General William Tecumseh Sherman's armies in Georgia. The Confederate forces were led by Lieutenant General Stephen Dill Lee, commander of the Department of Mississippi, Alabama, and East Louisiana. Lee and Forrest were friends, and their relationship appears to have been cordial, even though the uneducated Tennessee cavalry genius, who had grown rich as a slave trader and planter, had little in common with his commander, a West Point artillery officer from South Carolina. As large as Forrest loomed in Confederate mythology, he was larger still in the fears of the Federals. They knew of his flinty courage at Fort Donelson and of his daring and his swift recovery from a severe wound at Shiloh.

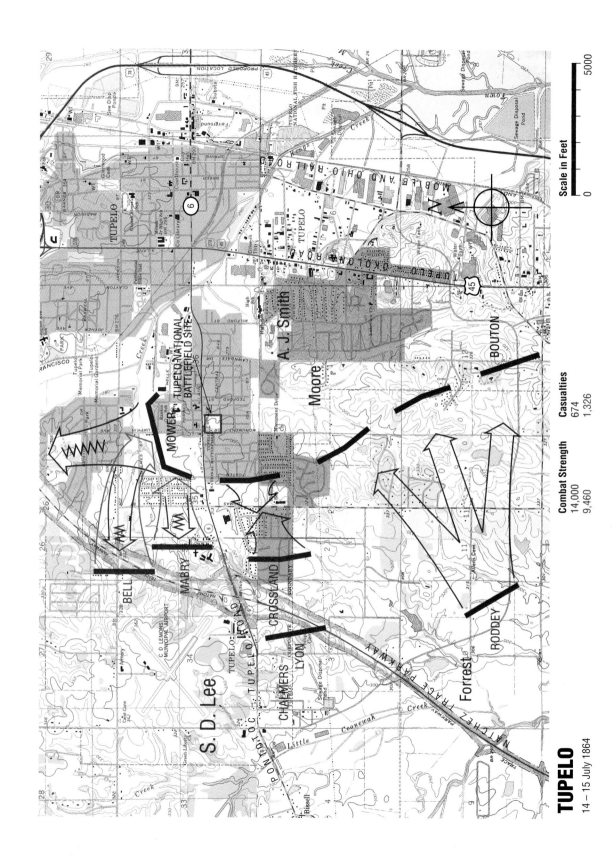

TUPELO

14 – 15 July 1864

Combat Strength	Casualties
14,000	674
9,460	1,326

Scale in Feet

0 — 5000

US Major General Cadwallader Colden Washburn, commander of the Federal District of West Tennessee, was ordered to "get" Forrest, and he therefore ordered US Major General Andrew Jackson Smith, a veteran of the Vicksburg and Red River campaigns, to move his 14,000 troops from Memphis fifty miles due east to La Grange, Tennessee. The Federals left La Grange on July 5 and headed toward a rendezvous with Forrest. It strains definition to call this movement a march; it was more like a tiptoe. Roll was called three times daily, allegedly to prevent stragglers, but more likely to prevent desertion. Memphis and La Grange were friendly places compared with Forrest's haunts in northeast Mississippi.

Sherman had authorized Smith to punish the area and its people. His forces burned much of Ripley, Mississippi, eighteen miles south of the Tennessee line, and then headed due south. They crossed the Tallahatchie River at New Albany and moved toward Pontotoc, seventeen miles west of Tupelo. Smith had two infantry divisions from his XVI Corps, commanded by US Brigadier General Joseph A. Mower and US Colonel David Moore. US Brigadier General Benjamin H. Grierson commanded a XVI Corps cavalry division, and US Colonel Edward Bouton led the 1st Brigade of U.S. Colored Troops (USCT). During the march, most of Smith's cavalry covered the march to the left (east) side, frequently fighting running skirmishes with Confederate scouts.

Meanwhile Forrest and Lee were responding to Smith's movements by hastily gathering their scattered forces. By the time the battle was joined at Tupelo on July 14, three cavalry divisions and one of infantry were on or near the field. CS Brigadier Generals James R. Chalmers, Abraham Buford, and Philip D. Roddey commanded the cavalry divisions, while CS Brigadier General Hylan B. Lyon directed a loose assortment of infantry, dismounted cavalry, and artillery. The total Confederate strength was 9,460.

Intelligence gathered by Confederate scouts during the Federal thrust was accurate. Forrest and Lee knew that the enemy strength was between 12,000 and 15,000; they knew the number of Union artillery pieces; and they even knew about the unusually tight control regarding roll calls and stragglers. What they did not know was exactly where the Federals were headed. For that matter, neither did Smith. Lee and Forrest knew that Smith's main assignment was to keep the Confederate cavalry away from Sherman's supply line, and they knew that Smith would do whatever damage he could to the Confederates' vital Mobile & Ohio Railroad, which ran through Tupelo and Okolona.

Lee's objective was to fight Smith quickly and whip him decisively so he could send reinforcements to CS Major General Dabney H. Maury to help him protect Mobile. Lee had an additional problem: Forrest was suffering intense pain from boils.

If Forrest could have picked his spot to fight, it would have been near Okolona, eighteen miles due south of Tupelo. Forrest knew the area well, and the route of Smith's march seemed to indicate that the Federals would head in that direction. Okolona was twenty-two miles southeast of Pontotoc, where Smith camped on the night of July 11–12. Anticipating that Smith would march toward Okolona, Lee and Forrest had positioned most of the Confederate troops closer to Okolona than to Tupelo. But when Smith abruptly turned east toward Tupelo on July 13, a race began. Grierson's cavalry, leading the Federal column, occupied Tupelo by noon and tore up portions of the Mobile & Ohio Railroad. The remainder of Smith's forces followed, tailed and flanked by Confederates.

Forrest termed Smith's movement toward Tupelo a "retreat." Smith, on the other hand, reported that he had found too many of the enemy along the Pontotoc-Okolona Road and had decided to move on Tupelo to damage the Confederates' railroad. By nightfall the main body of Smith's force had reached Harrisburg, a virtual ghost town one mile west of Tupelo. During the night the Federals constructed fortifications, which Forrest later called "impregnable," from rail fences, cotton bales, and pieces of buildings that had been destroyed at Harrisburg.

On the morning of July 14 the Federal battle line stretched almost two miles in a shallow arc along a low ridge from northwest to southwest of Tupelo, facing open territory dotted by a few cornfields. King's Creek was in the rear, Moore's division was on the left facing southwest, and Mower's division was on the right facing west and north. Bouton's USCT and Grierson's cavalry backed up Moore and guarded the Union left and rear. The Confederate line was in a similar arc, with Roddey's Division on the right, CS Colonel Edward Crossland's Kentucky Brigade in the center, backed by Chalmers and Lyon, and CS Colonels Tyree H. Bell's and Hinchie P. Mabry's Brigades on the left. Roddey's wing was recessed behind Crossland, Bell, and Mabry.

The Confederates attacked at about 7:00 A.M. Crossland slid toward Roddey to compensate for the ill-formed line and made a disastrous frontal attack. Mabry moved farther left, while Bell moved toward the center. A series of uncoordinated attacks, uncharacteristic of either Forrest or Lee, spent themselves against the well-defended Federal lines. By 1:00 P.M. the fighting had eased. That night, as the Federals burned what was left of Harrisburg, the flames silhouetted their positions, making them easy marks for Confederate artillery. Forrest even led a night attack against Moore's wing and Bouton's black troops, but he pulled back when the Federals, instead of panicking, opened well-aimed and heavy fire.

On July 15 Smith's forces began moving north toward La Grange from Harrisburg, harried closely by the undaunted Confederates. On a fork of Old Town Creek another confrontation occurred when Bell and Crossland attacked the Federal rear. While coordinating another assault against this position, Forrest was shot in the right foot. Despite his painful wound, he commandeered a buggy and rode among his men to dispel the rumor that he had been killed.

By July 21 Smith's men were back in La Grange. Although the Confederates held the field at Tupelo, the statistics reflect a decisive Federal victory. Estimates vary, but the most reliable figures are 1,326 Confederate casualties and 674 Union. The Confederate force was about two thirds that of the Federals.

The battle of Tupelo was over, and Smith had kept Forrest away from Sherman's supply line. But Forrest still lived.

Estimated Casualties: 674 US, 1,326 CS

Tupelo National Battlefield, administered by the Natchez Trace Parkway, is in Tupelo near Route 6 and includes one acre of the historic battlefield.

Memphis II, Tennessee (TN031), Memphis, August 21, 1864

CS General Forrest launched a daring raid on Memphis on the morning of August 21 to force the Federals to withdraw from northern Mississippi, to capture the three Union generals posted there, and to free Confederate prisoners from the Irving Block Prison. Striking northwestward with 2,000 troopers, his march was slowed by the loss of a quarter of his exhausted horses. The Confederates arrived in Memphis in a predawn fog and galloped through the streets, surprising the Union sentries. They sparred with Union soldiers as they split up for separate missions. US General Washburn's troops stalled the invaders at the State Female Prison.

After two hours Forrest withdrew, having failed to capture Union generals or release Confederate prisoners. He did succeed in cutting telegraph wires, taking prisoners and horses, and, most important, in drawing Union forces out of northern Mississippi. There are discrepancies between the two sides' reports of casualties, particularly in regard to prisoners.

Estimated Casualties: 80 (plus 400 prisoners) US, 62 CS

Dakota Territory: July 1864

Killdeer Mountain, North Dakota (ND005), Dunn County, July 28–29, 1864

US Major General John Pope's 1864 campaign against the Lakota (Sioux) was a response to the demands for protection by travelers to gold mines in the northern Rockies and by settlers claiming land as a result of the Homestead Act.

The Lakotas resisted the invasion of their lands with raids and killings that heightened the whites' fear of them. Pope sent US Brigadier General Alfred Sully with 1,800 men from Nebraska and Iowa volunteer regiments to establish forts to protect the emigrants' northern overland routes and the Missouri River route. After three Lakotas killed the brigade's topographical engineer, the cavalry killed them. Sully ordered their heads hoisted on poles as a warning, but his action increased the Lakotas' resolve to oppose the army.

In July Sully established Fort Rice above the mouth of the Cannonball River, then moved up the Heart River, escorting a wagon train of emigrants to the Yellowstone River in Montana Territory. He left the emigrants with a strong guard and rode in 110-degree heat toward the Killdeer Mountains with 2,200 soldiers, including 1,500 from Minnesota volunteer regiments, to attack a large Lakota camp. There were about 1,600 warriors, including Tetons (Hunkpapa, Sans Arc, Blackfeet, and Miniconjou), as well as Yanktonais and Santee Dakota from eastern Dakota Territory and Minnesota. One of the Tetons was Sitting Bull.

Sully formed his troops into a mile-long square, with their horses, wagons, and artillery in the center and skirmishers out in front. As they advanced, there were charges and feints by both sides until artillery fire and a charge by the Minnesota cavalry forced the Lakotas into the woods and ravines, where the soldiers shelled them. The Lakotas had to abandon their camp, and Sully captured their food stores, including about 400,000 pounds of dried buffalo meat and berries. The cavalry broke off their pursuit the next morning when the Lakotas found refuge in the Badlands of the Little Missouri River.

Sully's force escorted the emigrants through the Dakota Badlands — where they were harassed by the survivors of the Killdeer battle, reminders that the Lakotas were not defeated.

Estimated Casualties: 15 US, 31 Dakotas and Lakotas

Killdeer Mountain State Historic Park, ten miles northwest of Killdeer near Route 200, includes one acre of the historic battlefield.

Richmond-Petersburg Campaign: June 1864– March 1865

Petersburg I, Virginia (VA098), Petersburg, June 9, 1864

US Lieutenant General Ulysses S. Grant's tragic losses at Cold Harbor precluded another Federal assault there against CS General Robert E. Lee. Grant concluded that "the key to taking Richmond is Petersburg," a town on the southern bank of the Appomattox River where five railroads converged. Most of Lee's supplies came into Petersburg and were then shipped into Richmond on the Richmond & Petersburg Railroad. If the Federals could take Petersburg, Lee's only supply line would be from the southwest, the Richmond & Danville Railroad.

While Grant prepared to shift US Major General George Gordon Meade's Army of the Potomac south from Cold Harbor toward Petersburg, US Major General Benjamin F. Butler was at Bermuda Hundred, the area between the James and Appomattox Rivers. He sent US Major General Quincy A. Gillmore across the Appomattox River at Point of Rocks to attack Petersburg. The city was defended by only 2,500 Confederates commanded by former governor CS Brigadier General Henry A. Wise, but they were behind the Dimmock Line: fifty-five artillery batteries in an arc-shaped line of earthworks ten miles long, anchored on the Appomattox River.

On June 9 Gillmore ordered US Brigadier General Edward W. Hincks's division of U.S. Colored Troops to rush the outer line of entrenchments while US Brigadier General August V. Kautz's cavalry circled to the southeast to enter the city along the Jerusalem Plank Road. Gillmore's main body of 5,300 infantry advanced down the City Point Railroad. Hincks's 1,300 men probed the formidable defenses and, unaware that they were thinly manned, concluded that they were too strong to assault. South of town Kautz's 1,300 troopers pushed aside a scant force of militia defending Battery No. 27, but were stopped by Con-federate cavalry and artillery in an action called the "battle of old men and young boys."

North of the James River, Grant carried out a brilliant movement of his forces, combined with feints toward Richmond to confuse Lee. During the night of June 12–13 Grant began moving his carefully screened forces from the Cold Harbor trenches toward Petersburg. For several crucial days Lee was blind to the movement. US Major General William F. "Baldy" Smith's XVIII Corps of the Army of the James boarded transports at White House Landing and headed via the Pamunkey, York, and James Rivers to Bermuda Hundred. The corps crossed the Appomattox River on a pontoon bridge near Point of Rocks and was the first Federal corps to arrive in front of Petersburg. On June 14 US Major General Winfield Scott Hancock's II Corps crossed the James on transports from Wilcox Landing, upriver from Wyanoke Landing, where Union engineers were constructing a 2,100-foot pontoon bridge that would hold under the pressure of strong currents and four-foot tides. Beginning on June 15 US Major General Gouverneur K. Warren's V Corps, US Major General Horatio G. Wright's VI Corps, and US Major General Ambrose E. Burnside's IX Corps began crossing the river on the bridge. Grant's forces were converging on Petersburg while Lee was still defending Richmond.

Estimated Casualties: 120 total

Petersburg National Battlefield, off Interstate 95, includes 1,600 acres of the historic battlefield in the main unit; ninety of these acres are privately owned.

Petersburg II, Virginia (VA063), Prince George County and Petersburg, June 15–18, 1864

US General Grant's rapid movement of his forces enabled the Federals to attack Petersburg before

CS General Lee could reinforce his scant force. On June 15 US General Smith's XVIII Corps attacked seven Confederate batteries (numbers 5–11) with the commands of US Brigadier Generals John H. Martindale, William T. H. Brooks, and Edward W. Hincks. They pushed the Confederates back to Harrison Creek and captured more than a mile of the Dimmock Line held by CS General Wise. Smith responded to a rumor of reinforcements arriving from Lee and did not push on. CS General P. G. T. Beauregard was holding Petersburg with only 5,400 troops, many of whom were taken from the Bermuda Hundred front. After the war he wrote, "Petersburg at that hour was clearly at the mercy of the Federal commander, who had all but captured it."

That night Smith's corps was relieved by US General Hancock's II Corps, which captured more of the line the next day. US General Burnside's IX Corps attacked on June 17, while Beauregard withdrew the last of his troops from the Howlett Line on Bermuda Hundred to Petersburg, and Lee rushed elements of the Army of Northern Virginia to reinforce the defenses. Burnside's Second Division included the Indian unit, Company K of the 1st Michigan Sharpshooters, who distinguished themselves in Virginia in 1864–65. The unit included Ottawa (Odawa), Ojibwa (Chippewa), Ottawa-Ojibwa, Delaware, Huron, Oneida, and Potawatomi.

On June 18 the Confederates pulled back to their third line just outside the city limits. CS Lieutenant General Ambrose Powell Hill's Third Corps and units from CS Lieutenant General Richard H. Anderson's First Corps had arrived with more than 18,800 men. The final attacks were by three corps, US Major General David B. Birney's II, Burnside's IX, and US General Warren's V. Meade observed that the men were tired and their attacks lacked "the vigor and force which characterized our fighting in the Wilderness." They had suffered tragic losses in the assaults at Cold Harbor and 10,000 casualties since June 15.

Grant made City Point his headquarters. It was a small town ten miles east of Petersburg at the confluence of the James and Appomattox Rivers, but it became a small city, full of Union soldiers, sailors, and sutlers. Grant's U.S. Military Railroad hauled men and supplies from the ships and boats docked at the great wharf to the battlefield.

Estimated Casualties: 9,964–10,600 US, 2,974–4,700 CS

Petersburg National Battlefield, at Petersburg, off Interstate 95, includes 1,600 acres of the historic battlefield in the main unit; ninety of these acres are privately owned. The City Point unit of the Petersburg National Battlefield is at the confluence of the Appomattox and James Rivers in Hopewell, about ten miles east of Petersburg.

Jerusalem Plank Road, Virginia (VA065), Dinwiddie County and Petersburg, June 21–23, 1864

On June 21 US General Grant launched his plan "to envelop Petersburg" and sever the railroads supplying Richmond from the south. While US Major General Philip H. Sheridan diverted 5,000 Confederate cavalrymen with his raid against the Virginia Central Railroad northwest of Richmond, Grant ordered US Brigadier Generals James H. Wilson and August V. Kautz with 5,500 cavalrymen to attack Petersburg's two remaining rail lines, the South Side Railroad and the Weldon Railroad, which connected Petersburg to the Confederacy's only major port, Wilmington, North Carolina.

Grant also ordered the infantry to attack the Weldon. On June 21 the vanguard of the infantry clashed with the Confederate cavalry. US General Meade ordered US General Birney's II Corps and US General Wright's VI Corps to maintain a continuous line that would close like a door on the

Confederates and cut the railroad. When Wright was slowed by Confederate skirmishers in the difficult terrain, Meade ordered Birney to keep moving. This caused a gap to form between the II Corps and the VI Corps to the south. CS Major General William Mahone, a railroad engineer before the war, had surveyed the area and knew of a ravine that could hide the Confederates' approach. Lee approved Mahone's attack through the ravine on the II Corps's flank. On June 22, while CS Major General Cadmus M. Wilcox's Division pinned the VI Corps in position, Mahone's three brigades shattered the divisions of US Brigadier General Francis C. Barlow and US Major General John Gibbon and took 1,742 prisoners. One soldier reported, "The attack was to the Union troops more than a surprise. It was an astonishment."

The next day the II Corps advanced across the lost ground, but the Confederates had pulled back. When some of the Federals reached the Weldon, Mahone's troops drove them off and captured many of the Vermont Brigade. They then pulled back and dug in along the Jerusalem Plank Road. The Confederates had, for the time being, saved the Weldon Railroad, but the Federals had extended their siege lines farther to the west.

During these two days President Abraham Lincoln made a surprise visit to Grant that included the VI Corps headquarters.

Estimated Casualties: 2,962 US, 572 CS

Staunton River Bridge, Virginia (VA113), Halifax and Charlotte Counties, June 25, 1864

The Wilson-Kautz raid on Confederate railroads continued, and on June 23 the Federals arrived at Burke Station where the Richmond & Danville Railroad crossed the South Side Railroad. The troopers tore up miles of railroad before 900 Confederate Home Guards stopped their advance along the railroad at the strategic Staunton River Bridge on June 25. The Union cavalry skirmished with Confederates posted in two redoubts protecting the bridge, but small-arms fire pinned

them down, and they were unable to reach and destroy the bridge. US General Wilson decided to return to the Petersburg area after having penetrated one hundred miles behind Confederate lines.

Estimated Casualties: 150 total

Staunton River Bridge Battlefield Historic State Park, seventeen miles northeast of South Boston near Route 360, includes eighty-six acres of the historic battlefield.

Sappony Church, Virginia (VA067), Sussex County, June 28, 1864

While US General Wilson headed east toward the Union lines at Petersburg, CS Major General William H. F. "Rooney" Lee's Division rode on a parallel route to the north to cut him off. The Federals struck the Weldon Railroad on June 28 near Sappony Church where they were stopped by CS Brigadier General John R. Chambliss's cavalry brigade. Since CS Major Generals Wade Hampton and Fitzhugh Lee had crossed to the south side of the James River after the cavalry battle at Trevilian Station, Wilson and US General Kautz rode west and then north to join the Union infantrymen who were to have occupied Reams Station.

Estimated Casualties: see below

Reams Station I, Virginia (VA068), Dinwiddie County, June 29, 1864

On June 29 US General Kautz rode to Reams Station, where he found not the US infantry, as he expected, but CS General Mahone's Division. Kautz held off Mahone's attacks and was joined by US General Wilson. When the Confederate troopers blocked their escape on the north and the east, the Federals burned their wagons, abandoned their artillery and their wounded, and fought their way out. Kautz rode for seven hours to the south and then around the Confederates to reach the Union lines at Petersburg. Fitzhugh Lee defeated Wilson's rear guard, forcing them to break up to escape. Wilson slipped into Union lines on July 1. In the Wilson-Kautz raid the Federals destroyed more than sixty miles of railroad, but the Confederates quickly repaired the track and rebuilt the burned trestles and bridges.

Estimated Casualties: 1,445 total for the raid

First Deep Bottom, Virginia (VA069), Henrico County, July 27–29, 1864

During the night of July 26–27 US General Hancock's II Corps and two divisions of US General Sheridan's cavalry crossed to the north side of the James River on a pontoon bridge at Deep Bottom to threaten Richmond. US General Grant's objective was to lure Confederate forces away from Petersburg, where Union soldiers were preparing to detonate a mine on July 30. Hancock tried to turn the Confederate positions at New Market Heights and Fussell's Mill in a dawn attack on July 27 along Bailey's Creek. Learning of the movement, CS General Lee reinforced his lines north of the James to 16,500 men. The divisions of CS Major Generals Cadmus M. Wilcox and Joseph B. Kershaw drove Hancock back in a slashing counterattack. Sheridan's attempt to ride around Hancock's right flank to cross the creek to the north was blocked by Confederate infantry.

The next day the Federals abandoned their attack on the Confederate left when Lee reinforced the position with almost 10,000 men. Grant's diversion succeeded in drawing three Confederate divisions north of the James River. He left some of the X Corps troops to maintain the bridgehead at Deep Bottom while the remainder recrossed the James the night of July 29 to assist in the assault on Petersburg, defended by only 18,000 troops.

Estimated Casualties: 1,000 total

The Crater, Virginia (VA070), Petersburg, July 30, 1864

After weeks of digging, the former coal miners in US Lieutenant Colonel Henry Pleasants's 48th Pennsylvania Infantry completed a 510-foot tunnel extending from the Union lines to beneath Elliott's Salient, a Confederate stronghold protecting Petersburg. US General Burnside's IX Corps planned to detonate 8,000 pounds of black powder in the tunnel, destroy the enemy battery, and blast a hole in the defenses. A division of U.S. Colored Troops under US Brigadier General Edward Ferrero had trained for weeks to lead the assault by going around, not through, the resulting crater to penetrate the Confederate lines. At the last minute, Burnside, responding to the concerns of US Generals Grant and Meade, substituted US Brigadier General James H. Ledlie's division of white soldiers — to avoid being blamed for sacrificing black soldiers if the attack failed.

The Federals exploded the mine at 4:45 A.M. on July 30, resulting in nearly 300 Confederate casualties and a 170-foot gap in their line. The Union siege artillery followed with a massive bombardment, but the Federal charge went awry. Ledlie's division charged forward, but rather than moving around the crater, they jumped into it. When Burnside funneled two more white divisions into the crater, sharpshooters picked off their officers as they attempted to push their men forward. Some 15,000 men swarmed in confusion in and around the crater.

The Confederates quickly recovered. CS General Lee pulled brigades from CS General Mahone's Division from the line four miles southwest to counterattack. Mahone contained the breach at 8:00 A.M., positioned his artillery, and blasted the Union infantry. Burnside finally sent in Ferrero's division, and the black soldiers fanned out around the crater as instructed. They were soon pinned down by massed Confederate artillery and were unable to continue the advance. The Confederates finally took control of the crater in savage hand-to-hand fighting, and the isolated Federals in the crater surrendered at 1:00 P.M. Grant reported to US Major General

Henry W. Halleck, "It was the saddest affair I have witnessed in the war." Burnside was relieved of his command for his role in the debacle.

The soldiers settled in for another eight months of trench warfare. On August 6 Lee dispatched CS Lieutenant General Richard H. Anderson with CS Major General Fitzhugh Lee's cavalry division and CS Major General Joseph B. Kershaw's infantry division to reinforce CS Lieutenant General Jubal A. Early in the Shenandoah Valley.

Estimated Casualties: 3,798 US, 1,491 CS

The Crater is in Petersburg National Battlefield.

Second Deep Bottom, Virginia (VA071), Henrico County, August 13–20, 1864

Robert E. L. Krick

US Lieutenant General Ulysses S. Grant's strategy in central Virginia from July through October 1864 included two-pronged movements to apply pressure simultaneously on the Confederacy's defenses north of the James River and on its supply lines below Petersburg. The second battle at Deep Bottom between August 14 and 20 (known generally as Fussell's Mill in the South) differed from the other movements only in the extent of its failure.

When CS General Robert E. Lee detached more troops to aid CS Lieutenant General Jubal Early's army in the Shenandoah Valley, Grant extracted US Major General Winfield Scott Hancock's veteran II Corps from its entrenchments around Petersburg and allied it with US Major General David B. Birney's X Corps from the adjacent Army of the James. Grant ordered the two corps, under Hancock's overall supervision, to cross the James River at Deep Bottom and Jones's Neck on the evening of August 13–14. Surging north, they

were to flank and overwhelm the Richmond defenders from the south and east. The plan resembled Hancock's unsuccessful first Deep Bottom expedition of the previous month.

The movement began poorly for Hancock. The II Corps's delays in crossing the James robbed the Federals of the benefit of surprise. The X Corps was successful when US Brigadier General Robert S. Foster's brigade of US Brigadier General Alfred H. Terry's division of the X Corps stormed the Confederates' advanced picket lines. Infantry from the 100th New York captured the Rockbridge Artillery's four 8-inch howitzers, which had been poorly placed on the Confederate front. CS Major General Charles W. Field, in command of the Confederates north of the James River, saw the danger, contracted his lines, and established them on the more defensible New Market Heights.

Hancock developed a new plan for the fifteenth. Leaving his II Corps stationary, he shifted Birney's X Corps northward beyond the Darbytown Road to turn the left of Field's powerful position. The maneuver dragged out all day in the August heat and humidity. Sunstruck infantrymen cluttered the road along the X Corps's route. Hancock's failure to bring the Confederates to battle ruined his chances of a decisive expedition.

The unfinished plan of August 15 carried over into the next day. At about noon brigades from Terry's division stormed the Confederate entrenchments along the Darbytown Road near Fussell's Millpond. Terry's men easily shattered CS Brigadier General Victor J. B. Girardey's Brigade of Georgians. Lauded by Lee as "one of our boldest & most energetic officers," Girardey had been a brigadier for only two weeks. Observing the breach in his lines, he grabbed the flag of the 64th Georgia Infantry and tried to rally his brigade, only to fall amongst its folds, shot in the head. The Federals captured nearly 300 Confederates and jeopardized Richmond's primary line of defense.

Field quickly gathered reinforcements from all directions. CS Colonel William Flank Perry's Brigade (formerly Law's), joined by regiments from the brigades of CS Brigadier Generals James Henry Lane, Samuel McGowan, John Bratton, George Thomas Anderson, and Colonel Dudley McIver DuBose, sealed off the break and eventually recaptured the original line. Lee arrived late in the day and observed the restoration of his line.

To the north, on the Charles City Road, cavalry skirmishing reached unusual intensity. US Brigadier General David M. Gregg's division had orders to push around Richmond and disrupt Confederate communications on the Virginia Central Railroad. Early on the sixteenth Gregg found elements of CS Major General William H. Fitzhugh "Rooney" Lee's Division blocking the route. In the course of the fighting, troopers from the 16th Pennsylvania Cavalry killed CS Brigadier General John R. Chambliss. Scattered action continued during the day as Gregg pushed as far northwest as White's Tavern before Lee drove the Union cavalry back through Fishers' farm.

While nothing more than indecisive skirmishing marked August 17–20, Robert E. Lee felt compelled to transfer five brigades from the south side of the James River to the north side. That redistribution allowed Grant to attack the Weldon Railroad below Petersburg and saved Hancock's operation from utter failure.

Estimated Casualties: 2,900 US, 1,500 CS

Second Deep Bottom battlefield, near Darbytown Road three miles southeast of the Richmond International Airport, is privately owned. The James River landing is in the Henrico County Deep Bottom Park.

Globe Tavern, Virginia (VA072), Dinwiddie County, August 18–21, 1864

US General Grant ordered US General Warren's V Corps and elements of the IX and II Corps to cut the Weldon Railroad after CS General Lee had depleted the Petersburg defenses to oppose the Federals at Deep Bottom. They crossed the railroad at Globe Tavern, six miles south of Petersburg, and began tearing up track. At 2:00 P.M. on August 18 CS Major General Henry Heth's Division attacked US Brigadier General Romeyn B. Ayres's division and pushed it back. A counterattack by US Brigadier General Samuel W. Crawford's division halted Heth's advance, and the two sides engaged in heavy fighting. Union forces dug in north of Globe Tavern with a gap between them and the rest of the army.

On August 19 CS General Hill's 14,000-man Third Corps maneuvered through the woods around the Federal right flank and launched a flank attack from the northeast at 5:00 P.M. CS General Mahone's Division crashed into US General Crawford's flank and took nearly 2,700 prisoners. A counterattack from the IX Corps to the east stopped Mahone. Warren withdrew a short distance to a stronger position to the south. During the night his troops built earthworks to defend their hold on the Weldon Railroad.

On August 21 Mahone launched an attack to drive the Federals from the railroad. The Confederate artillery posted at the Davis house bombarded the Union lines beginning at 9:00 A.M. Four brigades advanced across open ground to assault the Federal left, which lay along the railroad. Union artillery devastated their ranks and decisively repulsed each attack. Many of CS Brigadier General Johnson Hagood's Brigade were casualties, and the fighting ended by 10:30 A.M. Grant extended his siege lines westward.

The increasing opposition to the war and the lack of notable Federal victories made President Abraham Lincoln think he would be defeated by George B. McClellan on a platform that would not end slavery and would not ensure the preservation of the Union. In the last week of August the

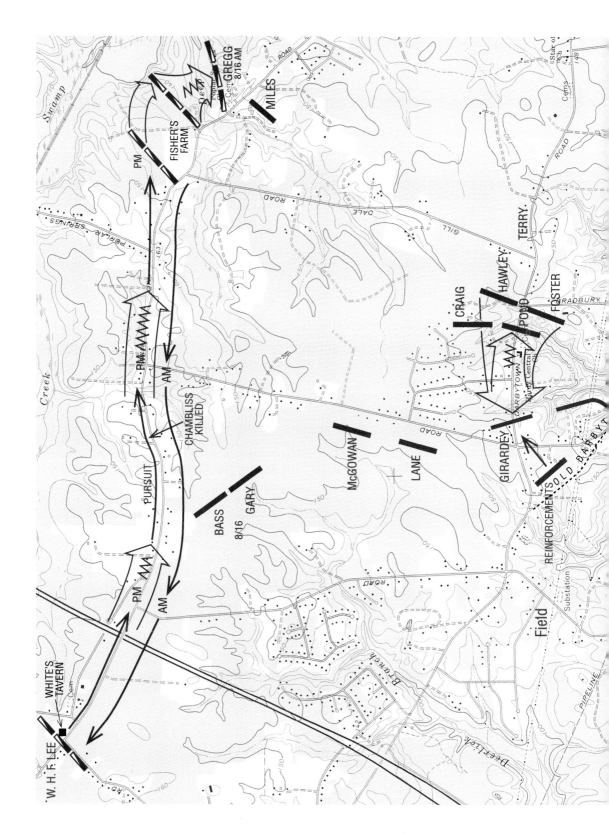

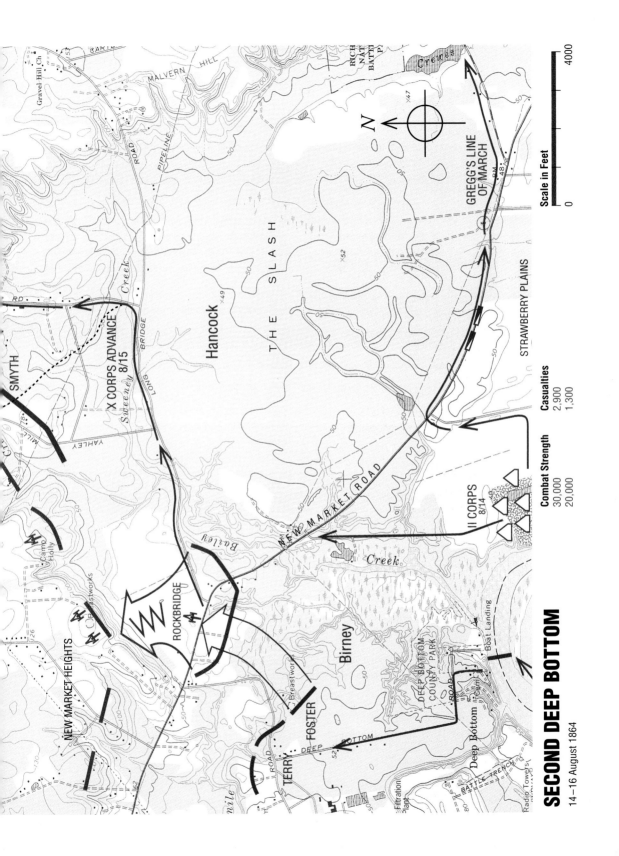

SECOND DEEP BOTTOM

14–16 August 1864

Scale in Feet

0   4000

	Combat Strength	Casualties
	30,000	2,900
	20,000	1,300

GREGG'S LINE OF MARCH

STRAWBERRY PLAINS

X CORPS ADVANCE

Sweeny 8/15

SMYTH

THE SLASH

Hancock

NEW MARKET ROAD

II CORPS 8/14

ROCKBRIDGE

Bailey

Creek

Birney

FOSTER

TERRY

NEW MARKET HEIGHTS

Deep Bottom

DEEP BOTTOM COUNTY PARK

Boat Landing

Breastworks

MALVERN HILL

Gravel Hill Ch

PIPELINE

LONG BRIDGE

Creek

president asked the members of his cabinet to sign a statement without reading it — to avoid revealing his expectation of defeat. It read: "This morning, as for some days past, it seems exceedingly probable that this Administration will not be re-elected. Then it will be my duty to so co-operate with the President elect, as to save the Union between the election and the inauguration; as he will have secured his election on such ground that he can not possibly save it afterwards."

Estimated Casualties: 4,455 US, 1,600 CS

Areas of the battlefield, but not the Globe Tavern site, are in the Petersburg National Battlefield.

Reams Station II, Virginia (VA073), Dinwiddie County, August 25, 1864

Christopher M. Calkins

The Weldon Railroad, one of CS General Robert E. Lee's lifelines, connected Petersburg, Virginia, with the Confederacy's last major port at Wilmington, North Carolina, via Weldon. The Federals' successful effort to cut that connection gave them control over the railroad from Reams Station to Petersburg, twelve miles to the north. In September the Federals built Fort Wadsworth to protect their gain. (The fort is on the Halifax Road and is in Petersburg National Battlefield.)

On August 24 US Major General Winfield Scott Hancock's 7,000-man II Corps was ordered to destroy the fourteen miles of Weldon Railroad track from Globe Tavern through Reams Station (burned by Union cavalry raiders in late June) to Rowanty Creek. Hancock took two of his divisions and US Brigadier General David M. Gregg's 2,000-man cavalry division, and by that evening, his men had destroyed the track to a point about three miles beyond Reams Station.

On August 25 the Federals were five miles short of Rowanty Creek when CS Lieutenant General Ambrose Powell Hill approached rapidly with 8,000–10,000 Confederate infantry. Hancock's men moved quickly back to Reams Station into an elliptical line of breastworks with an opening in the rear that provided inadequate protection for the soldiers. These poorly built works had been thrown up by Union soldiers of the VI Corps after the June 29 cavalry battle at Reams Station. Only about 700 yards of low parapet faced the enemy, with the returns extending approximately 800–1,000 yards and curving inward. The returns were so close together that the troops holding them were exposed to enfilading and rear fire. This parapet paralleled the railroad twenty to thirty yards behind the track, which ran through a cut, then up on an embankment. If the Union troops needed supplies or had to retreat along the rail line, they would be exposed to enemy view and fire. The Halifax Road was adjacent to the railroad. The Oak Grove Methodist Church at the north end of the parapet later served as a hospital.

The battle at Reams Station began when Gregg's cavalry was pushed in from its post at Malone's Crossing by CS Major General Wade Hampton's 5,000 troopers. At the same time Hancock's pickets were pressed from the west by the van of CS Major General Henry Heth's columns (Heth was in command because Hill reported himself sick) advancing on the Dinwiddie Stage Road. At 2:00 P.M. Hancock's two divisions, under US Major General John Gibbon and US Brigadier General Nelson Miles, readied themselves behind the breastworks for the enemy assault.

Three brigades under CS Major General Cadmus Wilcox arrived first, followed by two divisions of horsemen under Hampton. Wilcox's soldiers quickly made two stabs from the west, coming within yards of the parapet before being forced back. They were reinforced by Heth's Division and a detachment of CS Major General William Mahone's Division. At about 5:30 P.M., after Confederate artillery under CS Lieutenant Colonel William Pegram had peppered the Union

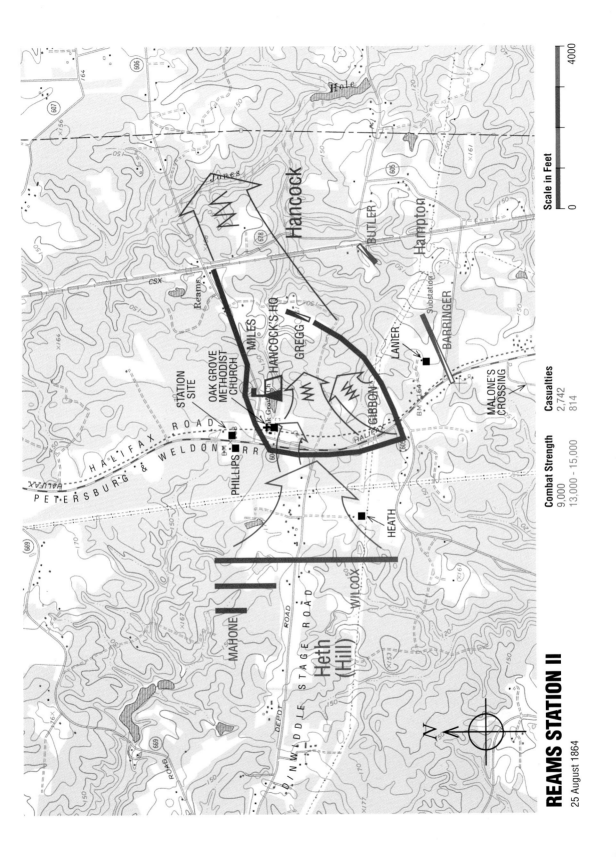

REAMS STATION II

25 August 1864

Scale in Feet

0   4000

Combat Strength	Casualties
9,000	2,742
13,000 – 15,000	814

troops, the final attack began. This time the Confederates were able to break through at the northwest angle of the Union line and carry the fighting into the nearby railroad cut. Simultaneously, Hampton's troopers assailed the lower return from the south. Miles held his line along the northern return, but Gibbon's men broke or were captured. Hancock tried to rally his fleeing troops and was partially successful in keeping the battle from turning into a rout. Nightfall and a heavy rainstorm brought an end to the inglorious defeat of Hancock's II Corps. The poor performance of the corps has been attributed to numerous factors, but especially to the men's exhaustion after their recent expedition north of the James River and to the large number of new draftees.

The Federals withdrew to the Petersburg entrenchments along the Jerusalem Plank Road after suffering 2,742 casualties, mostly men taken prisoner. The Confederates lost 814. The destruction of the railroad was stopped for a time, and Lee was able to use the line as far north as Stony Creek Depot, sixteen miles south of Petersburg and nine miles south of Reams Station. From that point, supplies had to be unloaded and carried by wagon train toward Dinwiddie Court House, then via the Boydton Plank Road into the besieged city. Even with the victory at Reams Station, the prospects for Lee's army and Petersburg were dimming.

Estimated Casualties: 2,742 US, 814 CS

Reams Station battlefield is near Route 604, ten miles south of Petersburg. No area of the battlefield is open to the public.

Chaffin's Farm and New Market Heights, Virginia (VA075), Henrico County, September 29–30, 1864

Chaffin's Farm

David R. Ruth

Between 1862 and 1864 three major Union drives reached dangerously close to the Confederate capital. Two of those, the Seven Days campaign and the battle of Cold Harbor, were checked by CS General Robert E. Lee's Army of Northern Virginia. The third came the closest of the three to victory when US Major General Benjamin F. Butler's Army of the James nearly broke through the Richmond defenses in September 1864 at New Market Heights and Chaffin's Farm.

Ten miles south of Richmond the countryside of farms, woodlots, and creeks on the north side of the James River was known as Chaffin's Farm, or Chaffin's Bluff. Beginning in 1862 Confederate soldiers, engineers, and slaves assigned to this area built an elaborate system of earthworks designed to protect the southern approaches to the capital.

On September 29 Butler launched two attacks, one against New Market Heights and the other against Fort Harrison. He ordered one wing of his army under US Major General Edward O. C. Ord with 8,000 men of the XVIII Corps to cross the James River at Aiken's Landing. They advanced north along the Varina Road, targeting the sparsely defended Confederate entrenched camp, Fort Harrison, near Chaffin's Farm. Fort Harrison was on the highest ground in the vicinity and was the most powerful work confronting the Federals. The trees in front of it had been felled to provide a field of fire, and the open space was cluttered with stumps. The parapets were nearly twenty feet tall, and six heavy guns including 8-inch columbiads, 32-pounders, and a large rifled Parrott faced the attackers. These powerful weapons should have compensated for the inadequate strength of the garrison — fewer than 300 soldiers — but four of the guns were inoperable. CS

Major Richard Taylor, assigned by CS Lieutenant General Richard S. Ewell to defend Fort Harrison, positioned the Goochland Artillery to help serve the guns, while portions of CS Colonel John M. Hughs's Tennesseans were placed behind the parapets of the fort. Additional help had arrived when CS Major James Moore's battalion of the 17th Georgia was rushed to the fort to man one of the large guns. On September 29 the Confederates had only 4,500 men to cover the entire Fort Harrison and New Market Heights lines.

By 6:00 A.M. US Brigadier General George Stannard's 3,000-man First Division of the XVIII Corps formed for the attack in a stretch of pine woods a mile southeast of Fort Harrison. Ord hesitated to order the assault since the defenses that flanked Harrison appeared more vulnerable. Stannard contended that if they took Harrison, the entire outer defense line would fall. Ord relented, and Stannard prepared his assaulting force, fifty ranks deep and rarely more than four companies wide.

As the Federal advance began, Taylor's artillery roared into action but fired too high. Jokes about Confederate marksmanship passed through the Union ranks, but the humor was silenced when the artillerymen corrected their range. A shell struck the column, killing or wounding a dozen or more men.

Stannard's men braved the fire, rushed across the open field, and took cover in a slight depression one hundred yards in front of the fort. After a few minutes of rest they were ordered forward. In one final effort the Federals clawed their way up the earthen ramparts and into Fort Harrison. Resistance was useless, and the Confederate defenders broke for the rear. The small force had fought gallantly, and the defeat was no disgrace. They had inflicted heavy casualties, particularly among the officers, which made further Federal gains difficult.

US Brigadier General Charles Heckman, commanding the Second Division of the XVIII Corps, was ordered to support Stannard, but his misdirected columns veered too far north to participate directly in the attack. Instead, his futile frontal as-saults against Forts Johnson, Gregg, and Gilmer were repulsed. The forces at Fort Gilmer stopped US Major General David Birney's corps, which had moved westward to Ord's sector after occupying New Market Heights. The Federal attacks against Gilmer were bloody and desperate. The last of three assaults was by men of the 7th U.S. Colored Troops, all but one of whom were casualties. The Confederate right, supported by iron-clads in the James River, stopped Stannard's drive toward Chaffin's Bluff.

Fort Harrison was vital to the Confederate defenses, and that night Lee rode to the front to direct the counterattack. Before he left his south-side headquarters, he ordered 10,000 men, two divisions commanded by CS Major General Charles W. Field and CS Major General Robert Hoke, as well as four regiments from CS General George Pickett's command, to the north side of the James to reinforce CS Brigadier General John Gregg, who had arrived from New Market Heights. At about noon on September 30 CS Brigadier General E. Porter Alexander's artillery, less than one mile northwest of Fort Harrison, opened a thirty-minute barrage, which was followed by two uncoordinated infantry attacks that ended in failure. Lee called off further assaults and ordered a new line constructed to face the Federals, who had strengthened Fort Harrison. The fort was renamed Fort Burnham, in honor of US Brigadier General Hiram Burnham, who fell in the fighting on September 29. The armies faced each other along this front until April 2, 1865, when the Richmond-Petersburg line was evacuated.

Estimated Casualties, Chaffin's Farm: 3,300 US, 1,700 CS

The Chaffin's Farm battlefield is south of Richmond near Route 5 and its intersection with Interstate 295. There are 310 acres of the historic battlefield

included in the Fort Harrison unit of the Richmond National Battlefield Park, which also includes the sites of Forts Gilmer, Hoke, and Johnson and a portion of Fort Gregg.

New Market Heights

William W. Gwaltney

In September 1864 US Lieutenant General Ulysses S. Grant ordered US Major General Benjamin F. Butler to prepare his Army of the James for an attack on Confederate defenses southeast of Richmond, using infantry, cavalry, and artillery. The objectives were to force CS General Robert E. Lee to weaken his Petersburg defenses by drawing troops from there to repel Butler's attacks (Lee was also shuttling troops back and forth between Richmond/Petersburg and the Shenandoah Valley) and to capture Richmond. Butler directed a two-pronged attack. While US Major General Edward O. C. Ord assaulted Fort Harrison, the bulwark of Richmond's eastern exterior defenses, Butler sent US Major General David Bell Birney's X Corps across the James to join US Brigadier General Charles J. Paine's black division from the XVIII Corps at Deep Bottom. From that bridgehead Birney and Paine's combined force was to strike north on farm roads against the formidable Confederate line that stretched west to east along the New Market Road.

Butler was an advocate of enlisting black soldiers, and his attacking columns included fourteen regiments of blacks, primarily U.S. Colored Troops (USCT) who were rested and reasonably well trained. For many of these soldiers the army was more than merely a job or a chance to show their gratitude for emancipation. They saw it as an opportunity to strike a blow against slavery and to demonstrate their willingness to fight and die for citizenship. Some of these men were free blacks and others were escaped slaves, known as "contrabands."

On the foggy morning of September 29, 13,000 troops left the staging area at Deep Bottom Landing in three columns. US Brigadier General Alfred H. Terry, on the right, marched his X Corps division north to take a position along Four Mile Creek, south of the New Market Road. In the middle a black brigade headed north and then filed in behind Terry. Birney's other two divisions advanced along a road west of Terry's line of march and parallel to it. Paine's USCT took the lead, followed by US Brigadier General Robert S. Foster's division. Paine's column turned as it approached Four Mile Creek and formed the Union line of battle facing the Confederate right. Dismounted black cavalry linked Paine's right to Terry's left. West of those troopers US Colonel Samuel A. Duncan's brigade of USCT formed Paine's spearhead. Foster's division halted along the Grover House Road, ready to serve as a reserve force.

North of Paine and Terry loomed the Confederate position at New Market Heights. Artillery was sited on top of the heights to command the approaches to the Confederate works. On the western end of the heights, Signal Hill, a well-prepared earthen fortification with cannons that commanded much of the ground below, became a focus of the battle. Confederate infantry entrenchments along the southern foot of the heights swept the gentle slopes descending from the New Market Road to Four Mile Creek. In addition to digging rifle pits, the Confederate soldiers had protected their front with a double line of *abatis* to delay and entangle the attacking soldiers.

CS Lieutenant Colonel Frederick S. Bass commanded the troops confronting Duncan's black brigade. Bass's troops were General Robert E. Lee's "grenadier guards" — the 1st, 4th, and 5th Texas and the 3rd Arkansas Regiments of infantry. To their left was CS Brigadier General Martin W. Gary's veteran cavalry brigade, prepared to fight dismounted. These soldiers, in the trenches at the foot of the heights, along with artillery units of the 3rd Richmond Howitzers and the 1st Rockbridge Artillery, were led by CS

Brigadier General John Gregg, the senior Confederate officer on the field. His command numbered fewer than 1,800 men.

At about 5:30 A.M. Duncan's infantry, having forded Four Mile Creek, attacked the Confederate positions to their front. Bass's infantry waited until the black soldiers reached the first line of *abatis* and struggled to move over, under, and around the obstructions. The long line of Confederate riflemen, supported by the artillery on the heights, sent a crashing volley into the USCT.

Gary's 24th Virginia Cavalry, fighting dismounted, enfiladed the Union right. The seasoned Confederates poured well-aimed volleys into the ranks of the black soldiers. After two color bearers were shot down, US Sergeant Major Christian Fleetwood of the 4th USCT seized the national colors. Duncan was wounded, and US Colonel John W. Ames, the senior regimental commander, called a retreat. Many blacks were killed or wounded, and some surrendered, only to be killed or imprisoned by the enraged Confederates. During this attack another of Paine's brigades, under US Colonel Alonzo Draper, moved forward, but before he could reach the Confederate lines, he was forced to cover Ames's retreat.

Stubbornly, Birney held to the initial plan for storming the Confederate works. The USCT under Draper moved forward again in a line six companies wide and ten ranks deep, while Terry's three brigades demonstrated on the USCT's right toward the Confederate works. Draper's soldiers of the 5th, 36th, and 38th USCT were supported on the left by the 22nd USCT deployed as skirmishers.

Draper moved out of the Four Mile Creek ravine and over the field of Duncan's attack. With the fog lifting, the Federals were easy targets as they were slowed at the marshy creek and by the *abatis*, where Bass's Texans blasted them with deadly volleys. For half an hour the soldiers fought a desperate, inconclusive battle, until the Confederate fire slackened. They continued the charge, stormed the Confederate rifle pits, drove off the few remaining defenders in hand-to-

hand fighting, and took the summit. After the officers of Company G, 5th USCT Regiment, had been killed, 1st Sergeant Powhatan Beaty took command of his company and led it into combat. To Draper's left, west of Four Mile Creek, the 22nd USCT consolidated into battle line and reached New Market Road. A charge by the 3rd New Hampshire and the 24th Massachusetts of Terry's division against the Confederate left, held by the 1st Rockbridge Artillery, sent the battery into retreat. When the fighting was over and the smoke cleared, it was only about 8:00 A.M.

The fighting at New Market had turned when word of Ord's forces, striking up the Varina Road, had compelled Gregg to withdraw troops from New Market Heights to strengthen the Confederate forces at Forts Gregg, Johnson, and Gilmer. This redeployment so weakened the forces opposing Birney that his men were able to overpower the few who remained and seize the heights. The Confederates, with 1,800 soldiers engaged, lost perhaps 50 men. The Federals lost 850 of their 13,000 men.

Following their victory at New Market Heights, Birney's X Corps marched west along the New Market Road. In unsuccessful assaults US Brigadier General Robert Foster and US Brigadier General William Birney tried to take the Confederate strongholds north of Fort Harrison, including Forts Gregg, Johnson, and Gilmer.

The men of the USCT proved themselves worthy soldiers in those hours of battle. Among the citations for gallantry in the assault none speaks more eloquently than the one granted for bravery to US Corporal James Miles of Company B, 36th USCT. "Having had his arm mutilated, making immediate amputation necessary, he loaded and discharged his piece with one hand and urged his men forward; this within thirty yards of the enemy's works." Miles was one of fourteen black soldiers and two white officers at the battle of New Market Heights who were later recipients of the nation's highest military accolade, the Medal of Honor, for actions at New Market Heights.

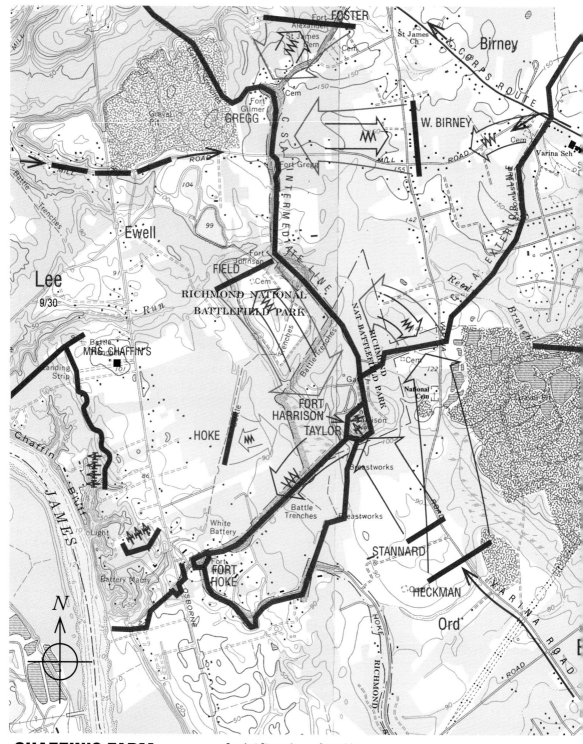

CHAFFIN'S FARM

29–30 September 1864

Combat Strength	Casualties
25,000	3,300
14,500	1,700

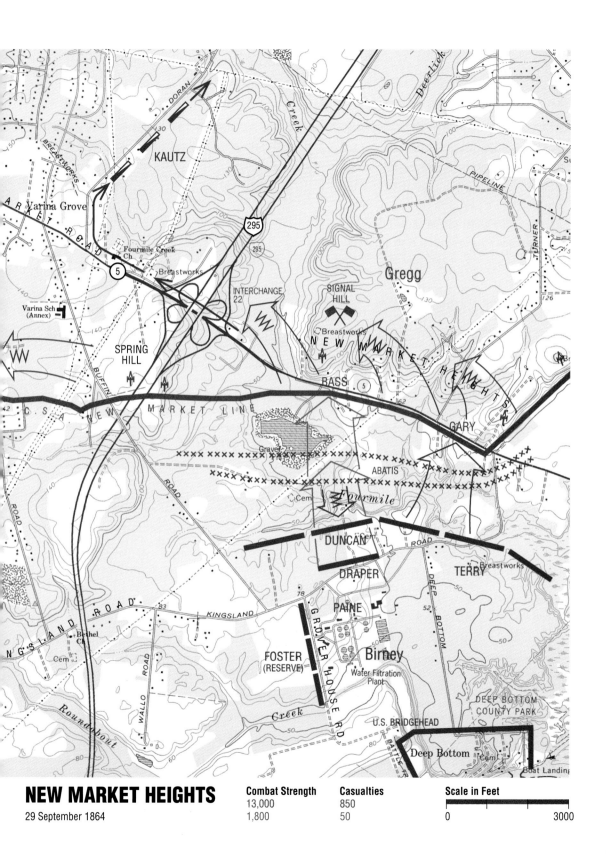

KAUTZ

DORAN

Creek

Deerlick

PIPELINE

Varina Grove

MARKET ROAD

295

295

Fourmile Creek Ch.

Breastworks

5

INTERCHANGE 22

Gregg

SIGNAL HILL

TURNER

Breastworks

Varina Sch (Annex)

SPRING HILL

N E W   M A R K E T   H E I G H T S

BASS

5

CSA   N E W   M A R K E T   L I N E

BUFFIN

GARY

Gravel

ABATIS

Fourmile

Cem

DUNCAN

ROAD

DEEP BOTTOM

DRAPER

TERRY

Breastworks

78

KINGSLAND

PAINE

52

GROVER HOUSE RD

KINGSLAND ROAD

83

Bethel Ch

Cem

FOSTER (RESERVE)

Birney

Water Filtration Plant

WALLO

ROAD

Roundabout

Creek

50

DEEP BOTTOM COUNTY PARK

U.S. BRIDGEHEAD

Deep Bottom

Cem

BATTLE

80

Boat Landing

NEW MARKET HEIGHTS

29 September 1864

Combat Strength	Casualties
13,000	850
1,800	50

Scale in Feet

0   3000

Estimated Casualties, New Market Heights: 850 US, 50 CS

New Market Heights battlefield is near Route 5 and Kingsland Road, four miles south of the Richmond International Airport. The James River landing is in the Henrico County Deep Bottom Park.

Peebles' Farm, Virginia (VA074), Dinwiddie County, September 30– October 2, 1864

The victories of the Union armies in Georgia and in the Shenandoah Valley diminished the chances of a Confederate victory in the Civil War and virtually assured President Lincoln's re-election in November. However, CS General Robert E. Lee continued to hold the Confederate capital, and the Virginia stalemate continued. Lee could not break out to save his army without surrendering Richmond. The determination to hold Richmond was fixed in place by May 1862 when the Virginia General Assembly declared that it must be defended "to the last extremity," and Lee stated in a cabinet meeting, "Richmond must not be given up; it shall not be given up!"

In late September, while continuing his siege, US General Grant struck once again with simultaneous punches—to the right against Richmond and to the left against Lee's supply lines. These blows forced Lee to rush troops to the Fort Harrison area to extend—and man—his already overextended lines from north of Richmond to southwest of Petersburg.

While Lee sent 10,000 men to attempt to recapture Fort Harrison, Grant used the opportunity to extend his left flank toward the South Side Railroad, the last Confederate railroad linking Petersburg with the west. He ordered two divisions of US General Warren's V Corps, two divisions of

the IX Corps commanded by US Major General John G. Parke, and US General Gregg's cavalry to cut the railroad and extend the Union siege lines westward. On September 30 the Federals marched toward the Poplar Spring Church and were opposed by a thin skirmish line held by CS General Wade Hampton's cavalry. At 1:00 P.M. US Brigadier General Charles Griffin's division stormed Fort Archer, north of Peebles' Farm, and forced the Confederates out of their line along the Squirrel Level Road. The Confederates retreated to their inner works at the Joneses' farm, which protected the Boydton Plank Road. Two divisions of CS General Hill's Third Corps raced to intercept Warren. They repulsed an attack by US Brigadier General Robert Potter's IX Corps division to the left of the V Corps. After dark Warren withdrew a mile to Peebles' Farm and entrenched along the former Confederate line.

The next day Hill assaulted the new Union works with four brigades. They captured the first line of pickets, but US General Ayres's V Corps division repelled them. Hampton's three cavalry brigades attempted to outflank the Union line from the south. US Brigadier General Henry E. Davies's cavalry brigade quickly dug in and blocked the attack. On October 2 US Brigadier General Gershom Mott's II Corps division reinforced Warren and moved on the Boydton Plank Road but did not attack the strong Confederate position. Hill contained the Federals' drive and prevented them from cutting both the Boydton Plank Road and the South Side Railroad.

Estimated Casualties: 2,869 US, 1,300 CS

Areas of the battlefield, including the U.S. Fort Wheaton (formerly the Confederate Fort Archer), but not the Peebles' Farm area, are in Petersburg National Battlefield at Petersburg, Virginia.

Darbytown and New Market Roads, Virginia (VA077), Henrico County, October 7, 1864

On October 7 CS General Lee launched his last offensive against US General Butler's forces north of the James River. He ordered the Confederate cavalry to sweep around the Federal right flank and attack US General Kautz's cavalry division along the Darbytown Road. The Confederates forced the Federals to retreat to the main defensive works held by US General Birney's X Corps. The divisions of CS Generals Hoke and Field assaulted the Union line along New Market Road. The Federals repulsed them and inflicted heavy losses, including that of CS Brigadier General John Gregg of the Texas Brigade. Lee withdrew into his Richmond defenses.

Estimated Casualties: 458 US, 700 CS

Darbytown Road, Virginia (VA078), Henrico County, October 13, 1864

On October 13 two X Corps divisions under US General Terry probed the new Confederate defensive lines at Richmond with a reconnaissance-in-force. Terry sent waves of skirmishers forward, then assaulted the left of the enemy line with a brigade. The Confederates repulsed the attack, inflicting casualties, and the Federals returned to their entrenched lines along the New Market Road.

Estimated Casualties: 437 US, 50 CS

Boydton Plank Road, Virginia (VA079), Dinwiddie County, October 27, 1864

Garrett C. Peck

By late October the Confederate line at Petersburg was thinning. It extended far beyond the city's defenses, curving to the southwest to Hatcher's Run to protect the vital South Side Railroad and the Boydton Plank Road. The plank road was CS General Robert E. Lee's link to the Weldon Railroad and Wilmington, the Confederacy's last major port.

US Major General George Gordon Meade, the commander of the Army of the Potomac, won US Lieutenant General Ulysses S. Grant's approval for a major turning movement to cut those roads. Union forces had just won a major victory at Cedar Creek, and the presidential election was less than two weeks away. The Federals needed another victory before winter halted all offensive operations.

Meade assembled a strike force of 42,823 men from three infantry corps and the cavalry. US Major General Winfield Scott Hancock's II Corps was to cross Hatcher's Run, then swing up the White Oak Road, on to the Boydton Plank Road, and then proceed cross-country to sever the railroad. Success hinged upon US Major General Gouverneur K. Warren's V and US Major General Ambrose E. Burnside's IX Corps' punching through the enemy's weak line along the run. If they failed, the II Corps would be isolated. The Army of the James was to undertake a simultaneous demonstration against Richmond to prevent the transfer of reinforcements.

Union forces began moving into position at 3:00 A.M. on October 27 in a drizzle that increased to rain. Muddy roads and Confederate skirmishers slowed the advance to a crawl, and many units got lost in the dense woods. Six hours later, when the IX Corps found the strongly manned Confederate lines, they had lost the element of surprise. They dug in without a fight. The V Corps also ground to a halt north of Armstrong Mill after discovering formidable Confederate earthworks. These lines were held by 15,386 veteran troops of CS Lieutenant General Ambrose Powell Hill's Third Corps.

Meanwhile two divisions of the II Corps crossed the swollen Hatcher's Run, with US Brigadier General David M. Gregg's 4,921-man cavalry division protecting the Federal left flank. Brushing aside skirmishers, Hancock headed west up Dabney Mill Road toward Burgess's Mill.

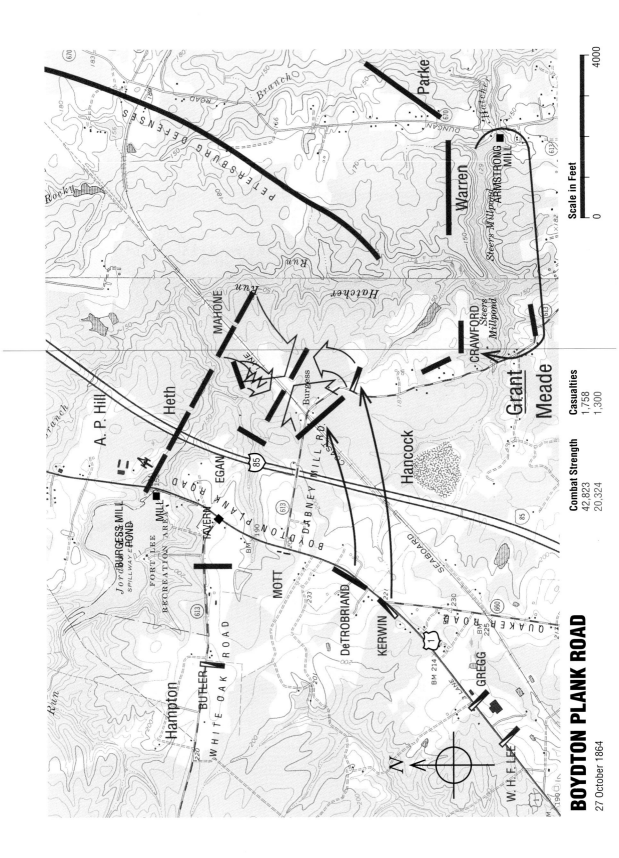

BOYDTON PLANK ROAD

27 October 1864

	Combat Strength	Casualties
	42,823	1,758
	20,324	1,300

Scale in Feet

0   4000

This movement threatened to cut off CS Major General Wade Hampton's two cavalry divisions (4,938 men), which patrolled the area south of the stream. After he held up Gregg's cavalry along Gravelly Run, Hampton retreated northward to block the White Oak Road.

The II Corps crossed the Boydton Plank Road where US Brigadier General Gershom Mott's force confronted Hampton's cavalry corps. Hill reacted quickly to the Union threat, but became ill and turned over the command of his corps to CS Major General Henry Heth. Soon Heth's and CS Major General William Mahone's Divisions occupied the north bank of Hatcher's Run. Hancock planned to push Heth aside and continue up the Boydton Plank Road, but at 1:00 P.M. General Meade ordered him to halt. Hancock's advance would further isolate the II Corps, and the South Side Railroad was still six miles away. Meade ordered US General Crawford's V Corps division to connect with Hancock's right, but that unit floundered in the thick woods. Grant made a personal reconnaissance of Heth's line and came under heavy small-arms fire at the bridge near Burgess's Mill. After escaping unharmed, he concluded that the enemy was too strong and called off the offensive.

The II Corps was left trapped in a pocket along the Boydton Plank Road without any support. Heth and Hampton planned to destroy it with an attack that would have been a humiliating repeat of Hancock's defeat in the battle of Reams Station. They ordered the cavalry to hold Gregg in place from the west and the southwest while the infantry swept around the Federals' right, seized the Dabney Mill Road, and cut their line of retreat. At 4:30 P.M. Mahone attacked across Hatcher's Run, shattered one Union brigade, overran two guns, and reached the Dabney Mill Road. Although they were hemmed in on three sides, the II Corps did not panic and offered fierce resistance. Hancock quickly grasped his opportunity. Mahone had advanced unsupported, and his flanks were unprotected. Hancock ordered one division to attack the enemy right, while another brigade and part of Gregg's cavalry hit Mahone from the front and left. This counterattack threatened the Confederates with encirclement, but they fought their way back across Hatcher's Run with heavy losses.

After routing Mahone, the Federal cavalry galloped off to oppose Hampton's attack. The Confederate cavalry pressed forward as planned but gained no ground. Two of Hampton's sons were wounded that day, one mortally. Gregg's cavalry prevented Federal disaster by protecting the II Corps's left flank from being overwhelmed.

Grant left to Hancock the decision of whether to remain in position or to retire. Hancock had won a tactical victory against an enemy equal in numbers and who threatened him with disaster; a section of the strategic Boydton Plank Road was in his hands; and he had restored his corps's reputation. However, the II Corps was isolated behind enemy lines, the men were short of ammunition, and the V Corps had not made contact. When Hancock ordered his men to dig earthworks, one asked, "General, which way will you have them face?"

Hancock decided to withdraw that night toward Dabney's Mill and to the army's original lines. He pulled out in a pouring rain, leaving wounded men and equipment on the field. Both sides settled in for a cold winter in the squalid trenches around Petersburg. The following week the election gave Abraham Lincoln a mandate to conclude the war. Then it was just a matter of time.

Estimated Casualties: 1,758 US, about 1,300 CS

Boydton Plank Road battlefield, seven miles southwest of Petersburg near Routes 1 and 613 and Interstate 85, is privately owned.

Fair Oaks and Darbytown Road, Virginia (VA080), Henrico County, October 27–28, 1864

While the Army of the Potomac attacked the Confederate works protecting the South Side Railroad and the Boydton Plank Road, US General Grant ordered US Major General Benjamin F. Butler's Army of the James to create a diversion north of the James River so that CS General Lee would not reinforce his Petersburg lines with troops from Richmond. Butler's plan was to march US Major General Godfrey Weitzel's XVIII Corps northward to the Williamsburg Road and flank the Confederate line while US General Terry's X Corps pinned the Confederates along the Charles City Road farther south.

At 1:00 P.M. on October 27 Weitzel's corps reached the Williamsburg Road after an eight-hour march and turned west. CS Lieutenant General James Longstreet, who had returned to duty after being wounded in the Wilderness battle the previous May, commanded the Confederate forces north of the James River. He recognized the threat and shifted CS General Field's Division to oppose the Federal advance up the Williamsburg Road. CS General Hoke's Division continued to hold the works opposite Terry. Weitzel spent two hours getting into position, giving Longstreet time to strengthen his new front with earthworks. At 3:30 P.M. Weitzel sent only two brigades out of his seven to attack across open ground. The Confederates repulsed them with heavy fire, flanked them, and took about 700 prisoners.

The Federals held their positions in front of the Confederate works that night and until the next afternoon, when they returned to their original lines. Artillery boomed and action flared sporadically on the skirmish line, but the Confederates continued to hold their Richmond line.

Estimated Casualties: 1,603 US, 100 CS

Hatcher's Run, Virginia (VA083), Dinwiddie County, February 5–7, 1865

In the relatively mild weather of early February 1865, US General Meade surprised the Confederates by launching an offensive to cut the Boydton Plank Road, the Confederate supply line from the Weldon Railroad. It was defended by CS General Hill's Third Corps. On February 5 the Federal cavalry under US General Gregg occupied Dinwiddie Court House, and US General Warren's V Corps deployed south of Hatcher's Run to support Gregg. US Major General Andrew A. Humphreys's II Corps took up a defensive position around Armstrong's Mill, west of the Vaughan Road and north of Hatcher's Run. At 4:00 P.M. CS General Mahone's Division attacked the II Corps from the north, but US Colonel Robert McAllister's brigade plugged a gap in the center and repulsed the Confederates after a ninety-minute fight. The V Corps and the cavalry were vulnerable, so Meade ordered them back to join the II Corps. The V Corps extended Humphreys's line south of Hatcher's Run, while Gregg's cavalry protected the left flank.

At about 1:00 P.M. on February 6 a reconnaissance of the V Corps lines by CS Major General John Pegram's Division developed into a fight with US Brigadier General Samuel W. Crawford's division. Crawford drove the Confederates back until CS Brigadier General Clement A. Evans's Division on Pegram's left counterattacked, stopping the Federals. At 5:00 P.M. Mahone's Division, led by CS Brigadier General Joseph Finegan, hit the Federal center near the site of Dabney's Mill. The Union line collapsed and reformed to the rear, parallel to Hatcher's Run. Pegram was killed in the attack.

On February 7 Warren launched an offensive at 10:00 A.M. that steadily drove back the outnumbered Confederates. The V Corps recaptured most of the lines around the mill site that they had lost the day before, and the winter offensive stalled. The Confederates kept the Boydton Plank

Road open but at the price of extending their thinning lines.

Estimated Casualties: 1,539 US, 1,000 CS

Fifty acres of the historic Hatcher's Run battlefield are owned by the Association for the Preservation of Civil War Sites and are open to the public.

Fort Stedman, Virginia (VA084), Petersburg, March 25, 1865

During the fall of 1864 US General Sheridan had destroyed the Confederacy's critical sources of food, the farms in the Shenandoah Valley, so that during the winter of 1865 the Confederates defending Petersburg and Richmond were weakened by food shortages and inadequate supplies. Thousands of CS General Lee's troops voluntarily surrendered or deserted and headed home. By the last week of March 1865 Lee knew that he had to get his army out of Richmond and Petersburg. US General Grant was preparing his attack against the Confederate defenses with a force of 125,000 men while Lee had fewer than 60,000.

On March 25 Lee massed nearly half of his army in Colquitt's Salient under the command of CS Major General John B. Gordon to threaten the Union supply depot at City Point, force Grant to contract his lines, and open an escape route from Petersburg to CS General Joseph E. Johnston in North Carolina. At 4:00 A.M. 50 Confederate axmen cut through the obstructions to Fort Stedman on the eastern side of Petersburg just north of the Crater battlefield, while assault troops quietly captured many of the 1,000-man garrison and Batteries X, XI, and XII. Gordon poured reinforcements into the thousand-foot gap in the Union line, but US Brigadier General John F. Hartranft's division of US Major General John Parke's IX Corps counterattacked and contained the breakthrough. Lee ordered a withdrawal. The Confederates tried to pull back, but the Federals caught them in a withering crossfire and a slashing counterattack. Many escaped, but more than 1,900 were trapped and forced to surrender.

Confederate prospects continued to dim during the day as US General Wright's VI Corps captured the entrenched picket lines north of Fort Fisher which Lee had weakened to provide soldiers for the Fort Stedman attack. Lee's effort to preempt Grant's spring offensive and force him to contract his lines was a failure.

Estimated Casualties: 1,017 US, 2,681 (including 1,949 captured) CS

Fort Stedman is in the Petersburg National Battlefield.

Mobile Bay: August 1864

Mobile Bay, Alabama (AL003),
Mobile and Baldwin Counties,
August 2–23, 1864

Arthur W. Bergeron, Jr.

The first line of defense for the strategic city of Mobile in the summer of 1864 consisted of three forts guarding the entrances to Mobile Bay. Fort Morgan, a pentagonal bastioned work built of brick on the western extremity of Mobile Point, commanded the main ship channel into the bay. An earthen water battery mounting seven heavy cannons stood at the base of the fort next to the channel. Fort Gaines, another old masonry work, was on the eastern end of Dauphin Island. Confederate engineers had constructed an earthen work at Grant's Pass on the Mississippi Sound and christened it Fort Powell. CS Brigadier General Richard L. Page commanded the garrisons of the three forts and had his headquarters in Fort Morgan.

To help obstruct all of the ship channels, Confederate engineers drove wooden pilings and floated mines (torpedoes) in the waters near the forts. The engineers left a gap of four hundred to five hundred yards between the easternmost torpedoes and Fort Morgan to allow blockade runners to pass in and out. A small naval squadron within the bay supported the forts. Commanded by CSN Admiral Franklin Buchanan, this squadron consisted of the ironclad ram *Tennessee* and three wooden gunboats: the *Morgan*, the *Gaines*, and the *Selma*. The forts, obstructions, and naval squadron combined gave Mobile defenses that would be a stern challenge to any attacking force.

In late July 1864, at USN Rear Admiral David G. Farragut's request, US Major General Edward R. S. Canby, commander of Union land forces on the Gulf, sent about 1,500 men under US Major General Gordon Granger to attack the forts in a joint operation. Farragut's objective was the reduction of the forts, sealing off blockade running in and out of the bay. At daylight on August 5 Farragut's fourteen wooden gunboats and four monitors entered the main ship channel. The squadron steamed up in pairs, lashed together, with the more powerful ships on the side facing Fort Morgan. The monitors were between the gunboats and the fort, creating a "wall of iron" to shield the wooden vessels. The Federal squadron took about forty-five minutes to pass the fort. Heavy smoke from the artillery obscured the Confederate gunners' vision, and their fire did little damage.

The leading monitor, the *Tecumseh*, was proceeding through the gap between the torpedoes and Fort Morgan when its commander directed the ship into the torpedo field so that he could engage the ram *Tennessee*. The *Tecumseh* struck a mine and sank. The commander of the *Brooklyn*, the leading wooden gunboat, ordered his vessel to back up to avoid the torpedoes. This maneuver threw confusion into the battle line and threatened either to force a retreat or to cause the gunboats to remain under the heavy Confederate artillery fire. While Farragut did not yell, "Damn the torpedoes, full speed ahead," he did utter some choice expletives and ordered his squadron to continue into the bay. He moved his flagship to the head of the line and through the torpedo field.

Farragut's vessels destroyed the Confederate naval squadron. They disabled the *Gaines*, and the *Selma* was surrendered. Of the wooden vessels, only the *Morgan* escaped. It reached safety under the guns of Fort Morgan and ran past the Union squadron to Mobile during the night. Once inside the bay, Farragut's vessels gathered about four miles from Fort Morgan and began to anchor. Buchanan decided to attack them with the *Tennessee* alone. All of the Federal gunboats joined in the hour-long battle in which the cannon fire cut the *Tennessee*'s steering chains so it could not be steered. When they shot the smokestack away, the ship filled with smoke, and its commander finally surrendered the ironclad.

Cut off from reinforcements and without the support of any naval vessels, the forts could not hold out. The 140-man garrison abandoned Fort Powell during the night of August 5 and blew up

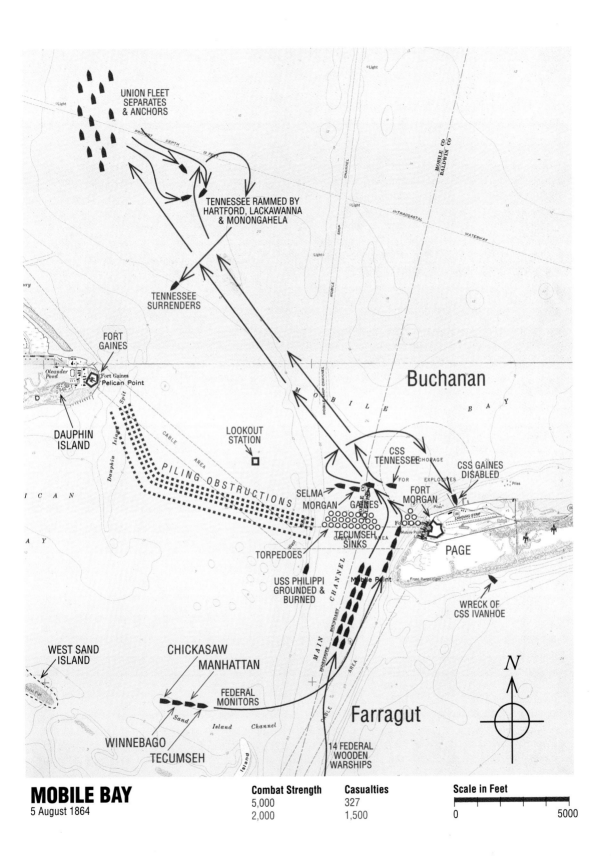

UNION FLEET
SEPARATES
& ANCHORS

TENNESSEE RAMMED BY
HARTFORD, LACKAWANNA
& MONONGAHELA

TENNESSEE
SURRENDERS

FORT
GAINES

Oleander
Pond

Fort Gaines
Pelican Point

DAUPHIN
ISLAND

LOOKOUT
STATION

Buchanan

BAY

CSS
TENNESSEE

CSS GAINES
DISABLED

PILING OBSTRUCTIONS

SELMA
MORGAN

GAINES

FORT
MORGAN

TECUMSEH
SINKS

TORPEDOES

PAGE

USS PHILIPPI
GROUNDED &
BURNED

WRECK OF
CSS IVANHOE

WEST SAND
ISLAND

CHICKASAW
MANHATTAN

FEDERAL
MONITORS

N

WINNEBAGO
TECUMSEH

Farragut

14 FEDERAL
WOODEN
WARSHIPS

MOBILE BAY
5 August 1864

Combat Strength	Casualties
5,000	327
2,000	1,500

Scale in Feet

0   5000

the fort's magazine. Fort Gaines surrendered on the morning of August 8. The next day the Federals turned on Fort Morgan. Granger's infantry, reinforced from New Orleans, landed at Navy Cove and moved toward the fort. When Page refused to surrender, the Federals began siege operations. By August 21 Granger had twenty-five cannons and sixteen mortars ready to bombard Fort Morgan. Joined by all the vessels in Farragut's squadron, the Federal artillerymen opened a tremendous fire on the fort. After a day-long bombardment, Page surrendered on the morning of the twenty-third.

The Federal victory stopped blockade running at the port but left Mobile under Confederate control. Farragut's fleet could not take the city without a strong infantry force. In March 1865 Canby moved against Mobile, and the city surrendered on April 12.

Estimated Casualties: 327 US, 1,500 CS

Fort Morgan State Park, twenty-two miles west of Gulf Shores on Route 180W, includes 439 acres of the historic battlefield.

Pro-Confederate Activity in Missouri

James M. McPherson

○

Whatever the true extent of pro-Confederate activity in the Old Northwest may have been, no one could deny its potency and danger in Missouri. There the shadowy "Order of American Knights" established connections with various guerrilla bands that ravaged the state. Confederate General Sterling Price was designated "military commander" of the O.A.K.[1] In September 1864, Price coordinated an invasion of Missouri with guerrilla attacks behind northern lines that represented a greater threat to Union control there than all the cloudy conspiracies in other parts of the Midwest.

Partisan warfare along the Kansas-Missouri border continued the violence that had begun in 1854. The vicious conflicts between Border Ruffians and Jayhawkers expanded a hundred-fold after 1861 as they gained sanction from Confederate and Union governments. The guerrilla fighting in Missouri produced a form of terrorism that exceeded anything else in the war. Jay-hawking Kansans and bushwhacking Missourians took no prisoners, killed in cold blood, plundered and pillaged and burned (but almost never raped) without stint. Jayhawkers initiated a scorched earth policy against rebel sympathizers three years before Sheridan practiced it in the Shenandoah Valley. Guerrilla chieftains, especially the infamous William Clarke Quantrill, initiated the slaughter of unarmed soldiers as well as civilians, whites as well as blacks, long before Confederate troops began murdering captured black soldiers elsewhere. Guerrilla bands in Missouri provided a training ground for outlaw gangs that emerged after the war — most notably the James and Younger brothers.

The war of raid and ambush in Missouri seemed often to have little relation to the larger conflict of which it was a part. But the hit-and-run tactics of the guerrillas, who numbered only a few thousand, tied down tens of thousands of Union soldiers and militia who might otherwise have fought elsewhere. The guerrillas' need for sanctuary in the countryside and the army's search and destroy missions forced civilians to choose sides or else suffer the consequences — usually both. Confederate generals frequently attached guerrilla bands to their commands or requested these bands to destroy Union supply lines and bases in conjunction with orthodox operations against northern forces. In August 1862, Quantrill's band captured Independence, Missouri, as part of a raid by rebel cavalry from Arkansas. As a reward Quantrill received a captain's commission in the Confederate army — and thereafter claimed to be a colonel.

1. When the O.A.K. changed its name to the Sons of Liberty elsewhere in early 1864, it appears to have retained the old name in Missouri. Frank L. Klement, "Phineas C. Wright, the Order of the American Knights, and the Sanderson Exposé," *Civil War History,* 18 (1972), 5–23, maintains that Sterling Price's alleged role in the Knights was invented by Union detectives and perjured witnesses. But Albert Castel, *General Sterling Price and the Civil War in the West* (Baton Rouge, 1968), 193–96, while conceding that the O.A.K. amounted to little, asserts that Price was indeed its military commander.

The motives of guerrillas and Jayhawkers alike sometimes seemed nothing more than robbery, revenge, or nihilistic love of violence. But ideology also played a part. Having battled proslavery Missourians for nearly a decade, many Jayhawkers were hardened abolitionists intent on destroying slavery and the social structure that it sustained. The notorious 7th Kansas Cavalry — "Jennison's Jayhawkers" — that plundered and killed their way across western Missouri were commanded by an abolitionist colonel with Susan B. Anthony's brother as lieutenant colonel and John Brown, Jr., as captain of a company. To a man the soldiers were determined to exterminate rebellion and slaveholders in the most literal manner possible. On the other side, guerrilla outlaws such as the James brothers have been celebrated in myth, by Hollywood films, and by some scholars as Robin-Hood types or "primitive rebels" who defended small farmers by attacking the agencies of Yankee capitalism — the Union army during the war, banks and railroads afterwards. But in reality, as a recent study has shown, the guerrillas tended to be the sons of farmers and planters of southern heritage who were three times more likely to own slaves and possessed twice as much wealth as the average Missourian. To the extent that ideology motivated their depredations, they fought for slavery and Confederate independence.[2]

The most notorious of their leaders was William Clarke Quantrill. The son of an Ohio schoolteacher, Quantrill had drifted around the West until the war came along to give full rein to his particular talents. Without any ties to the South or to slavery, he chose the Confederacy apparently because in Missouri this allowed him to attack all symbols of authority. He attracted to his gang some of the most psychopathic killers in American history. In kaleidoscopic fashion, groups of

these men would split off to form their own bands and then come together again for larger raids. An eruption of such activities along Missouri's western border in the spring of 1863 infuriated the Union commander there, Thomas Ewing. A brother-in-law of William T. Sherman, Ewing had learned what Sherman was learning — that this was a war between peoples, not simply between armies. The wives and sisters of Quantrill's men fed and sheltered the guerrillas. Ewing arrested these women and lodged them under guard in Kansas City. There on August 14 a building containing many of them collapsed, killing five of the women.

This tragedy set in motion a greater one. Inflamed by a passion for revenge, the raiders combined in one large band of 450 men under Quantrill (including the Younger brothers and Frank James) and headed for Lawrence, Kansas, the hated center of free soilism since Bleeding Kansas days. After crossing the Kansas line they kidnapped ten farmers to guide them toward Lawrence and murdered each one after his usefulness was over. Approaching the town at dawn on August 21, Quantrill ordered his followers: "Kill every male and burn every house." They almost did. The first to die was a United Brethren clergyman, shot through the head while he sat milking his cow. During the next three hours Quantrill's band murdered another 182 men and boys and burned 185 buildings in Lawrence. They rode out of town ahead of pursuing Union cavalry and after a harrowing chase made it back to their Missouri sanctuary, where they scattered to the woods.[3]

This shocking act roused the whole country. A manhunt for Quantrill's outlaws netted a few of them, who were promptly hanged or shot. An en-

2. Don Bowen, "Guerrilla Warfare in Western Missouri, 1862–1865: Historical Extensions of the Relative Deprivation Hypothesis," *Comparative Studies in Society and History* (1977), 30–51. I am indebted to my colleague Richard D. Challener for calling this article to my attention.

3. Jay Monaghan, *Civil War on the Western Border 1854–1865* (New York, 1955), 274–89; Richard S. Brownlee, *Gray Ghosts of the Confederacy: Guerrilla Warfare in the West, 1861–1865* (Baton Rouge, 1958), 110–57; Albert E. Castel, *A Frontier State at War: Kansas, 1861–1865* (Ithaca, 1950), 124–41. The best study of Quantrill is Albert E. Castel, *William Clarke Quantrill: His Life and Times* (New York, 1962).

raged General Ewing issued his famous Order No. 11 for the forcible removal of civilians from large parts of four Missouri counties bordering Kansas. Union soldiers ruthlessly enforced this banishment of ten thousand people, leaving these counties a wasteland for years. None of this stopped the guerrillas, however. Quite the contrary, their raids became more daring and destructive during the following year.

General Sterling Price, who longed to redeem Missouri from the Yankees, was impressed by Quantrill's prowess. In November 1863 Price sent him words of "high appreciation of the hardships you . . . and your gallant command . . . have so nobly endured and the gallant struggle you have made against despotism and the oppression of our State, with the confident hope that success will soon crown our efforts."[4] Guerrilla chieftains convinced Price that Missourians would rise *en masse* if a Confederate army invaded the state, which had been denuded of first-line Union troops to deal with Forrest in Tennessee. Scraping together 12,000 cavalry from the trans-Mississippi, Price moved northward through Arkansas and entered Missouri in September 1864.

4. O.R., Ser. 1, Vol. 53, P. 908.

He instructed partisan bands to spread chaos in the Union rear, while the O.A.K. mobilized civilians to welcome the invaders. The latter enterprise came to nothing, for when Union officers arrested the Order's leaders the organization proved to be an empty shell. The guerrillas were another matter. Raiding in small bands all over central Missouri they brought railroad and wagon transportation to a standstill and even halted boat traffic on the Missouri.

The most effective partisan was "Bloody Bill" Anderson who had split from Quantrill with about fifty followers — all of them pathological killers like their leader. Through August and September, Anderson's band struck isolated garrisons and posts, murdering and scalping teamsters, cooks, and other unarmed personnel as well as soldiers. The climax of this saturnalia came at Centralia on September 27. With thirty men including Frank and Jesse James, Bloody Bill rode into town, burned a train and robbed its passengers, and murdered twenty-four unarmed northern soldiers traveling home on furlough. Chased out of town by three companies of militia, the guerrillas picked up 175 allies from other bands, turned on their pursuers, and slaughtered 124 of the 147 men, including the wounded, whom they shot in the head.

Price in Missouri and Kansas: September– October 1864

Pilot Knob, Missouri (MO021), Iron County, September 26–28, 1864

Albert Castel

On September 19 CS Major General Sterling Price crossed into Missouri from Pocahontas, Arkansas, with 12,000 troops, all but 1,000 mounted, organized into three divisions commanded by CS Major General James F. Fagan and CS Brigadier Generals John S. Marmaduke and Joseph O. "Jo" Shelby. Price's goals were to seize St. Louis, gather recruits and supplies, and bring about an uprising against Union domination of Missouri. Unfortunately, many of his men were poorly armed — if armed at all — conscripts lacking adequate training and discipline.

On September 24 Price reached Fredericktown, where he was told that about 1,500 Union soldiers held Pilot Knob and the terminus of the St. Louis & Iron Mountain Railroad, eighty-six miles southwest of St. Louis. Unwilling to leave this force in his rear, and believing he could gain an easy victory, he decided to attack it. On September 26 he sent Shelby's Division to cut the railroad north of Pilot Knob while he marched on the town with Fagan's and Marmaduke's Divisions.

US Brigadier General Thomas Ewing, Jr., the brother-in-law of US Major General William Tecumseh Sherman, commanded the Federals at Pilot Knob, who actually numbered 1,456. There were 856 Federal troops, 450 Missouri State Militia Cavalry, commanded by Major James Wilson, and 150 civilian volunteers. Ewing's instructions from US Major General William S. Rosecrans, head of the Department of the Missouri, were to make a reconnaissance-in-force, but Ewing decided instead to hold the area as long as possible to delay the Confederate advance on St. Louis. He was successful on the evening of September 26 in

checking and then driving back Price's lead division, Fagan's, at Arcadia.

The superior Confederate strength compelled Ewing to withdraw most of his forces to Fort Davidson, a six-sided dirt parapet nine feet high, surrounded by a ditch ten feet wide and more than six feet deep. Mounted in the fort were eleven cannons, four of them 32-pounder siege guns, which were fired in the battle. Rifle pits about 150 yards long protected the fort's northern and southern flanks.

Price's chief of engineers proposed placing artillery atop Shepherd Mountain, which overlooked the fort, and bombarding the garrison into surrender. Instead, Price, at the urging of Fagan and Marmaduke, who insisted that they could take the fort in a matter of minutes, ordered it to be stormed. CS Brigadier General John B. Clark, Jr.'s Brigade of Marmaduke's 3,700-man division advanced over Shepherd Mountain. One of the four brigades of Fagan's 5,000-man division, CS Brigadier General William L. Cabell's, was along Knob Creek, while the brigades of CS Colonels W. F. Slemons and Thomas H. McCray ascended Pilot Knob Mountain. Troopers from Marmaduke's Division were also sent to attack the fort from the north.

Price demanded Ewing's surrender, but he refused. Ewing believed he could hold the fort, and he also feared that if he became a prisoner he would be killed by Confederate Missouri troops in retaliation for a decree, General Orders No. 11, he had issued in 1863 expelling civilians from four counties in western Missouri.

At dawn US Captain William J. Campbell and Wilson were in a line south of the mountains. When pressed, they withdrew to a new line extending from Pilot Knob to Shepherd Mountain and then over the summits of the two mountains and down the north slopes.

At about 2:00 P.M., following an ineffectual shelling of the fort by two cannons on Shepherd Mountain, the Confederates advanced on foot, with Clark's men leading the charge down from Shepherd Mountain, while Cabell attacked from the south. The Confederates on Pilot Knob at-

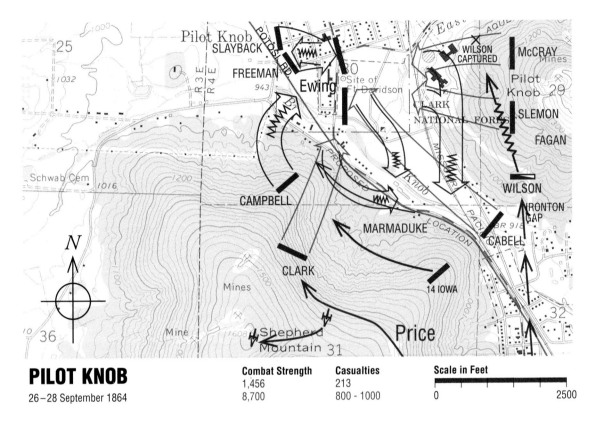

PILOT KNOB

26–28 September 1864

Combat Strength	Casualties	Scale in Feet
1,456	213	0 2500
8,700	800 - 1000	

tacked the fort from the southeast. Shot and shell, then bullets and canister ripped their ranks. Fagan's entire right wing broke in a "disgraceful manner," and most of Marmaduke's men took cover in a dry creek bed. Only Cabell's Brigade kept going until the men reached the fort's ditch. There they stopped, wavered, and fled, having suffered heavy losses. Wisely ignoring pleas from a humiliated Fagan to renew the assault, Price sent orders to the troops to prepare scaling ladders, and to Shelby to rejoin the rest of the army for an attack the next morning.

Ewing did not give Price another opportunity. At 3:00 A.M. on September 28, having accomplished all he had hoped to do and more with his stand at Pilot Knob, Ewing silently evacuated the fort and retreated northward by way of the Potosi Road. For some inexplicable reason, CS Colonel

Archibald S. Dobbins's Brigade of Fagan's Division, which Price had posted on that road to guard against this eventuality, neither detected nor blocked the Union escape. When the fort's powder magazine, touched off by a slow fuse, exploded at 3:30 A.M., the Confederates still failed to react.

Not until 8:00 A.M. did Price learn that Ewing had given him the slip. At once he sent Marmaduke and then Shelby in pursuit. On the evening of September 29 Shelby caught up with Ewing, entrenched thirty-five miles from Rolla, but concluded that an attack would cost more than it would be worth, so the Federals were able to proceed to Rolla and safety.

Price's bloody repulse at Fort Davidson revealed the poor quality of most of his army and impaired its already weak morale. It was the first in a series of defeats that turned his Missouri expedition into one of the worst military fiascos of the Civil War.

Estimated Casualties: 213 US, 800 – 1,000 CS

Fort Davidson State Historic Site is at Pilot Knob, north of Ironton and ninety miles south of St. Louis on County Road V, east of its junction with State Highway 21. It includes eighty-four acres of the historic Pilot Knob battlefield.

Glasgow, Missouri (MO022), Howard County, October 15, 1864

After the battle of Pilot Knob, CS General Price abandoned his plan to attack St. Louis and seize the supplies and armaments defended by US Major General Andrew Jackson Smith's 9,000 infantrymen. They had recently arrived from their service in the Red River campaign and in northern Mississippi. Price headed westward with his army across Missouri, driven in a carriage. He seldom rode his gray horse, Bucephalus, who had been given the same name as Alexander the Great's horse and was strong enough to carry the 290-pound Price. The Confederates looted and lived off the countryside. Because of the strong Federal force in Jefferson City, Price abandoned the plan to install Thomas C. Reynolds, a Confederate, as governor. In Boonville, a pro-Confederate town, thousands of unarmed volunteers as well as guerrilla bands joined Price.

On October 15 a detachment of two of Price's brigades of mounted infantry, cavalry, and artillery hit Glasgow on the Missouri River with an artillery bombardment and advanced on the town by several routes. The Federal garrison retreated to fortifications on Hereford Hill. US Colonel Chester Harding concluded that he could not withstand another attack and surrendered. The

Confederates paroled more than 600 Federal prisoners and rejoined Price's main column the next day at Marshall with supplies and weapons that boosted the soldiers' morale as they marched on toward Kansas City.

Estimated Casualties: 400 US, 50 CS

Lexington II, Missouri (MO023), Lafayette County, October 19, 1864

CS General Price's slow march along the Missouri River gave US Major General William S. Rosecrans, commander of the Department of the Missouri, time to order a pincer movement to trap him. Rosecrans sent 9,000 infantrymen under US General Smith across the state on Price's left flank and 7,000 cavalrymen under US Major General Alfred Pleasonton west in pursuit of Price. US Major General Samuel R. Curtis, commander of the Department of Kansas, was organizing his Army of the Border at Fort Leavenworth, Kansas. It included both Kansas State Militia and Federal troops. However, many of the 15,000 militiamen did not want to fight outside the state.

Curtis was able to send only 2,000 men under US Major General James G. Blunt toward Lexington to slow the Confederates. On October 19, as Price approached Lexington, CS General Shelby's cavalry collided with Union scouts and drove them back. The Confederates pushed the main force back through the town and forced them to retreat along the Independence Road while their cavalry held off Price until dark. The Confederates camped for the night on Fire Prairie Creek, while Blunt marched his men on to the Little Blue River. While the U.S. forces were not strong enough to stop Price's army, they slowed it and reported on its size and location.

Estimated Casualties: unknown

Little Blue River, Missouri (MO024), Jackson County, October 21, 1864

US General Blunt recommended to US General Curtis a defensive position on the Little Blue

River about nine miles east of Independence where the Federals could battle the Confederates. But the Kansas Militia would travel no farther east than the Big Blue River, so Curtis ordered Blunt to Independence. Blunt persuaded Curtis to let him return to support US Colonel Thomas Moonlight's force, left alone on the Little Blue. Before Blunt could reach him, Moonlight had engaged CS General Marmaduke's troopers. Moonlight held them off until CS General Shelby's Division joined the fight. The Federals retreated and burned the bridge as ordered. Blunt fought a delaying action but was outnumbered and had to retreat west toward Independence.

This battle prompted Kansas militiamen to head across the border to the Big Blue River to counter the threat Price posed to their state.

Estimated Casualties: unknown

Independence II, Missouri (MO025), Jackson County, October 22, 1864

CS General Price marched his army west while he considered two alternatives: to try to take Kansas City and Leavenworth, or to turn south after crossing the Big Blue River. CS Generals Shelby and Marmaduke were in the lead, and CS General Fagan's Division brought up the rear. On October 22 US General Pleasonton's cavalry crossed the Little Blue. They pressed the Confederate rear guard under CS General Cabell. In Independence they took prisoners and two cannons and occupied the town. Marmaduke's cavalry intervened two miles west of Independence, counterattacked, and drove Pleasonton back.

Estimated Casualties: unknown US, 140 CS

Big Blue River (Byram's Ford), Missouri (MO026), Jackson County, October 22–23, 1864

US General Curtis's Army of the Border established a strong defensive line along the Big Blue River, blocking CS General Price's advance into Kansas. Price feinted against Curtis at the main ford on the road between Independence and Kansas City while he sent CS General Shelby south to find another crossing. On October 22 Shelby's troopers stormed across Byram's Ford, southwest of Independence, flanked the Federals, and forced them to fall back to Westport, to a battle line along the north side of Brush Creek. Price led his forces, including more than five hundred wagons and a large herd of cattle, across the captured ford.

Price ordered his wagon train to head south the next morning on the Harrisonville Road. US General Pleasonton sent US Brigadier General John H. McNeil's brigade south on the east side of the river toward Little Santa Fe to intercept the wagon train. Pleasonton and his three other brigades attacked Marmaduke's troopers, who were defending Byram's Ford, and overpowered them. The Confederates fled west across the open prairie. The Federals pursued them and hit Price's rear and right flank. McNeil did not attack the train; he concluded that the 5,000-man guard was too strong to attack. Pleasonton later court-martialed him for not attacking since the guards were mostly unarmed recruits.

Estimated Casualties: unknown

One hundred acres of the Big Blue River battlefield are owned by Kansas City, Missouri, a gift of the Monnett Fund. The walking tour, in the area of the Byram's Ford Industrial Park, was established by the Monnett Battle of Westport Fund of the Civil War Round Table of Kansas City. Brochures are available through the Westport Historical Society in the Harris-Kearney House and through the Jackson County Historical Society in the Wornall House Museum.

Westport, Missouri (MO027), Jackson County, October 23, 1864

There were more soldiers in the battle of Westport than in any other Civil War engagement west of the Mississippi River. US General Curtis's Army of the Border included nearly 5,000 U.S. volunteers and 15,000 Kansas Militiamen. Price's Army of Missouri had about 9,000 men. The forces of US General Pleasonton, CS General Marmaduke, and the wagon train guards brought the total number of soldiers in the area to about 40,000.

CS General Price was threatened by three major forces. Curtis was covering the approaches to Kansas City from the south, Pleasonton was approaching the rear of the Confederates, and US General Smith's infantry was approaching on Price's left flank. Price began to retreat south to avoid being caught between them. On October 23 while Marmaduke and Pleasonton clashed at Byram's Ford on the Big Blue River, US General Blunt attacked CS Generals Shelby and Fagan across Brush Creek at Westport. The Confederates on the high ground south of the creek repulsed two charges before the Kansas Militia arrived from their Big Blue positions, and Pleasonton's troopers rode up after defeating Marmaduke at Byram's Ford. They overwhelmed the Confederates. Shelby's troopers protected the Confederates as they retreated south with heavy losses.

Estimated Casualties: 1,500 US, 1,500 CS

The Monnett Battle of Westport Fund of the Civil War Round Table of Kansas City has provided a self-guided thirty-two-mile driving tour of the battle of Westport, which includes twenty-five historical markers.

Marais des Cygnes, Kansas (KS004), Linn County, October 25, 1864

CS General Price's defeated army withdrew southward from Westport, pursued by US Generals Blunt and Pleasonton, and camped on the north bank of the Marais des Cygnes River. On October 25 both sides were exhausted from the march and from having slept on their weapons in a driving rainstorm. After a late afternoon artillery bombardment, the outnumbered Federal troopers charged and pushed the Confederates across the river.

Estimated Casualties: unknown

Mine Creek, Kansas (KS003), Linn County, October 25, 1864

Late on the morning of October 25, south of the Marais de Cygnes River, 2,600 cavalrymen under US Lieutenant Colonel Frederick W. Benteen and US Colonel John F. Philips of US General Pleasonton's division overtook CS General Price's columns at Mine Creek. Stalled by their wagons' crossing at the ford on the Fort Scott Road, about 7,000 Confederate troopers formed a line on the north side of the creek, with CS General Fagan's Division on the left and CS General Marmaduke on the right. They unlimbered eight cannons on the prairie. Although outnumbered, Benteen attacked Marmaduke's center, while Philips hit Fagan's left. The attack occurred so quickly that the cavalry on both sides remained mounted, making this one of the largest clashes between mounted cavalry during the Civil War. The Federals' rapid attack and their greater firepower — they had breechloading and magazine carbines, as well as revolvers — overwhelmed the Confederates' numerical superiority. In the half-hour battle the Federals captured about 500 Confederates, including CS Generals Marmaduke and Cabell, and their cannons. Price arrived with CS General Shelby's Division from south of Mine Creek in time to protect the retreat of the shattered Army of Missouri.

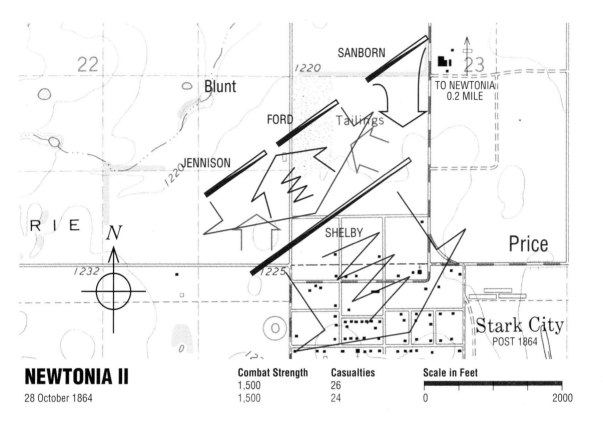

NEWTONIA II

28 October 1864

Combat Strength	Casualties
1,500	26
1,500	24

Scale in Feet

0   2000

Estimated Casualties: 150 US, 800 CS

Mine Creek Battlefield State Historic Site, two miles south of Pleasanton and west of Route 69, includes 280 acres of the historic battlefield.

Marmaton River, Missouri (MO028), Vernon County, October 25, 1864

Late in the afternoon of October 25 CS General Price's wagons were delayed at the Marmaton River ford. CS General Shelby deployed about 1,000 men and the unarmed recruits to save the wagons, and they skirmished with the Federals until dark. Near Deerfield Price burned all the wagons except those with army supplies. The army continued its march and arrived in Newtonia on October 28.

Estimated Casualties: unknown

Newtonia II, Missouri (MO029), Newton County, October 28, 1864

Albert Castel

CS Major General Sterling Price continued his retreat from Missouri. On October 28 he stopped to rest his command just south of Newtonia. While the Confederates were gathering corn in the fields near their camp, US Major General James G. Blunt approached at the head of 1,000 cavalrymen. Price, thinking that US Major General Samuel R. Curtis had caught up with him, ordered an instant retreat.

Blunt had fought well in the Union victory at Prairie Grove, Arkansas, in December 1862 but had damaged his reputation at the Baxter Springs massacre. His efforts earlier in the month at Little Blue River and Westport to re-establish his record were successful. At Newtonia, however, he attacked alone with only two brigades of his division, those of US Colonels Charles R. Jennison and James H. Ford. CS Brigadier General Joseph O. "Jo" Shelby, with his division and the remnant of CS Brigadier General William L. Cabell's Brigade of CS Major General James F. Fagan's Division, checked the Federals while Price with the rest of his army resumed the retreat toward Arkansas.

With his superior numbers, Shelby overlapped both of Blunt's flanks and pushed the Federals back. Just before sundown US Brigadier General John B. Sanborn arrived after a forced march of sixty-two miles from Fort Scott, Kansas. His fortunate arrival enabled him to take a position on Blunt's left, threaten the Confederates' right flank, and force them back to a defensive position.

Darkness put an end to the fighting. The Federals withdrew to Newtonia, and Shelby rode after the rest of Price's forces, having protected their retreat. Price's army began to disintegrate after Newtonia. Price fell back to Cane Hill, and Curtis pursued him to the Arkansas River on November 8. The Confederates continued their retreat across Indian Territory and on to Texas.

Price's expedition was the last large-scale operation west of the Mississippi River, and it was a strategic failure. Price lost men, weapons, and supplies while hardly damaging the Federal war effort. By mid-December Price had only 3,500 men, having lost as a result of battle, desertion, and illness more than two thirds of the 12,000 he had led into Missouri.

Estimated Casualties: 26 US, 24 CS

Newtonia is six miles east of Route 71 on Route 86. The Newtonia Battlefield Association owns nine historic acres.

Southwest Virginia and East Tennessee: September–December 1864

Saltville I, Virginia (VA076), Smyth County, October 2, 1864

US Brigadier General Stephen G. Burbridge defeated CS Brigadier General John Hunt Morgan at Cynthiana, Kentucky, in June. In October he began his own delayed raid without the threat of the wily raider, since Morgan had been killed on September 3 at Greeneville, Tennessee. Burbridge's objective was to destroy the vital salt works at Saltville. They were a source of the salt the armies used to preserve meat in the absence of refrigeration. Burbridge set out with 5,200 men, including 600 men of the 5th U.S. Colored Cavalry. At Clinch Mountain and Laurel Gap, 600 cavalrymen under CS Brigadier General John C. Vaughn delayed his raid, enabling CS Brigadier General Felix H. Robertson to concentrate 2,800 troops at Saltville.

Burbridge arrived before the Confederate works on October 1 and attacked the following day. Repeated assaults failed to overcome the defenses, and the Federals suffered 350 casualties. On October 3 Burbridge left his wounded on the field and retreated. The Confederate partisans led by Champ Ferguson killed more than 100 wounded black soldiers. Their cruel actions became infamous as the "Saltville Massacre." CS Major General John C. Breckinridge, the newly appointed commander of the Department of Western Virginia and Eastern Tennessee, arrived in the town too late to halt the massacre, but he ordered Ferguson arrested. Ferguson was hanged after the war.

Estimated Casualties: 350 US, 108 CS

Bull's Gap, Tennessee (TN033), Hamblen and Greene Counties, November 11–14, 1864

Bull's Gap in Bay Mountain was a critical area during the war because two vital communication lines ran through it, the East Tennessee & Virginia Railroad and the Knoxville Road. On October 16 CS General Vaughn's command cut the communications between Knoxville and the Federal garrison at the gap, twenty-five miles to the northeast. The Federals abandoned the gap. On October 29 they returned in strength to drive Vaughn out. The Confederacy needed the area's food and forage, so CS General Breckinridge led a force out from Abingdon, Virginia, to reoccupy the gap. They chased the Federals out of Greeneville. In command of about 3,000 men, Breckinridge approached the gap, defended by the 2,500-man "Governor's Guard" commanded by US Brigadier General Alvan C. Gillem.

On November 11 Breckinridge ordered his artillery to fire on the entrenched Federals, while he sent Vaughn's Brigade through Taylor's Gap to get behind Gillem and CS Brigadier General Basil W. Duke's Brigade to the crest of Bay Mountain to the east. The next morning at dawn Duke's men attacked along the ridge and advanced into the Federals' trenches. Gillem fought off both Duke on his left flank and Vaughn in his rear. Breckinridge avoided costly frontal assaults and skirmished throughout the thirteenth. Gillem was low on ammunition, so he withdrew that night and tried to reach Morristown, where he expected reinforcements. The Confederates rode hard and hit the Federals in a night attack in the early hours of November 14 which panicked the Federals. Gillem lost his artillery and his wagons, and had about 300 of his men taken prisoner near Strawberry Plains. Breckinridge soon returned to Virginia.

Estimated Casualties: 24 (plus 300 prisoners) US, 100 CS

Marion, Virginia (VA081), Smyth County, December 16–18, 1864

US Major General George Stoneman was taken prisoner in July 1864 during his disastrous raid in Georgia. Following his exchange he was given command of 5,700 Union cavalrymen in East Tennessee. He set out from Knoxville on December 1 for southwest Virginia, encountered some resistance at Kingsport, Tennessee, on the thirteenth, and occupied Bristol, Virginia, that night. The next day CS General Breckinridge ordered his 2,100-man command to concentrate in Saltville.

On December 16 US General Gillem's 1,500 cavalrymen routed CS General Vaughn's small force at Marion and drove the Confederates beyond Wytheville. The Federals captured the lead mines near the town and wrecked part of the Virginia & Tennessee Railroad. Meanwhile Stoneman held off Breckinridge in Saltville, twelve miles northwest of Marion, with a brigade of cavalry. That evening Breckinridge set out for Marion, leaving 400 men to defend Saltville.

The next day Breckinridge attacked when two Federal brigades under US General Burbridge blocked his advance one mile from Marion at a covered bridge over the Holston River. Stoneman ordered Gillem to capture Saltville. When Stoneman arrived at the river, he needed reinforcements and recalled Gillem. On the eighteenth Stoneman repeatedly hammered the Confederates until Breckinridge expended most of his ammunition and withdrew that night toward Wytheville.

Estimated Casualties: 300 total

Saltville II, Virginia (VA082), Smyth County, December 20–21, 1864

After the success at Marion, US General Stoneman rode to the northwest to capture the salt ponds at Saltville. CS General Breckinridge had left 400 men to defend the eastern Confederacy's primary remaining source of salt. Stoneman invested Saltville on December 20, skirmished with the outnumbered Confederates, and captured it the next day. He took 400 prisoners, nineteen cannons, three thousand horses, three thousand rifle-muskets, twenty-five thousand rounds of artillery ammunition, and thousands of bushels of salt. Stoneman damaged the salt works, the nearby railroad, and bridges in the area before retiring to Tennessee. Breckinridge reoccupied Saltville on the twenty-first. The mines were soon open, but the railroad was out of operation for two months.

Estimated Casualties: unknown

Forrest's Raid into West Tennessee: October–November 1864

Johnsonville, Tennessee (TN032), Benton County, November 3–4, 1864

In the fall of 1864, CS Major General Nathan Bedford Forrest led a twenty-three-day raid, culminating in his attack on the Union supply base at Johnsonville. The Federals shipped supplies up the Tennessee River to Johnsonville, where they offloaded them onto trains headed for Nashville. On the night of November 3 Forrest and CS Captain John Morton quietly planted their artillery across the wide river from the depot.

The next afternoon Forrest's attack with well-positioned guns surprised the Federals and disabled their three gunboats commanded by USN Lieutenant Edward M. King. King ordered the gunboats abandoned and burned, along with the valuable transports. Forrest then shelled the wharf area, including twenty-eight steamboats and barges, warehouses, and stacks of supplies. Forrest reported: "Having completed the work designed for the expedition, I moved my command six miles during the night by the light of the enemy's burning property."

The raid, Forrest's most successful, destroyed four gunboats, fourteen transports, twenty barges, and millions of dollars' worth of stockpiled supplies bound for Nashville and US Major General George H. Thomas's army.

Estimated Casualties: unknown

Johnsonville State Historic Area near Denver includes the Federal depot area. It is twenty-five miles north of I-40 off the Forrest exit; signs begin at Camden.

Hood's March to Tennessee: October–December 1864

Allatoona, Georgia (GA023), Bartow County, October 5, 1864

William R. Scaife

After the fall of Atlanta in early September 1864, the Confederates changed their strategy against US Major General William Tecumseh Sherman in Georgia. Instead of continuing to confront Sherman in open battle, they would attack his lines of supply and communications. Their new strategy called for CS General John Bell Hood to march his army northward, staying well to the west of the Western & Atlantic Railroad, Sherman's single-track supply line back to Chattanooga, and to launch a series of "hit-and-run" attacks against key bridges, passes, and other installations along the railroad.

Before the Atlanta campaign, Sherman's quartermaster and commissary officers had estimated that it would take 130 railroad cars containing 1,300 tons of material per day to supply his "army group" as it advanced into Georgia. The Confederates intended to disrupt this vital flow of supplies and force Sherman either to withdraw to Chattanooga or to pursue Hood over terrain the Federals had taken months before from CS General Joseph E. Johnston. If Sherman pursued Hood in force, Hood would withdraw before Sherman into the mountains of northern Alabama. If Sherman cut loose from Atlanta and headed for a seaport such as Charleston, Savannah, or Mobile, Hood would pursue and attack him from the rear.

It was not a bad plan, but it was doomed after President Jefferson Davis divulged it in speeches at Palmetto and Augusta, Georgia, and at Columbia, South Carolina, providing Sherman ample warning. Hood decided when he reached the mountains of north Georgia west of Dalton to embark instead on a campaign across Alabama to Franklin and Nashville, Tennessee.

On September 29 Hood crossed the Chattahoochee River at Phillips Ferry northwest of At-

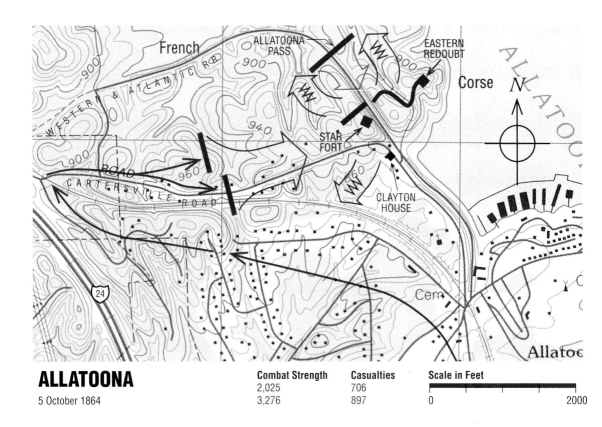

ALLATOONA

5 October 1864

Combat Strength	Casualties	Scale in Feet
2,025	706	0 2000
3,276	897	

lanta and marched northward. He sent CS Lieutenant General Alexander P. Stewart's Corps on the first "hit-and-run" attack against the railroad. Stewart overran small garrisons at Big Shanty, Moon's Station, and Acworth, north of Marietta, and by the evening of October 4 had destroyed about eight miles of track and taken about 600 prisoners. Hood next ordered Stewart to send one division six miles northward to Allatoona Pass, an important Federal supply base where the railroad ran through the Allatoona Mountain range in a cut 180 feet deep. This division was to fill the cut with earth and debris, then march northward about five miles to the railroad bridge over the Etowah River and burn it.

The dubious honor of leading this ambitious expedition was given, at Hood's suggestion, to CS Major General Samuel G. French. French's Division consisted of 3,276 men in three brigades under CS Brigadier Generals Claudius Sears, Francis M. Cockrell, and William Hugh Young. The force appeared adequate since Confederate intelligence reported only a few hundred Federal troops garrisoned at Allatoona.

Thanks to President Davis's forewarning, Sherman had ordered US Brigadier General John M. Corse to hurry his division from Rome, Georgia, to reinforce the small garrison at Allatoona. Corse and one brigade arrived there before French could begin his attack and swelled the defending garrison to 2,025 men. Although outnumbered three to two, Corse held a heavily fortified position anchored by large earthen forts on each side of the cut. Many of his men, including the entire 7th Illinois Regiment, were armed with sixteen-shot Henry repeating rifles, giving them equal, if not superior, firepower.

On the morning of October 5 French mounted

a fierce attack against a tenacious Federal defense. By noon most of the Federal troops had been driven back and pinned down in their main fort, Star Fort, and their surrender seemed imminent. Then, a false report from his cavalry led French to believe that a strong enemy force was approaching up the railroad from Acworth in his rear and threatening to cut him off from the army. French reluctantly withdrew, leaving Allatoona to the Federals. He later reported, "I determined to withdraw, however depressing the idea of not capturing the place after so many had fallen, and when in all probability we could force a surrender by night."

Federal casualties were 706 out of 2,025 present, and Confederate casualties were 897 out of 3,276 in a fiercely contested engagement.

After the war, the evangelist Philip P. Bliss of Chicago wrote a hymn entitled "Hold the Fort," and its resounding chorus, "Hold the fort; for we are coming, Union men be strong," did much to perpetuate the myth that Sherman signaled the garrison to hold out during the battle while a relief column rushed to assist them. However, Sherman later denied having sent such a message, and it was two days after the battle before a relief force arrived at Allatoona, under US Major General Jacob D. Cox.

On the day following the battle General Corse sent a rather dramatic message to Sherman: "I am short a cheekbone and one ear, but am able to lick all hell yet." When Sherman saw Corse a few days later, he expected to see a man with half his face shot away. Observing only a small bandage on Corse's cheek and no apparent damage to the ear he had claimed to have lost, the commanding general chided his subordinate, "Corse, they came damn near missing you, didn't they?"

Estimated Casualties: 706 US, 897 CS

Allatoona battlefield is on Old Allatoona Road one mile east of Exit 122 off I-75, about twenty-five miles north of Atlanta. Etowah Valley Historical Society markers

indicate the part of the battlefield that is administered by the U.S. Army Corps of Engineers and open to the public.

Dalton III, Georgia (GA024), Whitfield County and Dalton, October 13, 1864

On October 10 CS General Hood resumed his march northward to strike the Western & Atlantic Railroad again. He crossed the Coosa River near Rome and headed northeast toward Resaca. The town was too strongly fortified to attack, so his force destroyed twenty miles of track between Resaca and Tunnel Hill.

On October 13, when Hood's army surrounded the town of Dalton, US Major General John M. Schofield barely escaped by rail. Dalton's garrison, 751 men of the U.S. 44th Colored Infantry under US Colonel Lewis Johnson, barricaded themselves in Fort Hill. Johnson initially refused the demand to surrender but then agreed. CS Major General William Bate's men stripped the Federals of their shoes and personal belongings and threatened the officers' lives because they led black troops. The Confederates returned some of the African American soldiers to slavery. They paroled the officers and sent them back to the Union lines. The Federal garrisons at Tilton and Mill Creek Gap also surrendered.

Since Sherman's army was at Snake Creek Gap, Hood decided to move away from him and into Alabama to prepare his war-weary forces to move against the Federal supply lines and forces in Middle Tennessee. On October 14 they began the six-day march to Gadsden, Alabama. When Sherman concluded that Hood was determined to avoid battle with him, he decided to leave Hood to US Major General George H. Thomas in Tennessee, repair his railroads, and return to Atlanta to await Washington's approval of his plan to "cut a swath to the sea."

Estimated Casualties: 751 prisoners US, 0 CS

Decatur, Alabama (AL004), Morgan and Limestone Counties, October 26–29, 1864

On October 22 CS General Hood marched out from Gadsden to cross the Tennessee River at Decatur with an unrealistic plan approved by CS General P. G. T. Beauregard, commander of the Military Division of the West: defeat the Federals in Middle Tennessee and drive on to Virginia to join CS General Robert E. Lee.

On October 26–29 Hood demonstrated against US Brigadier General Robert S. Granger's 5,000-man garrison blocking the river crossing at Decatur. Hood concluded that he could not afford the losses that the victory would cost and marched on to the west to cross the river near Tuscumbia. He had to wait there for three weeks until the arrival of clothing, shoes, supplies, and CS Major General Nathan Bedford Forrest. On November 18 the cavalry commander arrived at Florence and took command of Hood's 5,000 troopers.

Estimated Casualties: 155 US, 200 CS

Columbia, Tennessee (TN034), Maury County, November 24–29, 1864

In mid-November US General Thomas, commander of the Army of the Cumberland, had planned to take the offensive against CS General Hood but did not receive his expected reinforcements, US Major General Andrew J. Smith's 10,000-man XVI Corps from Missouri. Thomas also lacked an effective cavalry. The new chief of cavalry, US Brigadier General James H. Wilson, had just begun reorganizing and equipping his troopers when he had to ride out of Nashville against CS General Forrest, who was leading Hood's advance into Tennessee. While Thomas prepared his defenses at Nashville, he ordered US Major General John M. Schofield with his XXIII Corps and US Major General David Stanley's IV Corps to Pulaski to delay Hood until Smith arrived, to avoid a battle, and to fall back fighting toward Nashville if Hood advanced.

Hood crossed the Tennessee River at Tuscumbia and upriver during November 16–21 with about 35,000 men. His Army of Tennessee advanced northeastward from Florence in three columns preceded by Forrest's cavalry. Schofield was isolated and outnumbered as he raced the thirty miles northward in cold weather to get to Columbia and the Duck River before Hood could cut him off from the road north through Spring Hill to Nashville. The 28,000 Federals arrived at the river on November 24, Thanksgiving Day, ahead of Forrest's cavalry. Hood arrived on November 26. Schofield withdrew across the river and destroyed the bridges to slow Hood's crossing. The Confederates, led by two Tennessee regiments, occupied Columbia on November 28. The skirmishing ended on the twenty-ninth with CS Lieutenant General Stephen D. Lee's artillery bombardment of the Federals north of Columbia. In the darkness of November 28–29 Hood launched a flanking movement to cut Schofield off from Nashville by racing around him to Spring Hill, recalling the "grand results achieved by the immortal Jackson in similar maneuvers."

Estimated Casualties: unknown

Spring Hill, Tennessee (TN035), Maury County and Spring Hill, November 29, 1864

Richard M. McMurry

On November 26 the Confederate army reached Columbia and found the town held by a 28,000-man northern force. The Federals were under orders to delay the southerners as long as possible to gain time for reinforcements to reach the great Union base at Nashville, some forty miles to the north. During the night of November 27–28 the Yankee commander at Columbia, Major General John M. Schofield, slipped his men across the rain-swollen Duck River to high ground a mile or so north of the stream. There, Schofield thought, he would be better positioned to carry out his assignment.

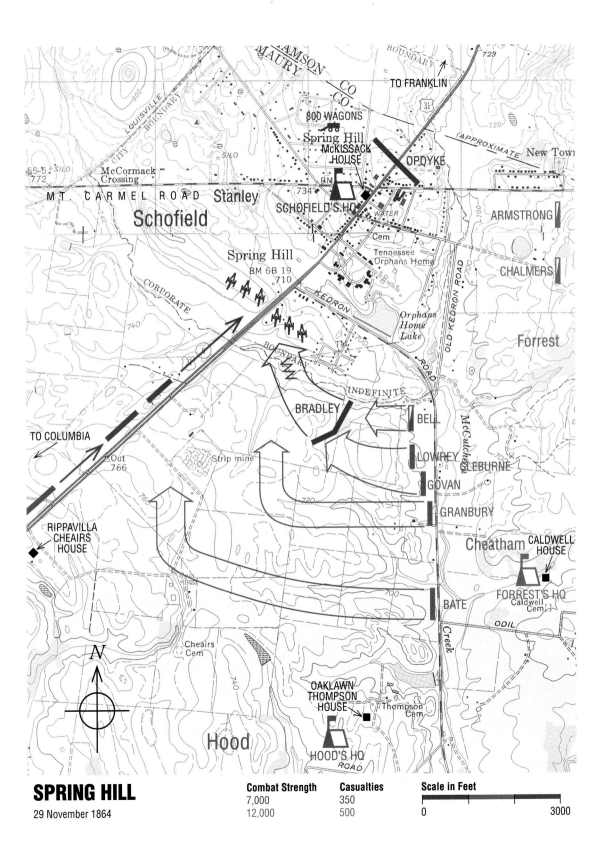

TO FRANKLIN

WILLIAMSON CO.
MAURY CO.

800 WAGONS
Spring Hill
McKISSACK
HOUSE

OPDYKE

New Town

LOUISVILLE
CITY BOUNDARY

SILO

McCormack
Crossing

BM 734

SCHOFIELD'S HQ

WATER

MT. CARMEL ROAD Stanley

Schofield

ARMSTRONG

Spring Hill
BM 6B 19
710

Cem

Tennessee
Orphans Home

CHALMERS

CORPORATE

KEDRON

Orphans
Home
Lake

OLD KEDRON ROAD

Forrest

ROGNAN

INDEFINITE

BRADLEY

BELL

LOWREY

CLEBURNE

TO COLUMBIA

Strip mine

Out
766

GOVAN

GRANBURY

McCutchen

RIPPAVILLA
CHEAIRS
HOUSE

Cheatham

CALDWELL
HOUSE

FORREST'S HQ
Caldwell
Cem

BATE

ODIL

N

Cheairs
Cem

Creek

OAKLAWN
THOMPSON
HOUSE

Thompson
Cem

Hood

HOOD'S HQ
ROAD

SPRING HILL

29 November 1864

Combat Strength	Casualties
7,000	350
12,000	500

Scale in Feet

0   3000

General John Bell Hood, commanding the 35,000 Rebel troops, could not rest content with having captured Columbia. He had to get across the river, fight or bypass Schofield, and continue northward. He soon developed a plan to do so.

Hood decided to cross the stream a few miles east of Columbia with all but two divisions of his army. He would then move northwest to regain the Columbia-Franklin Pike near Spring Hill, about ten miles north of the river. (The distance to be covered was about seventeen miles by the roads the Rebels would have to use.) Hood would leave his wagons and almost all of his artillery at Columbia lest they slow the march. The southern troops remaining at Columbia would demonstrate to threaten Schofield and, Hood hoped, fix him in position along the river.

Early on November 29 the Rebels were under way. Their cavalry had crossed the day before and driven the Union horsemen off to the north. By 7:30 A.M. on the twenty-ninth the leading Confederate division was over the river and stretched out on the road to Spring Hill. The other units followed as rapidly as possible. Whether Hood intended to try to trap the Yankees between the two wings of his army or slip around them and race for Nashville is unclear.

The crossing did not go unobserved by Federal eyes. On the twenty-eighth Schofield learned that Hood was doing something a few miles upriver. Schofield, however, did not know whether the Rebels off to his left were only a small cavalry force, a small body of infantry maneuvering to distract the Unionists from the important point at Columbia, or something more serious. He took the precaution of sending Major General David S. Stanley with the eight hundred valuable supply wagons, most of the artillery, and some of his infantry up the road toward Spring Hill.

Schofield already had a small garrison (about 1,300 men) at Spring Hill. In the late morning that force became engaged with the lead brigades of Major General Nathan Bedford Forrest's cavalrymen approaching from the east. A Yankee courier, dashing southward with word of the Rebel presence at Spring Hill, alerted Federal troops on the road between that place and Scho-

field's main force. Soon after noon Union reinforcements began to arrive at Spring Hill from the south. Their numbers were sufficient to hold the Confederate cavalry at bay.

By 4:00 P.M. the lead elements of Hood's infantry reached the area, moving under his orders to attack the Federals at Spring Hill. As the first troops deployed in the fields southeast of the village, Hood instructed Major General Patrick R. Cleburne's Division of Major General Benjamin Franklin Cheatham's Corps to go directly west to block the pike south of Spring Hill. Hood, however, did not inform Cheatham that Cleburne's mission had been changed. Cleburne's march was blocked by 2,000 men under Brigadier General Luther Prentice Bradley posted on a wooded knoll. Cleburne's 3,000 men — the brigades of Brigadier Generals Mark P. Lowrey, Daniel C. Govan, and Hiram B. Granbury — attacked, with Colonel Tyree H. Bell's troopers supporting their right and Major General William B. Bate's Division on their far left. They overpowered the Federals but were stopped short of the pike by artillery fire from high ground north of Bradley. As Cleburne approached the Columbia–Spring Hill Road, he received an order from corps headquarters to pull back and join Major General John Brown in an assault on the Federals at Spring Hill.

When Cheatham's Corps formed to attack, Brown, whose division was to begin the assault, panicked at reports of a Federal force on his right flank and refused to advance. Other units became confused in the rapidly falling darkness. Hood — the only one who might have straightened out the mess — had gone off to the nearby Absalom Thompson house. Owing to this command confusion, the Confederate advance came to a halt with its infantry units scattered over the countryside. In effect, seven divisions of fine troops were parked in the fields east of the Columbia–Spring Hill Pike, and there they spent the night.

While the Rebels milled around, the Yankees marched. Schofield, finally awake to the great danger he faced, bent every nerve to extract his men from the potential trap. All through the night he and his officers drove their exhausted troops northward, passing along the pike within a few hundred yards of the Rebel campfires.

During the night a number of Confederate generals made their way to the Thompson house to try to inform their commander of what was happening and to get instructions. Hood eventually came to understand that the pike had not been blocked, but he seems to have assumed that Schofield could not escape and that he could trap the Yankees at dawn. When he received a report that the Federals were marching up the pike, he sent an order for a unit to move a short distance to the west and fire at any force on the pike. The officer commanding the unit later reported that when he reached the pike he found it deserted and ordered his troops to their bivouac. (He either got to the pike after Schofield's men had all passed or he hit a long gap in the Federal column.)

When Hood awakened on the morning of November 30, he discovered that his enemy had escaped unscathed. In an angry meeting with his generals he blamed them for the failure. Then he ordered the army to march north toward Franklin.

The Spring Hill mystery has never been completely understood, and it never will be. The whole fiasco was typical of the command confusion and incompetence that characterized Confederate generalship in the West throughout the war.

The missed opportunity at Spring Hill cost the Rebels a chance to inflict a severe blow on the northerners. Such a success on November 29 would not have brought victory for the Confederacy, but it might well have given the secessionists enough leverage to negotiate their way back into the Union rather than having to surrender unconditionally.

Estimated Casualties: 350 US, 500 CS

Spring Hill battlefield, at Spring Hill, south of Franklin, is not open to the public but is marked by historical signs.

Franklin II, Tennessee (TN036), Williamson County and Franklin, November 30, 1864

US General Schofield's forces continued toward Nashville and halted on November 30 in Franklin at the Big Harpeth River eighteen miles south of the Nashville defenses held by US General Thomas. The turnpike bridge over the river was out, and the troops needed rest, having marched from Columbia with little sleep. They took positions behind previously constructed Union defenses and began to strengthen them. Their arc-shaped defensive line on the southern edge of town was protected on both flanks by the river. To their front was open ground stretching for two miles, commanded by strong Federal artillery. It was a formidable position to hold while the engineers rebuilt the pike bridge and planked the railroad bridge.

After his lost opportunity at Spring Hill, CS General Hood rushed his forces to battle the Federals at Franklin before they could reach the Nashville defenses and link up with Thomas's army. Against the advice of his subordinates and with little artillery support, Hood launched an attack at 4:00 P.M. Eighteen Confederate brigades, totaling about 20,000 men, made a frontal assault against the Union line.

US Brigadier General George D. Wagner had ordered two detached brigades, positioned one half mile in front of Union lines, to stay and fight. They stayed too long. After firing a deadly volley at the approaching divisions of CS General Cleburne and CS Major General John C. Brown, they were overrun by the Confederates. Their position also denied the Federal artillery a clear field of fire, so Cleburne's Division was able to penetrate the Union center until the brigades of US Brigadier General James W. Reilly and US Colonel Emerson Opdycke sealed the breach in a bloody counterattack. The battle continued for five hours, and the casualties were frightful. They included twelve Confederate generals — six killed or mortally wounded and one captured — and sixty-five other commanders.

The Federals began to pull out of Franklin at 11:00 P.M., and the lead elements of the exhausted army reached Nashville at dawn. Despite his losses, Hood marched on toward Nashville.

Estimated Casualties: 2,633 US, 7,300 CS

Fort Granger, a city park, and an area on Winstead Hill, owned by the Sons of Confederate Veterans, are open to the public.

Where this division defended, no odds broke its line; where it attacked, no numbers resisted its onslaught, save only once; and there is the grave of Cleburne.

— CS Lieutenant General William J. Hardee, after the death of CS Major General Patrick R. Cleburne in the battle of Franklin.

Murfreesboro II, Tennessee (TN037), Rutherford County, December 5–7, 1864

On December 2 CS General Hood ordered CS General Bate to move against the Nashville & Chattanooga Railroad, disrupt the Federal supply lines, and hit the depot at Murfreesboro. On December 3–5 CS General Forrest forced four blockhouse garrisons to surrender, those guarding railroad bridges between Mill Creek and La Vergne. Bate's Division, repulsed in a December 4 fight at Overall Creek, joined Forrest. They advanced on Murfreesboro, held by 8,000 Federals under US Major General Lovell H. Rousseau. The infantry brigades of CS Brigadier Generals Claudius Sears and Joseph B. Palmer reinforced Forrest, bringing his strength to about 6,000 men. Forrest concluded that Fortress Rosecrans was too strong to attack and prepared to draw Rousseau out and defeat him.

On December 7 Rousseau sent about 3,300 men — cavalry, infantry, and artillery — under US Major General Robert H. Milroy to find Forrest. They engaged the Confederates near the Wilkinson Pike in a sharp fight that ended in a rout, first of Bate's Floridians, likely as a result of Confederates firing at them — since some were wearing Union uniforms they had acquired on the Franklin battlefield — and then of Palmer's troops. (After the battle Forrest ordered all blues to be dyed gray.)

Hood ordered Bate back to the main army and Forrest to continue to harass the Federals at Murfreesboro. Forrest destroyed railroad tracks and disrupted Union supplies, but he had too few men to threaten Murfreesboro seriously.

Estimated Casualties: 208 US, 214 CS

Areas of the battlefield are within Stones River National Battlefield.

Nashville, Tennessee (TN038), Davidson County, December 15–16, 1864

The Federals had occupied Nashville since late February 1862 when it became the first Confederate state capital to fall under Union control. Because it was one of the South's important industrial centers, the loss was a major one. US Major General Andrew J. Smith, with years of military experience in the West, arrived the first week of December 1864 with his 10,000-man XVI Corps. With his and US General Schofield's commands, US General Thomas had about 55,000 troops and seven miles of trenches to protect them.

Despite his casualties at Franklin, CS General Hood led the Army of Tennessee north, reaching the outskirts of Nashville on December 2. The troops erected fieldworks between Montgomery Hill on their left at the Hillsboro Pike, and Rains Hill on their right, commanding the Nolensville

Pike and the Nashville & Chattanooga Railroad. The Franklin Road and the Tennessee & Alabama Railroad passed through the center of Hood's abbreviated front.

US Lieutenant General Ulysses S. Grant later stated, "I was never so anxious during the war as at that time." Grant, fearing that Hood would get past Thomas and north of the Cumberland River, had repeatedly ordered Thomas to attack Hood. Thomas had not carried out Grant's orders for several reasons: he was still assembling his command, US General Wilson's cavalry needed equipment and horses, and a major storm hit the night of December 8. Freezing rain covered the ground with ice, making it impossible for either army to move. Grant directed US Major General John A. Logan to go to Nashville with orders to replace Thomas if he had not attacked. So great was Grant's anxiety that he went to Washington with the intent of traveling to Nashville himself. Thomas had to wait until the weather improved to launch his attack: his left would hold the Confederates in place, while his reinforced right would swing around the enemy left.

December 15 dawned warm, but a dense fog covered Nashville. Thomas was finally able to launch the massive Federal attack at about 8:00 A.M. with US Major General James Steedman's division, which included two brigades of U.S. Colored Troops. In a heavy diversionary attack, they hit CS General Cheatham's Corps on the Confederate right at Rains Hill and took heavy losses. The Federal heavy artillery roared into action. The 13,500-man IV Corps, commanded by US Brigadier General Thomas J. Wood after US General Stanley was wounded at Franklin, had to delay their attack until Smith, with Wilson's cavalry protecting his flank, was in position to assault the Confederate left. When Wood stormed Montgomery Hill at noon, the Confederates were not there; they had pulled back their main line. The critical fighting was the assault by Smith and Wilson on the redoubts on the Confederate left. CS General Stewart's troops fought off the attack until they were flanked. The fighting continued until nightfall. Hood withdrew his battered troops

two miles to another, shorter line between Shy's Hill (named later to honor a Confederate officer who had died there) and Overton Hill.

On December 16, as soon as the fog burned off, Thomas began to advance toward the new entrenched Confederate line. He sent Wilson's cavalry around his right to the Confederate rear while Wood and Steedman pressured the Confederate right. Schofield feared an attack by Hood and delayed the Federal assault on Shy's Hill until, pressed by Smith's division commander, US Brigadier General John McArthur, Thomas ordered it at about 4:00 P.M. The infantry hit the Confederate front while Wilson's dismounted cavalry, armed with repeating carbines, attacked their rear and took Shy's Hill. Hood's left collapsed, Stewart and Cheatham's Corps disintegrated, and the Federals captured thousands of prisoners. CS General Stephen D. Lee's men repulsed the assault by Wood and Steedman on the Confederate stronghold on Overton Hill. The bravery of the U.S. Colored Troops, who were repulsed with heavy losses, was noted by a Confederate officer in his official report of the battle. The retreat of Cheatham and Stewart and the threat to his line of retreat — the road to Franklin — finally compelled Lee to abandon Overton Hill. Hood's army was beaten and could not be rallied.

Nashville was one of the most decisive and one-sided battles of the Civil War. It destroyed the Army of Tennessee as a fighting force. The remnants of the army, between 15,000 and 20,000 men — some of whom had no shoes — recrossed the Tennessee River on December 26–28 with the Federals in pursuit. Hood retreated to Tupelo and resigned his command on Friday the thirteenth of January 1865.

Estimated Casualties: 3,061 US, 6,500 CS

Sand Creek, Colorado Territory: November 1864

Sand Creek, Colorado (CO001), Kiowa and/or Cheyenne Counties, November 29, 1864

During the Civil War the reasons for killing Indians and restricting them to reservations included protecting the westward expansion of whites and preventing Indians from helping the Confederacy. The Plains tribes, however, were not involved with the Confederacy, as were, for example, the Cherokees.

The fate of the Indians in Colorado became inextricably mixed with the ambitions for high political office and financial gain of John Evans, the territorial governor of Colorado, and of US Colonel John M. Chivington, the hero of the battle of Glorieta Pass, a former Methodist minister, and the commander of the Military District of Colorado. Their personal goals required Colorado statehood, and they saw Indians as a major threat. Their policy was to exterminate Indians, whether they were peaceful or not, and their actions incited previously peaceful tribes to warfare. In April 1864 Chivington issued orders to "kill Cheyennes wherever and whenever found," and by midsummer there was a general uprising. By August the tribes had stopped the transport of all food and supplies to Denver via the Overland Trail.

When the men began hunting to prepare for winter, the Arapaho and Southern Cheyenne chiefs who were still advocating peace became more influential. After a council, Black Kettle (Southern Cheyenne) and Left Hand (Southern Arapaho) met with US Major Edward Wynkoop, the commander at Fort Lyon, released white captives, and went on to Denver with Wynkoop to discuss peace with Evans and Chivington. Since peaceful Cheyennes and Arapahos blocked the objectives of Evans and Chivington, they sent the chiefs back to Fort Lyon with the impression that peace had been advanced while continuing their extermination plans. Following military orders, the chiefs and about 500 Southern Cheyennes and 50 Southern Arapahos camped at Sand Creek.

Chivington rode to Fort Lyon with the 3rd Colorado Cavalry and three companies of the veteran 1st Colorado. Early on November 29 he led the attack against the sleeping families in their Sand Creek camp. Chivington ordered his 700-man column to take no prisoners. Black Kettle stood in front of his tipi, with a United States flag and a white flag hung over it, and assured his people that the soldiers would not harm them. Chivington's force used four howitzers to kill about 150 Cheyennes and Arapahos, including women and children, and mutilated the bodies of the dead. The soldiers burned the camp, including food, shelter, and supplies, and returned to Denver with scalps, which were hung in public places to the cheers of crowds. The survivors, including Black Kettle, headed north across the Plains without adequate food or winter clothing.

News of the massacre outraged the country. US Major General Henry W. Halleck called for Chivington to be court-martialed, but Chivington was mustered out of the army in early January 1865. President Andrew Johnson requested and received the resignation of Governor Evans. Investigations of the massacre described Sand Creek as "the scene of murder and barbarity."

Estimated Casualties: 48 US, 150 Southern Cheyenne and Southern Arapaho

Sherman's March to the Sea: November–December 1864

Griswoldville, Georgia (GA025), Twiggs and Jones Counties, November 22, 1864

After the fall of Atlanta, US Major General William Tecumseh Sherman reacted to CS General John Bell Hood's attacks upon his supply lines to Chattanooga until he decided that such actions were too costly and essentially defensive at a time when the Union needed a bold offensive. Sherman convinced US Lieutenant General Ulysses S. Grant, and Grant convinced President Abraham Lincoln, that US Major General George H. Thomas could handle Hood and that Sherman's forces could support themselves while they marched southeast from Atlanta to the Atlantic, cutting the Confederacy in two. Sherman described it as "a demonstration to the world, foreign and domestic, that we have a power which Davis cannot resist. I can make the march, and make Georgia howl!"

Sherman launched his march to the sea and his total-war philosophy on November 15, having stated his views to the mayor of Atlanta: "War is cruelty, and you cannot refine it; and those who brought war into our country deserve all the curses and maledictions a people can pour out. . . . But, my dear sirs, when peace does come, you may call on me for anything. Then I will share with you the last cracker, and watch with you to shield your homes and families against danger from every quarter." But until then everything of military value — broadly defined — would be destroyed.

While Thomas assembled his forces in Tennessee to stop Hood, Sherman left Atlanta and marched southeast with his 60,000 men in two wings. The Left Wing under US Major General Henry W. Slocum feinted toward Augusta, while the Right Wing, commanded by US Major General Oliver O. Howard, paralleled them to the south, threatening Macon. Their only opposition

was CS Major General Joseph Wheeler's 3,500 cavalrymen.

On November 22 the Federals occupied Milledgeville, the state capital, where the troops held a mock session in the legislature's assembly room. Howard left US Brigadier General Charles C. Walcutt in command of a 1,500-man rear guard about ten miles east of Macon near Griswoldville on the Central Georgia Railroad. They encountered some of Wheeler's cavalrymen, drove them off, and occupied a strong, entrenched position on the Duncan farm on a low hill with open fields to their front. Suddenly a force of about 1,500 Georgia militiamen charged across the open ground, supported by effective artillery fire. After three futile assaults they withdrew. The Federals' victory became a somber one when they saw that most of the dead and wounded were old men and boys. Griswoldville was the only significant infantry battle during Sherman's march to the sea.

Estimated Casualties: 62 US, 650 CS

Buck Head Creek, Georgia (GA026), Jenkins County, November 28, 1864

On November 24 US General Sherman sent his cavalry under US Brigadier General H. Judson Kilpatrick to destroy the railroad between Augusta and Millen, burn the railroad bridge near Briar Creek, and rescue the Federals held prisoner at Camp Lawton. The troopers feigned a dash toward Augusta and tricked CS General Wheeler into concentrating his cavalry there. When he realized his mistake, Wheeler rode off to find the Federals.

On November 26 Wheeler attacked two regiments in their camp and pursued them as they rode to join the rest of the Union force. Wheeler was successful in defending the bridge, and Kilpatrick was able to tear out only a mile of track. When Kilpatrick found out that the Union prisoners had been transferred from Camp Lawton, he headed southwest to rejoin Sherman.

Wheeler surprised the Union forces at their camp at Buck Head Creek on November 28 and almost captured Kilpatrick. As the main cavalry force crossed the creek, one regiment's artillery fire slowed the Confederates and inflicted many casualties. After burning the bridge the Federals headed for the Reynolds Plantation where they stopped Wheeler's force. When the Confederates retired, Kilpatrick rode on to rejoin Sherman at Louisville.

Estimated Casualties: 46 US, 600 CS

Honey Hill, South Carolina (SC010), Jasper County, November 30, 1864

US Major General John G. Foster, the commander of the Department of the South, ordered an expedition from Hilton Head to cut the Charleston & Savannah Railroad to prevent the Confederates from rushing reinforcements by rail to oppose US General Sherman's march. US Major General John P. Hatch set out with 5,500 men on November 28 and steamed up the Broad River in transports. The Federals disembarked at Boyd's Neck and marched inland toward Grahamville on November 30. At Honey Hill, three miles from the railroad depot, they hit 2,000 South Carolina and Georgia Confederate troops and Georgia militia — the survivors of Griswoldville — under CS Major General Gustavus W. Smith. Hatch's troops, including the 54th Massachusetts, made three determined frontal attacks against Smith's entrenched position but were driven back with heavy losses each time. The Federals failed to cut the railroad and retired to their transports.

Estimated Casualties: 746 US, 50 CS

Waynesborough, Georgia (GA027), Burke County, December 4, 1864

On December 4 US General Kilpatrick's cavalry attacked CS General Wheeler's cavalry at Waynesborough, thirty miles southeast of Augusta. At 7:30 A.M. US Colonel Smith D. Atkins's brigade drove Wheeler's advanced guard into their entrenchments south of Waynesborough.

Atkins rode around the Confederate position and hit their rear. When the Federals flanked their left, the Confederates fled north to the town, their second line of defense. Kilpatrick's division attacked the barricades in a frontal assault. In a twenty-minute battle, Union troopers broke Wheeler's line and sent the Confederates retreating to Augusta, well out of Sherman's way.

Estimated Casualties: 190 US, 250 CS

Fort McAllister II, Georgia (GA028), Bryan County, December 13, 1864

During US General Sherman's march the only information Washington received came through Confederate sources. When Sherman's forces approached Savannah on December 9, ahead of schedule, they had marched for nearly a month, covered about three hundred miles, and left a swath of destruction about sixty miles wide. They had ripped up more than two hundred miles of railroad track, stacked the ties, burned the ties with the rails centered on them until the metal became red hot at the midpoint of the rails, and then wrapped the rails around trees, creating "Sherman's Neckties."

On December 12 Sherman ordered US Brigadier General William B. Hazen's division to capture Fort McAllister, on a bluff on the south bank of the Ogeechee River, south of Savannah and open a supply line to the fleet. His need for supplies would increase the longer his large army remained immobile. If the Confederates' heavy seacoast artillery, which had a longer range than Sherman's field artillery, could hold the Federals off until they needed supplies, Sherman might have to move away from Savannah.

The fort was defended by 230 Confederates under CS Major George W. Anderson. On December 13, one hour before dusk, 3,500 of Hazen's troops stormed through the obstructions and over the barricades. Sharpshooters picked off the Confederate cannoneers, and the infantry captured Fort McAllister in less than fifteen minutes.

For the first time since leaving Atlanta, Sherman was in direct contact with the North. While he called for heavy artillery bombardment and prepared to besiege Savannah, US Major General George H. Thomas defeated CS General John Bell Hood at Nashville.

Savannah was defended by 10,000 men under CS Lieutenant General William J. Hardee. Sherman demanded the city's surrender on December 17, and Hardee refused. Sherman then began to tighten the siege lines and threaten the last land route out of the city. Hardee's force escaped to South Carolina over a floating planked span during the night of December 20, the fourth anniversary of South Carolina's secession. The Federals occupied Savannah on the twenty-first.

Sherman wired President Lincoln, "I beg to present you, as a Christmas gift, the city of Savannah, with 150 heavy guns and plenty of ammunition; also about 25,000 bales of cotton."

Estimated Casualties: 134 US, 230 CS

Fort McAllister State Historic Park, nine miles east of Richmond Hill off I-95 at Exit 15, includes five acres of the battlefield.

North Carolina: December 1864– February 1865

Fort Fisher I, North Carolina (NC014), New Hanover County, December 7–27, 1864

Wilmington, North Carolina, was the only remaining port through which blockade runners could supply CS General Robert E. Lee's army. To control this vital port the United States had to capture Fort Fisher, at the mouth of the Cape Fear River. The fort was a huge L-shaped earthen fortification more than two thousand yards long on the sea side, with a short northern front to protect it from a land attack. It had forty-seven guns and an 800-man garrison commanded by CS Colonel William Lamb which included North Carolina militia and Junior Reserves, ages sixteen to eighteen. The parapets were constructed of earth and sand, which absorbed artillery fire.

US Major General Benjamin F. Butler's political influence had led to his promotion so that he was second in seniority in the East only to US Lieutenant General Ulysses S. Grant. Butler saw the port as an opportunity for a decisive victory and launched a 6,500-man joint amphibious expedition with USN Rear Admiral David D. Porter, who despised him. Butler's opinion of Porter was similar. Butler's plan was to level the fort by creating a floating bomb out of a derelict ship loaded with two hundred tons of gunpowder. However, when the Federals set off the charge at 1:18 A.M. on December 24, the old ship was six hundred yards offshore, so the explosion did no damage. The fleet bombarded the fort, in preparation for the army's attack, but dismounted only a few guns.

On Christmas morning Butler landed 3,000 men, commanded by US Major General Godfrey Weitzel, through a high surf north of the fort. They approached to within fifty yards of the fort. Butler then enraged Porter by calling off the attack. As the troops boarded their transports and departed for Hampton Roads, CS Major General

Robert F. Hoke's troops arrived at Wilmington to bolster the Confederate defenses.

Estimated Casualties: 320 total

Fort Fisher, a state historic site on Route 421 near Kure Beach twenty miles south of Wilmington, includes about sixty acres of the historic battlefield.

Fort Fisher II, North Carolina (NC015), New Hanover County, January 13–15, 1865

President Lincoln's re-election diminished the political need to keep US General Butler in command, and the Fort Fisher fiasco simplified replacing him on the next mission with US Brigadier General Alfred H. Terry, an able young officer. Unlike Butler, Terry worked well with USN Admiral Porter, and the two men devised a plan to capture the fort. Terry's 8,000-man force included men from the XXIV Corps and the Third Division of the XXV Corps, U.S. Colored Troops. Porter's fifty-nine-vessel naval force was the United States' largest and strongest.

   Their combined forces arrived off Fort Fisher on January 12, and the infantry landed unopposed the next day. They dug trenches across the fort's land front, cutting off the garrison from relief by CS General Hoke's Division at Wilmington. On January 14 Porter's fleet delivered one of the most intense and concentrated bombardments of the war, inflicting about 300 casualties on the fort's garrison of 1,500 men.

   On January 15 the Confederates landed 250 reinforcements by boat during the naval bombardment. At 3:00 P.M. 1,500 marines and sailors under USN Lieutenant Commander K. Randolph Breese landed from the northeast in small boats and attacked at the L angle of the fort. They charged down the open beach, but the small-

arms, grape, and canister fire drove them back. They did, however, succeed in distracting the Confederates while 3,300 infantrymen in US Colonel Newton M. Curtis's brigade in US Brigadier General Adelbert Ames's division attacked the land side. The Federals swept down the road fronting the Cape Fear River, but CS Colonel Lamb counterattacked and drove them back in fierce hand-to-hand fighting. The navy opened fire again. The infantry broke into the fort and took it section by section from the determined Confederate defenders.

   CS General Braxton Bragg, the commander of the Department of North Carolina, refused to commit Hoke's Division, and the fort fell. Lamb was wounded in the final assault and taken prisoner along with the garrison and other Confederate troops on the peninsula. The coordinated assault by the U.S. Army and Navy was a success. It opened the way to Wilmington, closed the South's last Atlantic seaport, and completed the 1861 Anaconda Plan to cut the Confederacy off from world markets. Alexander Stevens, the vice president of the Confederacy, declared that the fall was "one of the greatest disasters that had befallen our cause."

Estimated Casualties: 1,059 US, 400–500 (plus 2,083 prisoners) CS

Fort Fisher, a state historic site on Route 421 near Kure Beach twenty miles south of Wilmington, includes about sixty acres of the historic battlefield.

Wilmington, North Carolina (NC016), New Hanover County, February 12–22, 1865

The port of Wilmington, twenty-eight miles up the Cape Fear River, was effectively closed after the fall of Fort Fisher. CS General Bragg withdrew his troops from the batteries at the mouth of the river. The Confederates on the west side of the river retreated to a line anchored at Fort Anderson, while CS General Hoke's 6,600 men on the east side held Sugar Loaf, a dune that they shaped for their defense and extended with earthworks from the river to the ocean. US Major General John M. Schofield had arrived at Fort Fisher from Tennessee in early February with the Second and Third Divisions of his XXIII Corps. His command included these two divisions under US Major General Jacob D. Cox, and US General Terry's force, a total of 12,000 infantrymen. Schofield's orders were to capture Wilmington. His plan was to march up the coast with two divisions, lay a pontoon bridge over Masonboro Sound, and cross behind the Confederate lines. However, the boggy terrain forced Schofield to cancel this movement on the fourteenth.

On February 16 Schofield ferried 8,000 men commanded by Cox to the west side of the Cape Fear River at Smithville. While USN Admiral Porter's fleet fired on Fort Anderson, silencing all twelve guns, Cox swung his troops to the west to envelop the Confederate works. CS Brigadier General Johnson Hagood evacuated Fort Anderson on the night of February 18–19 and formed a new defensive line eight miles to the north behind Town Creek east of the Cape Fear River. Hoke retreated to a position opposite the mouth of Town Creek. Cox relentlessly pressed the Confederates, forcing them to abandon their line on the nineteenth.

By the next day the Federals were within artillery range of Wilmington and were closing in on the city from the south. Porter's gunboats steamed up to Fort Strong, tightening the Federal noose around Wilmington. CS General Bragg saw that resistance was futile. During the night of February 21–22 the Confederates burned cotton, tobacco, and government stores, and evacuated Wilmington. Terry's column marched into the city from the south and took control of the Confederacy's last major port.

Estimated Casualties: 1,150 total

Fort Anderson is in the Brunswick Town State Historic Site at Winnabow, seventeen miles south of Wilmington off Route 133.

Second Inaugural Address

March 4, 1865

Abraham Lincoln

○

At this second appearing to take the oath of the presidential office, there is less occasion for an extended address than there was at the first. Then a statement, somewhat in detail, of a course to be pursued, seemed fitting and proper. Now, at the expiration of four years, during which public declarations have been constantly called forth on every point and phase of the great contest which still absorbs the attention, and engrosses the energies of the nation, little that is new could be presented. The progress of our arms, upon which all else chiefly depends, is as well known to the public as to myself; and it is, I trust, reasonably satisfactory and encouraging to all. With high hope for the future, no prediction in regard to it is ventured.

On the occasion corresponding to this four years ago, all thoughts were anxiously directed to an impending civil-war. All dreaded it — all sought to avert it. While the inaugeral address was being delivered from this place, devoted altogether to *saving* the Union without war, insurgent agents were in the city seeking to *destroy* it without war — seeking to dissolve the Union, and divide effects, by negotiation. Both parties deprecated war; but one of them would *make* war rather than let the nation survive; and the other would *accept* war rather than let it perish. And the war came.

One eighth of the whole population were colored slaves, not distributed generally over the Union, but localized in the Southern part of it.

These slaves constituted a peculiar and powerful interest. All knew that this interest was, somehow, the cause of the war. To strengthen, perpetuate, and extend this interest was the object for which the insurgents would rend the Union, even by war; while the government claimed no right to do more than to restrict the territorial enlargement of it. Neither party expected for the war, the magnitude, or the duration, which it has already attained. Neither anticipated that the *cause* of the conflict might cease with, or even before, the conflict itself should cease. Each looked for an easier triumph, and a result less fundamental and astounding. Both read the same Bible, and pray to the same God; and each invokes His aid against the other. It may seem strange that any men should dare to ask a just God's assistance in wringing their bread from the sweat of other men's faces; but let us judge not that we be not judged. The prayers of both could not be answered; that of neither has been answered fully. The Almighty has His own purposes. "Woe unto the world because of offences! for it must needs be that offences come; but woe to that man by whom the offence cometh!" If we shall suppose that American Slavery is one of those offences which, in the providence of God, must needs come, but which, having continued through His appointed time, He now wills to remove, and that He gives to both North and South, this terrible war, as the woe due to those by whom the offence came, shall we discern therein any departure from those divine attributes which the believers in a Living God always ascribe to Him? Fondly do we hope — fervently do we pray — that this mighty scourge of war may speedily pass away. Yet, if God wills that it continue, until all the wealth piled by the bond-man's two hundred and fifty years of unrequited toil shall be sunk, and until every drop of blood drawn with the lash, shall be paid by another drawn with the sword, as was said three thousand years ago, so still it must

be said "the judgments of the Lord, are true and righteous altogether."

With malice toward none; with charity for all; with firmness in the right, as God gives us to see the right, let us strive on to finish the work we are in; to bind up the nation's wounds; to care for him who shall have borne the battle, and for his widow and his orphan — to do all which may achieve and cherish a just, and lasting peace, among ourselves, and with all nations.

Sherman's Carolina Campaign: February–March 1865

Rivers Bridge, South Carolina (SC011), Bamberg County, February 2–3, 1865

After US Major General William Tecumseh Sherman captured Savannah, US Lieutenant General Ulysses S. Grant ordered him to embark his army on ships for City Point to reinforce the armies of the Potomac and the James. Sherman disagreed, and the capture of Fort Fisher convinced Grant that Sherman should march north through the Carolinas, destroying everything of military value on the way. Sherman specifically targeted South Carolina, the first state to secede.

In late January Sherman marched toward Columbia. His 60,000 men included US Major General Oliver O. Howard's Army of the Tennessee and US Major General Henry W. Slocum's force, the XIV and XX Corps, detached from US Major General George H. Thomas and later formally designated as the Army of Georgia. To oppose Sherman, CS General P. G. T. Beauregard, the

commander of the Military Division of the West, could muster only militia, remnants of the Army of Tennessee slowly assembling from Mississippi, CS Major General Wade Hampton's cavalry division, CS General Braxton Bragg's troops from Wilmington, and CS Lieutenant General William J. Hardee's two divisions after they evacuated Charleston.

Heavy rains throughout January slowed the Federals' preparations, but by February 1 they had constructed corduroy roads and bridges and were advancing north in two columns. Howard was on the right and Slocum on the left. Howard's vanguard pushed the Confederates across the mile-wide Salkehatchie River and prevented them from burning the only bridge. CS Major General Lafayette McLaws positioned his artillery to fire directly down on Rivers Bridge. US Major General Joseph A. Mower, commanding a division in US Major General Francis P. Blair, Jr.'s XVII Corps, pushed his 2nd Brigade to rush the Confederate works, but enemy artillery repulsed the attack. The following day Mower's troops built bridges across the swamp to bypass the Confederate roadblock while other columns moved on the Confederate flanks and rear. Two Union brigades assaulted McLaws's right on February 3, forcing him to retreat toward Branchville.

Estimated Casualties: 92 US, 170 CS

Rivers Bridge State Park, fifteen miles east of Allendale near State Route 641, includes areas of the historic battlefield.

Wyse Fork, North Carolina (NC017), Lenoir County, March 7–10, 1865

By February 17 US General Sherman had isolated Charleston, and CS General Hardee evacuated it on February 17–18 after the 567-day siege. Sherman sent out foragers, known as "bummers," in all directions to seize supplies, destroy property, and sever the railroad. When the Federals occupied Columbia, the state capital, areas of it were set on fire, by Confederates, who burned cotton and supplies to prevent their capture, as well as by vengeful Federals. Sherman ordered his troops to fight the fires throughout the night. Sherman then headed northeast toward Goldsboro via Fayetteville, with his cavalry under US Brigadier General H. Judson Kilpatrick riding on the left, feinting toward Charlotte. On March 3 the Federals captured Cheraw and quantities of supplies and valuables shipped there for safekeeping by Charlestonians.

Sherman's army crossed into North Carolina on March 8 virtually unopposed. In cooperation with Sherman's advance through the Carolinas, US Major General Alfred H. Terry's column of US Major General John M. Schofield's command had started moving inland from Wilmington in late February. Schofield ordered US Major General Jacob D. Cox — whom he had sent to New Bern on February 23 — and his 13,000-man Provisional Corps to march from New Bern up the Neuse River, repair the railroad supply line to the port, and meet Sherman at Goldsboro.

On March 7 Cox advanced to Wyse Fork (then Wise's Forks), where the Upper Trent Road intersected with the Dover Road, and deployed two divisions. CS General Bragg's 10,000 men were entrenched behind Southwest Creek, three miles east of Kinston. The next day Bragg ordered CS Major General Robert F. Hoke to cross the creek and hit the Federal left flank. Hoke threw back the brigade of US Colonel Charles L. Upham. CS Major General Daniel Harvey Hill attacked with his division at noon but retired when Federal cavalry threatened their line of retreat to the creek. The Confederates captured about 1,000 Federals that day but did not damage Cox's main force. That night Cox dug in and received reinforcements. The two sides engaged in minor skirmishing on the ninth.

On March 10 Hoke maneuvered around the Federals' left and attacked at 11:30 A.M. Hill hit the center of the U.S. line and captured part of it. The 66th North Carolina Regiment, organized in Kinston, fought under heavy fire to within fifty yards of the Union position. The Federals repulsed them, and they retreated across the Neuse River to Kinston. The Federals occupied the town four days later, but the Confederates had slowed their advance.

Among the Federal forces fighting at Wyse Fork were the Iroquois soldiers in the 132nd New York State Volunteer Infantry. During the war they were commended twice in the official records for meritorious service and were among the approximately 20,000 American Indians who fought for the United States and the Confederacy.

Estimated Casualties: 1,300 US, 1,500 CS

Monroe's Cross Roads, North Carolina (NC018), Hoke County, March 10, 1865

On March 6 US General Kilpatrick's cavalry division, screening the left flank of the Union advance, crossed into North Carolina. Kilpatrick learned from prisoners that CS Lieutenant General Wade Hampton's 4,000 cavalrymen were to his rear, retreating toward Fayetteville. Kilpatrick tried to trap Hampton by blocking the three roads through the area, but Hampton learned of the plan from a prisoner.

On March 10 CS Major General Matthew C. Butler, in command of 1,000 troopers, hit US Colonel George E. Spencer's brigade camped at Monroe's Cross Roads. Butler's surprise attack at dawn caught the Federals sleeping. Most of them fled on foot and rallied in the swamp, five hundred yards to the south. Kilpatrick barely escaped, and the Confederates captured the camp, including dozens of wagons and artillery. CS Major General Joseph Wheeler's 3,000 cavalrymen were unable to attack through the swamp to the west and south of the Federal camp. The Federals counterattacked and drove Butler out of the camp. Union reinforcements from the rest of Kilpatrick's division arrived, and the Confederates retreated. Hampton continued on to Fayetteville.

Estimated Casualties: 183 US, 86 CS

The battlefield is within Fort Bragg Military Reservation.

Averasboro, North Carolina (NC019), Harnett and Cumberland Counties, March 16, 1865

US General Sherman reached Fayetteville on March 11, rested his army, destroyed the large arsenal, reopened communications with the outside world, and sent to Wilmington the thousands of refugees who had been traveling with the army. Sherman's forces began crossing the Cape Fear River on March 13. Sherman sent his Right Wing, commanded by US General Howard, toward Goldsboro to link up with US General Schofield's columns that were advancing: US General Cox's from New Bern (later designated the XXIII

Corps), and US General Terry's from Wilmington (later designated the X Corps). The Left Wing under US General Slocum continued toward Averasboro on the east bank of the Cape Fear River about fifteen miles north of Fayetteville.

CS General Joseph E. Johnston, commander of the Confederate forces in the Carolinas, assembled his army at Smithfield, between Goldsboro and Raleigh, to strike the Union columns before they united. He ordered CS General Hardee's Corps of 6,000 men to block the left wing of Slocum's XX Corps at Averasboro. Hardee deployed astride the Raleigh Road with the Black River to his left and the Cape Fear River on his right. He built three defensive lines: one brigade of CS Brigadier General William B. Taliaferro's Division occupied the first line, while the rest of the division occupied the second line two hundred yards to the rear; CS General McLaws's Division constructed a third line six hundred yards behind that line.

On March 15 US General Kilpatrick's cavalry came up against the first Confederate line. After scouting the enemy defenses, Kilpatrick withdrew and called for infantry support. He attacked the next day at 6:00 A.M. Four hours later Taliaferro had outfought him and threatened his right. Kilpatrick was saved by the arrival of the XX Corps. Two brigades struck Hardee's front while a third brigade under US Colonel Henry Case maneuvered through the swamp to hit the Confederate right. Case's attack forced the Confederates to fall back to their second line.

Two divisions of the XX Corps advanced on Taliaferro's Division as the XIV Corps began to come up, forcing the Confederates to retreat to McLaws's position farther north, centered on the Raleigh Road. This line held all afternoon against successive Union attacks. At 8:00 P.M. Hardee retreated to Elevation after stopping Slocum's march for nearly two days.

Estimated Casualties: 682 US, 865 CS

Bentonville, North Carolina (NC020), Johnston County, March 19–21, 1865

John G. Barrett

On March 18 just before dawn the Confederate chief of cavalry, CS Lieutenant General Wade Hampton, notified CS General Joseph E. Johnston that the Union army was marching on Goldsboro, not Raleigh, and that US Major General William Tecumseh Sherman's Right Wing was approximately half a day's march in advance of the Left Wing. Johnston saw an opportunity to crush one of the Union columns while it was separated from the other. Johnston ordered his troops at Smithfield and Elevation to Bentonville, a village approximately twenty miles west of Goldsboro. CS General Braxton Bragg was at Smithfield with CS Major General Robert F. Hoke's Division of North Carolinians, as well as remnants of the once-proud Army of Tennessee, the survivors of Franklin and Nashville, now under the command of CS Lieutenant General Alexander P. Stewart. CS Lieutenant General William J. Hardee was encamped at Elevation with the divisions of CS Major General Lafayette McLaws and CS Brigadier General W. B. Taliaferro. When Bragg and Stewart reached Bentonville on the eighteenth, Hardee was still six miles away.

Johnston's combat strength was about 21,000, considerably fewer than the 45,000 Sherman thought opposed him. This paucity in manpower was offset, at least in part, by the large number of able Confederate commanders present. Besides Johnston and Bragg, who were full generals, three officers — Hampton, Hardee, and Stewart — carried the rank of lieutenant general. Also on the field were many seasoned officers of lesser rank, including Major Generals Daniel Harvey Hill, Joseph Wheeler, Robert F. Hoke, Lafayette McLaws, and William W. Loring. Bentonville was singular among Civil War battles for having so few men led in combat by so many veteran officers of high rank.

During the evening of the eighteenth, Hampton informed Johnston that Union troops — US Major General Henry W. Slocum's column, with the XIV

Corps in the lead, US Major General Jefferson C. Davis commanding — were moving down the Goldsboro Road. He recommended a surprise attack at the eastern end of the Cole plantation, about two miles south of Bentonville near the Goldsboro Road. The land there was marshy and covered with dense thickets of blackjack pine.

Sunday morning, March 19, dawned clear and beautiful, and the unsuspecting Union soldiers expected a day of peace and quiet. They thought little of the fact that the Confederate cavalry was giving ground grudgingly and even revived an expression of the Atlanta campaign, "They don't drive worth a damn." Slocum, who had no idea that Johnston's entire army was gathering only a few miles down the road, sent a dispatch to Sherman, who was with US Major General Oliver O. Howard, that only Confederate horsemen and a few pieces of artillery were in his front. Sherman did not anticipate an attack because he could not imagine that Johnston would risk a fight with the Neuse River in his rear.

The deployment of the Confederate troops was slow because only one road led through the dense woods and thickets between Bentonville and the battlefield. First, Hoke's Division was placed on the Confederate left with its line crossing the Goldsboro Road almost at right angles. Stewart's Army of Tennessee was to the right of Hoke, with its right strongly thrown forward to conform to the edge of an open field. The center of Johnston's position was at a corner of the Cole plantation approximately a mile north of the Goldsboro Road. The two wings went forward from the center, the left blocking the advance of US Brigadier General W. P. Carlin's division of the XIV Corps. The right was partially hidden in a thicket, ready to stop any flanking movements by the enemy. However, Hardee, who was to hold the ground between Hoke and Stewart, had not reached the field when the two commands went into position, so Johnston had to change the deposition of his troops. Hardee did not arrive until around 2:45 P.M., long after Hoke's artillery had opened fire on Carlin's advance troops, the brigades of US Brigadier Generals Harrison C. Hobart and George P. Buell, as they approached the Cole house.

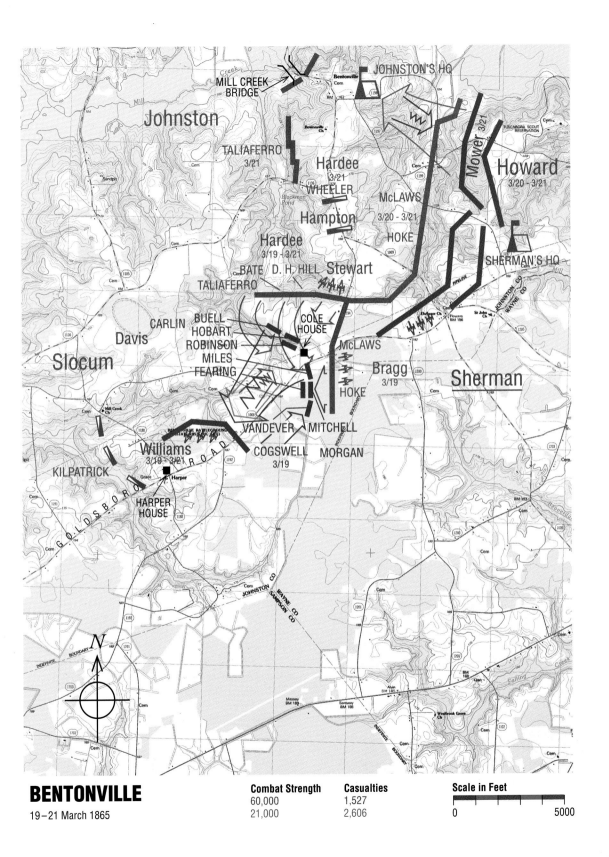

JOHNSTON'S HQ

MILL CREEK
BRIDGE

Johnston

TALIAFERRO
3/21

Hardee
3/21

WHEELER

Hampton

Hardee
3/19 - 3/21

BATE D. H. HILL Stewart

TALIAFERRO

CARLIN
BUELL
HOBART
ROBINSON
MILES
FEARING

Davis

Slocum

COLE
HOUSE

McLAWS

HOKE

VANDEVER MITCHELL

Williams
3/19 - 3/21

COGSWELL MORGAN
3/19

KILPATRICK

HARPER
HOUSE

Mower 3/21

Howard
3/20 - 3/21

McLAWS
3/20 - 3/21

HOKE

SHERMAN'S HQ

Bragg
3/19

Sherman

GOLDSBORO ROAD

N

BENTONVILLE

19–21 March 1865

Combat Strength	Casualties
60,000	1,527
21,000	2,606

Scale in Feet

0   5000

As the morning advanced, Slocum, still convinced that he faced only cavalry, sent word to Sherman that help was not needed. At the same time he ordered a general advance. The Confederate right responded fiercely to the assault, and in the words of a Union officer, "I tell you it was a tight place . . . [we] stood as long as man could stand . . . [then] we run like the duce." Carlin's men fell back to the vicinity of the Cole house, where they deployed carelessly into a weak defensive line. Soon they were joined by US Brigadier General James S. Robinson's brigade of the XX Corps. By this time US Brigadier General James D. Morgan's division of the XIV Corps and US Lieutenant Colonel David Miles's brigade of Carlin's division had moved into position south of the Goldsboro Road opposite Hoke and on Carlin's right. Log breastworks, thrown up in great haste by Morgan's brigade commanders, US Brigadier Generals John G. Mitchell and William Vandever, and US Colonel Benjamin D. Fearing, contributed to the Union success late in the day when the Confederates went on the offensive. One Federal officer said that those logs "saved Sherman's reputation." Slocum realized that he was in trouble at 1:30 P.M., called for reinforcements, and went on the defensive.

At about 3:00 P.M. Johnston ordered his right wing under Hardee to take the offensive. Hardee, Stewart, and Hill led the charge on horseback "across an open field . . . with colors flying and line of battle in . . . perfect order. . . . It was gallantly done but for those watching from Hoke's trenches it was . . . painful to see how close their battle flags were together, regiments being scarcely larger than companies and the division not much larger than a regiment should be." The Union left was crushed by this stirring, well-executed move and driven back in confusion upon the XX Corps under US Brigadier General Alpheus S. Williams, a mile to the rear.

The rout of Carlin's troops had exposed the Union right, enabling Hill to break through and strike Morgan's division in the rear while Hoke attacked from the front. The result was the bitterest fighting of the day, the crucial period of the battle. Veterans of the Army of Northern Virginia

thought "it was the hottest infantry fight they had been in except Cold Harbor." Only the timely arrival of US Brigadier General William Cogswell's brigade of the XX Corps saved Morgan from defeat. This was the turning point of the battle of Bentonville.

Later that afternoon, between 5:00 P.M. and sundown, McLaws's Division and the exhausted troops of Taliaferro and CS Major General William B. Bate tried five times without success to carry the formidable Union left. As dusk faded into darkness, the weary combatants gradually ceased their firing. After burying their dead, the Confederate soldiers withdrew to the position they had occupied earlier in the day. The Union wounded were taken to the home of John and Amy Harper, which had been converted into a field hospital.

The next morning Johnston, anticipating the arrival of Sherman's Right Wing, bent his left back to form a bridgehead, with the only bridge across Mill Creek to his rear. This put the Confederate line, in the shape of a large irregular V, entirely north of the Goldsboro Road.

On the late afternoon of March 20, Sherman's army of 60,000 was again united. Howard's troops, the last to arrive on the battlefield, dug in on the right. The Union left was held by the XIV and XX Corps. There was heavy skirmishing throughout the second day, which occasionally erupted into violent combat, some of it involving the three regiments of North Carolina Junior Reserves in Hoke's command.

On the twenty-first the only important action occurred on the Union right when US Major General Joseph A. Mower, without consulting his superiors, pushed two brigades around the Confederate left flank to within a mile of the Mill Creek bridge. Among the Confederate units helping to blunt this offensive was the skeletal 8th Texas Cavalry under Hardee's immediate command. In a gallant charge by the cavalrymen against the Union left, Hardee's sixteen-year-old son, Willie, was mortally wounded. A few hours earlier the father had reluctantly given his teenage son permission to join the Texans.

That night Johnston crossed Mill Creek and

moved on Smithfield, beginning a withdrawal that could have "but one end." Sherman, after burying the dead and removing the wounded, put his troops in motion for Goldsboro rather than in pursuit of his long-time antagonist.

Bentonville was a major contest, involving about 80,000 troops, and was the climax of Sherman's highly successful Carolinas campaign. At Goldsboro Sherman joined his army with US Major General John M. Schofield's two columns — US Major General Alfred H. Terry's and US Major General Jacob D. Cox's — and gained rail connections to the large supply bases on the North Carolina coast. Sherman's campaign had laid waste a forty-five-mile-wide swath of countryside from Savannah to Goldsboro. When morale among his troops began to wane badly with the rumors of Richmond's fall, Johnston directed that all executions for desertion be suspended. The time was almost at hand to end all killing.

Estimated Casualties: 1,527 US, 2,606 CS

Bentonville Battleground State Historic Site, west of Goldsboro near Route 1008 near Newton Grove, forty-five miles southeast of Raleigh, includes 130 acres of the historic battlefield.

When I learned that Sherman's army was marching through the Salk swamps, making its own corduroy roads at the rate of a dozen miles a day, I made up my mind that there had been no such army in existence since the days of Julius Caesar.

— General Joseph E. Johnston

No one ever has and may not agree with me as to the very great importance of the march north from Savannah. The march to the sea seems to have captured everybody, whereas it was child's play compared with the other.

— Major General William Tecumseh Sherman

Appomattox Campaign: March–April 1865

Lewis's Farm, Virginia (VA085), Dinwiddie County, March 29, 1865

On March 27 President Abraham Lincoln, who had come from Washington to visit the army, met on the *River Queen*, docked at City Point, with US Lieutenant General Ulysses S. Grant, US Major General William T. Sherman, and USN Rear Admiral David D. Porter. They discussed both war and peace. Sherman later recalled:

> Both General Grant and myself supposed that one or the other of us would have to fight one more bloody battle, and that it would be the *last*. Mr. Lincoln exclaimed, more than once, that there had been blood enough shed, and asked us if another battle could not be avoided. I remember well to have said that we could not control that event; that this necessarily rested with our enemy; . . . [President Lincoln] distinctly authorized me to assure Governor Vance and the people of North Carolina that, as soon as the rebel armies laid down their arms, and resumed their civil pursuits, they would at once be guaranteed all their rights as citizens of a common country; . . . I never saw him again. Of all the men I ever met, he seemed to possess more of the elements of greatness, combined with goodness, than any other.

US Major General Philip H. Sheridan arrived near City Point after his raid through central Virginia. Grant launched his spring offensive on March 29 and sent Sheridan with three cavalry divisions to turn the right flank of CS General Robert E. Lee's Petersburg defenses. Sheridan was to attack Lee if he moved out of his fortifications. If he did not, the cavalry commander was to wreck the Richmond & Danville Railroad and the South Side Railroad, Lee's last supply lines into Petersburg and Richmond. As the cavalrymen rode toward Dinwiddie Court House, they were supported by two infantry corps: the V Corps, under US Major General Gouverneur K. Warren, and the II Corps, under US Major General Andrew A. Humphreys.

The 17,000-man V Corps crossed Rowanty Creek on the Vaughan Road in the rain on March 29 and turned north on the Quaker Road, with US Brigadier General Joshua L. Chamberlain's brigade in the vanguard. Forcing passage across Gravelly Run, Chamberlain approached the fields of the Lewis farm. The brigades of CS Brigadier Generals Henry A. Wise and William H. Wallace were waiting on the other side, entrenched along the tree line. CS Lieutenant General Richard H. Anderson ordered them forward to crush Chamberlain before he could be reinforced. The Confederate attack pushed back the Federal left, but Chamberlain, although wounded, rallied his troops with the help of a four-gun battery. Reinforced, Chamberlain counterattacked and captured the enemy's earthworks. The Confederates retreated to White Oak Road where they had prepared a strong line of trenches.

Estimated Casualties: 381 US, 371 CS

Dinwiddie Court House, Virginia (VA086), Dinwiddie County, March 31, 1865

While US General Warren's V Corps battled the Confederates at the Lewis farm, US General Sheridan's 9,000 cavalrymen reached Dinwiddie Court House on muddy roads that seemed "almost bottomless." On the morning of March 30, Sheridan reconnoitered northwest toward the crossroads of Five Forks six miles away and met stubborn resistance from CS Major General Fitzhugh Lee's cavalry division. During the evening Fitzhugh Lee was reinforced by the rest of the Confederate cavalry under CS Major Generals William H. Fitzhugh "Rooney" Lee and Thomas L. Rosser and by five infantry brigades commanded by CS Major General George A. Pickett. Their orders were to drive Sheridan from the Boydton Plank Road.

On March 31 Pickett's combined force attacked to the east at 2:00 P.M. and forced a crossing over Chamberlain's Bed. The attack split Sheridan's troopers, driving some eastward toward the Boydton Plank Road and others to the south. The

Confederates then wheeled to the south and pushed Sheridan into Dinwiddie Court House. Sheridan admitted that Pickett had placed him in a "critical situation," but he rallied his men a mile north of the town. Pickett withdrew at 5:00 A.M. the next morning and entrenched at Five Forks.

Estimated Casualties: 354 US, 760 CS

White Oak Road, Virginia (VA087), Dinwiddie County, March 31, 1865

David W. Lowe

Through a steady, chilling rain on March 30, US Major General Gouverneur K. Warren's V Corps pressed north on the Quaker Road to its intersection with Boydton Plank Road. Across an open field loomed the main Confederate defense line, a formidable entrenchment paralleling White Oak Road, manned by CS Lieutenant General Richard H. Anderson's small corps. The II Corps, under US Major General Andrew A. Humphreys, worked through the woods on Warren's right, pressing Confederate skirmishers back to Hatcher's Run.

From his headquarters at Mrs. Butler's house, Warren dispatched US Brigadier General Romeyn B. Ayres to locate the Confederate right flank. Following a muddy farm road across a swampy branch of Gravelly Run and through the woods, Ayres came into an open field from which he could see White Oak Road and a column of infantry — CS Major General George E. Pickett's soldiers — trudging along it toward Five Forks just four miles away.

After Ayres's reconnaissance Warren reported to headquarters that he could throw his corps across White Oak Road to prevent reinforcements from reaching Five Forks. US Lieutenant General Ulysses S. Grant and US Major General George G. Meade approved Warren's plan and ordered the II Corps to cooperate. Before daylight on March 31 US Brigadier General Nelson A. Miles's division of the II Corps extended its left to cover the Quaker–Boydton Plank fork at the Stroud farm, freeing US Brigadier General Charles Griffin's V Corps division to join Warren's attack. While preparations were under way, an order from Meade arrived suspending operations for the day because of nearly impassable roads.

CS General Robert E. Lee had no intention of suspending operations. Confident that Pickett's force could handle US Major General Philip H. Sheridan's cavalry at Dinwiddie Court House, he rode out that morning to direct personally a thrust against Warren's flank. After thinning out his entrenchments, he had three brigades at hand — CS Brigadier Generals Samuel McGowan's, Archibald Gracie's (commanded by CS Colonel Martin L. Stansel), and Eppa Hunton's, numbering about 3,800 men. An attack with so few was a desperate gamble, but Lee's veterans had triumphed before against similar odds. Lee's strike force formed in the woods north of White Oak Road, fronting the W. Dabney and B. Butler fields.

When the rainfall slackened at about midmorning, Meade sent word for Warren to push his earlier proposal to occupy White Oak Road. Warren dispatched Ayres and his 4,000-man division back up the barely passable farm road to deploy in the open ground south of B. Butler's fields. US Brigadier General Samuel W. Crawford's division followed and massed near the Holliday house about five hundred yards in the rear of Ayres. Griffin's division remained east of the swampy ravine, with the artillery near Warren's headquarters at Mrs. Butler's house. At about 11:00 A.M., just as Ayres started his battle line forward, a long line of Confederate infantrymen stepped out of the woods, leveled their rifle-muskets, and delivered a volley that staggered the Federals. Order in Ayres's division collapsed from the shock, and a blue-clad rabble streamed back through Crawford's position at the Holliday house. Vainly, Crawford tried to redeploy his columns but found his own men confused and infected by the panic. Here and there isolated Federal units held their ground only to find themselves unsupported and outflanked by the determined attackers. Within an hour Lee's three brigades had routed two Federal divisions and herded them back on Griffin's reserve division like so many sheep.

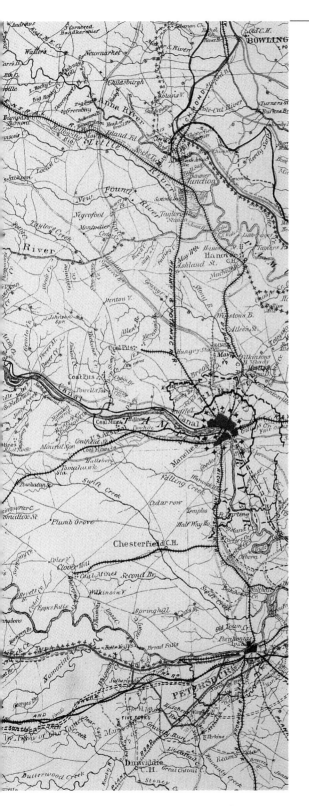

Thus far Lee's gamble had paid off. Lee then ordered CS Brigadier General Henry A. Wise's Brigade out of the White Oak Road trenches to fill the gap left by the precipitous advance, but his weakness in numbers became painfully apparent. The thin gray line paused to reform and began scratching a rifle trench across the Holliday fields, anticipating a counterattack.

Warren and Griffin worked feverishly to reform Ayres's and Crawford's men as they clambered out of the swamp. Warren rode up to US Brigadier General Joshua Lawrence Chamberlain's brigade of Griffin's division waiting in line of battle, and demanded, "General Chamberlain, will you save the honor of the Fifth Corps?" On command, Chamberlain's battle line waded down into the waist-deep water of the ravine with rifle-muskets and cartridge boxes held high, closely followed by US Colonel Edgar M. Gregory's and US Brigadier General Joseph J. Bartlett's brigades. From their shallow trench in the Holliday fields, the Confederates repulsed three assaults.

At about 1:00 P.M. Humphreys's II Corps came into action, demonstrating against the Confederate entrenchments at Burgess Mill and farther east at the Crow house redoubt. These attacks prevented Lee from detaching more reinforcements for his beleaguered right. When Miles's division forced Wise's Brigade back into the White Oak Road trenches, taking more than 200 prisoners, the Confederate line unraveled. Ayres's and Crawford's divisions reformed and returned to the front, adding weight to the Federal counterattacks. For several hours the Confederates resisted, but by late afternoon the V Corps had driven them back across White Oak Road. From astride his mount Lee watched somberly as his

Left: A portion of the map "Central Virginia showing Lieut. Gen'l. U.S. Grant's Campaign and Marches of the Armies under his Command in 1864–65," published by the Engineer Bureau of the U.S. War Department. Many maps such as this were produced during and after the war to illustrate campaigns and events of special significance. (Civil War map no. 516, Geography and Map Division, Library of Congress)

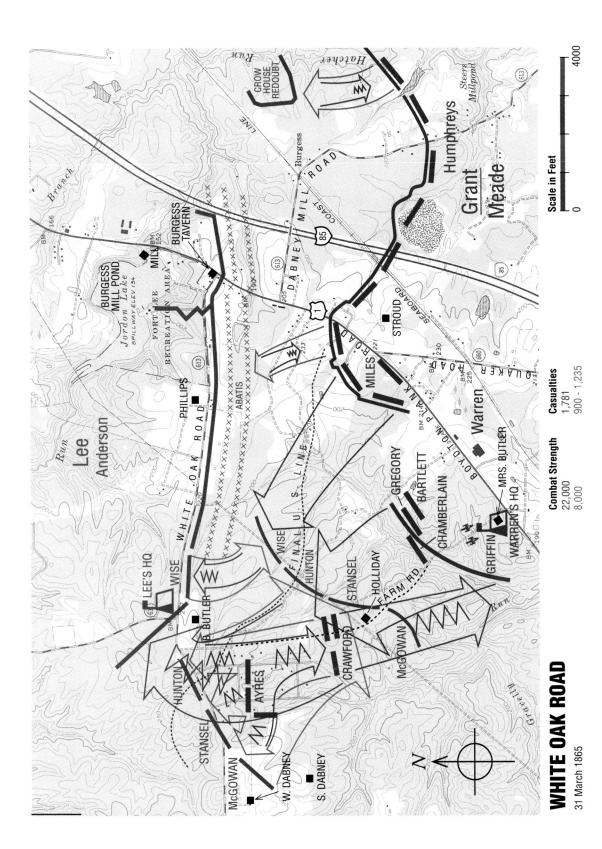

WHITE OAK ROAD

31 March 1865

Scale in Feet

0   4000

Combat Strength	Casualties
22,000	1,781
8,000	900 – 1,235

veterans filed back into their entrenchments. The attack had failed for want of numbers, but his main line had not been breached.

The V Corps suffered 1,406 casualties and the II Corps 375. Confederate losses were estimated at 900–1,235 killed, wounded, and captured. That night the men of the V Corps were ordered to abandon the road, the ground so dearly lost and reconquered, and march by a long detour to Five Forks "to rescue Sheridan's crowd," as some put it.

Estimated Casualties: 1,781 US, 900– 1,235 CS

White Oak Road battlefield is west of Route 1 at the intersection of Routes 613 and 631 (Claiborne Road). The thirty acres of the battlefield owned by the Association for the Preservation of Civil War Sites are open to the public.

Five Forks, Virginia (VA088), Dinwiddie County, April 1, 1865

Christopher M. Calkins

Five Forks was the intersection of the White Oak Road, Scott's Road, Ford's — or Church — Road, and the Dinwiddie Court House Road. Located six miles northwest of the Dinwiddie county seat, Five Forks was crucial in protecting CS General Robert E. Lee's last supply line into Petersburg, the South Side Railroad. Southeast of the junction stood a little white frame building called Gravelly Run Methodist Episcopal Church; nearby were the Barnes and Sydnor farmhouses. There were a few large plantations in the area, including those of the Gilliam and Boisseau families. Tangled thickets and pine woods were interspersed with swampy bogs, open spaces, and woods dotted with large outcroppings of granite.

While the battle of White Oak Road raged on March 31, CS Major General George E. Pickett's cavalry and infantry left their position at Five Forks, forced a passage over the swampy bottom-lands of Chamberlain's Bed, a branch of Stony Creek, and pushed US Major General Philip H. Sheridan's troopers back to Dinwiddie Court House. That night Sheridan's forces entrenched a mile north of the village, with Pickett's force interposed between them and Five Forks. US Lieutenant General Ulysses S. Grant responded to Sheridan's request for infantry to reinforce his 9,000 cavalrymen by ordering US Brigadier General Romeyn B. Ayres's division of US Major General Gouverneur K. Warren's V Corps to move quickly on March 31–April 1 by night march along the Boydton Plank Road to Dinwiddie Court House. (Warren's two other divisions took another route.) The soldiers' arrival was delayed because they had to build a forty-foot bridge to get across Gravelly Run.

Earlier on March 31, after gaining a foothold on the White Oak Road, Warren had dispatched a brigade to a position behind Pickett's left flank, facing Sheridan. Realizing that the Union army had him in check, the Confederate commander decided to withdraw his men to Five Forks. Soon the lead elements of Warren's V Corps column began arriving on the Dinwiddie Court House Road following Sheridan's troopers, who were pressing Pickett to the strategic crossroads.

When the Confederates arrived at Five Forks, Pickett set the men to strengthening their log and dirt fortifications. This line covered a one-and-three-fourths-mile front, with a return on the left flank about 150 yards long. The cavalry guarded each flank, and artillery was placed at key points along the works. Pickett had received instructions from CS General Robert E. Lee: "Hold Five Forks at all hazards. Protect road to Ford's Depot and prevent Union forces from striking the South-side Railroad. Regret exceedingly your forces' withdrawal, and your inability to hold the advantage you had gained."

While Sheridan impatiently awaited the arrival of the remainder of Warren's forces, he received a dispatch: "General Grant directs me to say to

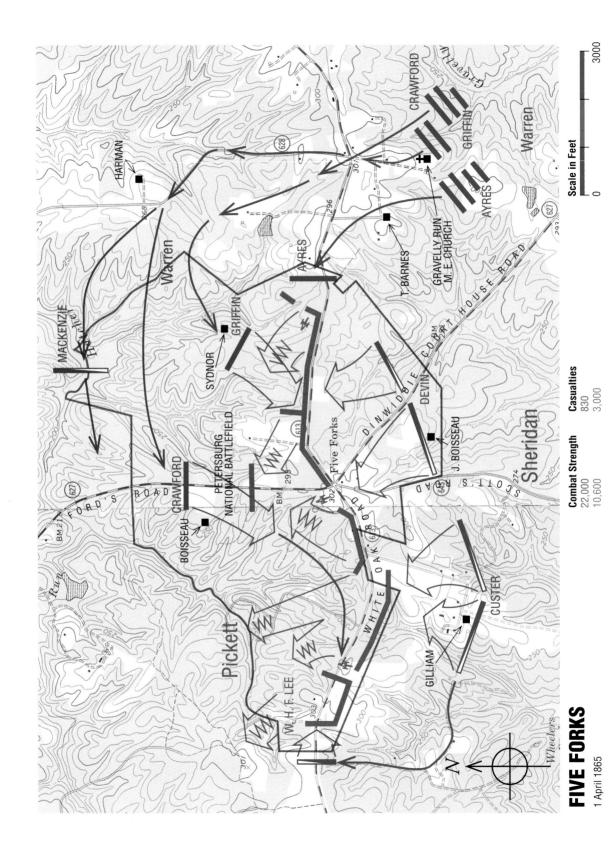

FIVE FORKS

1 April 1865

	Combat Strength	Casualties
	22,000	830
	10,600	3,000

Scale in Feet

0 — 3000

you, that if in your judgment the Fifth Corps would do better under one of the division commanders, you are authorized to relieve General Warren, and order him to report to General Grant, at headquarters." Warren's fate as a corps commander was in Sheridan's hands. Later that night, after the battle had ended, Sheridan replaced Warren with US Brigadier General Charles Griffin.

It was nearly 4:00 P.M. when Warren had his 12,000 men ready to attack. Because of faulty reconnaissance by Sheridan's staff, the map they drew for Warren erroneously showed Pickett's left flank as extending to the intersection of Gravelly Run Church Road and the White Oak Road. Warren formed his battle lines in a bottom near Gravelly Run Church and instructed his three division commanders to advance until they intersected with the White Oak Road. Sheridan's dismounted troopers were to press the Confederate line all along its front. Ayres formed the left of Warren's line, and US Brigadier General Samuel W. Crawford the right, with Griffin in support. When Warren's advancing columns reached that area and began to wheel, they found the Confederate flank was still three quarters of a mile to the west. Although the mapping and reconnaissance errors caused the three columns to diverge from the original intended alignment, they did overwhelm the Confederate angle and line. One of Warren's divisions swung around to the north of Pickett's position and attacked the Confederates in their rear at Five Forks. On the Confederate right flank US Brigadier General George A. Custer's troops battled with cavalry led by CS Major General William H. Fitzhugh "Rooney" Lee. CS Brigadier General Thomas C. Devin's dismounted troopers pushed forward between Custer and Warren.

Groups of Pickett's men formed pockets of resistance along the line but to no avail. Their commander did not arrive on the scene until the fighting was well under way, having spent most of the afternoon at a shad bake two miles in the rear with some of his officers. By the time he addressed the situation, it was too late. Those who were not taken prisoner scattered into the pine forests and escaped the best way they could. Dark-ness brought an end to the fighting, and Union campfires were lit around Five Forks, the key to the South Side Railroad.

Estimated Casualties: 830 US, 3,000 CS

Five Forks Battlefield, a unit of the Petersburg National Battlefield, is southwest of Petersburg at the intersection of Routes 613 and 627 between Route 460 and Interstate 85, and includes 1,115 acres of the historic battlefield.

Petersburg III, Virginia (VA089), Dinwiddie County and Petersburg, April 2, 1865

Emory Thomas

Five Forks began the end. US Lieutenant General Ulysses S. Grant knew it and "ordered a general assault along the lines." CS General Robert E. Lee likely also knew it; on the morning of April 2, he dressed himself in a new uniform, as though to be ready to surrender with dignity if so compelled.

Even before Lee was awake and dressed, the Federal attacks drove the Confederates. US Major General Horatio G. Wright's VI Corps launched an 18,000-man devastating assault at 4:40 A.M. in a wedge-shaped formation assembled during the night in silence. The Federals overran CS Major Generals Henry Heth's and Cadmus Wilcox's Divisions of CS Lieutenant General Ambrose Powell Hill's Third Corps and crossed the Boydton Plank Road on a broad front north of Hatcher's Run. US Major General John G. Parke's IX Corps (18,000 men) assaulted Fort Mahone. CS Major General John B. Gordon's troops prevented a breakthrough at this crucial point, but stasis was increasingly costly.

Lee awoke to meet Hill, who was alarmed

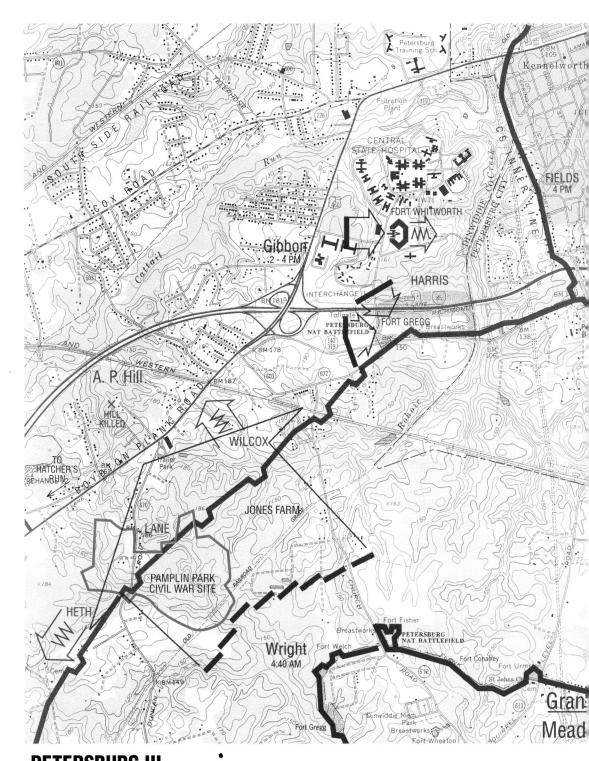

PETERSBURG III

2 April 1865

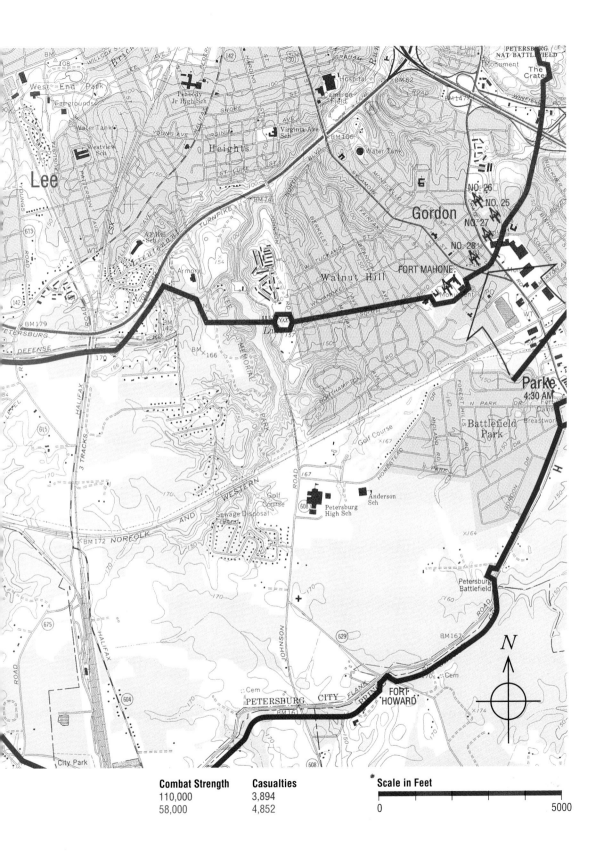

Combat Strength	Casualties	Scale in Feet
110,000	3,894	0 5000
58,000	4,852	

about reports from his command on the right. In the wake of more alarms Hill rode away to find and rally his corps. He found confusion and then Federal troops, one of whom shot him through the heart. Hill died as he fell from his horse to the ground.

By 10:00 A.M. Lee realized the magnitude of the disaster. He would have to abandon Petersburg and Richmond. The Army of Northern Virginia, which had occupied those lines and dug these trenches, would have to march once more. After being in place for nearly ten months the army would have to disengage and flee. Lee sent his telegram to Confederate President Jefferson Davis: "I see no prospect of doing more than holding our position here till night. I am not certain I can do that. . . . I advise that all preparation be made for leaving Richmond tonight."

Davis was at Saint Paul's Church in Richmond when Lee's message reached the Confederate War Department. The parish sexton walked quietly to Davis's pew and handed him the fateful paper. Davis left Saint Paul's before receiving communion. Soon officers of the Confederate government received similar summonses in churches and elsewhere. That evening the government left the capital and traveled by train to Danville. Fires set to destroy anything of potential use to the Federals spread to much of Richmond's business district, and hungry Richmonders mobbed government warehouses to reach the rations ahead of the flames.

Meanwhile Lee had to move his headquarters out of harm's way. Throughout the long day he issued orders and gave direction to his projected retreat. He had to coordinate his forces north of the James River with those holding his contracting lines around Petersburg and try to have them all marching in the same direction at approximately the same time. Already CS Lieutenant General James Longstreet, in command of the Confederates north of the James, was moving some of his troops, CS Major General Charles W. Fields's Division, into Petersburg to try to hold the inner defense line along Indian Town Creek. Necessity dictated that Lee cross the Appomattox River and then march west. Because of the

VI Corps breakthrough, the Confederates were split. Lee made Amelia Court House the common objective and ordered rations shipped to that rendezvous.

Even as the Army of Northern Virginia began scrambling to leave Petersburg, some of its soldiers had to stay and hold critical points or die trying. Most noble were the defenses for two critical hours of Fort Gregg and Fort Whitworth (Baldwin) in the afternoon against 5,000 men of US Major General John Gibbon's XXIV Corps. The loss of these forts would have jeopardized the entire operation and forced the Confederates to fight their way out of Petersburg. In each case very few defenders repulsed repeated attacks, and those who were able battled hand to hand before withdrawing. By the time the southerners succumbed, Longstreet had assembled an interior defensive line, and the long day was fading.

Lee appointed 8:00 P.M. as the time to commence the withdrawal. In the late afternoon, however, the commanding general received a bizarre request. CS Colonel Walter Herren Taylor had been with Lee from the very beginning of the war, when Lee was mobilizing Virginia volunteers. Taylor had served on every one of Lee's staffs and now was assistant adjutant general; he had charge of Lee's orders and correspondence. Young Taylor had not always appreciated his military patron. To his fiancée, Betty Saunders, he wrote, "He is so unreasonable and provoking at times"; "he is a queer old genius"; and "he is never so uncomfortable as when comfortable." Now, when Lee and his army were about to run for their lives, Taylor asked to be excused for the evening. He and Betty Saunders planned to marry that night. Taylor's request took Lee by surprise, which he expressed. But then Lee "promptly gave his consent."

Taylor and Betty Saunders did marry that night in Richmond, and Taylor made good his promise to overtake Lee and the army in retreat. When Taylor later told the story of his wedding in his memoirs, he wrote only of the bare facts of Lee's blessing his absence on that crucial night.

But what had Lee done here? That "unreasonable and provoking" man, the "queer old genius" who was "never so uncomfortable as when comfortable," instinctively acted to redeem a sad circumstance — he made April 2 a day to celebrate for the Taylor family. And in so doing Lee revealed a depth of humanity that very few people, certainly not Taylor, ever recognized. Somehow, even without his assistant adjutant general, Lee also extricated his army from its trenches in the face of a foe on the offensive. The Army of Northern Virginia was intact and on the move; the end was not yet.

Estimated Casualties: 3,894 US, 4,852 CS

Areas of the Petersburg battlefield are protected in Petersburg National Battlefield, including Fort Fisher, Fort Welch, Confederate Fort Gregg, and U.S. Fort Gregg. Pamplin Park Civil War Site at 6523 Duncan Road includes 173 acres of the historic battlefield.

Sutherland Station, Virginia (VA090), Dinwiddie County, April 2, 1865

While Union forces converged on Petersburg on April 2, US General Sheridan's cavalry and the V Corps cleared the Five Forks battlefield. US Major General Andrew A. Humphreys, commander of the II Corps, had orders to reinforce Sheridan with US Brigadier General Nelson A. Miles's division. When Sheridan returned the division to the II Corps, Humphreys advanced on the White Oak Road defenses. His troops found the trenches abandoned, and they continued northward up the Claiborne Road with Miles in the lead.

After CS General Hill was killed, CS General Robert E. Lee ordered CS Major General Henry Heth to take temporary command of the Third Corps. Heth left CS Brigadier General John R. Cooke in command of his division. Cooke posi-

tioned his four brigades at Sutherland Station to protect the South Side Railroad west of Petersburg. He anchored his left flank at the Ocran Methodist Church.

Beginning at 1:00 P.M. on April 2 Miles's division made two frontal assaults, which were repulsed with heavy losses. At 4:00 P.M. he attacked the Confederate left flank with artillery support, and the enemy line collapsed. The Federals captured 600 Confederates and the South Side Railroad, the Confederates' last supply line into Petersburg. After the loss of his escape route along the railroad, Lee crossed to the north bank of the Appomattox River after dark.

Estimated Casualties: 366 US, 600 CS

Namozine Church, Virginia (VA124), Amelia County, April 3, 1865

On April 3 US General Sheridan's cavalry pursued the remnants of the Confederate defenders of Five Forks and the White Oak Road defenses south of the Appomattox River. At noon a brigade of US General Custer's cavalry commanded by US Colonel William Wells engaged the Confederate rear-guard cavalry under CS Brigadier General Rufus Barringer at Namozine Church ten miles northwest of Sutherland Station. The Union cavalry quickly flanked the Confederate line and took 350 prisoners, including Barringer. Two days later Barringer became the first Confederate general to meet President Abraham Lincoln. His brother had served in Congress with Lincoln.

The day after the fall of Richmond and Petersburg, President Lincoln and US General Grant entered Petersburg together. The president said, "Thank God I have lived to see this. It seems to me that I have been dreaming a horrid dream for four years, and now the nightmare is gone. I want to see Richmond." Grant rode to join his advancing forces, and on April 4 USN Admiral Porter took the president upriver. Lincoln walked through Richmond, accompanied only by Porter, one White House guard, ten sailors, and his son, Tad — who was twelve years old that day. The president was greeted by freed slaves, one of whom knelt before him. "Don't kneel to me. That is not right. You must kneel to God only, and thank Him for the liberty you will enjoy hereafter." Among the Federal soldiers who had moved into Richmond to put out fires and restore order were XXV Corps black troopers, the 5th Massachusetts Cavalry, commanded by US Colonel Charles Francis Adams, and XXV Corps black infantry.

Estimated Casualties: 81 US, unknown CS

Amelia Springs, Virginia (VA091), Amelia County, April 5, 1865

Before the Federal victories at Five Forks, Petersburg, and Sutherland Station blocked his retreat, CS General Lee had planned to escape toward the southwest and join CS General Joseph E. Johnston in North Carolina. Instead he led the men of the Army of Northern Virginia from Petersburg along the north side of the Appomattox River and headed west to Amelia Court House to unite with his forces from Richmond. Lee expected to find rations at Amelia, but the trains arrived with ammunition. Foraging for food cost Lee a day — and his lead ahead of the Federals.

US General Grant pursued Lee with 112,500 men in two columns: one was behind Lee, primarily infantry, which constantly skirmished with Lee's rear guard; the other, Sheridan's cavalry, rode on a parallel route south of the shrinking Confederate forces. Sheridan's orders were to prevent Lee from turning toward North Carolina and to swing around their front to block their escape. On April 4 Sheridan rode with the V Corps to Jetersville, eight miles southwest of Amelia Springs, to block Lee's planned route southwest down the Richmond & Danville Railroad. Sheridan sent US Brigadier General Henry E. Davies's cavalrymen north to Paineville where they raided a wagon train and burned two hundred wagons. CS Brigadier General Martin W. Gary's Brigade held off the Federal advance. Reinforced by CS Major General Fitzhugh Lee's Division, the Confederates counterattacked and drove the Union

troopers back through Amelia Springs. The II and VI Corps reinforced Sheridan at Jetersville on April 5.

That night Sheridan asked Grant for his presence on the field, and Grant rode out more than twenty miles with a small escort to meet with him. Sheridan thought Lee was moving and disagreed with Meade, who had concluded that Lee would stop at Amelia Court House and fight. Grant stated that he wanted to get ahead of Lee, not follow him. Meade changed his orders.

Estimated Casualties: 158 US, unknown CS

Sailor's Creek, Virginia (VA093), Amelia, Nottaway, and Prince Edward Counties, April 6, 1865

Christopher M. Calkins

On April 5 CS General Robert E. Lee and his army left Amelia Court House and continued the march toward Danville, following the line of the Richmond & Danville Railroad. They were heading toward North Carolina, where Lee could combine his force with that of CS General Joseph E. Johnston. When CS Major General William H. Fitzhugh "Rooney" Lee (General Lee's son) reported Union cavalry entrenched across the road at Jetersville, Lee had to change his plans. Because the hour was late and his column was spread out, he decided to make a night march, passing to the north of the Union left flank and heading west for Farmville, twenty-three miles away on the South Side Railroad. There he could obtain supplies for his army, then march south, intersecting the Danville line near Keysville. His success depended once again upon outdistancing Grant's army.

The Confederates' planned route was across the ford at Flat Creek, past the resort of Amelia Springs, through the crossroads called Deatonville, and then through the bottomlands traversed by Little Sailor's Creek, which joins Big Sailor's Creek at Double Bridges. The rolling terrain is slashed by various watercourses: Flat Creek, Big

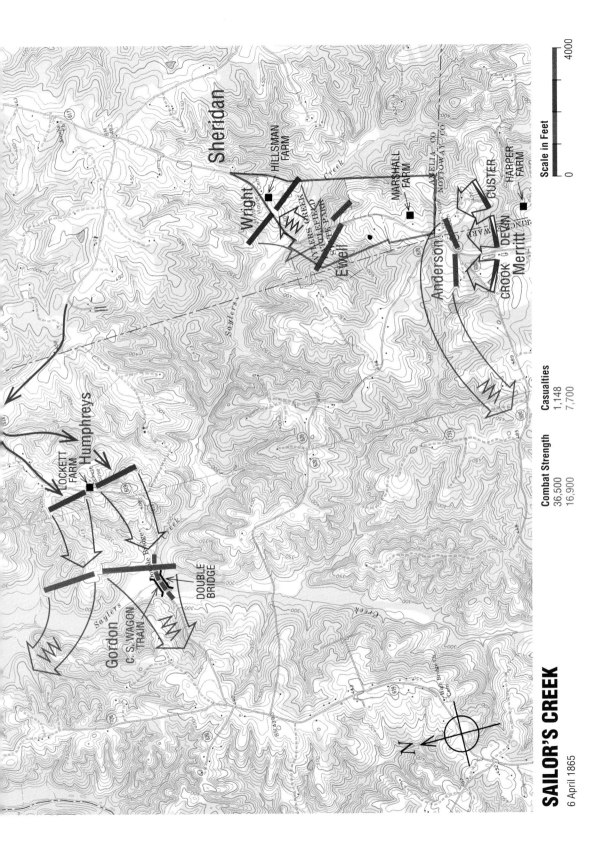

SAILOR'S CREEK

6 April 1865

	Combat Strength	Casualties
	36,500	1,148
	16,900	7,700

Scale in Feet

0   4000

and Little Sailor's Creeks, and Sandy and Bush Rivers. On the north is the Appomattox River, which had crossings only at Farmville and three miles northeast at the High Bridge — the South Side Railroad trestle.

CS Lieutenant General James Longstreet's combined First and Third Corps led Lee's column, followed by CS Lieutenant General Richard H. Anderson's small corps, then CS Lieutenant General Richard S. Ewell's reserve corps (made up of Richmond garrison troops), the main wagon train, and, finally, CS Lieutenant General John B. Gordon's Second Corps acting as rear guard.

The rear of Longstreet's column became separated from the head of Anderson's Corps. After noon on April 6 observant Union cavalry led by US Brigadier General George A. Custer charged into the gap and established a roadblock in front of Anderson, cutting him off from Longstreet. Close behind US Major General Philip H. Sheridan's fast-riding cavalry was US Major General Horatio G. Wright's VI Corps. Ewell realized that further attacks were imminent and decided to send the wagon train on a more northerly route. Gordon, who was heavily pressed by US Major General Andrew A. Humphreys's II Corps, followed the train. The stage was set for the battle of Sailor's Creek. The battle included three separate engagements: one between Wright and Ewell at the Hillsman farm, another between Humphreys and Gordon at the Lockett farm, and the third between US Brigadier General Wesley Merritt and Anderson at a crossroads bounded by the Harper and Marshall farms.

Ewell took his 5,200-man force to the southwest side of the creek, where he formed a battle line on a ridge parallel to the creek facing northeast, overlooking the Hillsman farm. The 10,000 Union soldiers occupied the high ground on the opposite side of the creek. Wright emplaced his artillery and at about 5:00 P.M. opened fire on Ewell's line. After bombarding the Confederates for a half hour, Wright's men formed their battle line and advanced to the creek. Because of spring rains, Little Sailor's Creek was out of its banks and was two to four feet deep. The men crossed

it with difficulty, reformed their lines, and began the assault upon the Confederates. When the Union troops came within easy range, Ewell's men rose and fired a volley into them, causing them to break and fall back. A group of Confederates made a counterattack, only to be thrown back with great losses. The Federals regrouped and again charged Ewell's line, this time overwhelming it. They captured more than 3,000 soldiers, including six generals. Confederate losses totaled 3,400; Union, 440.

When the wagons Gordon was following bogged down at Double Bridges, the crossing over the confluence of Big and Little Sailor's Creeks, Gordon's men were forced to protect them. Making a stand just before dusk on the high ground around the Lockett farm, the 7,000 Confederates awaited the arrival of Humphreys's 16,500-man corps. With the sound of fighting echoing from the south, the Union infantry gradually pushed the Confederates back into the low ground near the creek. Using the wagons as protection, Gordon's men fought desperately. When they saw a Union flanking column crossing farther to the north at Perkinson's Sawmill, they were forced to retreat up the opposite slope. At nightfall, when the fighting ended, the Confederate losses were 1,700; the Union, 536. Humphreys's men had taken more than two hundred wagons.

The third fight was to the south at a crossroads bounded by the Harper and Marshall farms, about a mile southwest of the road crossing Little Sailor's Creek. Merritt's cavalry, commanded by Custer, US Brigadier General Thomas Devin, and US Major General George Crook, overcame Anderson's stubborn resistance, led by CS Major Generals George E. Pickett and Bushrod Johnson. The Federals captured two more Confederate generals, although many of Anderson's men managed to escape through the woods. Anderson lost 2,600 of his 6,300 men. The Federals lost 172 of their 10,000 cavalrymen.

As the Confederate refugees fled the battlefield and headed west toward Rice's Station, they had to scramble through the valley of Big Sailor's Creek. General Lee had ridden to a knoll overlooking the creek and, seeing this disorganized mob, exclaimed, "My God! Has the army been dissolved?" The total casualties for the battle of Sailor's Creek were 7,700 Confederates and 1,148 Federals.

That night Lee's soldiers marched again. Gordon's men and those assembled by CS Major General William Mahone trudged on to the High Bridge and crossed the Appomattox River, planning to recross later into Farmville by another bridge. Lee took Longstreet's troops and Fitzhugh Lee's cavalry along the road running south of the river into Farmville, arriving there in the early morning hours. Awaiting them were at least three trainloads of supplies containing more than 80,000 rations. As the men began to receive their rations and prepare their meals, they heard the popping of carbine fire to the east: Union cavalry was approaching the outskirts of town. The Confederates quickly closed up the boxcars and sent the trains westward down the rail line. They intended to get the rest of their rations later, probably at Appomattox Station, thirty miles away.

Estimated Casualties: 1,148 US, 7,700 CS

Sailor's Creek Battlefield State Park, near Route 617 in Amelia County, fifty-six miles west of Petersburg near Route 460, includes 317 acres of the historic battlefield.

Rice's Station, Virginia (VA092), Prince Edward County, April 6, 1865

On April 6 CS General Longstreet's command led the vanguard of the retreating Army of Northern Virginia. When Longstreet learned that the vital High Bridge over the Appomattox River was being attacked by a "flying column" rushed forward by US Major General Edward O. C. Ord, he or-

dered his troops to entrench at Rice's Station, a depot on the South Side Railroad.

The Second Corps under CS General Gordon, followed by Mahone's Division moving cross-country, passed to the north of Longstreet and crossed the High Bridge to the north side of the Appomattox during the night. US Major General John Gibbon's XXIV Corps, spearheading Ord's march along the railroad from Burkeville Junction, approached Longstreet's position. After heavy skirmishing, Longstreet, satisfied that Gordon's column was safely across the Appomattox River, withdrew during the night toward Farmville.

Estimated Casualties: 66 US, unknown CS

High Bridge, Virginia (VA095), Prince Edward and Cumberland Counties, April 6–7, 1865

The High Bridge across the Appomattox River northwest of Burkeville was 2,500 feet long and carried the South Side Railroad. Underneath it was a wooden wagon bridge. On April 6 CS General Longstreet stopped to protect the South Side Railroad at Rice's Station on the south side of the river. When he learned that a Federal raiding party was heading for the High Bridge, he dispatched 1,200 cavalrymen commanded by CS General "Rooney" Lee and CS Major General Thomas L. Rosser to secure it. US General Ord had sent 900 men commanded by US Colonel Theodore Read, who reached the bridge first and captured the south end. When Rosser arrived, Read ordered a mounted charge by the 4th Massachusetts Cavalry. The troopers broke through, but the Confederates counterattacked and separated them from their supporting infantry. The Federal cavalrymen attacked once again and were surrounded. Read was killed, and his men, as well as the isolated infantry, were either killed, wounded, or captured in a short but bitter fight. CS Brigadier General James Dearing was mortally wounded, the last Confederate general to die in the war.

After escaping from Sailor's Creek, CS General Gordon's Second Corps crossed the High Bridge to the north side of the river, and CS General Mahone's Division secured the bridge. The rest of the Army of Northern Virginia moved on to Farmville that night, where trains of rations were waiting.

Early on April 7 US General Humphreys's II Corps advanced on the High Bridge while Mahone's troops were attempting to destroy it, to give the Confederates time to escape. US Brigadier General Francis Barlow's division charged the burning structure and saved a large section of the railroad bridge. The Federals put out the flames before they did major damage and crossed the lower wagon bridge to the north side of the river, enabling Humphreys's II Corps to move on Lee's flank and force the hungry Confederates away from their supply trains. Lee ordered the three supply trains to meet the army at Appomattox Station. His route along the north bank of the Appomattox River to the station was eight miles longer than the direct one available to the Union cavalry and two infantry corps.

Estimated Casualties: 847 (including 800 captured) US, 100 CS

Cumberland Church, Virginia (VA094), Cumberland County, April 7, 1865

US General Humphreys's II Corps crossed High Bridge on the morning of April 7, and US General Barlow's division, following the railroad west toward Farmville, hammered the rear guard of CS General Gordon's Second Corps. The Confederates turned on the Federals, checked their pursuit, took prisoners, and mortally wounded US Brigadier General Thomas A. Smyth, the last United States general to be killed in Civil War combat.

Meanwhile CS General Mahone's Division won the race to Cumberland Church, entrenched on the high ground east and north of the church,

and waited for the approach of Humphreys's other two divisions marching on the Jamestown Road. The Confederates headed off the probes of Humphreys, while Gordon's and CS General Longstreet's Corps arrived from Farmville and took the ground on Mahone's right.

US Major General George Crook's cavalry division forded the Appomattox River west of Farmville and rode north up the Maysville Plank Road to raid Lee's wagon trains. Crooks's troopers were driven off by Confederate cavalry and infantry in a fight witnessed by CS General Robert E. Lee.

The day's fighting shifted north to the Cumberland Church area where US Brigadier General Nelson Miles's division spearheaded an attack on Mahone's Division north of the church. Mahone's forces repulsed the Federals and kept the road to Appomattox Court House open.

Lee received US General Grant's first note that night asking him to surrender. Lee refused and led his men in a midnight march west, with Gordon's Corps in the lead and Longstreet's Corps as the rear guard.

Estimated Casualties: 571 US, unknown CS

Appomattox Station, Virginia (VA096), Appomattox County, April 8, 1865

While Confederates were straggling, abandoning their rifle-muskets, and leaving in groups, US General Grant became ill with a painful headache. US General Sheridan's cavalry pulled ahead of CS General Lee on the evening of April 8 and blocked his retreat toward Campbell Court House. US Brigadier General George A. Custer rode into Appomattox Station and captured three supply trains sent from Lynchburg. The Federals rode on a half mile toward Appomattox Court House where CS Brigadier General R. Lindsay Walker had parked Confederate artillery and wagons. Walker formed his guns in a semicircle and held off the Union cavalry for several hours. In Custer's overwhelming attack at 9:00 P.M., some of the artillerymen escaped with their guns, but Custer took more than twenty-five.

As Grant had ordered, the cavalry was staying ahead of Lee. The troopers had captured rations and cannons and had blocked the Confederates' retreat route west of the village of Appomattox.

Lee turned down Grant's second request by letter to surrender.

Estimated Casualties: 48 US, 1,000 captured, unknown killed and wounded CS

Appomattox Court House, Virginia (VA097), Appomattox County, April 9, 1865

William C. Davis

As the spring of 1865 blossomed, it was certain that the Civil War would end soon and that the Confederacy would fall. With armies spread over half the continent, the war could hardly cease all at once everywhere. The question was where the end would begin.

It started in Virginia. For ten months, since June 1864, US Lieutenant General Ulysses S. Grant's forces, chiefly the Army of the Potomac commanded by US Major General George Gordon Meade, had besieged CS General Robert E. Lee's Army of Northern Virginia in and around Petersburg and Richmond. Steadily the blue noose drew tighter until, by April 1, all but one of the supply routes into Petersburg were cut off. On that day the Confederate defeat at Five Forks, on the far right of Lee's line, threatened the South Side Railroad, the last lifeline. There was no choice for Lee but to abandon Petersburg and Richmond to Grant and retreat to the southwest.

On April 2 Lee pulled out of Petersburg one step ahead of his foes. President Jefferson Davis and his cabinet fled Richmond, and the Confederacy became a government truly on the run. Lee headed west to Amelia Court House, to Jetersville, then toward Farmville and the Appomattox River. In spite of the disaster at Sailor's Creek, Lee pushed on, pursued relentlessly by Meade's infantry and the Union cavalry, commanded by US Major General Philip H. Sheridan. Lee neared

Appomattox Court House at about nightfall on April 8, only to see the glow of Sheridan's campfires to the west, his route of retreat. Sheridan was ahead of him, and Meade and Grant were behind him.

Lee and the remnant of his once mighty army bivouacked for the last time near the village clustered around the Appomattox County courthouse. The village was important to Lee because it was on the road to Appomattox Station, where he had hoped to find supplies. But now that hope was fading. Lee's Second Corps, commanded by CS Major General John B. Gordon, occupied the town itself, assisted by the cavalry of CS Major General Fitzhugh Lee. To the southwest they faced portions of US Major General Charles Griffin's V Corps and, due west of them, more elements of US Major General John Gibbon's XXIV Corps of the Army of the James, commanded by US Major General E. O. C. Ord. At the same time Sheridan's cavalry had nearly encircled Lee. Two divisions under US Major General George A. Custer and US Brigadier General Thomas C. Devin cut off any escape to the southeast, where only a small Confederate cavalry brigade led by CS Brigadier General Martin Gary and the engineer battalions of CS Colonel T. M. R. Talcott could oppose them. Off to Gibbon's left the cavalry division of US Brigadier General Ranald S. Mackenzie stood poised to meet any attempt to move around Gibbon. About three miles away to the northeast, Lee and CS Lieutenant General James Longstreet, commanding what was left of the First and Third Corps, faced US Major General Andrew A. Humphreys's II Corps and behind it US Major General Horatio G. Wright's VI Corps of the Army of the Potomac. Lee made his headquarters to the rear of Longstreet, about a mile northeast of the village.

Grant had sent Lee a note on April 7 stating that the events of the past few days must have shown the futility of further resistance and suggesting surrender. Lee declined but kept the door open by asking what terms Grant would request. Grant responded on April 8 that peace was his "great desire." He asked the Confederates to give up their arms, give their parole not to fight again, and go

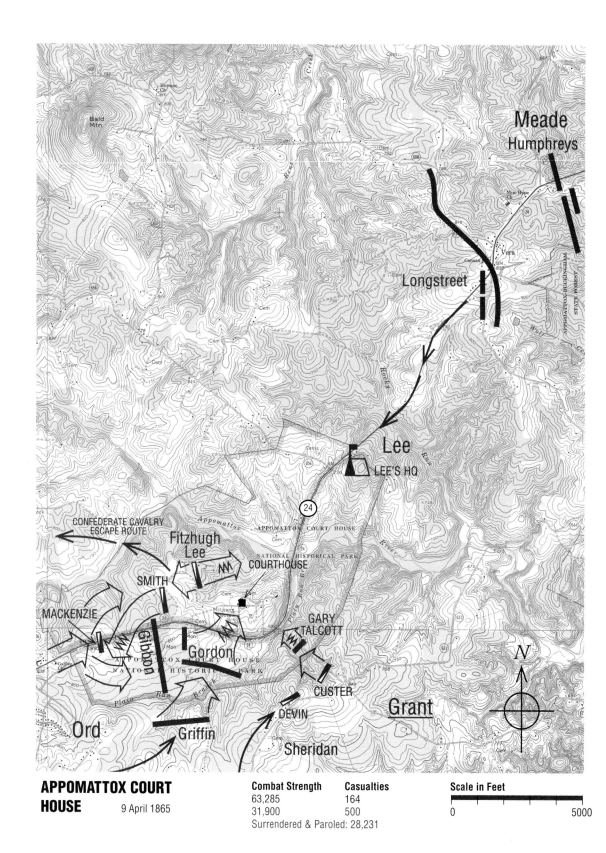

Meade
Humphreys

Longstreet

Lee
LEE'S HQ

24

CONFEDERATE CAVALRY
ESCAPE ROUTE
Fitzhugh
Lee
COURTHOUSE
SMITH
MACKENZIE
Gibbon
Gordon
GARY
TALCOTT

Ord
CUSTER
DEVIN
Grant
Griffin
Sheridan

N

APPOMATTOX COURT
HOUSE   9 April 1865

Combat Strength	Casualties
63,285	164
31,900	500

Surrendered & Paroled: 28,231

Scale in Feet

0   5000

home. In response, Lee suggested that they meet to talk. Grant declined to talk unless it was to discuss surrender.

Grant's refusal did not reach Lee until the morning of April 9, and by then something had happened to change Lee's mind about surrender. The evening before, when Lee learned that the Federals were ahead of him and were at Appomattox Station, he called together his few remaining corps commanders, Fitzhugh Lee, Longstreet, and Gordon, to discuss what could be done. Gordon and the younger Lee argued that if only cavalry was in their front, they could attack and perhaps break through, opening a route to continue the retreat. Should Sheridan have infantry with him, however, they would be trapped, with surrender the only alternative. Lee, with an ill-concealed lack of confidence, agreed and set the hour for attack at 5:00 A.M. He dressed in his finest uniform, commenting to a friend that "I have probably to be General Grant's prisoner. I must make my best appearance."

On Palm Sunday, April 9, the Confederates followed their battle flags into the Army of Northern Virginia's last assault. Gordon initially realized — or so he thought — some success as he pushed Sheridan's cavalry back before him, not knowing that Sheridan was pulling his troopers back to allow Gibbon's infantry to come into the fight. On Gordon's right Fitzhugh Lee seemed to make progress until they both came face to face with the infantry of the XXIV Corps. Lee and his cavalry fell back. Gordon, forced to withdraw, sent the commanding general a message: "I have fought my corps to a frazzle." Longstreet could not send reinforcements because he was engaged in holding off Humphreys and Wright. General Lee called off the engagement. "There is nothing left for me to do but to go and see General Grant," said the proud Virginian, "and I would rather die a thousand deaths."

At about 8:30 A.M. Lee rode for the meeting with Grant that he had proposed the previous day. Soon after, he received Grant's reply refusing the meeting. Lee wrote again, specifically requesting a meeting to discuss surrender. Word then came that Fitzhugh Lee's cavalry had succeeded

in breaking out after all but that Gordon was trapped. Lee ordered truce flags sent out and awaited Grant's reply.

It came just after noon; Grant agreed to the meeting. Lee sent a staff officer ahead to Appomattox Court House to find a suitable place, and the man chose the home of Wilmer McLean, about sixty yards down the road from the courthouse. It was ironic that McLean had lived near Manassas in 1861 at the time of the first major battle of the war. He had moved to the modest brick house in Appomattox Court House after the battle.

Lee arrived at the McLean home first and went into the parlor, where he sat at a table to await Grant, who came half an hour later. Grant had had a terrible headache that morning, but it disappeared when he received Lee's note. The two generals presented quite a contrast: Lee in full formal uniform, Grant in a private's dress with only the general's stars to denote his rank. They spoke briefly of mutual service in the Mexican War. Then Grant proposed the same terms he had mentioned in his note the day before. When Lee said that many of the Confederates owned the horses they rode, Grant allowed them to take the animals home with them. "This will have the best possible effect upon the men," said Lee. Grant also authorized 25,000 rations to feed Lee's men. The two generals signed the surrender documents, shook hands, and left.

A commission of six general officers from both armies was appointed to work out the actual details of the surrender, including the formal turning over of arms and flags. US Brigadier General Joshua L. Chamberlain of Maine was given the honor of formally receiving the surrender of the Confederate infantry.

On April 12 Chamberlain formed his command on either side of the Richmond-Lynchburg Stage Road leading out of town toward the Confederate camps. At the appointed hour the Confederates formed ranks as if on parade and marched off for the last time, Gordon's Corps in the lead. There were so few men and so many flags that when Chamberlain saw them approach, he thought that "the whole column seemed crowned with red."

Chamberlain ordered a bugler to signal their approach. The Federals snapped to "carry arms." Gordon, astride his horse, caught the spirit of the event, rose erect in his stirrups, wheeled his horse magnificently, and brought the point of his sword to his boot toe, at the same time ordering his men to the same position at arms, "honor answering honor."

And so the Confederates passed, only 22,000 infantry, to lay down their arms, furl their flags, and say their farewells. On the road to Richmond behind them another 13,800 had been captured and 6,300 killed or wounded. Only Fitzhugh Lee's 2,400 troopers escaped. Grant had a total available Federal force of 63,285 in the area, though only a portion was actually engaged. Fewer still were privileged to stand along the road to see the last moments of Lee's army. Chamberlain later wrote of "memories that bound us together as no other bond." Among the Union soldiers, he observed, "not a sound of trumpet more, nor roll of drum; not a cheer, nor whisper of vain-glorying, nor motion of man standing again at the order, but an awed stillness rather, and breath-holding, as if it were the passing of the dead."

Although the men in gray went home, Lee's surrender did not end the war. Other Confederate armies were still in the field, and it was more than two months before all had capitulated. But Appomattox would always symbolize the end for the South. For four years the indomitable Army of Northern Virginia had been the fighting standard by which all other armies, blue or gray, were measured. For most of that time Robert E. Lee stood as the unrivaled general of the war. When he and his army surrendered, the hopes of the Confederacy were over.

It had been a terrible ordeal for North and South. The structure of the old Union and the nature of the constitutional compact had been shaken to their core. The young men of the continent, nearly 3 million of them, had gone off to war, and more than 620,000 would never go home again. The questions of slavery and secession had been settled forever, but the old sectional feelings continued as the reunited nation began Reconstruction.

Still, out of that war experience came the ties that Chamberlain sensed as his old enemies filed past him at Appomattox. All that the men on both sides had endured bound them together. As the passions subsided, their common experiences helped to rebind the nation. In the terrible storm of fire and blood, millions of farm boys and clerks had participated in the greatest event of their century. It gave them a brotherhood that transcended even the ties of blood.

They are all gone now; the last of them died in the 1950s. Yet some participants in that conflict can still be seen today. Although Johnny Reb and Billy Yank now rest beneath the sod, the ground for which they fought yet endures. Alas, much of it has been altered or built over to the point that little remains to link it with the events of the 1860s, as is the case in Atlanta. Other hallowed places live in daily peril, unprotected from private exploitation. Many of the battlefields described in this book are privately owned, including Brandy Station, Port Gibson, and New Market Heights. So long as they remain in private hands, there is no surety that they will endure for future generations. Happily, however, grateful and committed citizens have preserved some of the great battlefields — Manassas, Antietam, Gettysburg, Shiloh, Vicksburg, Chickamauga, and others — so that today they are much as they were when the guns echoed across their hills and fields. Appomattox Court House too is set aside as a special place where blue met gray and created something greater than themselves. As long as these mute yet eloquent reminders remain to show us where men fought and for what, we cannot forget. So long as we preserve these fields and seek to save even more, we shall preserve ourselves.

Estimated Casualties: 164 US, 500 CS (surrendered and paroled: 28,231)

Appomattox Court House National Historical Park, on Route 24 at Appomattox, includes 1,775 acres of the historic battlefield and village in the park; 270 of these acres are privately owned.

Lee: I am glad to see one real American here.
Parker: We are all Americans.

— General Robert E. Lee to Lieutenant Colonel
   Ely Parker, a Seneca Indian who was General
   Ulysses S. Grant's military secretary

After four years of arduous service, marked by unsurpassed courage and fortitude, the Army of Northern Virginia has been compelled to yield to overwhelming numbers and resources.

I need not tell the brave survivors of so many hard fought battles, who have remained steadfast to the last, that I have consented to the result from no distrust of them.

But feeling that valor and devotion could accomplish nothing that would compensate for the loss that must have attended the continuance of the contest, I determined to avoid the useless sacrifice of those whose past services have endeared them to their countrymen.

By the terms of the agreement officers and men can return to their homes and remain until exchanged. You will take with you the satisfaction that proceeds from the consciousness of duty faithfully performed, and I earnestly pray that a Merciful God will extend to you His blessing and protection.

With an increasing admiration of your constancy and devotion to your country, and a grateful remembrance of your kind and generous considerations for myself, I bid you all an affectionate farewell.

— Robert E. Lee, General Order, No. 9, April 9, 1865

The momentous meaning of this occasion impressed me deeply. I resolved to mark it by some token of recognition which could be no other than a salute of arms. Well aware of the responsibility assumed, and of the criticisms that would follow, as the sequel proved, nothing of that kind could move me in the least. The act could be defended, if needful, by the suggestion that such a salute was not to the cause for which the flag of the Confederacy stood, but to its going down before the flag of the Union. My main reason, however, was one for which I sought no authority nor asked forgiveness. Before us in proud humiliation stood the embodiment of manhood: men whom neither toils and sufferings, nor the fact of death, nor disaster, nor hopelessness could bend from their resolve; standing before us now, thin, worn, and famished, but erect, and with eyes looking level into ours, waking memories that bound us together as no other bond;— was not such manhood to be welcomed back into a Union so tested and assured?

— US Brigadier General Joshua Lawrence
   Chamberlain

On April 14, 1865, John Wilkes Booth shot President Abraham Lincoln at Ford's Theater in Washington, D.C. The president died the next morning.

Florida: March 1865

Natural Bridge, Florida (FL006), Leon County, March 6, 1865

US Brigadier General John Newton and USN Lieutenant Commander William Gibson launched a joint expedition against the Confederates near St. Marks below Tallahassee under the overall command of CS Major General Sam Jones. Their objective was the Confederate-held fort/battery at the confluence of the Wakulla and St. Marks Rivers. On March 3 an advance force of 90 Federals captured the East River Bridge, four miles north of the St. Marks lighthouse but were unable to hold it. The expedition lost its advantage of surprise because the ships went aground. The St. Marks River was too shallow for the deep draft of the twelve steamers and four schooners. Newton disembarked with his 1,000-man force of the 2nd and 99th Regiments of U.S. Colored Troops, along with several dismounted companies of the 2nd Florida Cavalry Regiment. They recaptured the East River Bridge on March 5 and advanced until they were blocked at Newport Bridge by Confederate cavalry and volunteers from Tallahassee, including young cadets from the West Florida Seminary.

Leaving the cavalry to hold the Federal position on the east bank of the Newport Bridge, Newton advanced with approximately 600 U.S. Colored Troops on a night march to the narrow natural bridge crossing of the river, six miles to the north. On March 6 they were stopped at Natural Bridge by about 700 entrenched troops commanded by CS Brigadier General William Miller. The Federals initially pushed the Confederates back but not away from the bridge. After a day-long effort to dislodge the defenders, the unsuccessful Federals retreated to the protection of the fleet.

Estimated Casualties: 148 US, 25 CS

Natural Bridge Battlefield State Historic Site, six miles east of Woodville on Natural Bridge Road, includes seven acres of the historic battlefield. Woodville is six miles south of Tallahassee.

Mobile Campaign: March–April 1865

Spanish Fort, Alabama (AL005), Baldwin County, March 27–April 8, 1865

The Federal victory in the battle of Mobile Bay and the capture of Fort Gaines and Fort Morgan in August 1864 closed the port of Mobile to Confederate shipping. The city of Mobile, thirty miles up the bay, continued as a Confederate stronghold, ringed with fortifications and defended by 10,000 men under CS Major General Dabney H. Maury. In March 1865 US Major General Edward R. S. Canby, commanding the XIII and XVI Corps, advanced up the eastern shore of the bay to rendezvous with US Major General Frederick Steele's force from Pensacola, capture Spanish Fort and Fort Blakely on the eastern shore, and flank Mobile.

On March 17 Canby moved up the east side of Mobile Bay. He united with Steele at Danley's Ferry and with 45,000 troops initiated the siege of Spanish Fort on March 27. They prepared elaborate siege lines and emplaced dozens of batteries. Their constant sniping and shelling wore down the Confederates and destroyed their works faster than they could be repaired. On April 8 the Federals delivered a devastating bombardment with ninety guns, including those of USN Rear Admiral Henry K. Thatcher's six ironclads. The 8th Iowa broke through the Confederate line north of the fort, but the Confederate counterattack slowed the Federals until darkness ended the battle. With his escape route threatened, CS Brigadier General Randall L. Gibson evacuated the garrison after dark along a treadway only eighteen inches wide and about 1,200 yards long. The Confederates made their way to Mobile, and the Federals occupied Spanish Fort early the next morning.

Estimated Casualties: 657 US, 741 CS

Fort Blakely, Alabama (AL006), Baldwin County, April 2–9, 1865

While most of the Federal force besieged Spanish Fort, US General Canby detached US General Steele's force to blockade Fort Blakely, three miles up the Apalachee River. Steele cut off the fort on April 2 and began digging siege lines. After Spanish Fort fell on April 8, Canby concentrated 18,000 men to attack Blakely. The fort was garrisoned by about 3,800 men under CS Brigadier General St. John R. Liddell, defending its nine redoubts. At 5:30 P.M. on Sunday, April 9 — the day that CS General Robert E. Lee surrendered at Appomattox — the Federals stormed forward over a front more than two miles long. They charged at a full run through *abatis*, fields of mines, and heavy gunfire. Their numbers were overwhelming, and they quickly broke through the Confederate defenses. The attack included US Brigadier General John P. Hawkins's division of U.S. Colored Troops.

After Fort Blakely fell, Union troops were ferried to the western side of Mobile Bay for the attack on Mobile. On April 12, the same day that Lee's troops stacked their arms at Appomattox Court House, CS General Maury abandoned the indefensible city to save his troops.

Estimated Casualties: 775 US, 3,700 (including 3,200 prisoners) CS

Blakely State Park is on Route 225 near Spanish Fort, twelve miles northeast of Mobile, off Interstate 10. Areas of the historic battlefield are within the park.

Wilson's Raid in Alabama and Georgia: March–May 1865

Selma, Alabama (AL007), Dallas County, April 2, 1865

In late January 1865 US Brigadier General James H. Wilson, the twenty-seven-year-old commander of US Major General George H. Thomas's cavalry at Nashville, began concentrating the 13,500 men of three cavalry divisions in northwestern Alabama. On March 22 they rode to seize Selma, the site of large Confederate iron foundries, a navy yard, and ordnance shops. Their twelve-day raid took them more than three hundred miles into Confederate territory. At the same time Union forces were approaching Mobile, pinning down many of the forces the Confederacy still had in the region. CS Lieutenant General Nathan Bedford Forrest had only about half as many troopers as Wilson and had positioned them throughout the area to meet such threats. He needed to unite them quickly to carry forward his plan to trap Wilson between two of his columns at the Cahaba River. The Federals captured the courier carrying his orders and foiled his plan. Wilson immediately sent US Brigadier General Edward M. McCook to destroy the bridge at Centerville, preventing 3,000 veterans from riding with Forrest to Selma.

On April 1 Wilson battled Forrest at Ebenezer Church, eighteen miles north of Selma. Forrest was wounded by a U.S. captain in a saber attack that ended when Forrest shot and killed the man. The Confederates, including Alabama militia, fell back to a defensive line at the church, where they were beaten, and they retreated with Forrest to Selma. CS Lieutenant General Richard Taylor, the commander of the Department of Alabama, Mississippi, and East Louisiana, joined Forrest at Selma, which was ringed by more than three miles of extensive fieldworks manned by only 3,000 defenders, including Alabama militia.

In the April 2 attack, the 9,000 Federal cavalrymen had another advantage: they had one of the designers of the Selma defenses provide them with sketches of the works. Wilson split his troopers into three columns and captured most of the garrison as well as the guns, warehouses stockpiled with supplies, and the iron foundries. Although Forrest and Taylor escaped, Wilson had beaten Forrest and outfought him.

On April 12 Wilson continued his raid and captured Montgomery, the first capital of the Confederacy. On the same day the Army of Northern Virginia stacked arms at Appomattox Court House, and US Major General Edward R. S. Canby's forces occupied Mobile. Wilson then pushed east to Columbus, Georgia, another major center of Confederate industry, and occupied it on April 16. Wilson's next orders were to capture the president of the Confederacy, Jefferson Davis, who was fleeing through Georgia on his way to Texas to continue the war. Wilson's troops captured Davis on May 10 near Irwinville.

Davis was imprisoned for two years at Fort Monroe, Virginia, then released on bond and never brought to trial. There were no trials for treason after the Civil War. Though Davis lived until he was eighty-one, he never requested a pardon. He received one posthumously from President Jimmy Carter. CS General Robert E. Lee requested a pardon, but it was never forwarded to the president during Lee's lifetime. Gerald Ford granted the pardon during his presidency.

Estimated Casualties: 359 US, 2,700 CS

That we are beaten is a self-evident fact, and any further resistance on our part would be justly regarded as the height of folly and rashness. . . . Reason dictates and humanity demands that no more blood be shed. Fully realizing and feeling that such is the case, it is your duty and mine to lay down our arms, submit to the "powers that be," and to aid in restoring peace and establishing law and order throughout the land. The terms upon which you were surrendered are favorable, and should be satisfactory and acceptable to all. They manifest a spirit of magnanimity and liberality on the part of the Federal authorities which should be met on our part by a faithful compliance with all the stipulations and conditions therein expressed. . . .

Civil war, such as you have just passed through, naturally engenders feelings of animosity, hatred, and revenge. It is our duty to divest ourselves of all such feelings, and so far as in our power to do so to cultivate friendly feelings toward those with whom we have so long contested and heretofore so widely but honestly differed. Neighborhood feuds, personal animosities, and private differences should be blotted out, and when you return home a manly, straightforward course of conduct will secure the respect even of your enemies. Whatever your responsibilities may be to Government, to society, or to individuals, meet them like men. . . . I have never on the field of battle sent you where I was unwilling to go myself, nor would I now advise you to a course which I felt myself unwilling to pursue. You have been good soldiers, you can be good citizens. Obey the laws, preserve your honor, and the Government to which you have surrendered can afford to be and will be magnanimous.

— Lieutenant General Nathan Bedford Forrest in his
farewell to his soldiers, May 9, 1865

Texas: May 1865

Palmito Ranch (TX005), Cameron County, May 12–13, 1865

On November 2, 1863, 6,000 men of the XIII Corps commanded by US Major General Napoleon J. T. Dana had landed at Brazos Santiago Island, Texas, to stop the Confederates from sending cotton and other commodities to Brownsville, where they could easily move them across the Rio Grande into Mexico and load them onto ships bound for Europe. Accompanied by US Major General Nathaniel P. Banks, the troops had captured the town four days later. In July 1864 CS Colonel John S. "Rest in Peace" Ford, a former Texas Ranger, had recaptured Brownsville. The Federals had fled to the coast, where they entrenched in the sand dunes of Brazos Santiago Island, twenty-four miles away.

Although the forces had informally agreed in March 1865 not to fight along the river, the new commander, US Colonel Theodore H. Barrett, ordered his 800 men of the 62nd U.S. Colored Infantry Regiment and a company of the 2nd Texas Cavalry Regiment to the mainland on May 11.

On May 12 the Federals crossed at Boca Chica, found the outpost at White's Ranch deserted, and attacked the Confederate camp at Palmito Ranch, twelve miles from Brownsville. The next afternoon Ford's 350-man "Cavalry of the West" seized the initiative with a two-pronged attack on the Federal front and right flank. The firepower provided by their six 12-pounder cannons helped them drive Barrett back to Boca Chica that evening. The defeated Federals returned to Brazos Santiago. The last battle of the Civil War was won in Texas by the Confederates. Thirteen days later Ford disbanded his unit rather than surrender.

On April 26 CS General Joseph Johnston had surrendered all Confederate forces in the Southeast, including the Army of Tennessee at Durham Station, North Carolina, on the same terms as Lee at Appomattox Court House. CS Lieutenant General Richard Taylor, commanding the Department of Alabama, Mississippi, and East Louisiana, had signed a similar surrender with US

Major General Edward R. S. Canby on May 4 at Citronelle, Alabama, forty miles north of Mobile. The commander of the Trans-Mississippi, CS Lieutenant General E. Kirby Smith, authorized CS Lieutenant General Simon Bolivar Buckner to accept the terms of surrender offered by Canby. Buckner signed the agreement on May 26 in New Orleans, and Smith signed it on a Federal steamer in Galveston harbor on June 2. The final Confederate general to surrender was CS Brigadier General Stand Watie, the Cherokee leader, on June 23 at Doaksville in Indian Territory.

Estimated Casualties: 30 US, 118 CS

The Palmito Ranch battlefield is twelve miles east of Brownsville and south of a Texas Historical Commission interpretive plaque on Route 4. Areas of the battlefield are within the Lower Rio Grande Valley National Wildlife Refuge.

Appendixes

Glossary

About the Authors

Index

Appendix 1

The 384 Principal Battlefields

○

The battlefields are listed in alphabetical order by state and then by county or city. Those marked with an asterisk (*) were designated as Priority I on page 9 of the *Civil War Sites Advisory Commission Report*. Battlefields marked with a dagger (†) have areas open to the public (some require prior permission) or are marked by an information panel or are included in a tour brochure available locally. On the maps on pages 452–456, counties shown in white include terrain where one or more of the 384 principal battles were fought.

Alabama

Fort Blakely: AL006†
Baldwin County, April 2–9, 1865

Spanish Fort: AL005
Baldwin County, March 27–April 8, 1865

Day's Gap: AL001
Cullman County, April 30, 1863

Selma: AL007
Dallas County, April 2, 1865

Athens: AL002
Limestone County, January 26, 1864

Mobile Bay: AL003*†
Mobile and Baldwin Counties, August 2–23, 1864

Decatur: AL004
Morgan and Limestone Counties, October 26–29, 1864

Arkansas

Arkansas Post: AR006†
Arkansas County, January 9–11, 1863

St. Charles: AR002
Arkansas County, June 17, 1862

Pea Ridge: AR001†
Benton County, March 6–8, 1862

Ditch Bayou (Old River Lake): AR017
Chicot County, June 6, 1864

Elkin's Ferry: AR012
Clark and Nevada Counties, April 3–4, 1864

Chalk Bluff: AR007†
Clay County, May 1–2, 1863

Marks' Mills: AR015†
Cleveland County, April 25, 1864

Jenkins' Ferry: AR016†
Grant County, April 30, 1864

Pine Bluff: AR011
Jefferson County, October 25, 1863

Prairie D'Ane: AR013
Nevada County, April 10–13, 1864

Poison Spring: AR014†
Ouachita County, April 18, 1864

Helena: AR008
Phillips County, July 4, 1863

Bayou Fourche (Little Rock): AR010
Pulaski County, September 10, 1863

Devil's Backbone: AR009
Sebastian County, September 1, 1863

Cane Hill: AR004
Washington County, November 28, 1862

Prairie Grove: AR005*†
Washington County, December 7, 1862

Hill's Plantation: AR003
Woodruff County, July 7, 1862

Colorado

Sand Creek: CO001
Kiowa County and/or Cheyenne County,
November 29, 1864

District of Columbia

Fort Stevens: DC001†
District of Columbia, July 11–12, 1864

Florida

Olustee: FL005†
Baker County, February 20, 1864

St. Johns Bluff: FL003†
Duval County, October 1–3, 1862

Santa Rosa Island: FL001†
Escambia County, October 9, 1861

Natural Bridge: FL006†
Leon County, March 6, 1865

Fort Brooke: FL004
Tampa, October 16–18, 1863

Tampa: FL002
Tampa, June 30–July 1, 1862

Georgia

Allatoona: GA023*†
Bartow County, October 5, 1864

Adairsville: GA009
Bartow and Gordon Counties, May 17, 1864

Fort McAllister I: GA002†
Bryan County, January 27–March 3, 1863

Fort McAllister II: GA028†
Bryan County, December 13, 1864

Waynesborough: GA027
Burke County, December 4, 1864

Ringgold Gap: GA005*†
Catoosa County, November 27, 1863

Chickamauga: GA004*†
Catoosa and Walker Counties,
September 18–20, 1863

Fort Pulaski: GA001†
Chatham County, April 10–11, 1862

Jonesboro: GA022
Clayton County, August 31–September 1, 1864

Lovejoy's Station: GA021
Clayton County, August 20, 1864

Kennesaw Mountain: GA015*†
Cobb County, June 27, 1864

Kolb's Farm: GA014†
Cobb County, June 22, 1864

Davis' Cross Roads: GA003
Dade and Walker Counties, September 10–11,
1863

Atlanta: GA017
Fulton and De Kalb Counties, July 22, 1864

Ezra Church: GA018
Fulton County, July 28, 1864

Peachtree Creek: GA016
Fulton County, July 20, 1864

Utoy Creek: GA019
Fulton County, August 5–7, 1864

Buck Head Creek: GA026
Jenkins County, November 28, 1864

Dallas: GA011
Paulding County, May 28, 1864

New Hope Church: GA010
Paulding County, May 25–26, 1864

Pickett's Mill: GA012†
Paulding County, May 27, 1864

Lost Mountain–Brushy Mountain Line: GA013
Paulding and Cobb Counties, June 9–18, 1864

Griswoldville: GA025
Twiggs and Jones Counties, November 22, 1864

Rocky Face Ridge: GA007
Whitfield County and Dalton, May 7–13, 1864

Dalton I: GA006
Whitfield County and Dalton, February 22–27, 1864

Dalton II: GA020
Whitfield County and Dalton, August 14–15, 1864

Dalton III: GA024
Whitfield County and Dalton, October 13, 1864

Resaca: GA008†
Whitfield and Gordon Counties, May 13–15, 1864

Idaho

Bear River: ID001
Franklin County, January 29, 1863

Indiana

Corydon: IN001†
Harrison County, July 9, 1863

Kansas

Baxter Springs: KS002
Cherokee County, October 6, 1863

Lawrence: KS001
Douglas County, August 21, 1863

Marais des Cygnes: KS004
Linn County, October 25, 1864

Mine Creek: KS003†
Linn County, October 25, 1864

Kentucky

Perryville: KY009*†
Boyle County, October 8, 1862

Ivy Mountain: KY003
Floyd County, November 8–9, 1861

Middle Creek: KY005
Floyd County, January 10, 1862

Cynthiana: KY011†
Harrison County, June 11–12, 1864

Munfordville (Battle for the Bridge): KY008
Hart County, September 14–17, 1862

Rowlett's Station: KY004
Hart County, December 17, 1861

Barbourville: KY001
Knox County, September 19, 1861

Camp Wildcat: KY002†
Laurel County, October 21, 1861

Richmond: KY007†
Madison County, August 29–30, 1862

Paducah: KY010
McCracken County, March 25, 1864

Mill Springs: KY006*†
Pulaski and Wayne Counties, January 19, 1862

Louisiana

Donaldsonville I: LA004
Ascension Parish, August 9, 1862

Donaldsonville II: LA013
Ascension Parish, June 28, 1863

Kock's Plantation: LA015
Ascension Parish, July 12–13, 1863

Fort DeRussy: LA017
Avoyelles Parish, March 14, 1864

Mansura: LA022
Avoyelles Parish, May 16, 1864

Yellow Bayou: LA023
Avoyelles Parish, May 18, 1864

Mansfield: LA018†
DeSoto Parish, April 8, 1864

Pleasant Hill: LA019
DeSoto and Sabine Parishes, April 9, 1864

Baton Rouge: LA003
East Baton Rouge Parish, August 5, 1862

Plains Store: LA009
East Baton Rouge Parish, May 21, 1863

Siege of Port Hudson: LA010*†
East Baton Rouge and East Feliciana Parishes,
May 22 – July 9, 1863

Goodrich's Landing: LA014
East Carroll Parish, June 29 – 30, 1863

Vermillion Bayou: LA008
Lafayette Parish, April 17, 1863

Georgia Landing: LA005
Lafourche Parish, October 27, 1862

Lafourche Crossing: LA012
Lafourche Parish, June 20 – 21, 1863

Milliken's Bend: LA011
Madison Parish, June 7, 1863

Monett's Ferry: LA021
Natchitoches Parish, April 23, 1864

Fort Jackson and Fort St. Philip: LA001†
Plaquemines Parish, April 16 – 28, 1862

Stirling's Plantation: LA016
Pointe Coupee Parish, September 29, 1863

Blair's Landing: LA020
Red River Parish, April 12 – 13, 1864

New Orleans: LA002
St. Bernard and Orleans Parishes, April 25 –
May 1, 1862

Fort Bisland: LA006
St. Mary Parish, April 12 – 13, 1863

Irish Bend: LA007
St. Mary Parish, April 14, 1863

Maryland

Folck's Mill: MD008
Allegany County, August 1, 1864

Monocacy: MD007*†
Frederick County, July 9, 1864

Antietam: MD003*†
Washington County, September 17, 1862

Boonsboro-Funkstown – Falling Waters: MD006†
Washington County, July 8 – 14, 1863

Williamsport: MD004
Washington County, July 6, 1863

South Mountain: MD002*†
Washington and Frederick Counties,
September 14, 1862

Hancock: MD001†
Washington County, Maryland, and Morgan
County, West Virginia, January 5 – 6, 1862

Minnesota

Fort Ridgely: MN001†
Nicollet County, August 20 – 22, 1862

Wood Lake: MN002
Yellow Medicine County, September 23, 1862

Mississippi

Corinth: MS002†
Alcorn County and Corinth, October 3 – 4, 1862

Siege of Corinth: MS016*†
Alcorn County and Corinth, April 29 – May 30,
1862

Okolona: MS013
Chickasaw County, February 22, 1864

Grand Gulf: MS004†
Claiborne County, April 29, 1863

Port Gibson: MS006*†
Claiborne County, May 1, 1863

Champion Hill: MS009
Hinds County, May 16, 1863

Raymond: MS007*
Hinds County, May 12, 1863

Big Black River Bridge: MS010
Hinds and Warren Counties, May 17, 1863

Jackson: MS008
Hinds County and Jackson, May 14, 1863

Meridian: MS012
Lauderdale County, February 14–20, 1864

Tupelo: MS015†
Lee County and Tupelo, July 14–15, 1864

Iuka: MS001
Tishomingo County, September 19, 1862

Brices Cross Roads: MS014*†
Union, Prentiss, and Lee Counties, June 10, 1864

Chickasaw Bayou: MS003*
Warren County, December 26–29, 1862

Snyder's Bluff: MS005
Warren County, April 29–May 1, 1863

Battle and Siege of Vicksburg: MS011*†
Warren County and Vicksburg, May 18–July 4, 1863

Missouri
Kirksville: MO013
Adair County, August 6–9, 1862

Mount Zion Church: MO010
Boone County, December 28, 1861

Cape Girardeau: MO020
Cape Girardeau, April 26, 1863

Liberty (Blue Mills Landing): MO003
Clay County, September 17, 1861

Boonville: MO001
Cooper County, June 17, 1861

Clark's Mill: MO017
Douglas County, November 7, 1862

Springfield I: MO008
Greene County, October 25, 1861

Springfield II: MO018
Greene County, January 8, 1863

Wilson's Creek: MO004†
Greene and Christian Counties, August 10, 1861

Glasgow: MO022
Howard County, October 15, 1864

Pilot Knob: MO021*†
Iron County, September 26–28, 1864

Big Blue River (Byram's Ford): MO026†
Jackson County, October 22–23, 1864

Independence I: MO014
Jackson County, August 11, 1862

Independence II: MO025
Jackson County, October 22, 1864

Little Blue River: MO024
Jackson County, October 21, 1864

Lone Jack: MO015
Jackson County, August 15–16, 1862

Westport: MO027†
Jackson County, October 23, 1864

Carthage: MO002†
Jasper County, July 5, 1861

Lexington I: MO006†
Lafayette County, September 13–20, 1861

Lexington II: MO023
Lafayette County, October 19, 1864

Fredericktown: MO007
Madison County, October 21, 1861

Belmont: MO009†
Mississippi County, November 7, 1861

New Madrid/Island No. 10: MO012
New Madrid, Missouri, and Lake County, Tennessee, February 28–April 8, 1862

Newtonia I: MO016†
Newton County, September 30, 1862

Newtonia II: MO029*†
Newton County, October 28, 1864

Roan's Tan Yard: MO011
Randolph County, January 8, 1862

Dry Wood Creek: MO005
Vernon County, September 2, 1861

Marmaton River: MO028
Vernon County, October 25, 1864

Hartville: MO019
Wright County, January 9–11, 1863

New Mexico

Glorieta Pass: NM002*
Santa Fe and San Miguel Counties,
March 26–28, 1862

Valverde: NM001
Socorro County, February 20–21, 1862

North Carolina

Washington: NC011
Beaufort County, March 30–April 20, 1863

South Mills: NC005
Camden County, April 19, 1862

Fort Macon: NC004†
Carteret County, March 23–April 26, 1862

Albemarle Sound: NC013
Chowan and Washington Counties,
May 5, 1864

Fort Anderson: NC010
Craven County, March 13–15, 1863

New Bern: NC003
Craven County, March 14, 1862

Hatteras Inlet Forts: NC001†
Dare County, August 28–29, 1861

Roanoke Island: NC002
Dare County, February 7–8, 1862

Averasboro: NC019
Harnett and Cumberland Counties,
March 16, 1865

Monroe's Cross Roads: NC018
Hoke County, March 10, 1865

Bentonville: NC020*†
Johnston County, March 19–21, 1865

Kinston: NC007
Lenoir County, December 14, 1862

Wyse Fork: NC017
Lenoir County, March 7–10, 1865

Fort Fisher I: NC014†
New Hanover County, December 7–27, 1864

Fort Fisher II: NC015†
New Hanover County, January 13–15, 1865

Wilmington: NC016†
New Hanover County, February 12–22, 1865

Tranter's Creek: NC006
Pitt County, June 5, 1862

Plymouth: NC012
Washington County, April 17–20, 1864

Goldsboro Bridge: NC009
Wayne County, December 17, 1862

White Hall: NC008
Wayne County, December 16, 1862

North Dakota

Stony Lake: ND003
Burleigh County, July 28, 1863

Whitestone Hill: ND004†
Dickey County, September 3–4, 1863

Killdeer Mountain: ND005†
Dunn County, July 28–29, 1864

Big Mound: ND001†
Kidder County, July 24, 1863

Dead Buffalo Lake: ND002
Kidder County, July 26, 1863

Ohio

Salineville: OH002
Columbiana County, July 26, 1863

Buffington Island: OH001
Meigs County, July 19, 1863

Oklahoma

Middle Boggy: OK005
Atoka County, February 13, 1864

Round Mountain: OK001
County Unknown, November 19, 1861

Old Fort Wayne: OK004
Delaware County, October 22, 1862

Cabin Creek: OK006†
Mayes County, July 1–2, 1863

Honey Springs: OK007*†
Muskogee and McIntosh Counties,
July 17, 1863

Chustenahlah: OK003
Osage County, December 26, 1861

Chusto-Talasah: OK002
Tulsa County, December 9, 1861

Pennsylvania

Gettysburg: PA002*†
Adams County, July 1–3, 1863

Hanover: PA001
York County, June 30, 1863

South Carolina

Rivers Bridge: SC011†
Bamberg County, February 2–3, 1865

Charleston Harbor I: SC004
Charleston County, April 7, 1863

Charleston Harbor II: SC009
Charleston County, September 5–8, 1863

Fort Sumter I: SC001†
Charleston County, April 12–14, 1861

Fort Sumter II: SC008†
Charleston County, August 17–September 8,
1863

Fort Wagner I: SC005
Morris Island, Charleston County, July 10–11,
1863

Fort Wagner II: SC007
Morris Island, Charleston County, July 18, 1863

Secessionville: SC002*†
Charleston County, June 16, 1862

Simmons' Bluff: SC003
Charleston County, June 21, 1862

Grimball's Landing: SC006
James Island, Charleston County, July 16, 1863

Honey Hill: SC010
Jasper County, November 30, 1864

Tennessee

Hoover's Gap: TN017
Bedford and Rutherford Counties, June 24–26,
1863

Johnsonville: TN032†
Benton County, November 3–5, 1864

Nashville: TN038
Davidson County, December 15–16, 1864

Bean's Station: TN026
Grainger County, December 14, 1863

Blue Springs: TN020
Greene County, October 10, 1863

Bull's Gap: TN033
Hamblen and Greene Counties,
November 11–14, 1864

Chattanooga I: TN005
Hamilton County and Chattanooga,
June 7–8, 1862

Chattanooga II: TN018
Hamilton County and Chattanooga,
August 21, 1863

Chattanooga III: TN024*†
Hamilton County and Chattanooga,
November 23–25, 1863

Wauhatchie: TN021
Hamilton, Marion, and Dade Counties,
October 28–29, 1863

Davis Bridge (Hatchie Bridge): TN007†
Hardeman and McNairy Counties,
October 5, 1862

Shiloh: TN003†
Hardin County, April 6–7, 1862

Parker's Cross Roads: TN011†
Henderson County, December 31, 1862

Dandridge: TN028
Jefferson County, January 17, 1864

Mossy Creek: TN027
Jefferson County, December 29, 1863

Campbell's Station: TN023
Knox County, November 16, 1863

Fort Sanders: TN025
Knox County, November 29, 1863

Fort Pillow: TN030†
Lauderdale County, April 12, 1864

Jackson: TN009
Madison County, December 19, 1862

Columbia: TN034
Maury County, November 24–29, 1864

Spring Hill: TN035*†
Maury County and Spring Hill,
November 29, 1864

Memphis I: TN004
Memphis, June 6, 1862

Memphis II: TN031
Memphis, August 21, 1864

Murfreesboro I: TN006
Rutherford County, July 13, 1862

Murfreesboro II: TN037†
Rutherford County, December 5–7, 1864

Stones River: TN010†
Rutherford County, December 31, 1862–
January 2, 1863

Vaught's Hill: TN014
Rutherford County, March 20, 1863

Fair Garden: TN029
Sevier County, January 27–28, 1864

Collierville: TN022
Shelby County, November 3, 1863

Dover: TN012
Stewart County, February 3, 1863

Fort Donelson: TN002*†
Stewart County, February 12–16, 1862

Fort Henry: TN001
Stewart County, February 6, 1862

Blountville: TN019
Sullivan County, September 22, 1863

Hartsville: TN008†
Trousdale County, December 7, 1862

Brentwood: TN015
Williamson County, March 25, 1863

Thompson's Station: TN013
Williamson County, March 4–5, 1863

Franklin I: TN016
Williamson County and Franklin, April 10, 1863

Franklin II: TN036
Williamson County and Franklin,
November 30, 1864

Texas

Palmito Ranch: TX005†
Cameron County, May 12–13, 1865

Galveston I: TX002
Galveston County, October 4, 1862

Galveston II: TX003
Galveston County, January 1, 1863

Sabine Pass I: TX001†
Jefferson County, September 24–25, 1862

Sabine Pass II: TX006†
Jefferson County, September 8, 1863

Virginia

Amelia Springs: VA091
Amelia County, April 5, 1865

Namozine Church: VA124
Amelia County, April 3, 1865

Sailor's Creek: VA093†
Amelia, Nottaway, and Prince Edward Counties,
April 6, 1865

Appomattox Court House: VA097†
Appomattox County, April 9, 1865

Appomattox Station: VA096
Appomattox County, April 8, 1865

Piedmont: VA111
Augusta County, June 5, 1864

Waynesboro: VA123
Augusta County, March 2, 1865

Samaria Church (Saint Mary's Church): VA112
Charles City County, June 24, 1864

Wilson's Wharf: VA056†
Charles City County, May 24, 1864

Chester Station: VA051
Chesterfield County, May 10, 1864

Drewry's Bluff: VA012†
Chesterfield County, May 15, 1862

Port Walthall Junction: VA047
Chesterfield County, May 6–7, 1864

Proctor's Creek (Drewry's Bluff): VA053†
Chesterfield County, May 12–16, 1864

Swift Creek and Fort Clifton: VA050
Chesterfield County, May 9, 1864

Ware Bottom Church and Howlett Line: VA054†
Chesterfield County, May 20, 1864

Berryville: VA118
Clarke County, September 3–4, 1864

Cool Spring: VA114
Clarke County, July 17–18, 1864

Brandy Station: VA035*
Culpeper County, June 9, 1863

Cedar Mountain: VA022
Culpeper County, August 9, 1862

Kelly's Ford: VA029
Culpeper County, March 17, 1863

Rappahannock River: VA023
Culpeper and Fauquier Counties,
August 22–25, 1862

Rappahannock Station: VA043
Culpeper and Fauquier Counties,
November 7, 1863

Cumberland Church: VA094
Cumberland County, April 7, 1865

Boydton Plank Road: VA079*
Dinwiddie County, October 27, 1864

Dinwiddie Court House: VA086
Dinwiddie County, March 31, 1865

Five Forks: VA088†
Dinwiddie County, April 1, 1865

Globe Tavern: VA072†
Dinwiddie County, August 18–21, 1864

Hatcher's Run: VA083†
Dinwiddie County, February 5–7, 1865

Lewis's Farm: VA085
Dinwiddie County, March 29, 1865

Peebles' Farm: VA074†
Dinwiddie County, Sept. 30–Oct. 2, 1864

Reams Station I: VA068
Dinwiddie County, June 29, 1864

Reams Station II: VA073
Dinwiddie County, August 25, 1864

Sutherland Station: VA090
Dinwiddie County, April 2, 1865

White Oak Road: VA087*†
Dinwiddie County, March 31, 1865

Jerusalem Plank Road: VA065
Dinwiddie County and Petersburg, June 21–23,
1864

Petersburg III: VA089*†
Dinwiddie County and Petersburg, April 2, 1865

Chantilly: VA027†
Fairfax County, September 1, 1862

Dranesville: VA007
Fairfax County, December 20, 1861

Auburn I: VA039
Fauquier County, October 13, 1863

Auburn II: VA041
Fauquier County, October 14, 1863

Buckland Mills: VA042
Fauquier County, October 19, 1863

Fredericksburg II: VA034
Fredericksburg, May 3, 1863

First Kernstown: VA101*
Frederick County and Winchester,
March 23, 1862

Second Kernstown: VA116
Frederick County and Winchester, July 24, 1864

Rutherford's Farm: VA115
Frederick County and Winchester, July 20, 1864

First Winchester: VA104
Frederick County and Winchester, May 25, 1862

Second Winchester: VA107
Frederick County and Winchester,
June 13–15, 1863

Opequon (Third Winchester): VA119
Frederick and Clark Counties and Winchester,
September 19, 1864

Cedar Creek: VA122*†
Frederick, Shenandoah, and Warren Counties,
October 19, 1864

Staunton River Bridge: VA113†
Halifax and Charlotte Counties, June 25, 1864

Hampton Roads: VA008
Hampton Roads, March 8–9, 1862

Beaver Dam Creek (Mechanicsville/Ellerson's
Mill): VA016†
Hanover County, June 26, 1862

Cold Harbor: VA062*†
Hanover County, May 31–June 12, 1864

Gaines' Mill: VA017*†
Hanover County, June 27, 1862

Hanover Court House: VA013
Hanover County, May 27, 1862

Haw's Shop: VA058
Hanover County, May 28, 1864

Matadequin Creek (Old Church): VA059
Hanover County, May 30, 1864

Totopotomoy Creek and Bethesda Church:
VA057
Hanover County, May 28–30, 1864

North Anna: VA055*†
Hanover and Caroline Counties, May 23–26,
1864

Chaffin's Farm and New Market Heights:
VA075*†
Henrico County, September 29–30, 1864

Darbytown and New Market Roads: VA077
Henrico County, October 7, 1864

Darbytown Road: VA078
Henrico County, October 13, 1864

First Deep Bottom: VA069†
Henrico County, July 27–29, 1864

Second Deep Bottom: VA071*†
Henrico County, August 13–20, 1864

Fair Oaks and Darbytown Road: VA080
Henrico County, October 27–28, 1864

Garnett's and Golding's Farms: VA018
Henrico County, June 27–28, 1862

Glendale: VA020a*†
Henrico County, June 30, 1862

Malvern Hill: VA021*†
Henrico County, July 1, 1862

Oak Grove: VA015
Henrico County, June 25, 1862

Savage's Station: VA019
Henrico County, June 29, 1862

Seven Pines: VA014
Henrico County, May 31–June 1, 1862

White Oak Swamp: VA020b†
Henrico County, June 30, 1862

Yellow Tavern: VA052
Henrico County, May 11, 1864

McDowell: VA102†
Highland County, May 8, 1862

Walkerton: VA125
King and Queen County, March 2, 1864

Aldie: VA036
Loudoun County, June 17, 1863

Ball's Bluff: VA006
Loudoun County, October 21, 1861

Middleburg: VA037
Loudoun and Fauquier Counties,
June 17–19, 1863

Upperville: VA038
Loudoun and Fauquier Counties, June 21, 1863

Trevilian Station: VA099
Louisa County, June 11–12, 1864

Lynchburg: VA064
Lynchburg, June 17–18, 1864

Eltham's Landing: VA011
New Kent County, May 7, 1862

Sewell's Point: VA001
Norfolk, May 18–19, 1861

Mine Run: VA044*†
Orange County, November 26–
December 2, 1863

Morton's Ford: VA045
Orange and Culpeper Counties,
February 6–7, 1864

The Crater: VA070†
Petersburg, July 30, 1864

Fort Stedman: VA084†
Petersburg, March 25, 1865

Petersburg I: VA098†
Petersburg, June 9, 1864

Rice's Station: VA092
Prince Edward County, April 6, 1865

High Bridge: VA095
Prince Edward and Cumberland Counties,
April 6–7, 1865

Petersburg II: VA063†
Prince George County and Petersburg,
June 15–18, 1864

Bristoe Station: VA040*
Prince William County, October 14, 1863

Cockpit Point: VA100
Prince William County, January 3, 1862

First Manassas: VA005†
Prince William County, July 21, 1861

Second Manassas: VA026*†
Prince William County,
August 28–30, 1862

Manassas Station/Junction: VA024
Prince William County,
August 26–27, 1862

Blackburn's Ford: VA004
Prince William and Fairfax Counties,
July 18, 1861

Thoroughfare Gap: VA025
Prince William and Fauquier Counties,
August 28, 1862

Cloyd's Mountain: VA049
Pulaski County, May 9, 1864

Cross Keys: VA105†
Rockingham County, June 8, 1862

Port Republic: VA106†
Rockingham County, June 9, 1862

Fisher's Hill: VA120*†
Shenandoah County, September 21–22, 1864

New Market: VA110†
Shenandoah County, May 15, 1864

Tom's Brook: VA121†
Shenandoah County, October 9, 1864

Marion: VA081
Smyth County, December 16–18, 1864

Saltville I: VA076
Smyth County, October 2, 1864

Saltville II: VA082
Smyth County, December 20–21, 1864

Chancellorsville: VA032*†
Spotsylvania County, April 30-May 6, 1863

Salem Church: VA033†
Spotsylvania County, May 3–4, 1863

Spotsylvania Court House: VA048*†
Spotsylvania County, May 8–21, 1864

Wilderness: VA046*†
Spotsylvania County, May 5–6, 1864

Fredericksburg I: VA028†
Spotsylvania County and Fredericksburg,
December 11–15, 1862

Aquia Creek: VA002
Stafford County, May 29–June 1, 1861

Suffolk I: VA030
Suffolk, April 13–15, 1863

Suffolk II (Hill's Point): VA031
Suffolk, April 19, 1863

Sappony Church: VA067
Sussex County, June 28, 1864

Front Royal: VA103
Warren County, May 23, 1862

Guard Hill: VA117
Warren County, August 16, 1864

Manassas Gap: VA108
Warren and Fauquier Counties, July 23, 1863

Cove Mountain: VA109
Wythe County, May 10, 1864

Big Bethel: VA003
York County and Hampton, June 10, 1861

Siege of Yorktown: VA009†
York County and Newport News,
April 5–May 4, 1862

Williamsburg: VA010†
York County and Williamsburg, May 5, 1862

West Virginia

Philippi: WV001
Barbour County, June 3, 1861

Hoke's Run (Falling Waters): WV002
Berkeley County, July 2, 1861

Moorefield: WV013
Hardy County, August 7, 1864

Harpers Ferry: WV010*†
Jefferson County, September 12–15, 1862

Shepherdstown: WV016
Jefferson County, September 19–20, 1862

Summit Point and Cameron's Depot: WV014
Jefferson County, August 21, 1864

Smithfield Crossing: WV015
Jefferson and Berkeley Counties,
August 28–29, 1864

Princeton Courthouse: WV009
Mercer County, May 15–17, 1862

Carnifex Ferry: WV006†
Nicholas County, September 10, 1861

Kessler's Cross Lanes: WV004
Nicholas County, August 26, 1861

Camp Allegheny: WV008
Pocahontas County, December 13, 1861

Cheat Mountain: WV005
Pocahontas County, September 12–15, 1861

Droop Mountain: WV012†
Pocahontas County, November 6, 1863

Greenbrier River: WV007
Pocahontas County, October 3, 1861

Rich Mountain: WV003*†
Randolph County, July 11, 1861

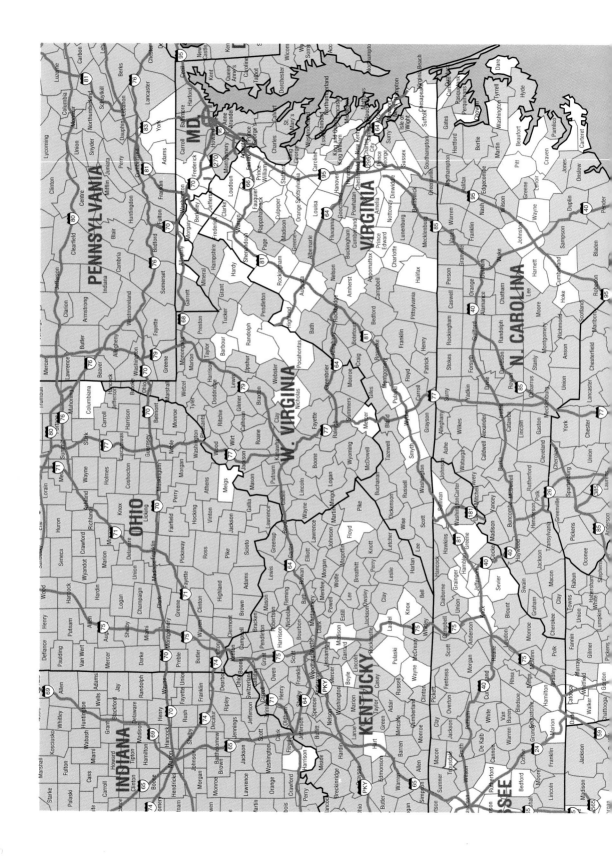

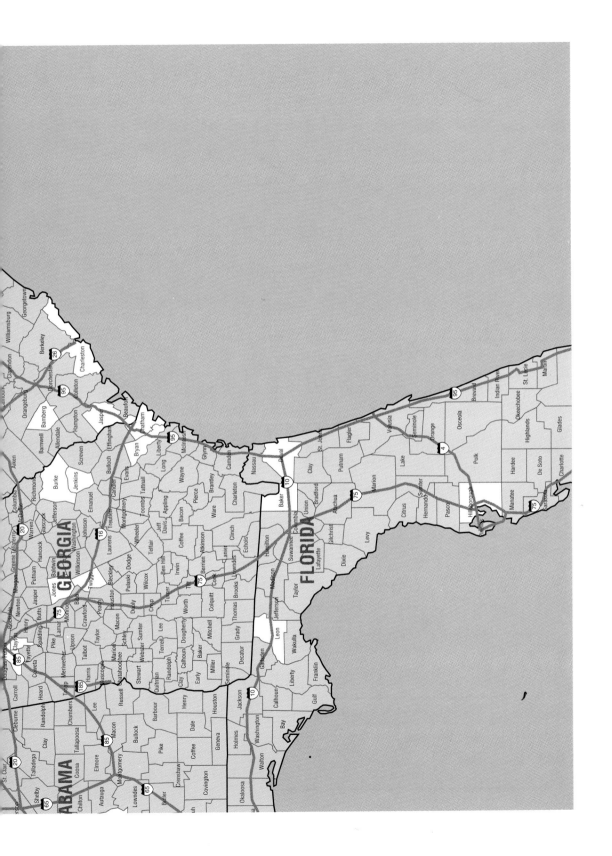

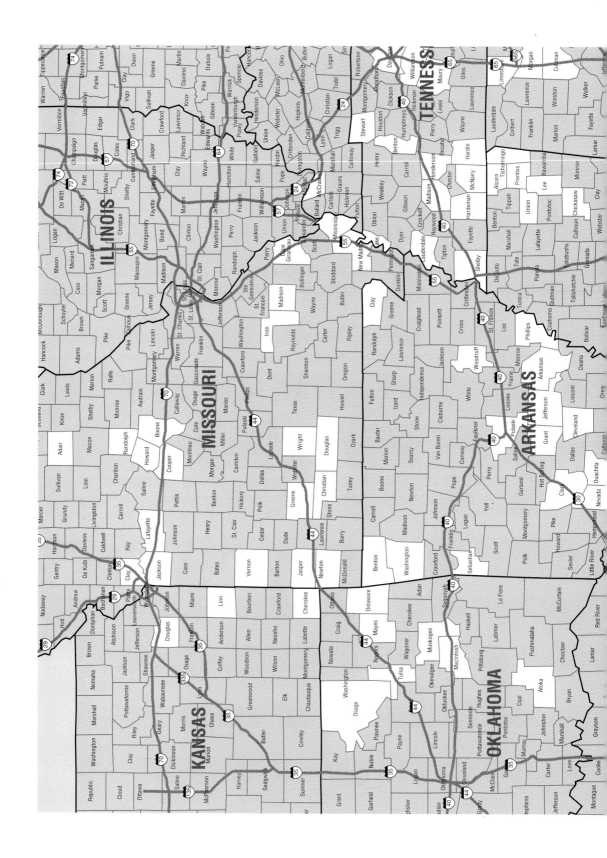

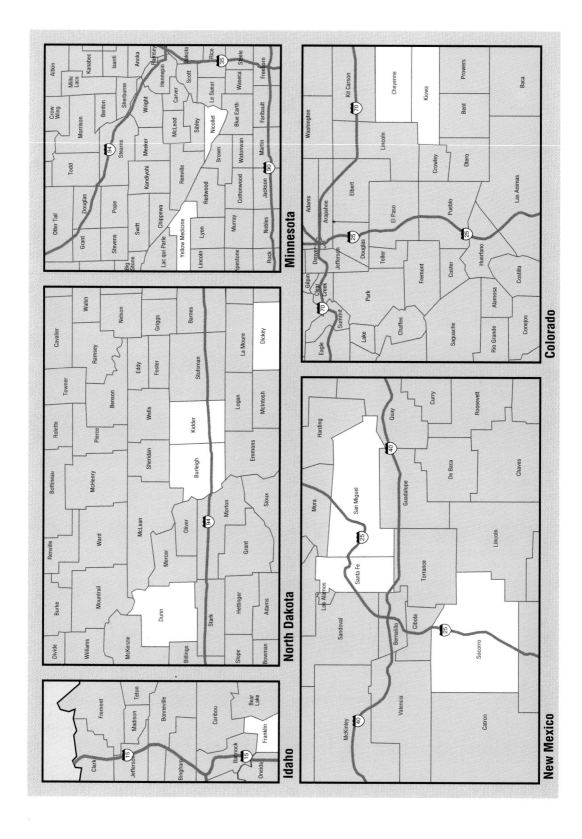

Minnesota

Colorado

North Dakota

New Mexico

Idaho

Appendix 2

An Excerpt from the

Civil War Sites Advisory Commission
Report on the Nation's Civil War Battlefields

❶

Dr. Holly A. Robinson, Chair (Georgia)

Mr. Hyde H. Murray, Vice-Chair (District of Columbia)

Mr. Edwin C. Bearss, ex-officio (District of Columbia)

Dr. Mary Frances Berry (Pennsylvania)

Mr. Ken Burns (New Hampshire)

Dr. Robert D. Bush, ex-officio (District of Columbia)

Mr. Howard J. Coffin (Vermont)

Dr. William J. Cooper, Jr. (Louisiana)

Hon. Frances "Peg" Lamont (South Dakota)

Mr. J. Roderick Heller III (District of Columbia)

Hon. Robert J. Mrazek (New York)

Dr. James M. McPherson (New Jersey)

Hon. Charles H. Taylor (North Carolina)

Hon. William J. Wright (Georgia)

Executive Summary

This nation's Civil War heritage is in grave danger. It is disappearing under buildings, parking lots, and highways. Recognizing this as a serious national problem, Congress established the Civil War Sites Advisory Commission in 1991. The Commission was to identify the significant Civil War sites, determine their condition, assess threats to their integrity, and offer alternatives for their preservation and interpretation. Because of limited time and resources, the Commission concentrated on battlefields as the central focus of the Civil War and of many contemporary historic preservation decisions.

Protecting these battlefields preserves an important educational asset for the nation because:

- Seeing the battlefield is basic to an understanding of military campaigns and battles while the latter are crucial to comprehending all other aspects of the Civil War.

- To be upon a battlefield is to experience an emotional empathy with the men and, in fact, the women who fought there.

- Clashing convictions and the determination to defend them cost the nation 620,000 lives.

- The values tested and clarified in that great conflict are what continue to bind the nation together today.

Today, more than one-third of all principal Civil War battlefields are either lost or are hanging onto existence by the slenderest of threads. It is not too late to protect the remaining battlefields if the nation acts swiftly. If it does not act now, however, within 10 years we may lose fully two-thirds of the principal battlefields.

The Primary Battlefield Findings

The Battlefield Sites: Some 10,500 armed conflicts occurred during the Civil War ranging from battles to minor skirmishes; 384 conflicts (3.7 percent) were identified as the principal battles and classified according to their historic significance.

Class A and B battlefields represent the principal strategic operations of the war. Class C and D battlefields usually represent operations with limited tactical objectives of enforcement and occupation.

- 45 sites (12%) were ranked "A" (having a decisive influence on a campaign and a direct impact on the course of the war);

- 104 sites (27%) were ranked "B" (having a direct and decisive influence on their campaign);

- 128 sites (33%) were ranked "C" (having observable influence on the outcome of a campaign);

- 107 sites (28%) were ranked "D" (having a limited influence on the outcome of their campaign or operation but achieving or affecting important local objectives).

The 384 principal battles occurred in 26 states. States with fifteen or more include: Virginia (123), Tennessee (38), Missouri (29), Georgia (28), Louisiana (23), North Carolina (20), Arkansas (17), and Mississippi (16).

Some counties, such as Henrico and Dinwiddie counties in Virginia and Charleston County in South Carolina, have a great concentration of battlefields. Yet, even in Virginia, where two great armies fought for most of four years, only one-third of the counties have any of the principal Civil War battlefields.

Forty-three percent of the battlefields are completely in private ownership. An additional 49 percent are under multiple kinds of ownership (e.g., private, state, and Federal). Only 4 percent of the principal battlefields are owned primarily by the Federal, state, or local governments.

Their Condition: Nineteen percent (71) of the Civil War battlefields are already lost as intact historic landscapes. Half of the 232 principal battlefields that currently are in good or fair condition are now experiencing high or moderate threats. Most of these sites will be lost or seriously fragmented within the coming 10 years, many very soon. Only one-third of the principal battlefields currently face low threats.

Their Preservation: Some 22 percent of the principal battlefields (84) have been listed in, or determined eligible for, the National Register of Historic Places.

Sixteen battlefields are designated National Historic Landmarks; 58 are partly or entirely included within the boundaries of National Park units; 37 principal battlefields have some state park ownership. Many of these parks protect only very small areas of the battlefield.

Appendix 3

Lost and Fragmented Civil War Battlefields

o

Appendix Q of the *Civil War Sites Advisory Commission Report* lists the following, of the 384 battlefields, as "lost as complete and coherent historic battlefields." The report urges the preservation of the surviving areas and, at a minimum, their commemoration with historical markers.

Alabama
Decatur AL004
Selma AL007
Spanish Fort AL005

Arkansas
Bayou Fourche (Little Rock) AR010
Pine Bluff AR011

District of Columbia
Fort Stevens DC001

Florida
Fort Brooke FL004
St. Johns Bluff FL003
Tampa FL002

Georgia
Atlanta GA017
Ezra Church GA018
Jonesboro GA022
Peachtree Creek GA016

Kansas
Baxter Springs KS002
Lawrence KS001

Kentucky
Barbourville KY001
Ivy Mountain KY003
Paducah KY010

Louisiana
Donaldsonville I LA004
Donaldsonville II LA013
Milliken's Bend LA011
Vermillion Bayou LA008

Mississippi
Jackson MS008
Meridian MS012
Tupelo MS015

Missouri
Cape Girardeau MO020
Carthage MO002
Independence II MO025

Kirksville MO013
New Madrid/Island No. 10 MO012
Springfield I MO008
Westport MO027

North Carolina
Goldsboro Bridge NC009
Kinston NC007
Plymouth NC012
Washington NC011
Wilmington NC016

Oklahoma
Chusto-Talasah OK002

South Carolina
Fort Wagner I SC005
Fort Wagner II SC007

Tennessee
Bean's Station TN026
Campbell's Station TN023
Chattanooga I TN005
Chattanooga III TN018
Columbia TN034

Dover TN012
Fort Henry TN001
Fort Sanders TN025
Johnsonville TN032
Memphis II TN031
Murfreesboro I TN006
Nashville TN038
Wauhatchie TN021

Virginia
Appomattox Station VA096
Beaver Dam Creek (Mechanicsville/Ellerson's
   Mill) VA016
Big Bethel VA003
Chantilly VA027
Chester Station VA051
Darbytown and New Market Roads VA077
First Winchester VA104
Garnett's and Golding's Farms VA018
Lynchburg VA064
Petersburg I VA098
Seven Pines VA014
Sewell's Point VA001
Waynesboro VA123

West Virginia
Princeton Courthouse WV009

Petersburg National Battlefield, Virginia. On April 2, 1865, Colonel George W. Gowen died leading the 48th Pennsylvania Regiment in a charge against Confederate fortifications. In 1907 Union and Confederate veterans gathered near the site to dedicate this monument (*left*) to the colonel and the regiment. During his address the adjutant general of Pennsylvania, Thomas J. Stewart, spoke of the importance of commemorating that place: "Round about us are heroic fields. Round about us the dead of both armies sleep, while the living survivors of the war-worn and veteran legions of Grant and Lee are gathered here fraternally, recalling the incidents of that great struggle. These men gaze again upon the unforgettable pictures that have hung these many years upon the chamber walls of their memory; and today, they and we thank God that the sword has been sheathed, the cannon silenced, the muskets stacked, the war flags furled, and that once again, in glorious Virginia, Pennsylvania is welcome." *Below:* The monument in 1989, at the intersection of Sycamore Street and Crater Road on the south side of Petersburg. (National Park Service)

Salem Church, in Fredericksburg and Spotsylvania National Military Park, Virginia. On May 3, 1863, Union and Confederate forces battled in the fields and woods surrounding Salem Church. The brick church was a fort for Confederate troops during the battle and a hospital afterward. Today only the church and its grounds are preserved. (© Patricia Lanza)

Appendix 4

War Statistics

Robert W. Meinhard

◑

Dead and wounded in the Civil War, 1861–1865*

	Dead	Wounded	Total
Federal	364,511	281,881	646,392
Confederate	260,000	194,000	454,000
Total	624,511	475,881	1,100,392

*The number of dead and wounded, especially for the Confederates, is not known exactly because many reports were incomplete or inaccurate, and records were lost. These figures are estimates from the evidence available. Sources include the Department of Defense; E. B. Long, *The Civil War Day by Day: An Almanac;* Thomas L. Livermore, *Numbers and Losses in the Civil War in America, 1861–1865;* and James M. McPherson, *Battle Cry of Freedom.*

American deaths in service in nine wars†

Revolutionary War‡, 1775–1783	4,435
War of 1812‡, 1812–1815	2,260
Mexican War, 1846–1848	13,283
Civil War, 1861–1865	624,511
Spanish-American War, 1898	2,446
World War I, 1917–1918	110,516
World War II, 1941–1945	404,399
Korean War, 1950–1953	33,916
Vietnam War, 1964–1973	58,184

†Figures, except those for the Confederates in the Civil War, are from the Department of Defense, Selected Manpower Statistics, Fiscal Year 1996. Another source for the Revolutionary War, *The Toll of Independence*, ed. Howard Peckham, gives the number of battle deaths as 7,174, and the number of probable deaths in service as 25,674.

‡Battle deaths only.

Glossary

○

Abatis. A network of felled trees in front of an entrenched position, with branches interlaced and facing the enemy's position to form an obstacle to attacking troops.

Angle and return. A turn made in a fortified line to provide covering fire for other parts of the line or to protect the line from enfilading fire and flank attack.

Army. The armies were composed of corps, which controlled divisions, composed of brigades, consisting of regiments. Two to ten (usually three to five) regiments were assigned to a brigade, two to six (usually three or four) brigades to a division, and two to five (usually two or three) divisions to a corps. In 1863, for example, the average Federal brigade contained about 2,000 men and the Confederate about 1,800.

Artillery. Field artillery maneuvered with troops, while heavy artillery was used to defend or attack fixed positions. Guns were either smoothbore or rifled; rifled guns had greater range and accuracy, while the smoothbore were more effective as close-range antipersonnel weapons. Types of artillery included:

Napoleon—a smoothbore 12-pounder with a range of about 1,600 yards.

Parrott—a rifled gun invented by R. P. Parrott in calibers for both field and heavy artillery. One such caliber, the 20-pounder, had a maximum range of about 3,500 yards. Ten- and 20-pounders were used by the field artillery, while Parrotts ranging from 30- to 300-pounders were used in fortifications and to bombard cities.

Ordnance (three-inch)—a rifled 10-pounder. The maximum effective range of rifled artillery was about 2,500 yards.

Columbiad—a large, smoothbore cannon (eight, ten, and fifteen inches) used in inland as well as coastal fortifications. Columbiads were occasionally rifled.

Break contact. To move away from the enemy intentionally for tactical or strategic reasons.

Breastworks. A barricade of logs, fence rails, stones, sandbags, or other material to protect troops fighting on the defensive. When erected in front of trenches, breastworks are covered with the dirt excavated from the trenches.

Cashier. To dismiss an officer from the service for disciplinary reasons.

Contraband. Technically, enemy property or goods subject to seizure by a belligerent power in war. During the Civil War "contrabands" became the popular name for freed slaves.

Countermarch. To reverse the direction of marching troops and return to or near the starting point.

Demonstrate. In military operations, to make a show of force on a given front without actually attacking in order to distract enemy attention from the actual point of attack. A demonstration is similar to a feint.

Earthworks. Military fortifications constructed of earth, sand, gravel, etc.

Echelon. To deploy troops in echelon is to arrange them in parallel lines to the side and rear of the

---

Note: The definitions for abatis, breastworks, cashier, contraband, countermarch, demonstrate, earthworks, enfilade, envelop, feint, flank, flotilla, forage, forced march, parole, picket, quartermaster, redan, regular, repeating firearm, salient, screen, solid shot, transport, trooper, volley, and works are reprinted by permission of McGraw-Hill Publishing Company from *Ordeal by Fire*, pages 651–53, by James M. McPherson (New York: Alfred A. Knopf, 1982).

front line, presenting the appearance of steps. To attack in echelon is to have each unit advance as soon as the unit next to it moves forward; such attacks were successive rather than simultaneous and often broke down if just one unit in the sequence failed to advance.

Enfilade. To bring an enemy position under fire from the side or end instead of directly or obliquely from the front. The advantage of enfilading fire is twofold: shots that miss the initial target may hit men farther down the line, and the enemy has difficulty returning the fire effectively without risk of hitting their own men.

Envelop. To undertake an attack on one or both flanks or the rear of an enemy position; to encircle or surround.

Face. Either of the two outer sides that form the foremost angle of a fort or breastworks.

Feint. A limited attack or movement of troops against one objective to mislead the enemy and cause him to weaken his defenses at the intended point of real attack. Similar to but more aggressive than a demonstration.

Flank. The side or end of a moving or stationary column or line of troops. To "flank" an enemy position is to get around to its side or rear in order to enfilade the position. A "flanking march" is the movement of troops to get on the enemy's flank or rear.

Flotilla. A group of warships and transports acting in concert for a specific purpose. A flotilla generally contains a smaller number of ships than a fleet.

Forage. As a noun, grass, hay, or grain for horses and mules. Forage was as necessary for a Civil War army as petroleum is for a modern army. The verb "to forage" means to seek food for humans as well as for animals.

Forced march. A long march of troops at a fast pace made necessary by an impending battle or other emergency.

Garrison. A force stationed at a fortified place. It can also mean the place where troops are stationed, usually a permanent facility. As a verb, *garrison* means to provide a fort with a force.

General officers. The Union army had three grades of general officer: lieutenant general (Ulysses S. Grant), major general, and brigadier general. The Confederate army grades included general (Samuel Cooper, Robert E. Lee, and six others), lieutenant general, major general, and brigadier general. Brevet rank, a higher rank, usually without an increase in pay and with a limited exercise of the higher rank, was granted as an honor when there was no vacancy for promotion to a higher substantive grade.

Lunette. A work consisting of a salient angle with two flanks open to the rear.

Parole. An oath by a captured soldier, given in return for release from captivity, not to bear arms against the captors until formally exchanged for one of the captor's soldiers. To parole a captured soldier is to exact such an oath as a condition of his release.

Picket. A soldier assigned to the perimeter of an army encampment or position to give warning of enemy movements.

Quartermaster. An officer responsible for supplying army units with uniforms, shoes, equipment (exclusive of ordnance), transportation, and forage. The Quartermaster Bureau or Quartermaster Corps is the army administrative department in charge of this function.

Redan. Earthworks or breastworks thrown up in front of a cannon in the form of an inverted V to protect the gun and its crew from enemy fire.

Refused. Describes a flank that is protected from enemy attack by being angled toward the rear or anchored on a difficult or impenetrable natural or manmade obstacle; also refers to troops deployed in echelon.

Regular. An officer or soldier in the peacetime army, or "regular army," as distinguished from a "volunteer" in the "volunteer army," who enlisted for the specific purpose of fighting in the Civil War.

Repeating firearm. A gun that can be fired two or more times before reloading.

Retrograde. A backward movement or retreat.

Return. The portion of a fortification (including trenches) that connects a salient (angle) with the main axis of the defenses.

Salient. A portion of a defensive line or trench that juts out toward the enemy.

Screen (cavalry). A patrol of the front and flanks of an army to prevent enemy cavalry or scouts from getting close enough to the main army for observation.

Solid shot. Round cannonballs that do not explode.

Stand of arms. A soldier's rifle-musket and cartridge belt or his complete set of equipment: rifle-musket, bayonet, cartridge belt, and box.

Transport. An unarmed ship carrying troops or supplies.

Trooper. A cavalryman.

Unlimber. To detach the artillery piece from the limber (a two-wheeled cart pulled by six horses or mules) and prepare it for use.

Van. The troops who march at the front of an army; the advance guard.

Volley. The simultaneous firing of guns by an entire unit of soldiers.

Works. A general term to describe defensive military fortifications of all kinds.

About the Authors

○

Don E. Alberts is president of Historical Research Consultants of Albuquerque and president of the Glorieta Battlefield Preservation Society. He was chief historian for Kirtland Air Force Base. He is the author of *Brandy Station to Manila Bay: The Biography of General Wesley Merritt; Rebels on the Rio Grande: The Civil War in New Mexico;* and *Balloons to Bombers: Albuquerque Aviation, 1928–1982.*

Stacy Allen is a National Park Service historian at Shiloh National Military Park and was a contributor to *The Atlas of the Civil War,* James M. McPherson, editor.

Michael J. Andrus was a park ranger at Manassas National Battlefield Park and at Fredericksburg and Spotsylvania National Military Park, and is now a park ranger at Richmond National Battlefield Park. He is a coauthor of *The Brooke, Fauquier, Loudoun and Alexandria Artillery* for the Virginia Regimental History Series.

John G. Barrett, professor of history emeritus, Virginia Military Institute, is the author of *Sherman's March Through the Carolinas; The Civil War in North Carolina;* and *North Carolina as a Civil War Battleground.* He is a coeditor with W. B. Yearns of *North Carolina Civil War Documentary.*

Edwin C. Bearss is chief historian emeritus of the National Park Service. He is the author and editor of fourteen books on the Civil War and western expansion and more than two hundred historical monographs, including *Forrest at Brice's Cross Roads and in North Mississippi in 1864; Hardluck Ironclad: The Sinking and Salvage of the Cairo;* and *The Vicksburg Campaign.*

Arthur W. Bergeron, Jr., is the historian for the Pamplin Park Civil War Site at Petersburg, Virginia. He is editor of *The Civil War Reminiscences of Major Silas T. Grisamore, C.S.A.* and the author of *Confederate Mobile, 1861–1865* and *Guide to Louisiana Confederate Military Units, 1861–1865.*

Bob L. Blackburn is deputy executive director of the Oklahoma Historical Society and editor of *The Chronicles of Oklahoma.* He is the author of twelve books on the history of Oklahoma and the West.

Keith S. Bohannon is a doctoral candidate in the history department at Pennsylvania State University and a former historian at the Fredericksburg and Spotsylvania National Military Park. He is on the staff of the Chattanooga Civil War Sites Assessment Project.

Daniel A. Brown began his work with the National Park Service at Fort Pulaski National Monument. He was the historian at Kennesaw Mountain National Battlefield and at Cumberland Gap National Historical Park. He is a priest in the Episcopal Church and the rector of Calvary Episcopal Church in Wadesboro and of All Souls' Episcopal Church in Ansonville, North Carolina.

Kent Masterson Brown is a lawyer in Danville, Kentucky, and Washington, D.C. He was chairman of the Gettysburg National Military Park Advisory Commission and was the chairman of the Perryville Battlefield Commission. He was founder and editor of *The Civil War,* the magazine of the Civil War Society. He is the author of *Cushing of Gettysburg: The Story of a Union Artillery Commander.*

Albert Castel is an author-historian specializing in the Civil War. His books include *A Frontier State at War: Kansas, 1861–1865; General Sterling Price and the Civil War in the West;* and *Decision in the West: The Atlanta Campaign of 1864.*

Christopher M. Calkins is a historian with the National Park Service at Petersburg National Battlefield, his third Civil War battlefield. He has written numerous articles and books dealing mainly with the final year of the war. He is also active in Civil War battlefield preservation efforts.

William C. Davis was the editor of *Civil War Times*

Illustrated magazine and is now a full-time writer. He has published more than thirty works of Civil War history, including *Fighting Men of the Civil War,* an illustrated history of the common soldier, North and South.

Frank Allen Dennis is professor of history and chair of the Department of History at Delta State University. He is the editor of *Kemper County Rebel: The Civil War Diary of Robert Masten Holmes, C.S.A.; Southern Miscellany: Essays in History in Honor of Glover Moore;* and *Recollections of the 4th Missouri Cavalry.* He is the compiler of a two-volume index to *The Journal of Mississippi History.*

LeRoy H. Fischer is Oppenheim Professor of History Emeritus at Oklahoma State University in Stillwater. He is the editor of *The Civil War Era in Indian Territory* and other books on the Civil War in the American West.

Dennis E. Frye is president of the Association for the Preservation of Civil War Sites and was formerly the chief historian at Harpers Ferry National Historical Park. He wrote *2nd Virginia Infantry* and *12th Virginia Cavalry.*

Gary W. Gallagher is professor of history at the University of Virginia. He is the author of *Stephen Dodson Ramseur: Lee's Gallant General; The Confederate War;* and *Lee and His Generals in War and Memory;* the editor of *Fighting for the Confederacy: The Personal Recollections of General Edward Porter Alexander;* and editor and coauthor of *The Third Day at Gettysburg and Beyond* and *Lee the Soldier.* He is editor of the Civil War America series at the University of North Carolina Press and past president of the Association for the Preservation of Civil War Sites.

A. Wilson Greene is executive director of the Pamplin Park Civil War Site at Petersburg, Virginia. His writings include *Whatever You Resolve to Be: Essays on Stonewall Jackson* and *The National Geographic Guide to Civil War Battlefield Parks.*

William W. Gwaltney is chief of interpretation at Rocky Mountain National Park. He was the superintendent of Fort Laramie National Historic Site and is interested in the history of African Americans during the nineteenth century, with an emphasis on the periods of the Civil War, westward expansion, and the Indian wars. He is a cofounder of Company B of the 54th Massachusetts Volunteer Infantry, an Afri-

can American Civil War interpretation and re-enactment group.

Clark B. Hall is an officer of the Chantilly Battlefield Association and serves on the board of the Brandy Station Foundation. He is completing a book on the battle of Brandy Station. He is a retired congressional investigator.

Richard W. Hatcher III was a historian with the National Park Service at Wilson's Creek National Battlefield and is currently at Fort Sumter National Monument. He is a contributor to *The Encyclopedia of the Confederacy.*

Herman Hattaway is professor of history at the University of Missouri–Kansas City and was visiting professor of military art at the U.S. Military Academy. He is the author of *General Stephen D. Lee* and coauthor of *How the North Won: A Military History of the Civil War.*

Paul Hawke is chief of interpretation and resource management at Shiloh National Military Park. He is also the secretary-treasurer of the Civil War Fortification Study Group. He has worked at Petersburg National Battlefield, Fredericksburg and Spotsylvania National Military Park, Independence National Historical Park, and Pea Ridge National Military Park.

John Heinz was the senior United States senator from Pennsylvania until his death in 1991. He was coauthor of "Project 88: Harnessing Market Forces to Protect Our Environment: Initiatives for the New President," an analysis of major conservation issues recommending new natural resources policies.

John J. Hennessy was a historian at Manassas Battlefield and the New York State Office of Historic Preservation, and is now the assistant superintendent at Fredericksburg and Spotsylvania National Military Park. He is the author of *The First Battle of Manassas: An End to Innocence* and *Return to Bull Run: The Campaign and Battle of Second Manassas.*

Earl J. Hess is assistant professor of history at Lincoln Memorial University. He is the coauthor with William L. Shea of *Pea Ridge: Civil War Campaign in the West* and is the author of several other books and articles on the military history of the Civil War.

Lawrence Lee Hewitt is the managing editor of *North and South.* He was a professor of history at Southeastern Louisiana University and the historic site manager of the Port Hudson State Commemorative Area. He is the author of *Port Hudson, Confederate Bastion on the Mississippi* and coauthor of *The Confederate High Command and Related Topics; Leadership During the Civil War; Miles Legion: A History and Roster;* and *Boone's Louisiana Battery: A History and Roster.*

James Oliver Horton is the Benjamin Banneker Professor of American Civilization and History at George Washington University and director of the African-American Communities Project of the National Museum of American History at the Smithsonian Institution. He was Senior Fulbright Professor of American Studies at the University of Munich in Germany (1988–89). Among his most recent books are *Free People of Color; A History of the African American People;* and *In Hope of Liberty.*

Ludwell H. Johnson is professor of history emeritus at the College of William and Mary and the author of *Red River Campaign: Politics and Cotton in the Civil War* and *Division and Reunion: America, 1848–1877.*

Robert E. L. Krick is a Civil War historian based in Richmond, Virginia, and the author of *The Fortieth Virginia Infantry* and numerous articles for journals and magazines.

Robert K. Krick is the author of more than one hundred published articles and ten books. His *Stonewall Jackson at Cedar Mountain* won the 1991 Douglas Southall Freeman Award for Best Book in Southern History. *Conquering the Valley: Stonewall Jackson at Port Republic* (1996) was a selection of the Book-of-the-Month Club and a main selection of the History Book Club.

Thomas A. Lewis writes about history and the environment from his home in the Shenandoah Valley. He has served as director and president of the Cedar Creek Battlefield Foundation. He is the author of *The Guns of Cedar Creek.*

Michael D. Litterst was a National Park Service ranger at Gettysburg National Military Park and Richmond National Battlefield Park, and is currently a historian with the Manassas National Battlefield Park.

David W. Lowe is a historian with the National Park Service. He was on the staff of the Civil War Sites Advisory Commission and was the principal researcher for the Civil War Sites in the Shenandoah Valley Report to Congress.

Jay Luvaas is retired professor of military history at the U.S. Army War College. He is coauthor of the U.S. Army War College series Guide to Civil War Battlefields and Campaigns; author of *The Military Legacy of the Civil War: The European Inheritance;* and editor of *The Civil War: A Soldier's View,* by G. R. Henderson.

William D. Matter is a retired United States Air Force pilot and the author of *If It Takes All Summer: The Battle of Spotsylvania.*

David McCullough is the author of *The Path Between the Seas; Mornings on Horseback; Brave Companions;* and *Truman.*

Richard M. McMurry is a historian who lives in Americus, Georgia. He specializes in the history of the Civil War in the West.

James M. McPherson is George Henry Davis 1886 Professor of American History at Princeton University. His books include *The Struggle for Equality; The Abolitionist Legacy; Ordeal by Fire; Battle Cry of Freedom;* and *What They Fought For, 1861–1865.*

Grady McWhiney is the Lyndon Baines Johnson Professor of History Emeritus at Texas Christian University and the Distinguished Visiting Professor of History at McMurry University. He is the author of *Cracker Culture; Attack and Die;* and *Braxton Bragg and Confederate Defeat.*

Robert W. Meinhard is professor of history emeritus at Winona State University and former department chairman. He has been active in battlefield preservation, was a founder of the Battlefield Preservation Advisory Coalition, and is a columnist for *The Civil War News.*

J. Michael Miller is senior archivist at the Marine Corps Research Center in Quantico, Virginia. He has published numerous articles on the Civil War and Marine Corps history, and is the author of *Even to Hell Itself: The North Anna River Campaign.*

Richard Moe is president of the National Trust for Historic Preservation, a director of the Civil War Trust, and author of *The Last Full Measure— The Life and Death of the First Minnesota Volunteers,* from which his essay is adapted.

Sam Nunn is a partner in the law firm of King & Spalding. He is a former United States senator from Georgia and former chairman of the Senate Armed Services Committee.

T. Michael Parrish is an archivist at the Lyndon Baines Johnson Library at the University of Texas. He is the author of *Richard Taylor: Soldier Prince of Dixie* and editor of *The Military Operations of General Beauregard,* by Alfred Roman.

Garrett C. Peck, a graduate of the Virginia Military Institute, served in the U.S. Army in Germany. He received his master's degree in international affairs at George Washington University. He was a research assistant for a second edition of *The Civil War Battlefield Guide.*

Donald C. Pfanz is the author of *Abraham Lincoln at City Point* and *General Richard S. Ewell: A Soldier's Life.*

Harry W. Pfanz was the historian at Gettysburg National Military Park for ten years and was the chief historian of the National Park Service at the time of his retirement in 1981. He is the author of *Gettysburg: The Second Day* and *Gettysburg: Culp's Hill and Cemetery Hill.*

Brian C. Pohanka has written numerous articles and several books dealing with Civil War subjects. An adviser for several films, and active in battlefield preservation, he served as series consultant for the History Channel's documentary, *Civil War Journal.*

Ethan S. Rafuse was on the staff of the Fort Ward Museum and Historic Site in Alexandria, Virginia, and is a doctoral candidate at the University of Missouri–Kansas City. He is the author of articles and reviews on Civil War topics.

George A. Reaves III was the National Park Service supervisor ranger at Shiloh National Military Park until his death in 1994. He wrote publications for Shiloh National Military Park, Manassas National Military Park, and Horseshoe Bend National Military Park. He was the coauthor of *Seeing the Elephant: The Raw Recruits at the Battle of Shiloh.*

James I. Robertson, Jr., is Alumni Distinguished Professor in history at Virginia Polytechnic Institute and State University. He is the author or editor of twenty-two books on the Civil War, including *Soldiers Blue and Gray; General A. P. Hill;* and *Civil War Sites in Virginia.*

William Glenn Robertson is a professor of military history at the U.S. Army Command and General Staff College, Fort Leavenworth, Kansas. He is the author of *Back Door to Richmond: The Bermuda Hundred Campaign, April–June, 1864* and *The Petersburg Campaign: The Battle of Old Men and Young Boys, June 9, 1864.* Forthcoming works include *River of Death: The Chickamauga Campaign* and *A Walking Guide to Chickamauga.*

Charles P. Roland is alumni professor emeritus at the University of Kentucky. He has been president of the Southern Historical Association and has served as the visiting professor of military history at the U.S. Army War College and the U.S. Military Academy. He is the author of *The Confederacy; Albert Sidney Johnston: Soldier of Three Republics; Reflections on Lee: A Historian's Assessment;* and *An American Iliad: The Story of the Civil War.*

David R. Ruth is the chief of interpretation at Richmond National Battlefield Park, and has served at Fort Sumter National Monument, Manassas National Battlefield, and Fredericksburg and Spotsylvania National Military Park. He is the author of articles and reviews on the Civil War.

William R. Scaife is an Atlanta architect and author of *Campaign for Atlanta,* which received the Richard Barksdale Harwell Award, and *Allatoona Pass, a Needless Effusion of Blood.* He is chairman of the board of the Kennesaw Mountain Historical Association, and is a planning and historical consultant.

Stephen W. Sears is the author of *Landscape Turned Red: The Battle of Antietam, George B. McClellan: The Young Napoleon; To the Gates of Richmond: The Peninsula Campaign;* and *Chancellorsville.* He is the editor of *The Civil War Papers of George B. McClellan* and *For Country, Cause & Leader: The Civil War Journal of Charles B. Haydon.*

William L. Shea is professor of history at the University of Arkansas at Monticello. He is coauthor of *Pea Ridge: Civil War Campaign in the West* and author of several books and articles on the trans-Mississippi theater of operations.

John Y. Simon is professor of history at Southern Illinois University at Carbondale, executive director of the Ulysses S. Grant Association, and editor of eighteen volumes of *The Papers of Ulysses S. Grant.*

Richard J. Sommers is assistant director for archives at the U.S. Army Military History Institute and author of *Richmond Redeemed: The Siege at Petersburg,* which was awarded the National Historical Society's Bell I. Wiley Prize. He is on the board of the Society of Civil War Historians and of the Jefferson Davis Association.

Richard W. Stephenson was the specialist in American cartographic history in the Geography and Map Division, Library of Congress. He is a part-time member of the faculty at George Mason University, where he teaches the history of cartography. His publications include *Civil War Maps: An Annotated List of Maps and Atlases in the Library of Congress* and *The Cartography of Northern Virginia.* His most recent publication is *A Plan Wholly New: Pierre Charles L'Enfant's Plan of the City of Washington.*

William A. Stofft (Major General, U.S. Army, Ret.) was commandant of the Army War College in Carlisle, Pennsylvania, director of management at the Headquarters of the Department of the Army, and chief of military history for the U.S. Army, supervising the staff ride program for the army leadership. He is coeditor of *America's First Battles, 1776–1965.*

Robert G. Tanner practices law in Atlanta, Georgia, and is the author of *Stonewall in the Valley,* which was recently reissued with extensive revisions.

Emory Thomas is Regents Professor of History at the University of Georgia. His most recent book is *Robert E. Lee: A Biography.*

Jan Townsend is the cultural resources program lead, Eastern States, Bureau of Land Management. She was formerly the chief of the American Battlefield Protection Program at the National Park Service and the project manager for the Civil War Sites Advisory Commission 1991–93 study. She has conducted research and written about the Civil War history of Prince William County, Virginia, and wrote the Bristoe Station Battlefield National Register of Historic Places nomination.

Noah Andre Trudeau is a producer in the cultural programming division of National Public Radio. He writes on American music and film music, as well as the Civil War. He is the author of an "end of the war" trilogy, covering campaigns in the 1864–65 period, consisting of *Bloody Roads South; The Last Citadel;* and *Out of the Storm.*

William H. Webster is senior partner in the law firm of Milbank, Tweed, Hadley & McCloy. He was the director of the Central Intelligence Agency, director of the Federal Bureau of Investigation, and judge of the United States Court of Appeals for the Eighth Circuit. He is a member of the board of directors of the Civil War Trust.

Joseph W. A. Whitehorne (Lieutenant Colonel, U. S. Army, Ret.) was staff historian for the inspector general of the army and is professor of history at Lord Fairfax Community College. His books and articles on military subjects include two guidebooks, *The Battle of Cedar Creek* and *The Battle of New Market.* His most recent book, *The Battle for Baltimore,* is about the war of 1812 in the Chesapeake Bay.

Terrence J. Winschel has served at Gettysburg National Military Park, Fredericksburg and Spotsylvania National Military Park, Valley Forge National Historical Park, and is the historian at Vicksburg National Military Park. He is the author of *The Corporal's Tale* and *Alice Shirley and the Story of Wexford Lodge* and coauthor of *Vicksburg, a Self-Guiding Tour of the Battlefield.* He has also written more than forty articles on the Civil War.

Stephen R. Wise is the director of the Parris Island Museum at the Marine Corps Recruit Depot in South Carolina and an adjunct professor at the University of South Carolina at Beaufort. He is the author of *Lifeline of the Confederacy: Blockade Running During the Civil War* and *Gate of Hell: Campaign for Charleston Harbor 1863.*

Index

o

Page numbers in italics refer to maps and photographs.

Abercrombie, John J., 11
A. B. Noyes, 263
Abolitionism, 133, 185–86, 188
Adairsville, Ga., battle of, 331
Adams, Charles Francis, Jr., 80, 424
Adams, Daniel W., 126
Adams, Emil, 261
Adams, Henry, 214
Adela, 263
African American troops. *See* Black troops
Albemarle, 277
Albemarle Sound, N.C., battle of, 277
Aldie, Va., battle of, 205
Alexander, E. Porter, 213, 363
Alexandria, La., 266, 272
Allatoona, Ga., battle of, 390–91, *390*
Allen, Robert O., 204
Amelia Springs, Va., battle of, 424
American Indians. *See* Native Americans
American (Know Nothing) Party, 224
Ames, Adelbert, 402
Ames, John W., 365
Ames, Nelson, *253, 254*
Anaconda Plan, 5, 58
Anacostia, 18
Anderson, "Bloody Bill," 379
Anderson, George Thomas, 357
Anderson, George W., 400
Anderson, Hiram, 195
Anderson, James Patton, 126
Anderson, Richard H.: at Chancellorsville, *198,* 199; at Cold Harbor, 291, *292,* 293–94; as Early's reinforcements, 313; at Fredericksburg I, 145, *146–47;* at

Gettysburg, *209–10,* 211; at Lewis's Farm, 412; at Manassas Gap, 213–14; at North Anna, *288,* 289; at Petersburg II, 353; to Richmond, 315; at Sailor's Creek, *425,* 426; at Santa Rosa Island, 27; to Shenandoah Valley, 356; at Smithfield Crossing, 314; at Spotsylvania Court House, *284;* at Summit Point, 314; at White Oak Road, 413
Anderson, Robert, 1, 3
Anderson, Samuel R., 10
Andrews, W. S., 61
Anthony, Susan B., 378
Antietam, Md., battle of, 118–21, *119,* 201, *236*
Appomattox campaign, 412–33, *414–16, 418, 420–21, 425, 430*
Appomattox Court House, Va., battle of, 429–33, *430*
Appomattox River, 324, 352, 426, 427
Appomattox Station, Va., battle of, 428–29
Aquia Creek, Va., battle of, 5–6
Archer, James J., 148
Arkansas, 58, 136
Arkansas Post, Ark., battle of, 157
Armistead, Lewis A. J., 103
Armstrong, Frank C., 250–51, 342, *393*
Army Corps of Topographical Engineers, 25, 71
Arnold, Richard, 271
Arnold, William, 252–54, *253*
Ashby, Turner, *75,* 76, 81, 82
Atchison, D. R., 24
Athens, Ala., battle of, 261
Atkins, Smith D., 400
Atkinson, C. F., 285
Atlanta, Ga., battle of, 340, 342, 343

Atlanta campaign, 261, 271, 275, 326–43, *327, 330, 333, 337,* 344
Atlantic & North Carolina Railroad, 60–61, 62, 194
Auburn I and II, Va., battles of, 251–52
Augur, Christopher C., *106,* 107, 181
Augustana, Alexander T., 188
Averasboro, N.C., battle of, 407
Averell, William W.: at Cove Mountain, 297–98; at Droop Mountain, 240; at Folck's Mill, 312; at Kelly's Ford, 196; at Moorefield, 313; at Opequon, 316; at Rutherford's Farm, 309; in Staunton area, 301
Ayres, Romeyn B.: at Five Forks, 417–19, *418;* at Globe Tavern, 357; at Peebles' Farm, 368; at White Oak Road, 413, 415, *416*

Bailey, Joseph, 272
Bailey, Theodorus, 263
Baird, Absalom, 227
B & O Railroad, 6, 18, 74, 205, 312, 314, 315
Baker, Edward D., 18
Baldwin, William E., 163–64
Balloon corps, 71
Ball's Bluff, Va., battle of, 18
Baltimore & Ohio Railroad. *See* B & O Railroad
Banks, Nathaniel P.: and Brashear City, 180; at Brownsville, 437; at Cedar Mountain, *106,* 107; in Congress, 224; at First Winchester, 81; at Fort Bisland, 179; Grant's orders to, 267; at Mansfield, 267–69, *268,* 326; at Mansura, 272; at Pleasant Hill, 269–71, *270;* at Port Hudson, 180; at Port Hudson siege, 181–84, *183;*

and Red River campaign, 265–72; relieved of command, 271; at Sabine Pass II, 232; and Shenandoah Valley campaign, 74, 76, 78, 80, 81, 90; to Shreveport, 273; at Vermillion Bayou, 179

Barbourville, Ky., battle of, 28

Barksdale, William, 145, *146–47*

Barlow, Francis C., *284,* 285–86, *292,* 293, 354, 428

Barrett, Theodore H., 437

Barringer, Rufus, 423

Barron, Samuel, 59

Barstow, Hiram E., 134

Barton, Seth, *155,* 156, 169

Bartow, Francis F., 14

Bass, Frederick S., 364–65, *367*

Bate, William B.: at Bentonville, *409,* 410; at Dallas, *333,* 334; at Dalton III, 391; at Murfreesboro II, 396; at Pine Mountain, 335; at Resaca, *330;* at Rocky Face Ridge, *327;* at Spring Hill, *393,* 394–95; at Utoy Creek, 341

Baton Rouge, La., battle of, 136–37

Battery Wagner. *See* Fort Wagner, S.C., battle of

Battle, Joel A., 28

Battle for the Bridge, Ky., 123

Baxter Springs, Kans., battle of, 224

Bayou Fourche (Little Rock), Ark., battle of, 233

Bean's Station, Tenn., battle of, 249

Bear Hunter, 217

Bear River, Idaho, battle of, 217–18

Beatty, Samuel, 153

Beaty, Powhatan, 365

Beauregard, P. G. T.: in Army of Mississippi, 48; and Bermuda Hundred campaign, 278–80; at Blackburn's Ford, 11; and Bull Run, 11; at Charleston Harbor I, 191; as commander of Department of North Carolina and Southern Virginia, 278; at Corinth, 52–56, *54–55;* at First Manassas, 12, *13,* 14–15; at Fort Sumter I, 1, 4; and Morris Island evacuation, 193; and New Madrid/Island No. 10, 56; at Petersburg II, 353; Petersburg position of, 278, 279; and plans for Hood, 392; and reinforcements

for Lee, 291; relieved of command, 122; and Sherman's Carolina campaign, 405; at Shiloh, 49–52, *50–51;* sick leave for, 129; withdrawal from Fort Pillow and Memphis, 57

Beaver Dam Creek (Mechanicsville/Ellerson's Mill), Va., battle of, 93–94

Beckham, Robert F., 202

Bee, Barnard E., 14

Bee, Hamilton P., 271–72

Bell, Sarah, 49

Bell, Tyree H.: at Brices Cross Road, *345,* 346; at Spring Hill, *393,* 394–95; at Tupelo, *348,* 350

Belmont, Mo., battle of, 26, 45

Benham, Henry W., 67, *68,* 69

Benjamin, Judah P., 61, 74

Benteen, Frederick W., 384

Benton, William, *159,* 164

Bentonville, N.C., battle of, 408–11, *409*

Bermuda Hundred campaign, 278–80, 287, 290

Bernard, Simon, 63

Berryville, Va., battle of, 315

Bethesda Church, Va., 290

Big Bethel, Va., battle of, 6

Big Black River Bridge, Miss., battle of, 170–71

Big Blue River (Byram's Ford), Mo., battle of, 383

Big Mound, N.D., battle of, 222

Birney, David B.: at Darbytown Road, 369; at Fort Gilmer, 363, *366;* at Jerusalem Plank Road, 353–54; at New Market Heights, 364–65, *367;* at Petersburg II, 353; at Second Deep Bottom, 356, *358–59*

Black, Isaac J., 28

Blackburn's Ford, Va., battle of, 11

Blackford, Eugene, 199

Black Kettle, 398

Black troops: casualty rate of, 188; in Confederate army, 188; Confederate policy on, 186; and the Crater, 355; at Dalton III, 391; Douglass on, 184; at Fort Blakely, 435; and Fort Clifton, 278; at Fort Fisher II, 402; at Fort Pillow, 276; at Fort Pocahontas, 290; at Fort

Wagner, 192, 193, 263; at Goodrich's Landing, 175; at Honey Springs, 221; Lincoln on, 186, 193, 264; at Milliken's Bend, 173, 175; at Nashville, 397; at Natural Bridge, 434; in navy, 188; at New Market Heights, 364–65; number of, 188; at Olustee, 263, 264; at Palmito Ranch, 437; photograph of, *238;* at Port Hudson, 182, 184, 264; recipients of Medal of Honor, *187,* 188; recruitment of, 186, 188; in Richmond, 424; at Saltville I, 387; under Sherman, 261; at Sol Legare Island, 192; training of, 173, 175; at Tupelo, 349–50; War Department's position on, 186

Blair, Francis P., Jr.: at Champion Hill, 169; and decision on war in Missouri, 20; at Kennesaw Mountain, *337;* at Lost Mountain–Brushy Mountain Line, 335; to Old Auburn, 166; at Rivers Bridge, 405; at Snyder's Bluff, 158

Blair, Montgomery, 3

Blair's Landing, La., battle of, 271

Bledsoe, H. M., *165,* 166

"Bleeding Kansas," 224

Bliss, Philip P., 391

Blockade: of Chesapeake Bay, 5–6; of James River, 88; of North Carolina coast, 59, 61; of Potomac River, 5–6, 18–19; of southern ports, 59; of Texas coast, 138–39, 232

Bloodgood, Edward, 190

Blountville, Tenn., battle of, 236, 238

Blue Mills Landing, Mo., 24

Blue Springs, Tenn., battle of, 239–40

Blunt, James G.: in Arkansas, 140, 141; at Baxter Springs, 224; at Cane Hill, 140, 141; as commander of Department of Kansas, 133; at Fort Smith, 221, 224; at Honey Springs, *219,* 220–21; and "Indian Expedition," 133, 218; at Lexington II, 382; at Little Blue River, 382–83; at Marais des Cygnes, 384; and Newtonia I, 134; at Newtonia II, *385,* 386; at

Blunt, James G. (*continued*)
Old Fort Wayne, 134; at Prairie
Grove, 141–43, *142;* at Westport,
384
Bohlen, Henry, 82, *83,* 84
Bombshell, 277
Bonham, Milledge L., 12
Boomer, George B., 170
Boonsboro, Md.: battle of
Boonsboro–Funkstown–Falling
Waters, 213
Boonville, Mo., battle of, 20
Booth, Lionel F., 276
Borcke, Heros von, 205
"Border Ruffians," 224, 377
Bouton, Edward, *348,* 349–50
Bowen, John S.: and Big Black
River Bridge, 171; at Champion
Hill, *168,* 169; at Grand Gulf, 158;
at Port Gibson, 158–64, *159;* at
Vicksburg, 171
Boydton Plank Road, Va., battle of,
369–71, *370,* 372
Bradford, William F., 276
Bradley, Luther Prentice, *393,* 394–
95
Bragg, Braxton: at Bentonville,
408–11, *409;* at Chattanooga I,
122; at Chattanooga II, 226, 227;
at Chattanooga III, 243–46, *244,*
245, 249; at Chickamauga,
226–31, *228–29;* as commander
of Army of Tennessee, 226; as
commander of Army of the Mississippi, 122, 129; as corps commander in Army of the Mississippi, 48; criticisms of, 226, 245,
246, 248; and Davis' Cross Roads,
227; defensive position in Middle
Tennessee, 224; and Fort Fisher
II, 402; at Hoover's Gap, 225; in
Kentucky, 124, 129; and Knoxville, 248; and Morgan's raid in
Indiana, 216; at Perryville, 124–
27, *125;* reinforcements for, 251;
relieved of command, 246; and
Ringgold's Gap, 246; and Santa
Rosa Island, 27; and Sherman's
Carolina campaign, 405; at
Shiloh, 48–49, *50–51;* at Smith-
field, 408; at Stones River, 151–
54, *152;* and Wilmington, 403; at
Wyse Fork, 406
Branch, Lawrence O'B., 60–61, 92

Brandy Station, Va., battle of, 202–
5, *203*
Brannan, John M., 139, *228,* 230
Bratton, John, 357
Brawner, John, 110
Brawner, M. H., 134
Breckinridge, John C.: at Baton
Rouge, 136–37; at Bull's Gap,
387; at Chattanooga III, *244,* 245;
at Cold Harbor, 291, *292;* at
Corinth, 53, *54–55;* corps commander in Army of the Missis-
sippi, 48; at Lynchburg, 304; to
Lynchburg and Shenandoah Val-
ley, 294; at Marion, 388; at Mar-
tinsburg, 312; at Monocacy, 305–
8, *306;* at New Market, 298–301,
299, 326; at Opequon, 315–16; at
Port Hudson, 182; and Saltville I
and II, 387, 388; at Second Kerns-
town, 310–12, *311;* at Shiloh, 48–
49, *50–51;* at Stones River, 153
Breese, K. Randolph, 158, 402
Brentwood, Tenn., battle of, 190
Brices Cross Roads, Miss., battle of,
344–47, *345*
Bristoe campaign, 251–55, *253*
Bristoe Station, Va., battle of, 252–
54, *253*
Brooklyn, 374
Brooks, T. H., 353
Brooks, William T. H., 278
Brown, Egbert B., 177
Brown, Harvey, 27
Brown, John C., 394, 395
Brown, John, Jr., 378
Brown, Joseph E., 64
Brown, T. F., 252–54, *253*
Brown, Williams Wells, 188
Brown's Ferry, Tenn., 241–42
Brushy Mountain Line, Ga.: battle
of Lost Mountain–Brushy Moun-
tain Line, 335–36
Bryan, Goode, 249
Buchanan, Franklin, 88, 374–76,
375
Buchanan, James, 1, 25, 45, 224
Buck Head Creek, Ga., battle of,
399–400
Buckingham, Catharinus Putnam,
144
Buckland Mills, Va., battle of,
254–55
Buckner, Simon B.: at Chicka-

mauga, *228–29,* 230–31; at Fort
Donelson, 45–47, *46;* at Munfordville, 123; at Perryville, 124,
126; surrender by, 438
Buel, James T., 133
Buell, Don Carlos: at Chattanooga I,
122; as commander of Army of
the Ohio, 29, 30, 48, 52, 58; at
Corinth, 53, *54–55;* in Kentucky,
124; and Mill Springs, 32; at Per-
ryville, 124–27, *125;* relieved of
command, 126; and Shiloh, 48–
52; in Tennessee Valley, 129
Buell, George P., 408–11, *409*
Buffington Island, Ohio, battle of,
216
Buford, Abraham, 275, 349–50
Buford, John: at Brandy Station,
202, *203,* 204; at Gettysburg, *208;*
and Upperville, 206; at
Williamsport, 212
Bull Run, 11, 12
Bull's Gap, Tenn., battle of, 387
Burbridge, John Q., 134
Burbridge, Stephen G., 344, 387,
388
Burks, Jesse, *75,* 76
Burnham, Hiram, 363
Burnside, Ambrose E.: at Antietam,
119, 120; at Blue Springs, 239–
40; at Boydton Plank Road, 369–
71; at Campbell's Station, 248–
49; at Cincinnati, 216; at Cold
Harbor, *292, 293;* as commander
of Army of the Potomac, 121, 144;
at the Crater, 355; at Fredericksburg I, 144–48, *147–48,* 197; and
Knoxville, 227, 236, 238, 245; and
Morgan's raid in Indiana, 216–
17; and "Mud March," 197; at
New Bern, 60–61; at North Anna,
288, 289; at Petersburg I and II,
352, 353; promotion to major
general, 61; relieved of command, 197, 249, 356; at Roanoke
Island, 60; and South Mills, 61; at
Spotsylvania Court House, *284,*
285–86; and Totopotomoy Creek,
290; in Virginia, 62; in Wilderness, 281
Burrell, Isaac S., 138
Butler, Benjamin F.: and Bermuda
Hundred campaign, 278–80, 287,
290; at Chaffin's Farm, 362–63,

366; at Fort Fisher I, 401–2; and Georgia Landing, 137; Grant's orders to, 267; at Hatteras Inlet Forts, 59–60; at New Orleans, 58, 59; and Petersburg I, 352; replaced by Terry, 402; and Richmond, 260, 326, 364; at Swift Creek, 278; at White House, 291; and Williamsburg Road, 372

Butler, Calbraith, 290

Butler, Matthew C., 407

Butterfield, Daniel: at Fredericksburg I, 148; at Lost Mountain–Brushy Mountain Line, 335; at New Hope Church, Pickett's Mill, and Dallas, 332–35, *333;* at Resaca, 331; at Rocky Face Ridge, *327*

Byram's Ford, Mo., 383

Cabell, William L.: and Cabin Creek, 218; at Honey Springs, 220–21; at Independence II, 383; at Mine Creek, 384; at Newtonia II, 386; at Pilot Knob, 380–82, *381*

Cabin Creek, Okla., battle of, 218, 220

Cahill, Thomas W., 136

Cailloux, André, 184

Cairo, 156

Calhoun, John C., 39

Camden, Ark., expedition, 273–75

Cameron, Robert Alexander, *268, 269*

Cameron's Depot, W.Va., battle of Summit Point and, 314

Camp Allegheny, W.Va., 10

Camp Andrew Johnson, Ky., 28

Campbell, Albert H., 72

Campbell, William J., 380–82, *381*

Campbell's Station, Tenn., battle of, 248–49

Camp Dick Robinson, Ky., 28

Camp Jackson, 20

Camp Johnston, 26

Camp Lawton, 399

Camp Wildcat, Ky., battle of, 29

Canby, Edward R. S., 39, 43, 374, 376, 435, 436, 438

Cane Hill, Ark., battle of, 140

Cane River, 266, 271

Cantey, James, 329–31, *330*

Cape Girardeau, Mo., battle of, 178

Carlin, William P.: at Bentonville,

408–11, *409;* at Fredericktown, 24–25; at Perryville, *125,* 126

Carolina campaign, 405–11, *409*

Carondelet, 44, 57, 136

Carr, Eugene A.: at Champion Hill, 169–70; at Mine Run, *256–57;* at Pea Ridge, 36–37; at Port Gibson, 164

Carroll, William, 32

Carson, Christopher "Kit," 39

Carter, James, 238

Carter, S. D., 32

Carthage, Mo., battle of, 20–21

Cartography. *See* Mapping of Civil War

Case, Henry, 407

Casey, Silas, 92

Casualties in Civil War, 4, 173, 188, 325, 343, 432, 464. *See also* specific battles

Cedar Creek, Va., battle of, 319–23, *320–21*

Cedar Mountain, Va., battle of, 105–7, *106*

Central Georgia Railroad, 399

Chaffin's Farm, Va., battle of, 362–64, *366*

Chalk Bluff, Ark., battle of, 178

Chalmers, James R.: at Collierville, 241; at Fort Pillow, 276; at Munfordville, 123; at Spring Hill, *393;* at Stones River, 153; at Tupelo, *348,* 349–50

Chamberlain, Joshua L., 17, 412, 415, *416,* 431–32, *433*

Chambersburg, Pa., 312, 341

Chambliss, John R.: death of, 357, *358–59;* at Hagerstown, 212; at Sappony Church, 354; at Shepherdstown, 213; at Thoroughfare Gap, 205, 206

Champion Hill, Miss., battle of, *162–63,* 167–70, *168*

Chancellorsville, Va., battle of, 196, 197–99, *198*

Chantilly, Va., battle of, 112

Charles City Crossroads, Va. *See* Glendale, Va., battle of

Charleston, S.C.: battles in June 1862, 67–70; battles in Sept. 1863, 191–94; under Beauregard, 191; fortifications of, 191; Sherman at, 406

Charleston & Savannah Railroad, 70, 192, 400

Charleston harbor, S.C.: first battle, 191–92; Fort Sumter I, 1–4, *2;* Fort Sumter II, 193–94; second battle, 193

Chattanooga, Tenn.: first battle of, 122; second battle of, 226–27; strategic significance of, 227, 243; third battle of, 243–46, *244*

Cheat Mountain, W.Va., battle of, 10

Cheatham, Benjamin Franklin: at Adairsville, 331; at Atlanta, 340; at Belmont, 26; at Kennesaw Mountain, *337,* 338–39; at Meridian, 261; at Nashville, 397; at Perryville, *125,* 126; at Resaca, *330;* at Rocky Face Ridge, *327,* 328; at Spring Hill, *393,* 394–95

Chesnut, Mary, 259

Chester Station, Va., battle of, 279

Chickahominy River, 92, 94, 295

Chickamauga, Ga., battle of, 226–31, *228–29*

Chickamauga campaign, 226–31, *228–29*

Chickasaw Bayou, Miss., 171; battle of, 154–57, *155*

Chicora, 194

Chivington, John M., *40–41,* 42–43, 218, 398

Choctaw, 173, 175

Churchill, James, 269–71, *270*

Churchill, Thomas J., 123, 157, 274–75

Churchill, Winston, 201

Chustenahlah, Okla., battle of, 34

Chusto-Talasah, Okla., battle of, 33–34

Cincinnati, 57

Civil War: casualties in, 4, 173, 188, 325, 343, 432, 464; end of, 431–33, 437–38; first general to die in, 8; impact of, 4, 325–26, 432; last generals to die in, 427–28; mapping of, 71–73; photography in, 201, 234–35, *235–39;* preservation of battlefields, 201–2, 325–26, 432, 458–59; privately owned battlefields, 432; and staff ride, 16–17

Civil War Sites Advisory Commission Report, 458–59

Clark, John B., Jr., 380

Clark's Mill, Mo., battle of, 134

Clayton, Powell, 233

Cleburne, Patrick R.: at Atlanta, 340; at Chattanooga

Clay, Henry, 39 III, *244*, 245–46; death of, 396; at Franklin II, 395; at Kennesaw Mountain, *337*, 338–39; at Lost Mountain–Brushy Mountain Line, 335; at Meridian, 261; at Perryville, 126; at Pickett's Mill, *333*, 334–35; at Resaca, 329, *330;* at Richmond, Ky., 123; at Ringgold Gap, 246–48, *247;* at Rocky Face Ridge, *327;* at Spring Hill, *393*, 394–95

Clifton, 232

Clingman, Thomas L., 63

Cloud, William F., 221

Cloyd's Mountain, Va., battle of, 296–97, *296*, 298

Cluseret, Gustave P., 82, *83*, 84

Cobb, Howell, 117

Cobb, Thomas R. R., *146–47*, 148

Cobham, George A., Jr., 247–48, *247*

Coburn, John, 189

Cockpit Point, Va., battle of, 18–19

Cockrell, Francis M., *159*, 164, 169, 390

Coffee, John T., 133–34

Cogswell, William, *409*, 410

Cold Harbor, Va., battle of, 280, 291–94, *292*

Collierville, Tenn., battle of, 241

Colorado, 27

Colquitt, Alfred H., *116*, 117, 192, 263–64

Colquitt, Peyton, 5

Colston, Raleigh E., 199

Columbia, S.C., 406

Columbia, Tenn., battle of, 392

Comstock, Cyrus B., 175

Conestoga (gunboat), 38

Confederate States of America, 1, 4, 5

Congress, 88

Congressional Joint Committee on the Conduct of War, 18

Connor, Patrick Edward, 217–18

Conservation Fund, 202

Constitutional amendments, 188

Cook, Joseph J., 138

Cooke, J. W., 277

Cooke, John R., 252–54, *253*, 423

Cooke, Philip St. George, 12, 97

Cool Spring, Va., battle of, 309

Cooper, Douglas H.: at Chusto-Talasah, 33–34; as commander of Indian Territory Confederates, 133; at Honey Springs, *219*, 220–21; at Newtonia I, 134; at Old Fort Wayne, 134; at Round Mountain, 33

Corcoran, Michael, 195

Corinth, Miss.: battle of, 129–32, *130;* siege of, 52–56, *54–55*

Corse, John M., 390–91

Corydon, Ind., battle of, 216

Cotton Plant, 277

Couch, Darius N., 103, 148

Cove Mountain, Va., battle of, 297–98

Cox, Jacob D.: at Allatoona, 391; at Goldsboro, 407, 411; at Princeton Courthouse, 80; at Resaca, 329, *330;* at Rocky Face Ridge, *327;* at South Mountain, *116*, 117; at Utoy Creek, 341; at Wilmington, 403; at Wyse Fork, 406

"Cracker Line," 241–42, 245, 255

Crampton's Gap, Md., 115, 117

Crane, Henry, 263

Crater, battle of the, Va., 341, 355–56

Crawford, Samuel W.: at Boydton Plank Road, *370*, 371; at Cedar Mountain, *106*, 107; at Five Forks, *418*, 419; at Globe Tavern, 357; at Hatcher's Run, 372; at White Oak Road, 413, 415, *416*

Creighton, William R., 247–48, *247*

Crittenden, George B., *31*, 32

Crittenden, Thomas L.: at Bradyville, 225; at Chickamauga, *228–29*, 230–31; on Cumberland plateau, 226; at Murfreesboro I, 122; at Perryville, 124, *125*, 126; at Stones River, 151–53, *152*

Crocker, Frederick, 138, 232

Crocker, Marcellus M., *165*, 166, *168*, 170

Crook, George R.: at Cedar Creek, 319, *320–21*, 322; at Cloyd's Mountain, 296–97, *296*, 298; at Cumberland Church, 428; and defense of Shenandoah Valley, 309; at Fisher's Hill, 316–18, *317;*

and Hunter, 304; at Opequon, 316; at Sailor's Creek, *425*, 426; at Second Kernstown, 310–12, *311;* at Snicker's Ford, 309; in Staunton area, 301

Cross Keys, Va., battle of, 82, *83*, 84, 85

Crossland, Edward, *348*, 350

Crusader, 70

Cumberland, 88

Cumberland Church, Va., battle of, 428

Cumberland Gap, Tenn., 239–40

Cumberland River, 45–48, 189

Cumming, Alfred, 169

Curtis, Henry Z., 224

Curtis, Newton M., 402

Curtis, Samuel R.: in Arkansas, 48; at Batesville, 38; at Big Blue River, 383; and death of son, 224; at Helena, 38; at Lexington II, 382; and Little Blue River, 382–83; at Pea Ridge, 34–37, *35;* at Westport, 384; along White River, 38

Cushing, William B., 277

Custer, George A.: at Appomattox Court House, 429–32, *430;* at Appomattox Station, 428; at Brandy Station, 204; at Buckland Mills, 254–55; at Five Forks, *418*, 419; at Guard Hill, 314; at Hanover, 206; at Haw's Shop, 290; and Namozine Church, 423; at Sailor's Creek, *425*, 426; at Tom's Brook, 319; at Trevilian Station, 295; at Waynesboro, 324; at Yellow Tavern, 286–87

Cutshaw, Wilfred E., 313, 315, 319

Cynthiana, Ky., battle of, 344

Dabney, Robert L., 85

Dahlgren, John A., 192, 193–94, 260

Dahlgren, Ulric, 260

Dakota Territory, 222, 223, 351

Dallas, Ga., battle of, *333*, 334–35

Dalton, Ga.: first battle of, 262; second battle of, 341–42; third battle of, 391

Dana, Napoleon J. T., 180–81, 437

Dandridge, Tenn., battle of, 250

Daniel, Junius, 194–95

Darbytown Road, Va.: battle of

Darbytown and New Market Roads, 369; battle of Fair Oaks and Darbytown Road, 372

*David*s, 191

Davidson, John W., 233

Davies, Henry E., 368, 424

Davies, Thomas A., *130,* 131

Davis, Benjamin F. "Grimes," 202

Davis, Charles H., 57, 136

Davis, Jefferson: assassination plans against, 260; and Beauregard, 129; and Bragg, 129, 151, 245, 246, 248; and Bristoe Station, 254; capture and imprisonment of, 436; on Confederacy's desires, 4; and Corinth, 56; and defense of slavery, 186; and Fort Sumter I, 1, 4; at Glendale, 100; and government's escape from Richmond, 422, 429; and Hood, 389; and Johnston, 339; and Lee as commander of army, 93; and Longstreet, 194, 249; and Meridian expedition, 261; and Missouri, 20; and Napoleon III, 265; and Petersburg III, 422; on Pillow in Kentucky, 45; and Port Hudson, 181; posthumous pardon of, 436; and Shenandoah Valley, 304; and Vicksburg battle and siege, 172

Davis, Jefferson C.: at Bentonville, 408–11, *409;* at Kennesaw Mountain, *337,* 338–39; at New Hope Church, 333–34; at Pea Ridge, 36; at Rocky Face Ridge, *327*

Davis Bridge (Hatchie Bridge), Tenn., battle of, 132

Davis' Cross Roads, Ga., battle of, 227

Dawn, 290

Day's Gap, Ala., battle of, 176

Dead Buffalo Lake, N.D., battle of, 222

Dearing, James, 427–28

Decatur, Ala., battle of, 392

DeCourcy, John, *155,* 156

Deep Bottom, Va.: first battle of, 355; second battle of, 356–57, *358–59*

Democratic Party, 224, 343

Dennis, Elias S., *165,* 166, 175

Devil's Backbone, Ark, battle of, 221

Devin, Thomas C.: at Appomattox Court House, 429–32, *430;* at Five Forks, *418,* 419; at Guard Hill, 314; at Sailor's Creek, *425,* 426

Diana, 179

Dibrell, George G., 149

Dinwiddie Court House, Va., battle of, 412–13

Ditch Bayou (Old River Lake), Ark., battle of, 275

Dobbins, Archibald S., 381

Dodge, Grenville M., 329–31, *330, 337,* 340

Donaldsonville, La.: first battle of, 137; second battle of, 180

Donelson, Daniel S., 153

Dorsey, Caleb, 27

Dot, 171

Doty, James J., 218

Doubleday, Abner, 145, *146–47*

Douglas, Stephen A., 224

Douglass, Frederick, 184, 185, 188

Dover, Tenn., battle of, 189

Dowling, Richard W. "Dick," 232

Drake, Francis M., 274

Dranesville, Va., battle of, 18

Draper, Alonzo, 365

Drayton, Percival, 18

Drew, John, 35

Drewry, Augustus, 91

Drewry's Bluff, Va., battle of, 91

Droop Mountain, W.Va., battle of, 240

Dry Wood Creek, Mo., battle of, 23–24

DuBose, Dudley McIver, 357

Dudley, N. A. M., 181

Duffié, Alfred N.: and Brandy Station, 204; at Droop Mountain, 240; at Middleburg, 205–6; at Snicker's Ford, 309

Duke, Basil W., 387

Dumont, Ebenezer, 6

Duncan, Johnson K., 58

Duncan, Samuel A., 364–65, *367*

Dunham, Cyrus L., 123, 150

du Pont, Henry A.: and burning of Virginia Military Institute, 304; at Cedar Creek, 322; at New Market, *299,* 300; at Opequon, 316; at Second Kernstown, 310–12, *311*

Du Pont, Samuel F.: at Charleston Harbor I, 191–92; at Fort McAllister I, 191; at Fort Pulaski, 64, 66; at James Island, 67

Duval, Isaac H., 310–12, *311*

Dwight, William, *183,* 184

Eads, James B., 44

Early, Jubal A.: and Berryville, 315; at Bethesda Church, 290; at Blackburn's Ford, 11; at Bristoe Station, *253;* at Cameron's Depot, 314; at Cedar Creek, 319–23, *320–21;* at Cedar Mountain, 105–7, *106;* and Chambersburg, 312, 341; at Cold Harbor, 291, *292,* 293; at Fisher's Hill, 316–18, *317;* at Fort Stevens, 308–9; at Fredericksburg I, 145, *146–47;* at Fredericksburg II, 199–200; at Gettysburg, 207, *208–9;* Lee's orders to, 304, 305; and Lynchburg, 294, 304; and Manassas campaign, 12; at Mine Run, *256–57,* 258–59; at Monocacy, 305–8, *306;* at Opequon, 316; at Rappahannock Station, 255; reinforcements for, 319, 356; and Richmond, 315; at Second Kernstown, 310–12, *311;* at Second Manassas, *109,* 111; at Second Winchester, 205; and 1864 Shenandoah Valley campaign, 304–13; at Smithfield Crossing, 314; at Staunton, 319; at Waynesboro, 324; and Wilderness, 283; at Williamsburg, 90; Winchester position of, 313–14

East Tennessee & Virginia Railroad, 80, 236, 250, 387

Echols, John, 240, *299,* 300–301

Eisenhower, Dwight D., 16

Elkin's Ferry, Ark., battle of, 273

Ellerson's Mill, Va., 93–94

Ellet, Alfred W., 175

Ellet, Charles, 57

Ellet, Charles, Jr., 57

Elliott, Stephen, 194

Eltham's Landing, Va., battle of, 91

Elzey, Arnold, 82, *83,* 84

Emancipation Proclamation, 120, 188, 189, *238*

Emory, William H.: at Cedar Creek, 319, *320–21;* at Fisher's Hill, 316; and Lafourche Crossing, 180; at

Emory, William H. (*continued*)
  Mansfield, *268*, 269; at Monett's
  Ferry, 271; at Opequon, 315–16;
  at Pleasant Hill, 269
Essex, 136
Evans, Clement A., *306*, 307–8, 372
Evans, John, 398
Evans, Nathan G. "Shanks": at
  Ball's Bluff, 18; at First Manassas,
  12, *13*, 14; at Kinston, 62; at Se-
  cessionville, 67, *68*, 69; at South
  Mountain, 117
Ewell, Richard S.: at Boonsboro–
  Funkstown-Falling Waters, 213;
  at Bristoe Station, 252–54, *253*; at
  Chaffin's Farm, *366*; as comman-
  der of Second Corps of Army of
  Northern Virginia, 200; at Cross
  Keys, 82, *83*, 84, *86*, 87; at First
  Winchester, 81; and Fort Harrison, 363; and Front Royal, 81; at
  Gaines' Mill, *95*, 96; at Gettysburg, 207–12, *208–10;* and
  Gettysburg campaign, 202, 206;
  at Gettysburg, 81; at Kettle Run,
  108; under Jackson, 81; and
  Manassas campaign, 12; at Morton's Ford, 260; at North Anna,
  288, 289; at Sailor's Creek, *425*,
  426; and Second Winchester,
  205; at Spotsylvania Court House,
  284, 285–86; in Wilderness, *281*,
  282–83
Ewing, Thomas, Jr., 224, 378, 379,
  380–82, *381*
Ezra Church, Ga., battle of, 341

Fagan, James F.: at Helena, 175–76;
  at Independence II, 383; at
  Marks' Mills, 274; at Mine Creek,
  384; at Newtonia II, 386; at Pilot
  Knob, 380–82, *381*
Fair Gardens, Tenn., battle of,
  250–51
Fair Oaks, Va.: battle of Fair Oaks
  and Darbytown Road, 372
Falling Waters, W.Va., 11
Falling Waters, Md.: battle of
  Boonsboro–Funkstown–Falling
  Waters, 213
Farnsworth, Elon J., 204, 206
Farragut, David G.: at Donald-
  sonville I, 137; at Forts Jackson
  and St. Philip, 58–59; on Missis-

sippi River, 136; at Mobile Bay,
  374–76, *375;* at New Orleans, 59;
  and Port Hudson, 182; promotion
  to rear admiral, 59, 137
Farrand, Ebenezer, 91
Fearing, Benjamin D., *409*, 410
Ferguson, Champ, 387
Ferrero, Edward, 239–40, 355
Field, Charles W.: at Chaffin's
  Farm, 363, *366;* at Darbytown
  and New Market Roads, 369; at
  Fair Oaks and Darbytown Roads,
  372; at Petersburg III, *420–21*,
  422; at Second Deep Bottom,
  356–57, *358–59*
Fifteenth amendment, 188
Finegan, Joseph, 139–40, 263–64,
  372
Fisher's Hill, Va., battle of, 316–18,
  317
Fitch, Graham N., 38, 57
Five Forks, Va., battle of, 417–19,
  418, 423, 429
Fleetwood, Christian, 365
Floyd, John B., 9, 10, 45–48, *46*
Flusser, Charles W., 277
Folck's Mill, Md., battle of, 312
Foote, Andrew H.: at Fort Donel-
  son, *46*, 47; at Fort Henry, 44; at
  New Madrid/Island No. 10, 48,
  56–57
Ford, James H., *385*, 386
Ford, John S., 437
Forrest, Jeffrey, 262
Forrest, Nathan Bedford: at Athens,
  261; at Brentwood, 190; at Brices
  Cross Roads, *345*, 346–47; at
  Chattanooga I, 122; at Columbia,
  Tenn., 392; and command of
  Hood's army, 392; cruel excesses
  of, 276; at Day's Gap, 176; de-
  fense of Mississippi by, 344–50;
  at Fort Donelson, 47; at Fort Pil-
  low, 275–76; at Franklin I, 190;
  friendship with S. D. Lee, 347;
  at Jackson, Tenn., 149; at Johnsonville, 389; at Memphis II,
  350; military genius of, 347; at
  Murfreesboro I, 122; at Murfreesboro II, 396; at Okolona, 262; at
  Paducah, 275; at Parker's Cross
  Roads, 149–50; raid along Cumberland River, 189; raid into West
  Tennessee, 389; at Selma, 436;

at Spring Hill, *393*, 394–95; and
  Streight's raid through Alabama,
  176; on surrender, 437; at
  Thompson's Station, 189; at Tu-
  pelo, *348*, 349–50; in West Ten-
  nessee, 149–50, 154; and Wil-
  son's raid in Alabama and
  Georgia, 436; wounds incurred
  by, 347, 350, 436
Fort Anderson, N.C., 275, 403; battle
  of, 194–95
Fort Archer, Va., 368
Fort Baldwin, Va., 422
Fort Barrancas, Fla., 27
Fort Bartow, N.C., 60
Fort Beauregard, S.C., 64
Fort Bisland, La., battle of, 179
Fort Blakely, Ala., battle of, 435
Fort Blanchard, N.C., 60
Fort Brooke, Fla., battle of, 263
Fort Burnham, Va., 363
Fort Butler, La., 180
Fort Clark, N.C., 59
Fort Clifton, Va., battle of Swift
  Creek and, 278
Fort Cobun, Miss., 158
Fort Craig, Ky., 123
Fort Craig, N.M., 39, 42
Fort Curtis, Ark., 176
Fort Darling, Va., 91
Fort Davidson, Mo., 380–81
Fort DeRussy, La., 265; battle of,
  267
Fort Desperate, La., 182
Fort Dix, Va., 195
Fort Donelson, Tenn., 10, 44, 189;
  battle of, 45–48, *46*, 56
Fort Douglas, Utah, 217
Fort Fillmore, N.M., 42
Fort Fisher, N.C.: first battle of,
  401–2; second battle of, 402
Fort Fisher, Va., 373
Fort Forrest, N.C., 60
Fort Gaines, Ala., 374, *375*, 376, 435
Fort Gibson, Okla., 218, 220, 221
Fort Gilmer, Va., 363, 365
Fort Gregg, Va., 363, 365, *420*, 422
Fort Griffin, Tex., 232
Fort Harrison, Va., 362–64, *366*, 368
Fort Hatteras, N.C., 59–60
Fort Henry, Tenn., 45, 47; battle of,
  44, 45, 56
Fort Hindman, Ark., 157
Fort Huger, N.C., 60

Fort Jackson, La.: battle of Fort Jackson and Fort St. Philip, 58

Fort Johnson, S.C., 193

Fort Johnson, Va., 363, 365

Fort Lamar, S.C., 69

Fort Leavenworth, Kans., 382

Fort Lyon, Colo., 398

Fort Macon, N.C., 60; battle of, 61

Fort Magruder, Va., 90

Fort Mahone, Va., 419, *421*

Fort McAllister, Ga.: first battle of, 191; second battle of, 400–401

Fort McRee, Fla., 27

Fort Monroe, Va., 6, 60, 88, 92, 436

Fort Morgan, Ala., 374, *375*, 376, 435

Fort Moultrie, S.C., 1, 191, 194

Fort Pickens, Fla., 27

Fort Pillow, Tenn., 56, 57, 186; battle of, 75–76

Fort Pocahontas, Va., 290

Fort Point, Tex., 138

Fort Powell, Ala., 374, 376

Fort Pulaski, Ga., 61; battle of, 63–67, *64–65*

Fortress Rosecrans, 396

Fort Rice, N.D., 351

Fort Ridgely, Minn., 135–36, 222

Fort St. Philip, battle of, 58

Fort Sanders, Tenn., battle of, 249

Fort Scott, Kans., 23, 24, 133, 134, 218, 220, 386

Fort Smith, Okla., 220, 221

Fort Stedman, Va., battle of, 373

Fort Stevens, D.C., battle of, 308–9

Fort Strong, N.C., 403

Fort Sumter, S.C.: and Du Pont's squadron, 191; first battle of, 1–4, *2;* second battle of, 193–94

Fort Terrill, Ky., 123

Fort Thompson, N.C., 60, 61

Fort Union, N.M., 39, 42, 43

Fort Wade, Miss., 158

Fort Wadsworth, Va., 360

Fort Wagner, S.C., battles of, 192–93, 263

Fort Walker, S.C., 64

Fort Wheaton, Va., 368

Fort Whitworth, Va., *420*, 422

Fort Williams, N.C., 277

Fort Willich, Ky., 123

Foster, Emory S., 133–34

Foster, John C., 60–63

Foster, John G., 195, 249, 400

Foster, John W., 236, 238

Foster, Robert S.: at Chaffin's Farm, *366;* at New Market Heights, 364–65, *367;* at Second Deep Bottom, 356, *358–59*

Fourteenth amendment, 188

Fox's Gap. *See* South Mountain, Md., battle of

Franklin, William B.: captured by Confederates, 309; at Eltham's Landing, 91; at Fredericksburg I, 144–48, *146–47;* at Glendale and White Oak Swamp, *99*, 100; at Sabine's Pass, 232; to Shreveport, 267; at South Mountain, 115–17, *116*

Franklin, La., battle of, 43

Franklin, Tenn.: first battle of, 190; second battle of, 395–96

Frayser's Farm, Va., 98

Frazier, Julian, 25

Fredericksburg, Va.: first battle of, 144–49, *146–47*, 197; second battle of, 199–200, 258–59

Fredericktown, Mo., battle of, 24–25

Freeman, Samuel L., 190

Free Soil Party, 185

Frémont, John C.: in Army Corps of Topographical Engineers, 25; as commander of Western Department, 21, 25, 78; at Cross Keys, 82, *83*, 84, 85; at Port Republic, 85, *86*, 87; as presidential candidate, 25; removed from command, 25; in Shenandoah Valley, 81, 90; at Springfield I, 25; at Strasburg, 82

French, Samuel G., 18, 195; at Allatoona, 390–91, *390*

French, William H.: at Auburn I, 251–52; at Gaines' Mill, *95*, 96; at Manassas Gap, 213; at Mine Run, *256–57*, 258–59; at Rappahannock Station, 255

Front Royal, Va., battle of, 80–81

Frost, Daniel M., *142*, 143

Fry, Joseph, 38

Fry, Speed S., 32

Fugitive slave law, 19, 39

Fulkerson, Samuel, *75*, 76, 78, 85

Fuller, John W., 150

Funkstown, Md.: battle of Boonsboro–Funkstown–Falling Water, 213

Fussell's Mill, Va., 355, 356

Gaines, 374, *375*

Gaines' Mill, Va., battle of, 94–97, *95*

Galena, 91, 100

Gallie, John B., 191

Galveston, Tex.: first battle of, 138; second battle of, 138–39

Gardner, Alexander, photographs by, *236*, *237*

Gardner, Franklin, 181–84, *183*

Garis, Conrad, 344

Garfield, James A., 30

Garland, Samuel, Jr., *116*, 117

Garnett, Richard, *75*, 76, 78, 195

Garnett, Robert Selden, 8

Garnett's Farm, Va.: battle of Garnett's and Golding's Farms, 97

Garrard, Kenner, *337*, 341–42

Garrard, T. T., 29

Garrott, Isham, *159*, 164

Gary, Martin W., 364–65, *367*, 424, 429, *430*

Geary, John W.: at Lost Mountain–Brushy Mountain Line, 335; at New Hope Church, Pickett's Mill, and Dallas, 332–35, *333;* at Resaca, 331; at Ringgold Gap, 247–48, *247;* at Rocky Face Ridge, *327*, 328; at Wauhatchie, 242

General Van Dorn, 57

Georgia Landing, La., battle of, 137

Gettysburg, Pa., battle of, 17, 173, 201, 207–12, *208–10*, 254, 297

Gettysburg address, 207, 215

Gettysburg campaign, 202–14, *203*, *208–10*

Gibbon, John: at Appomattox Court House, 429–32, *430;* at Cold Harbor, *292*, 293–94; at Fredericksburg I, 145, *146–47*, 148; at Fredericksburg II, 199–200; at Jerusalem Plank Road, 354; at Petersburg III, *420–21*, 422; at Reams Station II, 360–62, *361;* at Rice's Station, 427; at South Mountain, 117

Gibson, James F., photograph by, *235*

Gibson, Randall Lee, 49, *50–51*, 435

Gibson, William H., 334, 434

Gilbert, Charles C., 124, *125*, 126

Gillem, Alvan C., 387, 388

Gillmore, Quincy Adams: and Bermuda Hundred campaign, 278–80; at Charleston, 192–94; at Chester Station, 279; and Florida support for Union, 263; at Fort Pulaski, 65, 66; at Fort Wagner, 192–93; at Petersburg I, 352; at Port Walthall Junction, 278; at Proctor's Creek, 279

Gilmer, Jeremy F., 72

Gilmor, Harry W., 309

Girardey, Victor J. B., 356, 358–59

Glasgow, Mo., battle of, 382

Glendale, Va., battle of, 98–101, 99

Globe Tavern, Va., battle of, 357, 360

Glorieta Pass, N.M., battle of, 39–44, 40–41

Goddard, Charley, 259

Godwin, Archibald C., 255

Golding's Farm, Va.: battle of Garnett's and Golding's Farms, 97

Goldsboro Bridge, N.C., battle of, 63

Goldsborough, Louis M., 60

Gooding, Michael, 126

Goodrich's Landing, La., battle of, 175

Gordon, John B.: at Appomattox Court House, 429–32, 430; at Cedar Creek, 320–21, 322; at Cumberland Church, 428; at Fisher's Hill, 316–18, 317; at Fort Stedman, 373; at High Bridge, 428; at Monocacy, 305–8, 306; at Opequon, 315–16; at Petersburg III, 419–23, 420–21; at Rice's Station, 427; at Sailor's Creek, 425, 426; at Second Kernstown, 310–12, 311; at Smithfield Crossing, 314; in Wilderness, 281, 283

Gorgas, Josiah, 214

Govan, Daniel C., 246–48, 247, 393, 394–95

Gowen, George W., 462

Gracie, Archibald, 413

Graham, Robert F., 192

Granbury, Hiram B.: at Dug Gap, 262; at Pickett's Mill, 334; at Ringgold Gap, 246–48, 247; at Rocky Face Ridge, 327, 328; at Spring Hill, 393, 394–95

Grand Gulf, Miss., battle of, 157–58

Granger, Gordon: at Chickamauga,

229, 230; as corps commander in East Tennessee, 250; at Mobile Bay, 374, 376

Granger, Robert S., 392

Grant, Ulysses S.: at Amelia Springs, 424; and Atlanta campaign, 271; at Belmont, 26, 45; and Boydton Plank Road, 369; and Burnside, 248; at Champion Hill, 167–70, 168; at Chattanooga III, 244, 245–46; City Point as headquarters of, 353; at Cold Harbor, 291–94, 292; as commander of District of West Tennessee, 129; as commander of Division of Mississippi, 241, 243; and Corinth fortifications, 131; and Cracker Line, 241–42, 255; on the Crater, 355–56; and Dalton I, 262; under fire, 371; and First Deep Bottom, 355; and Five Forks, 417, 419; at Fort Donelson, 45–48, 46; at Fort Henry, 44, 45; as general-in-chief, 129, 259, 267; and Iuka, 129; and Jackson, Miss., 167; and Jackson, Tenn., 149; in Knoxville, 250; on Lincoln, 412; Lincoln's visit to, 354; map of campaigns and marches in 1864–65, 414–15; along Mississippi River, 26, 45, 58; and Nashville, 396–97; at North Anna, 287–89, 288; Overland campaign of, 280–95, 281, 284, 288, 292; at Paducah, 28, 45; near Petersburg, 326; in Petersburg and Richmond with Lincoln, 423–24; at Petersburg I and II, 352–53; and Piedmont, 301; at Pittsburg Landing, 48; at Port Gibson, 158–64, 159; at Ringgold Gap, 248; as second-in-command at Corinth, 52; and Sheridan, 286, 312, 313, 315; and Sherman, 261, 399, 405; at Shiloh, 48–52, 50–51; and Shreveport, 273; at Spotsylvania Court House, 283–86, 284; strategic planning in March 1865, 412; and surrender by Lee, 431–33; and surrender offers to Lee, 428, 429–30; at Tennessee River, 38; at Vicksburg battle and siege, 171–

73; Vicksburg campaign of, 154–76; and White Oak Road, 413; in Wilderness, 278, 280–83, 281

Green, Daniel, 204

Green, Martin E., 159, 163–64, 169

Green, Thomas: at Blair's Landing, 271; at Brashear City, 180; death of, 271; at Fort Butler, 180; at Galveston II, 138; at Kock's Plantation, 180; at Mansfield, 268; at Stirling's Plantation, 181; at Valverde, 39, 271

Greenbrier, River, W.Va., 10

Greene, Colton, 275

Green River, 123

Greer, Elkanah, 23

Gregg, David M.: at Boydton Plank Road, 369–71, 370; at Brandy Station, 202, 204; at Clayton's Store, 294–95; at Dinwiddie Court House, 372; at Gettysburg, 209–10, 212; at Hatcher's Run, 372; at Haw's Shop, 290; along Mount Defiance, 206; at Peebles' Farm, 368; at Reams Station II, 360–62, 361; at Samaria Church, 295; at Second Deep Bottom, 357, 358–59; at Shepherdstown, 213; at Upperville, 206

Gregg, John: at Chaffin's Farm, 363, 366; at Chickasaw Bayou, 155, 156; at Jackson, Miss., 167; at New Market Heights, 365, 367; at New Market Road, 369; at Raymond, 165–66, 165; in Wilderness, 281, 282–83

Gregg, Maxcy, 95, 96–97, 148

Gregory, Edgar M., 415, 416

Grierson, Benjamin H.: at Brices Cross Road, 345, 346; Mississippi raid of, 157–58, 160, 176; at Tupelo, 349–50

Griffin, Charles: at Appomattox Court House, 429–32, 430; as corps commander replacing Warren, 419; at Five Forks, 418, 419; at Peebles' Farm, 368; at White Oak Road, 413, 416

Grigsby, J. Warren, 327, 328

Grimball's Landing, S.C., battle of, 192

Griswoldville, Ga., battle of, 399

Grover, Cuvier: at Fort Bisland,

179; at Irish Bend, 179; at Kock's Plantation, 180; at Opequon, 315–16
Guard Hill, Va., battle of, 313–14
Gwynn, Walter, 5

Hagood, Johnson: at Fort Anderson, 403; at Globe Tavern, 357; at Grimball's Landing, 192; at Port Walthall Junction, 278; at Secessionville, 68, 69; at Swift Creek, 278
Hall, Albert, 189–90
Halleck, Henry W.: as chief-of-staff, 259; and Corinth, 52–56, 54–55, 131; and the Crater, 356; as general-in-chief, 157; Grant's instructions to, 313; on Sand Creek massacre, 398; and Sherman's Atlanta campaign, 342; in Tennessee, 45, 48, 57; and Texas blockade, 232
Halloran, Richard, 201
Hamilton, Charles S., 130, 131
Hampton, Wade: attack on Kilpatrick, 260; at Bentonville, 408–11, 409; at Boydton Plank Road, 370, 371; at Brandy Station, 202, 203, 204; and Buckland Mills, 254–55; at Gettysburg, 254; at Haw's Shop, 290; Kilpatrick's attempt to trap, 406–7; at Matadequin Creek, 291; at Monroe's Cross Roads, 406–7; at Peebles' Farm, 368; at Poplar Spring Church, 368; at Reams Station II, 360–62, 361; at Samaria Church, 295; and Sherman's Carolina campaign, 405; south of James River, 354; at Trevilian Station, 294–95; at Upperville, 206; wounded at Gettysburg, 254
Hampton Roads, Va., 5; battle of, 88
Hancock, Winfield Scott: at Boydton Plank Road, 369–71, 370; at Cold Harbor, 292, 293; at First Deep Bottom, 355; at Garnett's Farm, 97; at Gettysburg, 207, 209–10, 211–12; on Meade, 213; at North Anna, 287–89, 288; at Petersburg I and II, 352, 353; at Reams Station II, 360–62, 361; at Second Deep Bottom, 356–57,

358–59; at Spotsylvania Court House, 284, 285–86; and Stuart during Gettysburg campaign, 206; at Totopotomoy Creek, 290; in Wilderness, 281, 282–83; at Williamsburg, 90
Hancock, Md., battle of, 74
Hannon, Moses W., 261
Hanover, Pa., battle of, 206–7
Hanover Court House, Va., battle of, 91–92
Hardee, William J.: at Atlanta, 340; at Averasboro, 407; at Bentonville, 408–11, 409; at Chattanooga III, 244, 245; on Cleburne's death, 396; corps commander in Army of the Mississippi, 48; at Jonesboro, 343; at Kennesaw Mountain, 337; at Liberty Gap, 225; at Lost Mountain-Brushy Mountain Line, 335; at Meridian, 261; at Munfordville, 123; at New Hope Church, Pickett's Mill, and Dallas, 333, 334–35; at Peachtree Creek, 339–40; at Perryville, 124; at Resaca, 329–31, 330; at Rocky Face Ridge, 327; at Savannah, 401; and Sherman's Carolina campaign, 405; at Shiloh, 48, 50–51; at Stones River, 151–53, 152
Harding, A. C., 189
Harding, Chester, 382
Harker, Charles G., 327, 328, 337, 338
Harman, William, 75, 76, 78
Harpers Ferry, W.Va., 6, 82; battle of, 113–15, 114
Harriet Lane, 138
Harris, Thomas R., 263
Harrison, Thomas J., 262
Hartford, 58, 182
Hartranft, John F., 373
Hartsville, Tenn., battle of, 150–51
Hartville, Mo., battle of, 177–78
Hatch, Edward, 241
Hatch, John P., 400
Hatcher's Run, Va., battle of, 372–73
Hatchie Bridge, Tenn., 132
Hatteras Inlet Forts, N.C., battle of, 59–60

Hawes, James M., 173
Hawkins, John P., 435
Haw's Shop, Va., battle of, 290
Hay, John, 263
Hayes, Rutherford B.: at Cedar Creek, 320–21, 322; at Cloyd's Mountain, 296, 297; at Second Kernstown, 310–12, 311
Hays, Alexander, 260
Hays, Harry T., 255, 256–57
Hazen, William B., 334, 400
Heath, Francis E., 252–54, 253
Hébert, Louis, 36, 130, 131
Heckman, Charles: at Chaffin's Farm, 366; at Forts Johnson, Gregg, and Gilmer, 363; at Port Walthall Junction, 278; at Swift Creek, 278
Heintzelman, Samuel P.: at First Manassas, 12, 13, 14; at Malvern Hill, 101–4, 102; and Savage's Station, 98; at Seven Pines, 92
Helena, Ark., battle of, 175–76
Henry, Guy V., 263
Henry James, 138
Herron, Francis J., 141–43, 142
Heth, Henry: at Boonsboro, 213; at Boydton Plank Road, 370, 371; at Bristoe Station, 252–54, 253; at Cold Harbor, 292; as commander of Third Corps of Army of Northern Virginia, 423; at Gettysburg, 207–12, 208–9; at Globe Tavern, 357; at Mine Run, 256–57; at Petersburg III, 419–23, 420–21; at Reams Station II, 360–62, 361; at Spotsylvania Court House, 284, 285–86
Hicks, Stephen G., 275
High Bridge, Va., battle of, 427–28
Hill, Ambrose Powell: at Antietam, 119, 120; at Beaver Dam Creek, 93; at Boonsboro–Funkstown–Falling Waters, 213; at Boydton Plank Road, 369–71, 370; at Bristoe Station, 252–54, 253; at Cedar Mountain, 106, 107; at Chancellorsville, 199; at Cold Harbor, 292, 293; as commander of Third Corps of Army of Northern Virginia, 200; death of, 423; at Fredericksburg I, 145, 146–47; at Gaines' Mill, 95, 96–97; at

Hill, Ambrose Powell (*continued*)
Gettysburg, 207–12, *209–10;* at
Glendale, *99,* 100; at Globe Tavern, 357; at Harpers Ferry, *114,*
115; at Hatcher's Run, 372; and
Malvern Hill, 103; at Mine Run,
256–57, 258–59; at North Anna,
288, 289; at Peebles' Farm, 368; at
Petersburg II, 353; at Petersburg
III, 419–23, *420–21;* at Reams
Station II, 360–62, *361;* at Second
Manassas, *109,* 110–11; at Shepherdstown, 121; in Wilderness,
281, 282–83
Hill, Daniel Harvey: at Antietam,
119, 120; at Beaver Dam Creek,
93; at Bentonville, 408–11, *409;*
at Big Bethel, 6; at Fredericksburg I, 145, *146–47;* at Gaines'
Mill, *95,* 96; under Longstreet,
194; at Malvern Hill, 101–4, *102;*
at New Bern, 194–95; relieved of
command, 245; at Seven Pines,
92; at South Mountain, *116,* 117;
at Washington, N.C., 195; at
Williamsburg, 90; at Wyse Fork,
406
Hill's Plantation, Ark., battle of, 38
Hill's Point, Va., 195–96
Hincks, Edward W., 278, 352, 353
Hindman, Thomas C.: and Arkansas defense, 38, 133, 140; at Columbia, Ky., 32; at Kennesaw
Mountain, *337;* at Kolb's Farm,
336; and Marmaduke's raid
through Missouri, 177; at New
Hope Church, Pickett's Mill, and
Dallas, 332–35, *333;* at Prairie
Grove, 141–43, *142;* at Resaca,
329, *330;* at Rowlett's Station, 30
Hobart, Harrison C., 408–11, *409*
Hobson, Edward H., 216
Hoke, Robert F.: at Bentonville,
408–11, *409;* at Chaffin's Farm,
363, *366;* on Charles City Road,
372; at Chester Station, 279; at
Cold Harbor, 291, *292,* 293; at
New Market Road, 369; at Ply-
mouth, 277; at Smithfield, 408; at
Wilmington, 402–3; at Wyse
Fork, 406
Hoke's Run (Falling Waters), W.Va.,
battle of, 11

Holmes, Theophilus H., 61, 100,
175–76
Homestead Act, 351
Honey Hill, S.C., battle of, 400
Honey Springs, Okla., battle of,
219–21, *220*
Hood, John Bell: at Atlanta, 340; at
Chickamauga, 228–29, 230–31;
at Columbia, Tenn., 392; as commander of Army and Department
of Tennessee, 340, 343; at Dalton
III, 391; at Decatur, 392; at
Eltham's Landing, 91; at Franklin II, 395; at Fredericksburg I,
145, *146–47;* at Gaines' Mill, 96–
97; at Gettysburg, *209,* 211; at
Jonesboro, 342–43; at Kennesaw
Mountain, *337;* at Kolb's Farm,
336; under Longstreet, 194;
march to Tennessee by, 389–97;
at Nashville, 396–97, 401; at New
Hope Church, Pickett's Mill, and
Dallas, 332–35, *333;* at Peachtree
Creek, 339–40; at Resaca, 329–
31, *330;* resigns command, 397;
at Rocky Face Ridge, *327;* at
South Mountain, *116,* 117; at
Spring Hill, *393,* 394–95; at Suffolk, 195; supply line of, 341
Hooker, Joseph: and Aldie, 205; at
Antietam, 118–20, *119;* in
Bridgeport, 241; at Chancellorsville, 196; at Chattanooga III,
243–46, *244;* at Fort Magruder,
90; at Fredericksburg I, 144–48,
146–47; intelligence concerning
Culpeper County, 202; at Kennesaw Mountain, *337;* at Kettle
Run, 108; at Kolb's Farm, 336; in
Lookout Valley, 242; at New Hope
Church, Pickett's Mill, and Dallas, 332–35, *333;* at Oak Grove,
93; recalled to duty and ordered
to Tennessee, 251; at Resaca,
329–31, *330;* resigns command,
397; at Ringgold Gap, 247–48,
247; at Second Manassas, *109,*
110; at South Mountain, *116,* 117
Hoover's Gap, Tenn., battle of, 225–
26
Hopkins, Charles F., 139–40
Hotchkiss, Jedediah, 72–73, *76–77,*
322

House, Albert E., 223
Hovey, Alvin P., 164, *168,* 169–70
Hovey, Charles E., 38
Howard, Oliver O.: at Adairsville,
331; at Bentonville, 408, *409;*
at Brown's Ferry, 242; at Chancellorsville, *198,* 199; at Dalton,
328; at Ezra Church, 341; at
Gettysburg, 207–12, *208–10;*
to Goldsboro, 407; at Jonesboro,
343; at Kennesaw Mountain,
337; to Macon, 399; at New
Hope Church, Pickett's Mill,
and Dallas, 332–35, *333;* at
Resaca, 329–31, *330;* at Rocky
Face Ridge, *327,* 328; and
Sherman's Carolina campaign,
405
Howlett Line, Va., 280
Huger, Benjamin: at Glendale, *99,*
100; at Malvern Hill, 101–4, *102;*
at Oak Grove, 93; at Richmond,
97; and Roanoke Island, 60; at
Savage's Station, 98; at Seven
Pines, 92
Hughes, John T., 133
Hughs, John M., 363
Humphreys, Andrew A.: at Appo-
mattox Court House, 429–32,
430; at Cumberland Church,
428; at Hatcher's Run, 372; at
High Bridge, 428; at Lewis's
Farm, 412; at Sailor's Creek,
425, 426; at White Oak Road,
413, 415, *416,* 423
Humphreys, Benjamin G., 249
Hunter, David: at Charleston Harbor I, 191–92; as commander of
Western Division, 25; at First
Manassas, 12, *13,* 14; and James
Island, 67, 69; to Lexington, 304;
at Lynchburg, 304; at Martinsburg, 309; at Piedmont, 301–3,
302; relieved of command, 313;
to Richmond, 294; at Staunton,
304
Hunton, Eppa, 413, *416*
Hurlbut, Stephen A., 49, *50–51,*
132

Imboden, John D.: at New Market,
298–301, *299;* at Piedmont, 301–
3, *302;* at Williamsport, 212

Independence, Mo.: first battle of, 133, 377; second battle of, 383
"Indian Expedition," 133, 218
Indian Territory, 33–34, 133, 134, 141, 218, 220, 438. *See also* Native Americans
Ingersoll, Robert G., 149
Inkpaduta, 222, 223
Irish Bend, La., battle of, 179
Irvine, J. S., 138
Iuka, Miss., battle of, 129
Iverson, Alfred M., 212
Ivy Mountain, Ky., battle of, 29

Jackson, Andrew, 343
Jackson, Claiborne Fox, 20, 25
Jackson, Henry R., 9, 10
Jackson, James S., 126
Jackson, J. F. B., 169
Jackson, Thomas J. "Stonewall": achievements of, 199; at Antietam, *119*, 120; and B & O Railroad, 74; and Beaver Dam Creek, 93–94; at Cedar Mountain, 105–7, *106;* at Chancellorsville, 196, 197–99, *198;* at Chantilly, 112; at Cross Keys, 82, *83*, 84; death of, 199; delays and miscommunications during Peninsula campaign, 93–94, 96, 98; at First Kernstown, 74, *75*, 76, 78; at First Manassas, *13*, 14; at First Winchester, 81–82; at Fredericksburg I, 144–48, *146–47;* at Front Royal, 81; at Gaines' Mill, 94–97, *95;* near Gordonsville, 107; at Hancock, 74; at Harpers Ferry, 6, 113–15, *114;* at Hoke's Run, 11; and Jedediah Hotchkiss, 73: Loring's complaints against, 74; at Malvern Hill, 101–4, *102;* at Manassas Station/Junction, 108; at McDowell, 78–80, *79*, 90, 128; military genius of, 325; at Port Republic, 82, 84–87, *86;* at Second Manassas, *109*, 110–11; and Seven Days campaign, 93; 1862 Shenandoah Valley campaign of, 74–87, *75–77, 79, 83, 86*, 265, 267; threatened resignation of, 74; at White Oak Swamp, 98–101, *99*
Jackson, William H. "Red," 189

Jackson, William L., 240
Jackson, Miss., 166; battle of, 167
Jackson, Tenn., battle of, 149
James, Frank, 224, 377–79
James, Jesse, 224, 377–79
James River, 88, 91, 94, 100, 324, 363
"Jayhawkers," 23, 224, 377–78
Jenkins, Albert G., *296*, 297
Jenkins, Micah: at Campbell's Station, 249; at Glendale, 100; at Seven Pines, 92; at Wauhatchie Station, 242
Jenkins' Ferry, Ark., battle of, 44, 274–75
Jennison, Charles R., *385*, 386
Jerusalem Plank Road, Va., battle of, 353–54
Jobe, Isaac, 248
Johnson, Andrew, 398
Johnson, Bradley T., 308–9, 312, 313
Johnson, Bushrod R.: at Bean's Station, 249; at Bristoe Station, *253;* at Chickamauga, 230; at Fort Donelson, *46*, 47; at Perryville, 124, 126; at Port Walthall Junction, 278; at Sailor's Creek, 426; at Swift Creek, 278
Johnson, Edward "Allegheny": at Camp Allegheny, 10; at Gettysburg, *209–10*, 211; at McDowell, 79–80, *79;* at Mine Run, *256–57*, 258–59; at Second Winchester, 205
Johnson, Lewis, 391
Johnson, Richard W., *327, 333*, 334
Johnsonville, Tenn., battle of, 389
Johnston, Albert Sidney: at Barbourville, 28; as commander of Army of Mississippi, 45, 48; death of, 49; at Pittsburg Landing, 48; at Shiloh, 48–49, *50–51;* troops of, at Fort Donelson, 45
Johnston, Joseph E.: at Adairsville, 331; at Bentonville, 408–11, *409;* as commander in Georgia, 246; as commander of Army of Tennessee, 326–27, 343; and defensive line after First Manassas, 18–19; at Eltham's Landing, 91; at First Manassas, 12, *13*, 14–15; at Hoke's Run, 11; at Jackson,

Miss., 166, 167; at Kennesaw Mountain, 336–39, *337;* Lee's retreat from Petersburg toward, 424; at Lost Mountain–Brushy Mountain Line, 335–36; at New Hope Church, Pickett's Mill, and Dallas, 332–35, *333;* in north Georgia, 261, 266, 267, 278; at Peachtree Creek, 339–40; and Port Hudson, 181; relieved of command, 339; at Resaca, 329–31, *330*, 344; retreat into Jackson and across Pearl River, 175; at Rocky Face Ridge, 326–28, *327;* and Seven Pines, 92; on Sherman, 339, 411; and Sherman's Atlanta campaign, 326–43; at Smithfield, 407; and strength of Army of Tennessee, 262; surrender by, 437; and Vicksburg battle and siege, 172–73; at Yorktown, 90
Jones, David R., 12, 97, *116*, 117
Jones, Sam, 434
Jones, William E. "Grumble": at Bean's Station, 249; at Brandy Station, 202, *203*, 204; at Cove Mountain, 298; death of, 303; at Hagerstown, 212; at Piedmont, 301–3, *302*
Jonesboro, Ga., battle of, 342–43
Jordan, Lewis, 216
Juárez, Benito, 232
Judah, Henry M., 216
Judah, 27
Jumper, John, 33, 221

Kansas-Nebraska Act, 224–25
Kate Dale, 263
Kautz, August V.: at Darbytown Road, 369; at New Market Heights, *367;* at Petersburg I, 352; at Proctor's Creek, 279; raid against rail lines, 353–55; at Reams Station I, 354–55
Kearny, Philip: death of, at Chantilly, 112; at Glendale and White Oak Swamp, *99*, 101; at Oak Grove, 93; at Second Manassas, *109*, 111; at Seven Pines, 92; at Williamsburg, 90
Keitt, Laurence M., 193
Kelley, Benjamin F., 6, 312

Kelly, John H., *333*, 334
Kelly's Ford, Va., battle of, 196
Kenly, John R., 81
Kennard, Motey, 33
Kennesaw Mountain, Ga., battle of, 336–39, *337*
Kensington, 138
Kentucky, strategic importance of, 28, 124
Keokuk, 191
Kernstown, Va.: first battle of, 74, *75*, 76, 78; second battle of, 310–12, *311*
Kershaw, Joseph B.: at Berryville, 315; at Cedar Creek, 319–23, *320–21;* at Cold Harbor, 291, *292*, 293; as Early's reinforcements, 313; at First Deep Bottom, 355; and reinforcements for Early, 319; to Richmond, 315; to Shenandoah Valley, 356
Kessler's Cross Lanes, W.Va., battle of, 9
Keyes, Erasmus D., 92, 101–4, *102*
Killdeer Mountain, N.D., battle of, 351
Kilpatrick, H. Judson: at Aldie, 205; attempt to trap Hampton, 406–7; at Averasboro, 407; at Brandy Station, *203*, 204; at Buck Head Creek, 400; at Buckland Mills, 254–55; at Falling Waters, 213; feint toward Charlotte, 406; at Hagerstown, 212; and Hanover, 206; near Jonesboro, 342; at Lovejoy's Station, 342; at Monroe's Cross Roads, 407; raid on Richmond, 260; and Sherman's march to the sea, 399; at Walkerton, 260; at Waynesborough, 400
Kimball, Nathan, 10, *75*, 78
King, Edward M., 389
King, Rufus, 81, 91
Kinston, N.C., battle of, 62
Kirkland, William W., 252–54, *253*
Kirksville, Mo., battle of, 133
Knoxville, Tenn., 227, 236, 238, 245, 248–49
Kock's Plantation, La., battle of, 180
Kolb's Farm, Ga., battle of, 336
Koltes, John A., 82
Ku Klux Klan, 276

Lafourche Crossing, La., battle of, 180
Laiboldt, Bernard, 342
Lamar, Thomas, *68*, 69
Lamb, William, 401, 402
Lander, Frederick W., 74
Landrum, William J., *155*, 156, 268
Lane, James H.: at Fredericksburg I, 148; at Petersburg III, *420;* at Second Deep Bottom, 357, *358–59;* at Spotsylvania Court House, *284*, 285–86
Lane, James M. "Jim," 23–24, 133
Langston, John Mercer, 188
Law, Evander, 96–97
Lawler, Michael K., 171
Lawrence, Kans., battle of, 224
Lawton, Alexander R., *109*, 110
Leake, J. B., 181
Ledlie, James H., 355
Lee, Albert Lindley, 268
Lee, Fitzhugh: at Amelia Springs, 424; at Appomattox Court House, 429–32, *430;* at Buckland Mills, 254–55; at Dinwiddie Court House, 412–13; as Early's reinforcements, 303; escape of, 432; to Farmville, 427; at Guard Hill, 314; at Haw's Shop, 290; at Kelly's Ford, 196; at Louisa Court House, 294–95; at Opequon, 315–16, 319; and Sailor's Creek, 426–27; at Samaria Church, 295; to Shenandoah Valley, 356; at Shepherdstown, 213; south of James River, 354; at White House, 295; at Williamsport, 212; at Wilson's Wharf, 290; wounded at Opequon, 319
Lee, Robert E.: at Amelia Springs, 424; at Antietam, 118–21, *119;* at Appomattox Court House, 429–32, *430;* at Beaver Dam Creek, 93–94; on black troops in Confederate army, 188; and Brandy Station, 204; and Bristoe campaign, 251; at Bristoe Station, 252–54, *253;* at Chaffin's Farm, 363, *366;* at Chancellorsville, 197–99, *198;* at Cheat Mountain, 10; at Cold Harbor, 291–94, *292;* as commander of Army of Northern Virginia, 93; criticisms of,

422; at Cumberland Church, 428; at Darbytown and New Market Roads, 369; and Early, 319, 323–24; and Five Forks, 417, 419; and food rations, 194, 196; and Fort Pulaski, 63, 66; and Fort Stedman, 373; at Fredericksburg I, 144–49, *146–47;* at Gaines' Mill, 94–97, *95;* at Gettysburg, 173, 207–12, *208–10;* and Gettysburg campaign, 206; at Glendale and White Oak Swamp, 98–101, *99;* and Harpers Ferry, 113; health problems of, 196; and Jackson, 81; and Longstreet, 194, 195, 196; at Malvern Hill, 101–4, *102;* and mapping, 72; and marriage of Walter Herren Taylor, 422–23; military genius of, 325; at Mine Run, 255–59, *256–57;* at North Anna, 287–89, *288;* in northwest Virginia, 9; near Petersburg, 326; and Petersburg defenses, 412; at Petersburg III, 419–23, *420–21;* and plans for invasion of North in June 1863, 205; plans for removing army from Richmond and Petersburg, 373; posthumous pardon of, 436; along Rappahannock River, 107–8; at Rappahannock Station, 255; reinforcements for, 291; reorganization of Army of Northern Virginia, 200; retreat from Petersburg, 422–29; and Richmond, 74, 76, 368; at Savage's Station, 98; on secession, 4; at Second Manassas, 108–11, *109;* and Seven Days campaign, 93–104, *95*, *99*, *102;* and Shenandoah Valley, 304, 305; south of Rapidan River, 251; at Spotsylvania Court House, 283–86, *284;* and Stuart, 93; surrender by, 431–33; and surrender offers by Grant, 428, 429–30; at Totopotomoy Creek, 290; Union discovery of campaign plans of, 115, 118; at White Oak Road, 413, 415–17, *416;* in Wilderness, 278, 280–83, *281*
Lee, Stephen Dill: at Champion Hill, 169; at Chickasaw Bayou, *155*, 156; at Columbia, Tenn.,

392; as commander in Mississippi and Alabama, 344, 346; at Ezra Church, 341; friendship with Forrest, 347; at Nashville, 397; at Tupelo, *348*, 349–50

Lee, W. H. F. "Rooney": at Boydton Plank Road, *370;* at Brandy Station, 202, *203*, 204; and cutting off Wilson, 354; at Dinwiddie Court House, 412; at Five Forks, *418*, 419; at High Bridge, 427–28; intelligence on Union cavalry at Jetersville, 424; at Second Deep Bottom, 357, *358–59;* son of Robert E. Lee, 424

Left Hand, 398

Leggett, Mortimer D., 340

Lester, Henry C., 122

Letcher, John, 74

Lewis, W. Gaston, 309

Lewis's Farm, Va., battle of, 412

Lexington, 26, 38, 52, 175

Lexington, Mo.: first battle of, 24, 34; second battle of, 382

Liberty (Blue Mills Landing), Mo., battle of, 24

Liberty Party, 185

Liddell, St. John R., 124, 126, 435

Lieb, Hermann, 173

Lightburn, Joseph A. J., *337*, 338–39

Lincoln, Abraham: and Banks, 232; Barringer's meeting with, 423; on black troops, 186, 193, 264; and blockade of southern seaboard, 5; and Chattanooga, 243; and commanders of Union army, 91, 112, 121, 126, 129, 135, 241, 248, 251, 255, 267, 344, 354; death of, 433; and East Tennessee, 236; and Emancipation Proclamation, 120, 188, *238;* and Fort Sumter I, 3–4; and Frémont, 25; Gettysburg address by, 207, 215; Grant on, 412; inauguration of, 1, 3; on Kansas-Nebraska Act, 224–25; on Kentucky's strategic importance, 124; and loss at Front Royal, 81; and McClellan, 88, 121; on Meade's failure to end war after Gettysburg, 213; on Mississippi River, 173; and Native Americans, 133, 136; at Pe-

tersburg and Richmond, 423–24; photograph of, 201, *237;* Proclamation of Amnesty and Reconstruction by, 263, 265; and reelection, 341, 343, 357, 360, 368; and Rosecrans's victory at Stones River, 154; on secession as illegal, 263; second inaugural address of, 404–5; and Sheridan, 315; Sherman on, 412; and Sherman's march to the sea, 399, 401; on slavery and blacks, 185, 224–25, 424; and Texas, 265

Lincoln, Tad, 423–24

Little, Henry, 129

Little Blue River, Mo., battle of, 382–83

Little Crow, 135–36, 222

Little Rock, Ark., 233

Lockwood, Samuel, 61

Logan, John A.: at Atlanta, 340; at Champion Hill, *168*, 169–70; as commander of Army of the Tennessee, 340; at Kennesaw Mountain, *337*, 338–39; at Nashville, 397; at New Hope Church, Pickett's Mill, and Dallas, *333*, 334–35; at Raymond, *165*, 166; at Resaca, 329–31, *330*

Lone Jack, Mo., battle of, 133–34

Longstreet, James: at Antietam, *119*, 120; at Appomattox Court House, 429–32, *430;* at Bean's Station, 249; at Beaver Dam Creek, 93; at Blackburn's Ford, 11; at Boonsboro–Funkstown–Falling Waters, 213; on Bragg, 245; at Campbell's Station, 248–49; at Chickamauga, *229*, 230–31; as First Corps commander in Army of Northern Virginia, 194, 200; as commander of Department of East Tennessee, 250; at Cumberland Church, 428; at Dandridge, 250; to Farmville, 427; at Fort Sanders, 249; at Fredericksburg I, 144–48, *146–47;* at Gaines' Mill, *95*, 96; at Germantown, 112; at Gettysburg, *209–10*, 211; and Gettysburg campaign, 202, 206; at Glendale and White Oak Swamp, 98–101, *99;* near Gordonsville, 107; at Knoxville,

245, 249; and Lee, 245; in Lookout Valley, 242; and Malvern Hill, 101, 103; and Manassas campaign, 12; military genius of, 325; north of James River, 372; at Petersburg III, 422; and reinforcements for Bragg, 251; and retreat from Petersburg, 426; at Rice's Station, 427; at Second Manassas, *109*, 110–11; at Seven Pines, 92; and Thoroughfare Gap, 108; Tidewater campaign of, 194–96; at the Wilderness, *281*, 282–83; at Williamsburg, 90; wounded, 283

Longstreet's Tidewater campaign, 194–96

Loring, William W.: at Bentonville, 408–11; and Big Black River Bridge, 171; at Champion Hill, *168*, 169–70; at Cheat Mountain, 10; on Jackson, 74; at Kennesaw Mountain, *337;* in northwest Virginia, 9; Polk's Corps under command of, 336; at Port Gibson, 163; at Resaca, *330*

Lost Mountain–Brushy Mountain Line, Ga., battle of, 335–36

Louisiana, 58

Louisville & Nashville Railroad, 30, 123, 216

Lovejoy's Station, Ga., battle of, 342

Lovell, Mansfield, 59, 131

Lowe, Thaddeus S. C., 71

Lowrey, Mark P.: at Pickett's Mill, 334; at Ringgold Gap, 246–48, *247;* at Spring Hill, *393*, 394–95

Lynch, W. F., 60

Lynchburg, Va., battle of, 304, 309

Lynde, Edward, 154

Lyon, Hylan B., *348*, 349–50

Lyon, Nathaniel, 20, 21, *22*, 23, 34

Mabry, Hinchie P., *348*, 350

Mackall, William W., 57

Mackenzie, Ranald R., 429, *430*

Macon & Western Railroad, 341

Magruder, John B.: at Big Bethel, 6; at Galveston II, 138; at Glendale and White Oak Swamp, *99*, 100; at Malvern Hill, 101–4, *102;* at Richmond, 97; at Savage's Station, 98; at Yorktown, 88–90

Mahone, William: at Boydton Plank Road, *370*, 371; at the Crater, 355; at Cumberland Church, 428; to Farmville, 427; at Globe Tavern, 357; at Hatcher's Run, 372; at High Bridge, 428; at Jerusalem Plank Road, 354; at Reams Station I, 354–55; at Reams Station II, 360–62, *361;* at Rice's Station, 427; at Spotsylvania Court House, *284*, 285–86

Major, James P., 180

Mallon, James, 252–54, *253*

Malvern Hill, Va., battle of, 101–4, *102*

Manassas, 58

Manassas, Va.: first battle of, 11–15, *13;* second battle of, 108–11, *109*

Manassas campaign, 11–15, *13*

Manassas Gap, Va., battle of, 213–14

Manassas Station/Junction, Va., battle of, 108

Mansfield, K. F., 63

Mansfield, La., battle of, 266, 267–69, *268,* 326

Manson, Mahlon D., 32, 122–23

Mansura, La., battle of, 266, 272

Mapping of Civil War, 71–73

Marais des Cygnes, Kans., battle of, 384

March to the sea (Sherman), 391, 399–401

Marion, Va., battle of, 388

Marks' Mills, Ark., battle of, 274

Marmaduke, John S.: arrest of, 233; at Bayou Fourche, 233; at Big Blue River, 383; at Boonville, 20; at Cane Hill, 140; at Cape Girardeau, 178; at Chalk Bluff, 178; at Elkin's Ferry, 273; at Hartville, 177–78; at Independence II, 383; at Little Blue River, 383; at Mine Creek, 384; at Pilot Knob, 380–82, *381;* at Pine Bluff, 233; at Poison Spring, 274; at Prairie De Rohan, 273; at Prairie Grove, *142*, 143; at Springfield II, 177; at Westport, 384

Marmaton River, Mo., battle of, 385

Marsh, John S., 135

Marshall, Humphrey, 30, 80

Marshall, J. Foster, *95*, 96–97

Martha Washington, 18

Martin, William T., 249, 250

Martindale, John H., *292*, 294, 353

Maryland campaign, 113–21, *114*, *116, 119*

Matadequin Creek (Old Church), Va., battle of, 291

Maury, Dabney H., 129, *130*, 131, 349, 435

Maxey, Samuel B., 274

Maximilian, emperor of Mexico, 252

McAllister, Robert, 372

McArthur, John, 397

McCall, George A., 94–97, *95*, 100

McCausland, John, 297, 305–8, *306*, 312

McClellan, George B.: advance on Richmond, 74, 78, 81, 88, 92, 93; at Antietam, 118–21, *119;* and Ball's Bluff, 18; at Beaver Dam Creek, 93–94; as commander of Department of the Ohio, 6; as commander of Army of the Potomac, 9, 88, 112; Cumberland Landing encampment of army of, *235;* demotion from general-in-chief, 88; at Gaines' Mill, 94–97, *95;* and Grafton, 6; and Hanover Court House, 92; at Malvern Hill, 101–4, *102;* at Oak Grove, 93; and Peninsula campaign, 18–19; photograph of, *237;* as presidential candidate, 343, 357; relieved of command, 121, 144; at Rich Mountain, 8–9; and Seven Pines, 92–93; and South Mountain, 115, 117; Stuart's reconnaissance of, 93; and Williamsburg, 90; and Yorktown, 88, 90

McClennan, Matthew R., *306*, 307–8

McClernand, John A.: at Arkansas Post, 157; at Big Black River crossings, 165; and Big Black River Bridge, 171; at Fort Donelson, *46*, 47; to New Carthage, 157; at Port Gibson, 158–64, *159;* to Raymond, 166; at Shiloh, 49, *50–51;* at Vicksburg, 171

McComas, W. W., 62

McCook, Alexander McD.: to Bellfonte and Stevenson, 226; at Chickamauga, 226–31, *228–29;* at Liberty Gap, 225; at Perryville,

124, *125*, 126; at Rowlett's Station, 29–30; at Stones River, 151–53, *152*

McCook, Daniel, 124, 338

McCook, Edward M., 250–51, 341, 436

McCook, Robert L., 32

McCown, John P., 56

McCray, Thomas H., 380–82, *381*

McCulloch, Benjamin: in Boston Mountains, 34; at Carthage, 20; at Pea Ridge, 37; at Wilson's Creek, 21, *22*, 23

McCulloch, Henry E., 173, 175

McCullough, James, 70

McDowell, Irvin: at Blackburn's Ford, 11; at Bull Run, 11; at First Manassas, 12, *13*, 14–15; at Fredericksburg, 81, 90, 92, 93; and Iron Brigade, 110; redeployment to Shenandoah Valley, 91, 92, 93

McDowell, Va., battle of, 78–80, *79*, 90, 128

McGarry, Edward, 218

McGinnis, George F., 170

McGowan, Samuel, 357, *358–59*, 413, 415, *416*

McIntosh, Chilly, 33

McIntosh, Daniel N., 33

McIntosh, David G., *253*, 254

McIntosh, James, 21, *22*, 34, 36

McKean, Thomas J., *130*, 131

McKinley, William, 323

McLaws, Lafayette: at Averasboro, 407; at Bentonville, 408–11, *409;* at Campbell's Station, 248–49; at Chancellorsville, *198*, 199; at Gettysburg, *209*, 211; at Harpers Ferry, 113–15, *114;* at Richmond, 97; at Rivers Bridge, 405–6; at Savage's Station, 98; at South Mountain, 115

McLean, Nathaniel, 79–80, *79*

McLean, Wilmer, 431

McNeil, John H., 133, 178, 383

McPhail, Samuel, 222

McPherson, James B.: at Atlanta, 340; at Champion Hill, *168*, 169–70; as commander of Army of the Tennessee, 326; death of, 340; at Jackson, Miss., 167; at Kennesaw Mountain, 536–38, *337;* at Lost Mountain–Brushy Mountain Line, 335; to New Carthage, 157;

at New Hope Church, Pickett's
Mill, and Dallas, 332–35, *333;*
and Port Gibson, 158, 160; at Raymond, 165–66, *165;* at Resaca,
329–31, *330;* at Snake Creek
Gap, 262, 328, 329; at Vicksburg,
171–72

Meade, George G.: along Blue
Ridge Mountains, 213; at Boonsboro–Funkstown–Falling Waters,
213; at Boydton Plank Road,
369–71, *370;* and Bristoe campaign, 251, 252; at Cold Harbor,
291–94, *292;* as commander of
Army of the Potomac, 259; criticisms of, 259; on Davis assassination plans, 260; at Fredericksburg I, 145, *146–47,* 148; at
Gettysburg, 207–12, *209–10;* at
Glendale and White Oak Swamp,
100–101; Grant's orders to, 267;
Lincoln's assessment of, 213; at
Mine Run, 255–59, *256–57;* at
North Anna, 287–89, *288;* north
of Rappahannock River, 251; and
Petersburg I, 352; and reinforcements for Rosecrans, 241; at
Spotsylvania Court House, 283–
86, *284;* on tiredness of troops,
353; and White Oak Road, 413; in
Wilderness, *281,* 282–83

Meagher, Thomas F., *95,* 96

Mechanicsville, Va., 93–94

Memphis, Tenn.: first battle of, 56,
57, 58; second battle of, 350

Memphis & Charleston Railroad,
52, 122, 129, 241

Meridian, Miss., battle of, 261

Merrill, Samuel, 177–78

Merrimack, 88

Merritt, Wesley: at Brandy Station,
204; at Cedar Creek, *320–21;* at
Opequon, 316; at Sailor's Creek,
425, 426; at Smithfield Crossing,
314; at Tom's Brook, 319

Mexican War: casualties of, 464;
Grant and Lee in, 431; Price
in, 20

Mexico, 232, 265, 437

Miami, 277

Middle Boggy, Okla. , battle of, 221

Middleburg, Va., battle of, 205–6

Middle Creek, Ky., battle of, 30

Miles, David, *409,* 410

Miles, Dixon S., 12, 113–15, *114*

Miles, James, 365

Miles, Nelson A., 360–62, *361,* 413,
416, 423, 428

Miles, W. R., 181

Miller, David, 120

Miller, Robert, 90

Miller, William, 434

Milliken's Bend, La., battle of, 173,
175

Mill Springs, Ky., battle of, 30, *31,*
32

Milroy, Robert H.: at Camp Allegheny, 10; at Cross Keys, 82, *83,*
84; at McDowell, 78–80, *79;* at
Murfreesboro II, 396; at Second
Manassas, 110; at Second Winchester, 205; Winchester position
of, 312

Mine Creek, Kans., battle of, 384–
85

Mine Run, Va., battle of, 255–59,
256–57

Minnesota, 88

Missionary Ridge, Tenn., 243, 244,
245, 246

Mississippi, 59

Mississippi Central Railroad, 149

Mississippi River, 26, 45, 56–58,
136–37, 157, 173, 180, 182, 265,
267, 271, 275

Missouri: pro-Confederate activity
and guerrilla warfare in, 377–79;
as slave state, 19–20; strategic
importance of, 20, 21; two governments in, 20, 25

Missouri Compromise, 19, 224

Mitchel, Ormsby A., 122

Mitchell, John G., *337,* 338, *409,* 410

Mitchell, John K., 58

Mitchell, Robert B., *125,* 126

Mobile, Ala., fall of, 374, 376, 435

Mobile & Ohio Railroad, 53, 149,
261, 262, 346, 349

Mobile Bay, Ala.: battle of, 374–76,
375; fall of, 435

Mobile campaign, 435

Monett's Ferry, La., battle of, 271–
72

Monitor, 88, 91

Monocacy, Md., battle of, 305–8,
306

Monroe's Cross Roads, N.C., battle
of, 406–7

Montauk, 191

Montgomery, James E., 57

Monticello, 5

Moonlight, Thomas, 383

Moor, Augustus, 240, *302,* 303

Moore, Absalom B., 150

Moore, David, *348,* 349–50

Moore, James, 363

Moorefield, W.Va., battle of, 313

Moose, 216

Morell, George W., 94–97, *95,* 103

Morgan, 374, *375*

Morgan, James D., *409,* 410

Morgan, John Hunt: at Buffington
Island, 216; at Corydon, 216; at
Cove Mountain, 297–98; at Cynthiana, 344; death of, 216, 344,
387; at Hartsville, 150; Indiana
and Ohio raid by, 216–17; in
Kentucky, 149; at Murfreesboro I,
122; promotion to brigadier general, 150; at Salineville, 216; and
Third Kentucky ("Christmas")
Raid, 150; at Vaught's Hill, 189–
90

Morgan, Richard, 216

Morgan, Tom, 216

Morris, Thomas A., 6, 8

Morris Island, S.C., 192–93, *194*

Morton, John, 346, 389

Morton's Ford, Va., battle of, 260

Moses, Raphael, 195

Mossy Creek, Tenn., battle of, 250

Mott, Gershom, 368, *370,* 371

Mound City, 38, 57

Mount Washington, 195

Mount Zion Church, Mo., battle of,
27

Mouton, Alfred: at Brashear City,
180; at Georgia Landing, 137; at
Mansfield, 268–69, *268;* at Stirling's Plantation, 181

Mower, Joseph A.: at Bentonville,
409, 410; at Ditch Bayou, 275;
at Fort DeRussy, 267; at Rivers
Bridge, 403–404; at Tupelo,
348, 349–50; at Yellow Bayou,
272

Mulligan, James A., 24, 310–12,
311

Munford, Thomas T., 202, *203,* 204,
205

Munfordville, Ky., battle of (Battle
for the Bridge), 123

Murfreesboro, Tenn.: first battle of, 122; second battle of, 396
Myrick, Andrew, 135

Nagle, James, *109,* 111
Nahant, 191
Namozine Church, Va., battle of, 423–24
Napoleon III, Emperor, 、 ., 265
Nashville, Tenn., battle of, 396–97, 401
Nashville & Chattanooga Railroad, 122, 226, 242, 243, 346, 396
Nashville & Decatur Railroad, 190, 261
Native Americans, 33–34, 133–36, 217–21, 274, 351, 353, 398, 406, 433, 438
Natural Bridge, Fla., battle of, 434
Navy. *See* specific naval officers and names of ships
Navy Hydrographic Office, 71
Negley, James Scott, 122, 227
Nelson, William, 29, 49, *50–51,* 123
Nelson's Farm, Va., 98
Neptune, 138
New Bern, N.C.: battle of, 60–61; battle of Fort Anderson, 194–95
New Era, 276
New Hope Church, Ga., battle of, 332–34, *333*
New Ironsides, 191
New Madrid/Island No. 10, Mo., battle of, 48, 56–57
New Market, Va., battle of, 298–301, *299,* 326
New Market Crossroads, Va., 98
New Market Heights, Va.: battle of Chaffin's Farm and, 362–68, *367*
New Market Road, Va., battle of Darbytown and, 369
New Mexico campaign, 39–44
New Orleans, La., battle of, 59
Newton, John, *337,* 338–39, 340, 434
Newtonia, Mo.: first battle of, 134; second battle of, 385–86, *385*
Norfolk, Va., 5, 59, 88, 91, 195
North Anna, Va., battle of, 280, 287–90, *288*
Northern Virginia campaign, 105–12, *106, 109*
Northwest Ordinance, 19

OAK. *See* Order of American Knights (OAK)
Oak Grove, Va., battle of, 93
Okolona, Miss., battle of, 261–62
Old Church, Va., 291
Old Fort Wayne, Okla., battle of, 134
Old River Lake, Ark., 275
Olstead, Charles H., 66
Olustee, Fla., battle of, 263–64
Opdycke, Emerson, 395
Opequon (Third Winchester), Va., battle of, 315–16
Opothleyahola, Chief, 33–34
Orange & Alexandria Railroad, 108, 252
Ord, Edward O. C.: at Appomattox Court House, 429–32, *430;* at Chaffin's Farm, 362–63, 364, *366;* at Davis Bridge, 132; at Dranesville, 17–18; at High Bridge, 427; at Iuka, 129; in Shenandoah Valley, 81, 91
Order of American Knights (OAK), 377, 379
Osborne, F. A., 62
Osterhaus, Peter J.: at Champion Hill, *168,* 169–70; at Pea Ridge, 36; at Port Gibson, *159,* 163–64; at Ringgold Gap, 247–48, *247*
O'Sullivan, Timothy, photograph by, *237*
Owen, Joshua T., 252–54, *253*

Paducah, Ky., battle of, 275
Page, Richard L., 374, *375,* 376
Paine, Charles J., 364–65, *367*
Paine, Halbert E., *183,* 184
Palmer, John M.: at Kennesaw Mountain, *337;* at New Hope Church, Pickett's Mill, and Dallas, 332–35; relieved of command, 341; at Resaca, 329–31, *330;* at Rocky Face Ridge, *327*
Palmer, Joseph B., 396
Palmito Ranch, Tex., battle of, 437–38
Parham, William A., 115
Parke, John G.: at Bean's Station, 249; at Boydton Plank Road, *370;* at Dandridge, 250; at Fort Macon, 61; at Fort Stedman, 373; at New Bern, 61; at Petersburg III, 419–23, *420–21;* at Poplar Spring Church, 368

Parker, Ely, 433
Parker's Cross Roads, Tenn., battle of, 149–50
Parsons, Mosby M., 24, 274–75
Parsons, William H., 38, 175
Passaic, 191
Patapsco, 191
Patterson, Robert, 11, 12, 14
Patton, John M., 84
Pawnee, 5
Pea Ridge, Ark., battle of, 34–37, *35,* 133
Peachtree Creek, Ga., battle of, 339–40
Peck, John J., 195
Peebles' Farm, Va., battle of, 368
Pegram, John: at Cedar Creek, *320–21,* 322; death of, 372; at Fisher's Hill, 316–18, *317;* at Hatcher's Run, 372; at Rich Mountain, 8
Pegram, William, 362
Pelham, John, 145, 148, 196
Pemberton, John C.: and Big Black River Bridge, 171; at Champion Hill, 167–70, *168;* at Chickasaw Bayou, 154–56, *155;* force to Vicksburg, 156; at Grenada, 154; and Grierson's raid through Mississippi, 160, 176; and Port Gibson, 160; Secessionville forces, 67; at Vicksburg battle and siege, 171–73
Pender, William D., 207–12, *209–10*
Pendleton, Sandie, 318
Pendleton, William N., 121
Peninsula campaign, 88–104, *89, 95, 99, 102*
Perry, Edward A., *253,* 254
Perry, William Flank, 356–57
Perryville, Ky., battle of, 124–28, *125*
Petersburg, Va.: battle of the Crater, 341, 355–56; first battle of, 352; Lee's retreat from, 422–29; second battle of, 352–53; third battle of, 419–23, *420–21*
Pettigrew, James Johnston, 195, *210,* 212
Philippi, W.Va., battle of, 6–7
Philips, John F., 384
Phillips, William A., 218, 221
Photography in Civil War, 201, 234–35, *235–39*

Pickett, George E.: at Chaffin's Farm, 363; at Dinwiddie Court House, 412–13; at Five Forks, 417–19, *418;* at Fredericksburg I, 145, *146–47;* at Gettysburg, *210,* 212; under Longstreet, 194; and Petersburg defense, 278; at Sailor's Creek, 426; at Suffolk, 195; at Swift Creek, 278; at White Oak Road, 413

Pickett's Mill, Ga., battle of, *333,* 354

Pickins, Francis, 4

Piedmont, Va., battle of, 301–3, *302*

Pierce, Ebenezer W., 6

Pierpont, Francis, 7

Pike, Albert, 33, 133

Pillow, Gideon J., 26, 28, 45–48, *46*

Pilot Knob, Mo., battle of, 380–82, *381*

Pine Bluff, Ark., battle of, 233

Pittsburg, 57

Pittsburg Landing, Tenn., 48–49

Plains Store, La., battle of, 181–82

Planter, 67, 70

Pleasant Hill, La., battle of, 266, 269–71, *270*

Pleasants, Henry, 355

Pleasonton, Alfred: at Aldie, 205; and Big Blue River, 383; at Brandy Station, *203,* 204; at Independence II, 383; at Lexington II, 382; at Marais des Cygnes, 384; at Westport, 384

Plummer, Joseph B., 21, *22,* 24–25

Plymouth, N.C., battle of, 277

Poague, William T., 252–54, *253*

Pocahontas, 18

Poindexter, J. A., 27

Poison Spring, Ark., battle of, 273–74

Polk, Leonidas: in Army of the Mississippi, 48; near Bardstown, 124; at Cassville, 332; at Chickamauga, *228–29,* 230; at Columbus, Ky., 26; at Corinth, 53, *54–55;* death of, 335; in Johnston's Army of Tennessee, 326; at Meridian, 261; in Mississippi, 245; at Munfordville, 123; at New Hope Church, Pickett's Mill, and Dallas, 332–35, *333;* at Perryville, 124, 126; at Resaca, 329–31,

330; at Shelbyville, 225; at Shiloh, 48–49, *50–51;* at Stones River, 151–53, *152*

Polk, Lucius E., 246–48, *247*

Pook, Samuel, 44

"Pook's Turtles," 44

Poole, David, 224

Pope, John: at Centreville, 112; as commander of Army of the Mississippi, 52; as commander of Army of Virginia, 129; as commander of Military Department of the Northwest, 112, 135, 136; at Corinth, 53, *54–55;* in Dakota Territory, 222, 223, 351; force at Cedar Mountain, 105; and Manassas Station/Junction, 108; at New Madrid/Island No. 10, 56–57; at Rappahannock River, 107–8; at Second Manassas, *109,* 110–11; in Tennessee, 48

Porter, David D.: at Arkansas Post, 157; at Fort Anderson, 403; at Fort Fisher I and II, 401–2; at Forts Jackson and St. Philip, 58; at Grand Gulf, 158; at Milliken's Bend, 173; and Red River campaign, 265–66, 267, 271–72; in Richmond with Lincoln, 423–24; strategic planning in March 1865, 412; at Vicksburg, 171; on Yazoo River, 171

Porter, Fitz John: at Beaver Dam Creek, 93–94; at Gaines' Mill, 94–97, *95;* at Hanover Court House, 92; headquarters of, *237;* at Malvern Hill, 101–4, *102;* at Shepherdstown, 121

Porter, Joseph C., 133, 177–78

Porterfield, George A., 6

Port Gibson, Miss., battle of, 158–64, *159–61*

Port Hudson, La., 136–37, 173, 179, 181; siege of, 180, 182–84, *183,* 264

Port Republic, Va., battle of, 82, 84–87, *86*

Port Walthall Junction, Va., battle of, 278

Posey, Carnot, *253,* 254

Potomac River blockade, 5–6, 18–19

Potter, E. E., 62

Potter, Robert, 368

Powell, Samuel, *125,* 126

Powers, Frank P., 181

Prairie D'Ane, Ark., battle of, 273

Prairie Grove, Ark., battle of, 141–46, *142*

Prentiss, Benjamin M.: at Helena, 175–76; at Mount Zion Church, 27; at Shiloh, 48–49, *50–51*

Price, Sterling: at Bayou Fourche, 233; at Big Blue River, 383; at Carthage, 20; as commander of Missouri State Guard, 20, 21, 34; at Davis Bridge, 132; at Dry Wood Creek, 23–24; at Glasgow, 382; at Helena, 175–76; at Independence II, 383; at Iuka, 129; at Lexington I, 24, 34; at Lexington II, 382; at Marais des Cygnes, 384; at Marmaton River, 385; at Mine Creek, 384; at Newtonia II, 385–86, *385;* number of forces under, 273; in Order of American Knights, 377; at Pilot Knob, 380–82, *381;* at Prairie D'Ane, 273; and Quantrill, 379; and Springfield I, 25; at Westport, 384

Princess Royal, 180

Princeton Courthouse, W.Va., battle of, 80

Proclamation of Amnesty and Reconstruction, 263, 265

Proctor's Creek (Drewry's Bluff), Va., battle of, 279

Pulaski, Count Casimir, 63

Putnam, Haldiman S., 193

Pyron, Charles L., 42

Quantrill, William C., 133, 224, 377–79

Queen of the West, 57

Rachel Seaman, 138

Radical Abolitionist Party, 185

Raguet, Henry W., 39

Ramseur, Stephen D.: at Cedar Creek, *320–21,* 322; at Fisher's Hill, 316–18, *317;* at Monocacy, 305–8, *306;* at Opequon, 315–16; at Rutherford's Farm, 309; at Second Kernstown, 310–12, *311;* at Smithfield Crossing, 314

Ramsey, Alexander, 222

Randol, Alanson, 101

Ransom, Matt W., 277

Ransom, Robert, 103, 145, *146–47*, 279

Ransom, Thomas Edward Greenfield, *268*, 269

Rapidan River, 251, 260

Rappahannock River, Va., battle of, 107–8

Rappahannock Station, Va., battle of, 255

Rawlins, John A., 261

Raymond, Miss., battle of, *162–63*, 164–67, *165*

Read, Theodore, 427

Reams Station, Va.: first battle of, 354–55; second battle of, 360–62, *361*

Reconstruction, 188, 452

Red River, 179, 182

Red River campaigns, 43–44, 265–72, *268*, *270*

Reekie, John, photograph by, *239*

Reilly, James W., 395

Reno, Jesse L.: at Chantilly, 112; death of, 117; at New Bern, 61; at Roanoke Island, 60; at South Mills, 61–62; at South Mountain, *116*, 117

Renshaw, William B., 138

Republican Party, 224

Resaca, Ga., battle of, 329–31, *330*

Resolute, 18

Reynolds, Daniel H., *327*, 328

Reynolds, John F., 207, *208*

Reynolds, Joseph J., 10

Reynolds, Thomas C., 382

Rhind, A. C., 70

Rice's Station, Va., battle of, 427

Richardson, Israel, 11, *99*, 100

Richmond, Ky., battle of, 122–23

Richmond, Va.: food riot in, 196; government's escape from, 422, 429; Kilpatrick-Dahlgren raid on, 260; Lincoln in, 423–24; McClellan's advance on, 74, 78, 81, 88, 92, 93; Sheridan's raid on, 286

Richmond & Danville Railroad, 279, 352, 354, 412, 424

Richmond & Petersburg Railroad, 278, 279, 352

Richmond & York River Railroad, 92, 94, 98

Richmond–Petersburg campaign, 352–73, *358–59*, *361*, 366–67, *370*

Rich Mountain, W.Va., battle of, 7–9, *7*

Ricketts, James B.: at Fisher's Hill, *317*, 318; at Monocacy, 305–8, *306;* at Smithfield Crossing, 314; at Thoroughfare Gap, 108

Ricketts, Robert Bruce, 252–54, *253*

Ringgold Gap, Ga., battle of, 246–48, *249*

River Queen, 412

Rivers Bridge, S.C., battle of, 405–6

Roanoke Island, N.C., battle of, 60

Roan's Tan Yard, Mo., battle of, 27

Robertson, Beverly H.: at Brandy Station, 202; at Middleburg, 206; at Rectortown, 205; at Upperville, 206; at White Hall, 62

Robertson, Felix H., 387

Robinson, James S., *409*, 410

Rocky Face Ridge, Ga., battle of, 326–29, *327*

Roddey, Philip D., *348*, 349–50

Rodes, Robert E.: at Bethesda Church, 290; at Bristoe Station, *253*, 254; at Chancellorsville, 199; at Cool Spring, 309; death of, 316; at Gettysburg, 207, *208;* at Manassas Gap, 213–14; to Martinsburg, 205; at Mine Run, *256–57;* at Monocacy, 305–8, *306;* at Opequon, 316; at Second Kernstown, 310–12, *311;* at South Mountain, 117

Rodgers, John, 91

Rodman, Isaac P., 117

Rogers, William P., 131

Rosecrans, William S.: at Carnifex Ferry, 9; at Chattanooga II, 226; at Chattanooga III, 243; at Chickamauga, 226–31, *228–29;* as commander in northwest Virginia, 9; as commander of Army of the Cumberland, 127, 216, 224, 241; as commander of Army of the Mississippi, 129; at Corinth battle, *130*, 131–32; and Davis Bridge, 132; at Hoover's Gap, 225–26; at Iuka, 129; and Lexington II, 382; in Murfreesboro area, 225; in north Georgia, 227; and Pilot Knob, 380; relieved of command, 241, 243; at Rich Mountain, 8; at Stones River,

151–54, *152;* and Streight's raid through Alabama, 176

Ross, John, 33, 133

Rosser, Thomas L., 295, 319, 412, 427

Round Mountain, Okla., battle of, 33

Rousseau, Lovell H., 341, 396

Rowan, Stephen C., 60–61

Rowlett's Station, Ky., battle of, 29–30

Ruggles, Daniel, 5

Runyon, Theodore, 12

Russell, A. A., 149

Russell, David A., 316

Rust, Albert, 10, 38

Rutherford's Farm, Va., battle of, 309

Sabine Pass, Tex.: first battle of, 138; second battle of, 232

Sabine River, 265–66

Sachem, 232

Sagamore, 139

Sailor's Creek, Va., battle of, 424–27, *425*

St. Charles, Ark., battle of, 38

Saint Emma Plantation, La., 180

St. Johns Bluff, Fla., battle of, 139–40

St. Louis, 38

St. Louis & Iron Mountain Railroad, 380

Saint Mary's Church, Va., 295

Salem Church, Va., battle of, 200

Salineville, Ohio, battle of, 216–17

Salomon, Frederick, 134

Saltville, Va.: first battle of, 387; second battle of, 388

Samaria Church (Saint Mary's Church), Va., 295

Sanborn, John B., *165*, 166, *385*, 386

Sand Creek, Colo., battle of, 43, 398

Santa Rosa Island, Fla., battle of, 27–28

Sappony Church, Va., battle of, 354

Saunders, Betty, 422

Savage's Station, Va., battle of, 98

Savannah, Ga., 400–401

Schenck, Robert C., 79–80, *79*, *82*, *83*, 84

Schoepf, Albin F., 29, 32

Schofield, John M.: at Columbia, Tenn., 392; as commander of

Army of the Ohio, 326; at Dalton III, 391; at Fort Fisher, 403; at Franklin II, 395; at Goldsboro, 407, 411; at Kennesaw Mountain, 336–39, *337;* at Kolb's Farm, 336; at Lost Mountain–Brushy Mountain Line, 335; in Missouri, 133, 141; at Nashville, 396–97; at New Hope Church, Pickett's Mill, and Dallas, 332–35, *333;* at Peachtree Creek, 339–40; at Resaca, 329–31, *330;* at Rocky Face Ridge, *327,* 328; and Sherman's Carolina campaign, 406; at Spring Hill, 392–95, *393;* at Utoy Creek, 341; at Wilmington, 403

Schurz, Carl, 242

Scott, John S., 24, 122–23

Scott, Winfield, 5, 6, 12; as general-in-chief, 3

Scottish Chief, 263

Scribner, Benjamin F., 334

Scurry, William R., *41,* 42–44

Sears, Claudius, 390, 396

Secession, 4, 5, 6, 7, 19–20, 186, 263, 325

Secessionville, S.C., battle of, 67, *68,* 69

Seddon, James, 194

Sedgwick, John: death of, 286; at Fredericksburg II, 199–200; at Gettysburg, *209–10;* at Mine Run, *256–57;* at Rappahannock Station, 255; at Savage's Station, 98; at Seven Pines, 92; at Spotsylvania Court House, 286; in Wilderness, *281,* 282–83

Selma, Ala., battle of, 436

Selma, 374, *375*

Seminole, 18

Seven Pines, Va., battle of, 92–93

Seward, William H.: as U.S. secretary of state, 3; as U.S. senator, 39

Sewell's Point, Va., battle of, 5

Seymour, Truman A., 193, 263–64

Shackelford, James M., 249

Shaw, Henry M., 60

Shaw, Robert Gould, 193

Shelby, Joseph O. "Jo": at Big Blue River, 383; at Cane Hill, 140; at Cape Girardeau, 178; at Independence II, 383; at Lexington II, 382; at Marks' Mills, 274; at Marmaton River, 385; at Mine Creek,

384; in Missouri, 133; at Newtonia II, *385,* 386; near Okolona, 273; at Pilot Knob, 380–82, *381;* at Prairie De Rohan, 273; at Westport, 384

Shenandoah Valley: campaign in May–June 1864, 298–304; Early's campaign in June–August 1864, 304–13; Jackson's campaign in March–June 1862, 74–87, *75–77, 79, 83, 86,* 264, 267; Sheridan's campaign in August 1864–March 1865, 312, 313–24

Shepherdstown, W.Va., battle of, 121

Sheridan, Philip H.: at Amelia Springs, 424; at Appomattox Court House, 429–32, *430;* to Bermuda Hundred, 295; at Berryville, 315; and "The Burning," 319; at Cameron's Depot, 314; at Cedar Creek, 319–23, *320–21;* at Charles Town, 314; at Clayton's Store, 294–95; at Cold Harbor, 291, 293; as commander of Army of the Shenandoah, 313; at Dinwiddie Court House, 412–13; at First Deep Bottom, 355; at Fisher's Hill, 316–18, *317;* at Five Forks, 417–19, *418,* 423; Grant's orders to, 267; at Haw's Shop, 290; and Lee's retreat from Petersburg, 428, 429; at Opequon, 315–16; at Perryville, 124, *125,* 126; raids against rail lines, 353, 412; Richmond raid by, 286; at Sailor's Creek, *425,* 426; Shenandoah Valley campaign of, 312, 313–24; at Smithfield Crossing, 314; at Staunton, 319, 324; at Stones River, 151, 153; and Tom's Brook, 318–19; at Trevilian Station, 295; at White House, 295; at Wyanoke Neck, 295; at Yellow Tavern, 286–87

Sherman, Frank, 331

Sherman, Thomas W., 64, 66

Sherman, William Tecumseh: advance down river toward Vicksburg, 150; and Allatoona, 391; at Arkansas Post, 157; at Atlanta, 315, 340; Atlanta campaign of, 261, 271, 275, 326–43, *327, 330,*

333, 337, 344; at Bentonville, 408–11, *409;* Carolina campaign of, 405–11, *409;* at Charleston, 406; at Chattanooga III, 243–46, *244,* 275; at Chickasaw Bayou, 154–56, *155;* at Columbia, S.C., 194, 406; at Fayetteville, 407; at Goldsboro, 411; Grant's orders to, 267; at Jackson, Miss., 167; on Johnston, 339; at Kennesaw Mountain, 336–39, *337;* on Lincoln, 412; at Lost Mountain–Brushy Mountain Line, 335–36; and march to sea, 391, 399–401; at Meridian, 261; at New Hope Church, Pickett's Mill, and Dallas, 332–35, *333;* in north Georgia, 278; and Red River campaign, 265; redeployment to Chattanooga, 241; and Resaca, 329; at Rocky Face Ridge, 326–28, *327;* and Savannah, 400–401; at Shiloh, 49, *50–51;* at Snake Creek Gap, 391; at Snyder's Bluff, 158; strategic planning in March 1865, 412; supplies for, 347, 389; total-war philosophy of, 399; and Vicksburg campaign, 154, 164–66, 171, 175

Shields, James: at First Kernstown, 76; to Fredericksburg, 80; in Luray Valley, 85; at Port Republic, 85; and Shenandoah Valley campaign, 81, 91; at Strasburg, 82

Shiloh, Tenn., battle of, 48–52, *50–51,* 347

Shoup, Francis A., *142,* 143

Shreveport, La., 265, 267, 273

Sibley, Henry Hastings, 136, 222–23

Sibley, Henry Hopkins, 39–44, *40–41*

Sickles, Daniel E., *198,* 199, *209,* 211

Sigel, Franz: at Carthage, 20; and Fredericksburg I, 144; Grant's orders to, 267; at New Market, 298–301, *299,* 326; at Pea Ridge, 36; relieved of command, 301; at Staunton, 298; at Wilson's Creek, 21, *22, 23*

Sill, Joshua W., 29

Simmons' Bluff, S.C., battle of, 70

Singletary, George B., 62

Slack, James R., *159*, 164, 169

Slavery: Democratic Party on, 343; and 1850 compromise, 39; elimination of, due to Civil War, 325; and Emancipation Proclamation, 120, 188, 189, *238;* fugitive slave law, 19, 39; importance of, for South, 186; and Kansas-Nebraska Act, 224; Lincoln on, 185, 224–25; and Missouri Compromise, 19, 224; and U.S. Constitution, 19. *See also* Abolitionism

Slemons, W. F., 380–82, *381*

Slocum, Henry W.: at Averasboro, 407; at Bentonville, 408–11, *409;* as commander of Army of Georgia, 405; feint toward Augusta, 399; at Gaines' Mill, *95*, 96–97; at Glendale, *99*, 100; and Sherman's Carolina campaign, 405; at South Mountain, *116*, 117

Slough, John P., *41*, 42–43

Smalls, Robert, 67, 70

Smith, A. J.: at Alexandria, 266; and Atlanta campaign, 275; at Champion Hill, *168*, 169; at Chickasaw Bayou, 155, 156; at Ditch Bayou, 275; at Fort DeRussy, 267; at Glasgow, 382; in Missouri, 382, 384; at Nashville, 396; to Old Auburn, 166; at Petersburg II, 353; at Pleasant Hill, 269; and Red River campaign, 265, 267, 271; and reinforcements for Thomas, 392; at Tupelo, *348*, 349–50; to Vicksburg, 275

Smith, Charles F., *46*, 47

Smith, E. Kirby: to Arkansas, 271, 274; as commander of Trans-Mississippi Department, 265; near Harrodsburg, 126; at Jenkins' Ferry, 274–75; and Marks' Mills, 274; at Richmond, 122, 123; surrender by, 438

Smith, Gerrit, 185

Smith, Giles A., *155*, 156, *337*, 338–39

Smith, Gustavus W., 92, 400

Smith, John E., *165*, 166

Smith, Melancton, 277, 279

Smith, Morgan L., *155*, 156, *330*, 331

Smith, Thomas Kilby, *155*, 156

Smith, W. A., 280

Smith, William F. "Baldy": and Bermuda Hundred campaign, 278–80; at Cold Harbor, 291, *292*, 293–94; and Garnett's and Golding's Farms, 97; at Glendale and White Oak Swamp, *99*, 100; at Petersburg I, 352; and plan for supply line to Chattanooga, 241–42; at Port Walthall Junction, 278; at South Mountain, *116*, 117; at Yorktown, 90

Smith, William Sooy, 261–62

Smithfield Crossing, W.Va., battle of, 314

Smyth, Thomas A., *253*, 254, 428

Snyder's Bluff, Miss., 171; battle of, 158

Southfield, 277

South Mills, N.C., battle of, 61–62

South Mountain, Md., battle of, 115–18, *116*

South Side Railroad, 353, 368, 369, 412, 417, 419, 423, 427, 429

Spangenberg, Charles L., 175

Spanish Fort, Ala., battle of, 435

Spencer, George E., 407

Spotswood, Alexander, 280

Spotsylvania Court House, Va., battle of, 283–86, *284*

Springfield, Mo.: first battle of, 25; second battle of, 177

Spring Hill, Tenn., battle of, 392–95, *393*

Staff ride: and Civil War battlefields, 16–17

Stahel, Julius: at Cross Keys, 82–84, *83;* at New Market, *299*, 300; at Piedmont, 301–3, *302*

Standing Buffalo, 222

Stanley, David S., *130*, 131, 190, 392, *393*, 394, 397

Stannard, George, 363, *366*

Stansel, Martin L., 413, *416*

Stanton, Edwin M., 226, 347

Star Fort, *390*, 391

Star of the West, 1

Starke, William E., 110

Starkweather, John, 126

Starnes, James W., 190

Staunton River Bridge, Va., battle of, 354

Steedman, Charles, 139

Steedman, James B., *229*, 231, 342, 397

Steele, Frederick: at Bayou Fourche, 233; at Chickasaw Bayou, *155*, 156; along Deer Creek, 157; and food supplies, 273–74; at Fort Blakely, 435; in Little Rock, 275; at Prairie D'Ane, 273; and Red River campaign, 267, 271; to Shreveport, 265, 273; at Spanish Fort, 435

Stephens, Alexander, 185, 186

Steuart, George H., 82, *83*, 84

Stevens, Alexander, 402

Stevens, Isaac, 67, *68*, 69, 112

Stevenson, Carter L.: at Champion Hill, 169; at Chattanooga III, *244*, 245; at Kennesaw Mountain, *337;* at Kolb's Farm, 336; at Resaca, *330*, 331; at Rocky Face Ridge, *327*, 328; at Vicksburg, 171

Stewart, Alexander P.: and Allatoona, 390; Army of Tennessee under, 408; at Bentonville, 408–11, *409;* at Ezra Church, 341; at Nashville, 397; at New Hope Church, *333;* at Peachtree Creek, 339–40; at Resaca, *330*, 331; at Rocky Face Ridge, *327*

Stewart, Thomas J., 462

Stickney, Albert, 180

Stirling's Plantation, La., battle of, 180–81

Stone, Charles P., 18

Stone, William M., *159*, 164

Stoneman, George, 338, 341–42, 388

Stones River, Tenn., battle of, 151–54, *152*

Stones River campaign, 150–54, *152*

Stony Lake, N.D., battle of, 222–23

Streight, Abel, raid of, 158, 176–77

Stribling, Robert M., 195

Stringham, Silas H., 59

Strong, George C., 192–93

Strong, George T., 323

Stuart, David, 49, *50–51*

Stuart, J. E. B.: and Aldie, 205; at Antietam, *119*, 120; at Auburn I and II, 251–52; at Boonsboro–Funkstown–Falling Waters, 213; at Brandy Station, 202, *203*, 204; at Buckland Mills, 254–55; death of, 287; at Dranesville, 18; at Fredericksburg I, 145; at Gettysburg, 207, *210*, 212; at Hanover, 206; and Middleburg, 206; and Pelham's death, 196; and "Ride around McClellan," 93; at Upperville, 206; at Yellow Tavern, 286–87

Sturgis, Samuel D.: at Brices Cross Roads, *345*, 346; at Dandridge, 250; at Fair Garden, 250–51; at Lexington I, 24; from Memphis to Ripley and back, 344–45; at Mossy Creek, 250; at South Mountain, *116*, 117

Suffolk, Va.: first battle of, 195; second battle of, 195–96

Sullivan, Jeremiah C.: at First Kernstown, *75*, 78; at Jackson, Tenn., 149, 150; at Piedmont, 301–3, *302*

Sully, Alfred, 222, 223, 351

Summit Point and Cameron's Depot, W.Va., battle of, 314

Sumner, Edwin V.: at Antietam, *119*, 120; at Fredericksburg I, 144–48, *146–47;* at Malvern Hill, 101–4, *102;* at Savage's Station, 98

Sutherland Station, Va., battle of, 425

Sweeny, Thomas W., 329, 331

Swift Creek: battle of Swift Creek and Fort Clinton, Va., 278

Sykes, George: at Gaines' Mill, 94–97, *95;* at Gettysburg, *209–10*, 211; at Mine Run, *256–57*

Tahoma, 263

Talcott, T. M. R., 429, *430*

Taliaferro, William B.: at Averasboro, 407; at Bentonville, 408–11, *409;* at Fredericksburg I, 145, *146–47;* at McDowell, *79*, 80

Tampa, Fla., battle of, 139

Tappan, James C., 175

Taylor, George W., 108

Taylor, Richard, 363

Taylor, Richard: at Brashear City, 180; at Cross Keys, 84; at First Winchester, 81; at Fort Bisland, 179; at Fort Harrison, 363; at Irish Bend, 179; and Lafourche Crossing, 180; at Mansfield, 267–69, *268;* at Mansura, 272; at Pleasant Hill, 269–71, *270;* at

Port Republic, 85, *86*, 87; and Red River campaign, 265–72; at Selma, 436; surrender by, 437–38; west of Vicksburg, 172; at Yellow Bayou, 272

Taylor, Walter Herren, 422–23

Taylor, Zachary, 128, 265, 267

Tecumseh, 374, *375*

Tennessee, 374, *375*

Tennessee River, 44, 45, 48–52, 243, 389, 392

Terrill, William R., 126

Terry, Alfred H.: at Darbytown Road, 369; at Fair Oaks and Darbytown Road, 372; at Fort Fisher II, 402; at Goldsboro, 407, 411; at Grimball's Landing, 192; at New Market Heights, 364–65, *367;* at Second Deep Bottom, 356, *358–59;* and Sherman's Carolina campaign, 406; at Wilmington, 403

Terry, William, *306*, 307–308

Thatcher, Henry K., 435

Thayer, John M., *155*, 156, 273

Thoburn, Joseph: at Berryville, 315; at Cedar Creek, *320–21*, 322; at Cool Spring, 309; at Piedmont, *302*, 303; at Second Kernstown, 310–12, *311*

Thomas, George H.: at Adairsville, 331; at Camp Wildcat, 29; and Chattanooga, 241; at Chattanooga III, 243–46, *244;* at Chickamauga, 226–31, *228–29;* and Chickamauga campaign, 226, 227; as commander of Army of the Cumberland, 241, 243, 326; as commander of Army of the Tennessee, 52; at Corinth, 53, *54–55;* at Dalton I, 262; Forrest's destruction of supplies for, 389; at Hoke's Run, 11; at Hoover's Gap, 225; at Jonesboro, 343; at Kennesaw Mountain, 336–39, *337;* at Lost Mountain-Brushy Mountain Line, 336; at Mill Springs, *31*, 32; at Nashville, 392, 395, 396–97, 401; at New Hope Church, Pickett's Mill, and Dallas, 332–35, *333;* and opposition to Hood, 399; at Peachtree Creek, 339–40; at Resaca, *330;* at Rocky Face Ridge, *327*, 328; and Sher-

man, 391; at Stones River, 151–53, *152*

Thomas Freeborn, 5

Thompson, David L., 121

Thompson, Gideon W., 133

Thompson, Meriwether "Jeff," 25

Thompson's Station, Tenn., battle of, 189

Thoroughfare Gap, Va., battle of, 108

Tilghman, Lloyd, 44, *168;* death of, 170

Tom's Brook, Va., battle of, 318–19

Toombs, Robert, 4, 97

Torbert, Alfred T. A.: and "The Burning," 319; at Haw's Shop, 290; at Matadequin Creek, 291; at Tom's Brook, 318–19; at Trevilian Station, 294–95; near Westover Church, 295

Torrence, W. M. G., 27

Totopotomoy Creek, Va.: battle of Totopotomoy Creek and Bethesda Church, 290

Tracy, Edward D., 163–64

Tranter's Creek, N.C., battle of, 62

Treasury Department Coast Survey, 71–72

Trevilian Station, Va., battle of, 294–95

Trimble, Isaac R., 82, *83*, 84, *210*, 212

Truex, William S., *306*, 307–8

Tullahoma campaign, 225–26

Tupelo, Miss., battle of, 347–50, *348*

Turkey Bridge, Va., 98

Turner's Gap, Md., 115, 117

Tuscumbia, 158

Tyler, Daniel, 11, 12, *13*, 14

Tyler, Erastus B., 9, *75*, 78, 85, 87, 305–8, *306*

Tyler, John, 290

Tyler, Robert O., *284*, 286

Tyler, 26, 52, 176

U.S.-Dakota conflict, 135–36

U.S. Geological Survey, 71, 73

U.S. Sanitary Commission, 173

Upham, Charles L., 406

Upperville, Va., battle of, 206

Utoy Creek, Ga., battle of, 341

Valverde, N.M., battle of, 39, 271

Vandever, William, 178

Van Dorn, Earl: at Corinth battle, 129–32, *130;* at Corinth siege, 53, *54–55;* at Davis Bridge, 132; at Franklin I, 190; at Holly Springs, 150, 154; along Mississippi River, 156; at Pea Ridge, 34–37, *35;* at Thompson's Station, 189

Varuna, 58

Vaughn, John C.: at Big Black River Bridge, 171; at Bull's Gap, 387; at Chickasaw Bayou, *155,* 156; at Marion, 388; at Piedmont, *302,* 303; at Saltville I, 387

Vaught's Hill, Tenn., battle of, 189–90

Vermillion Bayou, La., battle of, 179

Vicksburg, Miss.: battle and siege of, 171–73, 175; campaign and siege, 154–76, *155, 159–63, 165, 168, 174*

Virginia, 88, 91

Virginia & Tennessee Railroad, 240, 296, 297, 301

Virginia Central Railroad, 92, 286, 294, 324, 353, 357

Virginia Military Institute (VMI), 298, 300, 304

Wagner, George D., *337,* 338–39, 395

Walcutt, Charles C., *337,* 338–39, 399

Walker, Henry H., 252–54, *253*

Walker, John G.: at Harpers Ferry, 113–15, *114;* at Jenkins' Ferry, 274–75; at Mansfield, 267–69, *268;* and Milliken's Bend, 173; at Pleasant Hill, 270–71, *270*

Walker, Lucius M., 233

Walker, R. Lindsay, 428

Walker, Tandy, 274

Walker, William H. T.: at Chickamauga, *228–29,* 230–31; at Meridian, 261; at Resaca, *330,* 331; at Snake Creek, 167

Walkerton, Va., battle of, 260

Wallace, Lewis: at Fort Donelson, *46,* 47; at Monocacy, 305–8, *306;* at Shiloh, 49–52, *50–51*

Wallace, William H., 412

Wallace, William H. L., *50–51;* death of, 49

Ward, James H., 5

Ware Bottom Church, Va.: battle of Ware Bottom Church and Howlett Line, 280

Warren, Gouverneur K.: at Auburn I and II, 252; at Boydton Plank Road, 369–71, *370;* at Bristoe Station, 252–54, *253;* at Cold Harbor, 292, 293; at Five Forks, 417–19, *418;* at Gaines' Mill, *95,* 96–97; at Globe Tavern, 357; at Hatcher's Run, 372; at Lewis's Farm, 412; at Mine Run, *256–57,* 258–59; at North Anna, 287–89, *288;* at Peebles' Farm, 368; at Petersburg I and II, 352, 353; at Poplar Spring Church, 368; relieved of command, 419; along Shady Grove Church Road, 290; at White Oak Road, 413, 415–17, *416;* at the Wilderness, *281,* 282–83

Washburn, Cadwallader Colden, 349, 350

Washington, George, 259

Washington, D.C., fortifications, 11–12, 308

Washington, N.C., battle of, 195

Watie, Stand, 33, 34, 133, 134, 218, 220, 438

Wauhatchie, Tenn., battle of, 241–42

Waynesboro, Va., battle of, 323–24

Waynesborough, Ga., battle of, 400

Webb, Alexander S., *253,* 260

Weber, Max, 59

Webster, George Penny, 126, 128

Webster, Joseph D., 49

Weer, William, 133

Weiser, Josiah, 222

Weisiger, David A., *284,* 285–86

Weitzel, Godfrey: at Fair Oaks and Darbytown Road, 372; at Fort Fisher I, 401–2; at Georgia Landing, 137; at Kock's Plantation, 180; at Port Hudson, *183,* 184

Weldon Railroad, 353, 354, 357, 360, 369, 372

Wells, William, 423

Wescott, John, 263

Wessells, Henry W., 277

Western & Atlantic Railroad, 158, 176, 226, 262, 389, 391

Westfield, 138

Westport, Mo., battle of, 384

West Virginia, statehood for, 7–8, 9, 240

Wharton, Gabriel C.: at Cedar Creek, *320–21,* 322; at Fisher's Hill, 316–18, *317;* at Monocacy, 305–8, *306;* at New Market, *299,* 300–301; at Opequon, 315–16; at Second Kernstown, 310–12, *311;* at Waynesboro, 323

Wharton, John A., *125,* 126

Wheat, R. C., 81

Wheeler, Joseph: at Atlanta, 340; at Bentonville, 408–11, *409;* at Buck Head Creek, 399–400; at Dalton II, 341–42; at Dover, 189; at Griswoldville, 399; at Kennesaw Mountain, *337;* and Monroe's Cross Roads, 407; at Peachtree Creek, 339–40; at Perryville, 124, *125;* raid into Tennessee by, 341; at Rocky Face Ridge, 328; and Stones River, 151; at Waynesborough, 400

Whig Party, 224

Whipple, Amiel W., 148

White, Frank J., 25

White, Moses J., 61

White Hall, N.C., battle of, 62

White Oak Road, Va., battle of, 413, 415–17, *416*

White Oak Swamp, Va., battle of, 98–101, *99*

Whitestone Hill, N.D., battle of, 223

Whiting, W. H. C.: and batteries along Potomac, 18; at Gaines' Mill, *95,* 96; and Malvern Hill, 103; and Proctor's Creek, 279; at Seven Pines, 92

Wilcox, Cadmus M.: at First Deep Bottom, 355; at Gettysburg, 212; at Glendale, 100–101; and Hopewell Gap, 108; at Jerusalem Plank Road, 354; at Mine Run, *256–57;* at Petersburg III, 419–23, *420–21;* at Reams Station II, 360–62, *361;* at Salem Church, 200

Wild, Edward, 290

Wilder, John T., 123, 225–26, 226

Wilderness, battle of the, Va., 278, 280–83, *281*

Willcox, Orlando B., *116,* 117, 148

Willette, Charles, 221

Williams, Alpheus S.: at Bentonville, *409*, 410; at First Winchester, 81–82; at Kennesaw Mountain, *337;* at New Hope Church, Pickett's Mill, and Dallas, 332–35, *333;* at Resaca, *330*, 331

Williams, James M., 218, 220, 274

Williams, John S., 29, 239–40

Williams, Robert, 67, *68*, 69

Williams, Thomas, 136

Williamsburg, Va., battle of, 90–91

Williamson, James A., 247–48, *247*

Williamsport, Md, battle of, 212–13

Willich, August, 29–30

Williston, Edward, *237*

Wilmington, N.C., battle of, 402–3

Wilmington & Weldon Railroad, 62, 63

Wilson, James, at Pilot Knob, 380–82, *381*

Wilson, James H.: capture of Jefferson Davis, 436; as cavalry chief, 392, 396–97; on Forrest, 276; maps by, *160–63, 174,* 175; at Nashville, 397; at Opequon, 315–16; raid against rail lines, 353–55; raid in Alabama and Georgia by, 436; at Reams Station I, 354–55; at Selma, 436

Wilson, William, 27

Wilson's Creek, Mo., battle of, 21, *22, 23,* 34

Wilson's Wharf, Va., battle of, 290

Winchester, Va.: first battle of, 81–82; second battle of, 205, 312; third battle of, 315–16

Winder, Charles, 85, *86,* 87, *95,* 96, *106,* 107

Winthrop, Theodore, 6

Wise, Henry A.: and Carnifex Ferry, 9; Charleston occupied by, 9; at Lewis's Farm, 412; in northwest Virginia, 9; at Petersburg I and II, 352, 353; and Roanoke Island, 60; at White Oak Road, 415, *416*

Wofford, William, 249, 314

Wolford, Frank, 32

Wolseley, Viscount Garnet J., 347

Wood, Sterling A. M., 124, 126

Wood, Thomas J., *327, 333,* 354, 397

Wood, William F., 175

Wood Lake, Minn., battle of, 135–36

Woodruff, William E., 21

Woods, Charles, 247–48, *247*

Worden, John L., 88

Wright, Ambrose R., 61–62

Wright, Horatio G.: at Appomattox Court House, 429–32; at Cedar Creek, 319, *320–21,* 322; at Cold Harbor, *292,* 293–94; crossing of James River by, 352; at Fisher's Hill, *317,* 318; at Fort Stevens, 308; to Hanover Court House, 290; at Jerusalem Plank Road, 353–54; at North Anna, *288,* 289; north of Fort Fisher, 373; at Opequon, 315–16; toward Petersburg front, 309; at Petersburg III, 419–23, *420–21;* pursuit of Early from Washington, 309; at Sailor's Creek, *425,* 426; at Secessionville, 67, *68,* 69; at Spotsylvania Court House, *284, 285–86;* at Summit Point and Cameron's Depot, 314

Wright, Rebecca, 315

Wyman, R. H., 18–19

Wyndham, Percy, 204

Wynkoop, Edward, 398

Wyse Fork, N.C., battle of, 406

Yankee, 18–19

Yazoo River, 154, 156

Yellow Bayou, La., battle of, 266, 272

Yellow Tavern, Va., battle of, 286–87

York, Zebulon, *306,* 307–8

York River, 91

Yorktown, Va., siege of, 88–90, *89*

Young, Brigham, 217

Young, William Hugh, 390

Younger brothers, 377, 378

Zagonyi, Charles, 25

Zollicoffer, Felix K., 28, 29, 30, *31,* 32

The Conservation Fund

Partners in Land and Water Conservation

●

The Conservation Fund seeks sustainable conservation solutions for the challenges of the twenty-first century, emphasizing the integration of economic and environmental goals. Through land conservation, demonstration projects, education, and community-based activities, the Fund seeks innovative long-term measures to conserve land and water resources.

Since its founding in 1985, the Fund has forged partnerships that have protected more than 1.4 million acres. The Fund's programs include the American Greenways Program, the Civil War Battlefield Campaign, Conservation Leadership Network, the Freshwater Institute, America's Land Legacy, and Sustainable Communities.

Committed to leadership, results, and efficiency, the Fund pursues new opportunities to advance land and water conservation. The Civil War Battlefield Campaign and its partners have protected more than 5,800 acres on twenty-eight battlefields in twelve states. These fifty-one preservation projects, valued at more than $10.6 million, honor the soldiers who fought and died on this hallowed ground. The campaign's educational initiatives extend beyond these great outdoor classrooms to include this guide and *The Dollar$ and Sense of Battlefield Preservation: The Economic Benefits of Preserving Civil War Battlefields.* This handbook for community leaders provides a foundation for the development of heritage tourism that benefits the economies of battlefield communities.

The Conservation Fund is a 501(c)(3) charitable organization, publicly supported by contributions from individuals, foundations, and corporations. The Conservation Fund is a member of Earth Share, the nation's leading federation of environmental and conservation charities for workplace giving.

Proceeds to The Conservation Fund from the sale of this book are dedicated to protecting Civil War battlefields. Please join the Civil War Battlefield Campaign to preserve our nation's hallowed ground.

The Conservation Fund
Civil War Battlefield Campaign
1800 North Kent Street, Suite 1120
Arlington, Virginia 22209
http://www.conservationfund.org